ABOUT THE AUTHOR

Jerome Clark, an investigator of anomalous claims and occurrences for nearly three decades, is vice president of the J. Allen Hynek Center for UFO Studies (CUFOS) and editor of its magazine, *International UFO Reporter*. CUFOS, one of the preeminent UFO organizations in the world, was founded in 1973 by Sherman J. Larsen and Northwestern University astronomer Hynek, for 20 years the chief scientific consultant on UFO matters to the U.S. Air Force's Project Blue Book. Clark formerly edited *Fate*, a popular monthly devoted to anomalies and the paranormal.

Clark was an early proponent of theories that sought psychological and social explanations for extraordinary events. In his first book, 1975's *The Unidentified*, written with Loren Coleman, he argued that encounters with extraordinary beings were more likely to be internally than externally generated. Although such ideas became widely popular among anomalists, Clark himself eventually rejected such theories for their "grand pronouncements and inattention to empirical evidence." Instead, he urges a cautious approach tied closely to documentable evidence — such as that recorded in *Unexplained!* — along with an intellectual modesty that acknowledges the limitations of human knowledge and an open-ended agnosticism about claims that, however interesting and suggestive, can be neither proven nor disproven.

Born November 27, 1946, in Canby, Minnesota, Clark was educated at South Dakota State University and Moorhead State University. His other books include *UFOs in the 1980s*, *The Emergence of a Phenomenon: UFOs from the Beginning through 1959*, *UFO Encounters: Sightings, Visitations, and Investigations*, and, with J. Gordon Melton and Aidan A. Kelly, *New Age Encyclopedia*. Clark also did consulting work for the Time-Life series *Mysteries of the Unexplained* and has contributed to *Omni* and *Cryptozoology*.

UNEXPLAINED!

347 Strange
Sightings,
Incredible
Occurrences,
and Puzzling
Physical
Phenomena

UNEXPLAINED!

347 Strange
Sightings,
Incredible
Occurrences,
and Puzzling
Physical
Phenomena

Jerome Clark

Detroit   Washington, D.C.   London

Unexplained! 347 Strange Sightings, Incredible Occurrences, and Puzzling Physical Phenomena

Art Director: Cynthia Baldwin
Graphic Services Supervisor: Barbara J. Yarrow
Cover and Page Design: Tracey Rowens
Typesetter: The Graphix Group

ISBN 0-8103-9436-7

CONTENTS

This book is dedicated to Loren Coleman,
old friend and fellow explorer of the wild country.

INTRODUCTION ON ANOMALOUS EXPERIENCES

Dismissing the Unexplained

The three hardest words for human beings to utter are *I don't know.* We demand an accounting for every claim or experience, and when no accounting is available, someone will invent one for us.

Thus a New Hampshire man, considered by those who know him to be a reliable and a veteran outdoorsman, reports a daylight encounter with a nine-foot-tall apelike creature. A game warden explains it, with neither investigation nor specific cause, as a moose. Or when a number of West Texas motorists, over a period of hours, independently tell of close-range sightings of a 200-foot-long, egg-shaped, brilliantly luminous structure, Air Force personnel conduct a brief inquiry and identify the phenomenon as ball lightning. What the witnesses had described bore no resemblance to this rare natural phenomenon, and the electrical storm that had given rise to it, according to the Air Force, did not exist, according to weather records.

In both of these cases, the proposed solutions are so flimsy that one thinks it would have been easier just to call the witnesses bald-faced liars and be done with it. Either that, or diagnose them as dangerous lunatics whose vivid hallucinations call for their immediate sedation and hospitalization.

Of course if these were isolated episodes, the sorts of stories told and heard rarely, and then usually from excitable or gullible souls, we could probably tell ourselves, "Yes, I suppose it is possible, once in a great while, for someone to see a moose and mistake it for a nine-foot-tall bipedal anthropoid, or for a person to have a close-up view of a globe of ball lightning, ordinarily the size of a basketball or smaller, and judge it to be 200 feet in diameter." After all, where human behavior is concerned, just about anything that could happen has happened at some time or another.

It's just that the sorts of colossal perceptual breakdowns being proposed here run as counter to the experience of most human beings as do encounters with hairy giants in New England woods. Suppose the New Hampshire witness had seen something else, say a fugitive on the lam, and reported it to the sheriff. We may safely assume that the latter would not have said — at least without investigation and specific cause — that the witness had mistaken a moose for a man. Far more likely, the sheriff and his deputies would have raced to the site in anticipation of an immediate arrest.

Yet if we allow ourselves to believe (still in the absence of specific evidence to the effect) that at times, even under what are ordinarily viewed as good viewing conditions, a moose can look like an ape, we will only be stymied if we try to employ this identification in the many places in the United States where similar "apes" have been reported and where moose (or, in many cases, any wild mammals larger than deer) do not exist.

It will not help us, either, to level indiscriminate charges of dishonesty against all witnesses wherever we find them — whether in New Hampshire or Indiana or Pennsylvania or South Dakota or Texas or British Columbia or Newfoundland, or just about any state or province you can name — and off-the-cuff speculations about perceptual disorders of so a radical character as to suggest profound mental illness take us only so far. At some point we are going to have to listen to what the witnesses say.

Old Hags
Let us consider the case of the Old Hag.

The victim wakes up unable to move. As he lies there helpless, he hears footsteps and sees a horrifying form. An invisible force presses on his chest, and he thinks he is going to die. At last he is able to shake off his paralysis, and the eerie attack ends.

Chances are you have never heard of an incident like this — unless it has happened to you. And if it has happened to you, you are not alone. There is reason to believe that one American in six has had this kind of experience; yet it is so little discussed in our culture that it has no name.

But in other cultures the same experience is the subject of a rich folk tradition. Newfoundlanders, for example, call it the "Old Hag," "The Hags," or "Hagging." When it was first used in connection with these experiences, the word "hag" referred to "witch," and a victim of hagging was thought to be hag- or witch-ridden. In fact the most common expression for the experience in English is "riding." Interestingly enough, the original name is one with which we are all familiar: nightmare. Nightmare, which to us means simply "bad dream," once had a far more specific definition; it referred to an incubus or succubus which came in the night to put a crushing weight on a victim's chest.

Are Firsthand Accounts Valid?
In a remarkable book, *The Terror That Comes in the Night* (published by University of Pennsylvania Press in 1982), Penn State folklorist and behav-

ioral scientist David J. Hufford used the Old Hag to address an important question: Do persons reporting firsthand encounters with anomalous and paranormal phenomena know what they are talking about?

Standard wisdom holds that such experiences are the product of perceptual errors, faulty memories, lies, psychotic episodes, and hallucinations shaped by ideas in the claimants' cultural environment. Hufford used the Old Hag experience to test this hypothesis, which — except in cases where consciously false testimony is alleged — might be phrased as the "believing-is-seeing" theory. According to this notion, individuals believe they have seen something extraordinary because society has provided them with the images that shape their imaginings.

After an in-depth examination of Old Hag accounts both in cultures in which such beliefs are widely known and in others (ours, for example) in which they are all but unknown, Hufford learned that descriptions of the core experience, by those who say they have had it, are strikingly consistent wherever they occur. Such events are *not* culturally determined. "Recognizable Old Hag attacks of great complexity can and do occur in the absence of explicit models," Hufford wrote.

He then considered psychologists' efforts to account for the phenomenon and found them hopelessly muddled. Of one famous psychoanalytic study Hufford said that "one can hardly distinguish the experiences themselves from their interpretations. The lack of scientific precision attributed to popular thought is found here in academic disguise." The consistent unwillingness of psychologists and other professionals to listen to those persons who have had these experiences has led them to engage in freewheeling speculation devoid of empirical justification. "The subject of supernatural belief somehow leads to a lot of forgetting about what constitutes serious scholarship," Hufford observed.

"It was just such a rejection of untutored observation that delayed for so long the 'scientific' discovery of giant squid, gorillas, meteors and any number of other wild and wonderful (but apparently unlikely) facts of this world. In those cases, *post hoc* scientific rationalization was used to explain how people came to believe in such things. Seasoned fishermen were said to mistake floating trees with large root systems for huge animals attacking their boats; farmers were said to have overlooked iron-bearing rocks in the midst of their fields until they were pointed out by lightning; and in this case [the Old Hag experience] 'children and savages' were said to have difficulty knowing when they were awake and when they were asleep" — even though the victims, people of all ages, cultures, and educational levels, insist they were not "dreaming," that they were fully conscious when they heard and saw weird things.

Hufford argued that we must take seriously "an experience with stable contents which is widespread, dramatic, realistic and bizarre" and which has been repeatedly reported "by large numbers of our fellow humans."

Nor did Hufford hesitate to consider the implications of his Old Hag research for other claims of strange experiences. "I think the present study has amply demonstrated that at least some apparently fantastic beliefs are in fact empirically grounded," he wrote, noting that nonetheless most scholars have acted more interested in explaining troublesome claims "out of existence" than in investigating them. The further they remove themselves from the data (the accounts of those who have had the experiences), the more exotic, facile, and irrelevant their theories become. In Hufford's blunt assessment this practice amounts to "careless thinking retroactively applied with little regard for evidence."

An empirically based, "experience-centered" approach such as the one Hufford used would show, he argued, that events such as the Old Hag are believed in because they really happen; they are not simply imagined by people who are so stupid, crazy, or credulous that they cannot tell the difference between a popular superstition and a personal experience. Inquirers would learn not to confuse "folk explanation" — for example the notion that witches cause Old Hag attacks — with "folk observation" — which, as Hufford demonstrated, can be quite accurate, consistent, and scientifically valuable.

Hufford's argument brings revolutionary implications in its assertion that rational persons are accurately reporting experiences that at least *seem* to be extraordinary and that those who have attempted to explain away such accounts have not made their case or even understood what they are trying to explain. As a consequence scholars have failed to come to grips with a significant part of human experience.

Can the Old Hag experience be explained in nonparanormal terms? Drawing on findings from sleep research conducted in the 1960s and 1970s, Hufford concluded that the "state in which this experience occurs is probably best described as sleep paralysis with a particular kind of hypnagogic hallucination." In other words, science can explain how someone could wake from sleep, be unable to move, and have a frightening experience. But it cannot explain the fact that the *contents* of the experience are consistent no matter to whom or in what cultural environment they occur. This mystery cannot be solved, according to Hufford, "on the basis of current knowledge."

Seeing Is Believing
Where the experience of hairy bipeds, UFOs, or other anomalous entities or objects is concerned, one need not believe in, or even have heard of, such to see one. The isolated folk of Newfoundland, for example, had never heard of "Sasquatch" or "Bigfoot" — names that did not come into currency until well into the present century — on the other side of the continent but nevertheless reported seeing manlike entities they called "Indians." Few of the Newfoundlanders knew what a real Indian looked like, but nonetheless that was the name they attached to creatures whom other North Americans, who had never heard of Bigfoot or Sasquatch either, were calling "wild men" or "gorillas."

In our time, even when such phenomena are staples of popular culture, it is still possible to find individuals who have never heard, for example, of UFOs; yet they report extraordinary experiences with what they may interpret as everything from "secret airplanes" to "demons." Their interpretations aside, they relate sights or occurrences that are in every way congruent with those experienced by more culturally sophisticated observers. Witnesses often say, "I wouldn't have believed it if I hadn't seen it myself" — a statement that resonates with meaning. There are some things people believe in not because they are ignorant, credulous, or crazy but because either they or persons they trust see them. Seeing is believing, indeed.

People also see things for which their ancestors once had a vocabulary now lost. A young Wisconsin man walking along a country road in the middle of the night comes upon a group of peculiarly dressed, mumbling, bald little men who march past him in single file, paying no attention. He realizes quickly that something about this is eerie beyond reason, but he does not know what, though the memory of the encounter will remain with him the rest of his life. If it had been a hundred years ago and he had been passing down a lane in the west of Ireland, he would have been no less frightened, but at least he would have had a name for what he saw: the trooping fairies.

Likewise, when another young Midwesterner encounters a mysterious dog that disappears in front of his eyes, he recalls it for decades afterwards as the strangest event of his life. Neither then nor later would he hear of "black dogs," the supernatural canines known in many folk traditions and the subject of numerous sighting reports.

Even when the phenomenon is known in a general way as the focus of numerous sighting reports, witnesses are unlikely to know about its more subtle aspects. For example, popular lore about the footprints of hairy bipeds is influenced by casts associated with the Bigfoot/Sasquatch of the Pacific Northwest. These casts are, or so appearances suggest, of a giant primate; like all primates, these have five toes. Practically no one except the several hundred anomaly buffs who pay attention to such matters knows that hairy bipeds seen outside the Pacific Northwest usually leave zoologically absurd tracks which evince only three toes, and these oddly fat and oversized.

In the same way investigators of the UFO-abduction phenomenon find striking consistency not only in its overt features (as by now, considering the vast publicity such reports have generated in recent years, one would expect) but also in its subtle, obscure details, some still unpublished.

Our culture provides an immense number of models from which those claiming anomalous experience can draw, were their experiences wholly imaginary. Yet anomalous events and appearances draw on a distinctly finite number of images and motifs. People of apparent sanity and sincerity who report close encounters of the third kind describe humanoid beings, not multitentacled extraterrestrial octopuses or giant arachnids. They report kangaroos in Midwestern states but not platypuses. They report black panthers but not woolly mammoths. Even where the most extreme anomalous claims are concerned, one hears reports of fairies, and even of merfolk and werewolves, but not of unicorns or vampires.

The Value of Skepticism
There is, on the other hand, much to be said for skepticism. Skepticism need not be synonymous with anomalyphobia, and it does not require us to form debunking committees and launch emotional crusades against heretical beliefs and unacceptable experiences. But a rational, balanced skepticism, one that is neither apologetic about its demand for persuasive evidence nor afraid to admit the limits of current knowledge, is to be preferred to mindless credulity. And where extraordinary claims are concerned, there is a great deal to be skeptical about.

As indicated earlier, even militant disbelievers have become reluctant to level hoax charges indiscriminately against persons who say they have had close encounters with unrecognized entities or phenomena. Nonetheless hoaxes do occur. Most are fairly clumsy affairs, but some are devilishly clever and aggravatingly difficult to crack.

The most remarkable hoax in the history of ufology, for example, concerned a document which purported to be a top-secret briefing paper prepared for President-elect Eisenhower by a classified operation called Majestic-12, or MJ-12. MJ-12 supposedly consisted of a dozen high-ranking government officials and military officers who oversaw the deepest UFO secrets, including physical evidence. The hoaxer loaded the document with obscure, hard-to-find information which investigators later were able to verify, with much difficulty, in the course of archival research in Washington. Such findings, of course, were thought to give the document credibility.

Eventually, after prolonged and furious debate, skeptics won the argument in undramatic fashion: they demonstrated that the dating formats and rank designations would not have been used in an authentic government briefing paper. Even today, however, a few diehards refuse to give up on the MJ-12 document, and the identity and motive of the hoaxer remain a mystery. All we know is that as hoaxes go, this is one for the books.

Bogus Photographs
Historically photographs of extraordinary anomalies are more likely than not to be bogus. Serious Bigfoot/Sasquatch researchers reject as inauthentic nearly all photographs and films said to depict the creature. Probably 95 percent of all "UFO" photos are of dubious provenance, and some of the most spectacular footage of the Loch Ness monster is known or suspected to be fake. The debate about photographic evidence of these kinds of phenomena centers on a surprisingly small number of recorded images.

Sometimes, in fact, critics act as if the paucity of arguably authentic photographs amounted to evidence against the reality of these sorts of anomalies, but this is a singularly uncompelling objection when one considers that (1) most people do not walk around with cameras at the ready; (2) nearly all anomalous encounters occur abruptly and occasion emotions ranging from deep shock to sheer terror; and (3) the duration of most such events can be measured in seconds. These are not conditions conducive to the creation of a big body of photographs. And that is why there are so few reputable pictures of ball lightning, a strange natural phenomenon whose reality most physicists and meteorologists no longer dispute.

It is one of the perversities of anomalies research that the fuzzier the image, the more likely it represents something real, inasmuch as the circumstances that cause photographs to be rare are the same ones that are likely to cause them to be unclear. Pictures taken hastily by individuals with shaking hands do not produce sharp images, and hoaxers who seek attention or profit know that photographs like these won't get them anywhere. Fuzzy images are such a feeble variety of evidence that witnesses who trumpet them are only asking for yet more ridicule to be heaped upon their heads.

Pseudomysteries: Disappearances, the Bermuda Triangle, and Cattle Mutilations

Some tales marketed as "true mysteries" began less as hoaxes than as jokes or science fiction — in other words, as tales that, though they may not have been intended to be taken seriously, took on lives of their own and over the decades reincarnated in print as records of events which, it was assumed, someone somewhere had validated. Two of the most famous are a couple of mysterious-disappearance cases, the victim usually identified as David Lang in one and as Oliver Lerch in the other. Like true folktales these sometimes changed in the telling. While their origins are murky (Lang) or unknown (Lerch), it is certain that neither man ever lived, much less left the earth in such singular fashion.

Other "mysteries" arise from imaginative interpretations of events which, if unusual, are not so bizarre as they are made to seem. The Bermuda Triangle and cattle mutilations, two modern legends, disintegrated not long after competent investigators turned their attention to them, but not before the two notions had enthralled and frightened impressionable souls in the countless thousands.

These sorts of pseudomysteries flourish in part, of course, because people are drawn to exotic novelties and, moreover, enjoy being scared in comfort and safety. Few people possess the specialized knowledge that would expose the foolishness of the assertions made by the mystery-mongers. It took concentrated research into Naval, Coast Guard, and other nautical archives to uncover the prosaic events behind Triangle lore, and only veterinary pathologists could pronounce with certainty on the causes of the cattle deaths that fired rumors of sinister "mutilations." Historians and archaeologists easily demolished nearly all the evidence Erich Von Däniken and other writers offered in support of early space visitors, but to a historically illiterate audience — a large one, unfortunately — Von Däniken's theories seemed perfectly reasonable.

Beyond the hoaxes and the legends are genuine misperceptions and honest mistakes. No conscientious investigator embarks on his or her labors without considering these possibilities and pursuing them actively. (Neither, however, will he or she force them on the data if they manifestly fail to fit.) Some witnesses, though not so many as one might think, are mentally unwell.

Cautious Belief
A deeper reason for skepticism has to do with the nature of the more fantastic claims. Many reports attest to beings, creatures, and occurrences which, if established to be real, would shake the scientific community. Some would shake the foundations of consensus reality. In short, what is being alleged here is nothing to be taken lightly. The implications are enormous.

Because the stakes are so high, we would do well to be cautious. *Very* cautious. After all, one does not redefine the world on no more than the word — however sincere it may appear to be — of sailors and shore-dwellers who say they have sighted merfolk. No biological principle, or even *conceivable* biological principle, allows us to believe in beings or animals that are half fish and half human, or even in creatures that *look* as if they could be half fish and half human. (The inadequacy of most naturalistic explanations for the reports is discussed in the entry on "Merfolk.") Unsurprisingly, in our time merfolk have virtually no defenders, even among anomalists.

Neither do fairies, though first-person sighting reports in no small number have been logged over the centuries. In a handful of cases these are preserved in affidavits sworn by presumably reputable and sober members of the clergy. No one collects these reports anymore except folklorists. Folklorists are interested in them because they represent survivals of older, traditional beliefs; as to their status as descriptions of real events, folklorists shrug and say this is a question for parapsychologists. Parapsychologists for their part say fairy sightings are of interest only to folklorists.

Who can blame anybody here? Even to raise the question of fairy (or merfolk) sightings is to raise multitudes of eyebrows. For any number of reasons no rational person can fail to think of, fairies cannot exist, and the descriptions of fairy realms and life preserved in traditional narratives are clearly fabulous; not only that, they are so wildly at variance that even a committed supernaturalist would be hard-pressed to fashion a geography of fairyland from such accounts. But could it be that fabulous elements attached themselves to experiences at least perceived as real, much in the way those who experienced Old Hag attacks, which really happened, attributed a folk (and false) cause (witch assaults) to them?

The question is worth asking, but the problems in answering it are many.

To start with, the Old Hag experience is at least partially explainable by known physiological mechanisms, which is to say its degree of strangeness may be more apparent than real. These are also, without exception, single-person events. If you were in a bedroom with someone who was undergoing an Old Hag attack, you would not see the approaching apparition; you would see no more than the victim lying motionless and staring with a fearful expression.

Sightings of fairies and merfolk, on the other hand, typically are said to occur in settings where hallucinations tied to sleep paralysis are not an issue. The witnesses are usually individuals otherwise deemed sane and well, and consequently not susceptible to dramatic delusions. ("In our society," Graham Reed writes in *The Psychology of Anomalous Experience* [1988], "hallucinatory content is usually concerned with the fears and conflicts which would be expected from people who are suffering from mental disorder or delirium due to physical health.") A number of these sightings, moreover, involve multiple witnesses.

That just about sums up the case for high-strangeness anomalies: credible persons reporting incredible things, and nothing but sincerity to show for it. This is not, in short, the stuff of a scientific revolution. Neither is it, however, occasion to rush into the vacuum with a naively reductionist explanation that renders the anomalous claim harmless by covering it with a "natural" cause pulled out of a hat. It is just as unwise to fill the explanatory vacuum with scientifically meaningless or overtly supernatural "theories" based on a host of unverifiable assumptions about the nature of reality.

It ought to be clear, though the literature on anomalous phenomena (whether written by proponents or debunkers) shows it is everything but that, that *we do not know* why honest individuals, in all times and places, claim to see things that all evidence and logic tell us do not and cannot exist. Nearly everybody who pays attention to such anomalous testimony gets him- or herself worked into an intellectual and emotional knot over it. Human nature abhors an explanatory vacuum; thus in the rhetoric of the debate that has raged in one form or another over the centuries, a strange entity or beast gets transformed either into a conventional object or animal to which it bears no resemblance or into an intruder from some magical dimension.

If neither explanation seems especially helpful, it is because the question has been framed wrongly. The question ought not to be, though it always is, "Do bizarre beasts and entities exist?" No sensible, all-encompassing answer is possible, and it is futile to pretend otherwise. The question really is this: "Is it possible to have the experience of encountering bizarre beasts and entities?" And the answer is yes.

To respond affirmatively is only to acknowledge modestly the obvious, which is, as folklorist Bill Ellis puts it, "Weird stuff happens." We are in no way conceding anything about what all this weird stuff *means*. We can grant that people "see" fairies or merfolk without for a moment believing that fairies or merfolk are "real." We simply acknowledge that such sightings are an experience it is possible to have, even though the actual dynamics of the experience remain unknown so far. Therefore science as currently constructed has little to offer in the way of elucidation, and occultism has only obfuscation. The nature of these experiences need not remain forever inexplicable. With the ever-accelerating accumulation of knowledge in all areas, we may presume it will be possible sooner or later to place these experiences in a rational perspective, either as heretofore-unsuspected perceptual anomalies or as glimpses of an otherwise-undetected larger reality. Whether the solution comes from the micro (subjective) or macro (objective) side of the existential ledger, it is sure to teach us something new.

Until then, these events should be regarded simply as curiosities that represent some of human experience's more peculiar and unclassifiable aspects and about which it is difficult to say more. In other words, they should not be seen as the foundation of a new science or a new religion, and they ought not to threaten anyone who does not need to believe late-twentieth-century science has accounted for all the interesting phenomena of mind and nature.

Less Peculiar Phenomena: Giant Octopuses and Ghost Lights
Not all, or even most, anomalous claims are of such an extreme variety. On the low side of the strangeness scale, we find ball lightning, Eastern cougars, ghost lights, giant octopuses, ice falls, surviving thylacines, and other things that, while undeniably intriguing mysteries, do not hint at world-shaking revelations. Physicists, meteorologists, wildlife specialists, and marine biologists will solve these riddles one day in the near future. Newspapers, television, and radio will take notice for a few days, and the phenomena will then sink from popular view, to be revived occasionally on cable TV's ubiquitous nature documentaries.

But if cryptozoologists were to produce a Bigfoot or a mokele-mbembe (a sauropod dinosaur alleged to survive in the remote reaches of the Congo), the consequences for anthropology, paleontology, and evolutionary theory would be immense, if only because their presence (while not *a priori* impossible) is so unexpected — not just by scientists but by everybody. It is hard to imagine anyone who would not be excited. On the other hand, once the serious research — on these animals' physiology, diet, and behavior — began, popular interest would slacken, and in time Bigfoot and mokele-mbembe would be just more fodder for nature documentaries. The same can be said of lake monsters and the like.

UFOs: Unexplained Mystery or Mass Credulity?
There is no doubt that the discovery of an extraterrestrial presence on earth would have far more profound consequences. Unidentified flying objects are, to some, the major scientific mystery of the century and, to others, the century's most annoyingly persistent manifestation of mass credulity. UFOs are the most extraordinary claim this side of those that defy consensus reality. Excepting that minority of astronomers of the "we-are-alone"

school, who reject the concept of extraterrestrial intelligence (ETI) altogether, most space scientists see visitation from other solar systems at least theoretically possible. Some of the more conservative ETI proponents have argued that the vast distances between stars would prevent travel between them, but this view is falling out of favor as other theorists have demonstrated mechanisms by which interstellar voyages could be effected in manageable periods of time.

Thus the serious debate about UFOs — and much of the debate on both sides has been anything but serious — centers on two issues: (1) the quality of the evidence and (2) the likely nature, appearance, and behavior of extraterrestrial visitors.

The first of these was memorably encapsulated in the words of onetime Project Blue Book head Edward J. Ruppelt in a memoir of his experiences, *The Report on Unidentified Flying Objects* (1956): "What constitutes proof? Does a UFO have to land at the River Entrance to the Pentagon, near the Joint Chiefs of Staff offices? Or is it proof when a ground radar station detects a UFO, sends a jet to intercept it, the jet pilot sees it, and locks on with his radar, only to have the UFO streak away at a phenomenal speed?" In his official capacity Ruppelt had investigated a number of the latter kinds of reports, and since the 1950s many comparable ones have been recorded. Most have resisted explanation even after intense study.

It is cases like these (as well as others involving physical traces associated with close encounters) that will eventually settle the UFO question, since by now it is clear that no amount of eyewitness (a.k.a. "anecdotal") testimony — which by now exists in staggering quantities — is going to persuade those in position to render the judgments to which all scientists will adhere. And it will probably take a new generation of elite scientists who, not having staked their positions in concrete, will be able to take not only a fresh look but the vital step of seeing to it that the funding for real scientific inquiry requires is at last made available for UFO research.

Close Encounters of the Third Kind
Nonetheless the eyewitness testimony is what has always gripped popular attention, for understandable reasons. As stories go, it is hard to beat tales of grotesque, gray-skinned humanoids who abduct people and do odd things to their bodies inside UFOs. This characterization of them is not intended to poke fun at such reports, some of which are genuinely puzzling, nor at the real trauma some "abductees" suffer. But abduction reports, like other high-strangeness narratives, make the most extraordinary sorts of claims in support of which they produce only circumstantial evidence. Such evidence, which never rises above the consistent-with-the-hypothesis variety, ranges from unaccounted-for marks on abductees' bodies to patterns in the data that appear explainable neither by chance nor by cultural contamination. Few knowledgeable investigators, whether ufologists or mental-health professionals, doubt that the abduction phenomenon is an enigma; neither would many argue that the evidence so far available is sufficient to do anything more than keep the question open.

Abductions are just one variety of a class of reports the late astronomer/ufologist J. Allen Hynek called "close encounters of the third kind." Such reports first surfaced in press accounts at the very beginning of the modern UFO era, in the summer of 1947, and eventually forced themselves on reluctant investigators who, even if sympathetic to the hypothesis of alien visitation, felt discomforted by these fantastic, even absurd-sounding accounts. In due course it became evident that witnesses to humanoids were for the most part no different from witnesses to safely distant nocturnal lights or daylight discs. Thus, where anecdotal reports were concerned, there was no *prima facie* reason to take the former any less seriously than the latter.

Furthermore, witnesses in the thousands, from bus drivers to nuclear physicists, were insisting that the "flying saucers" they saw looked like craft (structured vehicles built by somebody); that these crafts' performance characteristics indicated a technology far in advance of anything known on earth; and that these objects had windows, presumably so that somebody inside could look out. In short, if appearances were to be believed, these were extraterrestrial spacecraft with occupants.

And what of those occupants? In the sighting reports investigators deemed credible, they were, with practically no exceptions to speak of, humanoid in appearance — as indeed intelligent, technology-building extraterrestrials would almost certainly be. This is a conclusion shared by anti- and pro-UFO scientists alike. For example, skeptic John L. Casti writes (in *Paradigms Lost: Tackling the Unanswered Mysteries of Modern Science* [1989]) that "bilateralism and the presence of large ganglia of nerves near the front of the body and close to the primary sense organs are essential characteristics of intelligent creatures in the convergent evolution scheme of things.... [O]ne comes up with an ETI whose physical forms would be remarkably humanoid; in fact, remarkably like the kinds of forms reported by people who are abducted by the occupants of UFOs." And proponent Michael D. Swords, developing a similar argument but in much greater detail, contends that viewed in the context of current astronomical knowledge and evolutionary theory, ufology's extraterrestrial hypothesis, including witnesses' reports of humanoids, is "eminently defensible and scientifically respectable." (Dr. Swords's case is developed at length in "Science and the Extraterrestrial Hypothesis in Ufology," *Journal of UFO Studies* 1 [1989] and in "Does the ETH Make Sense?", *International UFO Reporter*, September/October 1992.)

Ufology as Science
Seen in this light, the UFO phenomenon looks like something science can deal with. Even those who insist that eyewitness testimony alone is insufficient to validate so fantastic a notion as extraterrestrial visitation cannot fail to wonder why, given the array of alien forms witnesses could have borrowed from popular culture, they so persistently report exobiologically credible entities. Beyond this suggestive testimony is intriguing hard evidence (radar trackings, soil samples from landing sites, photographs, and films) of a sort consistent with the hypothesis of anomalous, technologi-

cally advanced craft in the earth's atmosphere. One does not have to be a crackpot to deem it at least possible that somebody from somewhere far away may be calling on us.

If this seems sensible enough, be advised that this is not the end of it. Some phenomena associated with UFOs take us over the edge of reality and into a void of unreasonableness and surreality. Men in black — the not-quite-human, not entirely coherent agents who allegedly threaten some UFO witnesses and investigators, or at any rate babble at them, and who navigate the landscape of the twilight zone in shiny black Cadillacs — seem more demonological than ufological, and about as easy to believe in as fairies and merfolk.

There is also what British ufologist Jenny Randles has called the "Oz factor," recorded in a surprising number of UFO-sighting accounts; according to Randles, it is the "sensation of being isolated, or transported from the real world into a different environmental framework ... where reality is slightly different." For example, a witness may observe a spectacular UFO display on a well-traveled highway during rush hour and note the utter absence of other traffic. In at least one instance, of particular interest because the percipient was himself an academic folklorist (who later recounted the incident in a *Journal of American Folklore* paper in which he gave himself a pseudonym and treated the event as if it had happened to someone else), a man in black appears to a student in a university library, utters a short message about flying saucers, then walks away and seems to disappear mysteriously. The student is perplexed to find the library inexplicably deserted.

Loch Ness Monsters, Hairy Bipeds, and Other Cryptozoological Curiosities
Likewise cryptozoologists deal with questions that seem straightforward enough but become complicated by unwelcome intrusions of high-strangeness manifestations. Most investigators of Loch Ness's monsters, for example, concentrate on reports — and there are many — of creatures that could be real animals, even if ones usually thought extinct such as plesiosaurs and zeuglodons. They pay as little attention as possible to reported sightings (usually though not always on land) of things that look like aquatic camels, enormous crocodiles, mutated hippopotamuses, great salamanders, or — in one instance — a giant frog. Confronted with such reports, most of them related by individuals seemingly no less sane or sincere than those whose accounts of encounters with less exotic specimens are revered by Ness proponents, cryptozoologists resort to the same desperate rationalizations they complain about in their critics. Even the usually sensible Roy P. Mackal dismissed one bizarre land sighting as an encounter with what he speculated was a "congenitally deformed specimen of the highland cattle common in the area."

Scientific proponents of the Northwest's Bigfoot/Sasquatch rarely discuss or even acknowledge hairy-biped reports in Eastern and Midwestern states and provinces. The presence of such creatures in these places cannot be defended on biological or logical grounds. Even worse, some aspects of their appearance verge on the apparitional, and a few instances hint at an association with UFOs. A growing number of wildlife biologists believe, not unreasonably, that cougars, once thought extinct everywhere east of the Mississippi River except in the Florida Everglades, have reestablished a foothold in the Northeastern wilds. They do not know what to do with the many hundreds, possibly thousands, of reports of "black panthers" and comparably anomalous felines (including maned African lions) all across the continent.

Accepting Ambiguity

Not uncommonly, in other words, what is thought of as a single anomalous phenomenon may be two phenomena, one merely fantastic, the other utterly incredible. One seems potentially explainable, more or less, by current (or near-future) science; the other is absurd or inexplicable, or both. This peculiar duality is apparent even in such relatively sedate manifestations of nature as ball lightning. Small luminous spheres which in other contexts would be labeled ball lightning demonstrate, in the testimonies of not a few witnesses, a bewildering purposefulness and intelligence. In his *Deviant Science* (1984) sociologist of science James McClenon recounts an interview with a man who swore he had seen a small ball of light enter his bedroom after the closed window magically rose. After sailing about the house, it departed via the front door, which obligingly opened to permit it to escape.

What all this means is, of course, impossible to say, though we can be assured that this small consideration will stop no committed debunker or true believer from saying it anyway. The temptations to reductionism (the witness was dreaming it) or occultism (it was a paranormal being from the etheric realm) are hard to resist. Again, human nature abhors an explanatory vacuum. Real understanding, on the other hand, demands intellectual modesty and patience, not to mention a huge tolerance for ambiguity. Where the most extreme sorts of claims — excepting those that are demonstrably bogus or otherwise suspect, naturally — are concerned, we are required neither to believe nor to disbelieve, and absolutely nothing calls for us to pursue explanations that defy reason and experience.

Common decency and common sense compel us to be courteous to witnesses and to hear them out. They, after all, were there; we weren't. If we can provide a reasonable nonextraordinary explanation for what they tell us they have seen, fine. If not, we need not insult them by reinventing their sightings so as to trivialize them into crude misperceptions of ordinary phenomena. We need not ridicule them or call them, without evidence to the effect, liars. Yet the sincerest testimony to the most bizarre event or entity, even if we deem it accurately rendered, is not enough to remake the world on its own, in the absence of other, more compelling evidence. Of sightings of merfolk, fairies, hairy bipeds, aquatic camels, Mothman, thunderbirds, and the rest, all we can say is that these comprise some people's experience of the world.

Science will explain what it can explain, and the more science learns, the more it will be able to explain. If there are large, uncatalogued animals living in the earth's oceans and lakes, if *Gigantopithecus* lives on in the Northwestern wilderness, if extraterrestrial visitors are streaking through the earth's air space, or if sauropods and thylacines are not really extinct, we will know about them, once we bring the appropriate attention and resources to a serious effort to answer these questions. Presumably the answers will come in the form of actual specimens.

But where high-strangeness anomalous claims are concerned, probably no amount of funding and expertise will do much more than produce still more sighting reports. Funding will permit analyses of the few (often literal) threads of physical evidence (hairy-biped hair, for example), with results that will either disappoint (it was dog hair) or frustrate (sort of like dog hair but also sort of like human hair, yet not quite either). Psychologists who are participating in the investigation will develop psychological profiles of the witnesses and will find their subjects to be essentially indistinguishable from nonwitnesses. To wit: ordinary people reporting extraordinary experiences — something we already knew. In other words, the end of the investigation takes us back to its beginning. Present knowledge is an unhelpful guide through the thickets of extreme anomalous experience.

That makes such experience no less interesting, of course. The contrary, in fact. Whether taken as wonderfully strange stories, the makings of a future science, or intimations of hidden dimensions of matter or spirit, these accounts tell us, at the least, that the possibilities of experience are far more various than we are led to believe. No amount of rationalization can alter the simple truth that — whatever their ultimate nature — all sorts of incredibly odd things can be experienced. If that fact does nothing else, it should alert us to the folly of ridicule. After all, if sane and sincere Joe Smith can encounter something weird, presumably so can you and I. (Perhaps you already have.) If it happened to us, we would expect a courteous reception and be outraged if we got anything else — as we almost certainly would.

"Weird Stuff Happens"
In this book about weird stuff that happens to people, we hear the witnesses out. And why not? All other approaches, after all, have proven unhelpful and have done nothing but conceal, thinly, our ignorance. A radically objective approach which respects the testimony that deserves respect, even when it speaks of the incredible, is all that is left to us. This testimony may or may not tell us extraordinary truths about the world, but it does tell us something about the peculiar things people can experience in the world.

The causes, not the occurrences, ought ultimately to comprise the focus of investigations and debates. It seems futile by now to argue that all anomalous experiences must have demonstrable conventional causes; yet it is also unwise to extrapolate too broadly from such experiences — which may not mean at all what they appear to mean — to invent, with no other justification than a witness's account, an extraordinary phenomenological context in which the reported phenomenon is said to make sense. What we experience anomalously may not "exist" in the literal sense in which that verb is customarily used.

Anomalies of the highest strangeness dwell in a twilight zone of ambiguity. To say that you have "seen" one is not necessarily to say that the anomaly lives on in the world when it is not briefly occupying your vision and scaring the daylights out of you. We may experience unbelievable things, but our experiences of them may tell us nothing about them except that they can be experienced. You can "see" a mermaid or a werewolf, but however impressive the experience may be to you, the rest of us cannot infer from that that mermaids and werewolves are "real." In fact, we can be certain that they are not. And that is all we can be certain of, because all we have done here is to remove one explanation (that mermaids and werewolves live in the world) from consideration while failing to put another in its place.

Here at the fringes of reason and experience, we can only marvel at how little we understand about some kinds of human experiences. Whether their causes, when at last understood, turn out to be profound or trivial, these experiences are undeniably strange. Just as undeniably, they remind us what a mystery this world is, and what mysteries we ourselves are.

Jerome Clark
Minnesota
January 1993

WORDS OF APPRECIATION ————————————

I would like to thank these individuals for their kindness and consideration, which had much to do with making this book possible: Henry H.
Bauer, Janet Bord, William R. Corliss, George M. Eberhart, Lucius Farish, J.
Richard Greenwell, Roy P. Mackal, Mark Rodeghier, Don Schmitt, Gordon
Stein, and Marcello Truzzi. Special thanks to J. Gordon Melton, who suggested the idea to me and helped get the project started; to Dennis Stacy,
who wrote the entry on crop circles; to Rebecca Nelson, my editor, who
somehow kept her cool through it all; and to my wife Nancy, for all kinds
of reasons.

AIRSHIPS, UNIDENTIFIED

The first known printed reference to a mysterious "airship" was in the March 29, 1880, issue of the *Santa Fe Weekly New Mexican*. The newspaper reported that late on the evening of the twenty-sixth, observers in the village of Galisteo Junction had observed the passage of a "large balloon" and heard the merry shouts of its passengers. From the craft were dropped a cup of "very peculiar workmanship" and a "magnificent flower, with a slip of exceedingly fine silk-like paper, on which were some characters resembling those on Japanese tea chests." The next evening a Chinese-American visitor said he recognized the paper as a message from his girlfriend, a passenger on the ship, which he said was on its way to New York City.

Like many other airship tales reported in the late-nineteenth-century American press, this one is almost certainly wholly fictional, but in the years ahead more credible reports would be made in the United States and other countries. Though American papers in particular tended to treat such sightings as jokes — and were themselves responsible for many hoaxes — there seems no doubt that such "airships," had they been seen in the later decades of the twentieth century, would have passed as unidentified flying objects. In fact, sightings of airshiplike objects — cigar-shaped objects with multicolored lights along the sides and flashing searchlights — continue to the present.

An outbreak of airship reports occurred along the border of Germany and Russian Poland in early 1892. As would be the case with later airship scares, the Germans were thought to have developed advanced aircraft which could fly against the wind (unlike balloons) and hover for extended periods of time. No such aircraft existed at the time, nor had any been developed (despite numerous contemporary rumors to the contrary) by 1896, when the great American airship scare erupted in California.

Beginning in mid-November, numerous witnesses in both urban and rural portions of the state reported seeing fast-moving or stationary nocturnal

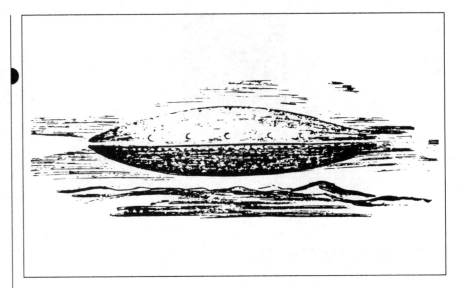

lights assumed to be connected to airships. Daylight sightings typically were of a device which "somewhat resembled a balloon traveling end on … and with what appeared to be wings both before and behind the [bottom] light," as the *San Francisco Call* of November 22 put it, or of a "great black cigar with a fishlike tail … at least 100 feet long" with a surface which "looked as if it were made of aluminum," as the *Oakland Tribune* of December 1 had it. In some cases, observers reported seeing propellers.

All the while much press attention was paid to the claims of San Francisco attorney George D. Collins, who swore on his "word of honor" (though he later denied it) that he not only represented the airship inventor but had seen the marvelous invention himself. The inventor was rumored to be one E. H. Benjamin, a dentist and Maine native who was known to be a habit-ual tinkerer. Benjamin told a *Call* reporter that his "inventions have to do with dentistry," but harassed by those who suspected he was not telling the entire truth, he went into hiding. Reporters who broke into his office found nothing but copper dental fillings.

By November 24, according to an article in the *Oakland Tribune*, former California attorney general W.H.H. Hart had claimed the role of the inven-tor's legal representative, Collins having been fired for talking too much. Hart, however, was if anything more gabby. He said two airships existed — the second had been built in an Eastern state — and his job was to "consolidate both interests." The airships would be used to bomb the Spanish fort in Havana, Cuba. Subsequently Hart, like Collins before him, did some backtracking and soon conceded he had not personally seen the invention, only met someone "who claims to be the inventor."

The California airship scare receded the following month. In February 1897 Nebraska newspapers began noting reports from rural districts of nocturnal lights moving at "most remarkable speed." On the fourth, wit-

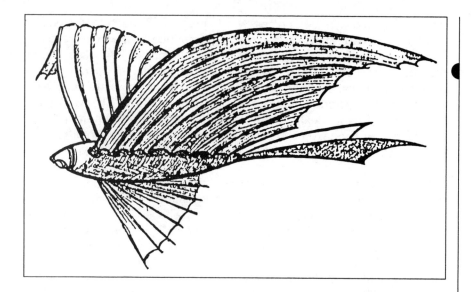

nesses at Inavale got a close-up view of the object to which the lights were attached. It was cone-shaped, 30 to 40 feet long, and had "two sets of wings on a side, with a large fan-shaped rudder" (*Omaha Daily Bee*, February 6). Over the following weeks a wave of sightings struck Nebraska and then neighboring Kansas. By early April airships were moving east, north, and south, and all that month's newspaper columns would be full of sightings, rumors, and tall tales.

Many of the dubious stories focused, as they had in California, on allegations about secret inventors. Some press accounts even alleged that airships had landed and their occupants, ordinary Americans, had confided their identities and plans to witnesses. The "conversations" with these aeronauts were recounted verbatim in newspaper stories, usually though not invariably presented as serious news but always invented out of whole cloth.

Other hoaxes reflected an undercurrent of speculation about extraterrestrial visitors. A Le Roy, Kansas, rancher swore in an affidavit that he, his son, and his hired man had seen strange-looking beings in an airship lasso and steal a calf from a corral outside his house. Though the tale attracted wide publicity (and was rediscovered and widely published in the UFO literature of the 1960s), it turned out to be a prank played by the rancher and fellow members of a local liars' club. At Aurora in north Texas an airship crashed, and its sole occupant, a Martian, was buried in the local cemetery, or so reported the *Dallas Morning News* of April 19. This tale, invented by an Aurora man as a joke, was rediscovered in the 1960s and 1970s and brought spade-bearing searchers to the tiny, fading village.

Amid all the hoaxes, however, were apparently authentic reports of cigar-shaped structures with or without wings as well as sightings of nocturnal lights variously described as pear-, egg-, ball-, or V-shaped — suggesting that beneath all the hoopla and silliness the first great modern UFO wave,

3

with the full variety of UFO types, was in progress. Though by the end of May the wave had run its course, sightings continued without interruption into the next century. For example, in the summer of 1900 two young Reedsburg, Wisconsin, men saw an enormous dirigible-shaped structure hovering in the night sky. As it passed over a grove of trees, the trees bent as if blown by a strong wind, though the night was still. The March 15, 1901, issue of New Mexico's *Silver City Enterprise* even reported that a local physician had taken a clear photograph of an airship. Unfortunately the photograph has not survived.

In 1909 a worldwide wave of airship sightings occurred in Great Britain, the United States, New Zealand, and Australia. In Britain the sightings, which began in March, were mostly of torpedo-shaped vessels moving at a "tremendous pace" and flashing lights and searchlights; they revived fears, first expressed 15 years earlier in eastern Europe and still unfounded, of high-flying German spies. In America secret inventors were the suspects, with most of the speculation directed toward a Worcester, Massachusetts, man named Wallace E. Tillinghast, though there was no real reason, then or now, to link him with the objects New Englanders and others were reporting. The New Zealand wave began in July at the southern end of the South Island, then moved northward. As with other airship scares, some witnesses claimed to have seen humanlike figures in passing craft. In one instance, said to have taken place on August 3, a Waipawa man said an airship occupant had shouted at him in an unknown language, and in another, "missiles" were fired from an airship and hit the water. The witness, a man in a boat, thought he was being attacked. Australia experienced a handful of sightings in August.

Another airship wave erupted in the fall of 1912, and reports were made all across Europe. The objects were typically described as large and cigar-shaped, with brilliant searchlights. Few if any reports mention wings. As before, the airships reportedly were capable of hovering and moving at great speeds, even against the wind. The wave had run its course by April, but the sightings continued periodically in Europe and elsewhere. On October 10, 1914, for example, a Manchester, England, man said he saw an "absolutely black, spindle-shaped object" cross the face of the sun. A cigar-shaped object at least 100 feet long flew over Rich Field, Waco, Texas, one evening in early 1918, leaving witnesses with, in the words of one, "the weirdest feeling of our lives." In the summer of 1927 an airship which one observer compared (as had some in 1896 and 1897) to a "perfectly shaped, huge fish, with big fins extended outward near the front and small, short ones near the rear," was seen over Wolfe County, Kentucky.

Though after the 1920s unidentified cigar-shaped objects were seldom called "airships," they continued to be reported. On October 9, 1946, observers in San Diego, California, saw an airshiplike object which they compared to a "huge bat with wings." A similar object was seen over Havana, Cuba, the following February. A Pittsburg, Kansas, radio musician driving to work at 5:50 A.M. on August 25, 1952, said he came upon a 75-foot-long object with windows, through which the head and shoulders of a

● SOURCES:

Bullard, Thomas E., ed. *The Airship File: A Collection of Texts Concerning Phantom Airships and Other UFOs, Gathered from Newspapers and Periodicals Mostly During the Hundred Years Prior to Kenneth Arnold's Sighting.* Bloomington, IN: The Author, 1982.

Chariton, Wallace O. *The Great Texas Airship Mystery.* Plano, TX: Wordware Publishing, 1991.

Clark, Jerome. *The Emergence of a Phenomenon: UFOs from the Beginning Through 1959 — The UFO Encyclopedia, Volume 2.* Detroit, MI: Omnigraphics, 1992.

Cohen, Daniel. *The Great Airship Mystery: A UFO of the 1890s.* New York: Dodd, Mead and Company, 1981.

Fort, Charles. *The Books of Charles Fort.* New York: Henry Holt and Company, 1941.

Gross, Loren E. *The UFO Wave of 1896.* Fremont, CA: The Author, 1974.

———. *Charles Fort, the Fortean Society, and Unidentified Flying Objects.* Fremont, CA: The Author, 1976.

4

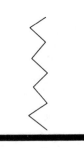

human figure were visible. Along the UFO's outer edges, according to investigators from the Air Force's Project Blue Book, "were a series of propellers about six inches to eight inches in diameter, spaced closely together." Driving between Deming and Las Cruces, New Mexico, on the morning of February 6, 1967, Ruth Ford sighted two fast-moving "cigar-shaped craft," each with two small propellers on it and a row of windows. She could see no one inside.

Lore, Gordon I. R., Jr., and Harold H. Deneault, Jr. *Mysteries of the Skies: UFOs in Perspective*. Englewood Cliffs, NJ: Prentice-Hall, 1968.

Menzel, Donald H. *Flying Saucers*. Cambridge, MA: Harvard University Press, 1953.

Shoemaker, Michael T. "UFO Saboteurs." *Fate* 38,12 (December 1985): 59–64.

Watson, Nigel. "Phantom Airships Over Britain in 1909, and Their Impact on Society." *Common Ground* 3 (November 1981): 18–23.

Watson, Nigel, Granville Oldroyd, and David Clarke. *The 1912–1913 British Phantom Airship Scare*. Althorpe, South Humberside, England: The Authors, n.d.

Welsch, Roger L. "'This Mysterious Light Called an Airship.' Nebraska 'Saucer' Sightings, 1897." *Nebraska History* 60,1 (Spring 1979): 92–113.

Whalen, Dwight. "Phantom Fliers." *Fate* 36,9 (September 1983): 89–93.

5

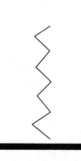

ALLIGATORS IN SEWERS ————————————————

A popular modern American urban legend has it that alligators dwell in the New York sewer system. They got there, it is said, when baby alligators purchased as pets grew too big for their owners' comfort and were dispatched down toilets. The animals reportedly survived under the city and became so large as to threaten the well-being of sewer workers. However, New York City officials deny that any such creatures currently exist.

Though the rumor was circulated most widely in the 1960s, its origins are in a forgotten series of events in the 1930s. The first of them took place on June 28, 1932, when "swarms" of alligators were seen in the Bronx River. A three-foot-long specimen was found dead along its banks. In March 1935 and June 1937 both live and dead alligators were recovered.

The most remarkable of these incidents was chronicled in the February 10, 1935 issue of the *New York Times.* Several teenage boys were shoveling snow into an open manhole near the Harlem River when they spotted something moving in the icy water 10 feet down. It turned out to be an alligator trying to free itself. The boys retrieved a rope, fashioned it into a lasso, and pulled the animal to the surface, but when one of them tried to take the rope off its neck, the alligator snapped at him. In response the young men beat it to death with their shovels.

The boys dragged the body to a nearby auto repair shop, where it was determined that the animal weighed 125 pounds and was seven and a half feet long. Later the police were notified, and a city Department of Sanitation employee drove the remains off to be incinerated.

Around that time Teddy May, New York City's superintendent of sewers, was receiving complaints about alligators. At first he thought they were the result of alcohol consumption on the job, and he even hired investigators to check on the drinking habits of his employees. When the investigators came up empty-handed, May himself went into the sewers with a flash-light, which soon enough revealed the presence of alligators. A shaken May subsequently had the animals killed by poison or gunshot.

It is not known how the animals got there, though it is generally assumed (as the folk explanation indicates) that they were abandoned or escaped pets. It is also true that alligators and crocodiles have a way of showing up in the most unexpected places. Between 1843 and 1983, according to anomalist Loren Coleman, no fewer than 84 such animals were seen or recovered dead or alive all across the United States and Canada. Coleman writes, "Pet escapee explanations cannot deal adequately with these accounts of alligators in northern waters — when it is caimans [Central or South American crocodilians similar to alligators but often superficially resembling crocodiles] that are being sold as pets."

● SOURCES:

"Alligator Found in Uptown Sewer." New York Times (February 10, 1935).

Coleman, Loren. Mysterious America. Boston, MA: Faber and Faber, 1983.

———. "Erratic Crocodilians and Other Things." INFO Journal 3, 4 (February 1974): 12–18.

———. "Alligators-in-the-Sewers: A Journalistic Origin." Journal of American Folklore 92, 365 (July/September 1979): 335–38.

Corliss, William R., ed. Strange Life: A Sourcebook on the Mysteries of Organic Nature, Volume B-1. Glen Arm, MD: The Sourcebook Project, 1976.

Michell, John, and Robert J. M. Rickard. Living Wonders: Mysteries and Curiosities of the Animal World. London: Thames and Hudson, 1982.

ALMAS ——————————————————————————————

In the Mongolian language Almas means "wildman." These strange creatures, half human, half ape, are reputed to dwell in the Altai mountains in western Mongolia and in the Tien Shan mountains of neighboring Sinkiang in the People's Republic of China. Related Eurasian traditions of wildmen, such as those reported in the Caucasus Mountains between the Black and Caspian Seas, are dealt with elsewhere in this book.

The earliest known printed reference to Almases is in a journal written by Bavarian nobleman Hans Schiltberger. In the 1420s, he traveled through the Tien Shan range as a prisoner of the Mongols. "In the mountains themselves live wild people, who have nothing in common with other human beings," he recorded. "A pelt covers the entire body of these creatures. Only the hands and face are free of hair. They run around in the hills like animals and eat foliage and grass and whatever else they can find." Schiltberger saw two of them himself, a man and a woman whom a local warlord had captured and given as presents to the Bavarian's captors.

A late-eighteenth-century Mongolian manuscript on natural history contains a drawing of a wildman. The caption, in the Tibetan, Chinese, and Mongolian languages, identifies the figure as a "man-animal." All of the other illustrations in the book are of undeniably real animals, indicating that the Almas was not viewed as a supernatural being. In fact, Almases are not an element of the otherworldly folklore of the Mongolian people; they are considered ordinary creatures of flesh and blood.

Prof. Tsyben Zhamtsarano conducted the first systematic scientific study of Almases, collecting reports mostly from nomads and others in the remote regions where the creatures — adults and children — were said to live. He plotted the sightings on maps and brought an artist with him on his field trips to interview witnesses. Unfortunately, while living in Leningrad in the 1930s, Zhamtsarano fell victim to the Stalinist terror (he was deemed a "bourgeois nationalist" for his interest in Mongolian folklore) and died in prison about 1940. The records of his Almas research have been lost.

Nonetheless, one of his associates, Dordji Meiren, has testified that their information indicates Almas sightings decreased significantly in number in the later decades of the nineteenth century. The Almases apparently largely disappeared from southern Outer Mongolia and Inner Mongolia (south of Outer Mongolia), perhaps suggesting that they were migrating westward to escape from encroaching civilization. Another early researcher, anatomist V. A. Khakhlov, submitted findings from his Almas studies to the Russian Imperial Academy of Sciences in 1913. These, too, seem no longer to exist.

In 1936 M. K. Rosenfeld's *The Ravine of the Almases* incorporated the creatures into the plot of an otherwise routine adventure novel. Rosenfeld had heard of the creatures during a trip across Mongolia in the 1920s. By this time another Mongolian scholar, Y. Rinchen, was conducting his own research, and in the 1950s, in the wake of renewed interest in the Himalayas's yeti ("abominable snowman"), the Soviet Academy of Sciences established a Commission for the Study of the Snowman Question. The commission's principal figure, Boris Porschnev (who later wrote a book dealing in part with Almases), encouraged Rinchen to publish some of his material. Rinchen concluded, as had his predecessors, that the Almas population was shrinking and retreating. Since then other Russian and Mongolian scholars have published Almas accounts gleaned from eyewitness accounts and literary sources.

Zhamtsarano's associate Meiren claimed to have seen an Almas skin being used as a ritual carpet in a Buddhist monastery in the southern Gobi region of Mongolia. The creature had been skinned by a straight cut down the spine, so its features were preserved. The body had red, curly hair and there was long hair on the head, but the face was hairless except for eyebrows. The nails at the ends of the toes and fingers were essentially human in appearance.

Adult Almases have been described as five feet or slightly taller, hairy, and shy, with prominent eyebrow ridges, a receding chin, and a jaw that juts out. They subsist on small mammals and wild plants and use simple tools, but have no language. According to British anthropologist Myra Shackley, their "very simple lifestyle and the nature of their appearance suggests strongly that Almas[es] might represent the survival of a prehistoric way of life, and perhaps even of an earlier form of man. The best candidate is undoubtedly Neanderthal man."*

Another British anthropologist, Chris Stringer, while remaining open-minded on the question of the Almases' existence, disputes this conclusion. He notes reports that "include mentions of bent knees, an unusual gait, turned-in feet (with six toes in one case), long arms, forearms, hands and fingers, small flat noses, 'Mongolian' cheekbones, and a lack of language, culture, meat-eating and fire. None of these readily matches accepted ideas about the Neanderthals."

● SOURCES:

Bord, Janet, and Colin Bord. *The Evidence for Bigfoot and Other Man-Beasts.* Wellingborough, Northamptonshire, England: The Aquarian Press, 1984.

Heaney, Michael. "The Mongolian Almas: A Historical Reevaluation of the Sighting by Baradiin." *Cryptozoology* 2 (1983): 40–52.

Sanderson, Ivan T. *Abominable Snowmen: Legend Come to Life.* Philadelphia, PA: Chilton Book Company, 1961.

Shackley, Myra. *Still Living?: Yeti, Sasquatch and the Neanderthal Enigma.* New York: Thames and London, 1983.

Stringer, Chris. "Wanted: One Wildman, Dead or Alive." *New Scientist* (August 11, 1983): 422.

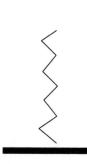

AREA 51

Area 51 is located at a corner of the Nevada Test Site, where highly classified national-security projects have been developed for several decades, including spy planes such as the U-2 and the SR-71, the Stealth aircraft, and the technology associated with the Strategic Defense Initiative (popularly known as "Star Wars").

In recent years many observers have reported seeing odd lights maneuvering in ways conventional aircraft do not and cannot: flying at great speeds, stopping abruptly, and hovering for periods of time. The early sightings were almost all at night, but in a few instances witnesses saw the objects reflected in the moonlight and were able to determine that they resembled huge triangles. In May 1990 daytime observers reported a craft of the same peculiar appearance. According to an article in the October 1, 1990, issue of *Aviation Week & Space Technology*, the triangles had "been spotted recently over the northern end of the Antelope Valley, near Edwards AFB and Mojave, California, as well as in central Nevada." The author of the article, *Aviation Week* editor John D. Morrocco, remarked that to all indications a "quantum leap in aviation," even beyond the Stealth technology, apparently had taken place, under conditions of great secrecy.

When interviewed on National Public Radio, Morrocco was asked what he thought of similar sightings (including films and radar trackings) of giant triangles over Belgium and other European countries. The Nevada/California sightings were "different than [sic] that," he insisted; the others were "mere sightings of UFOs."

Nonetheless, to at least some persons the two series of events were linked. What connected them was the belief that the technology that created the remarkable new aircraft was of unearthly origin. The breakthrough had emerged from studies of crashed extraterrestrial spacecraft which were stored at Area 51 of the Nevada Test Site. Such rumors are so rampant that scarcely a magazine or newspaper article on the site has failed to mention them. For example, an article in the *Las Vegas-Review Journal* had noted rumors that the "remains of an alien spacecraft are stored" there. Aviation writer James C. Goodall, who investigated the stories, wrote, "Rumor has it that some of these systems involve force field technology, gravity drive systems, and 'flying saucer' designs. Rumor further has it that these designs are not necessarily of Earth human origin, but of who might have designed them or helped us do it, there is less talk."

Other writers and researchers have interviewed persons who tell of secret projects based on extraterrestrial technology, but none of these informants has offered proof of his allegations. The one who attracted the most attention was Robert Scott Lazar, who in November 1989 appeared on a Las Vegas television news show. Lazar claimed that while working at Area 51 he became aware that the advanced propulsion systems under development there involved a nearly unimaginable technology, powered by what he described as an "anti-gravity reactor." He also said he had seen the crashed UFOs from which these technological secrets had been gleaned. According to Lazar, not even Congress knew anything about the project and it was unlikely it would ever be announced to the American people.

These revelations caused a stir for a short period, but information uncovered during follow-up investigations cast serious doubt on Lazar's credibility. His claims about his education and employment could not be verified, and he turned out to be a man of questionable character. In 1990 he was arrested for his involvement with a Nevada brothel.

Nonetheless, the rumors persist. They have given rise to a bizarre science-fictional folklore of government-extraterrestrial contacts, including a treaty in which aliens have provided the American government with their technology in exchange for permission to abduct citizens. Some tellers of such tales have added even more fantastic, conspiratorial speculations to this already unlikely scenario, claiming, for example, that a secret government run by the Central Intelligence Agency (CIA) and "international bankers" in alliance with evil aliens controls the world and already has established slave colonies on the moon and Mars.

● SOURCES:

Cameron, Grant R., T. Scott Crain, and Chris Rutkowski. "In the Land of Dreams." *International UFO Reporter* 15,5 (September/October 1990): 4–8.

Cooper, Milton William. *The Secret Government: The Origin, Identity, and Purpose of MJ-12*. Fullerton, CA: The Author, May 23, 1989.

Ecker, Don. "The Saucers and the Scientist." *UFO* 5,6 (November/December 1990): 16–19,40.

————. "Tales of the Bizarre." *UFO* 6,1 (January/February 1991): 7–8.

Good, Timothy. *Alien Liaison — The Ultimate Secret*. London: Random Century, 1991.

Howe, Linda Moulton. *An Alien Harvest: Further Evidence Linking Animal Mutilations and Human Abductions to Alien Life Forms*. Littleton, CO: Linda Moulton Howe Productions, 1989.

"Multiple Sightings of Secret Aircraft Hint at New Propulsion, Airframe Designs." *Aviation Week & Space Technology* (October 1, 1990): 22–23.

ATMOSPHERIC LIFE FORMS ────────────────

A once-popular theory held that unidentified flying objects were neither delusions nor spacecraft but "space animals" — life forms existing in the upper atmosphere. The idea was even entertained for a time by individuals in the Air Force's first UFO project, Sign, after it was suggested to them by John Philip Bessor, a Pennsylvania man interested in psychic phenomena. Bessor thought flying saucers were "of a highly attenuated (ectoplasmic?) substance, capable of materialization and dematerialization, whose propellant is a form of telekinetic energy." He even suspected these creatures were eating people; as evidence he pointed to reported falls from the sky of flesh and blood.

Bessor, however, was not the first to engage in speculation of this sort. In a science-fiction story published in the November 1913 issue of *The Strand*, Sir Arthur Conan Doyle imagined "The Horror of the Heights," atmospheric monsters which attacked and killed pilots. In a nonfiction context Charles Fort took note of reports of "unknown, luminous things" seen in the sky which may describe "living things that occasionally come from somewhere else."

In later years space animals were championed by no less than Kenneth Arnold, the pilot whose June 24, 1947, sighting over Mount Rainier, Washington, marked the beginning of the UFO age. In Arnold's view, expressed in a 1959 interview with a *Denver Post* reporter, UFOs are "living organisms ... in the atmosphere.... [T]hey have the power to change their density and appearance." Other champions of space animals were Countess Zoe Wassilko-Serecki, biologist Ivan T. Sanderson, and occultist/saucer contactee Trevor James Constable. Constable claimed to have photographed "critters," as he called them, using infrared film.

But if one rejected Constable's pictures as inconclusive, there was no compelling evidence, logical or material, for space animals. The closest thing to such evidence came in the form of a small number of reports in which witnesses reported seeing jellylike substances come out of the sky and plop in front of them.

One such incident occurred in Philadelphia on September 26, 1950, when two police officers saw what they thought was a UFO land in a field. When they and two other officers investigated, they found a six-foot-long gelatinous mass which evaporated within half an hour.

In Frisco, Texas, on the evening of August 10, 1979, a woman saw a bright light descend near a neighbor's house. The next morning the neighbor, Sybil Christian, found three purple blobs. One evaporated in the sunlight, and the other two were shipped off for analysis. After a cursory look the analysts claimed, in the face of the witnesses' protests, that the material was industrial waste, despite significant differences in appearance and consistency between the two substances.

● SOURCES:

Bessor, John Philip. "Are the Saucers Space Animals?" Fate 8,12 (December 1955): 6–12.

Constable, Trevor James. The Cosmic Pulse of Life: The Revolutionary Biological Power Behind UFOs. Santa Ana, CA: Merlin Press, 1976.

Gaddis, Vincent H. Mysterious Fires and Lights. New York: Dell, 1978.

Sanderson, Ivan T. Uninvited Visitors: A Biologist Looks at UFOs. New York: Cowles, 1967.

Schultz, Ted. "Blobs from Space?" Fate 34,12 (December 1981): 85–90, 92.

Wassilko-Serecki, Zoe. "Startling Theory on UFOs." American Astrology 23 (September 1955): 2–5.

"Who 'Discovered' Space Animals?" CSI News Letter 10 (December 15, 1957): 31.

BALL LIGHTNING ——————————————————

Moments after hearing a sound like a thunderclap, a Parisian man reportedly witnessed an extraordinary sight: a fireball the size of a human head emerging from the fireplace in his fourth-story Paris apartment. It pushed aside the frame covering and darted toward him "like a cat." He hastily withdrew his feet, and the ball moved to the center of the room. Though bright, it gave off no discernible heat. It ascended slightly, headed back to the fireplace, and rose up the chimney, exploding just before it escaped into the open air. It caused considerable damage to the chimney top.

This incident, which occurred on July 5, 1852, is one example of a strange and so far unexplained natural phenomenon, ball lightning, whose existence some scientists still dispute. The skeptics' objections are strikingly like those raised against reports of unidentified flying objects: the evidence is primarily anecdotal, most if not all of the photographs are open to question, and no conceivable scientific theory can make sense of the phenomenon.

The alternative (in other words, debunking) explanations also echo those voiced in the UFO debate. The "objects," the debunkers say, are either optical illusions — most likely visual afterimages formed by the observation of lightning strikes — or natural occurrences such as St. Elmo's Fire (a corona discharge from an object protruding above the ground during an electrical storm), misperceived or exaggerated. The former explanation requires witnesses possessed of breathtaking stupidity. The latter has the virtue of at least surface plausibility, but as James Dale Barry, a leading scientific authority on ball lightning, notes, "A characteristic distinction between St. Elmo's Fire and ball lightning is the apparently independent motion of the latter. Although St. Elmo's Fire has been observed to move about, it may move along a conductor, sometimes pulsating as it moves, but it does not free itself from the conductor. Thus, it does not exhibit the descending, hovering, or flying motions that are common to ball lightning."

The first investigator to describe ball lightning in the scientific literature was G. W. Richman, a Russian. Tragically and ironically, his interest led to his death. The incident took place in 1754 during a thunderstorm, when Richman was attempting to measure the energy of a lightning strike. As he stood behind his equipment, a small, blue, fist-sized sphere came out of the electrodes and floated toward his face. A moment later it exploded violently, killing him and knocking his assistant unconscious.

Fortunately, deaths related to ball-lightning manifestations are rare, but many observers have witnessed its destructive qualities. In Paris in July 1849, during an electric storm, a red ball hovered about 20 feet above a tree. Abruptly it caught fire, burned up, and burst open, freeing jagged streaks of lightning to shoot in all directions. One hit a nearby house and blew a cannon-sized hole in it. What remained of the ball started to spin and spark and then exploded with great force, knocking down three pedestrians.

At 6:30 P.M. on October 8, 1919, at a busy downtown intersection in Salina, Kansas, a "ball of fire as large as a washtub floating low in the air" struck the side of a building, ripped out bricks, and demolished a second-story window. It then exploded with a "bang that resembled the noise made by the discharge of a large pistol, filling the air with balls of fire as large as baseballs, which floated away in all directions," according to a *Monthly Weather Review* correspondent (October 1919 issue). "Some of these balls followed trolley and electric-light wires in a snaky sort of manner and some simply floated off through the air independently of any objects near by. An electric switch box across the street was ripped open and a transformer destroyed, leaving the east side of the town in darkness."

In the summer of 1960, as Louise Matthews of South Philadelphia, Pennsylvania, lay on her living room couch, she looked up to see a huge red ball coming through a window and the Venetian blinds, both closed and neither damaged in any way by the object's passage. When the ball, which was making a sizzling sound, passed by her, Mrs. Matthews felt a tingling on the back of her neck. She put her hand to the spot but felt nothing. The ball went through the living room and into the dining room, exiting — again without damage — through a closed window. She called her husband, who came home from work to find the back of her hand burned. The hair at the back of her head fell out, leaving the skin there as smooth as that in the front of her face.

During a violent early-evening thunderstorm on August 12, 1970, a "red ball of fire" appeared above Sidmouth, England, crackled for a few seconds, then exploded with a deafening roar. Jagged flashes of lightning shot from it toward the ground. At that moment 2,500 area television sets were cut off.

Ball lightning is not, of course, invariably harmful. It does not even always explode at the end of its manifestation. British scientist Alexander Russell saw ball lightning behaving both ways. He wrote in *Nature* (November 23, 1930):

> *Many years ago I saw two globes of lightning. They were reddish-yellow in color, and appeared to be rotating. One of them struck a building and burst with a loud report, causing the inhabitants to open the windows and look out to see what had happened, but as there was no trace of anything they looked bewildered. The other drifted slowly away. Globular lightning makes a slight noise as it drifts about. It has been compared with the purring of a cat.*

Theories.

Hard scientific data about ball lightning are rare — a major reason for some scientists' continuing doubts about the phenomenon's existence. Even Barry, a major proponent, acknowledges, "The unbiased examination of ball lightning reports leads one to conclude that a great percentage of the reports are highly questionable and could be interpreted in several ways." (Again, these words echo those that have been said of UFO reports.) Of the many photographs alleged to be of ball lightning, Barry believes that only three "are not obviously erroneous or highly suspect."

Much of the problem of explaining (as opposed to explaining away) the phenomenon has to do with the varying descriptions witnesses have given. The ball either explodes loudly or vanishes silently; it is white, orange, red, blue, or purple; it is small or it is large; it survives for a few seconds or a couple of minutes. "These may seem like trivial distinctions," science writer Gordon Stein observes, "but they cause theorists no end of difficulties. Explanations that will work for a ball of one second's duration, for example, cannot account for a 10-second ball." A ball that lasts one minute or more "requires an energy content so high that there is no known way for it to be formed."

Ball lightning also has the strange habit of penetrating the metal walls of in-flight aircraft. On March 19, 1963, R. C. Jennison, a professor of electrical energy, saw a ball-lightning globe first outside, then inside, an airliner he was taking from New York to Washington. An electrical storm was in progress. Of this report Stein notes, "Microwave, electric, radio or heat energy — all of these figure in the various theories — could not have gotten through the metal fuselage. We can also eliminate antimatter as a possible cause of ball lightning [an extraordinary hypothesis proposed by E.T.F. Ashby and C. Whitehead in *Nature*, March 19, 1971]. When antimatter (matter with exactly the opposite charges from those on normal matter on each of its subatomic particles) comes in contact with normal matter, both are annihilated.... Antimatter would have a difficult time getting through the body or window of an airplane without colliding with some regular matter, thus destroying itself."

If the evidence for ball lightning is almost all anecdotal and if it seems too bizarre for any so-far-imaginable physical theory to explain, why is it at least marginally acceptable to much of the scientific community when

● SOURCES:

Barry, James Dale. *Ball Lightning and Bead Lightning: Extreme Forms of Atmospheric Electricity.* New York: Plenum Press, 1980.

Constance, Arthur. *The Inexplicable Sky.* New York: The Citadel Press, 1957.

Corliss, William R., ed. *Strange Phenomena: A Sourcebook of Unusual Natural Phenomena, Volume G-1.* Glen Arm, MD: The Author, 1974.

———. *Strange Phenomena: A Sourcebook of Unusual Natural Phenomena, Volume G-2.* Glen Arm, MD: The Author, 1974.

Evans, Hilary, ed. *Frontiers of Reality: Where Science Meets the Paranormal.* Wellingborough, Northamptonshire, England: The Aquarian Press, 1989.

Fuller, Curtis. "I See by the Papers: Mysterious Burnings." *Fate* 13,11 (November 1960): 16, 18–19.

Gaddis, Vincent H. *Mysterious Fires and Lights.* New York: David McKay Company, 1967.

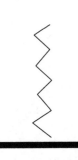

UFOs, the evidence for which shares many of the same problems, are not? If anything, the UFO evidence is better; no ball-lightning case is so well-documented as, for example, the January 1981 Trans-en-Province physical-trace case investigated by France's official UFO-investigative agency (discussed in the entry on unidentified flying objects).

The answer is not that no scientists have seen UFOs. In fact, many scientists, including some prominent ones, have seen UFOs, and some have acknowledged as much publicly. More likely, scientists see ball lightning as natural, even if deeply enigmatic, phenomena, whereas UFOs, if they exist, imply the operation of an alien intelligence in the earth's atmosphere — a prospect so incredible that it causes scientists, on some unconscious level, to see the ball-lightning evidence as a cup half full and the UFO evidence a cup half empty.

Gillmor, Daniel S., ed. *Scientific Study of Unidentified Flying Objects.* New York: Bantam Books, 1969.

Stein, Gordon. "Ball Lightning: The Impossible Enigma." *Fate* 41,10 (October 1988): 82–90.

17

BEAST OF EXMOOR ───────────────────────

The name "Beast of Exmoor" was coined in the spring of 1983, after a marauding animal killed a ewe belonging to Eric Ley of South Molton, Devonshire, England. In the next two and a half months Ley lost 100 of his sheep. The killer did not attack its prey at the hindquarters as would a dog or fox, but instead ripped out their throats.

The Beast of Exmoor is described by many people who say they have seen it as a huge, jet-black cat, eight feet long from nose to tail. Other witnesses — about one in five — report a tan- or fawn-colored pumalike feline. In a few instances two giant felines, one black and one tan, have been seen in each other's company. A smaller number of witnesses recount sightings of large animals which look like unusual dogs.

Sightings of the "Beast" go back at least to the early 1970s, but they made no impact on popular attention until the depredations occurred at the Ley farm. In early May Britain's Royal Marines descended on the area, and London's *Daily Express* offered a monetary reward of one thousand pounds. Marine sharpshooters hid in the hills, and some even said they saw a "black and powerful animal," but were unable to get a clear shot at it. The beast or beasts mostly lay low but as soon as the soldiers were withdrawn, the attacks started again.

One witness, local naturalist Trevor Beer, reported that he saw a beast in the summer of 1984 while watching birds in an area where deer carcasses had been found. "I saw the head and shoulders of a large animal appear out of the bushes," he wrote. "It looked black and rather otter-like, a first impression I shall always remember for the head was broad and sleek with small ears. The animal's eyes were clear greeny-yellow.... As it stared back at me I could clearly make out the thickish neck, the powerful looking forelegs and deep chest, and then without a sound it turned and moved swiftly away through the trees. That it was jet black I was sure, and long in the body and tail. I guessed at four and a half feet in body length, and about two feet at the shoulders."

Beer chased it to the edge of the woods. He recalled, "It ran like a greyhound, its forelegs pushing through the hind legs and they seeming to go forward in front of its round head as it raced away, then forcing back as the forelegs came forward to hit the ground together, a beautiful, very large black panther was my immediate thought."

In 1988 an area farmer reported he saw a "fantastic cat going at a hell of a speed. Every time it moved you could see the lights shine back across its ribs." Another time he saw a huge cat "jump a hedge, 15 feet from standing, with a fair-sized lamb in its mouth." Late one night in December 1991 a rural family watched a large pantherlike animal for some minutes as it prowled near their house. Several weeks earlier the son, 13, had seen it or a similar animal climbing a tree.

By now, a January 1992 article in London's *Daily Telegraph* said, a significant number of persons who live in the wild countryside of southwestern England allegedly have seen the beast or beasts.

Theories about the beasts range from misidentification (the cats are really dogs) to the paranormal (the creatures are intruders from another reality). The former view, once held by authority figures but hardly anyone else, has mostly been abandoned. The favorite conservative explanation is that witnesses have overestimated the sizes of the animals, which are domestic cats gone feral. Other theorists hold that a small breeding population of pumas, let loose by persons who once kept them as pets, populates England's wild West Country. A more extreme hypothesis, advanced by Di Francis but nearly universally rejected by zoologists, holds that large felines have secretly inhabited Britain since prehistoric times.

Complicating matters is the fact that giant cats have been reported all over the British Isles. Officially the only recognized nondomestic feline is *Felis silvestris grampia*, a small wild cat which lives in the rugged regions of northern England and Scotland.

● SOURCES:

"The Beast of Exmoor." *The ISC Newsletter* 2,3 (Fall 1983): 7–8.

Beer, Trevor. *The Beast of Exmoor: Fact or Legend?* Barnstaple, Devonshire, England: Countryside Productions, 1985.

Francis, Di. *Cat Country: The Quest for the British Big Cat.* North Pomfret, VT: David and Charles, 1983.

Martin, Andrew. "In the Grip of the Beast." London *Daily Telegraph* (January 4, 1992).

"Mystery Moggies." *Fortean Times* 59 (September 1991): 18–20.

Rickard, Bob. "The Exmoor Beast and Others." *Fortean Times* 40 (Summer 1983): 52–61.

———. "Out of Place: The Exmoor Beast, Continued." *Fortean Times* 42 (Autumn 1984): 40–41.

BEAST OF GEVAUDAN ————————————————

One day in June 1764, in a forest in Gevaudan, a region of southeastern France, a young woman tending cows looked up to see a hideous beast bearing down on her. The size of a cow or donkey, the creature resembled an enormous wolf. Her dogs fled, but the cattle drove the beast off with their horns. The woman would prove considerably more fortunate than most witnesses of what became known as the "Beast of Gevaudan."

Before long the mangled bodies of shepherd men, women, and — especially — children reportedly littered the landscape. The first victim apparently was a little girl who was found in July with her heart ripped from her body. The killings resumed in late August or early September, and soon the creature was fearlessly attacking groups of men. The terrified peasantry were certain that a *loup-garou* (a werewolf) was abroad in the land. These rumors gained credence when individuals who had shot or stabbed the creature reported that it seemed almost impervious to human weapons. On October 8, after two hunters pumped several rifle balls into it from a distance of 10 paces, the creature limped off. When word of the incident spread, it was believed, briefly, that the beast had gone off to die. But within a day or two it was killing again.

The *Paris Gazette* summarized witnesses' descriptions of the beast: It was "much higher than a wolf, low before, and his feet are armed with talons. His hair is reddish, his head large, and the muzzle of it is shaped like that of a greyhound; his ears are small and straight; his breast is wide and gray; his back streaked with black; his large mouth is provided with sharp teeth." On June 6, 1765, *St. James's Chronicle*, an English periodical, remarked "it appears that he is neither a Wolf, Tiger, nor Hyena, but probably a Mongrel, generated between the two last, and forming, as it were, a new Species."

After a frightening public attack on two children, who were bitten and torn even as older youths slashed at the creature with pitchforks and knives, an appeal was sent to the Royal Court at Versailles. King Louis XV dispatched a troop of light cavalry, under the direction of Capt. Duhamel, to the region. Duhamel ordered several of his men to dress as women, on the theory that the creature was especially attracted to females. The hunters spotted the beast a number of times and shot at it, but it always managed to escape. Finally, after the slaughter seemed to have ceased, Duhamel thought the beast had died of its wounds. After he and his dragoons departed, however, the killings resumed.

A large reward for the slaying of the beast then brought professional hunters and soldiers to the area. More than 100 wolves were killed, but the creature's rampage continued. Some hunters, including a professional wolf-tracker who had been sent personally by the king, reported that they had badly wounded the beast. But nothing seemed to stop it. During the summer of 1765 the massacre of children was especially fierce.

As the months dragged on, whole villages were abandoned after residents claimed they had seen the beast staring through their windows. Those who ventured out into the streets were attacked. Many peasants were too frightened to fire on the creature even when it presented an open target.

Events reached a climax in June 1767, when the Marquis d'Apcher, who lived in the western part of Gevaudan, brought together several hundred hunters and trackers who fanned out in smaller bands over the countryside. On the evening of the nineteenth, the beast charged members of one band. Jean Chastel, who had taken the precaution of loading his weapon with silver bullets on the assumption that the beast was a *loup-garou*, fired on it twice. The second shot hit it squarely in the heart and killed it. When the creature was gutted, the collar bone of a young girl was recovered from its stomach. By the time of its death, it had killed some 60 persons. The state had expended over 29,000 livres — a fortune for the period — in its effort to stop the beast.

After the monstrous carcass was paraded through the region for the next two weeks, it was packed up to be sent to Versailles. By that time the body had begun to putrefy, and before it got to the king's court, it was buried somewhere in the French countryside.

Though the story sounds like something out of a horror movie, there is no question that it happened. Many wildlife authorities believe reports of attacks on human beings by wolves (if the beast was indeed a wolf, as modern chroniclers assume) are sufficiently suspect that, as Roger A. Caras observes, "most can probably be discounted out of hand." Yet mythology and exaggeration notwithstanding, there are widespread and seemingly credible reports of rapacious wolves, especially in the days before firearms. In a study of the relationship of human-attacking wolf reports to werewolf legends, W.M.S. and Claire Russell write that "modern wolves have had many generations' experience of fire-arms, and are likely to be more cautious than their ancestors."

This is, on one level, an extraordinary event in the annals of animal behavior. On another, the sheer size of the creature pushes it into the realm of the cryptozoological. The episode raises many questions which, unfortunately, are unlikely to be answered over two centuries after its occurrence.

● SOURCES:

Caras, Roger A. *Dangerous to Man: The Definitive Story of Wildlife's Reputed Dangers*. New York: Holt, Rinehart and Winston, 1975.

Matheson, Colin. "The Grey Wolf." *Antiquity* 17 (1943): 11–18.

Pons, Gregory. "The Ravening Beast." *The Unexplained* 7, 84 (1982): 1678–80.

Rickard, R.J.M. "The 'Surrey Puma' and Friends: More Mystery Animals." *The News* 14 (January 1976): 3–8, 17, 24.

Rothovius, Andrew E. "Who or What Was the Beast of Le Gevaudan?" *Fate* 14,9 (September 1961): 32–37.

Russell, W.M.S., and Claire Russell. "The Social Biology of Werewolves." In J. R. Porter and W.M.S. Russell, eds. *Animals in Folklore*, 143–82. Totowa, NJ: Rowman and Littlefield, 1978.

BERMUDA TRIANGLE ——————————————

The genesis of the Bermuda Triangle legend is in an Associated Press dispatch of September 16, 1950, in which reporter E. V. W. Jones took note of what he characterized as mysterious disappearances of ships and planes between the Florida coast and Bermuda. Two years later, in an article in *Fate* magazine, George X. Sand recounted a "series of strange marine disappearances, each leaving no trace whatever, that have taken place in the past few years" in a "watery triangle bounded roughly by Florida, Bermuda and Puerto Rico."

M. K. Jessup picked up on some of the same stories in his 1955 book *The Case for the UFO*, which suggested that alien intelligences were responsible, a view echoed by Donald E. Keyhoe (*The Flying Saucer Conspiracy* [1955]) and Frank Edwards (*Stranger Than Science* [1959]). It took Vincent H. Gaddis to coin the catch-all phrase that would enter popular culture; his article in the February 1964 issue of *Argosy* (the following year incorporated into his book *Invisible Horizons*) was titled "The Deadly Bermuda Triangle." Soon nearly every popular book on "true mysteries" included sections on the Bermuda Triangle or, as some called it, the "Devil's triangle" or the "hoodoo sea." Ivan T. Sanderson, author of *Invisible Residents* (1970), cited it as evidence of an intelligent, technologically advanced underwater civilization which is responsible for, among other mysterious phenomena, UFOs.

The first book specifically on the subject was a self-published work by John Wallace Spencer, *Limbo of the Lost* (1969), which as a 1973 Bantam paperback found a huge readership. In 1970 a feature-film documentary, *The Devil's Triangle*, brought the subject a new, larger audience. The Bermuda Triangle fever peaked in 1974 with the publication of *The Bermuda Triangle*, a major bestseller (five million sales worldwide) written by Charles Berlitz with J. Manson Valentine. That year two paperbacks,

Richard Winer's *The Devil's Triangle* and John Wallace Spencer's *No Earthly Explanation*, also racked up impressive sales.

The articles and books on the subject betrayed little evidence of original research. Attentive readers could not help noticing that mostly the Triangle's chroniclers rewrote each other's work. In 1975 Larry Kusche, a librarian at Arizona State University, published a devastating debunking of what he called the "manufactured mystery." In the book, titled *The Bermuda Triangle Mystery — Solved*, he did the archival digging the other writers had neglected. Weather records, the reports of official investigating agencies, newspaper accounts, and other documents indicated that the Triangle literature had played fast and loose with the evidence. For example, calm seas in the literature turned into raging storms in reality; mysterious disappearances became conventionally caused sinkings and crashes; the remains of ships "never heard from again" turned out to have been found long since.

In an April 4, 1975, letter to Mary Margaret Fuller, editor of *Fate*, a spokesman for Lloyd's of London wrote, "According to Lloyd's Records, 428 vessels have been reported missing throughout the world since 1955, and it may interest you to know that our intelligence service can find no evidence to support the claim that the 'Bermuda Triangle' has more losses than elsewhere. This finding is upheld by the United States Coastguard [sic] whose computer-based records of casualties in the Atlantic go back to 1958."

If the Triangle's proponents had been able to mount any credible defense, the Triangle might have retained some claim to being an authentic anomaly. Instead there was virtual silence. An exchange in *Pursuit* between Berlitz and another Triangle critic, British writer Paul Begg, inspired little confidence in would-be believers. Berlitz's response to a long list of factual errors was to note that Kusche and Begg had not actually visited the Triangle and that Kusche had once asked him "whether *The New Yorker* was a New York newspaper."

Occasional reappearances in supermarket tabloids notwithstanding, the once-famous Bermuda Triangle survives for the most part as a footnote in the history of fads and passing sensations. In the mid-1970s another dubious "mystery," focused on allegedly enigmatic cattle mutilations, took its place in the popular imagination.

● SOURCES:

Begg, Paul. *Into Thin Air: People Who Disappear*. North Pomfret, VT: David and Charles, 1979.

Berlitz, Charles, with J. Manson Valentine. *The Bermuda Triangle*. Garden City, NY: Doubleday and Company, 1974.

———. *Without a Trace*. Garden City, NY: Doubleday and Company, 1977.

Gaddis, Vincent. *Invisible Horizons: True Mysteries of the Sea*. Philadelphia, PA: Chilton Books, 1965.

Kusche, Lawrence David. "The Bermuda Triangle and Other Hoaxes." *Fate* 28,10 (October 1975): 48–56.

———. *The Bermuda Triangle Mystery — Solved*. New York: Harper and Row, Publishers, 1975.

Sand, George X. "Sea Mystery at Our Back Door." *Fate* 5, 7 (October 1952): 11–17.

Sanderson, Ivan T. *Invisible Residents: A Disquisition Upon Certain Matters Maritime, and the Possibility of Intelligent Life Under the Waters of This Earth*. New York: World Publishing Company, 1970.

24

BIG BIRD

On January 1, 1976, Tracey Lawson, 11, and her cousin Jackie Davies, 14, were playing in Tracey's backyard five miles south of Harlingen in the Texas Rio Grande Valley. As they looked out on a plowed field beyond the yard, they noticed an unusual object standing some 100 yards away, near a borrow pit bordering an irrigation canal. Tracey went inside her house to get field glasses, through which she observed a "horrible-looking" black bird of extraordinary size: over five feet tall. Its wings were folded around its body, and the bird was staring at the girls through large, dark red eyes attached to a gray "gorillalike" face. Its head was bald, and it had a beak at least six inches long; it made a loud, shrill *eeeee* sound.

The bird, or whatever it was, was lost to view for a few moments, reappearing on the northeast corner of the property, its head poking above a small clump of trees. The girls fled inside and told Tracey's mother and father, who did not believe them.

But the next day Jackie's stepfather Tom Waldon found strange tracks: three-toed, eight inches across, square at the head, pressed an inch and a half into the hard ground. Tracey's father Stan Lawson, who weighed 170 pounds, found that he could not dent the ground with his own foot however hard he pressed down. He also noticed how oddly the family dog was behaving. It cowered inside the doghouse all day, leaving it only at suppertime, when it bolted into the house and had to be dragged out. That night Lawson thought he heard large wings scraping across the bedroom window, but whatever caused the sound, it left no trace of its passing.

An encounter with the same creature reportedly occurred on the evening of January 7, in nearby Brownsville, when Alverico Guajardo heard something hit his house trailer. Unnerved, he sneaked outside, got into his station wagon, and drove around to the south end of the trailer. His headlights caught "something from another planet." It was a huge bird, four feet tall, with black feathers, a long beak, and batlike wings. It had been lying on the ground when the lights hit it, but rose immediately. Its blazing red eyes, the size of silver dollars, focused on Guajardo, who for the next two or three minutes was literally paralyzed with fear. All the while a "horrible-sounding noise" emanated from its throat. Eventually the creature backed away and was lost in the darkness.

Exactly one week and two hours later, in the valley town of Raymondville, Armando Grimaldo sat smoking a cigarette in his mother-in-law's backyard when he said he heard a "sound like the flapping of batlike wings and a funny kind of whistling." As he got up to investigate, "I felt something grab me, something with big claws. I looked back and saw it and started running." "It" was a creature with a monkeylike face and leathery skin. It had large bright red eyes but no beak. Dashing for safety under a tree, he felt his pants, coat, and shirt being torn. The creature, breathing heavily, then flew off into the night.

These sightings, which the press humorously attributed to "Big Bird," after the *Sesame Street* character, were reported in valley and even national newspapers. As early as the previous November, however, rumors had circulated through Rio Grande City of the presence of a "man-bird" four feet tall, with a bird's body and a man's head. In San Benito, a small valley town inhabited almost entirely by Mexican Americans, residents had long believed in the existence of a large evil bird. According to one, it appeared at night, making a sound like "*tch-tch-tch*, with a whistle, very loud…. A lady around here was beaten by the bird. Another lady, she's dead now, saw it often through her window. Another woman said it has a cat face and no beak. The face is a foot in diameter, and it has a thick, foot-long neck. It has big eyes." One woman claimed to have been attacked from behind by a flying creature with enormous wings, black feathers, and no bill.

Theorists who sought conventional explanations pointed to great blue herons and pelicans as the likely cause of the scare, and some of the less impressive accounts were unquestionably of these familiar species. Nevertheless, if the witnesses to the better cases were telling the truth and, moreover, providing accurate descriptions of what they saw, the real Big Bird remains a real mystery.

● SOURCES:

Clark, Jerome, and Loren Coleman. *Creatures of the Outer Edge.* New York: Warner Books, 1978.

26

BIGFOOT

Bigfoot is unquestionably North America's biggest cryptozoological mystery. If its existence is ever proven — and nothing short of an actual specimen will satisfy most scientists — it would, at the very least, provide revolutionary insights into human evolution. If Bigfoot is there, it is almost certainly a relative of ours. In fact, Bigfoot proponents are divided on the question of whether it is an ape or a kind of early human being.

In what follows we define Bigfoot (or Sasquatch as it has traditionally been known in Canada) as the giant anthropoid reported in the northwestern United States (northern California, Oregon, Washington, and Idaho) and far western Canada (British Columbia and Alberta). In this vast region of mountains and forests, the idea that an undiscovered, extraordinary anthropoid could survive, undetected by all but the rare startled eyewitness, is at least conceivable — if still, of course, incredible. One can imagine, in other words, such creatures in the natural world.

It is necessary to say this because creatures of superficially similar appearance figure in reports in virtually every state and province of the continent. These are not imaginable in any conceivable natural world, and indeed many of the reports, with their intimations of the paranormal or at least of the zoologically nonsensical (three-toed tracks, for example), suggest phenomena not so much of nature as of the Goblin Universe. Though sometimes called "Bigfoot," these are not what we are concerned with here; these sorts of para-anthropoids are the subject of the entry hairy bipeds.

Bigfeet, according to their leading chronicler, Canadian journalist/investigator John Green, average — according to many hundreds of reports from eyewitness testimony — seven and a half feet in height. They are usually of solitary disposition and are seldom seen in the company of others. Hair covers almost all of their bodies, and their limbs are proportioned more like those people of than apes, though their broad shoulders, nonexistent necks, flat faces and noses, sloped foreheads, brow ridges, and cone-shaped heads are more characteristic of animals than of humans. They are omnivorous, largely nocturnal, and mostly inactive during cold weather.

Primatologist John Napier, one of the relatively few scientists to pay serious attention to the Bigfoot phenomenon, notes that in a number of the more credible reports the "Sasquatch is covered in reddish-brown or auburn hair.... Although auburn is the commonest overall color mentioned, black crops up, also beige, white and silvery-white.... Footprints range in size from 12 in.–22 in. In 66 percent of 33 reports the commonest quoted range is 14 in.–18 in., with a mode of 16 in.... [T]he most frequently reported width is 7 in."

The background.
If Bigfoot is a real animal or protohuman, it is not, it need hardly be said, a recent resident of the Northwestern wilderness. Thus students of the creature have sought evidence of its presence prior to the twentieth century — with ambiguous success.

In their attempt to give Bigfoot a long recorded history, Bigfoot proponents often cite American Indian traditions concerning oversized woodland bipeds, but usually such beliefs are taken out of context and selectively reported. The most popular proto-Bigfoot candidate is the Witiko (or Wendigo), known to the Algonkian Indians of the northern forests. Witikos were cannibalistic giants with supernatural powers, one of which was the ability to possess people and turn them into Witikos. Not surprisingly, much anthropological, as opposed to amateur Bigfootological, speculation on the roots of this belief focuses on psychiatric disorder. Comparable monsters loom large in a number of North American Indian mythologies; they warn members of the dangers of violating taboos and serve other, more complex functions within tribal society.

If Bigfoot lurks in here somewhere, its presence is fairly well disguised, though occasional details in otherwise nonresonant narratives (especially of the "Sasquatch," otherwise only generally identifiable with its modern counterpart) are intriguing. Most of the time, however, the woodland giants disqualify themselves from Bigfoot status either by being too aggressive and (often) cannibalistic or, conversely, by being too civilized and intelligent.

Trying to extract a tiny truth from a vast mythological fabric is a hopeless exercise. More productively, we can turn to early published reports which, first possibly and later certainly, refer to Bigfoot. In 1870 a correspondent to a California newspaper, the *Antioch Ledger*, reported that the year before, he had seen a "gorilla, or wild man, or whatever you choose to call it," in the bush. Its head, he wrote, "appeared to be set on [the creature's] shoulders without a neck" — a detail echoed by virtually every modern witness. On the other hand, the correspondent mentioned a decidedly uncharacteristic anatomical feature: "very short legs." If this animal existed outside the writer's imagination, it may well have been a (presumably escaped) gorilla; it could also have been a chimpanzee.

The next known contemporary account appears in a 1901 issue of the *Colonist,* a Victoria, British Columbia, newspaper, which tells of the experience of a lumberman working on Vancouver Island, near Campbell River. Mike King was alone because his Indian packers refused to accompany him for fear of the "monkey men" who they said lived in the forest. Late in the afternoon he observed a "man beast" washing roots in the water. Suddenly aware of King, the creature cried out and scooted up a hill, stopping at one point to look at him over its shoulder. The witness described it as "covered with reddish brown hair, and his arms were peculiarly long and were used freely in climbing and in brush running; while the trail showed a distinct human foot, but with phenomenally long and spreading toes."

On December 14, 1904, the *Colonist* related a sighting by "four credible witnesses" who saw a Bigfoot-like creature on Vancouver Island, and in 1907 it told of the abandonment of an Indian village, its inhabitants frightened into flight by a "monkey-like wild man who appears on the beach [near Bishop's Cove on the British Columbia coast] at night, who howls in an unearthly fashion."

By the early decades of the century, residents of western Canada were well aware of the hairy giants being called Sasquatches. The folkloric Sasquatch — the word is an Anglicization from a term used by the Coast Salish Indians — was introduced to the larger world in the writings of J. W. Burns, a schoolteacher at the Chehalis Indian Reserve near Harrison Hot Springs, British Columbia. Burns's Sasquatch, a mythological figure he learned of through native informants, was less an anthropoid than a fabulous superman, an intelligent "giant Indian" endowed with supernatural powers. Few believed such creatures were anything other than imaginary.

Dissenting from the skeptical consensus were individuals who said they had seen the hairy giants themselves. These included, most spectacularly, Albert Ostman, a British Columbia man who came forward in 1957 to recount an incident which he said had taken place in 1924. While on a prospecting trip at the head of Toba Inlet, opposite Vancouver Island, he was scooped up one night inside his sleeping bag and after many miles dumped out, to discover that he was the prisoner of a family — adult male and female, juvenile male and female — of giant apelike creatures. Though they were friendly, they clearly did not want him to escape, and he managed to do so only after the older male choked on his chewing tobacco. He was gone six days. Those who interviewed Ostman, including John Green and Ivan T. Sanderson, did not doubt his sincerity or sanity; writing from his professional viewpoint, Napier has remarked on a "convincing account ... which does not ring false in any particular."

Another intriguing anecdote concerns an attack by Bigfoot creatures on a party of miners in the Mount Saint Helens/Lewis River area of southwestern Washington. The episode began one evening in July 1924, when two of the miners — already unnerved by a week's worth of strange whistling and thumping sounds emanating from a couple of nearby ridges — spotted a seven-foot-tall apelike creature and fired on it. They fled to the cabin and with two other men endured a night-long assault, including thrown rocks and a concentrated effort to smash open the door, by a number of the creatures. *Portland Oregonian* reporters who came to the scene later found giant footprints. The spot where the episode occurred was thereafter named Ape Canyon, and so it is called to this day. In 1967 one of the participants, Fred Beck, and his son published a booklet, *I Fought the Apemen of Mt. St. Helens*, recalling the event.

In a 1982 interview with a Vancouver newspaper, Rant Mullens, 86, claimed responsibility for the episode. On their way home from a fishing trip, he reported, as a joke he and his uncle "rolled some rocks down over the edge. Then we got out of there fast." From that, he said, the "hairy ape stories" emerged. It is, however, easier to believe that Beck and the others invented the tale out of whole cloth than to credit the idea that this simple act precipitated the complex series of events that comprise the recorded incident. These events include repeated sightings, some at a distance of no more than a few feet, of Bigfoot creatures. Beck was dead by the time Mullens came forward, but the witness's son Ronald Beck rejected as "impossible" the notion that the incident "could have been caused by a common hoax — or even an uncommon one." As for his father's honesty, he added, "I was close to my father, and believe me, his account is straight and true. I once had the privilege of hearing him and another man [one of the other miners] discuss their mutual 1924 experience."

Sasquatch sightings continued and from time to time were noted in mostly Canadian newspaper accounts. At some point in the 1920s, the name "Bigfoot" entered the vocabulary of at least some locals, who were impressed by the size of the tracks they were coming upon in remote areas. Bigfoot entered the consciousness of all Americans in 1958, when heavy-equipment operators near Willow Creek in northwestern California discovered a large number of tracks, apparently left by a huge biped which had examined a land-clearing bulldozer left at the site overnight. After the tracks appeared on other occasions, casts were made, and the result was massive press attention. A few weeks later, in late October, two men driving down a wilderness road saw a huge hairy bipedal creature cross in front of them and disappear into the trees, leaving prints in its wake. Around this time a newspaper photographer following a set of tracks came upon a pile of fecal matter; it was, he told Ivan Sanderson, "of absolutely monumental proportions."

The Patterson film.
By the 1960s Bigfoot, sometimes called "America's abominable snowman," had a firm niche in the popular imagination. Though scientists refused even to consider the possibility that witnesses were actually seeing what they claimed (the skeptics attributed nearly all reports to hoaxes or bears even as they refrained from actual investigation or interviewing), several lay investigators, such as Green, Rene Dahinden, and Jim McClarin, sought out witnesses, ventured into the bush hoping to glimpse one of the elusive beasts, tried to discern patterns in the data, and wrote articles or books about their findings. Sanderson's *Abominable Snowmen: Legend Come to Life* (1961),

the first book to discuss Bigfoot/Sasquatch in any comprehensive manner, linked the North American reports with worldwide traditions of "wild men," Almas, and yeti.

Among those who went looking for Bigfoot in the wild was Roger Patterson, a onetime rodeo rider and author of an amateurish, self-published book, *Do Abominable Snowmen of America Really Exist?* (1966). In 1967, according to Green, Patterson was making a "precarious living as an inventor and promoter." A 1959 *True* magazine article had sparked his interest in Bigfoot, and from then on, when time permitted, he roamed the Pacific Northwest woods hoping for a glimpse of the creature. In due course, combining business and curiosity, he laid plans for a documentary film on the mystery. Consequently he took a motion-picture camera on his expeditions and shot footage that would be useful in his proposed movie.

At a little after 1:15 on the afternoon of October 20, 1967, he and a companion, Bob Gimlin, were riding north up the partly dry, 100-yard-wide bed of Bluff Creek in the Six Rivers National Forest of northern California. (This area had seen so much Bigfoot activity, both sightings and tracks, that it had become something of a weekend tourist attraction.) At one point a large, high pile of logs positioned in the center of the stream obstructed their approach, and they had to maneuver their horses around the east end. As they passed it and veered left to resume their original course, they saw — or would claim they saw — something that would engulf them in a controversy which, nearly three decades later, has yet to end.

A female Bigfoot stood up from the creek water in which she had been squatting and walked briskly away into the surrounding trees, swinging her arms all the while. In the course of this brief interlude, all three horses (the third being the pack horse Patterson and Gimlin had brought with them) panicked. Patterson's mount reared up and promptly fell over sideways on the rider's right leg. As his horse staggered to its feet, Patterson groped for the 16mm camera in the saddlebag, then jumped off to pursue the retreating creature on foot. Only 28 feet of film remained in the camera, and Patterson used it to record the Bigfoot's passage from three different positions.

Patterson died in 1972, swearing to the end to the authenticity of both sighting and film. Gimlin, still alive, sticks by the story. The first investigator on the site, Bob Titmus, found tracks corresponding exactly to the creature's route as depicted in the film and made casts of 10 of them. He also learned that it had gone up a hillside and sat down for a period, apparently to watch the two witnesses, who had opted to recover two of the horses rather than continue to pursue the Bigfoot.

Of course the film did not settle the thorny question of whether an abominable snowman of America really exists. The controversies swirling about it are many. One concerns the simple but crucial matter of the speed at which the film was shot. Patterson said he could not remember whether it was 24 feet or 16 feet per second. If the latter, one analyst, British biomechanics specialist D. W. Grieve, wrote, "the cycle time and the time of

Noted Sasquatch investigator John Green (left) with two companions and Bigfoot casts. (Courtesy of Loren Coleman.)

swing are in a typical human combination but much longer in duration than one would expect for the stride and the pattern of limb movement" — meaning that if this is the correct film speed, the figure's "neuromuscular system was very different to that of humans." In other words, the figure is not a man in an ape suit, and the "possibility of fakery is ruled out." At 24 feet per second, however, it "walked with a gait pattern very similar in most respects to a man walking at high speed."

Through painstaking on-site reconstruction the figure's height was found to be slightly under six feet, six inches, Patterson's seven feet-four inch estimate notwithstanding. To John Napier either height was inconsistent with the size of the footprints. Only an animal in the eight-foot range could have made 14-inch footprints, in his estimation. "The space (the step) between one footprint and the next is given at 41 in.," he further remarked. "A creature 6 ft. 5 in. in height should have a step of 45 in., particularly, as it is seen in the film, when striding out; in fact in view of the exaggerated nature of the walk, the step might be expected to be somewhat longer than the normal, say 50 in. The conclusion is inevitable. The footprints must be fakes or the film is."

Still, these and other problems (notably the bewildering mixture of human and ape features) notwithstanding, Napier backed off slightly from his "inevitable" conclusion, conceding that if this was not a "brilliantly executed hoax," it "was the first film of a new type of hominid, quite unknown to science, in which case Roger Patterson deserves to rank with Dubois, the discoverer of *Pithecanthropus erectus* or Java man; or with Raymond Dart of Johannesburg, the man who introduced the world to its immediate pre-human ancestor, *Australopithecus africanus*."

Green, who believes the film to be the genuine article, takes issue with the assertion that the creature's walk is humanlike. From a frame-by-frame

analysis he concluded that its "stride is actually much smoother than a normal man's, because the knee is bent as the weight comes on it. A walking man bobs up and down as his body goes over the top of his straightened leg. The Sasquatch in the film moves in a flowing fashion. It is much straighter when she is reaching out in full stride than when it is bearing her full weight."

After viewing the film with Bigfoot investigator Peter Byrne in 1973, the chief technician at Disney Studios declared that the "only place in the world a simulation of that quality could be created would be here, at Disney Studios, and this footage was not made here."

Because all observers agreed that the film, if faked, was brilliantly executed, speculation inevitably centered on the two witnesses. Some critics — excluding Napier (who regarded him as "very attractive and sincere") — pointed to Patterson's obvious financial interest in the creation of Bigfoot footage, and indeed he and Gimlin wasted no time in taking monetary advantage of their property.

Beyond that obvious consideration, however, there were problems. For one thing, the small community of Bigfoot investigators, though seldom agreeing about much else, spoke with one voice on one matter: Patterson and Gimlin simply were not bright enough to pull off a hoax of this magnitude. There were, moreover, financial considerations of another sort; neither man had the resources to pay for the construction of a suit that continues to defy, in Byrne's words, "the examination of 'where is the zipper' seekers all over the world." Only two companies in the United States could have fashioned a suit of such sophistication, and neither claims to have done so. The man in the suit, if he exists, has remained stone silent far longer than one presumes prudence requires. In fact, a confession to the right magazine or supermarket tabloid could reap an impressive financial reward.

The debate about the Patterson film goes on, probably not to remain resolved until the "man in the suit" confesses or someone produces a physical specimen of Bigfoot for comparison with the figure in the footage. At least everyone agrees that the Patterson film is worth debating, unlike other alleged Bigfoot films which are manifestly bogus.

Dermal ridges.
The next major controversy concerning alleged Bigfoot evidence erupted in 1982. Though initially it looked like the most promising development yet, it would come to a disappointing conclusion.

The episode begins with a story told by Paul Freeman, a seasonal employee of the U.S. Forest Service. On the morning of June 10, his story goes, he was driving through the Blue Mountains in the Walla Walla Ranger District of the Umatilla National Forest, which stretches across southeastern Washington and northeastern Oregon. Spotting some elk, he stopped his truck, jumped out, and pursued the animals on foot. He wanted to find out if there were any calves among them.

As he rounded a bend, he noticed a "stench" and at the other side of the turn saw something coming down a bank through thick vegetation. When the figure stepped into the clearing, Freeman froze and stared in disbelief at an "enormous creature" — an eight-and-a-half-foot-tall Bigfoot — which stared back at him. For a few seconds the two studied each other from a distance of 150 to 200 feet, then fled in opposite directions.

Freeman, apparently badly shaken, immediately notified his superiors in Walla Walla, Washington, and two hours later a group of Forest Service personnel arrived at the site, located in Oregon near the Washington border. They found 21 footprints measuring 14 inches long by seven inches wide. They took three casts and some pictures of the prints.

On June 14 the Walla Walla station released a statement recounting the details of Freeman's sighting and remarking that "no determination can be made" concerning the identity of the creature he claimed to have seen. The Forest Service said it had no further plans to investigate. Nonetheless four days later it reported that on the sixteenth Freeman and Patrolman Bill Epoch had discovered about 40 new tracks in the Mill Creek Watershed on the Washington side of the border. On the seventeenth Joel Hardin, a U.S. Border Patrol tracking expert and a Bigfoot skeptic, examined the prints and pronounced them hoaxes. Among other suspicious features, he said, they showed evidence of dermal ridges, which animals do not have. He failed to mention, however, that higher primates — monkeys, apes, and human beings — do have such ridges on their toes and fingers ("fingerprints").

The day after Freeman's sighting, the Umatilla County (Oregon) Sheriff's Department sent a five-person team of volunteers to the Tiger Creek area. The searchers were not looking for a Bigfoot but for the body of a boy who had disappeared the previous fall. They were brought to the site because the sheriff's officers noted Freeman's mention of a "stench," which they thought might be from a decaying corpse. Though the team found neither stench nor body, it did make another discovery.

According to Art Snow, a local businessman who headed the team, the search party was able to follow the tracks beyond the 21 found by the Forest Service people. In fact, Snow maintained, tracks were discernible for three-quarters of a mile. The team made a cast of one of the better prints.

"It would not be possible to fake the tracks without a helicopter," Snow said. "We assumed Freeman was telling the truth, and we could find no evidence whatsoever to contradict that assumption."

In July, citing stress from his experience and all the publicity it had received, Freeman left his job with the Forest Service.

Soon afterwards Washington State University anthropologist Grover Krantz, Bigfoot's leading scientific proponent, was provided with four casts from both the Tiger Creek and Mill Creek Watershed areas. Krantz also secured the print Snow had cast the day after Freeman's reported encounter.

● SOURCES:

Beck, Fred, and R. A. Beck. I Fought the Apemen of Mt. St. Helens. Kelso, WA: The Authors, 1967.

Beck, Ronald A. "Crypto-letters." The ISC Newsletter 1, 3 (Autumn 1982): 10.

Bord, Janet, and Colin Bord. The Bigfoot Casebook. Harrisburg, PA: Stackpole Books, 1982.

Byrne, Peter. The Search for Big Foot: Monster, Myth or Man? Washington, DC: Acropolis Books, 1976.

Coleman, Loren E., and Mark A. Hall. "Some Bigfoot Traditions of the North American Tribes." In Jacques Bergier and the editors of INFO, eds. Extraterrestrial Intervention: The Evidence, 73–83. Chicago: Henry Regnery Company, 1974.

Dahinden, Rene, and Grover S. Krantz. "Comments and Responses." Cryptozoology 3 (1984): 128–34.

Dennett, Michael R. "Evidence for Bigfoot?: An Investigation of the Mill Creek 'Sasquatch Prints'." Skeptical Inquirer 13 (Spring 1989): 264–72.

34

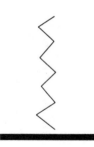

Some weeks later, in a summary of conclusions from his investigation, Krantz wrote that the prints were from "two individuals." The first of these, represented by two casts, one of each foot, had a big toe larger than that in the average Bigfoot track. The second specimen had a "splayed-out second toe."

Aside from these distinguishing features, the prints were much alike and typical of those associated with Bigfoot reports. The feet were about 15 inches long, and the toes were more nearly equal in size than a human being's would be. The arches were nearly flat, and a "double ball" was visible at the base of the big toe.

Adding to the prints' apparent credibility was the fact that there were no human prints around the Bigfoot tracks. The distance between them suggested that whoever made them had a *long* stride. Moreover, Krantz maintained, they were so deeply impressed into the ground that most investigators believed it would have taken over 600 pounds of force to make them; yet there was no evidence to suggest the presence of the kinds of mechanical devices necessary to fake this effect.

Krantz was particularly taken with the dermal ridges, visible, he thought, because of the unprecedented clarity of the prints. The dermal ridges were fine lines about half a millimeter apart in the skin of the feet. Krantz showed these to Benny D. Kling, a forensics expert at the Law Enforcement Academy in Douglas, Wyoming. From his examination Kling concluded that the dermal-ridge patterns were those of higher primates, but the foot and toe shapes were different from those of a human being or an ape. Some of the ridges were worn smooth, according to Kling, in exactly the places one would expect from someone or something that had walked barefoot for a long time.

If the story had ended here, it would have marked a significant advance in the case for Bigfoot's reality. It did not, however, end there.

Though Krantz remained convinced of the authenticity of both the prints and Freeman's testimony, other investigators saw serious problems. For one thing, the prints were too perfect. The stride did not vary, and there was no evidence of slippage up and down hillsides. When they were found in mud, they did not go nearly as deep as they should have, if the animal weighed, as estimated, between 800 and 1,000 pounds; in fact, they were shallower than the tracks left by searchers' boots. Moreover, according to wildlife biologist Rodney L. Johnson, "In several cases, it appeared that the foot may have been rocked from side to side to make the track." At one site where tracks were seen, he said, "it appeared that the fine forest litter (needles, etc.) had been brushed sideways from the track area in an unnatural manner."

There were also doubts about Freeman's credibility. Freeman would go on to claim other sightings and even take a photograph of an alleged Bigfoot. Veteran Bigfoot tracker Bob Titmus told of a suspicious experience with

Freeland, Deborah J., and Walter F. Rowe. "Alleged Pore Structure in Sasquatch (Bigfoot) Prints." *Skeptical Inquirer* 13 (Spring 1989): 273–76.

Green, John. *On the Track of the Sasquatch.* New York: Ballantine Books, 1973.

Greenwell, J. Richard. "Interview: Does the Sasquatch Exist and What Can Be Done About It? In a Wide-Ranging Interview, John Green Addresses the Problem." *The ISC Newsletter* 8, 2 (Summer 1989): 1–7.

Greenwell, J. Richard, and James E. King. "Attitudes of Physical Anthropologists Toward Reports of Bigfoot and Nessie." *Current Anthropology* 22, 1 (February 1981): 79–80.

Halpin, Marjorie, and Michael M. Ames, eds. *Manlike Monsters on Trial: Early Records and Modern Evidence.* Vancouver, British Columbia: University of British Columbia Press, 1980.

Hewkin, James A. "Investigating Sasquatch Evidence in the Pacific Northwest." *Cryptozoology* 5 (1986): 27–37.

———. "Observations of Two Lines of Sasquatch Tracks in Oregon." *Cryptozoology* 6 (1987): 78–84.

"Hoax Claimed for Ape Canyon Incident." *The ISC Newsletter* 1,1 (Spring 1982): 7–8.

Hunter, Don, with Rene Dahinden. *Sasquatch*. Toronto, Ontario: McClelland and Stewart, 1973.

Krantz, Grover S. "A Reconstruction of the Skull of Gigantopithecus Blacki and Its Comparison with a Living Form." *Cryptozoology* 6 (1987): 24–39.

Mannetje, Martien, and Grover S. Krantz. "Cryptoletters." *The ISC Newsletter* 8,2 (Summer 1989): 10–11.

Markotic, Vladimir, ed. Grover Krantz, associated ed. *The Sasquatch and Other Unknown Hominoids*. Calgary, Alberta: Western Publishers, 1984.

Napier, John. *Bigfoot: The Yeti and Sasquatch in Myth and Reality*. New York: E. P. Dutton and Company, 1973.

Penhale, Ed. "The Day Bob Gimlin Saw 'the Creature'." *Seattle Post-Intelligencer* (December 2, 1985).

"Pullman Symposium Reviews Sasquatch Evi-

Freeman. The two were in the woods, and Titmus said he had a hunch that creatures were in the area. Freeman got into his pickup, to return 20 minutes later with the news that he had found prints. When Titmus looked at them, he spotted dermal ridges immediately. He also noted the absence of any other evidence of a Bigfoot's presence beyond the footprints, conveniently located in the only terrain suitable for track-making. In a television interview Freeman admitted that in the past he had faked Bigfoot prints.

Some experts remarked that it would be easy, and inexpensive, to create a plaster foot showing dermal ridges, and they speculated that the hoaxer had simply used a specimen of a large human foot as the model.

Other evidence.
Though the Freeman prints may be of dubious provenance, other Bigfoot prints resist conventional explanation. Efforts to explain them seldom if ever go beyond glib dismissal, based on the sometimes explicitly stated assumption that the virtual impossibility of Bigfoot's existence renders such evidence moot. On the other hand, authorities who have examined them (or casts made from them) agree, nearly unanimously, that they comprise genuine evidence for an unknown anthropoid.

For all tracks to be fakes, Napier wrote,

> We must be prepared to accept the existence of Mafia-like ramifications with cells in practically every major township from San Francisco to Vancouver. Even if we accept the conspiracy angle there is still another hurdle to be jumped. How could footprints of such realism and functional consistency have been made? Rubber-latex molds bonded to a boot or shoe might explain how the footprints are reproduced, but the mechanical problems would be immense, particularly when it is borne in mind that the hoaxer would have to walk considerable distances over difficult terrain wearing such unwieldy contraptions. There is also the problem that footprints are found in conditions where an ordinary man is too light to make any impressions in the substrate. However, it is not impossible that some of the footprints were made in this way.

Napier was particularly impressed with tracks found near Bossburg, Washington, in October 1969. Measuring 17 1/2 by seven inches, they comprised 1,089 prints, according to Dahinden. But the most interesting feature was the right track, which indicated the creature had a clubfoot, evidently — so Napier's analysis indicated — as the result of injury in early childhood. "It is very difficult to conceive of a hoaxer so subtle, so knowledgeable — and so sick — who would deliberately fake a footprint of this nature," Napier declared. "I suppose it is possible, but it is so unlikely that I am prepared to discount it."

The occurrence of tracks in remote, seldom traveled areas also argues against the hoax hypothesis. James A. Hewkin of the Oregon Department of Fish and Wildlife reported finding Bigfoot tracks (as well as less direct

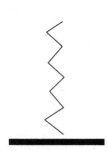

but nonetheless suggestive evidence) in remote, almost inaccessible regions of the Cascade Mountains. From his observations Hewkin, a biologist, concluded that a "species of giant, bipedal primate, weighing up to 800 pounds and standing as tall as 8 feet, and known as Sasquatch, does, in fact, exist. Its diet is probably omnivorous, with feeding habits similar to those of bears (grubbing for roots, larvae, etc.). It searches for rodents in stumps, logs, and rock slides. It might cache meat for winter use."

Other evidence consists of feces and hair samples associated either with sightings or with other indications of a Bigfoot's recent passage. Some of these have been identified and linked with human beings or known animals. In a few cases the samples seemed to resist such identification. There also have been analyses of recordings of alleged Bigfoot cries. One notable example is a recording made on October 21, 1972, at 8,500 feet altitude in northern California's High Sierras, where a number of sightings had been logged. That night investigators recorded a series of moans, whines, growls, grunts, and whistles. Two electronics specialists, one from the University of Wyoming and the other from Rockwell International, conducted an extensive analysis which led them to the conclusion that the sounds emanated from "more than one speaker, one or more of which is of larger physical size than an average human male. The formant frequencies found were clearly lower than for human data, and their distribution does not indicate that they were a product of human vocalizations and tape speed alteration."

Then, of course, there are the numerous sightings, by now in the low thousands, from all manner of human beings. Though these sightings amount to incredible claims, the claim that every witness without exception is lying or deluded is not a little incredible in itself. The only animal a person of average judgment and perception is likely to mistake for a Bigfoot is a bear, and bears are bipedal only for brief periods. And no knowledgeable observer would confuse bear tracks with Bigfoot tracks.

Yet the idea that such creatures, whether relic hominids or great apes, share the North American continent with us is indeed a fantastic one. One does not have to be a rigid, unbending dogmatist to resist it in the absence of a body or living specimen. This sort of skepticism, eminently defensible, is one thing, dogmatic denial quite another. In the meantime it seems safe to say that if the forests of the Northwest do harbor these extraordinary animals, they cannot remain hidden from us forever.

dence." *The ISC Newsletter* 8, 4 (Winter 1989): 1–5.

Riley, Sam G. "A Search for the Cultural Bigfoot." *Journal of Popular Culture* 10, 2 (Fall 1976): 377–87.

Sanderson, Ivan T. *Abominable Snowmen: Legend Come to Life.* Philadelphia, PA: Chilton Book Company, 1961.

"Sasquatch in Washington State: New Reports Involve Footprints." *The ISC Newsletter* 1,2 (Summer 1982): 7–9.

Shoemaker, Michael T. "Searching for the Historical Bigfoot." *Strange Magazine* 5 (1990): 18–23, 57–62.

Somer, Lonnie. "New Signs of Sasquatch Activity in the Blue Mountains of Washington State." *Cryptozoology* 6 (1987): 65–70.

Sprague, Roderick, and Grover S. Krantz, eds. *The Scientist Looks at the Sasquatch.* Moscow, ID: University Press of Idaho, 1977.

———. *The Scientist Looks at the Sasquatch (II).* Moscow, ID: University Press of Idaho, 1979.

"Walla Walla Casts Show Dermal Ridges." *The ISC Newsletter* 1, 3 (Autumn 1982): 1–4.

BLACK DOGS ————————————————————————

As he approached a crossroads on an autumn night in 1984, a Devonshire, England, man saw "this bloomin' great black thing.... I put on my anchors [brakes] and in the headlights it slowed down and walked right up to the car. I could see its eyes as plain as day, green and glassy they were, and he looked right over the bonnet [hood] at me, he was that tall, and then he went!... like a light going out. I just couldn't see it anymore. It isn't real like an ordinary dog. I could feel the hairs on my neck standing up."

This story was told to local naturalist Trevor Beer, who was investigating reports of large, livestock-killing cats in the area (see *Beast of Exmoor*). Beer apparently saw no reason to disbelieve the account even when he was told the encounter took place on October 31 (All Hallows' Eve). To every appearance the story is a fabrication consciously based on a world-wide folklore, known from England's West Country to the American South, about supernatural black dogs which frequently appear at crossroads and which are associated with the underworld.

In rural Mississippi in the early part of the twentieth century, black people told folklorist N. N. Puckett of huge black dogs with "big red eyes glowing like chunks of fire." In the 1930s Mississippian Robert Johnson, the great folk-blues singer/guitarist, did not deny rumors — spread by both those who resented his talents and those who held them in awe — that he had acquired his considerable musical skills in a midnight deal with a man in black (the devil) whom he met at a crossroads, an event hinted at in his 1936 recording "Cross Road Blues." He reported on the consequences of this pact the next year in another scary blues lyric:

> *I've got to keep movin' ...*
> *There's a hellhound on my trail.*

Theo Brown, a leading authority on black-dog lore, has written, "Oral tradition sometimes gives us a legend, but this has probably been invented to explain the ghost." In other words, black dogs exist not just in thricetold tales but also in firsthand reports, at least some of them from individuals meriting greater credence than Beer's informant. Brown adds that the black dog "if regarded purely as a symbol must represent some universal guardian of the threshold personified in various cultures."

A large and complex folklore surrounds black dogs. (Black dog is in some senses a generic term, meaning supernatural canine. Most tales and reports of such creatures describe them as black, but white, gray, and yellow "black dogs" figure in some stories.) Brown believes the legend is rooted in prehistory but acknowledges this conclusion is necessarily speculative. In historical time, especially in Britain where the lore is most fully documented, black dogs may encounter a traveler on a dark road and either guide him to safety or menace him, or their appearance may presage the death of the witness. They may also attach themselves to families; such a real-life family legend inspired Sir Arthur Conan Doyle to write the most celebrated of his Sherlock Holmes novels, *The Hound of the Baskervilles*. Black dogs are said to have glowing eyes and often to vanish, as did Devonshire's Halloween apparition, in an instant. Sometimes, especially in medieval and postmedieval chronicles of manifestations associated with witchcraft, the black dog is a shape-shifter, at some point revealing his true identity: the devil.

Sightings.

Traditional beliefs are one thing; however, actual (or alleged) events are another, and the latter are discussed here.

The first known example of a sighting event survives in a French manuscript, *Annales Franorum Regnum* (A.D. 856), wherein a chronicler records what happened after sudden darkness enveloped a provincial church midway through a service. A large black dog with fiercely glowing eyes appeared, dashed about as if searching for something, and vanished abruptly. On August 4, 1577, in Bongay, 10 miles from Norwich, England, a black dog showed up inside a church during a violent storm, ran through the aisle, killed two worshippers, and injured another, burning him severely. The same day a similar attack occurred inside a church in Blibery seven miles away, or so wrote one Abraham Fleming in a broadside titled *A Straunge Wunder in Bongay*, published not long afterwards. Fleming claimed to have been inside the Bongay church when the apparition went on its rampage. His account, he acknowledged, "to some will seem absurd."

Twentieth-century reports of black dogs tend not to share the wildly extravagant character of the older stories. Many seem simply to be a variety of ghost story. Typical of these is the account Theodore Ebert of Pottsville, Pennsylvania, gave to folklorist George Korson in the 1950s: "One night when I was a boy walking with friends along Seven Stars Road, a big black dog appeared from nowhere and came between me and one of

39

my pals. And I went to pet the dog, but it disappeared from right under me. Just like the snap of a finger it disappeared."

There is no shortage of modern black-dog sightings, at least through the early decades of the century. Ethel H. Rudkin collected a number of reports from her native Lincolnshire and published them in a 1938 paper in *Folklore*. "I have never yet had a Black Dog story from anyone who was weak either in body or mind," she wrote. "Perhaps it is because I have seen the Black Dog, and can therefore believe that the narrator has also seen him, that I have been able to get such good first-hand stories." Unfortunately Rudkin provided no details of her own encounter with this ghostly canine which, unlike its counterparts elsewhere, was of a gentle nature. According to her:

> *The spectator may be startled or annoyed, at first, by finding the huge creature trotting alongside, but fear of the Dog never enters into it, once he is recognized for what he is. He is always "table high," sometimes spoken of as being "as big as a caulf" which often produces a muddled idea as to whether he is a calf or a dog. In the story he is often associated with a woman. No matter how dark the night, the Dog can be seen because he is so much blacker. He seems to have a tendency to appear on the left hand side of the spectator, he crosses the road from left to right, and he is definitely looked on as a spirit of protection.... He is often heard, for when he disappears into a hedge the leaves rustle loudly.... In one description, his coat is wiry "like pig bristles" — in another he is "tall and thin with a long neck and pointed nose."*

More recently, something that looked like a "Great Dane" reportedly stepped in front of a moving car on Exeter Road in Okehampton, England, on October 25, 1969. Before the driver could stop, the car passed through the animal, which then disappeared. In April 1972 a member of Britain's Coastguard saw a "large, black hound-type dog on the beach" at Great Yarmouth. "It was about a quarter of a mile from me," he told the *London Evening News* (April 27, 1972). "What made me watch it was that it was running, then stopping, as if looking for someone. As I watched, it vanished before my eyes."

Witnesses often mention the creature's glowing eyes. In fact (or in allegation), they sometimes see little more than the eyes but infer for one or another reason that they belong to a ghostly dog. In the early 1920s young Delmer Clark of La Crosse, Wisconsin, saw "something that looked with shining eyes, with the face of a dog"; in the darkness he thought he could make out vaguely a "dark black body." When he saw it again a week later in the same location near his home, he kicked at it, only to find his foot inside its mouth as if it had been anticipating the action. When he screamed, the creature vanished. In 1976, when Clark recalled the incident for his son (the author of this book), he remarked, "I can still see it clearly as I talk now. It was the strangest experience I've ever had."

● SOURCES:

Beer, Trevor. *The Beast of Exmoor: Fact or Legend?* Barnstaple, Devonshire, England: Countryside Productions, 1985.

Bord, Janet, and Colin Bord. *Alien Animals.* Harrisburg, PA: Stackpole Books, 1981.

Brown, Theo. "The Black Dog in English Folklore." In J. R. Porter and W.M.S. Russell, eds. *Animals in Folklore*, 45–58. Totowa, NJ: Rowman and Littlefield, 1978.

Bunn, Ivan. "Black Dogs and Water." *The News* 17 (August 1976): 12–13.

Clark, Jerome, and Loren Coleman. *Creatures of the Outer Edge.* New York: Warner Books, 1978.

Gordon, Stan. "UFOs, in Relation to Creature Sightings in Pennsylvania." In Walter H. Andrus, Jr., ed. *MUFON 1974 UFO Symposium Proceedings*, 132–54. Quincy, IL: Mutual UFO Network, 1974.

Gurdon, Lady Eveline Camilla, ed. *County Folk-Lore: Suffolk.* Ipswich, England: D. Nutt, 1893.

Johnson, Robert. *The Complete Recordings.* Columbia Records, 1990.

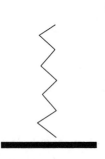

Black dogs, or creatures much like them, occasionally are reported during mystery-cat scares. In the spring of 1974 some residents of the English counties of Hampshire and Cheshire halved the difference; they said the creature looked "half cat, half dog."

In the curious (or inevitable) way in which seemingly separate categories of anomalous phenomena have of overlapping at the edges, the UFO literature contains a small number of reports in which black dogs are linked, directly or circumstantially, with flying saucers. None of these cases, it should be noted, is especially compelling or notably documented, but they do tell us something about the persistence of the black-dog image.

Among the circumstantial-link cases is one reported from South Africa in 1963. Two men driving at night on the Potchefstroom/Vereeniging road observed a large, doglike animal crossing the highway in front of them. Moments later a UFO showed up to buzz their vehicle several times, sending them on a frantic flight from the scene. Probably this was a large dog, and only coincidence tied it to the UFO. Several Georgia youths asserted a more direct association a decade later, when they claimed to have spotted "10 big, black hairy dogs" run from a landed UFO and through a cemetery in Savannah.

Like other supernatural manifestations, black dogs are phenomena which have to be seen to be believed. Those who have not seen them and who need to rationalize their skepticism can always counter, if not with entire accuracy, that black dogs have to be believed to be seen.

Keel, John A. *Strange Creatures from Time and Space.* Greenwich, CT: Fawcett Gold Medal, 1970.

Korson, George. *Black Rock: Mining Folklore of the Pennsylvania Dutch.* Baltimore, MD: Johns Hopkins University Press, 1960.

Rudkin, Ethel H. "The Black Dog." *Folklore* 49 (June 1938): 111–31.

Stein, Gordon. "Black Dogs: Fact or Fancy?" *Fate* 43,6 (June 1990): 65–73.

Tebbutt, L. F. "A Buckinghamshire Black Dog." *Folklore* 56 (March 1945): 222.

W.C.B. "Black Dogs: Gabriel Hounds." *Notes and Queries* 11, 5 (March 9, 1912): 185–86.

Watson, Nigel. "Notes on Lincolnshire Ghost Phenomena — 1." *The News* 1, 6 (September 1974): 18–19.

Webb, David, with Mimi Hynek, ed. 1973 — *Year of the Humanoids: An Analysis of the Fall 1973 UFO/Humanoid Wave.* Evanston, IL: Center for UFO Studies, 1976.

Woods, Barbara Allen. "The Devil in Dog Form." *Western Folklore* 13,4 (October 1954): 229–35.

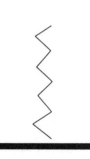

BLACK PANTHERS AND OTHER
ANOMALOUS FELINES ————————————————

Bill Chambers was driving near his Champaign County, Illinois, farm when he saw the animal 300 yards away in a field. It was just before sunset on June 2, 1963. The animal did not notice as Chambers pulled into a nearby lane and coasted down a grade which put him within 190 yards of it. Later he would give this account to anomalist Loren Coleman:

> I had a set of sandbags that I use on my shooting bench and I put them on top of the truck cab to give me a steady shooting position.... [Through the scope] the head was visible but seldom still enough for a target and the head is a poor place to shoot a cat anyway.

> The cat spent several minutes near a big weed clump with little show-ing until he jumped on something in the clover. When he did this I had laid my rifle down and was watching with my 8x binoculars and the tail was clearly visible.

> A little later, he sat up facing straight at me and with the sun down and directly at my back, I was looking at the lighted side all the time and he appeared jet black except for two tawny streaks under the jaws extending two to three inches down his neck. Before I could get the rifle on him again, he settled back in the clover.

> I was within an ounce of getting the shot off three different times in 10 or 15 minutes but the cat kept moving and I never got my shot off.

> The next day, I stepped the distance from the truck tracks to the weed clump and got 187 steps. The clover there averaged 12" tall which would make him about 15" tall at the shoulder. The fact that I was looking down on him a little might bring his shoulder height to about

14". Tail and all, I would say he was between four-and-a-half and five feet and probably closer to the four-and-a-half feet. The only tracks I could find measured two-and-five eighths inches in soft wet ground and had no claw marks like a dog would make.

In November 1945, at around 2 A.M., Wanda Dillard was driving between Franklin and Morgan City in southern Louisiana along Highway 90, then a narrow two-lane road, when she happened to notice a set of glowing red eyes at the edge of the woods ahead and to her right. Fearing that the animal might sprint into the middle of the road, she slowed down. She recalled what happened next:

As I braked, this huge black cat left the woods, and streaked across in front of the headlights and down the embankment on the left. It was such a beautiful thing that as soon as I could maneuver a turn, I went back to see if I could get another look at him, although I expected him to be at least over in the next parish [county] by then. But lo and behold, there he was, red eyes and all, crouched at the edge of the woods just as if he were waiting to play tag with the next motorist.

There being no traffic, I angled the car a bit with the motor running and the emergency brake on, and watched him. He seemed to become accustomed to the light, and simply sat down like any common old house cat and began to groom himself. I had no sense of fear of him.... I watched this animal for at least 10 minutes, possibly a bit longer, ... then had to move on because of oncoming traffic....

This cat was jet black, very sleek looking and well muscled, with a long black tail that he wrapped around himself as he sat there. His eyes glowed a sort of winey red in the light and as he turned his head during the process of grooming the eyes had more of a rainbow look to them — flashes of other color. Having seen the mountain lion and the bobcat both in the wild and in captivity, I would relate this black panther more to the mountain lion in both looks and movement, but sleek and more graceful. In size he would have been a bit smaller than the mountain lion, but much larger than the bobcat, and with a much more dignified looking head, and the ears were not pointed.

The animal known popularly as the panther, mountain lion, cougar, or puma and scientifically as *Felis concolor* was driven into extinction everywhere (except for a small population in Florida's Everglades) east of the Rocky Mountains in the latter half of the nineteenth century. Moreover, such animals were and are not prone to melanism, a condition caused by an overabundance of melanin pigment, resulting in black hair in mammals. Thus the two incidents above are rather more extraordinary than they seem.

What makes them even more interesting is that reports of black panthers number in the many hundreds, perhaps thousands, and they occur in places where neither *Felis concolor* nor any other big cat has ever existed:

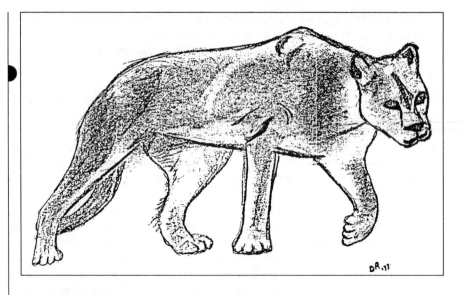

the British Isles and Australia, for example. Furthermore, black panthers sometimes appear in the same places that other kinds of anomalous felines, including maned "African lions," are reported. And yet, though some of the sightings — like the two recounted above — are so clear and detailed that misidentification seems out of the question, no skin or body of one has ever been produced. No clear and unambiguous photographs are known to exist. It has been said that black panthers and their equally shadowy cousins are the "flying saucers of the animal world."

An epidemic of panthers.

Persistent reports, including a number of claimed (albeit so far undocumented) kills, have led a number of wildlife specialists to conclude, at least tentatively, that a small population of panthers survives in the Eastern United States and Canada. If nothing else, the debate over whether people are seeing big cats or mistaking large dogs or feral housecats for them is largely ended; few doubt that big cats are out there. At issue is the question of their origin and of the likelihood of a breeding population. Skeptics contend that pet owners may have bought panthers as kittens and released them secretly in the wild when they grew up and out of control.

While interesting, this debate is only marginally relevant to the concerns of anomalists. Nonetheless biologists who have investigated the Eastern panther have all come upon black-panther reports, and all but a few reject such accounts out of hand. Robert L. Downing, who conducted a study of the Eastern-panther question for the U.S. Fish and Wildlife Service, expresses the conventional view: "Some black animals, such as Labrador retrievers, are reported to be black panthers because that's the color that panthers are supposed to be, according to folklore (the Asian 'black panther' is actually a melanistic leopard)." In fact, there is something to be said for this sort of caution. Many tracks attributed to black panthers actually were the prints of dogs.

Still, the first serious scientific investigator of the Eastern panther became convinced that some black-panther accounts merited attention. Biologist Bruce S. Wright, director of the Northeastern Wildlife Station of the University of New Brunswick, Canada, thought at first that witnesses were seeing normal panthers whose skin happened to be wet and therefore took on a darker cast. Experiments with a freshly killed panther on Vancouver Island convinced him of the inadequacy of this hypothesis. In the course of his research, he collected 20 black-panther reports he deemed reliable. All occurred in daylight and at close range.

One of the cases Wright judged credible is especially fantastic. It took place, according to the witness, in Queens County, New Brunswick, on November 22, 1951:

> I was returning home about 6 P.M. I came to a pole fence and before crossing it hit it with my axe…. Within seconds I heard five loud yells off in the woods…. I walked about 100 yards further … when I heard four or five more yells. I looked back and saw it coming leaping. I ran a short way when it overtook me, so I had to stop and face it. When I stopped it stopped and stood up on its rear legs with mouth open and "sizzling" and with forepaws waving it charged. I swung the axe at it but it jumped back and I missed, so I ran for it and whooped. It leaped off in the woods and I ran for the house but didn't run very far before I saw it coming again and had to stop and swing the axe at it. It jumped to one side so I ran for it and it ran off in the woods again…. It repeated the same thing over and over five or six times until I came to a field where I could see the lights of the houses; then it leaped off and never came back.
>
> The animal was black or dark grey in color. The tail was at least two and one-half feet long, and the animal was at least six feet long.

This story contains three fantastic elements: a panther that is (1) black, (2) erect, and (3) unafraid to attack a human being. "Real" panthers have learned through bitter experience to keep as far away as possible from their deadly enemy, the one that has very nearly destroyed their entire species. They are, in other words, anything but aggressive toward people.

Unlikely as the New Brunswick encounter may be, a report half a continent away and nearly two decades later contains all three of its predecessor's bizarre ingredients. It occurred a mile south of Olive Branch, Illinois, on a dark, mostly deserted road which runs along the edge of the vast Shawnee National Forest. Mike Busby of Cairo was on his way to pick up his wife when his car stalled. As he was releasing the hood latch, he heard something and looked to his left. When he turned to look, he was startled to see two quarter-sized, almond-shaped, greenish-glowing eyes staring at him.

Suddenly the strange form, six feet tall, black, and upright, hit him in the face with two padded front feet. Busby fell, the animal on top of him, and as the two rolled around, it ripped his shirt to pieces and used its dull, two-inch claws to cut his left arm, chest, and abdomen. Busby managed to keep its mouth open at arm's length and its long yellow feline teeth away from his throat. Though Busby never got a good look at the creature, he later said he felt what seemed to be whiskers around its mouth. It emitted deep, soft growls which sounded unlike anything Busby had heard before. Its body hair was short and wiry — "like steel wool," he told Loren Coleman — and though dry had the odor of wet hair.

In the lights of a passing diesel truck, the creature's colors looked a slick, shiny black, and for the first time Busby saw the "shadow of a tail." The light apparently frightened the animal, which loped across the road with "heavy footfalls" and vanished into the woods.

Disoriented and hurting, the young man crawled back to his car. To his relief it started without trouble. In Olive Branch Busby encountered truck driver John Hartsworth, who said he had seen Busby struggling with what looked like a "*big* cat." He claimed that he had been unable to brake his vehicle and stop to help. Later that evening Busby went to St. Mary's Hospital in Cairo to receive a tetanus shot and another for relief of pain. His brother Don would tell Coleman that for days afterwards Mike suffered dizzy spells and required aid in walking.

Black and other American mystery cats.
Busby's was only the most dramatic of a long series of anomalous-feline reports in Illinois and nearby states. Four years earlier, in its April 20, 1966, issue, the *Cairo Evening Citizen* had asked, "Does the black panther really roam the Shawnee Forest wilderness in Alexander County?" It took note of a rumor that "many years ago a circus train or truck was wrecked in the area and some black panthers escaped into the hills and were never found."

As an attempt to account for reports of anomalous beasts, the folk belief that on some occasion years ago a circus train wrecked and unleashed dangerous or exotic animals gets hauled out almost every time someone says he has seen a panther, kangaroo, or hairy biped. Investigations invariably reveal no substance to the rumor or else a considerably embellished version of a real event.

The Midwest has a particularly rich panther tradition. Black panthers figure prominently in these, but so do other kinds of big cats, including conventional-looking cougars and maned "African lions." (Of the latter Coleman, who has collected numerous reports from a variety of states, writes, "Besides being social, the mysterious maned lions appear to be more forthrightly venturesome, retreating less quickly than the black panthers, but then again not attacking as frequently either.") One of the early panther scares took place in central Illinois in July 1917, when posses searched fruitlessly for what a number of witnesses claimed were a male and female African lion. One witness, a butler on an estate near Monticello, claimed that one of the animals clawed him as he was working in a garden, and later that month two Decatur families reported that a lion lunged at their car as they drove down a country highway late in the evening.

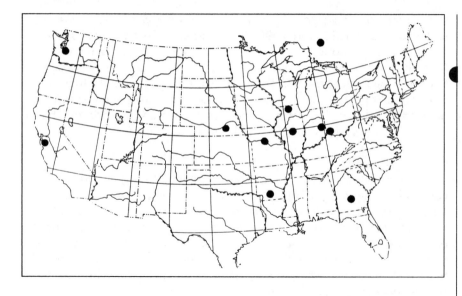

Locations where maned "African lions" have been reported in North America. (Courtesy of Loren Coleman.)

The two big cats disappeared as abruptly as they had arrived, but comparably mysterious felines would be heard from again. In 1948 a screeching "something" began killing livestock in east-central Indiana. Farmers, hunters, and law-enforcement officers who went looking for it told of seeing either an African lion or a black panther, and on at least one occasion witnesses said they had seen the two animals together. Members of a fishing party claimed that an "African lion" rushed them one evening near Elkhorn Falls.

On October 25, 1955, Game Warden Paul G. Myers fired on a black panther near Decatur, Illinois. He was certain that he had wounded the animal, but it escaped, and no body was ever found. In June 1962 a large tan-colored cat which others would compare to an African "lioness" clawed Monument City, Indiana, farmer Ed Moorman in the face. A few days later something killed 10 of his pigs, having ripped open their sides and devoured their hearts and livers. There were other sightings, the last of them by a group of armed hunters, including two television reporters from Indianapolis.

Reports like these are not confined to the Midwest but occur elsewhere in the United States as well. For example, near the tiny town of Direct in Lamar County, Texas, in the mid-1960s, residents described seeing a large pantherlike animal which left tracks like a cat's except that the claws showed. This curious detail appears in many anomalous-feline reports; "real" panthers have retractile claws which do not show in their prints. In at least some cases witnesses have mistaken dog or bear tracks for those of a big cat; but when a sighting and tracks are closely correlated, clawmarks still are reported.

Even in areas where the *Felis concolor* unquestionably exists, for example in northern California, or where it may exist, as in eastern and southern states, black-panther sightings are ubiquitous. Of 615 panther reports collected between 1983 and 1990, the editors of *Eastern Puma Network News* found that no fewer than 37 percent were of black panthers. As J. Richard Greenwell of the International Society of Cryptozoology observes, "Considering that not a single clear and indisputable photo of a living Eastern or Southern puma (except for the 'known' Florida panthers) has ever been obtained, and that zoology does not possess a single skin of a black puma from anywhere, this is a mind-boggling situation."

Britain's alien cats.

In the British Isles, according to orthodox opinion, there is one native wildcat — *Felis silvestris grampia* — or two, if feral domestic cats are counted. *Felis silvestris* is a small cat which once roamed much of the island but is now believed restricted to Scotland and possibly isolated regions of northern England. In the mid-1980s, in a Highlands area of northeastern Scotland, four recently killed wildcats puzzled zoologists until they were able to examine the specimens carefully. They proved to be the hybrid products of *Felis silvestris*/feral cat unions.

Even though all of these happened to be black, no one proposes that such creatures provide a blanket explanation for all, or even most, of the British mystery cats, dark-colored or otherwise, that have sparked debates and theories since the early 1960s, when the "Surrey puma" began to prowl the country lanes of southern England.

In the late summer of 1962, something described as "like a young lion cub — definitely not a fox or a dog" was seen near a reservoir in a Hampshire park. Other sightings occurred but got no more than local attention. All that changed on July 18, 1963, when a truck driver passing through Oxleas Wood, Shooters Hill, London, early that morning was startled to see a "leopard" leap across the road and into the trees on the other side. Later that day four police officers had an even closer encounter: a "large golden animal" jumped over the hood of their squad car before disappearing into the woods. A massive search involving dozens of officers, soldiers, and dogs found only large footprints of a catlike animal.

Other reports from southeastern England followed. Many of the tracks associated with the animals had claws in them, even as witnesses insisted on the cats' resemblance to large panthers or pumas, said to be either "fawn gold" or "black" in color. Deer, sheep, and cattle were found slaughtered, with huge claw marks on their sides. One woman claimed that a "puma" had struck her in the face with its two front paws as she was walking through a wooded area in Hampshire.

To wildlife biologists all of this seemed impossible. Reviewing these early reports, Maurice Burton wrote:

> Altogether, from September 1964 to August 1966, the official records show 362 sightings, and there were many more, possibly as many again, claimed but not officially reported. In other words this animal

[Felis concolor], declared by American experts to be "rarely seen by man," was showing itself on average once a day for a period of two years. The police ... reckon that some 47 of the 362 are "solid" sightings. Even this means that this animal belonging to a species characterized by its highly secretive nature was showing itself about once a fortnight throughout a period of two years. In two years it was reported from places as far apart as Cornwall and Norfolk, over an area of southern England of approximately 10,000 sq. miles. It has even been in two places many miles apart at the same time on the same day. It seems to have been particularly disturbed during one week when its presence was reported from 10 different places in half as many days.

Another wildlife authority, Victor Head, remarked that a single panther would need to eat 250 British roe deer a year to survive; yet there was no evidence of a corresponding reduction in the deer population.

Nonetheless in the years since, anomalous felines — along with associated tracks and slain livestock — reportedly have spread all over the British landscape, exhausting both the patience and the credibility of those who have sought to explain away the sightings as misidentifications, delusions, and hoaxes. They have taken heart, however, from a few incidents. For example, in August 1983 a Buckinghamshire woman saw a large pumalike black cat "wearing a studded collar" — suggesting, of course, that someone had once owned it before releasing it into the wild. In August 1975, in fact, a Manchester man had captured a leopard cub with a collar. In Iverness, Scotland, in 1980 a female puma was trapped. Examiners determined that it had been a pet for most of its life. On July 26, 1988, a hit-and-run driver on Hayling Island, Hampshire, killed a large cat. Another driver who witnessed the incident recovered the body, which proved to be that of a female North African swamp cat *(Felis chaus)*.

Still, if it is hard to believe that the wilds of Britain crawl with giant cats, neither is it easy to believe that they sustain a population of escaped pets and circus animals, which long experience has shown are poorly suited to the wild and usually either starve to death or are recaptured or killed not long after their release or escape. If feral large cats are out there, it is remarkable indeed that so few have been recovered.

Unfortunately, the alternative hypothesis — proposed by Di Francis, author of Cat Country (1983) — that a large, pantherlike cat has survived on the British Isles since Pleistocene times is implausible. Critic Lena G. Bottriell, remarking on the absence of evidence, asks, "[N]ot one skin in a period of some 1,000 years or more? No reports when the population of the same island reduced a smaller cat to the point of virtually killing it out? How much more so a bigger cat, supposedly the size of a puma, which doubtless wouldn't restrict its kills to the type favored by the smaller wildcat, its sheer size dictating a need every 2 to 3 days to bring down far bigger game than the rabbits, pheasants, or lambs sought by the wildcat. The potential depredation on large livestock, not least the stag and deer population, would have driven farmers and gamekeepers down the centuries to desperation, ever-vigilant as the British countryman has always been to the presence of marauding predators."

These problems have led some determined proponents to paranormal theories. One of these is teleportation. Here we are asked to believe that these big cats are real animals instantaneously transported to foreign shores from their traditional habitats; after a residence of anything from a few days to a few months, they return home, presumably in the same eye blink with which they arrived. One homeplace may be Africa, since some witnesses claim to have seen what they call "lions," "cheetahs," or "leopards" (though a careful reading of the reports suggests these words ought not necessarily to be taken literally; witnesses' descriptions almost always seem to be of pumas).

Another paranormal "explanation" draws on the paraphysical hypothesis to propose that the creatures are materialized psychic projections or intruders from parallel worlds. Even if such things are any more possible than teleportation — a long way from certain — such approaches ignore the virtual absence of paranormal elements from sighting reports. The only strange thing (and it is peculiar enough in its own right, no doubt) about such sightings is the presence of a big cat in a place where it has no right to be. But if no one disputed the existence of pumas, some of them melanistic, in Surrey or Nottinghamshire (home of the "Nottingham lion") or Devonshire (the Beast of Exmoor) or Scotland, the sightings would be unexceptional. In other words, appearances do not suggest that these are the feline equivalent of black dog encounters, with their undeniably otherworldly overtones.

Only one case even vaguely suggests something spooky, and it is susceptible to unextraordinary interpretations. It is presented here for what it is worth. In 1964 Charles Bowen of *Flying Saucer Review* interviewed a Godalming, Surrey, farmer named Edward Blanks about his repeated sightings, over a two-year period, of a "yowling" puma. According to Bowen, who had not mentioned his interest in UFOs to Blanks:

> *Part of Mr. Blanks' routine is to make the rounds of his farm before retiring for the night. On two occasions he suddenly became aware of a mysterious light on the roofs of the farm buildings. The light moved from roof to roof, yet he could not see the beam which produced the light. It was certainly not produced by car headlights from the Odiham Road: the local topography precluded that possibility. Mr. Blanks could not trace the source of the light, and he was puzzled and worried by the phenomenon, because on each occasion the mystery puma arrived on the scene afterwards!*

Continental cats.
Sightings of panthers and other anomalous felines have been noted in Western Europe since the 1970s. As in Britain and North America, at least some of the reports seem credible, coming from reliable individuals observing the animals under good viewing conditions, while other reports

● SOURCES:

Bord, Janet, and Colin Bord. *Alien Animals.* Harrisburg, PA: Stackpole Books, 1981.

Bottriell, Lena G. Review of Francis' *Cat Country. Cryptozoology* 4 (1985): 80–83.

Bowen, Charles. "Mystery Animals." *Flying Saucer Review* 10, 6 (November/December 1964): 15–17.

Brocke, Rainer H., Fred G. VanDyke, and Robert L. Downing. "Comments and Responses." *Cryptozoology* 4 (1985): 102–05.

Clark, Jerome, and Loren Coleman. *Creatures of the Outer Edge.* New York: Warner Books, 1978.

Coleman, Loren. *Mysterious America.* Boston, MA: Faber and Faber, 1983.

———. "Phantom Panther on the Prowl." *Fate* 30,11 (November 1977): 62–67.

———. "Black 'Mountain Lions' in California?" *Pursuit* 12, 2 (Spring 1979): 61–62.

———. "On the Trail." *Fortean Times* 32 (Summer 1980): 21–22.

Cropper, Paul. "The Pan-

are less deserving of a sympathetic hearing. In one of the latter instances, a German man claimed to have been attacked by a puma. He produced as evidence some of its hair, which analysis revealed to be from a rabbit.

On the other hand, in one especially impressive sighting which took place in the spring of 1977, several French witnesses, including a policeman with binoculars, saw two large black panthers at a range of 200 yards. Farmers in France and Italy lost livestock to such animals. Authorities attribute these events to the depredations of wolves and wild dogs, but witnesses reject these explanations. German cryptozoologist Ulrich Magin collected reports of all known big-cat escapes from zoos, circuses, or vehicles and found that "such animals are usually caught within hours after their escape, or at least days after."

Australian cats and pseudocats.
Officially no cats besides domestic ones (and feral members of the species) live in Australia. Nonetheless the supposedly, but far from certainly, extinct thylacine, a marsupial which looks something like a cross between a tiger and a dog, was and is sometimes called the "Tasmanian tiger." Though referred to as "tiger cats" or "quolls," dasyurids are also marsupials. These ferocious animals, which do not much resemble tigers, have reddish, spotted coats and at their maximum do not exceed four feet in length.

All this notwithstanding, black panthers are no strangers to the Australian landscape. Most reports have come from the southern coast of New South Wales, but cryptozoologist Paul Cropper, who has been investigating such matters for two decades, has collected others from "areas as far apart as the Dandenongs in Victoria, the New England area of NSW, and the Central Wheat Belt of Western Australia."

As with comparable sightings elsewhere in the world, some have occurred in daylight and at relatively close range; the animals have been linked with livestock slayings (between 1956 and 1957 one Uralla, New South Wales, farmer lost 340 sheep to a large black cat which managed to evade both individual hunters and massive hunting parties); and the prints usually contain claw marks. Also in common with other reports, none has ever been caught or killed. Cropper investigated one report of a killing on the Cambewarra Range in November 1977. When shown the skin, he found it to be from "nothing more than a large feral cat."

It is tempting to account for all sightings in this way, but descriptions and other details from the best reports do not easily accommodate such a hypothesis. Consider this incident, said to have taken place in mid-1975 in the Nowra area, in the Southern Highlands of New South Wales. Cropper writes:

> [A farmer] and his son had been out feeding their pigs around 5 o'clock when he … looked up and [saw] a large black animal unhurriedly ambling along a fence, past their sawmill for a couple of hundred yards. They both had watched this creature at a distance of 300 yards for at least 4 or 5 minutes. He estimated the animal weighed between 4

thers of Southern Australia." *Fortean Times* 32 (Summer 1980): 18–21.

Dash, Mike. "Mystery Moggies." *Fortean Times* 64 (August/September 1992): 44–45.

Downing, Robert L. "The Search for Cougars in the Eastern United States." *Cryptozoology* 3 (1984): 31–49.

"The Eastern Puma: Evidence Continues to Build." *The ISC Newsletter* 8, 3 (Autumn 1989): 1–8.

Eveland, Thomas E. "Cryptoletters." *The ISC Newsletter* 9,3 (Autumn 1990): 9–10.

Goss, Michael. "Britain's Phantom Cats." *Fate* 37, 4 (April 1984): 40–49.

———. "The Queensland Tiger." *Fate* 40, 3 (March 1987): 38–47.

Heuvelmans, Bernard. *On the Track of Unknown Animals.* New York: Hill and Wang, 1958.

"Lion at Large?" *Newsweek* (March 27, 1961): 31, 34.

Magin, Ulrich. "Continental European Big Cats." *Pursuit* 18,3 (Third Quarter 1985): 114–15.

Maloret, Nick. "Swamp Cat Fever." *Fortean Times*

or 5 hundred pounds and stood 2 foot 6 inches high at the shoulder and looked exactly like a black panther. As they watched, the animal sprang 9 ft. to clear a creek, and then disappeared into the bush, leaving a perfect set of pawprints in the soft soil of the creek bank.

The farmer told a neighbor, who had seen the animal earlier, as had his granddaughter in a separate sighting. The two farmers, with several others, went to the creek bank and took a cast of the best-preserved of the creature's tracks. It was huge: four inches by five inches.

Far better known is the so-called Queensland tiger, though reports have been logged as far south as Victoria on Australia's southeastern coast. The tiger was first noted in the zoological literature when Philip Lutley Sclater, secretary of the Zoological Society of London, received reports of what he termed an "undescribed animal about the size of a Dingo … of which no specimen had yet been obtained" around Queensland's Cardwell Bay district. One such letter was from police magistrate Brinsley G. Sheridan:

> *One evening strolling along a path close to the shore of Rockingham Bay, a small terrier, my son's companion, took a scent up from a piece of scrub near the beach, and followed, barking furiously, towards the coast-range westwards. My boy (thirteen years old, but an old bushman, who would put half those described in novels to the blush) followed and found in the long grass, about half a mile from the spot the scent was first taken up, an animal described by himself as follows: — "It was lying camped in the long grass and was as big as a native Dog [dingo]; its face was round like that of a Cat, it had a long tail, and its body was striped from the ribs under the belly with yellow and black. My Dog flew at it, but it could throw him. The animal then ran up a leaning tree, and the Dog barked at it. It then got savage and rushed down the tree at the Dog and then at me. I got frightened and came home."*

Later witnesses would include naturalist George Sharp, who in the early twentieth century saw a similar creature at twilight along the source of the Tully River. It was, he said, "larger and darker than the Tasmanian Tiger, with the stripes showing very distinctly." Not long afterwards a farmer killed one after it had attacked his goats. Sharp followed its tracks through the bush until he came upon the carcass. By then wild pigs had consumed the head and body, but just enough of it was left so that Sharp was able to determine that it had been five feet long. Unfortunately he had nothing with which to preserve the remains, which soon rotted away.

Ion L. Idriess, a longtime York Peninsula resident, once saw a "tiger" disembowel a fully grown kangaroo. On another occasion he found the body of one along the Alice River. It had died in combat with his staghound, which lay dead nearby. Idriess described the "tiger-cat" as the size of a "hefty, medium-sized dog. His body is lithe and sleek and beautifully striped in black and grey. His pads are armed with lance-like claws of

55 (Autumn 1990): 44–46.

"Out of Place." *Fortean Times* 18 (October 1976): 25–27.

"Out of Place." *Fortean Times* 20 (February 1977): 18–20; 25 (Spring 1978): 33–36; 26 (Summer 1978): 42–44; 28 (Winter 1979): 48–51; 30 (Summer 1979): 8–11; 40 (Autumn 1984): 40–44;

Rickard, R. J. M. "'If You Go Down to the Woods Today'…" *INFO Journal* 4, 1 (May 1974): 3–18.

———. "The 'Surrey Puma' and Friends: More Mystery Animals." *The News* 14 (January 1976): 3–8, 17.

———. "The Exmoor Beast and Others." *Fortean Times* 40 (Summer 1983): 52–61.

———. "Once More with Felines." *Fortean Times* 44 (Summer 1985): 28–31.

Rosen, Sven. "Out of Africa." *Fortean Times* 65 (October/November 1992): 44–45.

Sass, Herbert Ravenel. "The Panther Prowls the East Again!" *Saturday Evening Post* 226, 7 (March 13, 1954): 31, 133, 136.

Shuker, Karl P. N. *Mystery Cats of the World:*

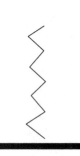

great tearing strength. His ears are sharp and pricked, and his head is shaped like that of a tiger."

In 1926, in their *The Wild Animals of Australasia*, A. S. Le Souef and H. Burrell counted among the fauna of North Australia a "large striped animal which has been aptly described as 'a cat just growing into a tiger.' The animal ... lives in country that man seldom penetrates.... Its stronghold appears to be the rough, rocky country on top of the ranges ... usually covered with heavy forest."

Sightings, though rare, continue virtually to the present. If the reports of slain specimens are true, and there is no particular reason to doubt them, we may assume they refer to a "real" animal, as opposed to the peculiarly elusive black panther. To Australian zoologists the black panther remains as outré as the yowie, that nation's version of Bigfoot or yeti, but the Queensland tiger is regarded as at least fit for discussion. It is, one chronicler notes, a "near-candidate for scientific recognition" — not as a big cat but as the marsupial or pouched "lion" known as *Thylacoleo*, richly documented in the fossil record and believed to have lapsed into extinction 10,000 years ago. Certainly that is the animal the strikingly consistent eyewitness testimony seems to describe, even down to the protruding fangs. If this is so, it probably is only a matter of time before a living or dead specimen falls into a zoologist's hands — assuming, of course, that the animals have not died out in recent years.

From Blue Tigers to Exmoor Beasts. London: Robert Hale, 1989.

————. "The Kellas Cat: Reviewing an Enigma." *Cryptozoology* 9 (1990): 26–40.

Tischendorf, Jay W. "Cryptoletters." *The ISC Newsletter* 10, 1 (Spring 1991): 11.

Wright, Bruce S. *The Ghost of North America.* New York: Vantage Press, 1959.

————. *The Eastern Panther — A Question of Survival.* Toronto, Canada: Clarke, Irwin, 1971.

BROWN MOUNTAIN LIGHTS

Brown Mountain (alt. 2600 feet), situated in the Blue Ridge Mountains of western North Carolina near Morganton, is celebrated in story and song (Scotty Wiseman's bluegrass standard "The Brown Mountain Light") as the location where luminous phenomena have baffled observers for — well, how long depends upon whom you believe and how much documentation you require.

In 1925 Robert Sparks Walker had this to say of the Brown Mountain mystery:

> The descriptions of the strange lights made by various observers do not agree. One person says that it is pale white, as is ordinarily observed through a ground-glass globe, with a faint, irregular halo encircling it. He claims that it is restricted to a prescribed circle, and appears from three to four times in rapid succession, then conceals itself for 20 minutes, when it reappears within the same circle. Another observer, who was standing about eight miles from Brown Mountain, says that suddenly after sunset there blazed into the sky above the mountain a steady glowing ball of light. To him, the light appeared yellowish, and it lasted about half a minute, when it disappeared rather abruptly. It appeared to him like a star from a bursting skyrocket, but much brighter.
>
> To some people it appears stationary; to others, it moves sometimes upward, downward, or horizontally. A minister says that it appeared like a ball of incandescent light in which he could observe a seething motion.

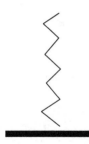

So far as is known, the first printed reference to the lights appeared in the *Charlotte Daily Observer* for September 13, 1913. Citing the testimony of a group of fishermen, the newspaper reported that the "mysterious light is seen just above the horizon almost every night…. With punctual regularity it rises in the southeasterly direction just over the lower slope of Brown Mountain…. It looks much like a toy fire balloon, a distinct ball, with no atmosphere about it … and very red." Not long afterwards D. B. Sterrett of the U.S. Geological Survey investigated and concluded that locomotive headlights were responsible. But participants in a 1916 expedition swore that they had seen the lights just below the summit and, moreover, floating to the southeast in a horizontal direction and in and out of the ravines.

Continuing sightings and debates about their meaning brought another Geological Survey scientist, George Rogers Mansfield, to the area in March and April 1922. He devoted seven evenings to personal observations and supplemented these with a survey of the mountains and with interviews of local residents. He attributed 44 percent of the lights to automobiles, 33 percent to trains, 10 percent to stationary lights, and 10 percent to brush fires. Besides leaving 3 percent unaccounted for, Mansfield was acknowledging what by now seemed obvious: no single explanation covered all the phenomena. He did speculate that the 1916 witnesses had seen nothing more than fireflies, even though he conceded that a government entomologist whom he had consulted held that identification to be "improbable" for various reasons.

In the years since then, witnesses have reported phenomena which they state resemble "toy balloons," "misty spheres," "flood lights," and "sky rockets." In a few instances, when witnesses believe they have been closest to the manifestations, they claim to have heard a sizzling noise. A 1977 experiment beamed a 500,000-candlepower arc from a town 22 miles away to a location west of the mountain where observers lay in wait. The blue-white beam looked like an "orange-red orb apparently hovering several degrees above Brown Mountain's crest." The investigators concluded that refractions of distant lights were largely responsible for the sightings.

Other theorists, such as Britain's Paul Devereux, hold that the lights are evidence of the presence of little-understood, so-far-unrecognized geophysical phenomena he calls "earthlights," but this explanation seems needlessly complex. Local folklore has it that people were seeing the light long before the age of trains and cars; the evidence for this, however, is exceedingly slight. Still, if this claim is ever validated, it would demonstrate that the Brown Mountain lights have not yet surrendered all their secrets.

● SOURCES:

Bessor, John Philip. "Mystery of Brown Mountain." Fate 4, 2 (March 1951): 13–15.

Devereux, Paul. Earth Lights Revelation: UFOs and Mystery Light form Phenomena: The Earth's Secret Energy Force. London: Blandford Press, 1989.

Walker, Robert Sparks. "The Queer Lights of Brown Mountain." Literary Digest 87 (November 7, 1925): 48–49.

CATTLE MUTILATIONS ─────────────────────

In the fall of 1973, farmers in Minnesota and Kansas reported that their cattle were dying under mysterious circumstances. To all appearances persons or forces unknown had killed the animals, though apparently without knife or bullet, and with surgical precision had removed various parts — usually eyes, ears, lips, sex organs, rectum, tail, or combinations thereof. Farmers also frequently claimed that the animals' blood had been drained. Strangest of all, the enigmatic killers accomplished all this without leaving footprints or other evidence of their presence.

Law-enforcement officers were mystified. According to Ottawa County, Kansas, Deputy Gary Dir, "The large majority of these mutilations occurred near occupied houses. In no instances were the animals found less than a quarter-mile from the roadside and none ... more than a quarter-mile from an all-weather, well-traveled road." One carcass in Cloud County was found in a mud hole. Even so, there were no footprints.

In December a dozen Kansas sheriffs met to discuss the problem. Though they had little to go on, most agreed that "cultists" were probably responsible. In southwestern Minnesota, however, authorities were expressing skepticism. Lincoln County Sheriff Albert Thompson, who investigated several deaths, was certain that the animals had died of ordinary cattle diseases and that the so-called cuts were left by small animals ("varmints") which had chewed on the soft parts of the carcasses. Nonetheless many rural people remained convinced that a group of Satanists rumored to exist in the area had killed the animals in bizarre sacrificial rites.

When Kansas authorities brought the carcasses to the Kansas State University Veterinary Laboratory, pathologists determined that the cause of death was blackleg, a bacterial disease often fatal to cattle. State Brand Commissioner Doyle Heft dismissed fears that something out of the ordinary was going on.

The "cattle mutilation" phenomenon had begun.

Satanists, secret services, and saucers.
Most of the essential elements were in place by early 1974: seemingly mysterious cattle deaths, a widespread conviction these were the acts of cultists, and prosaic findings from autopsies conducted by the veterinary pathologists.

The incidents, real or imagined, soon spread to other states in the Midwest and West and even into Canada's western provinces. By the late 1970s, newspapers claimed that several thousand unexplained cattle deaths had taken place even as clues to the perpetrators' identity remained elusive. Paranoia and speculation were running rampant. Four schools of thought emerged. The first blamed cultists for the depredations; a second suspected a conspiracy involving intelligence agents who were conducting secret chemical/biological-warfare experiments; a third pointed to UFOs and extraterrestrials; and the fourth laid the cause to hysteria about what were in fact ordinary deaths.

Police agencies in Alberta, Idaho, Montana, and Iowa found a few cases in which circumstantial evidence tied Satanist groups to cattle mutilations. Laboratory analysis confirmed that a small number of animals had been killed after being drugged. In Idaho a police informant infiltrated a group which claimed to have mutilated cattle, though he himself did not personally witness such an act. Some reliable sightings of black-hooded figures, presumably cultists in ritual garb, were recorded, though any connection between these and animals' deaths could only be speculative. Officers, farmers, and ranchers occasionally stumbled upon what they believed to be evidence of ritual activity, such as stone altars and the bodies of small animals.

In 1975 Donald Flickinger, a Minneapolis-based agent of the U.S. Treasury Department's Alcohol, Tobacco and Firearms division, was assigned to investigate reports of a nationwide Satanist network involved in animal and human mutilation. He found no supporting evidence, and his principal informant, convicted bank robber Albert Kenneth Bankston, proved untrustworthy. It turned out that Bankston had drawn on prison rumors and his own freewheeling imagination to get himself transferred from the federal penitentiary in Leavenworth, Kansas, to a small-town Minnesota jail where he supposedly would be safe to testify. Subsequently Bankston persuaded authorities to bring up a friend from Leavenworth, Dan Dugan. The two later broke out of jail — their intention all along — though the police recaptured them in short order.

Speculations concerning secret intelligence operations came out of Vietnam- and Watergate-era fears that the U.S. government could be counted on to be up to no good — which was not the logical conclusion from an abundance of evidence. In fact, the only arguably suggestive physical evidence consisted of a curious, if ultimately inconclusive, discovery made in Lincoln County, Colorado, in 1975. A rancher found a blue satchel —

● SOURCES:

Adams, Tom, and Gary Massey. *Mystery Helicopters and Animal Mutilations: Exploring a Connection.* Paris, TX: The Authors, 1979.

Bayles, Fred. "Scoffers, Believers Abound in Mutilated-Cattle Mystery." *Washington Post* (January 1, 1986).

Clark, Jerome. "Strange Case of the Cattle Killings." *Fate* 27, 8 (August 1974): 79–90.

———. *UFOs in the 1980s: The UFO Encyclopedia, Volume 1.* Detroit, MI: Apogee Books, 1990.

"The Cult Connection." *Stigmata* 11 (Fourth Quarter 1980): 10–21.

Donovan, Roberta, and Keith Wolverton. *Mystery Stalks the Prairie.* Raynesford, MT: T.H.A.R. Institute, 1976.

Ellis, Bill. "Cattle Mutilation: Contemporary Legends and Contemporary Mythologies." *Contemporary Legend* 1 (1991): 39–80.

assumed to be government issue — near his mailbox. Inside the satchel he discovered plastic artificial insemination gloves, a bloody scalpel, a cow's ear, and part of a tongue. The Colorado Bureau of Investigation unsuccessfully checked for fingerprints, and area law-enforcement officers were unable to connect the animal parts with any cattle-mutilation reports known to them.

Persistent reports of "mystery helicopters" also fueled speculations. Summarizing reports to 1979, "mutologists" Tom Adams and Gary Massey remarked that such aircraft "are almost entirely without identifying markings, or markings may appear to have been painted over or covered with something. The craft are frequently reported flying at abnormal, unsafe or illegal altitudes. The mystery choppers may shy away if witnesses or law officers try to approach. On the other hand, there are several accounts of aggressive behavior on the part of the helicopter occupants, with witnesses chased, 'buzzed,' hovered-over or even fired upon." No direct link between these reports and mutilations has ever been established, however.

In 1979 and 1980 a New Jersey investigator, Peter A. Jordan, gave photographs of mutilated New Mexico cattle to four East Coast psychics, who independently produced readings which seemed to describe an intelligence operation. None of their information checked out in any meaningful way.

Evil ETs.

To a number of mutologists, farmers, ranchers, and rural police officers, the apparently extraordinary features associated with the cattle deaths — notably the absence of footprints and the supposedly surgically precise cuttings on the carcasses — indicated that the mutilators must be of unearthly origin. *Strange Harvest*, a 1980 documentary produced and written by Denver filmmaker Linda Moulton Howe, attracted considerable

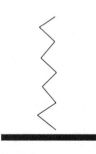

attention and was widely influential in shaping popular beliefs about UFO-generated cattle mutilations.

Belief in cattle-killing extraterrestrials spread quickly, even in the absence of compelling evidence. Few UFO reports suggested a direct connection with cattle deaths. One that did was recounted under hypnosis; a woman told University of Wyoming psychologist and ufologist R. Leo Sprinkle that she had seen a cow drawn up into a UFO "in a pale, yellow beam of light." She and her daughter also were taken into the object and saw aliens dismembering the animal.

Subsequently Sprinkle hypnotized a second woman who told a somewhat similar story. This woman reportedly was abducted with her son, and during the experience the two encountered aliens with "burning eyes, like the devil." Even more terrifying, the woman saw a vat containing blood and human body parts. This story bears a striking resemblance to one told in *Jay's Journal* (1979), a novelization of a young man's initiation into a Satanic cult that mutilates cattle.

From these small (and hardly conclusive) elements there grew a complex mythology which by the early 1990s had become a minor social movement based on the idea that evil UFO beings have entered into an agreement with America's "secret government" whereby the aliens are permitted to mutilate cattle and abduct human beings in exchange for extraterrestrial technology. Some versions of the tale have it that the government looks away as aliens mutilate people as well as animals. These yarns, for which no supporting evidence exists, have been spread through books, lectures, and videos by conspiracy theorists Milton William Cooper, William English, and others. All claim to have learned of these terrible secrets from unnamed intelligence informants and government documents. Critics have raised questions about the sincerity and motives of Cooper and English.

Conventional causes.

In 1979 the First Judicial District of New Mexico received a $40,000 grant from the Federal Law Enforcement Assistance Administration to investigate mutilations in that state. A former FBI agent, Kenneth Rommel, took charge. In April 1980, at the conclusion of his investigation, Rommel announced that he had found no evidence of cattle mutilations. He had worked on 24 cases in New Mexico and established extensive contacts in other states with law-enforcement officers whose own inquiries had led them to be skeptical. Rommel concluded that "all of the mutilations investigated by me were caused by and totally consistent with what one would expect to find from normal predation, scavenger activity, and decomposition of a dead animal."

Rommel blamed incompetent investigations, speculation, exaggeration, and ignorance for manufacturing a mystery which did not exist. His conclusions echoed those reached earlier by authorities in other states, though Rommel's received the most attention because he put them into a comprehensive official report. Academic social scientists who had investigated the

Grindstaff, Sharon. "Death of Heifer Ruled Due to Disease, Not Satanists, but UFO Investigators Sense Alien Involvement." *Berryville [Arkansas] Star Progress* (February 14, 1991).

Hall, Richard H. "Livestock Mutilations: A National Mystery." *Zetetic Scholar 7* (December 1980): 43–51.

Howe, Linda Moulton. *An Alien Harvest: Further Evidence Linking Animal Mutilations and Human Abductions to Alien Life Forms.* Littleton, CO: Linda Moulton Howe Productions, 1989.

Jordan, Peter A. "Psychometry and Cattle Mutilation: Four Psychics and Their Readings." *Fortean Times* 38 (Autumn 1982): 4–14.

Kagan, Daniel, and Ian Summers. *Mute Evidence.* New York: Bantam Books, 1984.

Owen, Nancy H. *Preliminary Analysis of the Impact of Livestock Mutilations on Rural Arkansas Communities.* Fayetteville, AR: University of Arkansas Department of Anthropology, January 1980.

Rommel, Kenneth M. *Operation Animal Mutilation.* Report of the District Attorney, First Judicial District, State of

mutilation panic's spread characterized the episode as a case of mass hysteria, fueled by exotic theories and unfounded statements which were quoted uncritically in press accounts.

In 1984 two New York writers, Daniel Kagan and Ian Summers, who had traveled the western United States and Canada researching the phenomenon and the individuals involved with it, wrote a thick book, *Mute Evidence*, which will probably remain the definitive account. In examining the origins and evolution of the legend, Kagan and Summers pointed to a small group of "mutology buffs," most of them also UFO enthusiasts, whom they held accountable. None of them, they charged, "had access to any experts in veterinary medicine, livestock, or any other fields that bore on the cattle mutilation question, and it was obvious there was not one seriously qualified investigator in their underground. They were all amateurs, all poorly trained to deal with the subject, and all seemingly uniquely ignorant of research procedures and methods of constructing proven cases.... They had nothing going for them, yet they controlled the opinions of literally hundreds of thousands, perhaps millions of people, regarding cattle mutilations. Not one of their testimonies would be acceptable as expert or even informed in a court of law."

By the early 1980s press accounts were asserting that as many as 10,000 mutilations had taken place. Kagan and Summers, who checked official cattle mortality rates, learned that cattle had died in normal numbers all through the most intense years of the mutilation scare. The 10,000 figure turned out to be the invention of a mutologist who conceded it had come essentially out of thin air. In 1991, reporting on a "mutilated" heifer calf which a veterinarian determined had died of blackleg and been chewed on by buzzards, an Arkansas newspaper quoted two "UFO investigators" who said 700,000 mutilations had occurred, and that the alien beings who performed them used "lasers" to do the cutting.

To all appearances the cattle-mutilation legend is one of the most durable myths of the late twentieth century.

New Mexico. Santa Fe, NM: District Attorney, June 1980.

Sanders, Ed. "The Mutilation Mystery." *Oui* 5, 9 (September 1976): 50–52, 92,113–22.

———. "On the Trail of the Night Surgeons." *Oui* 6, 5 (May 1977): 78–80, 121–30, 134.

Smith, Frederick W. *Cattle Mutilation: The Unthinkable Truth.* Cedaredge, CO: Freedland Publishers, 1976.

Sparks, Beatrice. *Jay's Journal.* New York: New York Times Book Company, 1979.

Stewart, James R. "Cattle Mutilations: An Episode of Collective Delusion." *The Zetetic* 1, 2 (Spring/Summer 1977): 55–66.

Vallee, Jacques. *Messengers of Deception: UFO Contacts and Cults.* Berkeley, CA: And/Or Press, 1979.

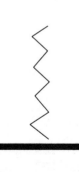

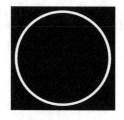

CHAMP

Champ is, at least according to some, Lake Champlain's version of the Loch Ness monster: a large, long-necked animal which bears a general resemblance to a plesiosaur, an aquatic reptile usually deemed extinct these past 65 million years. In fact, witnesses' accounts offer up a more complex picture than that. According to Joseph Zarzynski, who has investigated and written on the monster, there are over 300 recorded sightings.

Formed approximately 10,000 years ago out of melting glaciers, Lake Champlain is a deep, cold-water, 109-mile-long lake. It stretches north from Whitehall, New York, along the New York-Vermont border and ends a few miles into Quebec. There, at Sorel, it drains into the Saint Lawrence River; the Saint Lawrence flows into the North Atlantic Ocean, of which Champlain's parent Champlain Sea was once an estuary. The largest North American body of water outside the Great Lakes, it harbors some 80 different species of fish — more than enough to feed a family of monster-sized predators, if such exist.

In popular lore (traceable to an article by the late Marjorie L. Porter in the Summer 1970 issue of *Vermont Life*) the first white man to see the monster was Samuel de Champlain, after whom the lake is named. Champlain is supposed to have mentioned the creature in a 1609 chronicle of his explorations of the Saint Lawrence and associated rivers, but that source, which few writers on the subject seem to have consulted directly, indicates only that he saw large fish, identifiable from his description as garfish, whose undisputed presence in Champlain continues to this day.

(In using the singular "Champ" or "monster," we do not mean to imply that there is only one such creature. Obviously, if Champ is a real animal, it is part of a breeding population. Indeed, a handful of reports speak of two or more such entities. Thus "Champ" and "monster" are used here in something of a generic sense to represent the phenomenon in its totality.)

The Champ saga really begins, more or less, in 1873. The qualification has to do with a curious fact later many proponents of the monster would obscure: namely, the early monster and its modern version do not appear to be the same animal. The former, invariably described as a gigantic serpent, is no plesiosaur.

The earliest known newspaper story about a monster in Lake Champlain (*Whitehall* [New York] *Times,* July 9, 1873) recounts the adventure of a railroad work crew which, while laying track on the lake shore near Dresden, New York, "saw a head of an enormous serpent sticking out of the water and approaching them from the opposite shore." So terrified that at first they could not move, the crew stood paralyzed for some moments before scattering. The monster then turned toward the open water and departed. The *Times* reported:

> As he rapidly swam away, portions of his body, which seemed to be covered with bright silver-like scales, glistened in the sun like burnished metal. From his nostrils he would occasionally spurt stream of water above his head to an altitude of about 20 feet. The appearance of his head was round and flat, with a hood spreading out from the lower part of it like a rubber cap often worn by mariners with a cape to keep the rain from running down the neck. His eyes were small and piercing, his mouth board and provided with two rows of teeth, which he displayed to his beholders. As he moved off at a rate of 10 miles an hour, portions of his body appeared above the surface of the water, while his tail, which resembled that of a fish, was thrown out of the water quiteoften. Its head was said to be 20 inches in diameter. A quarter-mile into the lake, the creature sank suddenly out of sight.

Except for this last detail about the sinking (as opposed to diving), little of this story resembles twentieth-century reports. There is nothing mentioned here, for example, about the hump or humps most later witnesses would remark on, and the "scales" are a discordant detail which would, however, show up in subsequent early reports. (Seen in February 1880 by a group of Vermont men, it was said to be "covered with scales which glistened like the precious metals in the sun," according to the *Newport* [Vermont] *Express & Standard*, February 24.)

Within a few days of the Dresden sighting, farmers were complaining of missing livestock. Tracks and other marks in the ground indicated that something had dragged the animals into the lake. In caves along the waterside, locals claimed, "bright and hideous looking eyes" could sometimes be seen in the darkness. A few days later a young farmer saw the serpent in a lakeside marsh, with something that looked like a turtle in its mouth. He fired on it, and the creature disappeared into the water.

Other sightings and livestock kills followed, and search parties prowled the shoreline and surrounding farms. In early August a small steamship, *W. B. Eddy*, struck the serpent and nearly overturned. The head and neck of the creature surfaced 100 feet away. On August 9 the crew of the *Molyneaux* believed it had the monster trapped in the thick weeds of Axehelve Bay. Though no one could actually see it, the decision was made to fire into the thickets and await the result. According to the *Whitehall Times* (August 13):

> At a signal, the first three shots were sent. The smoke curled up from the muzzles of the guns as the contents went crackling in among the bushes. As three more muskets sent an echoing noise among the crags and peaks of Dresden, a terrible crackling and whistling noise greeted our ears. The noise was similar to that made by a great engine when it is discharging steam as its piston enters the steam chest. First, it was a low, suppressed bass whistle; then it gradually rose in strength and tone until our ears were greeted by a most unearthly noise.... The order was given (by Captain Belden) to steam away as the head of the mammoth snake appeared through the tangled vines and brushwood. The greyish hood upon his head flopped backwards and forwards like the immense ears of an elephant when being punished by his keeper. Great ridges of silver appeared above the surface of the water, undulating and scintillating in the bright sun like the highly polished surface of a warrior's silver helmet. The fanlike tail of the horrid monster was waved in the air about six feet above the water's surface. His eyes resembled two burning coals, fairly snapping fire, as its rage increased, while the rows of long and formidable teeth, pearly white and wicked looking, sent an indescribable thrill through us, which we shall never forget. The body seemed to be about 18 to 20 inches thick in the middle, and 36 to 40 feet long while it gradually tapered off to both extremes.... Our vessel began moving downstream. Shots were discharged at the great moving, waving mass of silver. Two streams of water arose high above the monster's head, the wind blowing the spray over us all on the boat.... Shots were sent toward the monster by members of the party, and as he lashed the water with his fishlike tail and gave great spasmodic, powerful lurches with his broad flat head, we were confident that the shots were telling.... Only about 25 feet was between us and the infuriated serpent. Hon. Charles Hughes and General Barrett discharged each a shot at it, when the head was seen to turn, the immense body begin to curve.... Streams of red blood spurted from its head.... At last the excited party observed the serpent give one spasmodic twist of its immense length, forming a circle by bringing its head toward its tail; then the great serpent, which had caused so much excitement in this vicinity, disappeared beneath the red sea of blood, never to rise more by its own exertions.

Attempts to raise the body proved unsuccessful, though searchers hoping to collect a $50,000 reward from P. T. Barnum, who wired the Whitehall newspaper to express his interest in the "hide of the great Champlain serpent to add to my mammoth World's Fair Show."

These events, or alleged events, took place in the Dresden area at the southwestern edge of the lake. When the monster or a relative returned a few years later, it had moved north to the shore near Plattsburgh along Champlain's northwest side.

On July 31, 1883, the *Plattsburgh Morning Telegram* reported Clinton County Sheriff Nathan H. Mooney's sighting of an "enormous snake or water serpent ... 25 to 35 feet in length." Beginning in the summer of 1886, sightings were registered almost daily from just about every part of the lake. One man fishing near Plattsburgh claimed to have hooked what he first thought was an enormous fish, but when its head reared out of the water, he and three other witnesses saw it was a "horrible creature." The line snapped, and the unwanted catch disappeared underwater.

Around this time a Saint Albans, Vermont, man hunting ducks along the Mississquoi River, which flows out of the lake, said he came upon an "enormous serpent coiled up on the swampy shore and asleep ... as large around as a man's thigh." When he reached back to get his gun, the slight noise he made was enough to awaken the creature, which shot toward the underbrush "making as much noise ... as a large hound would."

Sightings continued into the next year. At two o'clock one morning in May 1887, for example, a farm boy heard strange noises and went out to the shore. A mile out in the water a big serpent was "making noises like a steamboat." In several cases witnesses claimed the creature had acted aggressively, swimming menacingly toward them and causing them to beat a hasty retreat. Most spectacularly, it reportedly appeared in the view of a party of Charlotte, Vermont, picnickers who were on an early July outing near the lake. Seventy-five feet long and as big around as a barrel, it bore down on the group until several women screamed and the creature turned around and swam off.

Shortly afterwards this report was published in *Plattsburgh Morning Telegram*:

> The sea serpent ... has left the lake and is making his way overland in the direction of Lake George [New York]. He was seen last night about five o'clock by a farmer driving to his barn with a load of hay. Chancing to look behind him ... he saw ... not five rods behind him, gliding along like a snake with its head raised about four feet from the ground ... an immense monster anywhere from 25 to 75 feet in length, with gray and black streaks, running lengthwise of its body which was covered with scales.

In September 1889 a party of fishermen on the lake chased the creature. Fifteen feet of it was visible, and they made out an unserpentlike detail: it had, they said, "many large fins" (*Essex County Republican*, September 26). In the summer of 1899, a witness described only as a "wealthy New Yorker" reported seeing a 35-foot-long serpent with an arched back, a head "like an inverted platter" (whatever that means), and a broad flat tail raised a few feet out of the water (*Plattsburgh Republican*, August 5). This last detail indicates the animal — assuming for the moment that this report is not a hoax — was a mammal, not a reptile. Perhaps, as some have proposed, it was a zeuglodon, a snakelike whale which supposedly went out of existence 20 million years ago.

The twentieth-century monster.

If anything, the confusion about Champ's identity grows in our century. The plesiosaurlike Champ would emerge as the "classic" monster only in the 1970s. So far as we know, not a single sighting *recorded at the time of its occurrence* refers to a long, thin neck attached to a bulky reptilian body. The few early reports of this sort of animal are from testimony collected years afterwards, as in an account related at least four decades later by an elderly woman. She claimed that sometime in the 1920s or 1930s she and her brother had witnessed the sudden surfacing of a creature with three camel-like humps and a head like a boa constrictor's. Skeptics will argue, with reason if not with a certain grasp of the truth, that memories of such events have been contaminated by a monster image of recent invention.

In fact, many pre-1970s reports are so devoid of detail that it is difficult to understand just what the witnesses thought they were seeing. In those in which an adequate description is offered, the animal is often said to look like a huge snake, as in the nineteenth-century accounts. Some mention scales, which snakes do not possess. Some sightings apparently are of large fish, presumably sturgeons, and in a few instances the appearances are likened to (nonprehistoric) whales and eels.

In one of the very rare twentieth-century land sightings, this one made from a passing car in the spring of 1961, Thomas E. Morse reported what "appeared to be a monstrous eel with white teeth that raked rearward in the mouth." It was resting on the shore of Champlain's North West Bay in Westport, New York.

A sighting from the summer of 1970 is of particular interest for two reasons: one, it involves not only multiple but independent witnesses and, two, it tells us something of how a serpentlike entity is transformed into a Ness-style plesiosaur in the imaginations of those who want them to be the same animal. In the August 9, 1978, issue of the *Plattsburgh Valley News*, two accounts appear, written by Champ witnesses who had not spoken in the eight years since their mutual sighting. One of them, Richard Spear, tells of seeing the creature with his 13-year-old daughter Susanne as the two of them sat atop a ferry heading toward the Essex, New York, shore midway down the lake.

Spear writes that the creature, 90 yards or so from shore and "dark brownish-olive" in color, was "the size and shape of a barrel in cross-section. When first seen two 'bumps' were in evidence, each rising to about three feet above the surface and four feet in length, separated by about the same distance." As he helped his daughter with binoculars, she saw its head, which she said looked like a horse's. By the time Spear turned his head back, the creature was disappearing below the surface.

An enthusiastic theorist would have no trouble equating "bumps" with "humps" and noting, correctly, that many witnesses at Ness have said the animal's head looked like a horse's. But another ferry witness, Happy Marsh, who gave her separate testimony in the same issue of the newspaper (and who said that she had seen an identical creature in 1965 or 1966), said "it was a large snakelike creature, swimming with her head above water, held as snakes do, with coils behind. I am no judge of size, but I should say she was between 18 and 20 feet long. It was black, and swimming slowly. Her head was about three feet long, wrinkled like a raisin, with a small ridge down the back, a snake body[,] and was blackish-brown."

This more detailed description hardly resolves the issue. The animal Mrs. Marsh evokes has the features generally of a giant snake, eel, and zeuglodon without being any one of them in particular. In any case, it is not a plesiosaur or anything like one.

Reviewing Joseph W. Zarzynski's *Champ — Beyond the Legend* (1984), Henry H. Bauer, a leading academic authority on the Ness phenomenon, complained that the author's effort to link the two has "little specific justification. The listed sightings include a goodly number of descriptions as 'snake-like', which has never been said of Nessie; smooth skin is reported whereas Nessie's is rough, warty; eyes are featured several times, and fins and manes, which are almost totally lacking in reports from Loch Ness."

Still, some clear and specific reports of a Ness-like animal do exist. For example, Orville Wells's sketch of the "prehistoric monster" he claims to have seen in Champlain's Treadwell Bay in 1976 could easily have been drawn from a Loch Ness experience. Several witnesses have said specifically that what they saw looked like a "dinosaur." Perhaps such cases could be explained or rationalized away if it were not for the fact of the Mansi photograph — the one most substantive item of evidence for the reality of Champ as an extraordinary animal.

The Mansi photograph.
In early July 1977 a Connecticut couple, Anthony and Sandra Mansi, were vacationing in Vermont. Just past Saint Alban's Bay and somewhere near the Canadian border (they would never be able to recall the exact site), they stopped so that Sandra's two small children from a previous marriage could play in Champlain's water.

They parked their car and walked 100 to 200 feet across a field, then descended a six-foot bank to the waterline. As the children waded near the shore, Mansi went back to the car to retrieve his sunglasses and a camera.

Some moments later Mrs. Mansi noticed bubbles in the water about 150 feet away. In short order a huge animal with a small head, long neck, and humped back rose to the surface. As it moved its head from right to left, Mrs. Mansi thought it resembled a creature from a prehistoric age.

By this time her husband had returned, and he, too, watched the thing with mounting alarm. He and Sandra called the children (who, unaware of what was happening in the water behind them, never saw the creature), and Anthony tossed the camera to Sandra, instructing her to take a picture.

66

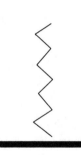

She took one photograph before the animal sank — it did not dive — under the water. The sighting had lasted between two and four minutes.

Fearing ridicule, the Mansis did not publicize their experience. Instead they placed the photograph, which had turned out remarkably well, into a family album. In time they lost the negative. Eventually Mrs. Mansi showed the picture to friends at her place of work, and by 1980 rumors of it reached Zarzynski, a Wilton, New York, social studies teacher. Zarzynski won the couple's trust and commenced an investigation.

He showed the photograph to a number of experts, including George Zug of the Department of Vertebrate Zoology at the Smithsonian Institution's National Museum of Natural History. Zug said it bore no resemblance to any known animal in the lake or anywhere else. Roy Mackal, biologist and vice president of the International Society of Cryptozoology (ISC), also examined it. Soon afterwards B. Roy Frieden of the University of Arizona's Optical Sciences Center conducted a careful analysis.

He determined that the photograph was not a montage. In other words, it had not been doctored by someone's pasting the image of Champ over a photograph of the lake. The wave patterns around the object purporting to be Champ suggested vertical rather than horizontal disturbance, which indicate that the "object" had come up from under the surface instead of moving along the surface as would be the case if it were an artificial device being pulled by a rope.

Frieden could not determine its size because the photograph provided no clear points of reference. It did not, for example, show precisely where the shoreline began, which would have helped investigators determine the dimensions of the object and its distance from the observers. But University of British Columbia oceanographer Paul LeBlond found another method of determining at least an approximate size: by measuring the length of the waves around the object. Using a formula which relates the speed of the wind and the distance of the open water over which the wind blows to wave properties, LeBlond estimated the waves to be between 16 and 39 feet in length. When he compared the "unknown object" with the waves in its vicinity, he found that it occupied one and a half to two wavelengths. Therefore, he concluded, the part of the object that was above water could not be less than 24 feet or more than 78 feet. In short, the object was enormous.

If this was a hoax, it is truly an extraordinary one, and also an enormously expensive one. But if that were the case, why did Mrs. Mansi wait for well over three years before allowing it to become public? Even more to the point, why did she take only *one* photograph? Over a decade later, evidence for the hoax hypothesis had yet to emerge. By any standard the Mansi photograph remains a genuine mystery and a serious obstacle to any effort to reduce the Champ phenomenon to mundane causes.

● SOURCES:

Bauer, Henry H. Review of Zarzynski's Champ — Beyond the Legend. Zetetic Scholar 12/13 (1987): 176–77.

Coleman, Loren. Mysterious America. Boston: Faber and Faber, 1983.

Greenwell, J. Richard. "Comments and Responses: Tracing Monsters." Cryptozoology 6 (1987): 137–40.

Hall, Robert F., ed. The Natural History of the Lake Champlain Monster. Supplement to Elizabethtown [New York] Valley News (August 10, 1978).

"Lake Champlain Monster Draws Worldwide Attention." The ISC Newsletter 1, 2 (Summer 1982): 1–4.

LeBlond, Paul H. "An Estimate of the Dimensions of the Lake Champlain Monster from the Length of Adjacent Wind Waves in the Mansi Photograph." Cryptozoology 1 (1982): 54–61.

Smith, Richard D. "Testing an Underwater Video System at Lake Champlain." Cryptozoology 3 (1984): 89–93.

———. "Investigations and Systems Tests in the Lake Champlain Basin,

67

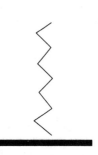

It also lends credence to the otherwise-debatable Nessie/Champ link. ISC secretary J. Richard Greenwell noted the striking resemblances between the famous surgeon's photograph (taken at the loch in April 1934) and the Mansi photograph. When tracings of the two profiles are compared, the relative neck/head proportions "are very similar," the few dissimilarities the likely result of "differences in angle and posture" rather than "taxonomic differences."

The continuing investigation.

In the 1970s Zarzynski formed the Lake Champlain Phenomena Investigation. The LCPI interviews witnesses and conducts archival searches for historical references to Champ. It also conducts extensive surveillance — visual and electronic — at the lake, so far with minimal results. Updates on the investigation appear regularly in the ISC's *Newsletter* and journal *Cryptozoology*. Zarzynski has also lobbied, with some success, for legal protection for Champ.

"Champ" may, however, not exist. If it is not a make-believe mystery created by hoaxes and misperceptions — which is certainly a possible, if not necessarily overwhelmingly compelling, conclusion to be drawn from the available evidence — it may be a catchall name for a variety of animals, some known but out of place, some conventional if unusual, and one or two genuine unknowns. Because Champlain is linked with the ocean, possibly such animals wander in and out. But until or unless the evidence gets better, just about anything we can say about Lake Champlain's fabled monster is almost wholly speculative.

1986." *Cryptozoology* 5 (1986): 85–88.

Smith, Richard D., and William L. Konrad. "Investigations and Sonar Testing at Lake Champlain, 1987." *Cryptozoology* 6 (1987): 85–87.

"Update on Sightings." *Champ Channels* 4, 3 (1986): 1–3.

Zarzynski, Joseph W. *Champ: Beyond the Legend.* Port Henry, NY: Bannister Publications, 1984.

———. "LCPI Work at Lake Champlain, 1984." *Cryptozoology* 3 (1984): 80–83.

———. "LCPI Work at Lake Champlain, 1986." *Cryptozoology* 5 (1986): 77–80.

———. "LCPI Work at Lake Champlain, 1987." *Cryptozoology* 6 (1987): 71–77.

———. "Lake Champlain's Monster Fossil." *Strange Magazine* 5 (1990): 30–31.

CLOUDS, ANOMALOUS ————————————

One pleasant summer morning in 1975, an Oyster Bay, New York, science teacher named Tom D'Ercole was in his driveway about to enter his car when he took a last glance up at the sky. There, hovering above the roof of his house, he saw a small dark cloud unlike the occasional cumulocirrus clouds that were floating by at a much higher altitude.

"The 'cloud' seemed to move and slightly enlarge as I watched it," D'Ercole related. "This basketball-sized 'cloud' floated back and forth across the peak of the roof, changing in shape from a small globular mass to a larger ovoid and finally becoming an abstract, multicurved, dark, vaporous 'something.' It finally measured about six feet in height and 1 1/2 feet in width."

Stunned and unable to think of a rational explanation, he continued to watch in disbelief as events took an even stranger turn. The cloud seemed to inhale, purse its "lips," and direct a stream of water toward him and the car, soaking both. After a minute the spray stopped, and the cloud vanished instantly.

After changing his clothes, D'Ercole took his wet shirt to Garden City Junior High School, where he worked, and ran a pH test on it. The precipitation was simply water.

This event, which sounds like nature's idea of a prank, may or may not be beyond current science's ability to explain. Clouds are capable of peculiar appearance and behavior. In his *Tornados, Dark Days, Anomalous Precipitation, and Related Weather Phenomena* (1983) William R. Corliss culls from the scientific literature reports of cloud arches, luminous clouds, rumbling clouds, clouds with holes in them, and more. Though unusual, these are, no doubt, mostly or entirely of more interest to meteorologists than to those seeking evidence of truly inexplicable events in the atmosphere. This entry concerns the latter: instances of clouds so peculiar that some of them, in fact, may not have been clouds at all.

Falls from clouds.
Falls from the sky of organic or inorganic materials sometimes are associated with unusual clouds.

One interesting case, reported in scientific journals of the period, concerned a small, slow-moving, perfectly spherical white cloud which suddenly appeared in an otherwise clear sky northwest of Agen, France, at 11 A.M. on September 5, 1814. Within a few minutes it stopped and remained motionless for a period of time, then abruptly sped southward, all the while revolving on its own axis and emitting ear-shattering rumbling noises. These climaxed with an explosion and the expulsion of a variety of stones, some of them of impressive dimensions. The cloud then ceased its movement and faded slowly away.

Comparable events are recorded at Sienna, Italy (1794), Chassigny, France (1815), Noblesville, Indiana (1823), and elsewhere.

In a letter published in a 1932 issue of *Science*, John Zeleny recalled a strange sight he had witnessed "on a clear summer night at Hutchinson, Minnesota, some 35 years ago." A solitary brightly luminous cumulus cloud "rose majestically from the eastern horizon," he recalled, "shone with a uniform, steady, vivid, whitish light and passed directly over the town. When the cloud was overhead a great shower of insects descended to earth covering the ground all around to the number of about 50 to 100 per square foot. These insects proved to be a species of hemiptera and were nonluminous."

That same summer (if Zeleny was correct in thinking the episode to have taken place in 1897) numerous small, blood-colored clouds filled the sky over Macerata, Italy. An hour later a storm broke, during which thousands of seeds fell. Unfamiliar to local people, they were eventually identified as being those of a kind of tree found only in central Africa and the Antilles.

Cigars in clouds.
"Although I have studied the skies for many years," Charles Tilden Smith wrote in the British scientific journal *Nature*, "I have never seen anything like it before." "It" was two triangle-shaped shadows in the clouds. These dark patches maintained their stationary position even as the clouds rolled on. To all appearances, he said, each was a "heavy shadow cast upon a thin veil of clouds by some unseen object."

This sighting took place on April 8, 1912, at Chisbury, Wiltshire, England. After the commencement of the flying-saucer era 35 years later, it would have been noted in the UFO literature as yet another instance in which UFOs had hidden themselves in clouds. As early as 1919, in The Book of the Damned, anomalies chronicler Charles Fort was speculating, "If a large substantial mass, or super-construction, should enter this earth's atmosphere, it is our acceptance that it would sometimes … look like a cloud."

Fort's prescient remark anticipated a later phenomenon which would be dubbed the "cloud cigar." Cloud cigars figured in a number of UFO reports from the late 1940s (what may have been the first was reported in Toronto in November 1947) into the 1960s but, for some reason, few if any after that. Usually such objects were associated with smaller disc-shaped structures; thus cloud cigars were also known as "motherships."

Just before the onset of the great autumn 1954 UFO wave in France, several witnesses, among them a businessman, two police officers, and an Army engineer, recounted a spectacular observation of an extraordinary object over the town of Vernon. Businessman Bernard Miserey, who watched it from his driveway at 1 A.M. on August 23, described it as an enormous vertical cigar, 300 feet long, hovering above the north bank of the Seine River 1,000 feet away. According to his testimony, "Suddenly from the bottom of the cigar came an object like a horizontal disc, which dropped at first in free fall, then slowed, and suddenly swayed and dived horizontally across the river toward me, becoming very luminous" before vanishing in the southwest. Over the next 45 minutes other, similar discs dropped out of the cigar. By this time the mother craft had lost its luminosity and disappeared into the darkness.

Though no clouds are mentioned in connection with this sighting, it set the scene for an even more spectacular event. This one, with hundreds of witnesses, took place three weeks later on September 14, in the southwest of France along the Atlantic coast. At 5 P.M., while working with his men in a field, a wealthy farmer who lived near St-Prouant saw a "regular shape something like a cigar or a carrot" drop rapidly out of a thick layer of clouds. The object, essentially horizontal though tipped slightly toward the earth, was luminous and rigid, and its movements did not correlate with the clouds just above it. It looked, Georges Fortin said, like a "gigantic machine surrounded by mists." It ceased its descent, then moved into a vertical position and became motionless.

By now citizens of half a dozen local villages, as well as farmers living in the region, were watching in awe. White smoke like a vapor trail began to pour out of the bottom of the object and head straight down before slowing and ascending to circle the cigar in ascending spirals. By the time it got to the top, the wind had blown away all the smoke or vapor, revealing its source: a small metallic disc which shone like a mirror and reflected light from the larger object. The disc darted about the area, sometimes moving with great speed, sometimes stopping abruptly, before finally streaking toward the cigar and disappearing into its lower part.

"Perhaps a minute later, the 'carrot' leaned over as it began to move, accelerated, and disappeared into the clouds in the distance," Fortin told investigators, "having resumed its original position, point forward. The whole thing had lasted about half an hour." Other witnesses up and down the valley confirmed this account. Meteorologists confirmed that no tornado or other unusual meteorological activity was occurring at the time of the sighting.

A 300-foot-long, dull-gray, cigar-shaped machine emerged from a cloud during a rainstorm over Cressy, Tasmania, Australia, on October 4, 1960. Among those who saw it was the Rev. Lionel Browning, an Anglican minister and Tasmanian Secretary of the World Council of Churches. As he and his wife watched this extraordinary sight — they estimated the object to be four miles away and 300 feet off the ground — five or six domed discs, approximately 30 feet in diameter, shot out of the clouds just above and behind the cigar. They headed toward it "like flat stones skipping along water" — exactly how Kenneth Arnold described the motion of the discs he saw over Mount Rainier, Washington, on June 24, 1947, in the sighting that ushered in the UFO age.

"After several seconds the ship, accompanied by the saucers, reversed the way it came," Browning reported. "It … was gone from sight after 30 seconds.… It appears the ship sailed on for some seconds unaware that it had shed its protection. Possibly when this was discovered, the saucers were called to the mother ship. The objects then moved back into the cover of the rain storm."

UFO-like clouds.

This incident, which took place on the Atlantic Ocean, off the coast of West Africa, south of Cape Verde, on March 22, 1870, is from the log of the barque *Lady of the Lake*:

> At from 6:30 to 7 P.M. a curious-shaped cloud appeared in the S.S.E. quarter, first appearing distinct at about 25 degrees from the horizon, from where it moved steadily forward, or rather upward, to about 80 degrees, when it settled down bodily to the N.E. Its form was circular, with a semicircle to the northern face near its center, and with four rays or arms extending from center to edge of circle. From the center to about six degrees beyond the circle was a fifth ray border and more distinct than the others, with a curved end: — diameter of circle 11 degrees, and of semicircle 2 1/2 degrees. The weather was fine, and the atmosphere remarkably clear, with the usual Trade sky. It was of a light grey color, and though distinctly defined in shape, the patches of cirro-cumulus at the back could be clearly seen through. It was very much lower than the other clouds; the shape was plainest seen when about 55 degrees to 60 degrees high. The wind at the time was N.N.E., so that it came up obliquely against the wind, and finally settled down right in the wind's eye; finally lost sight of it through darkness, about 30 degrees from the horizon at about 7:20 P.M. Its tail was very similar to that of a comet. The men forward saw it nearly 10 minutes before I [Capt. F. W. Banner] did, and came aft to tell me of it.… [I]ts general appearance was similar to that of a halo around the sun or moon.

A pair of clouds resembling "puffy-like daubs of cotton" passed in an eastward direction over Sunset, Utah, late on the afternoon of October 14, 1961. The clouds were linked by a cord of long, stringy material. Immediately behind them were two smooth, metallic, disc-shaped structures. All four

● SOURCES:

Banner, Frederick William. "Extract from Log of Barque 'Lady of the Lake'." *Quarterly Journal of the Royal Meteorological Society* 1 (1873): 157.

Bowers, Brent, and Ana Westley. "Spanish Farmers Say Barren Land Victim of Buzz of Darkling Planes." *Wall Street Journal* (August 6, 1985).

Brodu, Jean Louis. "Cloud-Chasing Planes." *Fortean Times* 60 (December 1991): 50–53.

Corliss, William R., ed. *Handbook of Unusual Natural Phenomena*. Glen Arm, MD: The Sourcebook Project, 1977.

———. *Tornados, Dark Days, Anomalous Precipitation, and Related Weather Phenomena: A Catalog of Geophysical Anomalies*. Glen Arm, MD: The Sourcebook Project, 1983.

D'Ercole, Tom, as told to Rene Decker. "True Mystic Experiences: My Own Little Cloud." *Fate* 32, 2 (February 1979): 54–55.

Delair, J. B. "UFOs, Clouds and Pseudo-Planes." *Fortean Times* 24 (Winter 1978): 42–46.

objects disappeared over the horizon. The next day Ronald Miskin, an investigator for the Aerial Phenomena Research Organization, interviewed the witnesses. One was Sunset's mayor, who was pointing upward and illustrating the objects' trajectory when suddenly a "puffy" white object flew overhead, joined soon after by another, and the two proceeded to streak across the sky in the same direction as the objects of the previous day.

Aliens in clouds.

Looking out the window of a clifftop house along the seashore at Sydney, Australia, late one afternoon in the spring of 1965, a tourist noticed a beautiful stationary pink cloud. An hour later, when she looked again, the cloud was moving in her direction and soon was actually below her eye-level, enabling her to look down on it and see, to her amazement, a round, white object. Vents along the object's side emitted gray steam which, as it enveloped all but the top portion of the object, turned pink. The "cloud," in short, was an artificial creation.

As if this were not mind-boggling enough, an engine sound came from the still-descending object. A luminous ladder was lowered from the underside, and a humanlike figure climbed down to a lower rung. There he sat down and directed a searchlight toward the sea below. Some distance out on the water a pink flare shot into the air. Immediately the ladder retracted, and the object shot off in the direction of the flare. The witness then noticed a long but not clearly visible shape in the water from which the flare had ascended. Both the UFO and the underwater shape vanished in a "vivid pink flash."

On the afternoon of January 7, 1970, two Finnish ski enthusiasts reportedly encountered a mysterious luminous red "cloud" which, when it got within 50 feet of them, turned out to contain a smoke-spewing domed disc at its center. The object hovered near them, and in the light it cast, they could see a three-foot-tall humanoid with a waxy, pale face and a hooklike nose but no visible eyes. The creature was standing on the ground just under the UFO. After about 20 seconds the red fog reappeared suddenly, and by the time it dissipated, both the object and the being were gone.

These are not the only close encounters of the third kind in which "clouds" or "fogs" play a role, though these are infrequent features of such reports.

Phantom planes and vanishing clouds.

A drought that began in 1973 and continued for well over a decade gave rise to a curious episode which, though its details are different, nonetheless is reminiscent in its effect of stories about "mad gassers." In other words, a person or persons unknown are said to be afflicting weird havoc on a community; yet the assailants' existence cannot be proved, and neither can their nonexistence.

In the early 1980s farmers in three southern Spanish provinces which drought had reduced to almost a desert landscape began charging that the absence of rainfall was not a sorry condition of nature but a sinister con-

"Flying Saucers over Tasmania." *Flying Saucer Review* 7, 2 (March/April 1961): 27–28.

Fort, Charles. *The Books of Charles Fort.* New York: Henry Holt and Company, 1941.

Jessup, M. K. *The Case for the UFO.* New York: The Citadel Press, 1955.

Lorenzen, Coral, and Jim Lorenzen. *UFOs: The Whole Story.* New York: Signet, 1969.

———. *Encounters with UFO Occupants.* New York: Berkley Medallion, 1976.

"Meteorological Curiosities." *Fortean Times* 8 (February 1975): 6–8, 20.

Michel, Aime. *The Truth About Flying Saucers.* New York: Criterion Books, 1956.

———. *Flying Saucers and the Straight-Line Mystery.* New York: Criterion Books, 1958.

Michell, John, and Robert J. M. Rickard. *Phenomena: A Book of Wonders.* New York: Pantheon Books, 1977.

Smith, Charles Tilden. "Clouds and Shadows." *Nature* 89 (1912): 168.

Vallee, Jacques. *Anatomy of a Phenomenon: Unidentified Objects in*

spiracy. The principal, though not the only, suspects were big tomato growers who, small farmers asserted without discernible logic, did not want precipitation to fall on their crops. Farmers claimed, moreover, that the conspirators had hired pilots to destroy rain clouds.

Space — A Scientific Appraisal. Chicago: Henry Regnery Company, 1965.

Zeleny, John. "Rumbling Clouds and Luminous Clouds." *Science 75* (1932): 80–81.

If there is a technology that can break up rain clouds, no meteorologist is aware of it. Despite repeated denials by atmospheric scientists, legal authorities, and aviation experts (who swore that small planes could not fly into storm clouds without serious risk of crashing), the farmers refused to back down. They said they had seen, on quite a number of occasions, the appearance of a thunderhead on the western horizon, followed within minutes by the approach of an unmarked aircraft. The aircraft would fly into the cloud, spew out chemicals, and reduce it to mere wisps.

A drought in southwestern France in 1986 produced identical claims. This time the villains were said to be corporate interests financing anti-hail seeding experiments. It did no good for the experts to retort that nothing can be done to prevent hail. Again some farmers insisted they had seen, or at least heard, the mysterious aircraft. The affair ended when heavy rain fell that summer.

Though social scientists laid the episode to mass hysteria, even some individuals not directly affected by the drought said they had seen the planes in action. One of them, Agriculture Ministry engineer Francisco Moreno Sastre, insisted, "It's not just the collective imagination." He told *Wall Street Journal* reporters that witnesses numbered in the "thousands." A priest, Father Manuel Prados Munoz of the mountain village of Maria, claimed repeated sightings, sometimes as many as a dozen a month. He said the planes would show up whenever his desktop barometer and his eyes indicated an imminent storm. After local people began to report their sightings to him, he learned of hundreds.

In cases such as these, no explanation really makes sense, and any speculation brought to bear on the episode is simply guesswork. No one suggested another possibility, for which no evidence whatever exists either, that a supersecret military or intelligence weather-control operation was responsible. One suspects that had these events occurred in the United States, where paranoia about such things is intense, this would have been the (non)explanation of choice. Fortunately for all concerned except those who wanted answers, the drought's passing put the mystery planes, real or imagined, out of sight and soon out of mind.

COTTINGLEY FAIRY PHOTOGRAPHS —————

In 1917 two young English girls, Frances Griffiths, 10, and her 13-year-old cousin Elsie Wright, shared a house in Cottingley, near Bradford, Yorkshire. Frances and her mother had moved there from Cape Town, South Africa; her father was serving as a British soldier in the great war. One day Frances returned home soaking wet and offered the excuse that she had fallen into the brook while playing with the fairies they had befriended in a nearby glen. Her mother was unmoved, and Frances was punished.

Feeling sorry for her cousin and best friend, Elsie hit upon an idea: they would borrow her father Arthur Wright's camera and photograph the fairies. After the parents believed them, the girls would announce that the picture was fake; they had lied about fairies just as their parents had lied to them about Father Christmas. Thus a kind of vengeance could be extracted for Frances's current misery.

Elsie approached her father and asked to borrow his camera, on the excuse that she wanted to take a picture of her cousin. He provided her with a single plate. An hour later the girls returned and said they now had proof of fairies. When the skeptical elder Wright developed the picture, he saw an image of Frances's facing the camera as four miniature winged women dressed in filmy clothing danced in front of her.

The girls refused to admit that they had, as their elders were certain they had, photographed paper cutouts — or, as Elsie's father suspected specifically, "sandwich papers." Still, one month later Wright again reluctantly gave the girls access to a camera and a single plate, and they returned with a second picture, this one showing a sitting Elsie bidding a gnomish figure to jump up on her lap. Convinced that this was a joke that was getting out of hand, Wright forbade the girls further use of the camera.

The following year, when Frances's father returned from service, the Griffithses moved to Scarborough, Yorkshire. Just prior to the move, Frances wrote a South African friend and enclosed copies of the two fairy photographs. On the back of one, she noted, "Elsie and I are very freindly [sic] with the beck fairies. It is funny I did not see them in Africa. It must be to [sic] hot for them there." In the letter she referred to the fairies only briefly and in passing. When rediscovered and published (in the *Cape Town Argus*, November 25, 1922), Frances's words would be cited as evidence of the girls' sincerity and of the photographs' authenticity.

The affair.
What would prove to be one of the most bizarre controversies in the history of photography began in 1920 when Polly Wright, Elsie's mother, attended a lecture on folklore, including fairy beliefs. Afterwards Mrs. Wright mentioned the photographs, and the lecturer asked for prints, which subsequently she sent to Edward L. Gardner, a prominent London Theosophist. Gardner entered into correspondence with the Wrights. In time they loaned him the original plates, which he took to an acquaintance, H. Snelling, an authority on photography. Snelling's positive assessment of the pictures would be widely quoted for decades afterwards, though it would not be known until 1983 that he retouched the first photograph — badly overexposed — and transformed it into the clear one with which all who knew of the Cottingley photographs would be familiar.

Gardner showed the pictures at a public lecture in May, and an audience member alerted Sir Arthur Conan Doyle, the prominent author, now an ardent Spiritualist. Doyle urged Gardner to take the photos to the Kodak laboratory in London. There, as Doyle would write later, "two experts were unable to find any flaw, but refused to testify to the genuineness of them, in view of some possible trap." Gardner finally met the Wrights that summer. He supplied Elsie with a modern camera, and subsequently she and Frances provided three more photographs of fairies.

In December *The Strand* magazine published Doyle's article on the first two pictures, and the following March a follow-up included the later three. The story received worldwide publicity, much of it unfavorable and centering on the question of how the creator of Sherlock Holmes could have fallen for what most saw as an obvious hoax.

Yet attempts to debunk it were not notably successful. A claim by Harry Houdini and others that the fairy figures were patterned after those in a certain advertising poster proved groundless once the poster was produced. By this time Doyle had written an entire book on the case, *The Coming of the Fairies* (1922). The previous year Theosophist and clairvoyant Geoffrey Hodson had visited the beck in the girls' company and reportedly saw numerous fairies, though efforts to photograph them subsequently proved unsuccessful.

There would be no more Cottingley fairy photographs, but the controversy would live on. In 1945 Gardner published a book-length account of the case, and the photographs were revived periodically in newspapers and magazines. Elsie and Frances seemed to stand by the pictures, or at least

● SOURCES:

Bord, Janet. "Cottingley Unmasked." *Fortean Times* 43 (Spring 1985): 48–53.

Clapham, Walter. "There Were Fairies at the Bottom of the Garden." *Woman* (October 1975): 42–43, 45.

Cooper, Joe. "Cottingley: At Last the Truth." *The Unexplained* 117 (1982): 2338–340.

Crawley, Geoffrey. "That Astonishing Affair of the Cottingley Fairies." *British Journal of Photography* Pt. One (December 24, 1982): 1375–80; Pt. Two (December 31, 1982): 1406–11, 1413–14; Pt. Three (January 7, 1983): 9–15; Pt. Four (January 21, 1983): 66–71; Pt. Five (January 28, 1983): 91–96; Pt. Six (February 4, 1983): 117–21; Pt. Seven (February 11, 1983): 142–45, 153, 159; Pt. Eight (February 18, 1983): 170–71; Pt. Nine (April 1, 1983): 332–38; Pt. Ten (April 8, 1983): 362–66.

Doyle, Arthur Conan. *The Coming of the Fairies.* New York: George H. Doran Company, 1922.

———. "Fairies Photographed." *The Strand Magazine* 60 (December 1920): 462–67.

refused to admit their phoniness. When asked, they responded with the ambiguous assertion that the photographs were of "figments of our imaginations," which believers interpreted as meaning "thought forms" (paranormal entities formed out of the perceiver's psychic energy) and doubters as a virtual admission that the girls had made them up. In 1972, however, Elsie sent the two cameras, along with other materials related to the case, to Sotheby's for sale; with them went a letter confessing for the first time ever that the photographs were unauthentic. Sotheby's returned the letter, apparently failing to understand what it had, on the grounds that it dealt only with antique documents.

Yet in 1975, when interviewed by a writer for *Woman* magazine, Elsie and Frances gave the impression (though without stating so explicitly) that the photographs were real. The first public acknowledgement to the contrary appeared in a 1982 issue of *The Unexplained*. At the same time, the *British Journal of Photography* was in the early installments of a major reappraisal of the case, based on an extensive investigation by editor Geoffrey Crawley. Frances and Elsie complained that the confessions cited by Joe Cooper in his *Unexplained* article were "unauthorized" (Cooper had been working with Frances on her [never published] autobiography). Their first signed, formal confessions were given to Crawley in early 1983.

It was revealed that the two had agreed that the truth — that the pictures were a "practical joke" which "fell flat on its face" — be withheld until the deaths of the major advocates, Doyle, Gardner, and Gardner's son Leslie. Elsie, a gifted young artist, had created the figures, using as her models fairies depicted in a popular children's book of the period, *Princess Mary's Gift Book*. According to Cooper, the first four photographs were all simple, single-exposure, open-air shots, but in Crawley's view the latter two were intentional double-exposures. The fifth, showing a "fairy bower," was an unintentional double-exposure. But even to the end the two women would not reveal the techniques they used, promising to reveal them in books they were writing. Both died, however, before finishing them. Interestingly, Frances would always insist, and reiterated her views in her communications with Crawley, that while the photographs were fake, she had seen real fairies in the beck.

Gardner, Edward L. Fairies: *The Cottingley Photographs and Their Sequel*. London: Theosophical Publishing House, 1945.

Hodson, Geoffrey. *Fairies at Work and at Play*. London: Theosophical Publishing House, 1925.

Sanderson, S. F. "The Cottingley Fairy Photographs: A Re-Appraisal of the Evidence." *Folklore* 84 (Summer 1973): 89–103.

Shepard, Leslie. "The Fairies Were Real." *Fortean Times* 44 (1985): 61–62.

CRAWFORDSVILLE MONSTER ────────────

Among the most fantastic of all UFO reports is one that came out of Crawfordsville, Indiana, in early September 1891.

According to a story in the *Indianapolis Journal* for September 5, at 2 o'clock the previous morning a "horrible apparition" appeared in the western sky, where two men hitching up a wagon saw it. One hundred feet in the air, 20 feet long and 8 feet wide, the headless, oblong thing — apparently some bizarre variety of living creature — propelled itself with several pairs of fins and circled a nearby house. It disappeared to the east for a short time and then returned. The two men, their curiosity exhausted, gave vent to an understandable impulse to take to their heels. They were not, however, the only witnesses. A Methodist pastor, the Rev. G. W. Switzer, and his wife also observed the phenomenon.

The creature was back the following evening, and this time hundreds of Crawfordsville's citizens saw its violently flapping fins and flaming red "eye." The creature "squirmed as if in agony" and made a "wheezing, plaintive sound" as it hovered at 300 feet. At one point it swooped over a band of onlookers, who swore they felt its "hot breath."

Years later, when Charles Fort came upon the story in the September 10, 1891, issue of the *Brooklyn Eagle*, he was suspicious, "convinced that there had probably never been a Rev. G. W. Switzer, of Crawfordsville." Curious almost in spite of himself, he investigated and, to his surprise, "learned that the Rev. G. W. Switzer had lived in Crawfordsville, in September, 1891." He wrote him at his present address in Michigan. Rev. Switzer replied that he would send a full account of his sighting as soon as he got back from current travels. Unfortunately, Fort added, "I have been unable to get him to send that account.... The problem is: Did a 'headless monster' appear in Crawfordsville, in September, 1891? And I publish the results of my researches: 'Yes, a Rev. G. W. Switzer did live in Craw-fordsville, at the time.'"

But in time Vincent Gaddis, a Crawfordsville newspaper reporter and member of the Fortean Society, was able to do better than that. He inter-viewed the town's older residents, who said the story was true and told him about the September 6 mass sighting, which had not been reported in the press. Gaddis wrote, "All the reports refer to this object as a living thing" — in other words, one of the hypothetical atmospheric life forms that would figure in early theories about unidentified flying objects.

● SOURCES:

Fort, Charles. *The Books of Charles Fort*. New York: Henry Holt and Company, 1941.

Gaddis, Vincent H. "Indiana's Sky Mon-ster." *Doubt* 14 (Spring 1946): 209–10.

———. *Mysterious Fires and Lights*. New York: Dell, 1968.

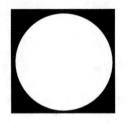

CROP CIRCLES

Crop circles are so called because they originally appeared as circular, swirled-flat cut-outs in various crops of growing grain, including wheat, rye, and barley. Over the years they have seemingly "evolved" in both number and complexity, and the term now refers to a variety of patterns, from simple single circles to quintuplets (a central circle ringed by four smaller satellites) to dumbbell shapes and complex arrays of all of the above (involving straight lines, bars, runged ladders, and so on). The latter are also referred to as "pictograms" because of their at least superficial resemblance to primitive rock paintings.

No one knows with certainty when the first such crop circle surfaced, but "cereology," the study of the phenomenon, can definitely be dated to an article and photographs which appeared in the August 15, 1980, issue of the *Wiltshire Times*, detailing flattened circles found in a field of oats worked by John Scull near Bratton, Wiltshire, England. Each was about 60 feet in diameter and swirled flat in a clockwise direction. The Bratton circles attracted the attention of both a meteorologist, George Terence Meaden of the Tornado and Storm Research Organization (TORO), and a ufologist, Ian Mrzyglod, editor of the now defunct *PROBE Report*. Mrzyglod made two important discoveries: he determined that the circles showed no obvious evidence of either beta or gamma radiation as measured by a geiger counter and, perhaps as importantly, that they were not really circles at all; in fact, the formations were slightly elliptical in shape, an unexpected characteristic which seemingly argues against hoaxing.

A year later, on August 19, 1981, three more circles were found in neighboring Hampshire county at the bottom of a natural bowl-shaped depression below Cheesefoot Head, alongside and easily visible from the A272 highway. Where the Bratton circles appeared random, the ones at Cheesefoot Head looked as if they had been laid out along a straight line. On either side of the main circle, again 60 feet in diameter, was a smaller circle 25 feet across, all again swirled clockwise, all created slightly off-center.

While dramatic developments would emerge, the basic pattern of the phenomenon appeared to be in place. Crop circles, whatever they were, seemed to form primarily during the spring and summer growing season in the rolling grain fields west and southwest of London. In fact, their "favored" haunt was an enchanted landscape already long marked by such previous mysteries as the monoliths of Stonehenge and Avebury, the pyramidlike peak of Silbury Hill, Europe's largest artificial mound, and numerous nearby carvings cut out of the chalk hills; of all of these, the White Horse of Westbury, overlooking the Bratton circles, is probably the most famous. The debate continues to rage as to whether this proximity of one mystery to another is coincidental or significant.

Unfortunately, no reliable and complete database for the number and types of crop circles appearing annually has yet been made public. The best available information suggests that between 100 and 120 circles formed in the Wessex area west of London in the years 1980 to 1987. During that same period the phenomenon displayed several "mutations." Circles which were swirled anti-clockwise as well as clockwise appeared. Rings around circles developed, and so did a disparity in the size of the circles reported. (They grew both considerably smaller and larger.)

In 1988, at least 112 circles were recorded, matching the previous eight-year "output." The following year the number almost tripled to 305, tripling again in the summer of 1990 to approximately 1,000. After a slow start in 1991, some 200 to 300 circles were eventually catalogued; many were of the more complex pictogram type.

What had begun with a few simple circles a decade before had mushroomed into an avalanche of global proportions, with well over 2,000 circles now on record worldwide. Similar circles — though rarely comparing in complexity or number with the English formations — were now being seen in the former Soviet Union, the United States, Canada, Australia, Japan, and a few other countries.

Characteristically, a crop circle occurs overnight, by all best guesses in the hour or two before dawn and normally in a matter of seconds, usually 60 or less. The demarcation line between affected and non-affected crop is almost always abrupt and dramatic. The flattened area is inevitably laid down in spiral fashion from the center outwards, though variations on almost all of these themes are not unknown. Moreover, the crop is frequently flattened in layers lying in opposite or varying directions. On occasion the plant stalks appear to have been braided together, one bunch or clump overlapping or intertwined with another. If a crop circle forms early in the growing season, the affected plants continue to mature and will "bounce back" to nearly normal height. Flattened later in the year, the stalks remain horizontal.

In a true crop circle the individual stalks are laid over without breaking or other obvious overt damage, even in the case of notoriously fragile plants such as rape, the source of canola oil. That is, the plant stalks appear to go limp, almost as if they had been steamed or rendered elastic, before returning to their previous state. An encircling ring may run counterclockwise to the central circle and vice versa, or both may be laid in the same direction. The smallest crop circle on record measured a mere eight inches in diameter. At Alton Barnes in 1990, a pictogram, or complex of crop circles, stretched for nearly an eighth of a mile. The sheer scope of such formations, both large and small, augurs against human involvement, as does the absence of any large pictograms obviously interrupted in *media res*, for whatever reason or reasons.

Daytime witnesses of the formation of simple circles are relatively rare and currently stand at about three dozen, most collected well after the fact by Dr. Meaden and his colleagues at the Circles Effect Research Group (CERES), a part of TORO. Typical is the account given by Gary and Vivienne Tomlinson and published in the *Mail on Sunday* of August 25, 1991 — a full year after the event. The Tomlinsons were walking alongside a field of corn (the generic English word for any cereal grain crop) near the village of Hambledon, when the plants to their right suddenly started rustling. "There was a mist hovering above, and we heard a high-pitched sound," said Mrs. Tomlinson. "Then we felt a wind pushing us from the side and above. It was forcing down on our heads so that we could hardly stay upright; yet my husband's hair was standing on end. It was incredible. Then the whirling air seemed to branch into two and zig-zagged off into the distance. We could still see it like a light mist or fog, shimmering as it moved."

Meaden quickly gave the Tomlinson account his seal of approval. He has postulated that crop circles, or at least the simple ones, are formed by the energetic breakdown of a standing, electrically charged whirlwind, a plasma-vortex. Unlike traditional whirlwinds such as dust devils and waterspouts, which suck in surrounding air at the base of a column of vertically rising air and which are driven by convection heating, Meaden's proposed plasma-vortex falls apart, or collapses, in a descending burst of violent wind. Theoretically, it is this collapsing wind-form, surrounded on occasion by a ring of electrically charged air, that quickly cuts out crop circles in the waiting medium below.

Meaden has suggested, in general, that calm atmospheric conditions are required for these standing vortices to form, along with an undulating landscape like that found in Wiltshire and the Wessex area. Air flowing over these low-lying hills tends to form vortices in the lee, or downwind, direction of such obstacles. A low-density charged plasma consisting of free electrons and positive ions might at first resemble a vague ball of light. The more rapidly a plasma spins, however, the more it would flatten toward a discoid platter typical of some "flying saucer" reports. In his most controversial book, *The Goddess of the Stones* (1991), Meaden has even argued that the local ancient stone works such as Stonehenge were actually raised in the wake of descending plasma-vortices, thus accounting for the unexplained ellipticity of many of these mysterious rock monuments. According to Meaden, our ancestors would have viewed crop circles as sacred fertility symbols, suitable sites for burials and other rites of rebirth.

The question of whether crop circles have occurred throughout history is thus crucial to any interpretation of the phenomenon, especially the meteorological one proposed by Meaden. If crop circles can be shown to be a recurring feature of the natural environment, then a weather-based theory is thereby strengthened, especially if one assumes, as Meaden now does, that all complex pictograms are indeed the product of human hoaxing. Conversely, such a theory is weakened if crop circles should emerge as a uniquely modern anomaly, particularly one seen as rapidly and unexpectedly evolving in terms of both occurrence and basic structure. How crop circles might have been reported in the past, then, is an issue worth considering.

Fairy rings and saucer nests.
Unexpected circular shapes in crops or grasses have long been associated with so-called fairy rings and, more recently, "saucer nests." The typical fairy ring is caused by a mushroom fungus, *Marasmius oreades*, and exhibits two stages. In the first, the fungi decompose organic matter and actually facilitate the growth off plants in the affected area; in the second they become so abundant that the plant growth is choked out, giving the appearance of a ring worn down by the patter of many little feet belonging to fairies.

While generally circular, fairy rings remain a random organic phenomenon wholly lacking the precise definition and complexity of a typical crop circle. They are also characterized by either the presence or absence of growing plants, whereas in a true crop circle the affected plants have simply "fallen over" in place. Still, historical accounts of fairy and other rings are often couched in such vague terms that they hold out the intriguing possibility that what was actually witnessed was a real crop-circle event, overlaid with local cultural considerations.

The earliest report dates to August 8 (19 by the modern calendar), 1590, and is found in Robert Plott's *The Natural History of Stafford-Shire*, published in 1686. Plott recounts the story of one Nicolaea Lang-Berhand who, returning home about noon, saw a circle of people dancing in an adjacent field. Observing more closely, she noticed that some of the dancers had *"cloven* feet like *Oxen* and *Goats"* (Plott's italics). Of a sudden, all vanished except Petter-Gross-Petter, "whom quickly after she saw snatch up into the Air ... and *Herself* was also driven so forcibly with the wind, that it made her almost lose her breath, and when she was got home to keep her bed no less than three days." At the same time a local herdsman, John Michael, sitting in an oak tree, slipped and was "presently catcht up again with a *whirlwind,"* only to be deposited, apparently safely, in a nearby meadow. Plott continues that "there was found in the place where they danced a round circle." Many people later went to see it, and it remained in place "till the next winter when the Plow cut it out."

This certainly *sounds* like a contemporary crop circle, with a major proviso: the whirlwind involved was apparently of the normal, ascending type, as opposed to Meaden's descending variety. More intriguing, in light of the high-pitched sound and static electricity sometimes associated with crop-circle formation, is this account from John Aubrey's *Natural History of Wiltshire* (spelling modernized):

> In the year 1633–34, soon after I had entered into my grammar at the Latin School at Yatton Keynal, our curate, Mr. Hart, was annoyed one night by these elves or fairies coming over the downs, it being nearly dark and approaching one of the fairy dances as the common people call them in these parts, viz. the green circles made by those spirits on the grass, he all at once saw an innumerable quantity of pygmies or very small people dancing round and round, and singing and making all manner of small odd noises. So being very greatly amazed and yet not being able, as he says, to run away from them, being as he supposes kept there in a kind of enchantment. They no sooner perceive him but they surround him on all sides, and what betwixt fear and amazement, he fell down scarcely knowing what he did; and thereupon these little creatures pinched him all over, and made a sort of quick humming noise all the time; but at length they left him, and when the sun rose he found himself exactly in the midst of one of these fairy dances. This relation I had from him myself a few days after he was so tormented; but when I and by bedfellow Stump went soon afterwards at night time to the dances on the downs, we saw none of the elves or fairies. But indeed it is said that they seldom appear to any persons who go to seek for them.

The time of year (August) is right, and conceivably the "sort of quick humming noise" Hart heard could be favorably compared (minus the "pygmies," of course!) to the high-pitched sound reported by the Tomlinsons some three and a half centuries later in the same general area. Moreover, there is the suggestion, however remote, that Hart's feeling of being "pinched … all over" might be analogous to the prickling sensation caused by static electricity or some other electromagnetic effect. While no strong wind is reported in the earlier case, there is mention of a sense of paralysis, Hart "being there as he supposes kept there in a kind of enchantment." There is, furthermore, the direct indication of a loss of consciousness, comparable, perhaps, to the period of "missing time" reported by some UFO abductees.

Compare the general circumstances and physical effects of these historical accounts with reports of saucer nests founded in the UFO literature, so called because such circular depressions resemble the sort of indentation that one could imagine might be left by a hovering or landed UFO. Two of the most notable saucer-nest cases occurred at Tully, Queensland, Australia, in January 1966, and near Langenburg, Saskatchewan, Canada, on September 1, 1974. Both involved daytime UFO sightings. The Langenburg case is particularly worth examining in detail for several reasons. Not only did it precede the current crop-circle craze, but it involved a credible witness, photographs, and investigations by both the Royal Canadian Mountain Police and Ted Phillips, a Center for UFO Studies researcher then specializing in physical-trace cases.

About 11 A.M. that September Sunday, 36-year-old Edwin Fuhr was swathing his family's rape crop with a mechanical harvester. The day was overcast and cool (43 degrees F.), with a falling mist and light showers in the area. Nearing a slough at the end of the field, Fuhr noticed what appeared to be a metallic dome some 50 feet distant. He left the swather idling and approached on foot to within 15 feet of the object, which now appeared as an inverted, stainless-steel bowl with lip, some 11 feet in diameter and approximately five feet high, spinning rapidly. It appeared to be hovering a mere 12 or 18 inches above the ground.

After a brief period of indecision, Fuhr retreated to the harvester. Now he could see four similar objects nested in the slough, all arranged in a semi-circle, all rapidly rotating. Because the harvester was still running, he could not tell whether the spinning domes were creating any noise on their own or not. At this point all five objects suddenly rose in the air to a height of about 200 feet, where they hovered momentarily in stair-step formation. Curiously they stopped spinning at this point. Eventually each emitted a puff of gray vapor or smoke and then instantaneously disappeared into the low overcast. Their departure, Fuhr told Phillips, was accompanied by a "pressure that flattened the rape that was standing, and I thought, 'Oh, hell, here goes my crop,' and there was just a downward wind, no twirling wind. I had to hold onto my hat."

Fuhr was confused about the exact duration of the entire episode, though he estimated it could have been "15 to 20 minutes," acknowledging "it could have lasted more or less, I can't be sure." Interestingly, Fuhr also

reported a period of momentary paralysis while in the presence of the phenomenon. He told Phillips that when he "got close [to the first object], my head wanted to go back fast, but my feet didn't want to move." Eventually he was able to retreat to the still-running swather, but when he "sat down … that's when I saw the other four, and that's when I couldn't move…. I sat there like I was froze. I couldn't move nothing."

After the objects departed, Fuhr found five depressed circular areas spiraled flat in a clockwise direction. "I checked for burns," he said, "but I couldn't find any. *The grass wasn't broken off, it was flat, pressed down.* It didn't seem different from the other grass except it was flattened. It wasn't dead or burnt or anything. Some sprouts are coming up there now." (Fuhr's emphasis.)

Other effects frequently mentioned in the UFO close-encounter literature were also noted. At approximately the same time as Fuhr's experience, the cattle in a neighboring field broke through their fencing in four places. The night before, Fuhr's own farm dogs had barked wildly. On Monday night they acted up again, and the following morning a sixth depressed circle was found in the field, a situation that repeated itself on the night of September 14 and the morning of the fifteenth. In all, seven swirled circles eventually were found on the Fuhr farm.

Still, the connection, if any, between a few historical fairy rings and saucer nests with the current crop-circle phenomenon remains tenuous and circumstantial at best. Nocturnal lights have been reported in the immediate vicinities of locations where crop circles were subsequently found. At least two daytime videos of small lights sailing just over or diving into existing crop circles are known to exist. What these light sources are cannot now be determined from the available evidence. In both cases the light sources appear to be only a foot or two in diameter.

Physical effects.

Anecdotal accounts of physical effects on human beings in close proximity to crop circles abound but remain difficult to confirm. Often they are based on highly idiosyncratic dowsing techniques or subjective feelings and impressions. Yet the Center for Crop Circle Studies has instituted a special study group concentrating on such reports. Thus far the most commonly reported aftereffect of visiting a crop circle in place is nausea, followed by headache and extreme fatigue. All of these sensations are short-lived. Some visitors tell of pleasant feelings, others negative ones. Since these sensations have also been associated with claimed hoaxed formations, it is obvious that more detailed data are required before any true conclusions are possible.

Interference with electronic equipment has been noticed on several occasions, most prominently in the failure of still and video cameras, but also including audio tape recorders. High-pitched warbling sounds have been reported and recorded in at least one instance by investigators Colin Andrews and Pat Delgado while in the company of a BBC video crew.

Actual instrumented anomalies are harder to come by, but several recent approaches now show promise and will no doubt be put to additional testing by future researchers. The American biophysicist W. C. Levengood has identified a number of areas in which these investigations may conceivably bear fruit. Compared to control samples, for examples, the nodes or knuckles of plant stalks taken from within crop circles appear visually larger — slightly swollen, in other words. Examination of the microscopic cell-wall holes through which the plant cells pass nutrients reveals stretched or larger pits suggestive of rapid microwave heating. In addition, seeds selected from an affected crop appear to germinate somewhat more vigorously than their control counterparts. Whether these preliminary findings will hold up under closer and repeated scrutiny, and if so what they may actually signify, remains to be determined.

Hoaxing.

Some circles are known to be the product of hoaxing. The current debate centers on just how many and which ones. Some cereologists accept the pictograms and other complex patterns and formations as authentic "circles," whereas the meteorological camp now tends to view with suspicion anything much more complex than a ringed quintuplet. Considerable activity is being devoted to agreement on guidelines and an instrumented methodology that would reduce the subjectivity factor and allow researchers to come to consensus on what characteristics comprise an authentic formation. Dowsing frequently is used as a means of determining authenticity, but the technique remains in dispute because of its controversial and indeterminate nature. Readings can vary from individual to individual, and the interpretations of the nature of the "energy" being dowsed remain in dispute. In addition, the occasional crop circle authenticated by dowsing has subsequently been shown to have been hoaxed.

In the majority of cases, "authentification" still depends on a visual inspection of the formation and the experience of the individual making the inspection. Aerial flyovers help to a degree, because especially crude or ragged hoaxes can be readily determined. Still, ground-level viewing of a circle is to be preferred if at all possible.

The involvement of hoaxers probably climaxed on September 9, 1991, when the British tabloid *Today* published the first of two articles by reporter Graham Brough detailing the confessions of Doug Bower and David Chorley — two English sexagenarians — who claimed to have hoaxed approximately 250 of the more complex crop-circle formations. According to Bower and Chorley, their career as professional hoaxers began in the summer of 1978 when the two created their first simple circle as a lark near Cheesefoot Head, Wiltshire, site of a prominent natural amphitheater easily visible from a major road. Bower, who had lived in Australia from 1958 to 1966, said he got the idea from the saucer nests that had appeared during that time in Queensland. "We had a good giggle about the first one," Chorley recalled. "It was nice being out on a summer night, so we decided to do some more. But for three rotten years [the papers] never noticed what we were doing."

Once the press and public did take note, Bower and Chorley said, they proceeded to improve their techniques and to create ever more elaborate circles, including a series of abstract-shaped "insectograms" which first appeared in the summer of 1991. Frequently they would incorporate their initials — in the form of a double-D — into their handiwork. The two claimed they finally came forward and confessed because others — primarily Colin Andrews and Pat Delgado, co-authors of the two best-selling books on the subject, *Circular Evidence and Crop Circles: The Latest Evidence* — were reaping the profits of their anonymous labors. With the assistance of the tabloid they created a complex formation by day, and Delgado was called in to inspect it. When he prematurely pronounced the formation authentic, Bower and Chorley stepped out of the background into the limelight.

When the cereologists recovered from their initial embarrassment, they promptly staged a rally. In their favor, another daytime circle created by Bower and Chorley before assembled media turned out to be a ragged and poorly constructed affair, by all accounts and photographs. Besides, the critics contended, Bower and Chorley's means seemed to fall considerably short of the claimed ends. The two said they wrought their original creations using deceptively simple tools: string, rope, four-foot-long wooden planks, and a crude Rube Goldberg-like sighting device fashioned from a piece of wire attached to the bill of a baseball cap, the latter designed to create straight lines by maintaining focus on a distant object — a tree, say — on the far horizon. Perhaps most significantly, Bower and Chorley have yet to demonstrate convincingly their ability to fashion a complex crop-circle formation by night, when most circles routinely appear. Other groups, including the local Wessex Skeptics, have also constructed semi-complicated hoaxes which initially caught out the crop-circle experts.

Yet many questions about human involvement in the crop-circle phenomenon remain unanswered. Several formations — such as the immense pic-

● SOURCES:

Brough, Graham. "How We Made the Circles That Fooled the World." *Today* (September 9, 1991).

———— with Wayne Francis and Richard Creasy. "Come on, Pat, Admit You Were Had." *Today* (September 10, 1991).

Chorost, Michael. "The Summer 1991 Crop Circles." MUFON UFO Journal 282 (October 1991): 3–15.

Clift, Diana, and Lucy Pringle. *CCCS Human Effects Working Group: Preliminary Findings.* London: Center for Crop Circle Studies, January 1992.

Delgado, Pat, and Colin Andrews. *Circular Evidence.* London: Bloomsbury, 1989.

————. *Crop Circles: The Latest Evidence.* London: Bloomsbury, 1990.

Hynek, J. Allen, and Jacques Vallee. *The Edge of Reality: A Progress Report on Unidentified Flying Objects.* Chicago: Henry Regnery Company, 1975.

Meaden, George Terence. *The Circles Effect and Its Mysteries.* Bradford-on-Avon, England: Artetech, 1989.

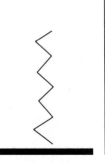

———, ed. Circles from the Sky. London: Souvenir Press, 1991.

———. The Goddess of the Stones. London: Souvenir Press, 1991.

———. "Circles in the Corn." New Scientist (June 23, 1990): 47–49.

Nickell, Joe, and John F. Fischer. "The Crop-Circle Phenomenon: An Investigative Report." Skeptical Inquirer 16,2 (Winter 1992): 136–49.

Noyes, Ralph, ed. The Crop Circle Enigma. Bath, England: Gateway Books, 1990.

Randles, Jenny, and Paul Fuller. Crop Circles: A Mystery Solved. London: Robert Hale, 1990.

Reynolds, David J. "Possibility of a Crop Circle from 1590." Journal of Meteorology (November 1990): 347–52.

tograms that appeared at Alton Barnes in 1990 and the massive Mandle-brot fractal near Cambridge the following year — are constructed on a monumental scale, measuring up to an eighth of a mile across. Assuming these and similar formations are indeed hoaxes, why has no massive crop circle ever been discovered obviously interrupted or abandoned — for whatever reason — halfway through completion?

On at least one well-documented occasion in the summer of 1991, Meaden and a team of visiting Japanese scientists had a field under surveillance with electronic equipment that included radar, magnetometers, night-vision video, and motion sensors. Obscured by mist, a small dumbbell formation appeared; yet none of the sensing equipment registered any obvious intruders, humans most of all. In addition, trespass and property damage remain punishable crimes under British law. As the cerelogists have increased their own vigilance in the affected areas, so have the local farmers and landowners; nonetheless the number of apprehended hoaxers caught in the act remains fairly modest. Finally, Bower and Chorley claim but a "mere" 250 or so crop circles as their own. During the same period of time, however, more than 2,000 crop circles were reported worldwide.

Competing theories.
While Meaden's plasma-vortex theory remains the only "mainstream" meteorological thesis, many critics within the cereological community contend that it simply does not account for all of the reported "behavior" of the phenomenon, which they deem indicative of some unknown intelligence. Two former colleagues, Delgado and Andrews, broke openly and acrimoniously with Meaden after claiming that "we looked at the meteorological correlations and they just weren't there." The two have since formed their own study group, Circles Phenomenon Research (CPR). George Wingfield, director of field research for the Center for Crop Circle Studies (CCCS), has also been highly critical of any weather-based hypoth-

esis. Richard Andrews, a dowser with the CCCS, has asserted that crop-circle patterns, or their energy fields, can be dowsed a year or more before the actual circle appears.

Unfortunately, few of the currently competing hypotheses are comprehensive in their own right. In general, they refer, in what are at best vague terms, to the intelligent nature of various and subtle energy fields, ranging from ley lines and other "telluric" earth currents all the way up to the spirit of the goddess Gaia herself, the hypothetical all-embracing Earth Mother. Many of these alternative theories depend on a subjective "interpretation" of the symbolic language supposedly spoken by the circles. The "message" thus being conveyed is usually interpreted in terms of dire environmental warnings of impending ecological disasters — a tortured planet's plaintive cries for help. Such pronouncements are more likely to indicate the concerns of the individual cereologists involved, however, than those of the "circle makers" themselves.

Other theories that would account for the phenomenon have included the almost ubiquitous UFO, collective psychokinesis, beamed microwave or laster radiation (as a by-product of secret military experiments), and so on. Dyed-in-the-wool debunkers have suggested that the vast majority of all crop circles can be attributed to nothing more mysterious than human behavior — hoaxing, in other words.

What is known is that the English crop circles in particular continue to attract sizeable crowds of curious onlookers. They also continue to generate a considerable cottage industry of their own, resulting in various organizations, newsletters, books, videos, and organized tourist tours, not to mention the usual assortment of T-shirts, postcards, jewelry, and souvenirs.

With so much attention focused on the phenomenon, the prospect of a significant breakthrough would appear imminent. In the meantime, in the words of Hilary Evans, author of *Intrusions: Society and the Paranormal* (1982), "Whatever else the crop circles may be, they are undoubtedly the most democratic anomaly ever. True, they challenge our current paradigms, but unlike ghosts, poltergeists, or even UFOs, the circles are absolutely there for anyone to examine at will. It's no longer a question of whether they exist or not, but rather of what they are." *Dennis Stacy*

Rutkowski, Chris, and John P. Timmerman. "Langenburg, 1974: A Classic Historical CE2 and a Crop Circle Progenitor?" *International UFO Reporter* 17,2 (March/April 1992): 4–11.

Skinner, R. M. "A Seventeenth-Century Report of an Encounter with an Ionized Vortex?" *Journal of Meteorology* (November 1990): 346–47.

Stacy, Dennis. "Graffiti of the Gods?" *New Age Journal* (January/February 1991): 38–44,103.

———. "The Circle Game." *New Age Journal* (November/December 1991): 12–13.

Tyrrel, Rebecca. "Shock Encounter as a Crop Circle Is Born." *Mail on Sunday* (August 25, 1991).

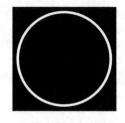

DAVID LANG DISAPPEARANCE —————————

On the afternoon of September 23, 1880, David Lang of Sumner County, Tennessee, was crossing a field near his home. His wife was watching him from the porch while his children, George and Sarah, played in the front yard. A Gallatin lawyer, "Judge" August Peck, and his brother-in-law were approaching in a buggy. Suddenly Mrs. Lang screamed, and the two visitors gaped in disbelief. David Lang had just vanished in front of their eyes.

Extensive searches in the days ahead failed to find a trace of him. Nonetheless an irregular circle 15 feet in diameter marked the spot of his disappearance for years afterwards. Nothing would grow there, and even insects avoided it. Once the children ventured into the circle and heard their father's tormented voice echoing from another dimension.

This is the substance of an enduring "true mystery" legend which attained its widest popularity in the 1950s and 1960s, owing largely to a story in the July 1953 issue of *Fate*. The piece, titled "How Lost Was My Father?", was supposedly a firsthand account of the event by Sarah Lang, based on a 1931 interview with writer Stuart Palmer. It further claimed that in April 1929 Sarah received a message via automatic writing. The message, in her father's handwriting, said, "Together now. Together now and forever ... after many years ... God bless you." To Sarah these words meant, "Mother and Father are together now in the World Beyond, after the nightmare years of separation."

Hershel G. Payne, a Nashville librarian who spent years trying to validate the story, found no archival evidence that a Lang family or an August Peck had ever lived in the area. Eventually he concluded that the tale's genesis was in a journalistic hoax engineered by traveling salesman Joseph M. Mulholland, who in the late nineteenth century contributed far-fetched yarns to various papers under the pseudonym Orange Blossom. In Payne's view, Mulholland probably had based his joke on a science-fiction story,

● SOURCES:

Edwards, Frank. *Stranger Than Science*. New York: Lyle Stuart, 1959.

"Fortean Corrigenda: The Disappearance of David Lang." *Fortean Times* 18 (October 1976): 6–7.

Nash, Jay Robert. *Among the Missing*. New York: Simon and Schuster, 1978.

Nickell, Joe, with John F. Fischer. *Secrets of the Supernatural: Investigating the World's Occult Mysteries*. Buffalo, NY: Prometheus Books, 1988.

Palmer, Stuart. "How Lost Was My Father?" *Fate* 6,7 (July 1953): 75–85.

Schadewald, Robert. "David Lang Vanishes... Forever." *Fate* 30, 12 (December 1977): 54–60.

Wilkins, Harold T. *Strange Mysteries of Time and Space*. New York: The Citadel Press, 1958.

"The Difficulty of Crossing a Field," by Ambrose Bierce. One later chronicler, Jay Robert Nash, added to the confusion by suggesting that Bierce's story (set in 1854 in Selma, Alabama, and concerning a "planter named Williamson") was the true one. In fact, there is no more reason to believe the Williamson story — which Bierce never pretended was authentic — than its Lang variant.

Palmer's *Fate* account credited to Lang's daughter contains what are represented as samples of the victim's handwriting, automatic writing, and signatures by Sarah and a notary public. Investigator Robert Schadewald showed these to Minneapolis handwriting expert Ann B. Hooten, who studied them and declared all "were authored by one individual" — presumably Palmer. Sarah Lang, in other words, was as much a figment of a hoaxer's imagination as was her father.

DEVIL'S FOOTPRINTS ——————————————————

Among the world's great mysteries is the case of the devil's footprints. Unfortunately, the documentation is not entirely satisfactory, but no one disputes that something out of the ordinary took place just after a snowfall on the night of February 7–8, 1855, in Devonshire, England.

As *The Times* of London reported on February 16:

> Considerable sensation has been evoked in the towns of Topsham, Lympstone, Exmouth, Teignmouth, and Dawlish, in the south of Devon, in consequence of the discovery of a vast number of foot-tracks of a most strange and mysterious description. The superstitious go so far as to believe that they are the marks of Satan himself; and that great excitement has been produced among all classes may be judged from the fact that the subject has been descanted on from the pulpit.

> It appears that on Thursday night last there was a very heavy fall of snow in the neighborhood of Exeter and the south of Devon. On the following morning, the inhabitants of the above towns were surprised at discovering the tracks of some strange and mysterious animal, endowed with the power of ubiquity, as the foot-prints were to be seen in all kinds of inaccessible places — on the tops of houses and narrow walls, in gardens and courtyards enclosed by high walls and palings, as well as in open fields. There was hardly a garden in Lympstone where the foot-prints were not observed.

> The track appeared more like that of a biped than a quadruped, and the steps were generally eight inches in advance of each other. The impressions of the feet closely resembled that of a donkey's shoe, and measured from an inch and a half to (in some instances) two and a half inches across. Here and there it appeared as if cloven, but in the generality of the steps the shoe was continuous, and, from the snow in the

center remaining entire, merely showing the outer crest of the foot, it must have been convex [concave?].

The creature seems to have approached the doors of several houses and then to have retreated, but no one has been able to discover the standing or resting point of this mysterious visitor. On Sunday last the Rev. Mr. Musgrave alluded to the subject in his sermon, and suggested the possibility of the foot-prints being those of a kangaroo; but this could scarcely have been the case, as they were found on both sides of the estuary of the Exe.

At present it remains a mystery, and many superstitious people in the above towns are actually afraid to go outside their doors after night.

● SOURCES:

Gould, Rupert T. *Oddities: A Book of Unexplained Facts.* New Hyde Park, NY: University Books, 1965.

Stein, Gordon. "The Devil's Footprints." *Fate* 38, 8 (August 1985): 88–95.

The *Times* had nothing more to say on the subject. The most detailed accounts, in fact virtually the only detailed accounts, are to be found in letters to the editor of *Illustrated London News* from locals who reported on what they saw, heard about, or believed about the enigmatic prints, which covered some 100 miles over a zigzag course. Of a general horseshoe shape, each track was, correspondents claimed, exactly eight and a half inches apart.

Then and later theorists would offer all kinds of candidates for print-maker: mouse, rat, swan, rabbit, deer, badger, otter, toad, donkey, and kangaroo. But if the accounts — never investigated by any independent authority — of what the tracks looked like and where they went are accurate, none of these candidates works.

The only other known instance of such tracks was reported by Captain Sir James Clark Ross, commander of two ships which were exploring the southern polar regions and which landed at Kerguelen Island in May 1840. The captain wrote in his *Voyage of Discovery and Research in the Southern and Antarctic Regions* (1847), "Of land animals we saw none; and the only traces we could discover of there being any on this island were the singular foot-steps of a pony or ass, found by the party detached for surveying purposes, under the command of Lieutenant Bird, and described by Dr. Robertson as 'being 3 inches in length and 2 1/2 in breadth, having a small and deeper depression on each side, and shaped like a horseshoe.'

"It is by no means improbable that the animal has been cast on shore from some wrecked vessel. They traced its footsteps for some distance in the recently fallen snow, in hopes of getting a sight of it, but lost the tracks on reaching a large space of rocky ground which was free from snow."

Rupert T. Gould asks the obvious question: "One wonders, if they had 'got a sight of it,' what they would have seen."

DEVIL'S SEA

During the Bermuda Triangle fad of the 1970s, several writers contended that this fabled region of lost planes and ships had a counterpart off the eastern or southeastern coast of Japan, site of the "devil's sea," where vanishings allegedly took place so suddenly that affected craft usually were unable to sound a distress call.

As with the Bermuda Triangle, it was speculated that space-time, magnetic, or gravitational anomalies — or else extraterrestrial kidnappers or even, as in a theory proposed by Ivan T. Sanderson, an intelligent, earth-dwelling, underwater race — were behind the disappearances. It also was claimed that the Japanese government viewed the situation with alarm.

After a period of celebrityhood in tabloid newspapers, pulp magazines, and sensationalistic books, the devil's sea fell victim to the first real research into the legend, conducted by Arizona State University librarian Larry Kusche. Kusche traced the story back to September 27 and 30, 1952, *New York Times* stories about an unusual oceanic disaster, the sinking of two Japanese ships via tidal wave from an underwater volcano. A January 15, 1955, *Times* report of another ship disaster used the term "devil's sea" and called it the "mystery graveyard of nine ships in the last five years."

In the early 1970s Kusche corresponded extensively with officials from Japan and nearby islands. None had ever heard the term "devil's sea," and all insisted the sinkings were not mysterious or unexplainable. The absence of radio messages in some events from the early 1950s could be attributed to the simple fact that many smaller fishing vessels did not have radios, owing to their owners' poverty.

Writing in 1975, Kusche concluded, "The story is based on nothing more than the loss of a few fishing boats 20 years ago in a 750-mile stretch of ocean over a period of five years. The tale has been reported so many times that it has come to be accepted as fact."

● SOURCES:

Bigham, Barbara J. "The Devil's Sea ... Another Bermuda Triangle?" *Fate* 28,7 (July 1975): 32–39.

Binder, Otto O. "Devil's Sea: Flying Saucer Death Trap." *Saga* (March 1970): 22–25, 68–74.

Drake, Rufus. "The Deadly Mystery of Japan's 'Bermuda Triangle'." *Saga* (April 1976): 20–23, 54–57.

Kusche, Larry. *The Bermuda Triangle Mystery — Solved.* Buffalo, NY: Prometheus Books, 1986.

————. "The Bermuda Triangle and Other Hoaxes." *Fate* 28,10 (October 1975): 48–56.

Nichols, Elizabeth. *The Devil's Sea.* New York: Award Books, 1975.

Sanderson, Ivan T. *Invisible Residents: A Disquisition Upon Certain Matters Maritime, and the Possibility of Intelligent Life Under the Waters of This Earth.* New York: World Publishing Company, 1970.

DINOSAURS, LIVING

Do dinosaurs still exist? The question may sound absurd. After all, conventional wisdom holds that these giant reptiles lapsed into extinction some 65 million years ago. Still, occasional reports from remote regions of the earth have kept the issue alive, if only to readers of tabloid newspapers and to the handful of scientists, adventurers, and nature writers who have tried to make sense of the accounts and, where possible, to investigate them.

Much of the investigation has centered on a legendary creature generally referred to as mokele-mbembe and described as a sauropodlike animal, with a long neck, small head, bulky body, and tail. The first printed mention of the huge, plate-shaped tracks associated with the beast appears in a 1776 history of French missionaries in west-central Africa. In the next two centuries missionaries, colonial authorities, hunters, explorers, and natives would provide strikingly consistent descriptions of the animals supposedly responsible for tracks of this kind. Sighting reports in recent years have been confined to the swampy, remote Likouala region of the Congo.

In 1980 and 1981 University of Chicago biologist Roy P. Mackal led two expeditions to the area, the first in the company of herpetologist James H. Powell, Jr., who had heard mokele-mbembe stories while doing crocodile research in west-central Africa. Neither expedition produced a sighting, though Mackal and his companions interviewed a number of native witnesses. The creatures, greatly feared, were said to live in the swamps and rivers. A band of pygmies supposedly killed one at Lake Tele around 1959.

Though the Mackal expeditions were unable to reach the nearly inaccessible Tele, a rival group, headed by American engineer Herman Regusters, successfully made the journey. Over a period of two to three weeks, he and his wife Kia Van Dusen would claim, huge long-necked animals came into view on several occasions, both in the water and in the swampy areas around the lake. Congolese government biologist Marcellin Agagna, who had participated in Mackal's second expedition, arrived there in the spring of 1982 and reported a single sighting. Both Regusters and Agagna said that camera problems frustrated their attempts to obtain photographic evidence of these fantastic sights. Three subsequent expeditions, one English and two Japanese, produced no sightings.

If there is such a thing as a living dinosaur, mokele-mbembe is it. Other claimed candidates cannot marshal a comparably compelling case. There is no *a priori* reason why dinosaurs could not survive in the Congo basin, where the climate and the geography have not changed since the age of reptiles. Its known fauna include such ancient animals as crocodiles, which coexisted with dinosaurs and whose form has remained stable over tens of millions of years. Of course, absent flesh, skin, or bones, mokele-mbembe's existence remains unproved — an intriguing possibility at best, an absurdly inflated legend at worst.

Enigma of the sirrush.

Around 600 B.C., during the reign of King Nebuchadnezzar, a Babylonian artist fashioned bas reliefs on bricks used in the enormous archway of the Ishtar Gate and the high walls of the approach road. The bas reliefs consist of three animals, and each row of bricks displays numerous images of one of them. The rows alternate, some showing lions, others rimis (as the Babylonians called them), and still others sirrushes (dragons).

Though extinct in Mesopotamia, the rimi was a real animal which was either remembered or known through specimens brought over from Eurasia, where these wild oxen (usually called urus or aurochs) lived on until 1627. The dragon, of course, was a purely imaginary animal. Or was it?

Willy Ley has described the sirrush, which he considered a "zoological puzzle of fantastic dimensions," thus:

> ... a slender body covered with scales, a long slender scaly tail, and a long slim scaly neck bearing a serpent's head. Although the mouth is closed, a long forked tongue protrudes. There are flaps of skin attached to the back of the head, which is adorned (and armed) with a straight horn....

The *Apocrypha's* Book of Bel and the Dragon relates a curious story: that in the temple of Bel, Lord of the World, Nebuchadnezzar's favored god, the priests kept a "great dragon or serpent, which they of Babylon worshipped." The king challenged the Hebrew prophet Daniel, who had been going about sneering about nonliving gods of brass, to dispute this god, who "liveth, and eateth and drinketh; you canst not say that he is no living god; therefore worship him." To remove himself from this quandary, Daniel poisoned the animal.

The fortieth chapter of Job in the Old Testament, though written anywhere from 100 to 1300 years earlier than the Ishtar Gate's construction, may refer to the sirrush by another name:

Behold now Behemoth ... he eateth grass as an ox. Lo now his strength is in his loins, and his force is in the navel of his belly. He moveth his tail like a cedar: the sinews of his stones are wrapped together. His bones are as strong pieces of brass, his bones are like bars of iron.... He lieth under the shady trees, in the cover of the reed, and fens. The shady trees cover him with their shadow; the willows of the brook compass him about.... [H]is nose pierceth through snares.

The behemoth's identity has long puzzled biblical scholars, who have not doubted that Job was writing of a real animal, even if no satisfactory candidate among known animals seems to exist. Mackal offers this interpretation: "The behemoth's tail is compared to a cedar, which suggests a sauropod. This identification is reinforced by other factors. Not only the behemoth's physical nature, but also its habits and food preferences are compatible with a sauropod's. Both live in swampy areas with trees, reeds and fins (a jungle swamp)."

The discoverer of the Ishtar Gate, German archaeologist Robert Koldeway, gave serious thought to the possibility that the sirrush may have been an actual animal. Unlike other fantastic beasts in Babylonian art, he noted, images of the sirrush remained unchanged over centuries. What struck him about these depictions was the "uniformity of [the sirrush's] physiological conceptions."

The sirrush, he said, was more like a saurian than any other animal. Such creatures did not coexist with human beings, he wrote, and the Babylonians, who were not paleontologists, could not have reconstructed a saurian from fossil remains; yet the Old Testament states explicitly that the sirrush was real. All this considered, he was reduced to speculating that the Babylonian priests kept "some reptile" in a dark temple and led the unsuspecting to believe it was a living sirrush.

The Babylonians are known to have penetrated equatorial Africa, home of the mokele-mbembe, and Ley, Bernard Heuvelmans, and Mackal have all suggested that in the course of their travels they heard of such creatures, perhaps sighted them, or even brought a specimen home with them. This is not an unreasonable hypothesis, if we assume that mokele-mbembe exists.

On the other hand, some modern scholars, for example Adrienne Mayor, dispute the assumption that the ancients did not know of, or had no interest in, prehistoric animals. Mayor has written, "Reliable ancient sources relate that, when fossils were discovered in antiquity, they were transported with great care, identified, preserved, and sometimes traded. Reconstructed models or the remains of 'unknown' species were displayed in Greece and Rome." She adds that ancient writings seem to indicate that "some representations and descriptions of crypto-animals in antiquity were based on reconstructions from skeletons of living or extinct animals." If such was the case with the sirrush, however, the fossilized remains would have had to be brought in from elsewhere. Dinosaur fossils did not exist in Mesopotamia.

Other dinosaurs in Africa.

While at Lake Tele, Herman Regusters reported, he and his companions heard a peculiar story. A few months earlier, in February 1981, according to local people, the bodies of three adult male elephants had been found floating in the water. The cause of death seemed to be two large puncture marks in the abdomen of each. These were not bullet holes, and the elephants still had their tusks, indicating that poachers had not killed them. The natives attributed the deaths to a mysterious horned creature which lived in the nearby forests.

This creature is called emela ntouka ("killer of elephants"). Reports consistently describe it as the size of an elephant, or larger, with heavy legs which support the body from beneath (as opposed to the side, as in crocodiles) and a long, thick tail. Its face is said to be generally rhinoceroslike, with a single horn which protrudes from the front of the head. It is semiaquatic in habit, eats foliage, and kills elephants and buffaloes with its great horn.

In *A Living Dinosaur?* (1987) Mackal suggests that such animals, if they exist, are likely to be a kind of prehistoric rhinoceros or a horned dinosaur of the triceratops variety. If the former, it is a mammal.

Mackal also has collected a handful of vague reports of mbielu mbielu mbielu, "the animal with planks growing out of its back," said to resemble a stegosaur. More compelling were sightings of nguma monene, an enormous serpentlike reptile with a serrated ridge along its back and four legs situated along its sides. Among the witnesses was American missionary Joseph Ellis, who in November 1971 said he saw such a creature emerge from the Mataba River and disappear into the tall grass. Ellis did not get a good look at its entire body, though he was only 200 feet away and had the creature under observation for two minutes. He never saw its head and neck, but from the portions of the body above water, he determined that it had to be over 30 feet long.

As one well familiar with the Congo's fauna, he was positive that the animal could not have been a crocodile. Native reports, which do include descriptions of a head and extended tail, suggest to Mackal that "we may be dealing with a living link between lizards and snakes," perhaps a "lizard type ... derived from a primitive, semi-aquatic group known as dolichosaurs, rather than more advanced monitors."

In 1932 biologist Ivan T. Sanderson and animal collector W. M. (Gerald) Russell had a bizarre and frightening experience in the Mamfe Pool, part of the Mainyu River in West Cameroon. The two men, with native guides, were in separate boats and passing clifflike river banks dotted with deep caves when suddenly they heard ear-shattering roars, as if huge animals were fighting in one of the caves.

Swirling currents sucked both boats near the cave's mouth. At that point, Sanderson would recall, there "came another gargantuan gurgling roar and something enormous rose out of the water, turned it to sherry-colored foam and then, again roaring, plunged below. This 'thing' was shiny black and was the *head* of something, shaped like a seal but flattened from above to below. It was about the size of a full-grown hippopotamus — this head, I mean."

Sanderson and Russell chose not to stick around to see anything more. Upstream they found big tracks which could not have been placed there by a hippopotamus because hippos did not live in the area. This was because the creatures had killed them all, the natives said. The creatures were not carnivorous, however; their diet consisted of the liana fruits that grew along the rivers. The natives called these creatures, in Sanderson's phonetic rendering, "m'kuoo m'bemboo."

If, however, the part of the animal the party saw really was its head, the animal was not the sauropodlike mokele-mbembe. Sauropods by definition have small heads. Mackal found during his own expeditions 50 years later that some local people used "mokele mbembe" as something of a generic description of any large, dangerous animal — including those described above — living in rivers, lakes, or swamps.

Dinosaurs in the lost world.
In his 1912 novel *The Lost World* Sir Arthur Conan Doyle imagined the discovery, by a band of hardy English explorers, of a plateau on the Amazon basin where prehistoric monsters lived on millions of years past their time. Considering the enduring popularity of this romantic tale, which one biographer calls "perhaps his finest work in fiction," it is perhaps surprising that relatively few claims of relic dinosaurs in South America have been made in real life.

One such account was published in the January 11, 1911, issue of the *New York Herald*. Its author, a German named Franz Herrmann Schmidt, of whom little is known, claimed that one day in October 1907 he and a companion, Capt. Rudolph Pfleng, along with Indian guides, entered a valley composed of swamps and lakes in a remote region of the Peruvian interior. There they discovered some strange, huge tracks, indicating the presence of more than one unknown animal in the waters, and crushed trees and vegetation. They also noticed the "queer" absence of alligators, iguanas, and water snakes.

Despite the guides' visible fear the party camped in the valley that night. The next morning expedition members got back into their boat and resumed their search for the animals. Just before noon they found fresh tracks along the shore. Pfleng declared that he was going to follow them inland, however dangerous the quest. Just then they heard the screams of a troop of monkeys which had been gathering berries from some trees nearby. According to Schmidt's account:

> ... [A] large dark something half hidden among the branches shot up among [the monkeys] and there was a great commotion.

● SOURCES:

Doyle, Sir Arthur Conan. *The Lost World.* London: Hodder and Stoughton, 1912.

Fulahn [William Hichens]. "On the Trail of the Brontosaurus: Encounters with Africa's Mystery Animals." *Chambers's Journal* 7, 17 (1927): 692–95.

Heuvelmans, Bernard. *On the Track of Unknown Animals.* New York: Hill and Wang, 1958.

Higham, Charles. *The Adventures of Conan Doyle: The Life of the Creator of Sherlock Holmes.* New York: W. W. Norton and Company, 1976.

Keel, John A. *Strange Creatures from Time and Space.* Greenwich, CT: Fawcett Gold Medal, 1970.

Ley, Willy. *Exotic Zoology.* New York: Viking Press, 1959.

Lorenzoni, Silvano. "Extant Dinosaurs: A Distinct Possibility." *Pursuit* 10, 2 (Spring 1977): 60–61.

———. "More on Extant Dinosaurs." *Pursuit* 12, 3 (Summer 1979): 105–09.

Mackal, Roy P. *Searching for Hidden Animals.* Garden City, NY: Dou-

One of the excited Indians began to paddle the boat away from the shore, and before we could stop him we were 100 feet from the water-line. Now we could see nothing and the Indians absolutely refused to put in again, while neither Pflug nor myself [sic] cared to lay down our rifles to paddle. There was a great moving of plants and a sound like heavy slaps of a great paddle, mingled with the cries of some of the monkeys moving rapidly away from the lake.... For a full 10 minutes there was silence, then the green growth began to stir again, and coming back to the lake we beheld the frightful monster that I shall now describe.

The head appeared over bushes 10 feet tall. It was about the size of a beer keg and was shaped like that of a tapir, as if the snout was used for pulling things or taking hold of them. The eyes were small and dull and set in like those of an alligator. Despite the half dried mud we could see that the neck, which was very snakelike, only thicker in proportion, was rough knotted like an alligator's side rather than his back.

Evidently the animal saw nothing odd in us, if he noticed us, and advanced till he was no more than 150 feet away. We could see part of the body, which I should judge to have been eight or nine feet thick at the shoulders, if that word may be used, since there were no fore legs, only some great heavy clawed flippers. The surface was like that of the neck....

As far as I was concerned, I would have waited a little longer, but Pfleng threw up his rifle and let drive at the head. I am sure that he struck between the eyes and that the bullet must have struck something bony, horny or very tough, for it cut twigs from a tree higher up and further on after it glanced. I shot as Pfleng shot again and aimed for the base of the neck.

The animal had remained perfectly still till now. It dropped its nose to the spot at which I had aimed and seemed to bite at it, but there was not blood or any sign of real hurt. As quickly as we could fire we pumped seven shots into it, and I believe all struck. They seemed to annoy the creature but not to work any injury. Suddenly it plunged forward in a silly clumsy fashion. The Indians nearly upset the dugout getting away, and both Pfleng and I missed the sight as it entered the water. I was very anxious to see its hind legs, if it had any. I looked again only in time to see the last of it leave the land — a heavy blunt tail with rough horny lumps. The head was visible still, though the body was hidden by the splash. From the instant's opportunity I should say that the creature was 35 feet long, with at least 12 of this devoted to head and neck.

In three seconds there was nothing to be seen except the waves of the muddy water, the movements of the waterside growth and a monkey with its hind parts useless hauling himself up a tree top. As the Indians paddled frantically away I put a bullet through the poor thing to let it *out of its misery. We had not gone a hundred yards before Pfleng called to me and pointed to the right. Above the water an eighth of a mile away appeared the head and neck of the monster. It must have dived and gone right under us. After a few seconds' gaze it began to swim toward us, and as our bullets seemed to have no effect we took flight in earnest. Losing sight of it behind an island, we did not pick it up again and were just as well pleased.*

This story appears in the course of an otherwise credible-sounding narrative about an expedition along the Solimes River. Schmidt writes that a few months later, on March 4, 1908, his companion Pfleng died of fever. Thus the story cannot be checked. Of the tale Mackal remarks, "The details ... seem to ring true and probably reflect the experiences of an actual expedition. It does not necessarily follow that the encounter with the alleged creature also occurred and may be nothing more than a clever addition to an otherwise authentic expedition."

Still, Schmidt's is not the only reference to a huge swamp-dwelling beast in the South American backwaters. In the early twentieth century Lt. Col. Percy H. Fawcett surveyed jungles for the Britain's Royal Geographical Society. A careful, accurate reporter, Fawcett wrote that native informants had told him of "tracks of some gigantic animal" seen in the swamps along the Acre River, near where the borders of Peru, Bolivia, and Brazil intersect (and 500 to 600 miles from the site of Schmidt and Pfleng's alleged encounter). The natives said they had never actually seen the creature responsible for the tracks.

Farther south, according to Fawcett, along the Peru-Bolivian border "some mysterious and enormous beast has frequently been disturbed in the swamps — possibly a primeval monster like those reported in other parts of the continent. Certainly tracks have been found belonging to no known animals — huge tracks, far greater than could have been made by any species we know."

Since then few reports or rumors of South American dinosaurs have found their way into print. In two articles published in *Pursuit* between 1977 and 1980 Silvano Lorenzoni suggested that the flat-topped, steep mountains of the Guayana Massif, which have remained geologically and ecologically stable for tens of millions of years, may harbor surviving dinosaurs. For his intriguing idea, however, Lorenzoni had only the thinnest supporting evidence: a trader's report of three "plesiosaur like things" in a lake on one such plateau, Auyantepuy, in southeastern Venezuela where Angel Falls originates. He also noted reports of exceptionally large, lizardlike reptiles in mountain valleys near the Venezuelan coast.

Dinosaurs from the twilight zone.

If living dinosaurs in Africa and South America seem at least marginally conceivable, the presence of such creatures in the United States or Europe is — it hardly need be stated — flatly impossible, at least this side of the twilight zone. Probably unsurprisingly, this consideration has not entirely

bleday and Company, 1980.

———. *A Living Dinosaur?: In Search of Mokele-Mbembe.* New York: E. J. Brill, 1987.

Magin, Ulrich. "A Brief Survey of Lake Monsters of Continental Europe." *Fortean Times* 46 (Spring 1986): 52–59.

Mayor, Adrienne. "Paleocryptozoology: A Call for Collaboration Between Classicists and Cryptozoologists." *Cryptozoology* 8 (1989): 12–26.

"Personal Glimpses: To Bring Home a Dinosaur Dead or Alive." *The Literary Digest* 64, 9 (February 28, 1920): 76–77, 80.

Powell, James. "Some Field Notes on African Neodinosaurs." *Pursuit* 9, 1 (January 1976): 8.

Rickard, Bob. "A Reprise for 'Living Wonders'." *Fortean Times* 40 (Summer 1983): 4–15.

Russo, Edoardo. "Meanwhile in Italy — The Goro Monster." *Pursuit* 9,3 (Summer 1976): 62.

Sanderson, Ivan T. *More "Things".* New York: Pyramid Books, 1969.

———. "There Could Be Dinosaurs." *Saturday Evening Post* 220 (January 3, 1948): 17, 53–56.

prevented the occurrence of a few reports anyway. A couple of examples are offered here for their curiosity and entertainment value.

In a letter published in the August 22, 1982, issue of *Empire Magazine*, a Sunday supplement, Myrtle Snow of Pagosa Springs, Colorado, wrote that in May 1935, when she was three years old, she saw "five baby dinosaurs" near her hometown. A few months later a local farmer shot one after it took some of his sheep. "My grandfather took us to see it the next morning," she said. "It was about seven feet tall, was gray, had a head like a snake, short front legs with claws that resembled chicken feet, large stout back legs and a long tail."

But these were not her only sightings. There were two more: (1) "I saw another one in a cave in 1937, but it was dark green." And (2) "On October 23, 1978, as I was returning from Chama, New Mexico, about 7:30 P.M., in a driving rain, I saw another one going through the field towards the place where I had seen the one in 1937."

In 1934 a South Dakota farmer claimed that a giant, four-legged reptile forced his tractor off the road before disappearing into nearby Campbell Lake. Investigators found huge tracks on the shore. Prior to this sighting sheep and other small animals had been disappearing mysteriously.

An Italian man reported being attacked by a "15-foot reptile, like a dinosaur," at Forli in December 1970. Fifty miles northwest of there, in June 1975, a monster appeared in a tomato field near Goro and badly frightened a farmer named Maurizio Tombini, who press accounts said "has a reputation for seriousness."

The story was widely publicized but poorly reported in the Italian press; no entirely coherent or comprehensive description of the creature emerges from any of it. A careful reading indicates that the creature was about 10 feet long and eight inches around, with legs and feet which left impressive-looking tracks. Tombini likened it to a "gigantic lizard" and denied it was a crocodile. According to police, several other people also reported sightings. They declared that the creature had a wolflike howl.

German anomalist Ulrich Magin asks, at least semiseriously, "Could it have been the most southerly sighting of the Austrian 'Tatzelwurm'?" The tatzelwurm ("worm with claws") is a strange, sometimes dangerous animal which, though unrecognized by zoology, figures in a number of sighting reports in the Alps and in one dubious photograph. Some theorists have suggested it is an unrecognized species of large lizard.

Schmidt, Franz Hermann. "Prehistoric Monsters in Jungles of the Amazon." *New York Herald* (January 11, 1911).

"Unidentifieds: On Land." *The News* 15 (April 1976): 9–11, 5.

104

DOVER DEMON

The scare began at 10:30 on the evening of April 21, 1977, as three 17-year-old boys were driving north through Dover, Massachusetts, Boston's most affluent suburb. One of them, Bill Barlett, thought he spotted something creeping along a low wall of loose stones on the left side of the road.

As the figure turned its head and stared into the headlights of the car, Bartlett said he saw two large, round, glassy, lidless eyes shining brightly "like orange marbles." Its head, resting atop a thin neck, was big and watermelon-shaped and fully as large as the rest of the body. Except for its oversized head, the creature was thin, with long spindly arms and legs and large hands and feet. The skin was hairless and peach-colored and appeared to have a rough, sandpaperlike texture. No more than four feet tall, it had been making its way uncertainly along the wall, its long fingers curled around the rocks, when the car lights surprised it.

Neither of Bartlett's companions, whose attention was elsewhere, noticed the creature, which was visible for only a few seconds. They testified later, however, that their friend had seemed genuinely upset. When Bartlett arrived at his home, his father noticed his distraught state and heard the story from his son, who drew a sketch of what he had seen.

Around 12:30 A.M. 15-year-old John Baxter, walking home from his girlfriend's house, reportedly saw a short figure approaching him. Thinking it was a small-statured friend, he called out his name but got no response. When the figure got closer, it stopped, causing Baxter to do the same. Trying to get a better look, Baxter took one step forward, and the figure scurried off to the left, running down a shallow wooded gully and up the opposite bank.

Baxter followed it down the slope, then stopped and looked across the gully. The figure — which looked like nothing he had ever seen or heard

John Baxter's sketch of the Dover Demon. (Courtesy of Loren Coleman.)

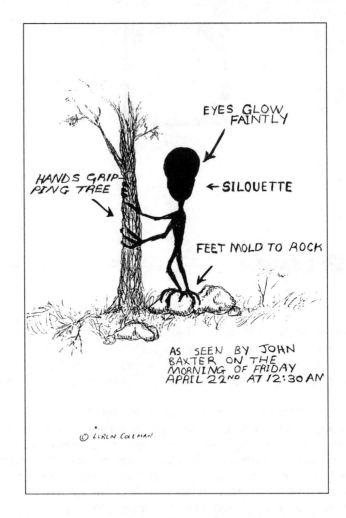

EYES GLOW FAINTLY

HANDS GRIP-PING TREE

← SILOUETTE

FEET MOLD TO ROCK

AS SEEN BY JOHN BAXTER ON THE MORNING OF FRIDAY APRIL 22ND AT 12:30 AM

© LOREN COLEMAN

of — stood in silhouette about 30 feet away, its feet "molded" around the top of a rock a few feet from a tree. It was leaning toward the tree with the long fingers of both hands entwined around the trunk. Though he would claim not to have heard of Bartlett's report at that point, his description of it would be exactly the same. Baxter backed carefully up the slope and walked quickly away from the scene.

The next day Bartlett told his close friend Will Taintor, 18, about his experience. That night, while Taintor was driving Abby Brabham, 15, home, Brabham said she spotted something in the car's headlights. On the left side of the road was a hairless creature crouched on all fours, facing the car. Its body was thin and monkeylike, its head large, oblong, and devoid of nose, ears, and mouth. The facial area around the eyes was lighter, and the eyes glowed green. Brabham insisted on this last detail even after investigators informed her that Bartlett had said the eyes were orange. Taintor said he caught only a brief glimpse.

Anomalist Loren Coleman, then living in the area, learned of Bartlett's report through an acquaintance who knew the teenager. Subsequently he, along with ufologists Walter N. Webb and Ed Fogg, interviewed Bartlett and the other witnesses, along with their parents, school officials and teachers, and police officers. They uncovered no evidence of a hoax; to the contrary, those who knew the teenagers described them as credible. A local newspaper dubbed the creature the "Dover demon."

● **SOURCES:**

Clark, Jerome. "The Dover Humanoid." *Fate* 31,3 (March 1978): 50–55.

Coleman, Loren. *Mysterious America*. Boston, MA: Faber and Faber, 1983.

"The Dover Demon." *Real Paper* [Cambridge, MA] (May 21, 1977).

EARTHLIGHTS AND TECTONIC STRESS THEORY ─────────

Two theorists, Michael Persinger and Paul Devereux, have independently proposed geophysical explanations for anomalous phenomena. Persinger's idea, called the tectonic stress theory (TST), argues that strain fields within the earth's crust produce electromagnetic charges which create bodies of light or generate hallucinations, based on images from popular culture, of alien craft, beings, communications, or creatures. A variant of the theory is Devereux's notion of "earthlights."

Devereux's approach differs from Persinger's in holding triboluminescence rather than piezoelectricity to be the "more likely candidate" for the production of naturally occurring UFOs. Whereas Persinger contends that UFO-like lights may manifest hundreds of miles away from an area of seismic activity, Devereux generally restricts such effects to the immediate vicinity of a fault line.

Beyond this, however, Devereux's is the more radical hypothesis. In his view earthlights may possess intelligence and even be able to read witnesses' thoughts. He ties this putative energy — which he calls an "unfamiliar form of electromagnetism or ... of a completely unknown order ... a secret force" — to a transformative, New Age vision. Earthlights research, according to Devereux, "holds the potential of creating a whole new area of human study, one of evolutionary significance, one that can help heal the fragmentation that bedevils our contemporary way of thinking about so many matters."

Persinger's theory has been published — and criticized — in the scientific literature. Its empirical base is weak, and its critics complain that Persinger tries to explain one unknown, UFOs, with another. They also note that UFO and "monster" sightings occur in seismically inactive areas. To skeptics such as Chris Rutkowski and Greg Long, alleged TST effects and earthlights are as likely to be known natural phenomena — ball lightning, earthquake lights, will-o'-the-wisp — as the extraordinary counterparts Persinger and Devereux suggest.

Concerning Devereux's attempt to explain UFOs, Long writes, "Devereux fails to recognize that when the various reports of 'earthlights' are carefully studied, a wide variety of lightforms is quickly noted; but even more, the reports describe objects so artificial in appearance, so intelligent in their behavior, so purposeful, that it is impossible to conceive that the objects are anything other than technological machines. Nothing in these accounts remotely suggests a ball or mass of energy." Rutkowski says, "Although the *hypothesis* that the lights represent a kind of EM [electromagnetic] phenomenon is supported by some circumstantial and observational evidence, the empirical question of whether or not such energy can actually exist needs further study."

● SOURCES:

Devereux, Paul. *Earth Lights: Towards an Understanding of the UFO Enigma.* Wellingborough, Northamptonshire, England: Turnstone Press Limited, 1982.

———. *Earth Lights Revelation: UFOs and Mystery Lightform Phenomena: The Earth's Secret Energy Force.* London: Blandford, 1989.

Long, Greg. *Examining the Earthlight Theory: The Yakima UFO Microcosm.* Chicago: J. Allen Hynek Center for UFO Studies, 1990.

———. "Earthlights: Science or Revelation?" *International UFO Reporter* 15, 3 (May/June 1990): 13–14, 23.

Persinger, Michael, and Gyslaine F. Lefreniere. *Space-Time Transients and Unusual Events.* Chicago: Nelson-Hall, 1977.

Rutkowski, Chris. "Earthlights, Earthquakes, UFOs and TST; or Who Is Michael Persinger and Why Is He Saying Those Things About Me?" *International UFO Reporter* 11, 1 (January/February 1986): 4–8.

ENTOMBED ANIMALS ───────────────────

"Many well authenticated stories of the finding of live toads and frogs in solid rock are on record," a writer for *Scientific American* declared in 1890. Twenty years later a *Nature* editor snarled, "It matters little to tell the reporters of such occurrences that the thing is absolutely impossible, and that our believing it would involve the conclusion that the whole science of geology (not speak of biology also) is a mass of nonsense."

Both are right. The thing is absolutely impossible, and there are many well authenticated stories of it. Trying to reconcile these conflicting realities, William R. Corliss, probably the world's leading authority on anomalies of nature, remarks, "If miracles do happen, then toads can be found in solid rocks. It may be that nature operates this way, violating the 'logical' laws we try to impose with some low frequency, after the fashion of the 'forbidden transitions' in quantum physics."

Because of its outrageousness the phenomenon of entombed toads, frogs, and other animals is seldom discussed in the scientific literature of our time, but it made frequent appearances in learned journals of the nineteenth and earlier centuries. An early example is this account, related by a sixteenth-century figure, Ambroise Pare, chief surgeon to Henry III of France, and reprinted in the 1761 edition of the *Annual Register*:

> *Being at my seat near the village of Meudon, and overlooking a quarryman whom I had set to break some very large and hard stones, in the middle of one we found a huge toad, full of life and without any visible aperture by which it could get there.... The laborer told me it was not the first time he had met with a toad and the like creatures within huge blocks of stone.*

At Hartlepool, England, on April 7, 1865, laborers doing excavation work found, 25 feet below the surface, a block of magnesium limestone. As they were breaking it up, it split open to reveal a cavity in which, to their astonishment, they saw a living toad. "The cavity was no larger than its body, and presented the appearance of being a cast of it," the *Hartlepool Free Press* reported on April 15. "The toad's eyes shone with unusual brilliancy, and it was full of vivacity on its liberation."

It seemed at first to be experiencing difficulty breathing, probably because its mouth was sealed shut. At first a "barking" sound came out of its nostrils, possibly related to inhalation and exhalation problems. Soon this ceased, though it would emit a startled bark whenever it was touched. When discovered, the toad was of a pale color indistinguishable from that of the stone in which it had been embedded, but in short order it grew darker until it became olive-brown. "The claws of its fore feet are turned inwards," the newspaper noted, "and its hind ones are of extraordinary length and unlike the present English toad."

S. Horner, president of the Natural History Society, took possession of it. The *Zoologist* reported that it had also been examined by a local clergyman and geologist, the Rev. Robert Taylor, who confirmed the strange circumstances of its recovery. The *Free Press* appended this commentary to its original article:

> The world now had another story of a toad in a hole.... Illustrations of the toad's perilous passion for holes abound in our literature and, if we turn over the leaves of our local chronicles, numerous examples present themselves.
>
> We read of the discovery within the last hundred years of live toads in all sorts of possible and impossible situations; in the solid slate of a quarry in Barnard Castle, in a block of freestone at Blyth, in a limestone block at Saeham and at Ryhope, and in a seam of coal down a deep pit at Sunderland.
>
> Another of his race, profiting by repairs, emerged from the battlements of Flambard's Bridge in 1828, and gave rise to unavailing speculation as to his antiquity. A beech tree at Shawdon and an American oak at Blyth fell into the hands of sawyers, when a "living toad" started out of each of them, and exchanged a life of solitude for the publicity of a paragraph in Sykes or Latimer.

As these words indicate, embeddings have been reported not only in rocks but in trees. In 1719 the *Memoires* of the French Academy of Sciences related that "in the foot of an elm, of the bigness of a pretty corpulent man, three or four feet above the root and exactly in the center, has been found a live toad, middle-sized but lean and filling up the whole vacant space." In the fall of 1876, according to the *Uitenhage Times* (a South African newspaper) of December 10, sawyers cutting a 16-foot trunk into lumber had just removed the bark and the first plank when a hole the size of a wine glass was uncovered. Inside this space were 68 small toads, each the size of the upper joint of a human little finger. "They were ... of a light brown, almost yellow color, and perfectly healthy, hopping about and away as if nothing had happened. All about them was sold yellow wood, with nothing to indicate how they could have got there, how long they had been there, or how they could have lived without food, drink or air."

Next to toads, frogs are the most popular stars of entombed-animals stories. One example was made known to the eminent twentieth-century biologist-philosopher Sir Julian Huxley in a letter from gas fitter Eric G. Mackley of Barnstaple, Devonshire, England. Mackley wrote:

> It became desirable to widen the Barnstaple-Ilfracombe road some years ago, taking in part of the long gardens in front of a row of bungalows which had gas meters housed just inside the front gates; these of course had to be moved back to the new front wall line. The meterhouses were brick-walled but rather massively concrete-floored, and the concrete had to be broken up to allow me to get at the pipes for extension. My mate was at work with a sledge hammer when he dropped it suddenly and said, "That looks like a frog's leg." We both bent down and there was the frog.... [T]he sledge was set aside and I cut the rest of the block carefully. We released 23 perfectly formed but minute frogs which all hopped away to the flower garden.

Tilloch's Philosophical Magazine told this lizard-in-stone story in 1821:

> A short time since, as David Virtue, mason, at Auchtertool, a village four miles from Kirkaldy, in Scotland, was dressing a barley millstone from a large block, after cutting away a part, he found a lizard imbedded in the stone. It was about an inch and a quarter long, of a brownish yellow color, and had a round head, with bright sparkling projecting eyes. It was apparently dead, but after being about five minutes exposed to the air it showed signs of life. One of the workmen, very cruelly, put snuff in its eyes, which seemed to cause it much pain. It soon after ran about with much celerity; and after half an hour was brushed off the stone and killed. When found, it was coiled up in a round cavity of its own form, being an exact impression of the animal. This stone is naturally a little damp; and about half an inch all round the lizard was a soft sand, the same color as the animal. There were about 14 feet of earth above the rock, and the block in which the lizard was found was seven or eight feet deep in the rock; so that the whole depth of the animal from the surface was 21 or 22 feet. The stone had no fissure, was quite hard, and one of the best to be got from the quarry of Cullaloe — reckoned perhaps the best in Scotland.

Attempts to explain.
To human beings mysteries may be appealing, but they are also abhorrent. Thus, inevitably, in common with other mysteries, entombed-animal reports have faced as much disbelief and ridicule as wonder and excitement. Unable to mock such things out of existence, critics have concocted "solutions" so patently inadequate as to make outright hoax accusations a more plausible alternative.

● SOURCES:

Corliss, William R., ed. *The Unexplained: A Sourcebook of Strange Phenomena.* New York: Bantam Books, 1976.

———. *Unknown Earth: A Handbook of Geological Enigmas.* Glen Arm, MD: The Sourcebook Project, 1980.

Daniels, C. "Toads in a Tree." *Zoologist* 2, 11 (1876): 4805.

"Embeddings." *Fortean Times* 36 (Winter 1982): 17–19.

Hricenak, David. "The Mystery of Entombed Animals." *INFO Journal* 8, 1 (May/June 1979): 5–6.

Michell, John, and Robert J. M. *Phenomena: A Book of Wonders.* New York: Pantheon Books, 1977.

———. *Living Wonders: Mysteries and Curiosities of the Animal World.* New York: Thames and Hudson, 1982.

Rickard, Bob. "Embeddings." *Fortean Times* 40 (Summer 1983): 17–18.

Sanderson, Sabina W. "Entombed Toads." *Pursuit* 6,3 (July 1973): 60–64.

Screeton, Paul. "The

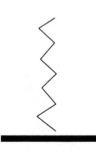

"The true interpretation of these alleged occurrences," wrote the same *Nature* writer who had relegated entombment tales to the realm of the absolutely impossible, "appears to be simply this — a frog or toad is hopping about while a stone is being broken, and the non-scientific observer immediately rushes to the conclusion that he has seen the creature dropping out of the stone itself."

There is no way to square such an "explanation" with most of the reports (try applying it, for instance, to Mackley's experience). Aside from its complacent implicit assumption that reporters of the phenomenon go through the world trying to function with what amounts to a chimpanzee's level of intelligence, it fails to consider a consistent feature of the phenomenon: the presence of a "smooth" or "polished" cavity, only slightly larger than the creature's body, inside the rock, concrete, or tree; as often as not, the animal is seen within that cavity before liberating itself or being liberated from it. There is also the fact that in many cases the toad or frog is decidedly unusual, its general appearance suggesting that it has indeed been confined somewhere for a period of time.

It is not hard to imagine how animals could get embedded in concrete. An indulged imagination conceives of ways they could meet such a fate within trees. Rocks, however, are quite another matter. The animals' survival, too, seems inexplicable. How could they have breathed, and what could they have eaten? Amphibians, the most frequent embedding victims, have, at the outer extreme and under the best of circumstances, a lifespan of three decades. How old are embedded animals?

In rare cases we have an answer. In August 1975, as they broke up concrete that had been laid over a year earlier, Fort Worth, Texas, construction workers were startled to find a living green turtle within it, the smooth, body-shaped cavity in which it had resided during its imprisonment clearly visible. The animal's rescue, alas, proved its undoing. It died within 96 hours of its liberation.

Where rocks are concerned, we seem indeed to be dealing with an event not significantly short of miraculous, as Corliss says. Occasionally conventionalists have speculated that the animals were able to sustain themselves by drinking water which seeped through cracks. Even if we discard testimony which specifically denies the presence of such openings, we still leave unanswered the monumental question of how the animal got there in the first place. The implication, it need hardly be emphasized, is that it was there a *long* time.

Nothing about this phenomenon makes any kind of sense. It seems to defy not only natural but even any conceivable paranormal explanation. Of the phenomenon all we can do is to acknowledge that while it is entirely impossible, it happens anyway.

Enigma of Entombed Toads." *Fortean Times* 39 (Spring 1983): 36–39.

Splitter, Henry Winfred. "The Impossible Fossils." *Fate* 7, 1 (January 1954): 65–72.

Thorn, Marjorie. "Fossils That Came Alive." *Fate* 19, 3 (March 1966): 71–72.

"Toads and Frogs in Stones." *Nature* 83 (1910): 406–07.

"Toads in Rocks." *Scientific American* 63 (1890): 180.

FAIRIES

As he walked down an isolated country road near Barron, Wisconsin, one summer night in 1919, 13-year-old Harry Anderson saw something distinctly odd. Twenty little men, trooped in single file and heading in his direction, were visible in the bright moonlight. Even as they passed him, they paid him no attention. Young Anderson noticed they were dressed in leather knee pants held up by suspenders. They wore no shirts, they were bald, and their skin was pale white. Though all were making "mumbling" sounds, they did not appear to be communicating with each other. Terrified, Anderson continued on his way and did not look back. The bizarre encounter remained vivid in his memory for the rest of his life.

To Americans, indeed to most people in the modern Western world, fairies are no more than figments of the sentimental imagination, suitable only for children's entertainment, in which they are portrayed almost invariably as tiny, winged, and good-hearted. This version of the fairy is rooted in romantic literature, not in the worldwide folk traditions in which beliefs concerning hidden races which share the earth with us have resided for most of human history.

The tradition and its mysteries.

A century or two ago Harry Anderson, who knew no more than that the figures he encountered were strange in the extreme, would have had little doubt about their identity. This would be especially true if he had lived in a Celtic country, whose roads, rocks, caves, fields, rivers, lakes, and forests — so common opinion attested — were infested with entities of such volatile temperament that only the unwise and unwary called them "fairies," for they did not like to hear their proper name spoken. Because one of them could be listening at any time, rural people employed various euphemisms — such as the "good people," the "Gentry," the "honest folk," the "fair tribe," and others — calculated to praise rather than to risk offense. As the Rev. Robert Kirk, a seventeenth-century chronicler of the fairy-faith, wrote, the "Irish ... bless all they fear harm of."

The fairy-faith populated the world with a bewildering variety of entities, even within a single region. Nonetheless fairies could be counted on to be more or less human in form, though sometimes taller or shorter (never, however, bearing wings), and much of their behavior was recognizably human. They had governments, societies, divisions of labor, art and music, and conflicts. They married, had children, waged war, and died. At the same time they possessed supernatural powers which made them, at best, unpredictable and, at worst, dangerous. Few people sought out the company of fairies, and most went out of their way to avoid it.

The origins of the fairy-faith are obscure and by now unknowable. (Stewart Sanderson characterizes belief in fairies as "one of the most difficult problems in the study of folklore.") Folklorists and anthropologists have theorized that the original fairies were members of conquered races who took to the hills and whose descendants were sighted on rare occasion, to be mistaken for supernatural beings. It also has been suggested that fairies were remnants of the old gods and spirits whom Christianity displaced but who survived in popular belief as immaterial beings of a lesser rank than God, Jesus, and the Holy Ghost. Some writers have suggested the fairy-faith is all that remains of an ancient cult of the dead; indeed, the dead sometimes were said to appear in the company of fairies. A fashionable modern view, expressed by folklorist Alan Bruford, holds that fairies "represent in anthropomorphic form the mysterious and numinous in wild nature, the part of the world which is beyond mankind's understanding."

Aside from the speculations of scholars, folk explanation, especially in Christian countries, often associated fairies with fallen angels. All that is known with any certainty is that wherever they come from, fairy beliefs exist in every traditional society.

Fairies figure most prominently in myths, legends, and tales which folklorists have collected in the field or uncovered in archaic printed sources. One of the great early studies was Robert Kirk's *The Secret Common-Wealth* (1691). Kirk, a Presbyterian clergyman who served in Scotland's Highlands and who had a keen interest in the supernatural lore of the region, was convinced of the reality of fairies. After all, he asked, how could such a widespread belief, even if "not the tenth part true, yet could not spring of nothing?" He conducted his inquiries on the assumption that once he had enough information, he could accurately describe the nature of fairy life down to its smallest details.

According to Kirk, fairies were of a "middle nature between man and angel" with bodies "somewhat of the nature of a condensed cloud." They dressed and spoke "like the people and country under which they live." Sometimes passing fairies could be heard but not seen. They traveled often, frequently through the air, could steal anything they liked (from food to human babies), and had no particular religion. Mortals with "second sight" (clairvoyance) were most likely to see them, since they were usually invisible to the human eye. In fact, the word "fairy" comes from a much earlier word, *fai-erie*, which meant a state of enchantment rather than an individual supernatural entity.

Few modern scholars have admitted to a belief in fairies. The major exception was W. Y. Evans-Wentz, author of the well-regarded *The Fairy-Faith in Celtic Countries*, originally published in 1911. Evans-Wentz, an anthropologist of religion with a Ph.D. from Oxford University, traveled through the British Isles and Brittany on France's northwest coast and reported the results in a thick book which remains a classic of folklore studies. Besides documenting what remained of an oral tradition of fairy belief, the author, who was also interested in Eastern religion and Western occultism, declared that "we can postulate scientifically, on the showing of the data of psychical research, the existence of such invisible intelligences as gods, genii, daemons, all kinds of true fairies, and disembodied men."

But even those possessed of the will to make this leap of faith — not a small one — usually find themselves brought up short by the fact that when considered in their entirety, fairy traditions are too wildly complex, various, and fantastic to add up to anything coherent. As one reads the vast literature of fairylore, one thinks more readily of the vagaries of the human imagination than of the mysteries of the invisible world. Moreover, anyone willing to embrace fairies also has to entertain the possibility, from "evidence" not a lot worse, that gods, merfolk, giants, shape-shifting monsters, werewolves, vampires, and other folkloric creatures may exist. Common sense warns us it may be better to draw the line sooner than later.

Yet mysteries remain. Even if these do not amount to evidence for the ultra-extraordinary and innately unbelievable claim that a fairy realm exists, they do not necessarily reduce to simple answers either. People see, or think they see, all kinds of strange things, and among the strange things people think they see are fairies. These "sightings" continue even in the absence of an accompanying fairy-faith, as Harry Anderson's story indicates. It is probable that in traditional societies fairies were believed in, at least in part, because they were "seen." Fairies did not exist, in other words, solely in stories; they also existed in what were believed to be experiences.

As the great Irish folklorist Douglas Hyde wrote, "The folk-tale ... must not be confounded with the folk-belief.... The ... story is something much more intricate, complicated, and thought-out than the belief. One can quite easily distinguish between the two. One (the belief) is short, conversational, chiefly relating to real people, and contains no great sequence of incidents, while the other (the folk-tale) is long, complicated, more or less conventional, and above all has its interest grouped around a central figure, that of the hero or heroine." What Hyde calls "beliefs" others would call "sightings."

To Evans-Wentz, to the poet W. B. Yeats (who wrote eloquently of Irish fairy traditions and encounters in *The Celtic Twilight* [1893,1902] and elsewhere), and to modern occult historian Leslie Shepard, these "sightings" suffice to establish the existence of a fairy world, located in a kind of fourth dimension or parallel reality. To folklorists such as Stewart Sanderson and Katharine Briggs, "sightings" are shrugged off and passed on, without further printed reflection, to parapsychologists, who for their part have shown approximately zero interest in the question.

To behavioral scientist David J. Hufford, a radical skepticism, which sees even "scientific" attempts to explain supernatural beliefs as contaminated by unexamined cultural prejudices which may themselves be no more than expressions of faith, demands that we acknowledge the limitations of our knowledge of some aspects of human experience. In a critique of academic literature which seeks to debunk testimony about anomalous encounters, Hufford writes that "one readily finds appeals to authority, post hoc fallacies, ad hominem arguments and a whole host of other informal errors. Nonetheless, because this inductive dimension of scholarship is less often explicitly presented for scrutiny, and because so much of the work of framing questions and establishing the boundaries of scholarly discourse about 'the supernatural' were largely set anywhere from several generations ago … to a number of centuries ago … the systematic bias of this tradition operates almost invisibly today."

In short, no explanation, whether conventionally "credulous" or "skeptical," that purports to offer a blanket explanation for these accounts, answers all the questions in a wholly convincing fashion. Even if we do not understand the underlying causes — be they psychological or paranormal — of these stories, there is nothing to stop us from marveling at them simply as stories. For now, after all, that is all we can do with them.

Sightings and hearings.
One example of the kinds of first-hand accounts folklorists collected while the fairy-faith still lived was related to Lady Campbell by an old, blind Irish farmer. The farmer claimed that some years earlier he had captured a fairy, a two-foot-high figure wearing a red cap, green clothes, and boots and having a dark but clear complexion.

"I gripped him close in my arms and took him home," the farmer related. "I called to the woman [his wife] to look at what I had got. 'What doll is it you have there?' she cried. 'A living one,' I said, and put it on the dresser. We feared to lose it; we kept the door locked. It talked and muttered to itself queer words.… It might have been near a fortnight since we had the fairy, when I said to the woman, 'Sure, if we show it in the great city we will be made up [rich]. So we put it in a cage. At night we would leave the cage door open, and we would hear it stirring through the house.… We fed it on bread and rice and milk out of a cup at the end of a spoon."

Soon, however, the fairy escaped. Not long afterwards the man lost his sight, and the couple's fortunes further declined — a situation he blamed on fairy retribution.

Another, earlier fairy episode had a happier ending. The following is the text of a sworn statement by a seventeenth-century Swedish clergyman, P. Rahm:

In the year 1660, when I and my wife had gone to my farm, which is three quarters of a mile from Ragunda parsonage, and we were sitting there and talking awhile, late in the evening, there came a little man in at the door, who begged of my wife to go and aid his wife, who was just in the pains of labor. The fellow was of small size, of a dark complexion, and dressed in old gray clothes. My wife and I sat awhile, and wondered at the man; for we were aware that he was a Troll, and we had heard tell that such like, called by the peasantry Vettar [spirits], always used to keep in the farmhouses, when people left them in harvest-time. But when he had urged his request four or five times, and we thought on what evil the country folk say that they have at times suffered from the Vettar, when they have chanced to swear at them, or with uncivil words bid them to go to hell, I took the resolution to read some prayers over my wife, and to bless her, and bid her in God's name go with him. She took in haste some old linen with her, and went along with him, and I remained sitting there. When she returned, she told me that when she went with the man out at the gate, it seemed to her as if she was carried for a time along in the wind, and so she came to a room, on one side of which was a little dark chamber, in which his wife lay in bed in great agony. My wife went up to her, and, after a little while, aided her till she brought forth the child after the same manner as other human beings. The man then offered her food, and when she refused it, he thanked her, and accompanied her out, and then she was carried along, in the same way in the wind, and after a while came again to the gate, just at 10 o'clock. Meanwhile, a quantity of old pieces and clippings of silver were laid on a shelf, in the sitting-room, and my wife found them next day, when she was putting the room in order. It is supposed that they were laid there by the Vettar. That it in truth so happened, I witness, by inscribing my name. Ragunda, the 12th of April, 1671.

Mari Sion of Llanddeusant, Anglesey, Wales, told a folklorist of her own early-twentieth-century experience with a fairy family. One moonlit night, she related, she, her husband, and their children heard a knocking at the door as they sat by the fire. The callers proved to be a tiny man, woman, and baby. The tallest of them, the man, was only two feet high. "I should be thankful for the loan of a bowl with water and a coal of fire," the woman said. "I should like to wash this little child. I do not want them at once. We shall come again after you have gone to bed."

Mrs. Sion left the requested materials before she and her family retired. During the night they could hear the comings and goings of the little people. In the morning the family found everything in order, except for the bowl, which lay upside down. Underneath it the family found four shillings.

Edward Williams, a prominent eighteenth-century British cleric, wrote that in 1757, when he was seven years old, he and other children were playing in a field in Wales when they saw, at a distance of 100 yards, seven or eight tiny couples dressed in red, each carrying a white kerchief in his or her hand. One of the little men chased the children and nearly caught one who, according to Williams, got a "full and clear view of his ancient, swarthy, grim complexion" just before effecting his escape. During the chase another of the figures shouted at the pursuer in an unknown language. The incident puzzled Dr. Williams all his life, and he concluded, "I am forced to class it among my unknowables."

The Rev. Sabine Baring-Gould, the Victorian historian and folklorist, wrote that when he was four years old and traveling in a carriage with his parents, "I saw legions of dwarfs of about two feet high running along beside the horses; some sat laughing on the pole, some were scrambling up the harness to get on the backs of the horses." His parents saw nothing. Baring-Gould also recorded an encounter his wife experienced when she was 15 and walking down a lane in Yorkshire. There she spotted a "little green man, perfectly well made, who looked at her with his beady black eyes. She was so frightened that she ran home." Fairy sightings evidently ran in the family. One of his sons had gone to fetch peapods in the garden when, so he informed his parents, he observed a "little man wearing a red cap, a green jacket, and brown knee-breeches, whose face was old and wan, and who had a gray beard and eyes as black and hard as sloes [blackthorn fruit]. He stared so intently at the boy that the latter took to his heels."

T. C. Kermode, a member of the Isle of Man's parliament, told Evans-Wentz, "About 40 years ago, one October night, I and another young man were going to a kind of Manx harvest-home at Cronk-a-Voddy. On the Glen Helen road, just at the Beary Farm, as we walked along talking, my friend happened to look across the river (a small brook), and said: 'Oh look, there are the fairies. Did you ever see them?' I looked across the river and saw a circle of supernatural light.... The spot where the light appeared was a flat space surrounded on the sides away from the river by banks formed by low hills; and into this space and the circle of light, from the surround sides apparently, I saw come in twos and threes a great crowd of little beings smaller than Tom Thumb and his wife. They moved back and forth amid the circle of light, as they formed into order like troops drilling. I advised getting nearer to them, but my friend said, 'No, I'm going to the party.' Then after we had looked at them a few minutes my friend struck the roadside wall with a stick and shouted, and we lost the vision and the light vanished."

One night in 1842, according to an account he gave to a local historian, a Stowmarket, England, man was passing through a meadow on his way home when he saw fairies in the moonlight. There might be a dozen of them, the biggest about three feet high, and small ones like dolls. Their dresses sparkled as if with spangles.... They were moving round hand in hand in a ring, no noise came from them. They seemed light and shadowy, not like solid bodies. I passed on, saying, the Lord have mercy on me, but them must be the fairies, and being alone then on the patch over the field could seem them as plain as I do you. I looked after them when I got over the style, and they were there, just the same moving round and round. I ran home and called three women to come back with me and see them. But when we got to the place they were all gone. I could not make out any particular things about their faces. I might be 40 rods from them and I did not like to stop and stare at them. I was quite sober at the time.

Over a century later, on April 30, 1973, an educated London woman named Mary Treadgold was traveling by bus through the Highlands. Near the town of Mull, the bus pulled over to the side of a narrow road to let an oncoming car pass by, and Treadgold idly looked out the window to an expanse of peat. There, standing in front of a clump of heather, stood a "small figure, about 18 inches high, a young man with his foot on a spade, arrested (frozen like a bird or a squirrel on the approach of something alien) in the act of digging," she reported. "He had a thin, keen face (which I would know again), tight, brown, curly hair, was dressed in bright blue bib-and-braces, with a very white shirt, with rolled-up sleeves. An open sack, also miniature, stood at his side. He was emphatically not a dwarf, nor a child, nor (last desperate suggestion of a skeptic) a plastic garden gnome. He was a perfectly formed living being like any of us, only in miniature." The figure was lost to view after the bus resumed its journey.

"When I got home," Treadgold wrote, "I inquired from a Highland acquaintance who told me friends of hers had seen similar small people on Mull, and that Mull was known for this. She added the small people were generally pale (I don't recall this particularly) and very bright. This last I do recollect in the brightness of the hair and clothes, and the general appearance of energy and alertness."

On occasion folklore collectors have had experiences consistent with local fairy manifestations. Sir Walter Scott complained of an educated correspondent who, though "a scholar and a gentleman," had confessed that "frequently" he had seen the "impression of small feet among the snow" and once "thought I heard a whistle, as though in my ear, when nobody that could make it was near me." Scott laid these presumed delusions to the "contagious effects of a superstitious atmosphere. [Antiquarian George] Waldron [the correspondent] had lived so long among the Manx that he was almost persuaded to believe their legends." John Cuthbert Lawson, who studied turn-of-the-century rural Greek traditions including beliefs in tall fairy women known as Nereids, remarked on the "wonderful agreement among the witnesses in the description of their appearance and dress. I myself once had a Nereid pointed out to me by my guide, and there certainly was the semblance of a female figure draped in white and tall beyond human stature sitting in the dusk between the gnarled and twisted boles of an old olive yard. What the apparition was, I had no leisure to investigate; for my guide with many signs of the cross and muttered invocations of the Virgin ordered my mule to perilous haste along the rough mountain path."

Many people claim to have heard fairy music. Manx fiddler William Cain swore he heard music emanating from a brightly lit glass palace which he

● SOURCES:

Barry, John. "Fairies in Eire." The Living Age 355 (November 1938): 265–66.

Briggs, Katharine. An Encyclopedia of Fairies: Hobgoblins, Brownies, Bogies, and Other Supernatural Creatures. New York: Pantheon Books, 1976.

Calder, Rev. George, ed. Highland Fairy Legends: Collected from Oral Tradition by Rev. James MacDougall. Totowa, NJ: Rowman and Littlefield, 1978.

Evans, Alex. "Encounters with Little Men." Fate 31, 11 (November 1978): 83–86.

Evans, Hilary. Gods, Spirits, Cosmic Guardians: A Comparative Study of the Encounter Experience. Wellingborough, Northamptonshire, England: The Aquarian Press, 1987.

Evans-Wentz, W. Y. The Fairy-Faith in Celtic Countries. New York: University Books, 1966.

Horwitz, Tony. "Iceland Has Elves, Who Live in Rocks, Nowhere to Be Seen." Wall Street Journal (July 13, 1990).

Hufford, David J. "Reason, Rhetoric, and Religion: Academic

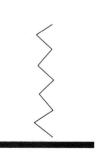

encountered one night in a mountain glen. He stopped and listened, then went home and learned the tune which he thereafter performed widely. In the summer of 1922, while sitting on the banks of the Teign River in Dartmoor, England, composer Thomas Wood heard a strange voice calling him by his first name. Though he searched with field glasses, he could find no source. Then he heard "overhead, faint as a breath," then ever louder, "music in the air. It lasted 20 minutes," he told writer Harold T. Wilkins. "Portable wireless sets were unknown in 1922.... This music was essentially harmonic, not a melody nor an air. It sounded like the weaving together of tenuous fairy sounds." Listening intently, he wrote down the notes. In 1972, while strolling along the shore of a peninsula in Scotland's Western Highlands, American folk singer Artie Traum heard disembodied voices chanting "Run, man, run" in a strange harmony to the sound of fiddles and pipes. When Traum fled into a nearby woods, he heard crackling sounds and "great motion." All the while, he recalled, "my head was swarming with thousands of voices, thousands of words making no sense." The voices ceased once he found his way back to the open air.

Though nearly extinct elsewhere in the West, the fairy-faith in its most traditional form lives on in Iceland, where a University of Iceland survey a few years ago indicated that as much as 55 percent of the population considers the reality of elves (*huldufolk*, or "hidden people") certain, probable, or possible, and only 10 percent rejects the notion as flatly out of the question. Belief is so strong that construction and road projects are sometimes delayed to accommodate the wishes of the invisible folk who dwell in fields, forests, rocks, and harbors. In such cases psychics are called in to negotiate. As with other fairies, the entities are not always invisible to normal perception. A 1990 *Wall Street Journal* article observes that "humans and huldufolk usually get on well. Midwives have told [folklorist Hallfredur] Eiriksson about delivering elf babies. Farmers say they have milked elf cows. Sometimes, the two peoples fall in love, though affairs of the heart often end badly."

Fairies or humanoids?

In 1938 Dublin's Irish Press reported, "Watching for fairies has leaped into sudden popularity in West Limerick." There a number of men and boys said they had seen groups of fairies and even chased them, to no avail; "they jumped the ditches as fast as a greyhound," one witness stated. All the while, "though they passed through hedges, ditches, and marshes, they appeared neat and clean all the time." The figures had "hard, hairy faces like men, and no ears."

The excitement began when a schoolboy named John Keely encountered a two-foot-tall man, dressed in red clothing, on a road. Asked where he was from, the gnome responded curtly, "I'm from the mountains, and it's all equal to you what my business is." The boy alerted friends and acquaintances, who the next day returned with Keely and hid in the bushes as he approached a company of fairies, letting one of them take his hand. They walked together for a short time until the fairies spotted the human beings in the bush and shot away.

Ideology Versus Folk Belief." *New York Folklore* 11,1–4 (1985): 177–94.

Jones, T. Gwynn. *Welsh Folklore and Folk-Custom.* Totowa, NJ: Rowman and Littlefield, 1979.

Keightley, Thomas. *The Fairy Mythology.* London: G. Bell, 1878.

Lake, E. F. Coote. "Folk Life and Traditions." *Folklore* 71 (March 1960): 52–58.

Lawson, John Cuthbert. *Modern Greek Folklore and Ancient Greek Religion: A Study in Survivals.* New Hyde Park, NY: University Books, 1964.

Lorenzen, Coral, and Jim Lorenzen. *Encounters with UFO Occupants.* New York: Berkley Medallion Books, 1976.

McKerracher, Archie. "The Minister of Fairyland." *Fate* 43, 1 (January 1990): 59–64.

"Nordic News." *Fortean Times* 43 (Spring 1985): 45–47.

Sanderson, Stewart, ed. *The Secret Commonwealth & A Short Treatise of Charms and Spels by Robert Kirk.* Totowa, NJ: Rowman and Littlefield, 1976.

Scott, Sir Walter. *Letters*

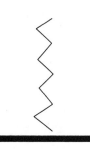

on Demonology and Witchcraft. New York: Ace Books, 1970.

Traum, Artie. "Rollin' and Tumblin': The Cambridge Festival." *Crawdaddy* (November 1972): 20–22.

———. Letter to Jerome Clark (December 27, 1972).

Treadgold, Mary. "Correspondence." *Journal of the Society for Psychical Research* 48, 765 (September 1975): 186–87.

"Trends." *Fortean Times* 31 (Spring 1980): 42–43.

Vallee, Jacques. Passport to Magonia: From Folklore to Flying Saucers. Chicago: Henry Regnery Company, 1969.

Wilkins, Harold T. "Pixie-Haunted Moor." *Fate* 5, 5 (July/August 1952): 110–16.

Winder, R.H.B. "The Little Blue Man on Studham Common." *Flying Saucer Review* 13, 4 (July/August 1967): 3–4.

If this incident had occurred a decade later and been reported somewhere other than Ireland, it probably would have been treated as an encounter with UFO occupants. (In November 1959, according to the *Belfast Telegraph* [November 9], a man moving a large bush with a bulldozer on a farm in County Carlow was startled to see a three-foot-tall red man run out from underneath the machine, "about 100 yards across the field, over a fence into the field adjoining." Three other men observed the fleeing figure. Only the Irish locale kept this from being treated as a UFO incident, though no UFO was seen.) Indeed, the UFO literature contains a handful of incidents in which someone conversant in the fairy-faith might find familiar elements. In April 1950 Kenneth Arnold, whose much-publicized June 24, 1947, sighting brought the UFO age into being, interviewed a Canby, Oregon, woman, Ellen Jonerson, who recently had seen a 12-inch little man with dark features, stocky build, and a plaid shirt. Walking with a "waddling" motion, he passed under a car and disappeared.

Inevitably some writers have suggested that UFO phenomena and fairy manifestations are related. Sometimes, notably in debunker Robert Sheaffer's sarcastic *The UFO Verdict* (1981), the connection is made as a way of heaping ridicule on UFO reports. Sometimes, as in Jacques Vallee's *Passport to Magonia* (1969), it is made to support an occult view that assumes the reality of paranormal shape-shifting entities that can appear, depending on the observer's preconceptions, as fairies or extraterrestrials. More recent theorists, for example Hilary Evans in *Gods, Spirits, Cosmic Guardians* (1987), argue that all "entity" encounters occur in altered states of consciousness and are hallucinatory. But despite their surface attractiveness, theories like Evans's are hardly more persuasive than Vallee's; psychosocial approaches suffer from an absence of empirical evidence and are open to the sorts of criticisms David Hufford has made (see above).

In any case, links between UFO lore and fairylore are weak and require the theorist to read the respective literatures with great selectivity. Folklorist Thomas E. Bullard calls proposed connections "oblique and speculative" at best — a point readers can easily establish for themselves by comparing the contexts of two books coincidentally published in the same year (1976): Coral and Jim Lorenzen's *Encounters with UFO Occupants* and Katharine Briggs's *An Encyclopedia of Fairies*.

Another important difference is that at least some "close encounters of the third kind" have been well investigated and documented by civilian or official inquirers, whereas fairy "sightings," however provocative, are no more than simple anecdotes. No doubt this is so because those who heard them saw no reason to investigate; either they believed in fairies and so implicitly assumed the stories to be true, or they did not believe in fairies, or they were collecting what they thought of as "folklore" whose reality status was irrelevant. In all of these cases, no further inquiry was deemed necessary.

Perhaps real investigation would turn belief or disbelief into a response based on information rather than on supposition. But fairy "sightings" are likely to remain where they always have been: at the fringes of human experience.

FALLS FROM THE SKY (INORGANIC MATTER)

For as long as human beings have been keeping historical records, all kinds of phenomena, living and otherwise, have been reported to fall out of the sky. Usually, though not always, these falls take place in the midst of a furious storm. On occasion, however, a fall may occur out of a clear sky.

The first skeptics "explained" falls as a misunderstanding of a fundamental process of nature, which was that rain triggered the spontaneous generation, out of mud, slime, and dust, of things (especially living things) already on the ground. This view, held for example by Pliny (who proposed it in *Natural History* [A.D. 77]), eventually evolved into a more realistic hypothesis, namely that naive witnesses falsely associated the fall of rain with the appearances of animals, vegetable matter, artifacts, or other inorganic materials in the rain's aftermath. These things had been there all along, but the rain had driven or washed them into view.

In due course, after it finally proved futile to dispute reliable observations (some by scientists) of objects falling, conventional opinion bowed to the superiority of witness testimony over armchair dismissal. But conventionalists were ready with another explanation. This one held that waterspouts, tornados, and whirlwinds pick up materials and deposit them somewhere else; consequently, though falls are real enough, they are merely curious, not extraordinary.

That strong winds rip objects off the ground and drop them somewhere else is, of course, beyond dispute. That such weather phenomena account for the most anomalous falls, on the other hand, is decidedly less certain. What makes anomalous falls so puzzling is their strange selectivity. Violent storms drop everything they pick up; most falls drop only one thing and the rest only a very few things. Often, too, the volume of material is so staggering that its disappearance from one place, even if a place could be found where much of it was held, would not go unnoticed. Some falls go on for hours, with the material falling in a steady stream over a significant area of ground.

Of the two types of falls (inorganic and organic; the latter is discussed in the next entry), however, those involving inorganic matter, especially if that matter consists of dust or ash, are the more amenable to mundane accounting. Such falls will not concern us here.

Fire in the sky.
Though many falls of "sulphur" turn out to be of pollen, a few reports, if they are to be believed, cannot be so explained. In other words, they really may be of sulphur or a sulphur compound. William R. Corliss of the Sourcebook Project remarks that a storm-driven fall of sulphur, a substance "rarely found in surface deposits where winds could pick it up, would seem to be very unlikely although not impossible"; yet "tales of burning sulphur," if true, pose a "significant anomaly." One such case was reported in the *American Journal of Science*:

> In March last [1832], there fell in the fields of the village of Kourianof [Russia] ... a combustible substance of a yellowish color, at least two inches thick, and covering a superficies of between six and seven hundred square feet. The inhabitants, at first, thought it was snow, but on examination, it appeared to have the properties of cotton, having, on being torn, the same tenacity; but, on being put into a vessel full of water, it assumed the consistency of rosin. On being put into the first, in its primitive state, it burnt and sent forth a flame like spirits of wine; but in its resinous state, it boiled on the fire, without becoming inflamed, probably because it was mixed with some portion of snow, from which it had been taken. After a more minute examination, the rosin had the color of amber, was elastic like indian [sic] rubber, and smelt like prepared oil, mixed with wax.

An even stranger event took place on October 18, 1867, when residents of Thames Ditton, Surrey, England, were startled by the appearance of a "shower of fire" in the evening sky. The light it cast was "brilliant" for the 10 minutes it lasted. "Next morning it was found that the waterbutts and puddles in the upper part of the village were thickly covered with a deposit of sulphur," *Symons's Monthly Meteorological Magazine* recounted.

Stones.
A larger, more significant category of anomalous falls of inorganic materials concerns nonmeteoritic rocks and stones. Vast numbers of small black stones are said to have fallen on Birmingham, England, in August 1858 and again at Wolverhampton, England, in June 1860. Both incidents took place during violent storms. But events of this sort, while clearly out of the ordinary and possibly (if far from certainly) of extraordinary cause, do not unambiguously challenge consensus-reality notions in the way that other kinds of stone and rock falls do.

Consider, for example, the events that occurred in Chico, California, in the spring of 1922 and for a period of weeks thrilled and perplexed the nation. These events comprise probably the most widely witnessed rock fall in history.

In November 1921 J. W. Charge, the owner of a grain warehouse along the Southern Pacific railroad tracks in Chico, complained to City Marshal J. A. Peck that an unseen someone was daily throwing rocks at the building. Taking this to be a harmless prank, Peck paid no attention — until March 8, 1922, when stones and rocks ranging in size from peas to baseballs came down on the warehouse. The fall continued intermittently all day. The *Chico Record* noted that "one can hear the impact of rocks striking the warehouse roof and they may be seen bouncing from the eaves to the ground." A dragnet through several surrounding blocks failed to flush out the rock-thrower.

In the days ahead Charge's building suffered considerable damage. Stones fell not just there but elsewhere in the cluster of houses near the tracks. Individuals standing in the open were hit, and searchers and investigators themselves became targets. In one such instance, which occurred on March 9, the *Record* related:

> Fire Chief C. E. Tovee and Traffic Officer J. J. Corbett had the scare of their lives while prowling about the Charge warehouse in an endeavor to sight the direction from which the rocks come. They had just approached the south end of the warehouse and were looking skyward when a fair-sized boulder struck the wooden wall above them with a mighty force and rebounded to the ground at their feet, leaving a dent where it had struck the timber.

By the end of the month, the episode had run its course, but not before attracting huge publicity and large numbers of curiosity-seekers. The great anomaly chronicler Charles Fort asked a friend, writer Miriam Allen deFord, to go to Chico and investigate personally. There she, in her words, "saw a stone fall from some invisible point in the sky and land gently at my feet." Fort noted that, whether by coincidence or inexplicable design, fish had fallen out of a clear sky in great numbers and landed on a roof and surrounding streets in Chico on August 20, 1878.

Comparable rock falls have been recorded (see *phantom attackers*), and the Chico events are remembered largely because of the publicity attending them. Anthony Boucher, a writer and critic, remarked that he met deFord "when I investigated a similar stone-fall case in Oakland, California, in 1943. We compared our notes and found our experiences almost identical." Showers of stones, described as warm to the touch, rained down on the pavement outside the office of the *Charleston News and Courier*, a South Carolina newspaper, on three occasions —at 2:30 and 7:30 A.M. and 1:30 P.M. — on September 4, 1886. According to witnesses, they fell straight down from some undetermined point in the sky and confined themselves to a ground area of 75 square feet. A case that took place in a housing development on the outskirts of Tucson, Arizona, lasted for four months, between September and December 1983, and was the sub-

● SOURCES:

Aldrich, Hal R. "Rainbows Keep Falling on My Head." *INFO Journal* 6, 2 (July/August 1977): 2–6.

———. "Fireballs and Rockfalls." *INFO Journal* 8, 4 (January/February 1981): 4–5.

Arnold, Larry E. "Money from Heaven." *Fate* 31, 12 (December 1978): 65–71.

"Chico's 1920s Mystery of Falling Rocks Remains Unsolved." *San Jose [California] Mercury News* (October 27, 1985).

Chorvinsky, Mark. "Our Strange World: It Came from the Skies." *Fate* 45,9 (September 1992): 31–35.

Corliss, William R., ed. *Handbook of Unusual Natural Phenomena.* Glen Arm, MD: The Sourcebook Project, 1977.

———. *Tornados, Dark Days, Anomalous Precipitation, and Related Weather Phenomena: A Catalog of Geophysical Anomalies.* Glen Arm, MD: The Sourcebook Project, 1983.

"Falls!" *INFO Journal* 4,2 (November 1974): 22–30.

125

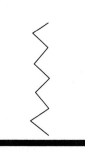

ject of extensive investigations both by police and by an experienced para-psychologist, the late D. Scott Rogo.

Falls of artifacts.

The most fantastic claims are those concerning falls of manufactured objects, most famously thunderstones, the subject of a worldwide folklore which has it that shaped stones (ax heads, for example) sometimes come down during storms, and especially in the wake of a spectacular roar of thunder and bolt of lightning. In the modern developed world thunderstones are all but forgotten, but no less improbable things are said to drop out of the atmosphere.

On the morning of May 28, 1982, a young girl was walking through the yard of St. Elisabeth's Church in Redding, a small town near Manchester, England, when, or so she later told the Rev. Graham Marshall, she spotted a 50-pence coin fall "from nowhere." As the day went on, children discovered numerous other coins at the same spot. Finally the owner of a local candy store, concerned that the children were stealing from the poor box, informed the clergymen of the sudden rush in business at his establishment. No money was missing, but the children all swore, when Marshall interviewed them, that the coins seemed to be coming from the sky. Or so they inferred from the fact that they would hear a tinkling sound on the sidewalk and, on looking, see a coin.

Marshall conducted his own investigation and eliminated some obvious explanations, such as that a prankster was tossing coins over the church wall (the wall was too high and bare for a coin-tosser not to be easily visible to passersby) or that birds were dropping them (too many coins clustered together and no nests overhead). Some of the coins were imbedded edgewise into the ground, suggesting a fall from some height. Marshall experimented by hurling a handful of coins to earth, and they made no impression.

An incident like this is insufficient to prove anything one way or another, but it is not unprecedented. One day in December 1968 shoppers in another English town, Ramsgate, Kent, heard pennies bouncing off the pavement. "Between 40 and 50 of them came down in short scattered bursts for about 15 minutes," one witness, Jean Clements, told the *London Daily Mirror*. "You could not see them falling — all you heard was the sound of them hitting the ground." They hit hard enough so that dents registered on them. There were "no tall buildings nearby," Clements said, "and no one heard a plane go overhead." Among other coin falls are those said to have happened in Meshehera, Russia, summer 1940 (during a storm); Bristol, England, in September 1956; Bourges, France, April 15, 1957 ("thousands" of 1000-franc notes, never claimed); and Limburg, West Germany, January 1976 (2000 marks, seen falling by two clergymen).

Usually artifacts (including, as legend has it, thunderstones) fall not in clusters but by themselves. On April 17, 1969, the *New York Times* reported the bizarre experience of a California woman, Ruth Stevens, who was dri-

Fort, Charles. *The Books of Charles Fort.* New York: Henry Holt and Company, 1941.

Jessup, M. K. *The Case for the UFO.* New York: The Citadel Press, 1955.

Knight, Damon. *Charles Fort: Prophet of the Unexplained.* Garden City, NY: Doubleday and Company, 1970.

Koenig, Vernon E., Jr. "Glob of Glass from the Sky." *Fate* 34,2 (February 1981): 81–83.

Magin, Ulrich. "Fortean Falls in Germany, Austria and Switzerland." *INFO Journal* 13,3 (March 1990): 12–14, iii.

Michell, John, and Robert J. M. Rickard. *Phenomena: A Book of Wonders.* New York: Pantheon Books, 1977.

Olmsted, Denison. "Observations on the Meteors of November 13th, 1833." *American Journal of Science* 1, 26 (1834): 132.

Quast, Thelma Hall. "Rocks Rain on Chico, California." *Fate* 29, 1 (January 1976): 73–81.

Rickard, Robert J. M. "Falls." *Fortean Times* 36 (Winter 1982): 26–27, 41.

Rogo, D. Scott. *On the Track of the Poltergeist.*

ving in Palm Springs when a wheel sailed out of the sky and onto her car's hood, where it left a one-foot dent. The account does not tell us what kind of wheel it was, but it does note that no local airport received a report of a missing wheel from any pilot.

Such instances of artifact falls are poorly documented on the whole, and only the foolhardy would rush in to wave wild paranormal "theories" on the assumption that no other explanation is possible. Without real investigations and firm reasons to dismiss mundane alternatives, these events should be viewed cautiously.

Englewood Cliffs, NJ: Prentice-Hall, 1986.

"Shower of Sulphur." *Symons's Monthly Meteorological Magazine* 2 (1867): 130.

Splitter, Henry Winfred. "Wonders from the Sky." *Fate* 6, 10 (October 1953): 33–40.

Vembos, Thanassis. "Some Accounts of Fortean Falls in Greece." *Strange Magazine* 4 (1989): 20–22.

Whitley, Gilbert. "Falls: Fishes, Ice, Straw." *INFO Journal* 3,2 (Spring 1973): 22–25.

FALLS FROM THE SKY (ORGANIC MATTER) —

As a heavy rain fell and a strong wind blew, a curious event took place at Mountain Ash, Glamorganshire, Wales, late on the morning of February 9, 1859. Numerous residents, including members of the clergy, witnessed it. One observer, John Lewis, provided this account not long afterwards to a correspondent for the *Annual Register*:

> *I was getting out a piece of timber, for the purpose of setting it for the saw, when I was startled by something falling all over me — down my neck, on my head, and on my back. On putting my hand down my neck I was surprised to find they were little fish. By this time I saw the whole ground covered with them. I took off my hat, the brim of which was full of them. They were jumping all about. They covered the ground in a long strip of about 80 yards by 12, as we measured afterwards. [The] shed was covered with them, and the shoots were quite full of them. My mates and I might have gathered bucketsful of them, scraping with our hands. We did gather a great many, about a bucketful, and threw them into the rain pool, where some of them now are. There were two showers, with an interval of about 10 minutes, and each shower lasted about two minutes or thereabouts. The time was 11 A.M. The morning up-train to Aberdare was just then passing. It was not blowing very hard, but uncommon wet…. They came down with the rain [as if] in a body.*

Another witness, the Rev. John Griffith, collected some specimens, the largest of which was five inches long.

Falls of fish — and, as we shall see, of other animals as well as organic matter generally — have been remarked on for many centuries. The first known printed reference appears in Pliny's *Natural History* (A.D. 77). In common with some subsequent would-be explainers, he doubted that living things actually fell, presumably reasoning that since fish do not live in the sky, fish cannot fall from the sky. In his view the creatures were already present, on the ground — where, in point of fact, they do not live either — as dust and slime which, when exposed to a vigorous spring rain, sprouted into animals (which then return to dust and slime with the onset of winter). In recent centuries, including the present one, some theorists have held that a hard rain drives small animals from their usual hiding places; thus the impression that the animals fell in the rain is a delusion. No doubt that happens sometimes, and that is why we here concern ourselves only with witnessed falls. Other "explanations" need not concern the serious inquirer. A particularly notorious example is a British Museum scientist's suggestion that the Mountain Ash fall recounted above resulted from the dumping of a pail of fish on someone's head. A mass fall of crabs and periwinkles near Worcester, England, in 1881 was attributed to a crazed, though untraceable, fishmonger.

Today hardly anyone disputes the occurrence of falls. The debate instead centers on how anomalous their causes are. For those to whom falls are a mere curiosity of nature, such events happen when waterspouts or tornadoes carry animals from a nearby body of water and dump them on land. While superficially plausible, this explanation does not begin to deal with some of the central and thoroughly bizarre aspects of the phenomenon. Charles Fort succinctly defined the shortcomings thus:

> Coffins have come down from the sky; also, as everybody knows, silk hats and horse collars and pajamas. But these things have come down at the time of a whirlwind. The two statements that I start with are that no shower exclusively of coffins, nor of marriage certificates, nor of alarm clocks has been recorded; but that showers exclusively of living things are common. And yet the explanation by orthodox scientists who accept that showers of living things have occurred is that the creatures were the products of whirlwinds. The explanation is that little frogs, for instance, fall from the sky, unmixed with anything else, because, in a whirlwind, the creatures were segregated, by differences in specific gravity. But when a whirlwind strikes a town, away go detachables in a monstrous mixture, and there's no findable record of washtubs coming down in one place, all the town's cats in one falling battle that lumps its infelicities in one place, and all the kittens coming down together somewhere else, in a distant bunch that meows for its lump of mothers.

The truly anomalous falls usually consist of one species of animal or organic material. In other words, other species of animals do not rain down with fish or frogs (and if they do, it is only a very small number of other species); mud, sand, weeds, and debris such as a whirlwind picks up as it passes over a lake, creek, river, or sea are not to be found. The selectivity is such that often the falling animals are not only of the same species but of the same age.

In many cases, moreover, there are vast numbers of them. On September 23, 1973, for example, *tens of thousands* of toads fell on Brignoles, France, during what was described as a "freak storm." And they were all *young* toads. In September 1922 young toads fell for two days on another French village, Chalon-sur-Saone. Between 7 and 8 A.M. on October 23, 1947, wildlife biologist A. D. Bajkov and residents of Marksville, Louisiana, witnessed the fall of many *thousands* of fish, which landed — cold and even frozen in some cases — on a strip 75 feet wide and 1,000 feet long. Weather conditions were foggy but otherwise calm, which makes this episode unusual but not unprecedented; most falls take place during storms. (Another fall of a frozen fish occurred on December 22, 1955, when one smashed through the windshield of a car occupied by two men driving to work near Alexandria, Virginia. Traffic was light, and they were nowhere near an underpass. From the damage done — a photograph appears in the same day's *Washington Evening Star* — the fish, apparently a large carp, fell from some considerable height.)

The animals that fall may or may not be known to the area. The Marksville fish were, according to Bajkov, identical to those found in local waters. In *Science* J. Hedgepath recorded a brief fall he had witnessed in Guam in 1936, noting that "one of the specimens ... was identified as the tench (*Tinca tinca*) which, to my knowledge, is common only to the fresh waters of Europe. The presence of this species at a locale so remote from its normal habitat is worthy of note." Sometimes the animals cannot be identified. When fish fell on Montgomery County, California, in February 1890, they proved to be of, according to one who saw them and wrote up the event, "a species altogether unknown here" (*Philadelphia Public Ledger*, February 6). The people of Clifton, Indiana, did not recognize the brown worms that fell on them one day in February 1892, and neither did the editor of *Insect Life*.

On occasion the falling animals arrive in a peculiar condition. At Nokulhatty Factory, India, on February 19, 1830, a great quantity of fish descended from the sky. Writing in the *American Journal of Science*, M. Prinsep reported, "The fish were all dead; most of them were large; some were fresh, others rotted and mutilated. They were seen at first in the sky like a flock of birds descending rapidly to the ground. There was rain drizzling at the time, but no storm." Some of the fish had no heads. Thousands of dead and dry fish landed on Futtehpur, India, in mid-May 1831. In a fall which lasted 10 minutes, sand-eels, stiff, hard, and dead, plummeted to earth near Hendon, England, on August 24, 1918, and some even broke when they hit the ground.

Fort, who found the phenomenon endlessly fascinating, collected some 294 accounts of the falls of organic matter. Since his death in 1932, of course, many more have occurred. Here are some examples of the kinds of materials that figure in fall reports, followed by a representative incident. It should be noted, incidentally, that with the sole exception of the turtle in ice, none of these is a one-of-a-kind event. Nor does this list exhaust the varieties of stuff reported to have fallen.

Mussels. August 9, 1892: A rapidly moving yellow cloud suddenly unleashed a torrential rain, dropping hundreds of mussels on the streets of Paderborn, Germany.

Worms. July 25, 1872: At 9:15 P.M., on a hot evening with a heretofore clear sky, "a small cloud appeared on the horizon," *Nature* reported, "and a quarter of an hour afterwards rain began to fall, when, to the horror of everybody, it was found to consist of black worms the size of an ordinary fly. All the streets were strewn with these curious animals."

Lizards. December 1857: During a shower lizards were observed to fall on streets and sidewalks of Montreal, Quebec.

Turtle. May 11, 1894: A gopher turtle, six by eight inches, fell during a hailstorm at Bovina, Mississippi.

Alligators. December 1877: "Dr. J. L. Smith, of Silvertown Township [South Carolina], while opening up a new turpentine farm, noticed something fall to the ground and commence to crawl toward the tent where he was sitting. On examining the object he found it to be an alligator. In the course of a few moments a second one made its appearance. This so excited the curiosity of the Doctor that he looked around to see if he could discover any more, and found six others within a space of 200 yards. The animals were all quite lively, and about 12 inches in length. The place whereon they fell is situated on high sandy ground about six miles north of the Savannah River" (*New York Times*, December 26).

Salamanders. June 1911: A girl walking along the banks of the Sandy River near Boring, Oregon, got caught in a sudden rain storm. Feeling large objects pelting her on the head and shoulders, she stopped and looked around her to see hundreds of salamanders "falling from the sky, literally covering the ground and wriggling and crawling all over," Arlene Meyer recalled as an adult.

Blood and flesh. July 1869: As mourners prepared for a funeral at a farm near Los Angeles, blood and meat rained out of a clear sky for three minutes. The substances blanketed two acres of a corn field. On examination the blood was found to be mixed with what looked like hairs from animal fur. The flesh ranged in size from small particles to six- and eight-inch strips and included what witnesses took to be pieces of kidney, liver, and heart. One witness brought samples to the *Los Angeles News*, whose editor subsequently declared (in the August 3 issue), "That the meat fell, we cannot doubt. Even the parsons in the neighborhood are willing to vouch for that. Where it came from, we cannot even conjecture."

Grain. March 24, 1840: During a thunderstorm a shower of grain covered Rajket, India, and a considerable area of surrounding countryside. According to the *American Journal of Science*, a British captain named Aston collected samples and sent them to England. "The natives flocked to Capt. A. to ask for his opinion of this phenomenon: for not only did the raining of grain upon them from heaven, excite terror, but the omen was aggravated by the fact that the seed was not one of the cultivated grains of the country, but was entirely unknown to them," the *Journal* stated.

Straw. August 1963: Straw in huge quantity began falling from clouds over Dartford, Kent, England, and did not stop for an hour. "I looked up," one witness said, "and the sky was full of it." The fall ceased as suddenly as it started. "We are mystified," a government meteorologist told Associated Press. A police officer said, "There was far too much of it for it to have been dropped from an airplane."

Leaves. April 7 and 11, 1894: On two clear, still days leaves fell for half an hour at two French villages, first at Clairvaux, then at Pontcarre. Though it was spring and trees were just starting to bud, the fully grown leaves were dried and dead — autumn leaves, in other words.

Seeds. Summer 1897: Half an hour before sunset, a large number of small, dark-red clouds abruptly filled the sky over Macerata, Italy, and an hour later a powerful storm erupted. Immediately "the air became filled with myriads of small seeds," R. Hedger Wallace reported in *Notes and Queries*. "The seeds fell over town and country, covering the ground to a depth of about half an inch. The next day the whole of the scientists at Macerata were abroad in order to find some explanation. Prof. Cardinali, a celebrated Italian naturalist, stated that the seeds were of the genus Cercis, commonly called Judas Tree, and that they belonged to an order of Leguminosae found only in Central Africa or the Antilles. It was found, upon examination, that a great number of the seeds were actually in the first stage of germination."

Hazelnuts. May 9, 1867: Hazelnuts "fell in great quantities and with great force" over a small area of Dublin, Ireland. "I am informed that so violent was the force with which they descended that even the police, protected by unusually strong head covering, were obliged to seek shelter from the aerial fusillade!" a correspondent told *Symons's Monthly Meteorological Magazine*.

Green slime. September 5 and 6, 1978: An "unexplained green slime," in the words of the *Journal of Meteorology*, splattered an area of Washington, D.C., injuring animals and plants and soiling automobiles. The roof of a 12-story building was coated with the substance, suggesting it had fallen from a considerable height. The authorities did not even try to explain it.

Theories.
If we eliminate waterspouts, whirlwinds, and earthbound animals and plants mistakenly assumed to have fallen as adequate explanations for the most anomalous falls, we are left with a mystery with no plausible answers. That, of course, has not stopped some writers from proposing their own implausible answers.

Fort at least had his tongue in his cheek when he put forth his own. His favorite "theory," which he cheerfully acknowledged to be preposterous

● SOURCES:

Bajkov, A. D. "Do Fish Fall from the Sky?" *Science* 109 (1949): 402.

Bessor, John Philip. "Are the Saucers Space Animals?" *Fate* 8,12 (December 1955): 6–12.

"Black Worms Fall from Sky." *Nature* 6 (1872): 356.

Chorvinsky, Mark. "Our Strange World: It Came from the Skies." *Fate* 45, 9 (September 1992): 31–35.

Corliss, William R., ed. *Handbook of Unusual Natural Phenomena.* Glen Arm, MD: The Sourcebook Project, 1977.

———. *Tornados, Dark Days, Anomalous Precipitation, and Related Weather Phenomena: A Catalog of Geophysical Anomalies.* Glen Arm, MD: The Sourcebook Project, 1983.

Dobbins, Ron. "The 'Fish Falls' of Yoro, Honduras." *Pursuit* 8,4 (October 1975): 93–95.

"A Fall of Green Slime." *Journal of Meteorology* 4 (1979): 312.

Fort, Charles. *The Books of Charles Fort.* New York: Henry Holt and Company, 1941.

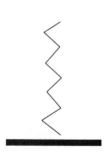

and outrageously pseudoscientific, was that giant land masses float above the earth. Tornadoes, hurricanes, and cyclones on the earth's surface carry all sorts of items upward and dump them on these lands. Some fall into the "Super-Sargasso Sea," to join other junk from other times and even other worlds. In that vast atmospheric ocean can be found almost anything conceivable:

> *Derelicts, rubbish, old cargoes from inter-planetary wrecks; things cast out into what is called space by convulsions of other planets, things from the times of the Alexanders, Caesars and Napoleons of Mars and Jupiter and Neptune; things raised by this earth's cyclones; horses and barns and elephants and flies and dodoes, moas, and pterodactyls; leaves from modern trees and leaves of the Carboniferous era — all, however, tending to disintegrate into homogenous-looking muds or dusts, red or black or yellow — treasure-troves for the palaeontologists and for the archaeologists — accumulations of centuries — cyclones of Egypt, Greece, and Assyria — fishes dried and hard, there a short time; others there long enough to putrefy ... or living fishes, also — ponds of fresh water; oceans of salt water.*

Violent terrestrial storms not only dump things into the Super-Sargasso Sea but cause disturbances there so that sometimes things drop from it — thus falls of all sorts of organic and inorganic matter.

Unlike Fort, John Philip Bessor actually meant his alarming "theory." According to Bessor, the "many falls of flesh and blood from the sky in times past" constitute evidence that UFOs are carnivorous atmospheric life forms, otherwise known as "space animals"; how else to explain mysterious disappearances of people? Relatively more prosaically, another 1950s-era UFO writer, Morris K. Jessup, thought the answer fairly obvious. The live things that have fallen from the skies are

> *the inhabitants of celestial hydroponic tanks and ... their falls come from one of two things: (1) when the tanks are dumped and cleared for refilling, for whatever reason there might be, (2) that the falls may be the residue from the collection from earth while the monitors of the tanks are replenishing their supplies.*

In other efforts to make sense of falls, writers of a Fortean disposition are inclined to draw on the concept of teleportation — the paranormal transporation of an object from one place to another — as a sort of blanket explanation. But even if teleportation is a real phenomenon of nature, which is by no means certain, it begs the same sorts of questions more conventional approaches do; in other words, it does not address the selectivity of falls and the staggering volume that falls in many of the cases.

Damon Knight formulated what amounts to a nonsatirical reworking of Fort's satirical hypothesis. A sober, scientifically sophisticated man and the author of the one biography so far published of Fort, Knight charted weather records and matched them against reports of falls and unusual

"Frozen Flying Fish Sails Out of Sky to Smack Car." *Washington Evening Star* (December 22, 1955).

Hedgepath, J. "Rainfall of Fish." *Science* 110 (1949): 482.

Jessup, M. K. *The Case for the UFO.* New York: The Citadel Press, 1955.

Knight, Damon. *Charles Fort: Prophet of the Unexplained.* Garden City, NY: Doubleday and Company, 1970.

Little, Gregory L. "Snakes Fell on Memphis." *Fate* 38, 2 (February 1985): 74–77.

Meyer, Arlene O. "Report from the Readers: Raining Dogs." *Fate* 21, 12 (December 1968): 131–32.

Michell, John, and Robert J. M. Rickard. *Phenomena: A Book of Wonders.* New York: Pantheon Books, 1977.

———. *Living Wonders: Mysteries and Curiosities of the Animal World.* New York: Thames and Hudson, 1982.

Pim, Arthur. "A Shower of Hazel Nuts." *Symons's Monthly Meteorological Magazine* 2 (1867): 59.

Prinsep, M. "Fall of Fishes from the Atmosphere in India." *American Journal of Science* 1, 32 (1837): 199.

space and aerial phenomena in Fort's books. From 1877 through 1892, a period of unusually intense anomalous activity, he found what seem to be striking correlations. He reviewed other kinds of evidence from physics and astronomy on the effects of extraterrestrial energies on everything from weather to behavior as well as scientific theories about parallel universes. These led him to suggest that

> under certain conditions of gravidic and electromagnetic strain in the solar system, channels open through which material objects can reach the Earth from parts unknown, or can be transferred from one part of the Earth's surface to another.... Let us suppose that a channel opens between this Earth and another, where the surface is a few hundred feet, or a few thousand feet higher. Then things fall, from that Earth to this. Frogs, minding their own affairs in a pond, feel the bottom drop out....

Falls certainly seem an extraordinary enough phenomenon to require an explanation this extraordinary, but the problem here is, ironically, the same one that makes the waterspout hypothesis unsatisfactory: the selectivity and the volume. Knight does make some slight effort to deal with at least the first issue: "If these channels are electromagnetic in nature, we may approach an answer to the puzzling question of selectivity.... All living things have electric charges, and it is possible to imagine that an electromagnetic field would discriminate between them." Perhaps wisely, he takes this vague idea no further.

"Remarkable Hail." *Monthly Weather Review* 22 (1894): 215.

Sanderson, Ivan T. *Uninvited Visitors: A Biologist Looks at UFOs.* New York: Cowles, 1967.

Schadewald, Robert. "The Great Fish Fall of 1859." *Fortean Times* 30 (Fall 1979): 38–42.

Shoemaker, Michael T. "Back from Limbo: The California Candy Falls." *Strange Magazine* 4 (1989): 23.

"Shower of Grain." *American Journal of Science* 1, 41 (1841): 40.

Splitter, Henry Winfred. "Wonders from the Sky." *Fate* 6, 10 (October 1953): 33–40.

Vembos, Thanassis. "Some Accounts of Fortean Falls in Greece." *Strange Magazine* 4 (1989): 20–22.

Wallace, R. Hedger. "A Marvelous 'Rainfall' of Seeds." *Notes and Queries* 8, 12 (1897): 228.

Whalen, Dwight. "Niagara Fishfalls." *Pursuit* 16, 2 (Second Quarter 1983): 64–67.

Whitley, Gilbert. "Falls: Fishes, Ice, Straw." *INFO Journal* 3,2 (Spring 1973): 22–25.

FLATWOODS MONSTER —————————————

On September 12, 1952, three boys in the tiny West Virginia town of Flat-woods (pop. 300) saw a slow-moving, reddish sphere sail around a hill, hover briefly, and drop behind the crest of another hill. From the other side a bright glow shone, as if from a landed object. On their way to investigate, the boys were joined by beautician Kathleen May, her two young sons, their friend Tommy Hyer, 17-year-old Eugene Lemon, and Lemon's dog.

The dog ran ahead of the group and was briefly out of sight. Suddenly it was heard barking furiously and, moments later, seen fleeing with its tail tucked between its legs. A foul-smelling mist covered the ground and caused the searchers' eyes to water. The two leading the group, Lemon and Neil Nunley, who got to the top first, looked down and observed a "big ball of fire" 50 feet to their right. Another of the witnesses reported it was the size of a house.

To the group's left, on the hilltop and just under the branch of an oak tree, were two small lights. At Mrs. May's suggestion, Lemon turned his flash-light on them. To everyone's considerable astonishment, the beam high-lighted a grotesque-looking creature with a head shaped like the "ace of spades," as several of the observers independently described it. Inside the head was a circular "window," dark except for the two lights from which pale blue beams extended straight ahead. In their short observation of the creature, the group saw nothing that looked like arms or legs.

The creature, which appeared to be over six feet tall, moved toward the witnesses; it seemed to be gliding rather than walking. Seconds later it changed direction, turning toward the glowing ball down the hill.

All of this allegedly took place in a matter of seconds, during which Lemon fainted. The others dragged him away as they ran from the scene.

When interviewed half an hour later by A. Lee Stewart, Jr., of *The Braxton Democrat*, most of the witnesses were barely able to speak. Some sought first aid. Stewart thought there was no question they had seen something that badly frightened them. Soon afterwards, he was able to get Lemon to accompany him to the hillside, where Stewart noticed an unusual odor in the grass that irritated his nose and throat. Returning to the site alone at seven o'clock the following morning, he found "skid marks" going down the hill and toward an area of matted grass, indicating the recent presence of a large object.

The encounter with what the press would quickly dub the "Flatwoods monster" took place during a flurry of sightings of unusual flying objects in the area. One man, Bailey Frame of nearby Birch River, told of seeing a bright orange ball circling over the area where the monster was reported. The object was visible for 15 minutes before shooting toward the airport at Sutton, where it was also seen.

According to one account, a week before the Flatwoods event and 11 miles away, a Weston woman and her mother encountered the same or a similar creature as they were driving to church. Both reported it emitted a foul odor, and the younger woman was so frightened that she required hospitalization. This report, if true, never made the newspapers. It was uncovered by two investigators associated with the Los Angeles-based Civilian Saucer Investigation.

Skeptics theorized that May and her companions had seen a meteor and an owl, and only hysteria had caused them to think they had observed anything else. Nonetheless, when interviewed separately shortly after the incident, the witnesses told a story investigators found strikingly consistent. Skeptical hypotheses have necessarily had to reject *a priori* the witnesses' descriptions of what they saw.

A Joliette, Quebec, woman reported seeing a similar creature as it gazed through a window of her home in the early morning hours of November 22, 1973. She roused her husband, who went outside to investigate, finding only a dog which acted as if "scared to death." The local police said they thought the woman was sincere.

● SOURCES:

Barker, Gray. "The Monster and the Saucer." *Fate* 6,1 (January 1953): 12–17.

Macduff, Claude. "The November 1973 UFO-Invasion of Quebec." *The UFO Register* 7,1 (December 1976): 3–18.

"More on the 'Green Monster.'" *Civilian Saucer Investigation Quarterly Bulletin* 1,2 (Winter 1953): 3.

Sanderson, Ivan T. *Uninvited Guests: A Biologist Looks at UFOs.* New York: Cowles, 1967.

FLIGHT 19

Of all the "mysterious disappearances" associated with the Bermuda Triangle, none is more famous than Flight 19. As with many of the stories that comprise the legend, however, there are serious discrepancies between what can be verified and what Triangle chroniclers have claimed.

The tragedy.
At 2:10 on the afternoon of December 5, 1945, five Avenger torpedo bombers left the Naval Air Station (NAS) at Fort Lauderdale, Florida, and headed east. Flight 19 was made up of 14 men, all students in the last stages of training except for the commander, Lt. Charles Taylor. The five pilots had been transferred only recently from the Miami Naval Air Station. Taylor knew the Florida Keys well; he did not know the Bahamas, in whose direction he and the others were heading.

The purpose of the exercise was to conduct a practice bombing at Hens and Chicken Shoals 56 miles away. Once that was accomplished, the Avengers were to continue eastward for another 67 miles, then head north 73 miles. After that they would turn west-southwest and take the remaining 120 miles straight home. In short, they were flying a triangular flight path through what would be called the Bermuda Triangle.

At 3:40 P.M. a pilot and flight instructor, Lt. Robert Cox, who was about to land at Fort Lauderdale, overheard a radio transmission addressed to someone named Powers. Powers replied, "I don't know where we are. We must have got lost after that last turn." Fort Lauderdale attempted to communicate with Powers (in fact Marine Capt. Edward Powers, Jr.) but got no immediate response. A few minutes later Cox established contact with Taylor, the pilot who had spoken to Powers. The pilot was Lt. Taylor. Taylor told Cox that his compasses were not working, but "I'm sure I'm in the Keys, but ... I don't know how to get to Fort Lauderdale." Cox urged him to fly north toward Miami "if you are in the Keys."

Taylor was not, however, in the Keys. He was in the Bahamas. By flying north he would only go farther out to sea. Efforts by Cox and others to establish just the location of Flight 19 were hampered by poor communications. At one point Taylor was urged to turn over control of the flight to one of the students, though apparently he did not do so; the occasional overheard exchange between him and other Flight 19 pilots suggested some degree of dissension. Just after 4:30 P.M. Taylor radioed a question to Port Everglades Boat Facility, an Air Sea Rescue Unit near Fort Lauderdale: "Do you think, as my student does, that we should fly west?" Not knowing where he was, Port Everglades simply acknowledged receiving his transmission. If Flight 19 had flown west at this stage, it would have been saved.

At 4:45 P.M. Taylor indicated that the Avengers were going to go north-northeast for a short time, then head north "to make sure we are not over the Gulf of Mexico." By now the people on the ground were seriously concerned; it was clear that Taylor, far from being temporarily lost as happens to many pilots, had no idea where he was. As dusk approached, atmospheric interference with the radio signals increased. Through the static, two of the student pilots could be heard complaining that "if we would just fly west, we would get home." Nonetheless they flew north, then veered off slightly to the east, for a few minutes. At 5:15 P.M. Taylor called in to Port Everglades, "We are now heading west." Taylor addressed his companions, telling them that they should join up; as soon as one of them ran out of fuel, they would all go down together.

The sun set at 5:29 P.M. With bad weather moving in from the north, the situation was growing ever more urgent, but no one on the ground knew where Flight 19 was. Around 6 P.M. reception improved for a short time. Taylor was urged to switch to 3000 kilocycles, the emergency frequency, but refused to do so for fear he and the other planes would fall out of communication; unfortunately, interference from Cuban commercial stations and the inability of other coastal stations to translate the Fort Lauderdale training signal easily would effectively shut off Flight 19 from the rest of the world.

A few minutes earlier, at 5:50 P.M., the ComGulf Sea Frontier Evaluation Center thought it had pinpointed the flight's approximate position: east of New Smyrna Beach, Florida, and far to the north of the Bahamas. At 6:04 P.M. Taylor was heard ordering the others to "turn around and go east again." Two minutes later he repeated the order, explaining, "I think we would have a better chance of being picked up." Apparently he still believed the flight was over the Gulf.

So far no rescue aircraft had gone out because the position fix had not yet been passed on to all affected parties, not the least of them Taylor and his companions. But finally a Dumbo flying boat based at the Dinner Key seaplane base left Miami, heading northeast, at 6:20 P.M. on what amounted to a blind effort to reestablish contact. The Dumbo itself soon fell out of contact with shore, however, and for a while it was feared that it, too, was lost. The problem turned out to be icing on the antenna, and the Dumbo continued on what proved to be a futile search.

Within the hour other aircraft joined it, including two Martin Mariners (Training 32 and Training 49), the second of which departed from the Banana River NAS at 7:27 P.M. This Mariner was to join up with the first, which had taken off about 20 minutes earlier, east of New Smyrna Beach. Lt. Gerald Bammerlin, 32's pilot, later told Naval investigators, "When we arrived in the area of Flight 19's 5:50 position fix, about 8:15, the overcast was at approximately 800 to 1200 feet. There were occasional showers. The estimated wind was west-southwest 25 to 30 knots. The air was very turbulent and the sea very rough. We flew manually on instruments throughout the night, though whitecaps were visible below."

In the meantime 49 had failed to make its scheduled rendezvous, and it was not answering radio calls. At 7:50 P.M. the crew of the *SS Gaines Mill* observed an enormous sheet of fire caused by the explosion of an airplane. A few minutes later the ship passed through a big pool of oil and looked with no success for survivors or bodies. Though they saw some debris, crew members did not try to retrieve any of it because of the ocean turbulence. Weather conditions were deteriorating rapidly.

The Flight 19 aircraft now had exhausted their fuel and were assumed to be down. Taylor's last transmission was heard at 7:04 P.M. The search continued through the night, though at a diminished rate because of turbulence in the air and on the ocean. The next day hundreds of planes and ships looked in vain, on heavy seas, for the missing Avengers and Mariner. No trace of them turned up then, later, or ever.

On April 3, 1946, at the conclusion of an intensive investigation of this much-publicized air disaster, the Navy declared that the "flight leader's false assurance of identifying as the Florida Keys, islands he sighted, plagued his future decisions and confused his reasoning.... [H]e was directing his flight to fly east ... even though he was undoubtedly east of Florida." When Taylor's mother and aunt refused to accept this verdict, the Navy set up a panel to review the report. In August this panel announced it could only agree with the original conclusion. Furious, the two women hired an attorney and secured a hearing the following October. On November 19 the Board for Correction of Naval Records retracted the original verdict and officially laid the disaster to "causes or reasons unknown."

The Mariner's fate seemed relatively clear. The Mariners were known as "flying gas bombs," which even something so small as a lighted cigarette or an electrical spark could ignite. As for the Avengers, none of the investigating authorities doubted that the 50-foot-high waves tearing across the ocean surface had chewed them up and sent what remained to the bottom, in no more than seconds.

Myth and mystification.
In September 1950 Associated Press reporter E.V.W. Jones sent a story out on the wires. Its echoes would be heard for decades to come. In it he wrote

that a triangular area connecting Florida, Bermuda, and Puerto Rico comprised a "limbo of the lost" where planes and ships often "vanished in the thin air." An especially baffling mystery was the disappearance of Flight 19 and the Martin Mariner which had gone in search of it. An October 1952 article in *Fate*, a popular digest-sized magazine on "true mysteries," drew heavily on the AP piece, citing the Flight 19 story along with others which by the 1960s would evolve into the "Bermuda Triangle" concept.

In a 1955 book, *The Flying Saucer Conspiracy*, Donald E. Keyhoe, a retired Marine Corps major and leading proponent of UFOs as extraterrestrial visitors, suggested that a "giant mother ship" from space had snatched the planes. Like many other writers who would follow, Keyhoe claimed that the sea had been calm all during the episode. More influential, however, was an *American Legion Magazine* article by Allan W. Eckert, who contributed fictitious dialogue other Triangle chroniclers would repeat endlessly. According to Eckert, Taylor had radioed Fort Lauderdale that "everything is wrong ... strange ... the ocean doesn't look as it should."

A later writer, Art Ford, reported he had interviewed a radio operator who heard Taylor say, "They look like they're from outer space — don't come after me." Nothing in the transcript of Taylor's exchanges with others during the flight substantiates this claim, though at one point, during his mid-afternoon conversation with Cox, Taylor had said not to come after him, most believe he meant that he would be fine, not that spaceships were pursuing him.

In a February 1964 *Argosy* article and the next year in a book, *Invisible Horizons*, Vincent Gaddis, coiner of the phrase "Bermuda Triangle," called Flight 19's fate the "most incredible mystery in the history of aviation." Other authors such as Charles Berlitz, Richard Winer, Alan and Sally Lansberg, and John Wallace Spencer told comparably fantastic and misleading versions of the episode. Having rejected all possible mundane explanations for the tragedy, these writers were free to speculate about marauding aliens, the fourth dimension, space-time warps, and extraordinary magnetic anomalies. At the conclusion of Steven Spielberg's 1977 science-fiction film *Close Encounters of the Third Kind*, the Flight 19 crew returns to earth via UFO.

In time more cautious investigators revived, and sometimes expanded on, the Navy's original findings. Larry Kusche wrote an entire book, *The Disappearance of Flight 19* (1980), based on considerable original research. Kusche contended that the Navy's Correction Board ought not to have exonerated Taylor. Though the "decision was a kindness to Mrs. [Kathleen] Taylor [Charles's mother] ... it was incorrect. The conclusion of the original Board of Investigation, that Charles Taylor was at fault, was correct."

Flight 19 was back in the headlines in the spring of 1991 when the crew of the salvage ship *Deep See*, hunting for sunken Spanish galleons, found the intact remains of five Avengers at 600 feet on the ocean bottom 10 miles northeast of Fort Lauderdale. One plane bore the number 28, the same as of Taylor's aircraft. But on June 4 Graham Hawkes, who had headed the search, conceded that further investigation had proved the craft were not from Flight 19. The numbers on the other planes were different from those on the fabled flight. Moreover, the craft were an older generation of Avenger.

In 1985, reminiscing about the event, Willard Stoll, who had led Flight 18 half an hour in front of Taylor's flight, remarked, "What the hell happened to Charlie? Well, they didn't call those planes 'Iron Birds' for nothing. They weighed 14,000 pounds empty. So when they ditched, they went down pretty fast. But they found the *Titanic*, and maybe one day they'll find him and the others. Wherever they are, they're together."

● SOURCES:

Begg, Paul. *Into Thin Air: People Who Disappear.* North Pomfret, VT: David and Charles, 1979.

Christensen, Dan. "After 40 Years, Story of Flight 19 Still Unknown." *West Palm Beach* [Florida] *Post* (December 8, 1985).

Clary, Mike. "Mystery of 'Lost Patrol' May Be Solved." *Los Angeles Times* (May 18, 1991).

Eckert, Allan W. "The Mystery of the Lost Patrol." *The American Legion Magazine* (April 1962): 12–23, 39–41.

"Explorers Say Planes Aren't Lost Squadron." *Staunton* [Virginia] *Daily News Leader* (June 5, 1991).

Kusche, Larry. *The Disappearance of Flight 19.* New York: Harper and Row, Publishers, 1980.

Kusche, Lawrence David. *The Bermuda Triangle Mystery — Solved.* New York: Harper and Row, Publishers, 1975.

McDonell, Michael. "Lost Patrol." *Naval Aviation News* (June 1973): 8, 10–16.

Sand, George X. "Sea Mystery at Our Back Door." *Fate* 5, 7 (October 1952): 11–17.

141

FLYING HUMANOIDS

When a mysterious object passed over Mount Vernon, Illinois, on the evening of April 14, 1897, 100 citizens, including Mayor B. C. Wells, saw something that, as press accounts had it, "resembled the body of a huge man swimming through the air with an electric light on his back."

Reports of flying beings of human or generally human appearance are among the rarer anomalous phenomena, but they occur periodically. A "winged human form" was observed over Brooklyn on September 18, 1877, according to W. H. Smith (*New York Sun*, September 21). Almost exactly three years later the *New York Times* (September 12, 1880) remarked on reports from Coney Island of a "man with bat's wings and improved frog's legs … at least a thousand feet in the air … flying toward the New Jersey coast … [with] a cruel and determined expression." In a 1947 book Russian writer V. K. Arsenyev recounted this July 11, 1908, experience in the Sikhote Mountains near Vladivostok in the far eastern region of what would be the USSR:

> The rain stopped, the temperature of the air remained low and the mist appeared over the water. It was then that I saw the mark on the path that was very similar to a man's footprint. My dog Alpha bristled up, snarled, and then something rushed about nearby trampling among the bushes. However, it didn't go away, but stopped nearby, standing stock-still. We had been standing like that for some minutes.... Then I stooped, picked up a stone and threw it towards the unknown animal. Then something happened that was quite unexpected: I heard the beating of wings. Something large and dark emerged from the fog and flew over the river. A moment later it disappeared in the dense mist. My dog, badly frightened, pressed itself to my feet.

> After supper I told the Udehe-men about this incident. They broke into a vivid story about a man who could fly in the air. Hunters often saw

his tracks, tracks that appeared suddenly and vanished suddenly, in such a way that they could only be possible if the "man" alighted on the ground, then took off again into the air.

One night in 1952 U.S. Air Force Pvt. Sinclair Taylor, on guard duty at Camp Okubo, Kyoto, Japan, said he heard a loud flapping noise. Looking up, he saw an enormous "bird" in the moonlight. When it approached, he got frightened and put a round into the chamber of his carbine. The "bird" now had stopped its flight and was hovering not far away, staring at the soldier.

"The thing, which now had started slowly to descend again, had the body of a man," Taylor recalled. "It was well over seven feet from head to feet, and its wingspread was almost equal to its height. I started to fire and emptied my carbine where the thing hit the ground. But when I looked up to see if my bullets had found home there was nothing there." When the sergeant of the guard came to investigate and heard the story, he told Taylor that he believed him because a year earlier another guard had seen the same thing.

Another soldier's tale of a flying humanoid came to ufologist Don Worley from Earl Morrison, who served with the First Marine Division in Vietnam. While stationed near Da Nang in August 1969, he and two other guards reportedly saw an extraordinary sight just after 1 o'clock in the morning. They were sitting atop a bunker and talking when they noticed something approaching them in the sky. Morrison told Worley:

> *We saw what looked like wings, like a bat's, only it was gigantic compared to what a regular bat would be. After it got close enough so we could see what it was, it looked like a woman. A naked woman. She was black. Her skin was black, her body was black, the wings were black, everything was black. But it glowed. It glowed in the night — kind of a greenish cast to it.... She started going over us, and we still didn't hear anything. She was right above us, and when she got over the top of our heads, she was maybe six or seven feet up.... We watched her go straight over the top of us, and still she didn't make any noise flapping her wings. She blotted out the moon once — that's how close she was to us. And dark — looked like pitch black then, but we could still define her because she just glowed. Real bright like. And she started going past us straight towards our encampment. As we watched her — she had got about 10 feet or so away from us — we started hearing her wings flap. And it sounded, you know, like regular wings flapping. And she just started flying off and we watched her for quite a while.*

Morrison thought the covering on her skin was more like fur than feathers. "The skin of her wings looked like it was molded on to her hands," he said, and the movement of her arms suggested they had no bones in them.

And UFOs.
The Mount Vernon sighting took place in the midst of the great American UFO wave of spring 1897, and in the modern UFO age (which began in

143

June 1947) reports of winged humanoids usually occur, or are interpreted, in a UFO context.

Some sightings are not of winged figures but of humans or humanoids flying through the air with the aid of mechanical devices attached to their bodies. The first known report of this kind was recorded near Louisville, Kentucky, on July 29, 1880 (*Louisville Courier-Journal*, August 6). UFO-age incidents include one from Chehalis, Washington, on January 6, 1948, when an elderly woman and a group of children allegedly saw a man with long mechanical wings which he manipulated with instruments on his chest as he flew in an upright position. Six and a half years later a 12-year-old Coldwater, Kansas, farm boy reportedly saw a dark-complected little man, with pointed nose and ears, float toward a UFO which was hovering nearby (*Wichita Evening Eagle*, September 8, 1954).

Three Houston residents reported what may or may not have been a winged UFO being in the early morning hours of June 18, 1953. As they sat on the front porch of their apartment building trying to escape the heat, an enormous shadow fell across the lawn, then appeared to bounce into a pecan tree. They saw the "figure of a man ... dressed in gray or black-fitting clothes" and bathed in a "dim gray light." Witnesses differed on whether he was wearing a cape or bearing wings. After 15 minutes he "just melted away," and shortly a "loud swoosh" sounded across the street, and a rocket-shaped object shot upward and disappeared along the northeastern horizon.

Even by the bizarre standards of flying-humanoid stories, the Mothman scare that hit the Ohio River Valley in 1966 and 1967 stands out in its sheer weirdness. Mothman's association with UFOs is speculative, resting on the fact that UFOs were manifesting in unusual numbers in the area all during the period of the creature's activity. The dozens of witnesses who saw it said it had batlike wings, humanlike legs, and a broad trunk, at the top of which two big "hypnotic" eyes were set. Oddly, the wings did not flap, and on occasion, when Mothman (or a Mothman) got close to observers, they could hear a mechanical humming sound emanating from it. Otherwise it made a "squeaking" sound.

● SOURCES:

Bord, Janet, and Colin Bord. *Alien Animals*. Harrisburg, PA: Stackpole Books, 1981.

Clark, Jerome, and Loren Coleman. *Creatures of the Outer Edge*. New York: Warner Books, 1978.

Fort, Charles. *The Books of Charles Fort*. New York: Henry Holt and Company, 1941.

Keel, John A. *Strange Creatures from Time and Space*. Greenwich, CT: Fawcett Gold Medal, 1970.

————. *The Mothman Prophecies*. New York: E. P. Dutton and Company, 1975.

Petrenko, Yurij B. "Mail Bag: Forerunner of the Flying 'Lady' of Vietnam?" *Flying Saucer Review* 19,2 (March/April 1973): 29–30.

Taylor, Sinclair. "True Mystic Experiences: The Bird Thing." *Fate* 13, 12 (December 1960): 53–54.

Worley, Don. "The Winged Lady in Black." *Flying Saucer Review Case Histories* 10 (June 1972): 14–16.

GHOST LIGHTS

Ghost lights are luminous phenomena, usually either points of lights or spheres, whose appearance, behavior, location, or regular manifestation puts them, at least ostensibly, into a separate category from ball lightning or unidentified flying objects. Ghost lights are often taken to be supernatural or paranormal, and in many cases, especially those in which they appear regularly over a period of time in one place (as with the famous Brown Mountain lights and the Marfa lights), legends have grown around them, typically associating the lights with apparitions of the dead.

Lights in folk tradition.
Over three hundred years ago Nathaniel Crouch wrote in *The English Empire in America* (1685) that the Indians "have a remarkable observation of a flame that appears before the death of an Indian or English upon their wigwams in the dead of night; I was called out once about twelve a clock ... and plainly perceived it mounting into the air over a church.... You may certainly expect a dead corpse in two or three days."

Three decades earlier, in 1656, John Davis, vicar of Geneu'r Glyn, Cardiganshire, Wales, recorded his and others' observations of varyingly colored lights which foretold deaths. These lights could be encountered anywhere: in the open air, on their way through a door, or inside a house. A small light presaged the death of a child, a bigger light that of an adult. Several lights together meant as many deaths. His wife's sister, Davis said, had observed five lights in a room; that night, in that very room, five servants suffocated to death in a freak accident.

In 1897 R. C. Maclagan published a long survey of ghost-light traditions, stories, and reports from Scotland's West Highlands. Typical of them are these tales told by an Islay man:

> One time lights were seen moving about at night on the rocks on the shore near Kilchearan. Shortly after that, a vessel was wrecked there,

and the body of a man was washed ashore at the spot where the lights had been seen. One time lights were seen on Lochandaal, between Bowmore and Blackrock. Not long after that, two young men were crossing the loch on a small boat, and at the place at which the lights had been seen the boat was capsized and the two lads drowned.

Such widespread traditions of "corpse candles" continued into the twentieth century. As a Welsh informant told W. Y. Evans-Wentz early in the century, "The death-candle appears like a patch of bright light; and no matter how dark the room or place is, everything in it is as clear as day. The candle is not a flame, but a luminous mass, lightish blue in color, which dances as though borne by an invisible agency, and sometimes it rolls over and over. If you go up to the light, it is nothing, for it is a spirit."

In February 1909, for example, newspaper accounts told of the excitement generated in Stockton, Pennsylvania, over the "appearance at night of an arrow of flame, which hovers over the spot on the mountain where the dismembered body of a woman was found in a barrel two years ago.... The light appears every night at about 9 o'clock and hovers over the spot until midnight, but it disappears when anyone approaches the spot to investigate. The superstitious villagers say it is the avenging spirit of the slain woman come back to keep alive the history of the crime so that the murderers may some day be apprehended."

Lights also were associated with appearances of fairies. A young Irishman who attended Oxford University with Evans-Wentz provided him with this account:

Some few weeks before Christmas, 1910, at midnight on a very dark night, I and another young man (who like myself was then about twenty-three years of age) were on horseback on our way home from

Limerick. When near Listowel, we noticed a light about half a mile ahead. At first it seemed to be no more than a light in some house; but as we came nearer to it and it was passing out of our direct line of vision we saw that it was moving up and down, to and fro, diminishing to a spark, then expanding into a yellow luminous flame. Before we came to Listowel we noticed two lights, about one hundred yards to our right, resembling the light seen first. Suddenly each of these lights expanded into the same sort of yellow luminous flame, about six feet high by four feet broad. In the midst of each flame we saw a radiant being having human form. Presently the lights moved toward one another and made contact, whereupon the two beings in them were seen to be walking side by side. The beings' bodies were formed of a pure dazzling radiance, white like the radiance of the sun, and much brighter than the yellow light or aura surrounding them. So dazzling was the radiance, like a halo, round their heads that we could not distinguish the countenance of the beings; we could only distinguish the general shape of their bodies; though their heads were very clearly outlined because this halo-like radiance, which was the brightest light about them, seemed to radiate from or rest upon the head of each being. As we travelled on, a house intervened between us and the lights, and we saw no more of them.

Lights in Wales.

In early December 1904 a 38-year-old Welsh housewife, Mary Jones of Egryn, Merionethshire, allegedly experienced a vision of Jesus, and in short order she became the leading figure in a Christian revival which in the weeks and months ahead attracted international attention — not because of her message, which was simply the tried and true one, but because of the peculiar phenomena that accompanied it.

The lights themselves were not unusual, but they had an odd quality: sometimes — though not always — they were visible to some persons but not to others who should have been able to observe them.

A *London Daily Mirror* reporter related a sighting he experienced in the company of the newspaper's photographer. The two had stationed themselves one evening in Egryn, where they hoped to see the lights. At 10 P.M., after a three-and-a-half-hour vigil, a light resembling an "unusually brilliant carriage lamp" appeared at a distance of 400 yards. As the reporter approached it,

it took the form of a bar of light quite four feet wide, within a few yards of the chapel [from which Mrs. Jones conducted her ministry]. For half a moment it lay across the road, and then extended itself up the wall on either side. It did not rise above the walls. As I stared, fascinated, a kind of quivering radiance flashed with lightning speed from one end of the bar to the other, and the whole thing disappeared. "Look! Look!" cried two women standing just behind me; "Look at the Light!" I found they had seen exactly what had appeared to me. Now comes a startling sequel. Within ten yards of where that band of vivid light had

flashed across the road, stood a little group of fifteen or twenty persons. I went up to them, all agog to hear exactly what they thought of the manifestations — but not one of those I questioned had seen anything at all!

The witness does not say what, if anything, his photographer saw, or why the latter took no photographs. (No photographs of the lights are known to exist, and some contemporary accounts even assert, improbably, that the lights could not be photographed.) Arguably the climate of excitement and expectation caused the reporter to hallucinate, but the *Daily Telegraph* writer was not the only journalist to report such an experience. If anything, the incident recounted by Beriah G. Evans of the *Barmouth Advertiser* is more puzzling.

Evans wrote that while walking with Mrs. Jones and three other persons early on the evening of January 31, 1905, he saw "three brilliant rays of light strike across the road from mountain to sea, throwing the stone wall twenty or thirty yards in front into bold relief, every stone plainly visible. There was not a living soul there, nor house, from which it could have come." Half a mile later, a "blood-red light" appeared in the middle of the village street a foot above the ground and immediately in front of them. It vanished suddenly. Only the reporter and the evangelist saw these things.

"I may add," Evans wrote in a subsequent magazine article, "that a fortnight later a London journalist had an almost identical experience. He, and a woman standing near, saw the white light, now a broad band, crossing the road near the chapel, and climbing and resting upon the wall. A group of half a dozen other people present at the same time saw nothing. Others have had an almost precisely similar experience."

Still, other light manifestations claimed not only multiple but independent witnesses. Once, as Mrs. Jones was holding a revival meeting in a chapel in Bryncrug, a ball of fire casting rays downward illuminated the church. It was also observed by passers-by. On another occasion, Mrs. Jones and three companions were traveling in a carriage in broad daylight when a bright light with no apparent source suddenly shone on them. The occupants of two trailing carriages including two skeptical journalists, witnessed the sight as did Barmouth residents who were awaiting her arrival.

Some representative sightings:

December 22, 1904, 5:18 P.M.: Three observers saw a large light "about half way from the earth to the sky, on the south side of Capel Egryn, and in the middle of it something like [a] bottle or black person, also some little lights scattering around the large light in many colors." January 2, 1905, 10:40 P.M.: "[H]overing above a certain farmhouse ... it appeared to me as three lamps about three yards apart ... very brilliant and dazzling, moving and jumping like a sea-wave under the influence of the sun on a very hot day. The light continued so for ten minutes. All my family saw it the same time." Early January, between 10 and 10:30 P.M.: "I saw two very bright lights, about half a mile away, one a big white light, the other smaller and red in color. The latter flashed backwards and forwards, and finally seemed in the same place again, but a few minutes after[,] we saw another light which seemed to be a few yards above the ground. It now looked like one big flame, and all around it seemed like one big glare of light. It flamed up and went out alternately for about ten minutes."

On February 23 the *Advertiser* took note of a recent report by two men, one a prominent farmer, of a "gigantic human form rising over a hedgerow. Then a ball of fire appeared above and a long ray of light pierced the figure, which vanished."

In the midst of all of this, Mrs. Jones and some of her followers were also encountering Christ and angels, who would manifest themselves in dreams and visions. One dark night, as she walked along a country road, Mrs. Jones said she encountered a shadowy figure who turned into a black dog and charged her, only to be dissuaded when she broke into a hymn. The attacker was, of course, Satan. These sorts of experiences are invariably personal and subjective and thus susceptible, to those so disposed, to secular psychological explanations. The lights, on the other hand, remain a mystery nearly a century later.

The appearance of the lights in the context of an evangelical revival may or may not be coincidental. Certainly it is true, if we look at the broader historical view, that anomalous luminosities are usually observed in a purely secular context. Still, there are precedents. During a religious revival in Ireland in 1859, a "cloud of fire" was seen to descend from the sky and then hover over open-air assemblies of the faithful.

Lights in one place.
In hundreds, possibly even thousands, of places around the world, "strange lights haunt the earth," anomaly chronicler Vincent H. Gaddis has written. "These types of UFOs are not flying saucers or balls of light-

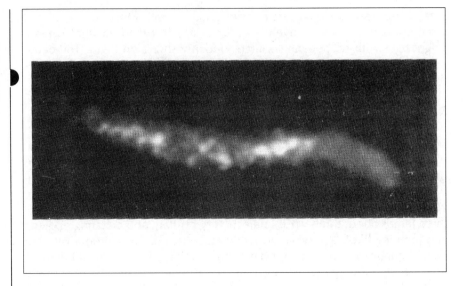

These two Hessdalen photographs were snapped just a few seconds apart, showing light's abrupt change in shape.

ning. They are usually small in size and appear close to the ground. Their outstanding characteristic is that they are localized to one area or place."

Such lights become the focus of legends, not infrequently of lantern-bearing ghosts searching for something they lost in life, such as (in not a few of the more morbid traditions) a head. Not many of these have ever been properly investigated, but on those rare occasions when scientists or other serious researchers have addressed themselves to the task, the results generally have been disappointing — at least to those who wish to have their mysteries remain forever enigmatic or who, on the other hand, have their own more exotic explanatory hobbyhorses to ride.

Many of the lights turn out, for example, to emanate from the headlights of cars on distant highways, or from stars and planets refracted through layers of air of varying temperatures. Sometimes the claim that the lights were a part of folklore even before the invention of the automobile or the locomotive proves itself to be folklore. Yet even ghost lights which are convincingly explainable in prosaic terms yield up occasionally puzzling reports, as if to confuse those of us who want to keep things simple. It may be that these are only anomalies of human perception, of course, but sometimes the witnesses are scientists and other trained observers.

There are, however, unambiguously mysterious lights which serious, sustained investigations by sober field researchers have not been able to lay to rest. The two major current examples are the lights at the Yakima Indian Reservation of south-central Washington and in the Hessdalen Valley of Norway.

Yakima.
The thinly populated reservation is 3500 miles square, divided between rugged wilderness in the west and flat lands in the east. Beginning in the late 1960s (though sporadic sightings had occurred before then), forest

rangers, fire-control personnel, and others began reporting the movement of bright white lights low in the sky over rough terrain on both the north and south sides of Toppenish Ridge, which cuts through the reservation's east-central section.

When these reports came to the attention of W. J. (Bill) Vogel, chief fire-control officer, by his own account he would greet them "with knowing smiles, an embarrassed shuffling of papers, and advisement to 'keep us informed'." Then late one night, as he was on patrol south of Toppenish, he saw something above a hill. "It was easy to see then that the object most certainly was no aircraft," he said. "Also there was no discernible lateral movement. Even without binoculars the object's teardrop shape, with the small, pointed end above, was obvious. Brilliantly white in the center, the outer edges were fluorescent tan or light orange with a surrounding halolike glow. Its most awe-inspiring feature was a mouselike tail or antenna protruding from the small end and pointing upward. The antenna, as long as the object itself, was segmented into colors of red, blue, green, and white which were constantly changing brilliancy and hue."

Over the next 90 minutes Vogel took a series of photographs of the object, which eventually vanished to the south over the Simcoe Mountains. It would be only the first of a number of sightings he would make. Soon Vogel was busy collecting and investigating sightings on the reservation. Most of the reports he gathered were from his own fire lookouts, all trained and reliable observers, but he also interviewed many local people who had seen the lights.

Later investigators included astronomer and former Air Force UFO consultant J. Allen Hynek. Hynek persuaded the Tribal Council to allow an observer to set up equipment on the reservation and to monitor the lights' activity. The observer, David Akers of the Aerial Phenomena Research Organization (APRO), brought with him cameras and other devices. On August 19, 1972, his first night on the reservation, Akers, accompanied by Vogel, saw two round, glowing, reddish-orange lights circling, changing places, and going on and off as they maneuvered beneath the tops of hills west of White Swan, a town at the reservation's north-central region. He took four photographs. Other sightings and other photographs followed until Akers left the reservation at the end of the month.

Unfortunately, technical problems with his equipment prevented him from getting the other kinds of hard data he was seeking, but Akers left convinced that "something very strange and unusual is taking place." He returned to the reservation over the next few days to interview witnesses and to see and photograph more strange aerial phenomena.

In later years Greg Long (who would write a book on his research) would join the investigation, working closely with Vogel (since deceased). Examining the detailed records of Vogel and Akers, Long found lights that appeared at ground level, above ground level, and at high altitudes.

Some of the strangest cases reported by fire lookouts involved apparent mental communications. Though most of their sightings were of distant lights, on occasion lookouts saw the phenomena at no more than several hundred yards, yet somehow were prevented from getting closer. Lookouts reported "hearing" a voice inside their heads saying, "Stay back, or you'll get hurt," and feeling restrained. One lookout saw a shaft of bright, purple-colored light shining down around her cabin. When she tried to go outside to investigate, she felt as if "two magnets [were] repelling each other" and blocking her exit. Puzzled but determined, she even ran at the entrance several times but could not get through.

Observers often reported feeling as if they were seeing something they were not meant to see, and more often than not they removed themselves from the presences of the lights or objects they had come to investigate.

It must be noted that some reports were of craftlike structures and a few were of alien beings (described as skinny and long-haired and -nosed). Consequently the Yakima phenomena may have more to do with UFOs than with the sorts of pure-light manifestations with which we are concerned here. Still, as UFOs, those at Yakima are out of the ordinary in being bound to one place and in looking like — at least in most of their appearances — ghost lights. In any case, the sightings have subsided substantially since 1986.

The Hessdalen lights also subsided in 1986, but for a period of several years they were the target of a determined investigation which combined the efforts of ufologists, scientists, and locals. The Hessdalen Valley, stretching across 12 kilometers of central Norway near the Swedish border and holding no more than 150 inhabitants, began to experience odd luminous phenomena in November 1981.

The lights sometimes appeared as often as four times a day, often below the horizon along mountain tops, near the ground, or on the roofs of houses. Usually white or yellow-white, they typically were shaped like cigars, spheres, or an "upside-down Christmas tree." In this last instance, according to miner Bjarne Lillevold, the light was "bigger than the cottage beside it. It was about four meters above the hill and had a red blinking light on it; there seemed also to be a curious 'blanket' over the whole thing. The object moved up and down like a yo-yo for about 20 minutes. When it was close to the ground, the light faded, but at the height of the maneuver it was so bright that I could not look at it for long. When the light was near the ground, I could see through it as though it was made of glass."

Occasionally, according to other witnesses, a red light maintained a position in front. The lights hovered, sometimes for an hour, then shot off at extraordinary speed. Most of the time they traveled from north to south.

Investigators from UFO-Norge brought valley residents together to discuss their sightings on March 26, 1982. Of the 130 who attended, 35 said they had seen the lights. Soon afterwards two Norwegian Air Force officers interviewed natives and later told reporters that the "people of Hessdalen have been seeing luminous objects since 1944, but many years passed before they dared to talk about the sightings." It is unclear what the 1944 reference means; numerous sightings of what would come to be called UFOs occurred in northern Europe during World War II, but such sporadic, seemingly random reports should not be confused with the phenomena that took place with great frequency in Hessdalen in the early to mid-1980s. The 1944 reference may be to one of the former. No one else was told of such recurring lights prior to 1981.

Though sightings declined for a time in 1983, that summer Scandinavian ufologists formed Project Hessdalen and secured technical assistance, including the active participation of scientists, from the Universities of Oslo and Bergen. A variety of equipment was set up on three mountains. The results from the month-long winter vigil (January 21 to February 26, 1984) were interesting but inconclusive: some sightings, radar trackings, and photographs. When laser beams were aimed at passing lights, the lights seemed to respond. Once, on February 12, one such object "changed its flashing sequence from a regular flashing light to a regular double flashing light, i.e.,

● SOURCES:

Clark, Jerome. "UFO Update." *Omni* 11,10 (July 1989): 73.

Corliss, William R., ed. *Strange Phenomena: A Sourcebook of Unusual Natural Phenomena, Volume G-1.* Glen Arm, MD: The Author, 1974.

Devereux, Paul. *Earth Lights: Towards an Understanding of the UFO Enigma.* Wellingborough, Northamptonshire, England: Turnstone Press, 1982.

———. *Earth Lights Revelation: UFOs and Mystery Lightform Phenomena: The Earth's Secret Energy Force.* London: Blandford, 1989.

Evans, Beriah G. "Merionethshire Mysteries." *Occult Review* Pt. I, 1,3 (March 1905): 113–20; Pt. II 1, 4 (April 1905): 179–86; Pt. III (June 1905): 287–95.

Evans, Hilary, ed. *Frontiers of Reality: Where Science Meets the Paranormal.* Wellingborough, Northamptonshire, England: The Aquarian Press, 1989.

———. "Seeing the Lights." *Fate* Pt. I. 38, 10 (October 1985): 82–87; Pt. II. 38, 11 (November 1985): 87–92.

153

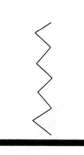

flash-flash … flash-flash … flash-flash. After about ten seconds we stopped the laser and the light immediately changed back to its previous flashing sequence. After about another ten seconds we repeated the exercise and again the light responded by changing to a double-flash sequence. In all we repeated this exercise four times and every time we got the same reaction from the light."

The investigators disagreed on what the phenomena could be, with some holding forth for a geophysical explanation and others suspecting some guiding intelligence. Erling Strand, one of Project Hessdalen's directors, thought it "strange that they [the lights] existed for a five-year period" to be "recorded in Hessdalen and nowhere else." Another investigator, Leif Havik, wrote of the "coincidences" that enlivened the investigation:

> On four separate occasions, it happened that we came to the top of Varuskjolen, stopped the car, went outside, and there "it" came immediately and passed by us. The same thing happened once on Aspaskjolen. All these instances happened at different times of the day and most of the time it was an impulse which made us take an evening trip to Hessdalen by car.... On some occasions other observers had been looking for hours without success.... "Coincidences" also happened to the video equipment which recorded the radar screen. One evening the pen of the magnetograph failed to work. At the same time the video tape had come to an end, and the phenomenon appeared less than one minute later. The next evening we made certain that the pen had sufficient ink and turned on the video recorder ten minutes later than the night before. We thought that now everything was ready for the usual 10:47 "message." [One light appeared regularly at 10:47 P.M.] The video tape ran out at 10:57 P.M. and we thought that tonight "it" had failed us. But at 10:58 the usual phenomenon appeared.

In terms of hard scientific data, the results were disappointing. Project investigators logged 188 sightings. Some, they determined, were of passing aircraft. Of four photographs taken through special lens gratings, only two showed light spectra of sufficient clarity to be analyzed. Project adviser Paul Devereux said of these, "One spectrum of one 'high strangeness' object was analyzed and showed a wavelength range from 560nm [nanometers] to the maximum the film could respond to — 630nm.... The spectrum analyzer did not register anything unusual while lights were being seen, but odd readings were obtained at times.... These showed up as 'spikes' at approximately 80mHz [megaHertz]." In 40 percent of the sightings, changes in the magnetic field registered on the instruments.

Looking back on the episode, University of Oslo physicist Elvand Thrane, who had participated in the research, remarked, "I'm sure the lights were real. It's a pity we cannot explain them."

Other luminous anomalies.

Writing of anomalous lights, sociologist of science James McClenon observes that the "circumstances of a report frequently determine its inter-

Evans-Wentz, W. Y. *The Fairy-Faith in Celtic Countries.* Hyde Park, NY: University Books, 1966.

Gaddis, Vincent H. *Mysterious Fires and Lights.* New York: David McKay Company, 1967.

Havik, Leif. "Project Hessdalen." *MUFON UFO Journal* 237 (January 1988): 4–7.

Jones, T. Gwynn. *Welsh Folklore and Folk-Custom.* Totowa, NJ: Rowman and Littlefield, 1979.

"Lights and Fireballs." *The News* 9 (April 1975): 9–11, 14, 20.

Long, Greg. *Examining the Earthlight Theory: The Yakima UFO Microcosm.* Chicago: J. Allen Hynek Center for UFO Studies, 1990.

McClenon, James. *Deviant Science: The Case of Parapsychology.* Philadelphia, PA: University of Pennsylvania Press, 1984.

Maclagan, R. C. "Ghost Lights of the West Highlands." *Folk-Lore* 8 (1897): 203–56.

Stacy, Dennis. *The Marfa Lights: A Viewer's Guide.* San Antonio, TX: Seale and Stacy, 1989.

pretation. A ball lightning effect that occurred during an electrical storm would be termed 'ball lightning'.... Other cases with the exact same appearance but occurring in other circumstances would be called UFOs, psychic lights, or will-o'-the-wisps depending on the context and the observer's assumptions and interpretation." He then relates a story, which the informant "solemnly affirms to be true" of a ball of light witnessed during his youth. The ball, one foot in diameter, approached the boy's bedroom from outside, magically opened a window, sailed around the house, and left via the front door, which also opened. "The respondent has not previously reported this observation," according to McClenon, "because it seems to defy classification."

Ball lightning, whose existence most physicists and meteorologists now accept, continues to defy explanation, at least in the sense that so far no one has been able to find a physical mechanism that accounts for all its features. We do know that ball lightning nearly always appears during thunderstorm activity, is seen just after and near a lightning strike, lasts a few seconds to (rarely) a minute or two, and often disappears in an explosion which leaves a sulfurlike odor. Clearly, whatever the surface similarity in shape and luminosity, true ghost lights are not examples of ball lightning.

Other hypotheses, notably Paul Devereux's "earthlights" and Michael Persinger's "tectonic stress theory," propose geophysical explanations for such luminous phenomena, but neither explanation has won any significant scientific acceptance. Devereux's in particular seems a thin scientific veneer for a kind of British nature mysticism, and Persinger's has been criticized on a number of methodological grounds. Both hold that ghost lights are the product of subterranean processes which not only create luminous energy on the surface but generate hallucinations in observers.

Probably ghost lights are a number of different things, from the ridiculously mundane, to the exotically natural, to the certifiably enigmatic.

Stein, Gordon. "Ball Lightning: The Impossible Enigma." *Fate* 41, 10 (October 1988): 82–90.

Strand, Erling. *Project Hessdalen 1984: Final Technical Report, Part One.* Duken, Norway: Project Hessdalen, 1985.

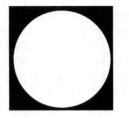

GIANT OCTOPUS ─────────────────────────────

On a southbound bicycle trip on Anastasia Island, Florida, on the evening of November 30, 1896, two young Saint Augustine cyclists, Herbert Coles and Dunham Coretter, made a discovery which set in motion one of the sorrier episodes in the history of marine biology. An event of enormous potential zoological interest would be rationalized away, ignored, ridiculed, and generally damned into oblivion.

The object that started the commotion was an immense carcass which, owing to its great weight, had sunk far into the sand when Coles and Coretter spotted it and braked quickly to a stop. They did not take measurements, but they knew immediately that it was bigger than anything they had ever heard of.

The next day DeWitt Webb, a physician and founder of the St. Augustine Historical Society and Institute of Science, came to the site with several associates. The group concluded that the creature, which apparently had been beached just days before, weighed something like five tons. The visible portions measured 23 feet in length, four feet high, and 18 feet across the widest part of the back. The skin, of a light pink, nearly white color, had a silvery cast to it. It was not a whale, Webb decided. It could only be some kind of octopus, albeit one of heretofore-unrecorded dimensions.

Webb and his assistants returned to the beach as schedules and weather permitted over the next few days and took photographs (since lost) of the decayed, mutilated remains. One assistant, while on a solo trip, reportedly found fragments of arms while digging in the vicinity of the carcass. According to an account in the April 1897 issue of *American Naturalist*, "one arm was lying west of the body, 23 feet long; one stump of arm, west of body, about four feet; three arms lying south of body and from appearance attached to same, longest one measured over 32 feet, the other arms were three to five feet shorter." Evidently the animal had been attacked and partially dismembered before its body washed to land.

Soon afterwards a severe storm arose, and the carcass floated out to sea, to resurface two miles to the south, far from the arms which apparently only the one assistant saw.

Webb began writing letters to scientists who he thought would be interested. One, dated December 8, 1896, came into the hands of A. E. Verrill, a Yale University zoologist known for his pioneering work on the once legendary but now recognized giant squid, known in Scandinavian folklore as the kraken. Verrill rejected Webb's suggestion that the carcass was of an octopus; conventional wisdom holds the largest specimens do not exceed 25 feet. In a brief notice in *American Journal of Science* for January 1897, he noted the discovery of a giant squid's remains on the Anastasia beach. On receiving further information, however, he embraced the giant-octopus identification. From comparing the sizes of the arm fragments to those of known octopus specimens, he came to a fantastic estimate: the creature's full arm length must be at least 75 feet, which meant it was a true monster: 200 feet from tentacle tip to tentacle tip. Though Webb had done all the work, Verrill named the new animal after himself: *Octopus giganteus Verrill*.

Meanwhile the stormy weather conditions had moved the carcass once again. By the time it settled in its third location, even more of its body was missing. Still, enough of it remained to frustrate, for a time anyway, any human-engineered effort to move or raise it. In a January 17, 1897, letter to W. H. Dall, curator of mollusks at the National Museum in Washington, D.C., Webb reported success:

> Yesterday I took four horses, six men, three sets tackle, a lot of heavy planking, and a rigger to superintend the work and succeeded in rolling the Invertebrate out of the pit and placing it about 40 feet higher upon the beach where it now rests on the flooring of heavy plank ... on being straightened out to measure 21 feet instead of 18.... A good part of the mantle or head remains attached near to the more slender part of the body.... The body was then opened for the entire length of 21 feet.... The slender part of the body was entirely empty of internal organs. And the organs of the remainder were not large and did not look as if the animal had been long dead.... The muscular coat which seems to be all there is of the invertebrate is from two and three to six inches in thickness. The fibers of the external coat are longitudinal and the inner transverse ... no caudal fin or any appearance if there had been any ... no beak or head or eyes remaining ... no pen to be found nor any evidence of any bony structure whatever.

The "pen" to which Webb referred is quill-pen-shaped cartilage material found in all squids. The absence of bones should have eliminated — but, as we shall see, did not eliminate — any speculation that the remains were from a whale.

Though he urged them to do so, neither Dall nor Verrill came down to inspect the carcass personally. Instead they instructed Webb, whom they treated essentially as their servant, to continue his efforts and to keep providing them with data. But as would soon be clear, they would feel free to ignore those data if they did not serve the purposes of eminent scientists. Dall continually referred to the creature as a "cuttlefish" (a cephalopod mollusk related to squids and octopuses, but with 10 arms and a calcified internal shell).

On February 23, the same day he received samples from the carcass, Verrill composed letters of retraction to both Science and the *New York Herald*. The carcass, he declared, was probably from the "upper part of the head and nose of a sperm whale." Prof. Frederic Augustus Lucas of the National Museum examined other samples, pronounced them "blubber, nothing more nor [sic] less," and took a swipe at the "imaginative eye of the average untrained observer." Webb protested vigorously in correspondence, which went unanswered. For his part Webb quietly expressed credulity at this unlikely explanation, as did several other cephalopod specialists, but they kept their dissent out of public print.

Meanwhile the remains of *Octopus giganteus Verrill* rotted away, and the brief controversy would be forgotten for six decades.

Return of the monster.
In 1957 Forrest G. Wood, Jr., curator of the research laboratories of Marineland, Florida, came upon a yellowed newspaper clipping concerning the affair. Though an authority on octopuses, Wood had never heard of it.

Intrigued, he launched an investigation which in due course disclosed that the Smithsonian Institution harbored samples. Subsequently they were examined by University of Florida octopus specialist Joseph F. Gennaro, Jr., who concluded, "The evidence appears unmistakable that the St. Augustine sea monster was in fact an octopus."

But when Wood and Gennaro published their findings in a trilogy of articles in the March 1971 issue of *Natural History*, the editors of that magazine surrounded them with whimsical commentary which led some readers to think they were an elaborate spoof. A *Wall Street Journal* article on the response reported that the editors had not done this accidentally. Wood, furious, wrote a letter of complaint to the magazine, which refused to publish it. A further insult came from the *Ocean Citation Journal Index* whose abstract incorrectly, though apparently intentionally, had Wood and Gennaro concluding the animal was a giant squid.

In the mid-1980s an independent analysis conducted by Roy P. Mackal, a University of Chicago biologist, determined that the tissue "was essentially a huge mass of collagenous protein" and "not blubber. I interpret these results as consistent with, and supportive of, Webb and Verrill's identification of the carcass as that of a gigantic cephalopod, probably an octopus, not referable to any known species."

Mystery of the globsters.

A carcass discovered on a beach in desolate northwestern Tasmania in August 1960 may conceivably have been of an animal similar to the one in Florida, but the investigation here was even more badly botched than the one that greeted the St. Augustine creature. In the latter case no fully qualified scientist examined the specimen personally. Where the Tasmanian "globster" (a word coined by zoologist/anomalist Ivan T. Sanderson) was concerned, scientists did investigate on site; the problem is that their pronouncements contradicted each other, and before the differences could be resolved, or even debated, all concerned dropped the matter.

Word of the find, made by a rancher and two drovers (cowboys) in his employ, did not reach Hobart, the provincial capital of Australia's southern island state, until months later. G. C. Cramp, a businessman and amateur naturalist, financed an aerial search which located the carcass. Once that had been accomplished, a four-man scientific team led by zoologist Bruce Mollison of the Commonwealth Scientific and Industrial Research Organization (CSIRO) ventured to the site in early March 1962. Mollison subsequently reported, "One is always seeking some explanation, and you try to add up everything, but this does not add up yet."

The carcass was indeed peculiar. Devoid of eyes, discernible head, or bones, it had an exterior skin that looked "creamy" and felt "rubbery." It was also "hairy."

Over the next week and a half newspapers all over the world gave the Tasmanian globster headline treatment, and the Australian government was inundated with inquiries. The subject was even discussed in Parliament. Under intense pressure for answers, the government flew a team of zoologists from Hobart to the site for what was billed as an extensive investigation. Nonetheless the party returned the very next day.

Its official report, written immediately afterwards, acknowledged that because of the length of time that had passed between the beaching and its examination, "it is not possible to specifically identify it from our investigations so far. But our investigations lead us to believe that the so-called monster is a decomposing portion of a large marine animal. It is not inconsistent with blubber." The same day he received the report, Sen. John Gorton, Minister for the Commonwealth of Australia, wasted no time in informing the press that "your monster is a large lump of decomposing blubber, probably torn off a whale."

Mollison disputed this conclusion, as did one of the globster's discoverers, drover Jack Boote, who said, "They had to say it was nothing new to cover up the fact they hadn't done anything about it before.... They were too late and too slow. By the time they got there, the thing had decomposed. The thing I saw was not a whale or any part of a whale." Mollison remarked that the samples he had taken "could not be identified" under analysis, and University of Tasmania zoologist A. M. Clark, who thought the animal might be a "giant ray," declared that "it was clearly not a whale."

● SOURCES:

"Bermuda Blob Remains Unidentified." The ISC Newsletter 7,3 (Autumn 1988): 1–6.

Breland, Osmond P. "Devils of the Deep." Science Digest 32, 4 (October 1952): 31–33.

Gennaro, Joseph F., Jr. "The Creature Revealed." Natural History 80, 3 (March 1971): 24, 84.

Lucas, Frederic Augustus. "The Florida Monster." Science 5, 116 (March 19, 1897): 467.

Mackal, Roy P. Searching for Hidden Animals. Garden City, NY: Doubleday and Company, 1980.

———. "Biochemical Analyses of Preserved Octopus giganteus Tissue." Cryptozoology 5 (1986): 55–62.

Mangiacopra, Gary S. "Octopus Giganteus Verrill: A New Species of Cephalopod." Of Sea and Shore (Spring 1975): 3–10.

———. "Octopus Giganteus Verrill." Pursuit 8, 4 (October 1975): 95–101.

———. "Monster on the Florida Beach." INFO Journal Pt. I. 5, 1 (May 1976): 2–6; Pt. II. 5, 2 (July 1976): 2–6.

Moffitt, Donald. "A 200 Foot Octopus Washes up in Florida, Two Scientists Claim." *Wall Street Journal* (April 8, 1971).

Sanderson, Ivan T. *"Things."* New York: Pyramid Books, 1967.

Smith, Malcolm, Martien't Mannetje, and Gerald L. Wood. "Cryptoletters." *The ISC Newsletter* 9, 1 (Spring 1990): 9–10.

"Terrors from the Deep." *Fortean Times* 56 (Winter 1990): 14.

Verrill, A. E. "The Florida Sea-Monster." *American Naturalist* 31 (April 1897): 304–07.

———. "The Supposed Great Octopus of Florida: Certainly Not a Cephalopod." *American Journal of Science* 4,3 (1897): 355–56.

"What Is This Creature?" *New York Herald* (March 7, 1897).

Wood, F. G. "In Which Bahamian Fishermen Recount Their Adventures with the Beast." *Natural History* 80, 3 (March 1971): 84, 86–87.

———. "Stupefying Colossus of the Deep." *Natural History* 80, 3 (March 1971): 14, 16, 18, 20–24.

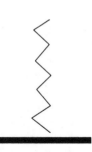

Unfortunately none of the laboratory analyses, including either those that allegedly supported the whale hypothesis or those that allegedly refuted it, ever was published. The affair ended in contradictions and ambiguities.

Perhaps these issues could have been settled in 1970, when another globster washed up onto the beach in the same general area of northwestern Tasmania. It was found, ironically, by the same ranch owner who had come upon the first one: Ben Fenton. Fenton, who remembered all too well the blistering ridicule to which he had been subjected 10 years earlier, was not pleased at his discovery. He told a reporter for a local newspaper, "Be careful you don't quote me as saying it is a monster. I don't know what it is, and I'm making no guesses — not after the last lot."

This time no scientists rushed, or even shuffled hesitantly, to investigate.

In March 1965 a globster appeared on Muriwai Beach on the eastern shore of New Zealand's North Island. It was 30 feet long, eight feet high, and "hairy," according to press accounts. Auckland University zoologist J. E. Morton was quoted as saying, "I can't think of anything it resembles." No further details have been published in either popular or scientific literature. Another globster washed up on a Mangrove Bay beach in Bermuda in May 1988. Samples were taken, but the results from the laboratory analyses have yet to be published.

Reviewing the cases, J. Richard Greenwell of the International Society of Cryptozoology observes that the "descriptions — and photos — are similar in all cases. All the carcasses were described as tough and hard to cut, usually odorless, and very 'stringy,' which is often called 'hairy.' And, curiously, all seem to be more or less unidentifiable by experts."

Until more is known, we cannot state with certainty that globsters and the St. Augustine beast represent the same kind of animal or that this animal is the giant octopus. It is, however, at least a possibility.

Sightings.

If giant octopuses are real, they would not often be seen for the simple reason that octopuses are bottom-dwelling animals. Nonetheless sightings, though infrequent, do occur or at least are claimed. Bahamian fishermen speak of sightings of "giant scuttles," and cephalopod specialist Forrest Wood finds such testimony credible.

In late December 1989 press accounts told of a frightening Christmas Eve encounter off Manticao in the southern Philippines. As the story had it, a party in a boat carrying an infant's body which was to be buried on a nearby island saw an octopus tentacle flop over the side of the craft. "At its thickest it was as big as a muscular man's upper arm," the boat's owner, Eleuterio Sarino, said. "It had bumps along it, and one of these hooked on to the edge of the boat." Another passenger, Jerry Alverez, said, "I saw other huge tentacles under the water and, though the light was poor even when I used my torch [flashlight], I'm convinced I saw a head down there with big eyes." The tentacles, he claimed, were eight feet long.

The boat began to rock from side to side and then capsized. The passengers waded safely to shore 200 yards away.

In recent years, marine biologists have turned their attention to the extraordinary and largely unknown fauna of the ocean depths, and so perhaps the giant octopus will finally get its due.

Yoon, Carol Kaesuk. "In Dark Seas, Biologists Sight a Riot of Life." *New York Times* (June 2, 1992).

161

GREEN CHILDREN

The tale of the green children dates from the middle of the twelfth century, in the realm of either King Stephen or his successor King Henry II. In Suffolk, England, according to medieval chroniclers, two green children, weeping inconsolably, were found wandering in a field. Seized by reapers, they were taken to the nearest village, Woolpit, and held in captivity at the home of Sir Richard de Calne where local people came to gape.

According to William of Newburgh, the children were clad in "garments of strange color and unknown materials." They could speak no English and refused all food offered them. A few days later, on the brink of starvation, they were brought "beans cut off or torn from stalks," wrote Abbot Ralph of Coggeshall, who allegedly had the story from de Calne himself. The children "broke open the beanstalks, *not* the pod or shell of the beans, evidently supposing that the beans were contained in the hollows of the stalks. But not finding beans within the stalks they again began to weep, which, when the bystanders noticed, they opened the shells and showed them the beans themselves. Whereupon, with great joyfulness, they ate beans for a long time, entirely, and would touch no other food."

Soon the children were baptized, and not long afterwards the boy weakened and died. The girl learned to eat other foods and was restored both to health and to normal skin color. She learned to speak English and took employment in service to a knight and his family. She "was rather loose and wanton in her conduct," Ralph of Coggeshall wrote.

Asked about her native country, "she asserted that the inhabitants, and all that they had in that country, were of a green color; and that they saw no sun, but enjoyed a degree of light like what is after sunset. Being asked how she came into this country with the aforesaid boy, she replied, that as they were following their flocks they came to a certain cavern, until they came to its mouth. When they came out of it, they were struck senseless by the excessive light of the sun, and the unusual temperature of the air; and they thus lay for a long time. Being terrified by the noise of those who came on them, they wished to fly, but they could not find the entrance of the cavern before they were caught."

In William of Newburgh's account, the children said their country was called St. Martin's Land. Its people were Christians. There was no sun there, but across a broad river a bright, shining land could be seen. Eventually the woman married and reportedly lived for years at Lenna in Suffolk.

Newburgh remarked, "Although the thing is asserted by many, yet I have long been in doubt about the matter, deeming it ridiculous to credit a thing supported by no rational foundation, or at least one of a mysterious character; yet, in the end, I was so overwhelmed by the weight of so many competent witnesses that I have been compelled to believe and wonder over a matter I was unable to comprehend and unravel by the powers of my intellect." A modern writer, British folklorist Katharine Briggs, says, "This is one of those curiously convincing and realistic fairy anecdotes which are occasionally to be found in the medieval chronicles."

Another recent chronicler, Paul Harris, speculates that the children were not aliens from another realm but simply lost, undernourished children who had wandered into flint mines in the vicinity of Thetford Forest, near the village of Fordham St. Martin. "Perhaps from the twilight of the thick woodlands the children could see a less forested and therefore sunnier land across the river Lark," he writes. They may have spoken in an English dialect "unintelligible to the insular 12th Century farmworkers of Woolpit."

● SOURCES:

Briggs, Katharine. *British Folktales*. New York: Dorset Press, 1977.

Briggs, Katharine. *An Encyclopedia of Fairies: Hobgoblins, Brownies, Bogies, and Other Supernatural Creatures*. New York: Pantheon Books, 1976.

Harris, Paul. "The Green Children of Woolpit." *Fortean Times 57* (Spring 1991): 39, 41.

Keightley, Thomas. *The Fairy Mythology*. London: G. Bell, 1878.

Wilkins, Harold T. *Strange Mysteries of Time and Space*. New York: The Citadel Press, 1958.

GREEN FIREBALLS

A strange aerial phenomenon briefly appeared in the earth's lower atmosphere for a three-year period between late 1948 and 1951. For a time sightings, virtually all of which occurred in the southwestern United States, were taking place with such intensity that military and civilian government agencies feared enemy agents had penetrated some of America's most sensitive national-security bases.

The epidemic of "green fireballs" first attracted official attention on the evening of December 5, 1948, when pilots flying over New Mexico reported two separate observations, 22 minutes apart, of a pale green light which was visible for no more than a few seconds. The witnesses insisted these were not meteors but flares of a decidedly peculiar kind. On the sixth, a similar "greenish flare" was sighted for three seconds over the supersecret atomic installation Sandia Base, part of the Kirtland Air Force Base complex in New Mexico.

That same day the Seventh District Air Force Office of Special Investigations (AFOSI), at Kirtland, commenced a probe. On the evening of the eighth, the two investigators, both pilots, saw one of the objects from their T-7 aircraft. They described it this way: "At an estimated altitude of 2000 feet higher than the airplane ... [t]he object was similar in appearance to a burning green flare of common use in the Air Forces. However, the light was much more intense and the object appeared to be considerably larger than a normal flare. No estimate can be made of the distance or the size of the object since no other object was visible upon which to base a comparison. The object was definitely larger and more brilliant than a shooting star, meteor, or flare. The trajectory of the object was almost flat and parallel to the earth. The phenomenon lasted approximately two seconds at the end of which the object seemed to burn out. The trajectory then dropped off rapidly and a trail of glowing fragments reddish orange in color was observed falling toward the ground. The fragments were visible

165

The spectacular "green fireballs" observed in the Southwestern United States in the late 1940s and early 1950s remain one of the great puzzles of the UFO age. (Courtesy of Don Schmitt.)

less than a second before disappearing. The phenomenon was of such intensity as to be visible from the very moment it ignited and was observed a split second later."

The next day one of the officers, Capt. Melvin E. Neef, conferred with Lincoln La Paz, director of the University of New Mexico's Institute of Meteoritics and an Air Force consultant with Top Secret clearance. La Paz said these were unlike any meteors he had ever heard of. Within days La Paz had seen one of the objects himself. Two inspectors from the Atomic Energy Security Service (AESS) independently witnessed it; from their observation and his own, La Paz was able to establish that it had flown too slowly and too silently to be a meteor. He wrote in a confidential letter to the Seventh District AFOSI commanding officer that "none of the green fireballs has a train of sparks or a dust cloud.... This contrasts sharply with the behavior noted in cases of meteoritic fireballs — particularly those that penetrate to the very low levels where the green fireball of December 12 was observed."

Acting on La Paz's suggestion, the AESS organized patrols to try to photograph the fireballs. As the sightings continued, scientists and engineers at New Mexico's Los Alamos Scientific Laboratory set up an informal group to evaluate the reports, and the Army and the Air Force grew increasingly concerned. By late January, 1949, La Paz, who had interviewed witnesses to some of the sightings, was convinced the objects were artificial.

On February 16, a "Conference on Aerial Phenomena" brought military officers and scientists to Los Alamos, where they were told that whatever the nature of the objects, they were not the product of a "classified training exercise." La Paz challenged conference participants to "find anywhere among meteorites examples of conventional meteorites that move over long horizontal paths reserving nearly constant angular velocities and therefore, on the average, constant linear velocities, at elevations of the order of eight to 10 miles."

● SOURCES:

Clark, Jerome. *The Emergence of a Phenomenon: UFOs from the Beginning Through 1959 — The UFO Encyclopedia, Volume 2.* Detroit, MI: Omnigraphics, 1992.

Gross, Loren E. *UFOs: A History — 1950: January–March.* Fremont, CA: The Author, 1983.

———. *UFOs: A History, Vol. 1 — July 1947–December 1948.* Fremont, CA: The Author, 1982.

———. *UFOs: A History, Vol. 2 — 1949.* Fremont, CA: The Author, 1982.

Moore, William L., ed. *The Mystery of the Green Fireballs.* Prescott, AZ: William L. Moore Publications and Research, 1983.

Ruppelt, Edward J. *The Report on Unidentified Flying Objects.* Garden City, NY: Doubleday and Company, 1956.

Sparks, Brad, and Jerome Clark. "The Southwestern Lights." *International UFO Reporter* Pt. I, 10, 3 (May/June 1985): 10–13; Pt. II, 10, 4 (July/August 1985): 12–14; Pt. III, 10, 5 (September/October 1985): 7–12, 15–16,18.

Late in April Major Charles Cabell, director of Air Force Intelligence in the Pentagon, and Theodore von Karman, chairman of the Air Force Scientific Advisory Board, dispatched physicist Joseph Kaplan to Kirtland. Kaplan, La Paz, and others discussed plans to establish an observational and instrumental network around several New Mexico installations. Meanwhile, since early March tiny white lights or "flares" had appeared regularly near Killeen Base, a nuclear-weapons storage site inside Camp Hood in central Texas, leading both to high-level alarm and to efforts to set up observation posts. Col. Reid Lumsden, commander of AFOSI at Kelly AFB, San Antonio, declared that the "unknown phenomena in the Camp Hood area could not be attributed to natural causes."

The testimonies of virtually all local experts and witnesses notwithstanding, the word came down from Washington: the fireballs and lights were natural even if they had features that were, as Kaplan acknowledged, "difficult to explain." Yet the sightings continued, and in the summer analyses of samples of the New Mexico atmosphere revealed an unusually large and unexplained quantity of copper particles, apparently associated with the fireball sightings. "I know of no case in which even the tiniest particle of copper has been reported in a dust collection supposedly of meteoritic origin," La Paz wrote Lt. Col. Doyle Rees.

After meeting with high-ranking Air Force intelligence and scientific personnel, Kaplan urged the creation of a photographic and spectrographic patrol whose purpose would be to obtain quantitative data on the fireballs and lights. A Los Alamos conference discussed the situation and backed the plan, to be run by the Air Materiel Command's Cambridge Research Laboratories. Project Twinkle was established, and it set up shop with an operations post manned by two observers at Holloman AFB in New Mexico. One of its critics was La Paz, who thought the matter was of sufficient gravity to deserve a far more "intensive, systematic investigation."

Despite some interesting sightings, Twinkle shut down in December 1951, owing to the incompetence of its personnel, poor funding, bureaucratic infighting, and inadequate instrumentation. It was a tragically missed opportunity to obtain solid information on at least one kind of unidentified flying object. Many of the scientists who participated in the investigation remained convinced that the fireballs were artificially created. In 1953, when Capt. Edward J. Ruppelt, head of the Air Force's Project Blue Book, talked with Los Alamos scientists about the episode, they expressed the conviction that the objects were projectiles fired from extraterrestrial spacecraft.

HAIRY BIPEDS

One night in January 1992 two men driving on a dark country road were startled to see two figures illuminated in their headlights. The larger figure stood seven to eight feet tall and appeared to weigh over 500 pounds; the shorter was five feet and 300 pounds. The creatures were advancing in the car's direction. Frightened, the driver backed up the vehicle, all the while keeping the figures in the lights, until he found a place to turn around. Looking over their shoulders on the way out, the witnesses saw that the larger creature was still heading in their direction.

This story sounds as if it came out of the Pacific Northwest, reputed home of Bigfoot (otherwise known as Sasquatch), the giant hominoid which proponents think represents an apelike human or a humanlike ape and which somehow has managed to escape scientific verification. If from some points of view Bigfoot's existence seems improbable, even the hardest skeptics do not deem it flatly impossible; the wilderness area that comprises northern California, Oregon, Washington, and British Columbia is vast, and it is at least dimly imaginable that a small population of such creatures, especially if they possess a degree of intelligence, could survive, to be glimpsed only rarely.

The above report, however, comes from Tuscola County in eastern Michigan. It is, according to local monster buff Wayne King, the county's thirty-eighth hairy-biped report since 1977. In fact, similar sightings have been chronicled in virtually every state and province in the United States and Canada. No one argues seriously that great numbers, or for that matter small numbers, of unknown apelike animals could exist, at least in any conventionally biological sense, in the Midwest, East, or South — or even southern California, site of a number of extraordinary reports.

Despite a number of surface similarities, the Bigfoot reports and (as we shall call them here) hairy-biped (HB) stories harbor some fundamental differences. Whatever their cause, Bigfoot sightings and attendant physical evidence (primarily footprints) do not challenge the most hallowed precepts of consensus reality; to all indications, in other words, the phenomena act as if they were answerable to the laws of zoology, and in fact several well-credentialed anthropologists and primatologists (most notably Grover Krantz and John Napier) have written at length on the creatures' possible place in the natural order. But where HBs are concerned, just about anything goes, as we shall see. As we leave Bigfoot's Pacific Northwest and head east and south, we enter the Goblin Universe.

Before Bigfoot.
The Bigfoot/Sasquatch stepped outside regional folklore and into international consciousness in the late 1950s. In common with its HB counterpart, evidence of its presence prior to the twentieth century is somewhat ambiguous, though Bigfoot's proponents would argue that the creature escaped detection because the wilderness in which it resided was vast and largely unexplored and thus it was able to keep itself well hidden. No such argument, of course, can be made for those regions that were settled long before and where wildernesses, if indeed they were part of the landscape to start with, were cleared many decades ago. Actually, though the evidence in neither case is overwhelming, that for a pre-1900 Bigfoot is clearly better.

Nineteenth-century American newspapers printed a number of accounts of "wild men." These are sometimes cited as evidence of early HBs, but a careful study of primary sources by Michael T. Shoemaker lays the stories, with a couple of possible exceptions, to hoaxes or prosaic causes, usually deranged individuals who lived as animals in the woods. Unless indications to the contrary come to light, we shall assume that, for some curious reason, HBs are creatures of the twentieth century.

Whatever that reason may be, it certainly is not that the Bigfoot of popular culture gave those prone to hallucinations the material from which to fashion an imaginary monster. Americans were reporting HBs before they had ever heard of Bigfoot. For example, in 1946 *Hoosier Folklore* noted a 1941 report from Mount Vernon, Illinois, where the Rev. Lepton Harpole was hunting squirrels along a creek when a "large animal that looked something like a baboon" leaped out of a tree and approached him on two legs. The reverend struck it with his gun barrel, then fired a couple of shots into the air. The creature fled. Over the next months hunters and rural families heard terrifying shrieks and found mysterious footprints. There were other sightings, some of them as much as 40 or 50 miles from the Mount Vernon area.

A letter published in an Illinois newspaper, the *Decatur Review*, on August 2, 1972, suggests a long tradition of such creatures in south-central Illinois. A woman named Beulah Schroat wrote:

> I am 76 years old. My home used to be south of Effingham [50 miles due north of Mount Vernon]. My two brothers saw the creatures when they were children. My brothers have since passed away.

They are hairy, stand on their hind legs, have large eyes and are about as large as an average person or shorter, and are harmless as they ran away from the children. They walk, they do not jump.

They were seen on a farm near a branch of water. The boys waded and fished in the creek every day and once in a while they would run to the house scared and tell the story.... This occurred about 60 years ago or a little less.

According to the *Washington Post* of July 26, 1929, a "huge gorilla" had been seen wandering in woods near Elizabeth, Illinois, the day before.

In *Wild Talents* (1932) Charles Fort took note of press accounts of a hunt for an "apelike animal — hairy creature, about four feet tall," coupled with denials by circus and zoo spokesmen that any ape was missing. The scare, which lasted about three weeks in June and July 1931, featured "gorilla" sightings, police searches, and tracks which "seemed to be solely of those of the hind feet." The following January, in a rural area north of Downington, Pennsylvania, John McCandless heard a moaning sound in a bush. Its source, he told a reporter, was a "hideous form, half-man, half-beast, on all fours and covered with dirt or hair." Soon afterwards other persons told of encounters with the creature, which managed subsequently to evade armed search parties.

In Ontario in the early decades of the century, newspapers chronicled occasional sightings of "Yellow Top," an apelike creature with a light-colored mane. Near Goose Bay, Labrador, between the winters of 1913 and 1914, according to Elliott Merrick's *True North* (1933), a seven-foot-tall apelike creature with a white mane on its head evaded hunters and left tracks in mud, sand, and snow. In the early 1970s, while teaching at Newfoundland's Memorial University, American folklorist David J. Hufford found a late-nineteenth-century book which indicated that such traditions predated 1913. The book recounted sightings of the "Traverspine gorilla," so called because of the name of the settlement near which it was seen on a number of occasions. Hufford also collected a story from the nearby island of Newfoundland. According to an elderly man who claimed to have participated in the event early in this century, a party of men had gone to Trinity Bay on a fishing expedition. They set up camp, only to find it in disarray every time they returned. They ascribed the trouble to "Indians," even though no Indians had lived on the island for a century and, Hufford said, it is "very unlikely that any of the men had ever seen an Indian." Finally they saw "two Indians" sitting on a log and opened fire on them, killing one.

"They described this dead 'Indian' as being seven feet tall, covered with short reddish brown fur and wearing no clothes," Hufford wrote. "There was no room to put the corpse in the boat so they towed it behind with a rope, taking it to their home community where they buried it after showing it to others in the community. As a result, the spot where the killing took place is now called Red Indian Point."

Other reports of HBs figure in contemporary published accounts in New Jersey, Maryland, Missouri, Indiana, Michigan, Alabama, and other states between the 1920s and the 1950s.

Later, during the Bigfoot era (late 1950s to the present), a number of persons came forward to testify to sightings earlier in the century. A woman wrote Ivan T. Sanderson, a biologist and the first writer to give the Bigfoot phenomenon wide publicity, to relate a 1911 incident which occurred when she was living in far northern Minnesota; there, she said, two hunters saw a "human giant which had long arms and short, light hair" and which left strange prints. A man remembered that in 1942, while he was cutting spruce in a New Hampshire forest, a "gorilla-looking" creature followed him for some 20 minutes. In 1914, according to an account given in 1975, a boy saw a gorillalike creature sitting on a log in his backyard in Churchville, Maryland.

The age of HBs.
From the 1950s to the present (though there are some small indications of a decline in sightings in recent years) HB reports have been catalogued in startling numbers. Some representative reports:

Monroe, Michigan, August 11, 1965: As they rounded a curve in a wooded area, Christine Van Acker, 17, and her mother gaped in astonishment as a hairy giant stepped out into the road. In her panic Christine hit the brakes instead of the accelerator. As she frantically tried to restart the car, the creature, seven feet tall and smelly, reached through the open window and grabbed the top of her head. The screams of Christine and her mother, not to mention the honking of the car horn, may have caused the HB to withdraw into the woods. Nearby workmen came on the scene moments later, finding the two nearly incoherent with fear. Somehow in the course of the incident — it is not clear how — Christine contracted a black eye. The story received national publicity, with a photograph of Christine's bruised face appearing in hundreds of newspapers around the country.

Rising Sun, Indiana, May 19, 1969: At 7:30 P.M., as George Kaiser was crossing the farmyard on his way to the tractor, he spotted a strange figure standing 25 feet away. "I watched it for about two minutes before it saw me," he reported. "It stood in a fairly upright position, although it was bent over about in the middle of its back, with arms about the same length as a normal human being's. I'd say it was about five-eight or so and it had a very muscular structure. The head sat directly on the shoulders, and the face was black, with hair that stuck out of the back of its head. It had eyes set close together, and with a very short forehead. It was covered with hair except for the back of the hands and the face. The hands looked like normal hands, not claws." The creature made a grunting sound, turned around, leaped over a ditch, and dashed off at great speed down the road. Plaster casts of the tracks it left show three toes plus a big toe.

Putnam County, Indiana, August 1972: Randy and Lou Rogers, a young couple living outside tiny Roachdale (pop. 950), 40 miles west of Indi-

171

anapolis, became recipients of regular late-night visitations from a shadowy creature. Occasional brief glimpses revealed it to be a large, hairy "gorilla." Most of the time it was bipedal, but when it ran, it did so on all fours. Mrs. Rogers reported that "we could never find tracks, even when it ran over mud. It would run and jump, but it was like somehow it wasn't touching anything. When it ran through weeds, you couldn't hear anything. And sometimes when you looked at it, it seemed you could see *through* it." Nonetheless an area farmer, Carter Burdine, allegedly lost all but 30 of his 200 chickens to the creature, which literally ripped them apart. Burdine, his father, and his uncle saw the HB in the chickenhouse and chased it into the barn. The uncle opened fire on it as it fled from there to a nearby field. "I shot four times with a pump shotgun," Bill ("Junior") Burdine said. "The thing was only about 100 feet away when I started shooting. I must have hit it. I've killed a lot of rabbits at that distance." Nonetheless the HB seemed unaffected. At least 40 persons claimed to have seen the HB before sightings ceased late in the month.

Noxie, Oklahoma, September 1975: Farmer Kenneth Tosh and his neighbors reported seeing and hearing at least two HBs. First seen on the first of the month 20 feet from Tosh's house, it stood six or seven feet tall and had dark brown hair all over its body except around the eyes and nose. "The eyes glowed in the dark, reddish-pink eyes," Tosh said. "They glow without a light bein' on 'em." On three occasions over the next days, Marion Parret would fire on the creature with a .30-hunting rifle. He was convinced he hit it each time, but only once did it respond: by swatting its arm as if at a fly. The HB smelled "like rotten eggs or sulphur." It left a three-toed track (all primates have five toes). Toward the end of the episode, Tosh and his brother-in-law found themselves between two HBs as they called to each other. "One of 'em had red eyes, and the other one had yellow," he said. "They was about 300 yards away from each other.... One of 'em, the one with red eyes, was more like a woman screamin'. The other one sounded more like a baby bawlin'. The one with the yellow eyes was more of a grayish color than the other one. And it was about half a foot shorter. They probably weighed between 300 and 500 pounds."

Southeastern Nebraska, August 1976: Near dusk a woman sitting on the back porch of a farmhouse south of Lincoln said she noticed a sudden eerie silence among the animals. Three hundred yards away, silhouetted against the sky, stood a huge, hairy figure. The figure moved rapidly through the pasture toward her, panicking the dogs, which knocked her down in their frantic effort to get inside the house. The HB broke down the wire fence and was only 30 feet from her when it vanished in front of her eyes. Nonetheless this cryptozoological ghost managed to leave hair samples on the fence. When the witness brought these into the state's Game and Parks Commission for analysis, however, it refused them.

Vaughn, Montana, December 26, 1975: In the late afternoon two teenaged girls went to check on the horses, which seemed agitated. They observed, 200 yards from them and 25 yards from a thicket, a huge figure seven and a half feet tall and twice as wide as a man. Intending to frighten it off, one of the girls fired a .22 rifle into the air. When nothing happened, she fired again, and this time the creature dropped to all fours, walked a short distance, then resumed its original bipedal stance. The girls took off running. One looked over her shoulder and saw three or four similar creatures with the first one, all heading toward the thicket. Law-enforcement officers asked the girls to take a polygraph test, which they passed. Other sightings, hearings, and tracks of HBs were chronicled in Montana in the mid-1970s.

Salisbury, New Hampshire, October 1987: Two or three days after a hunter had told him of seeing two strange beasts walking across a field next to Mill Brook, Walter Bowers, Sr., hunting at the same location, sensed that he was being watched. Between two stands of trees he saw a "thing ... at least nine feet" tall, "maybe less, maybe more." He said, "The whole body was covered with hair.... kind of a grayish color." Because the sun was in his eyes, he could not make out the creature's face, but he noted that the "hands were like yours or mine, only three times bigger, with pads on the front paws, like a dog.... Long legs, long arms. It was just like ... a gorilla, but this here wasn't a gorilla." The HB ran into a swamp, and Bowers ran to his car and sped away. A reporter characterized him as a "man of sound mind and sober spirit."

Furry objects and flying objects.

Late one evening in August 1972 a luminous object hovered briefly over a cornfield in rural Roachdale, Indiana, before seeming to "blow up," according to an observer. An hour and a half later the Roachdale HB (see above) allegedly made its presence known to a young woman, Lou Rogers, who lived on the other side of the field.

Taken in isolation, this incident tells us little if anything. The witness could, after all, have been mistaken about the object's proximity to the cornfield. It could have been much higher in the atmosphere and only seemed to be close by — a common optical illusion in meteor sightings. Perhaps this was a bolide, an exploding meteor.

Or perhaps not. A handful of cases link HBs with UFOs in more straightforward fashion, and several investigators, notably Stan Gordon and Don Worley, have held that HBs are a variety of UFO occupant. Even by the generally thin nature of HB evidence, this is a slender thread indeed, and most of the cases Gordon and Worley cite are poorly documented; moreover, the alleged link is highly circumstantial, usually no more than a UFO sighting in the same general vicinity of an HB report. Still, a few provocative incidents have been logged, including this one:

Uniontown, Pennsylvania, October 25, 1973: Having observed a red light hovering above a field just outside town, a 22-year-old man and two 10-year-old boys rushed to the site in a pickup truck. The light, now revealed to be a dome-shaped UFO, had turned white and now rested on the ground "making a sound like a lawn mower." "Screaming sounds" could be heard nearby. Two large apelike creatures with glowing green eyes were walking along a fence. The taller, eight-foot HB was running its left hand along the fence while the other nearly dragged the ground; behind it a shorter, seven-foot creature tried to keep up with the first. A whining sound emanating from both seemed to be a method of communication between the two. The oldest witness, who was bearing a rifle, fired three times directly into the larger HB, which reacted by whining and reaching out to its companion. At that moment the UFO vanished. The two creatures disappeared into the trees. A state trooper summoned to the scene soon afterwards noticed a 150-foot luminous area where the UFO had sat. He also heard loud crashing sounds in the woods, apparently made by someone or something big and heavy. The 22-year-old witness suffered an emotional breakdown at this juncture.

High strangeness.

On March 28, 1987, at 11:45 P.M., Dan Masias of Green Mountain Falls, Colorado, happened to look out his window to see "these creatures ... running down the road right in front of my house, which at one point is 30 feet from my front window. The whole road there was covered with about a quarter of an inch of fresh, cold snow that had fallen. They ran down the

● SOURCES:

"Bipedal Humanoids in Nebraska: A Chronology of Events." *Journal of the Fortean Research Center* 2, 1 (April 1987): 4–6.

Bord, Janet, and Colin Bord. *Alien Animals.* Harrisburg, PA: Stackpole Books, 1981.

———. *The Bigfoot Casebook.* Harrisburg, PA: Stackpole Books, 1982.

———. *The Evidence for Bigfoot and Other Man-Beasts.* Wellingborough, Northamptonshire, England: The Aquarian Press, 1984.

Brandon, Craig. "Bigfoot!!! Apeman Stalks Woods Near Us, Book Claims." *Albany* [New York] *Times Union* (February 16, 1992).

Chorvinsky, Mark, and Mark Opsasnick. "A Field Guide to the Monsters and Mystery Animals of Maryland." *Strange Magazine* 5 (1990): 41–46.

Clark, Jerome. "On the Trail of Unidentified Furry Objects." *Fate* 26, 8 (August 1973): 56–64.

Clark, Jerome, and Loren Coleman. *Creatures of the Outer Edge.* New York: Warner Books, 1978.

road in a manner with their arms hanging down, swinging in a pendulum motion. The first impression I got was that they were covered with hair. It was the most incredible thing I've ever seen."

After Masias's sighting was recounted in the newspapers, other residents of the area, near the Pike National Forest, came forward with their own reports, about which they had kept quiet for fear of ridicule. Sightings and hearings (of unearthly howls and growls) continued, and persons who followed HB tracks in snow swore they vanished in midstride.

As befits creatures whose mere presence in Colorado, Oklahoma, Indiana, New Hampshire, or elsewhere in populated America is a biological absurdity, HBs give every indication of *being* biologically absurd. When they leave tracks, which (as we have seen) they do not always seem to do, these tracks may be two-, three-, four-, five-, or even six-toed. In a handful of accounts, we are told that HBs were shot and killed; more often, witnesses allege that bullets either did not affect the creatures at all or simply elicited mild expressions of complaint from them. Creatures that are supposed to disappear instantaneously like ghosts (or hallucinations) also are said to shed strands of hair while crossing a fence.

Even worse, the phrase "hairy biped" is in some ways generic. It does not always denote a paranormal version of Bigfoot. In a small but persistent minority of reports, beings with fangs and vaguely wolflike facial features are described — werewolves to the superstitious. Such were among the five varieties of HBs reported in western Pennsylvania during a wave of reports in the early 1970s. In the spring of 1973, during a spate of sightings in the Enfield, Illinois, area, some witnesses reported seeing an apelike creature; others claimed to have encountered, as did one farmer who said he saw it from a distance of several feet, a three-legged creature with a "short body, two little short arms coming out of its breast area, and two pink eyes as big as flashlights." (He swore it was not a kangaroo. Hissing like a wildcat, it bounded away and covered 75 feet in three steps.)

Some witnesses, in locations as far apart as southern California and South Dakota, have even reported invisible HBs. During a spate of sightings at an Indian reservation in South Dakota in 1977, a creature was seen intermittently from the afternoon of November 3 into the evening, by which time locals and law-enforcement officers had the area staked out. One of them, rancher Lyle Maxon, reported this weird event: "We were out there walking in the dark, and I could hear very plainly something out of breath from running.... I put my flashlight right where I could plainly hear it, only where it should have been, there was nothing in sight. Now what I'm wondering is, can this thing make itself invisible when things get too close for comfort?" In their book on HB sightings in southern California, *Bigfoot* (1976), B. Ann Slate and Alan Berry tell of similar events.

At least some reports are surely hoaxes — stories told by the less than sincere, in other words, or by those sincerely fooled by pranksters wearing masks. Other HBs (for example, a figure observed by a number of Lawton,

Donovan, Roberta, and Keith Wolverton. *Mystery Stalks the Prairie.* Raynesford, MT: T.H.A.R. Institute, 1976.

Drier, Mary. "'Bigfoot' Returns, Area Men Maintain." *Bay City* [Michigan] *Times* (March 24, 1992).

French, Scot. "The Man Who Spied Bigfoot Comes Forward." *Concord* [New Hampshire] *Monitor* (November 13, 1987).

Gordon, Stan. "UFOs, in Relation to Creature Sightings in Pennsylvania." In Walter H. Andrus, Jr., ed. *MUFON 1974 UFO Symposium Proceedings,* 132–54. Seguin, TX: Mutual UFO Network, 1974.

Harris, Jesse W. "Myths and Legends from Southern Illinois." *Hoosier Folklore* 5 (March 1946): 14–20.

Hufford, David J. "Humanoids and Anomalous Lights: Taxonomic and Epistemological Problems." *Fabula* 18 3/4 (1977): 234–41.

Keel, John A. *Strange Creatures from Time and Space.* Greenwich, CT: Fawcett, 1970.

Lake, Bonnie. "Bigfoot on the Buttes: The Invasion of Little Eagle." *UFO Report* 5, 6 (June

Oklahoma, residents in February 1971) apparently are disheveled, bearded, deranged but entirely human individuals like the "wild men" of so many nineteenth-century accounts. In some cases the HBs were probably bears.

Unfortunately, explanations such as these are of limited utility. Unless one is prepared to reject the testimony — which by now is considerable — wholesale, rewrite the witnesses' descriptions, and then "explain" what one has invented, we can only be modest about what we do and do not know. The conundrum is a familiar one: credible people report incredible things, and thus far no theory, whether mundane or extraordinary, convincingly answers any of the interesting questions.

Yet it is undeniably true that the evidence is fairly modest: enough to leave the question open but not even remotely enough to inspire a scientific revolution. This, it should be added, has nothing to do with the question of whether three-toed, glowing-eyed Midwestern apelike bipeds are seen or exist in some sense; it has to do instead with the kind of evidence science requires to take a question into consideration to start with — the kind of evidence that is sufficient, in other words, to make that question appear ultimately resolvable. Where HBs are concerned, the implications are staggering, but the evidence, such as it is, is simply not enough to go on, much less to use as a stick with which to beat conservative scientists into confessing that the late-twentieth-century map of reality has ignored some of the landscape's most interesting features.

Still, scientists could do better. They could look at such evidence as has been collected more often than they do. It seems a shame that the Nebraska woman could not interest authorities in her samples of HB hair. On the other hand, if on analysis the hair proved genuinely anomalous, where could the scientists go from there? The experiences of scientists investigating the relatively "conventional" Bigfoot offer little encouragement here. Anomalous hair samples of this hairy biped abound, and that fact has served neither to change many minds nor to mount a serious challenge to orthodoxly skeptical views.

Perhaps what scientists can do — in fact, by ignoring the question for the most part, that is what they are doing in effect — is to refrain from making any pronouncements that are based on ignorance. The proper answer to the question of whether HBs are real, or what the observers' reports really mean, is not that all witnesses are liars, or that people are too stupid and hysterical to be able to tell the difference between a monstrous biped and a passing moose (a scientist's proposed explanation for the Salisbury, New Hampshire, episode above). Neither of these propositions is based in overwhelming evidence or logic.

At the same time, the believers' enthusiastic endorsement of the most extraordinary hypotheses is just as unwarranted. To claim, as some do, that HBs are dropping here out of another reality or dimension is to say nothing at all. Not, of course, that this could not be true; it is just that, given our present state of knowledge, we have no reason to believe it *is*

1978): 28–31, 67, 69, 71–72, 74.

MacDougall, Curtis D. *Hoaxes.* New York: Dover Publications, 1958.

Opsasnick, Mark. *The Maryland Bigfoot Reference Guide.* Greenbelt, MD: The Author, 1987.

Osborne, Augusta Knapp. "Counties (Duchess): The Green Fly Monster." *New York Folklore Quarterly* 11, 3 (Autumn 1955): 213–16.

Robbins, David L. "Colorado Bigfoot." *Fate* 41, 11 (November 1988): 70–77.

Roberts, Leonard. "Notes and Queries: Curious Legend of the Kentucky Mountains." *Western Folklore* 16, 1 (January 1957): 48–51.

Sanderson, Ivan T. *"Things."* New York: Pyramid Books, 1967.

Schwarz, Berthold Eric. "Berserk: A UFO-Creature Encounter." *Flying Saucer Review* 20, 1 (July 1974): 3–11.

Shoemaker, Michael T. "Searching for the Historical Bigfoot." *Strange Magazine* 5 (1990): 18–23, 57–62.

Slate, B. Ann, and Alan Berry. *Bigfoot.* New York: Bantam Books, 1976.

true either. It is the intellectual equivalent of "explaining" HBs by declaring them to be visitors from Cxkoikjlkfyl or any other fanciful place you want to make up.

The proper answer to the HB question is this: We don't know. And we probably aren't going to find out for a very long time.

Worley, Don. "The UFO-Related Anthropoids — An Important New Opportunity for Investigator-Researchers with Courage." In *Proceedings of the 1976 CUFOS Conference*, 287–94. Evanston, IL: Center for UFO Studies, 1976.

HAIRY DWARFS

During the fall of 1954, a worldwide UFO wave erupted. Among the many reports were a striking number involving humanoid occupants, sometimes described as hairy dwarfs. On October 9, for example, three rural French children out roller-skating reported that a "round shiny machine came down very close to us. Out of it came a kind of man, four feet tall, dressed in a black sack like the cassock M. le Cure wears. His head was hairy, and he had big eyes. He said things to us that we couldn't understand, and we ran away. When we stopped and looked back, the machine was going up into the sky very fast." Five days later a French miner encountered a humanoid with a squat, furry body and oversized, slanted, protruding eyes. It was wearing a skull cap and had a flat nose and thick lips.

In Venezuela in early December several reports recounted nocturnal encounters with three-foot-tall hairy dwarfs of aggressive disposition. In one instance, said to have taken place on December 10, four such beings stepped out of a hovering UFO and attempted to abduct a young man. His companion, who happened to be armed because the two were hunting at the time of the encounter, struck one of the entities on the head with his gun butt. The butt splintered as if it had collided with solid rock. The two men, bruised, cut, and clearly terrified, told their story to the police soon afterwards. Nine days later, at Valencia, a jockey on a late-night training ride said he saw six hairy dwarfs hauling rocks into a nearby UFO. When they noticed him, one fired a beam of violet light and paralyzed him, even though he had been trying to flee. Police found footprints at the scene. They looked, they said, "neither human nor animal."

Though accounts of encounters with UFO occupants continue to the present, hairy dwarfs faded from the scene by the end of 1954 and were seen, or at least reported, no more.

● SOURCES:

Bowen, Charles, ed. *The Humanoids: A Survey of Worldwide Reports of Landings of Unconventional Aerial Objects and Their Alleged Occupants.* Chicago: Henry Regnery Company, 1969.

Keyhoe, Donald E. *The Flying Saucer Conspiracy.* New York: Henry Holt and Company, 1955.

Lorenzen, Coral, and Jim Lorenzen. *Encounters with UFO Occupants.* New York: Berkley Publishing, 1976.

Michel, Aime. *Flying Saucers and the Straight-Line Mystery.* New York: Criterion Books, 1958.

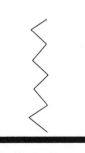

HANGAR 18 ———————————————————

In the 1960s Sen. Barry Goldwater, Republican of Arizona and a brigadier general in the U.S. Air Force Reserve, asked a friend, Gen. Curtis LeMay, for a favor. Senator Goldwater wanted access to a room at Wright-Patterson Air Force Base, Dayton, Ohio, where he had long heard that UFO wreckage and bodies were stored. As the Senator recalled years later in a *New Yorker* profile, General LeMay "just gave me holy hell. He said, 'Not only can't you get into it but don't you ever mention it to me again'."

Within days of the inception of the UFO age in the early summer of 1947, the world press reported that representatives of the Army Air Force had recovered the remains of a "flying disc" which crashed in remote Lincoln County, New Mexico. Within hours a "correction" went out on the wires, with officials at Eighth Army Headquarters in Fort Worth, Texas, assuring reporters that through a ludicrous misunderstanding the wreckage of a weather balloon had been mistaken for something extraordinary. (Meanwhile the material reportedly was secretly flown to Wright Field, subsequently renamed Wright-Patterson AFB at Dayton, Ohio.) This identification, now known not to be true, was widely accepted, and the story died a quick death. The episode would survive only as a small footnote in UFO history until the late 1970s, when ufologists commenced a reinvestigation which continues to this day. By 1992 four books had been written about the "Roswell incident," so called because the recovery operation took place out of the Army Air Force base in Roswell, New Mexico.

According to some informants, searchers found the bodies of four gray-skinned humanoid beings at a location two miles from the main crash site. Authorities allegedly swore all who knew of the episode, military or civilian, to secrecy. Decades later investigators encountered witnesses and participants who still would not discuss what they knew. Nonetheless by the early 1990s ufologists such as William Moore, Stanton Friedman, Kevin Randle, and Don Schmitt had collected the testimonies of several hundred persons, from local ranchers to Air Force generals, and from them meticulously reconstructed a complex series of events. By now the Roswell incident is one of the best-documented cases in UFO history.

Unearthly rumors.
Until latter-day inquiries brought the Roswell incident out of obscurity, even ufologists who thought UFOs to be extraterrestrial spacecraft — and who suspected the U.S. government knew as much — were largely skeptical of rumors of what were called, derisively, "little men in pickle jars." Such tales emerged early on, and some no doubt took their inspiration from the Roswell incident. But ufologists, few of whom questioned the official explanation, knew little if anything about the case, and they assumed the stories were nothing but folk variations on fabricated testimony such as that chronicled in a notorious book, Frank Scully's *Behind the Flying Saucers* (1950).

Scully, a *Variety* columnist, had naively reported and endorsed yarns told him by Silas Newton and Leo A. GeBauer (whom the book identifies as a mysterious "Dr. Gee"), who claimed to know of spaceship crashes in the Southwest. Other, more critical-minded investigators determined that Newton and GeBauer, life-long confidence artists, had concocted the story as part of an elaborate swindle. The two were peddling bogus oil-detection devices based on extraterrestrial technology to wealthy investors.

The Scully/Newton/GeBauer fiasco, along with the apparent absence of evidence for other claimed crashes and recoveries, rendered such stories unacceptable to all but fringe ufologists. More conservative UFO proponents agreed with Ed J. Sullivan who, writing in the September 1952 issue of *Civilian Saucer Investigation Quarterly Bulletin*, remarked that crash stories "are damned for the simple reason, that after years of circulation, not one soul has come forward with a single concrete fact to support the assertions. If there were one single iota of fact, certainly someone, somewhere, would be willing to bring it into the open."

The ufologists' doubts notwithstanding, the rumors continued to circulate. According to this UFO-age urban folklore, one or more extraterrestrial spacecraft had crash-landed in the Southwest. Supposedly military personnel transferred the wreckage and bodies to Wright-Patterson Air Force Base. In some instances individuals said they had seen the evidence personally; either they had participated in a recovery on site, or they had encountered it — by accident or in the course of classified work — in a secret room at Wright-Patterson. At some point the phrase "Hangar 18" or "Blue Room" came to denote this place, though it is not clear whether these names originated in someone's alleged firsthand testimony or in the sort of elaboration that inevitably occurs as stories pass from person to person. A 1980 science-fiction film, directed by James L. Conway and starring Darren McGavin and Robert Vaughan, dramatized the story. By this time many Americans did not have to be told what the title, *Hangar 18*, meant. In any case, the Air Force has long denied any such room exists.

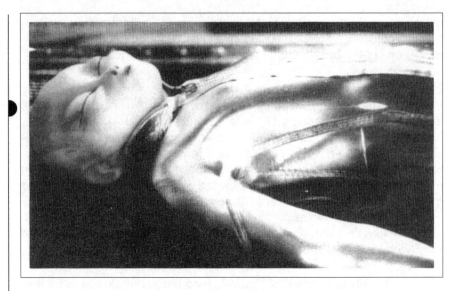

To impressionable UFO buffs this widely circulated photograph represents a picture of an extraterrestrial in a secret U.S. government vault. In fact, it is a wax dummy displayed in Canada in the early 1980s.

In the 1970s one prominent ufologist, Leonard H. Stringfield, broke ranks with his skeptical colleagues and began actively seeking out crash testimony, including Hangar 18 stories, which he published in a series of monographs. The most interesting of these were those from firsthand informants. Some examples:

A former Army pilot said he had been inside a Wright-Patterson hangar one day in 1953 when a DC-7 arrived bearing five crates. These crates were moved via forklift. The informant saw three of them opened, and inside each lay the body of a small humanoid on a fabric stretched over a bed of dry ice. Four feet tall, the entities had large, hairless heads with small mouths; the bodies were thin and looked brown under the hangar lights. They were dressed in tight-fitting uniforms, and one, so two bumps on the chest suggested, appeared to be female. He said crew members from the DC-7 later told him that a flying saucer had crashed in the Arizona desert and that one of the humanoids was still alive when a recovery team arrived and attempted unsuccessfully to save it. According to Stringfield, the man "impressed me as a person who is sincere and forthright, possessing a no-nonsense character."

A retired Army intelligence officer stationed at Wright-Patterson in 1966 allegedly saw nine alien bodies in a heavily guarded location at the base. They were four feet tall and gray-skinned. He was told that the facility held a total of 30 such bodies, along with the wreckage of spacecraft. He said, "Since 1948 secret information concerning UFO activity involving the U.S. military has been contained in a computer center at Wright-Patterson AFB. At this base a master computer file is maintained with duplicate support backup files secreted at other military installations." The source also claimed to have been at the base when Senator Goldwater showed up and General LeMay denied him access to the UFO-storage areas. "This refusal caused quite a fiasco on the base," the man said.

Another source, a retired Air Force pilot, told Stringfield that in 1952, while attending a "high-level secret meeting" at Wright-Patterson, he saw an alien body deep-frozen in an underground chamber. Four feet tall and hairless, it had a big head and long arms. He said he learned that some of the Wright-Patterson UFO material was eventually transferred to the Air Force's underground complex at Colorado Springs, Colorado.

The most remarkable of Stringfield's informants was a medical doctor associated with a major hospital. The physician claimed to have performed an autopsy on an alien body while serving in the military in the early 1950s. In a statement prepared for Stringfield in July 1979, he reported:

> The specimen observed was four feet three inches in length. I can't remember the weight. It has been so long and my files do not contain the weight. I recall the length well, because we had a disagreement and everyone took their turn at measuring. The head was pear-shaped in appearance and oversized by human standards for the body. The eyes were Mongoloid in appearance. The ends of the eyes furthest from the nasal cavity slanted upward at about a 10-degree angle. The eyes were recessed into the head. There seemed to be no visible eyelids, only what seemed like a fold. The nose consisted of a small fold-like protrusion above the nasal orifices. The mouth seemed to be a wrinkle-like fold. There were no human type lips as such — just a slit that opened into an oral cavity about two inches deep. A membrane along the rear of the cavity separated it from what would be the digestive tract. The tongue seemed to be atrophied into almost a membrane. No teeth were observed. X-rays revealed a maxilla and mandible as well as cranial bone structure. The outer "ear lobes" didn't exist. The auditory orifices present were similar to our middle and inner ear canals. The head contained no hair follicles. The skin seemed grayish in color and seemed mobile when moved.

What is striking about this description is its anticipation of the type of being that would figure in the UFO-abduction lore of the 1980s and beyond. (Sketches of such beings appear in two books by Budd Hopkins, *Missing Time* [1981] and *Intruders* [1987].) Humanoids of this sort are rare in the early UFO literature of occupant reports. Pre-abduction-era "close encounters of the third kind" generally characterized UFO beings as humans and near-humans, dwarfs in diving suits, and human dwarfs; there are also a few accounts of "monsters" (see *Flatwoods Monster*). The first book to carry a sketch of such an entity is Raymond E. Fowler's *The Andreasson Affair*, published in 1979. That was the same year the medical doctor had given Stringfield his statement; but Stringfield had met the man a year earlier and interviewed him at length. The quoted statement simply summarizes what the informant told the ufologist months prior to the publication of Fowler's book.

Stringfield had other medical informants who gave generally similar accounts of alien physiology. As with most of his material, however, whether concerning Hangar 18 or on-site recoveries, its credibility is not helped by his policy of keeping the informants' names anonymous. No one questions Stringfield's honesty, but independent checking of his sources' accounts is not possible.

More than rumors?

In other instances, however, names are known, and these individuals tell tales not unlike the ones related above. Norma Gardner worked at Wright-Patterson for a number of years. Her high security clearance gave her access to sensitive materials, including, she confided to a young acquaintance and UFO enthusiast, Charles Wilhelm, items recovered from crashed UFOs. She was responsible for cataloging, photographing, and tagging them. Once, she said, she saw two humanoid bodies being carted from one room to the next. They were of generally human appearance, though with large heads and slanted eyes. She told Wilhelm that she was passing on the information only because she was dying of cancer and "Uncle Sam can't do anything to me once I'm in my grave."

One evening in July 1952 Pan American pilot William Nash and co-pilot William Fortenberry had a dramatic UFO encounter over Virginia. The next morning, as they waited for investigators from the Air Force's Project Blue Book to interview them, they agreed to ask if the rumors about crashed discs at Wright-Patterson were true. In the subsequent excitement Nash forgot to say anything, but Fortenberry got an affirmative answer from one of his interviewers. When the pilots were brought together again, Nash suddenly remembered the question. When he addressed the officers, Nash related, they "all opened their mouths to answer the question, whereupon Maj. [John H.] Sharpe looked at them, not me, and said very quickly, 'NO!' It appeared as if he were telling them to shut up rather than addressing the answer to me."

Two well-placed informants did not claim themselves to have seen wreckage or bodies at Wright-Patterson, but they did say they knew of the existence of such things.

One was physicist Robert Sarbacher, who in the late 1940s and early 1950s served as a consultant to the Defense Department's Research and Development Board (RDB). On September 15, 1950, during a meeting in his office with a group of Canadian government scientists and engineers, Sarbacher was asked if there were any truth to persistent rumors that the U.S. government was holding UFO remains. He answered yes, adding, "We have not been able to duplicate their performance.... All we know is, we didn't make them, and it's pretty certain they didn't originate on the earth." The subject, he said, "is classified two points higher even than the H-bomb." He would say little more, except that a top-secret project had been formed to study the materials.

A memo recounting this remarkable conversation surfaced three decades later when ufologist Arthur Bray found it in the personal papers of Wilbert B. Smith, a deceased Canadian radio engineer and UFO buff who had asked the questions. Subsequently several investigators interviewed Sar-

● SOURCES:

Beckley, Timothy Green. *MJ-12 and the Riddle of Hangar 18*. New Brunswick, NJ: Inner Light Publications, 1989.

Berlitz, Charles, and William L. Moore. *The Roswell Incident*. New York: Grosset and Dunlap, 1980.

Bernstein, Burton. "Profiles: AuH2O." *The New Yorker* 64, 10 (April 25, 1988): 43–73.

Clark, Jerome. "Confessions of a Fortean Skeptic." *Zetetic Scholar* 11 (August 1983): 7–14.

———. *The Emergence of a Phenomenon: UFOs from the Beginning Through 1959 — The UFO Encyclopedia, Volume 2*. Detroit, MI: Omnigraphics, 1992.

Eberhart, George M., ed. *The Roswell Report: A Historical Perspective*. Chicago: J. Allen Hynek Center for UFO Studies, 1991.

Friedman, Stanton T., and Don Berliner. *Crash at Corona*. New York: Paragon Books, 1992.

Randle, Kevin D., and Donald R. Schmitt. *UFO Crash at Roswell*. New York: Avon Books, 1991.

Scully, Frank. *Behind the Flying Saucers*. New

bacher, then living in Florida (he died in 1986); he was located through the address listed after his long *Who's Who in America* entry, attesting to a distinguished career in science, government, and business. Sarbacher said his knowledge of the recoveries was limited to what he read in official reports he had seen in his RDB office. He recalled that "certain materials reported to have come from flying saucer crashes were extremely light and very tough" — which is how the material recovered in Lincoln County, New Mexico, in 1947 has been consistently described. "There were reports that instruments or people operating these machines were also of very light weight, sufficient to withstand the tremendous deceleration and acceleration associated with their machinery," he said.

Sarbacher also said that on one occasion he had been invited to a high-level conference at Wright-Patterson, where Air Force analysts were to discuss what they had learned from their work on wreckage and bodies stored at the base. (Note the reference by one of Stringfield's informants to a "high level secret meeting" at the base in the early 1950s.)

An even more impressive informant, retired Air Force officer Arthur Exon, has testified that in July 1947, when he was a lieutenant colonel at Wright Field, the remains of a flying saucer and its occupants recovered in New Mexico were flown in from Eighth Army Headquarters to undergo analysis at the base's laboratories. Lieutenant Colonel Exon told investigators Randle and Schmitt that some of the material from the craft was "very thin but awfully strong and couldn't be dented with heavy hammers" — again consistent with other people's experience of the material. "The overall consensus," he said, "was that the pieces were from space." The bodies "were in fairly good condition." A top-secret committee took over the investigation of this and other sensitive UFO incidents.

In 1964 Exon, by now a general, became base commander at Wright-Patterson. Even so, the area where the classified UFO studies were being conducted was off-limits to him and consequently his knowledge of its operations was limited. From time to time a "team of uniformed officers would arrive on a commercial flight" to confer with project operatives at the base, prior to their going out to investigate an important case. Then eight to fifteen men would board a "T-39 and occasionally a Convair 240" which General Exon made available to them. After three days to a week they would return, but according to the general, "We were never informed about any reports. They all went to Washington."

Clearly stories of this sort — these are only a few of many that could be cited — constitute a genuine mystery and cannot simply be shrugged off. Though none in and of itself comes close to proving the extraordinary claim it makes, these reports follow logically from the Roswell incident, which has been massively documented and intensively investigated. If something other than artifacts of extraterrestrial visitation were being claimed, evidence of this sort would raise both eyebrows and questions. It will be interesting to see where the story of Hangar 18 goes from here.

York: Henry Holt and Company, 1950.

Stringfield, Leonard H. *Situation Red, the UFO Siege!* Garden City, NY: Doubleday and Company, 1977.

————. *The UFO Crash/Retrieval Syndrome: Status Report II: New Sources, New Data.* Seguin, TX: Mutual UFO Network, 1980.

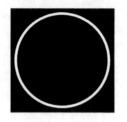

HOLLOW EARTH ─────────────────────────────

The idea that the earth possesses a hollow interior which houses an underground civilization is an old one — the widespread religious belief in hell is one expression of this notion — but the first American to try to prove it was the eccentric John Cleves Symmes (1779-1829). Symmes believed that the earth is made up of a series of concentric spheres, with 4,000-mile-wide holes at the north and south poles. In spite of massive ridicule, Symmes wrote, lectured, and lobbied vigorously for funding to mount an expedition through the poles to the interior, where he and his party would meet the inner-earth people and open "new sources of trade and commerce."

To the rest of the world, Symmes is remembered, if at all, as the inspiration for Edgar Allan Poe's early science-fiction tale of a hollow earth, *The Narrative of Arthur Gordon Pym* (1838). Yet Symmes was a pioneer of sorts, a man who encouraged generations of independent thinkers to imagine a new earthly geology and to dream of a fabulous race which secretly shares the planet with surface humanity.

Among the first to be infected was Symmes's own son Americus, who kept in touch with other hollow-earth disciples and in 1878 published an anthology of his father's lectures. By this time even the spirit world had picked up on the theme. In 1871 medium M. L. Sherman brought out *The Hollow Globe*, based on supposed communications from the dead. H. P. Blavatsky, founder of an influential school of occultism called Theosophy, wrote of the hollow earth in two classic works, *Isis Unveiled* (1877) and *The Secret Doctrine* (1888). Frederick Culmer weighed in with The Inner World in 1886, and exactly 20 years later William Reed released his *The Phantom of the Poles*. In a 1931 book, *Lemuria: The Lost Continent of the Pacific*, H. Spencer Lewis added a new ingredient to the mix when he reported that remnants of a super race dwell within Mount Shasta in northern California.

Late in the nineteenth century a religion based on hollow-earth doctrines came into being under the leadership of Cyrus Teed (1839–1908). Teed claimed to have been contacted by no less than the Mother of the Universe, who imparted some important news: he was to be the savior of the world. Teed founded a utopian community, based in Fort Myers, Florida, and dedicated to "Koreshanity," according to which the "universe is a cell, a hollow globe, the physical body of which is the earth; the sun is at the center. We live on the inside of the cell; and the sun, moon, planets and stars are all within the globe." In other words, the universe is inside out.

Less radical, relatively speaking, was a 1913 book, *A Journey to the Earth's Interior*, by Marshall B. Gardner, who returned to the Symmes model of the hollow earth (though speaking ill of his mentor at every turn). Gardner thought there was an interior sun, though it was not the sun. This sun, 600 miles in diameter, gave the underworld a pleasant climate, allowing its inhabitants to live in tropical splendor.

By this time the hollow earth concept, though disparaged by scientists as preposterous and physically impossible, had taken a firm hold in the imagination of many occultists. The next major occult figure to pick it up was Guy Warren Ballard (1878–1939), whose *Unveiled Mysteries* (1934), written under the pseudonym Godfre Ray King, told of an extraordinary experience the author had undergone four years earlier. Ballard wrote that while on an outing at Mount Shasta, he met a stranger who gave him a creamy liquid to drink. Once he had done so, Ballard saw the man as he "truly" was: Count Saint Germaine, an eighteenth-century occult figure who, Blavatsky had written, lived on as an immortal Tibetan Master.

Ballard said he met the count many times after that and in his company took numerous out-of-body tours under the earth, where he explored a beautiful world of scientific and spiritual marvels. In time he even started meeting space people under the earth. Under Wyoming's Grand Teton Mountains he attended a conference with 12 Venusian masters. He told comparable tales in a follow-up book, *The Magic Presence* (1935), and until his death he, his wife Edna, and son Donald toured the United States and spoke to large audiences of seekers who soon joined the Ballards' occult group, The "I AM" Activity.

The Shaver mystery.
Until Richard Sharpe Shaver came along, nearly all nineteenth- and twentieth-century hollow-earth proponents spoke of the inner world's inhabitants as members of an advanced, benevolent race whom it would be desirable for human beings to meet and befriend. Shaver, however, had another story to tell. Shaver technologized hell.

In September 1943, in Chicago, *Amazing Stories* editor Ray Palmer read a letter from a Barto, Pennsylvania, reader who claimed to know of an ancient alphabet from Lemuria, a continent said to have sunk in the Pacific Ocean thousands of years ago, taking a mighty civilization with it. (In fact, the idea of "Lemuria" was invented in the nineteenth century, first by biologist Ernst

Haekel as a hypothetical home for the original *Homo sapiens*, then elaborated by Blavatsky in her imaginative "history" of the human race. There is no geological or biological evidence that such a place ever existed.) Palmer reprinted the alphabet in the January 1944 issue, and soon he and the reader, Shaver, were corresponding regularly.

Shaver alleged that for years evil creatures known as "deros" — short for "detrimental robots" (who were not robots as the term is ordinarily understood but "robots" in the sense of being slaves to their passions) — had tormented him. Deros were the degenerate remnants of the "Titans," the people of Lemuria, who 12,000 years ago were forced to escape into great caverns under the earth to avoid deadly radiation from the sun. (Some Titans, however, stayed on the surface, adjusted, and became the present human race. Others fled to distant planets.) Deros — demons in all but name and close to it even there — were sadistic idiots who had access to the advanced Titan technology, which they used to increase sexual pleasure during the orgies to which they were addicted. They also used the machines in marathon torture sessions on kidnapped surface people and also on the "teros" (integrative robots, who were not robots but good Titans who, though vastly outnumbered, were fighting the deros); they also employed the machines to cause accidents, madness, and other miseries in the world above the caves.

Soon *Amazing* and its companion pulp *Fantastic Adventures* were filled with exciting and terrifying tales of the underworld. Most of these stories bore Shaver's by-line, but Palmer was writing them. The first, "I Remember Lemuria!", all 31,000 words of it, appeared in *Amazing*'s March 1945 issue, and in the introduction Shaver told readers of his vivid memories of life as "Mutan Mion, who lived many thousands of years ago in Sub Atlan, one of the great cities of ancient Lemuria!"

A flood of letters crossed Palmer's desk, some from individuals who claimed they, too, had met with the deros and barely lived to tell *Amazing* about it. Chester S. Geier, one of the magazine's regular contributors, started the Shaver Mystery Club as a way both of handling the mail and of "investigating" the "evidence" for the deros. Palmer and Shaver had caused quite a stir.

Not all readers were happy about it, however. Many were furious; convinced that some sort of swindle was afoot, they feared that the Shaver mystery would make all science-fiction fans look like fools or worse. By 1948 their protests led Ziff-Davis, *Amazing*'s parent company, to order the series stopped.

After co-founding *Fate* with Curtis Fuller in 1948, Palmer left Ziff-Davis and moved to tiny Amherst, Wisconsin, to produce his own magazines, notably *Flying Saucers and Mystic* (later Search), which regularly featured Shaver material. In 1961 he started *The Hidden World*, a series of magazines in trade-paperback format, and over the next three years reprinted Shaver's original articles and ran new contributions from a diminishing band of enthusiasts.

Shaver died in Arkansas in November 1975, Palmer in Florida two years later.

Other hollow earthers.
Another *Amazing* reader who claimed to have met the deros was Maurice Doreal (born Claude Doggins). Like Ballard, he said he was friends with the Masters who lived inside Mount Shasta, though unlike Ballard he said they were from Atlantis, not Lemuria. According to him, the Atlanteans and the Lemurians lived in great caverns under the earth and regularly visited, and received visits from, other star systems. His own occult group, the Brotherhood of the White Temple, was headquartered in the Pleiades and involved in complex interstellar diplomacy and warfare, which Doreal detailed at length in his various writings.

W. C. Hefferlin wrote *Amazing* about his adventures in Rainbow City, an abandoned extraterrestrial metropolis under the Antarctic ice. Though its inhabitants were long gone, they had left their advanced technology in place. Hefferlin's account of the space people's secrets failed to impress those readers who knew something about science; they wrote to jeer at the Rainbow City man's elementary errors, causing Hefferlin to drop out of sight for a year. He reappeared under the sponsorship of Borderland Sciences Research Associates, an occult-oriented group headquartered in Vista, California. In various BSRA publications Hefferlin and his wife Gladys related that Rainbow City's inhabitants were a race that had settled on Mars to escape the evil Snake People. When the atmosphere of Mars become unbreathable, they emigrated to earth and settled in seven great cities (Rainbow City being the greatest of all) on the continent of Antarctica, then a tropical paradise. Unfortunately, the Snake People found out where they were and attacked, scattering the settlers all over the earth and, incidentally, tipping the earth over on its axis, which is how Antarctica got to be such a frigid place.

Rainbow City was revived in 1951, in Robert Ernst Dickhoff's self-published *Agharta: The Subterranean World*, and again in 1960, in *Rainbow City and the Inner Earth People*, by Michael Barton, writing as Michael X. Barton also revived the Shaver mystery, reporting that Venusians and Masters were allied in a struggle to wipe out the deros. He further claimed to be receiving psychic communications from the long-deceased Marshall Gardner, who enthusiastically endorsed Barton's book.

Far and away the most popular of all such books was *The Hollow Earth* (1964), by Raymond Bernard, the pseudonym of Walter Siegmeister. Siegmeister was a strange character who had operated on the fringes of the occult scene since the 1930s, promoting assorted enterprises such as a South American utopian colony (which the U.S. Post Office concluded did not exist) and publishing his bizarre theories about sexual intercourse (which he believed to be unhealthy) and the male sex (a mutation that ought to be eliminated). *The Hollow Earth* contributed little new to the inner-earth legends and in fact quoted at length from nineteenth-century texts on the subject; the rest of the book focused on Ray Palmer's ruminations as well as

● SOURCES:

Bernard, Raymond [pseudonym of Walter Siegmeister]. *The Hollow Earth: The Greatest Geographical Discovery in History.* New York: Fieldcrest Publishing, 1964.

Cox, Norma. *Kingdoms Within Earth.* Marshall, AR: The Author, 1985.

Crabb, Riley. *The Reality of the Underground.* Vista, CA: Borderland Sciences Research Associates, 1960.

Fitch, Theodore. *Our Paradise Inside the Earth.* Council Bluffs, IA: The Author, 1960.

Friedrich, Christof [pseudonym of Ernst Zundel]. *UFOs — Nazi Secret Weapons?* Toronto, Ontario: Samisdat, 1976.

————. *Secret Nazi Polar Expeditions.* Toronto: Samisdat, 1978.

Kafton-Minkel, Walter. *Subterranean Worlds: 100,000 Years of Dragons, Dwarfs, the Dead, Lost Races and UFOs from Inside the Earth.* Port Townsend, WA: Loompanics Unlimited, 1989.

Michell, John. *Eccentric Lives and Peculiar*

speculations about the alleged conspiracy to hide the truth about the hollow earth, flying saucers, and pole holes. Yet the book sold well, went through numerous printings, and introduced many readers to the subject.

Notions. San Diego, CA: Harcourt Brace Jovanovich, 1984.

Trench, Brinsley le Poer. Secret of the Ages: UFOs from Inside the Earth. London: Souvenir Press, 1974.

Walton, Bruce A. A Guide to the Inner Earth. Jane Lew, WV: New Age Books, 1983.

X, Michael [pseudonym of Michael Barton]. Rainbow City and the Inner Earth People. Los Angeles: Futura, 1960.

Shaver's version of the inner earth dominated *Secret of the Ages*, a 1974 book by Brinsley le Poer Trench (later Lord Clancarty). According to Trench, an occult-oriented saucer enthusiast, evil inner-earthers regularly kidnapped surface people and brainwashed them into becoming their agents. Now, he said, the "ground work has ... been prepared for a takeover of this planet by those who live inside it."

Nazis inside the earth.

Some hollow-earth believers exhibit not just fascination with but open sympathy for Nazi Germany. The chief figure in the Nazi hollow-earth movement is a Toronto man named Ernst Zundel, who writes under the name Christof Friedrich. Zundel operates a clearinghouse for Nazi materials and contends, as do other neo-Nazis, that the Holocaust never took place. In *UFOs — Nazi Secret Weapons?* (1976) he claimed that when World War II ended, Hitler and his Last Battalion boarded a submarine and escaped to Argentina; they then established a base for advanced saucer-shaped aircraft inside the hole at the South Pole. When the Allies learned what had happened, they dispatched Adm. Richard E. Byrd and a "scientific expedition" — in fact an army — to attack the Nazi base, but they were no match for the superior Nazi weapons.

To Zundel the Nazis were "outer earth representatives of the 'inner earth'." This in his view accounted for their racial superiority. In 1978, with the publication of his *Secret Nazi Polar Expeditions*, Zundel solicited funds for his own polar expedition, for which he planned to charter an airliner with a large swastika painted on its fuselage. The swastika not only would bear witness to Zundel's ideological loyalties but also let the inner-earthers know that their visitors were friendly.

Around the same an expedition to the opposite pole, the northern one, was being planned by Tawani Shoush of Houston, Missouri. Shoush, a retired U.S. Marine Corps pilot and head of the International Society for a Complete Earth, wanted to fly a dirigible through the pole, where he and his companions would meet the "Nordic" inner-earthers and possibly join them permanently in their realm. "The hollow earth is better than our own world," he told *Chicago Tribune* columnist Bob Greene (October 31, 1978). Though he denied harboring Nazi sympathies, his stationery prominently featured a swastika. Neither Zundel's nor Shoush's expedition ever got off the ground, literally or figuratively.

An unambiguously pro-Nazi work, Norma Cox's self-published *Kingdoms Within Earth* (1985), held that an international Zionist conspiracy has hidden the truth about the hollow earth as part of a plot to enslave the human race. Identical themes figure in literature published by Cosmic Awareness Communications of Olympia, Washington. The organization claims to have its information from spirit beings who channel through the group's representatives.

ICE FALLS

Dominick Bacigalupo stood up from a kitchen chair and took a step or two just before his roof caved in. When he managed to recover his senses and get back on his feet, he was able to reconstruct what had happened, and it still did not make much sense. A 70-pound chunk of ice had crashed through both the top of his house and the attic and had fallen in three big pieces in the cooking area.

It was not storming on Madison Township, New Jersey, on the evening of September 2, 1958. Bacigalupo's 14-year-old son Richard said he had seen two airliners flying by just before the bizarre fall, but airport officials denied that the craft were carrying ice. The Rutgers University meteorology department said atmospheric conditions could not have created ice of such size and weight. So where did it come from?

Falls of ice comprise one of meteorology's great mysteries, though meteorologists have only reluctantly addressed the question, and usually only when asked. Most often the falls are "explained" as resulting from the accumulation of ice on aircraft. This explanation, however, is a nonstarter for several reasons. One is that electrical heating systems on most modern aircraft prevent ice build-ups on wings or other surfaces. Moreover, even on older planes without such heating systems, speed and construction ensure, according to the Federal Aviation Agency, that "the possibility of accumulating" significant amounts of ice — here the FAA was referring specifically to a fall of a 10-pound block — "is extremely rare." Finally, some of the fallen ice is of such enormous proportions that were a plane carrying it even for a short time, it would be in serious danger of an imminent crash.

Large blocks of ice were raining out of the sky long before the invention of the airplane. Late in the eighteenth century, for example, a block "as big as an elephant" reportedly fell on Seringapatam, India, and took three days to melt. Though poorly documented, it is not inherently incredible, inasmuch as later accounts of similarly oversized ice blocks are not exactly rare. In 1849 the *Edinburgh New Philosophical Journal* took note of the following event, in August of the same year, in Scotland:

> *A curious phenomenon occurred at the farm of Balvullich, on the estate of Ord, occupied by Mr. Moffat, on the evening of Monday last. Immediately after one of the loudest peals of thunder heard there, a large and irregularly shaped mass of ice, reckoned to be nearly 20 feet in circumference, and of a proportionate thickness, fell near the farmhouse. It had a beautiful crystalline appearance being nearly all quite transparent, if we except a small portion of it which consisted of hailstones of uncommon size, fixed together. It was principally composed of small squares, diamond-shaped, of from 1 to 3 inches in size, all firmly congealed together. The weight of this large piece of ice could not be ascertained; but it is a most fortunate circumstance, that it did not fall on Mr. Moffat's house, or it would have crushed it, and undoubtedly have caused the death of some of the inmates. No appearance whatever of either hail or snow was discernible in the surrounding district.*

On December 26, 1950, another Scottish man, driving near Dumbarton, watched a mass of ice rain out of the sky, nearly hitting him, and crashed on the road. When the police got there and weighed the pieces, they came to 112 pounds. This was only one of a number of ice falls that occurred in Great Britain over a two-month period between November 1950 and January 1951. In Kempten, West Germany, in 1951 a block of ice six feet long and six inches around fell on a carpenter working on a roof and killed him. In February 1965 a 50-pound mass of ice smashed through the Phillips Petroleum Plant roof in Woods Cross, Utah.

The largest recognized hailstones are slightly over five inches in diameter and weigh a little more than two pounds. They fall, of course, during storms, held aloft prior to their descent by vertical winds or updrafts. Ice falls, on the other hand, as often as not come out of a clear sky.

Scientists investigate.
Among the best documented cases is one witnessed by British meteorologist R. F. Griffiths. While waiting at a street junction in Manchester on April 2, 1973, he saw a large object strike the road 10 feet to his left and shatter on impact. He picked up the largest chunk, weighing three and a half pounds, and rushed home to store it in the freezing compartment of his refrigerator. He later wrote, "The ice sample displays a puzzling collection of features. Whilst it is clearly composed of cloud water, there is no conclusive evidence enabling one to decide precisely how it grew…. In some respects it is very much like a hailstone, in others it is not." A review of flight records determined that no aircraft were passing overhead at the time.

The fall took place nine minutes after another meteorological oddity with which it may or may not have been linked. While walking down the street, Griffiths saw a "single flash of lightning. This was noted by many people,"

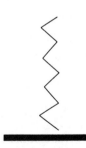

he remarked, both "because of its severity, and because there were no further flashes."

There were, Griffiths found, "unusual meteorological conditions" in England that day, including gales and heavy rains. Snow had fallen on Manchester that morning but had cleared by early afternoon, when the ice came down. Not long after the ice fall, sleet arrived, accompanied by a breeze too slight for its direction to be determined. He concluded (in an article in *Meteorological Magazine*, 1975): "[T]he lightning was triggered off an aeroplane which flew into the storm [in progress to the east, over Liverpool]. No definite conclusion as to the origin of the sample has been arrived at, except that it was composed of cloud water."

A less well known, but in many ways even stranger, occurrence was investigated by Pennsylvania meteorologists in 1957. Early on the evening of July 30, farmer Edwin Groff of Bernville, hearing a "whooshing noise," looked up and saw a large white, round object sailing out of the southern sky. After it crashed and shattered a few yards from him, another, similar object struck a flower bed near him and his wife. The first of these was a 50-pound ice cake; the second was half the size and weight of the first.

The witnesses immediately notified Matthew Peacock, a meteorologist who lived in nearby Reading. Peacock had a colleague, Malcolm J. Reider, examine it in detail. It was cloudy and white, as if it had been frozen rapidly, and permeated with "sediment" — dust, fibers, algae — and was put together like a "popcorn ball." In other words, it was made up of numerous one-inch hailstones frozen together in a single mass. Yet the chemical contaminants were not those associated with conventional ice or hailstones. According to one account, "Iron and nitrate were entirely absent, which is never true of ordinary 'ground water' or ice made by rapidly freezing such water; in contrast, salt and other dissolved minerals were present in an amount that would be excessive in drinking water, and the ice was *alkaline*."

191

Reider was perplexed, and another scientist who examined the material, Paul Sutton, chief of the U.S. Weather Bureau station at Harrisburg, declared that the ice "was not formed by any natural process known to meteorology."

Theories.
Charles Fort, the great anomaly collector, first brought together, from a wide range of scientific journals, the many reports of extraordinary ice falls. He as much as anyone showed that these were not isolated events but manifestations of a larger, continuing, and not infrequent phenomenon. Typically, Fort could not resist the temptation to indulge in extravagant, if tongue-in-cheek, speculation about the cause: "I shall have to accept that, floating in the sky of this earth, there are fields of ice as extensive as those on the Arctic Ocean." During violent thunderstorms some of this ice would get dislodged and plummet to earth.

The UFO age brought these sorts of "explanations" to the mystery:

> *It seems most natural that a space contrivance, if made of metal, and coming from cold space [wrote ufologist M. K. Jessup], would soon become coated with ice. That the ice should fall off, or be pushed off by de-icing mechanisms, or even melt off when the space ships are heated by friction with the air, or become stationary in the sunshine, seems equally natural. If these contrivances are drawing power from surrounding media via an endothermic process, the space structure will become colder and colder the more power it draws, and, in the atmosphere, ice would tend to form on it, just like the frosting of the coils in a refrigerator.*

In fact, few ice falls are associated with UFO sightings. Fort noted one rare, though arguable, exception, recorded in an 1887 issue of *Monthly Weather Review*. On March 19 of that year, at 5 P.M., the Dutch bark *J.P.A.* found itself in the middle of a severe storm in the North Atlantic. Capt. C. D. Swart noticed

> *a meteor in the shape of two balls, one of them very black and the other illuminated. The illuminated ball was oblong, and appeared as if ready to drop on deck amidships. In a moment it became dark as night above, but below, on board and surrounding the vessel, everything appeared like a sea of fire. The ball fell into the water very close alongside the vessel with a roar, and caused the sea to make tremendous breakers which swept over the vessel. A suffocating atmosphere prevailed, and the perspiration ran down every person's face on board and caused everyone to gasp for fresh air. Immediately after this solid lumps of ice fell on deck, and everything on deck and in the rigging became iced, notwithstanding that the thermometer registered 19 degrees Centigrade. The barometer during this time oscillated so as to make it impossible to obtain a correct reading. Upon an examination of the vessel and rigging no damage was noticed, but on that side of the vessel where the meteor fell into the water the ship's side appeared black and the copper plating was found to be blistered. After this phenomenon the wind increased to hurricane force.*

If the captain's description is even generally accurate, the object could not have been a "meteor." It may have been a particularly extraordinary manifestation of ball lightning. It may also have been a genuine unidentified flying object. Whatever it was, no incident like it has been reported since, and consequently it tells us almost nothing at all about the cause or nature of ice falls.

Ice falls are almost certainly some strange variety of natural phenomenon. William R. Corliss suggests that "some unappreciated mechanism in hailstorms permits the sudden aggregation of many hailstones." More likely, as some theorists — once ridiculed, now being taken more seriously (though still skeptically) — have proposed, the ice chunks are true meteorites. Unfortunately, as critic Ronald J. Willis observes, "there is little indication

● SOURCES:

Corliss, William R., ed. *Handbook of Unusual Natural Phenomena*. Glen Arm, MD: The Sourcebook Project, 1977.

———. *Tornados, Dark Days, Anomalous Precipitation, and Related Weather Phenomena: A Catalog of Geophysical Anomalies*. Glen Arm, MD: The Sourcebook Project, 1983.

"Falls." *The News* 3 (March 1974): 8–10.

"Falls." *The News* 13 (December 1975): 7–11.

Foght, Paul. "Ice-Falls Continueth." *Fate* 13, 2 (February 1960): 27–31.

Fort, Charles. *The Books of Charles Fort*. New York: Henry Holt and Company, 1941.

Hitching, Francis. *The Mysterious World: An Atlas of the Unexplained*. New York: Holt, Rinehart and Winston, 1978.

"Ice Cold in Portsmouth." *Fortean Times* (Autumn 1984): 18–19.

"Ice Falls." *Fortean Times* 43 (Spring 1985): 20–21.

"Ice Falls." *Fortean Times* 45 (Winter 1985): 16.

192

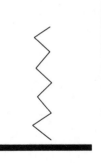

of high speed entry into the atmosphere that we would expect from any meteorite, whatever its origin." Also, the sample studied by Griffiths was composed of "cloud water," suggesting an atmospheric origin.

It is always possible that the falls are of diverse origin. There is enough variety in the reports to sustain this interpretation, if not to prove it. Meanwhile the falls continue — and continue to confound the explainers.

Jessup, M. K. *The Case for the UFO*. New York: The Citadel Press, 1955.

Laprade, Armand, ed. *Shapes in the Sky*. Marshall, AR: Would-You-Believe Publications, 1985.

Lorenzen, Coral E. *The Shadow of the Unknown*. New York: Signet, 1970.

Martin, M. W. "Are There Icebergs in the Sky?" *Fate* 23, 9 (September 1970): 54–58.

Rickard, Bob. "Falls." *Fortean Times* 39 (Spring 1983): 22–23.

———. "Falls." *Fortean Times* 40 (Summer 1983): 31–33.

———. "Falls." *Fortean Times* 27 (Autumn 1978): 3–5.

———. "Falls." *Fortean Times* 36 (Winter 1982): 26–27, 41.

Wilkins, Harold T. "Mystery of the Falling Ice." *Fate* 4, 4 (May/June 1951): 22–27.

Willis, Ronald J. "Ice Falls." *INFO Journal* 1, 3 (Spring 1968): 12–23.

JACKO

On June 30, 1884, a strange creature was captured near the village of Yale in south-central British Columbia. It was glimpsed from a passing British Columbia Express train by engineer Ned Austin, who thought it was a man lying dangerously near the tracks. He brought the train to a near-immediate standstill. Suddenly the "man" stood up and uttered a barking sound, then scrambled up one of the bluffs along the Fraser River. The crew chased the "Indian" — which is what they thought the figure to be — until finally they trapped it on a rocky ledge. The conductor, R. J. Craig, climbed to a point about 40 feet above it and dropped a rock on its head, knocking it unconscious. The crew were then able to tie it up and bring it to town, where it was harbored at the jail.

According to the *Daily British Colonist* for July 4, the creature, quickly dubbed Jacko, turned out to be "something of the gorilla type standing about 4 feet 7 inches in height and weighing 127 pounds. He has long, black, strong hair and resembles a human being with one exception, his entire body, excepting his hands (or paws) and feet are covered with glossy hair about one inch long. His forearm is much longer than a man's forearm, and he possesses extraordinary strength." Noting that some locals had reported seeing a "curious creature" in the past two years, the *Colonist* asked, "Who can unravel the mystery that now surrounds Jacko? Does he belong to a species hitherto unknown in this part of the country?"

In the 1950s, after Sasquatch reports in the Pacific Northwest became the focus of popular interest and speculation, newspaperman Brian McKelvie searched for earlier press accounts and found the Jacko story. He pointed it out to John Green and Rene Dahinden, who were just embarking on what would be lifelong careers as Sasquatch hunters. He told them that this was the only surviving record of the incident; other area papers, which could have confirmed the story, had been lost in a fire. In 1958 Green interviewed an elderly Yale man, August Castle, who said he remembered the incident, though his parents had not taken him to the jail to see Jacko.

The Jacko story made its first appearance between book covers in Ivan T. Sanderson's *Abominable Snowmen: Legend Come to Life* (1961). Sanderson wrote, "Now, whatever you may think of the press, you cannot just write off anything and everything reported by it that you don't like, don't believe in, and don't want." The article, he said, was "excellent ... factual ... hardly being at all speculative." Thereafter hardly a book on Sasquatch failed to mention Jacko. In 1973 Dahinden and coauthor Don Hunter reported that according to the grandson of a man who had been a judge in Yale in 1884, Jacko "was shipped east by rail in a cage, on the way to an English sideshow." No more was heard of him, and locals assumed that he had died in transit.

Primatologist John Napier thought "the description [of Jacko] would fit an adult chimpanzee or even a juvenile male or adult female gorilla, but unless it was an escapee from a circus it is difficult to imagine what an African ape was doing swanning about in the middle of British Columbia. At that time chimpanzees were still fairly rare creatures in captivity."

Meanwhile Green was continuing his effort to get to the bottom of the matter. He learned that microfilms of contemporary British Columbia newspapers did exist, not in the British Columbia Archives, where McKelvie had looked, but at the University of British Columbia. In the July 9, 1884, issue of the *Mainland Guardian*, published in New Westminster, he found a story datelined two days earlier, from a reporter passing through Yale. "The 'What Is it' is the subject of conversation in town," he wrote. "How the story originated, and by whom, is hard for one to conjecture. Absurdity is written on the face it. The fact of the matter is, that no such animal was caught, and how the Colonist was duped in such a manner, and by such a story, is strange." Two days later another paper, the *British Columbian*, reported that the Jacko story had sent some 200 persons scurrying to the jail. There the "only wild man visible was Mr. Murphy, governor of the gaol [jail], who completely exhausted his patience" answering questions about the nonexistent beast.

Though Green now was satisfied that Jacko was a piece of fiction, those unwilling to abandon the story of a captured Sasquatch could take heart from *Pursuit* contributor Russ Kinne's argument that rival newspapers were simply trying to discredit the *Colonist*. Green noted, however, that the *Colonist* did not dispute its critics. To all appearances it was as much a victim of the joke as its readers.

● SOURCES:

Green, John. *On the Track of the Sasquatch*. Agassiz, British Columbia: Cheam Publishing, 1968.

Green, John, and Sabina W. Sanderson. "Alas, Poor Jacko." *Pursuit* 8, 1 (January 1975): 18–19.

Hunter, Don, and Rene Dahinden. *Sasquatch*. Toronto, Ontario: McClelland and Stewart, 1973.

Kinne, Russ. "Jacko Reconsidered." *Pursuit* 9, 2 (April 1976): 43.

Napier, John. *Bigfoot: The Yeti and Sasquatch in Myth and Reality*. New York: E. P. Dutton and Company, 1973.

Sanderson, Ivan T. *Abominable Snowmen: Legend Come to Life*. Philadelphia, PA: Chilton Books, 1961.

195

JERSEY DEVIL

The Jersey Devil's origins are a matter of dispute. The most popular version lists its birthplace as Leeds Point, New Jersey, and the year of its birth 1735. It came into the world, it is said, when a Mrs. Leeds, learning she was pregnant for the thirteenth time, declared that her offspring might just as well be a devil, which it turned out to be. A grotesque creature possessing bat's wings, horse's head, cloven hoofs, and tail, it flew off into the remote pine barrens of South Jersey and has lived there ever since, as evidenced by mysterious livestock deaths, enigmatic footprints, eerie cries in the night, and — on rare occasions — sightings. First known as the Leeds Devil, by the nineteenth century the beast was being referred to as the Jersey Devil.

Stories of the Jersey Devil read more like a folk joke than anything meant to be believed, though this may be a misleading impression an outsider gets from the invariably tongue-in-cheek reporting of the legend by journalists and even folklorists. Still, the Jersey Devil is inherently even more unbelievable than other strange creatures chronicled here; at least these latter manifestations can lay claim to named witnesses and investigated reports. The Jersey Devil appears here only because of what two folklorists have called its "finest hour," when — if press accounts are to be credited — 100 persons in 30 different towns saw the thing as it rampaged through eastern Pennsylvania and southern New Jersey.

The first sighting reportedly took place at 2 A.M. Sunday, January 17, 1909, when Bristol, Pennsylvania, postmaster E. W. Minister saw a glowing monster flying over the Delaware River. It had, he said, a ramlike head, with curled horns, and stayed aloft with long, thin wings. It had short legs, the rear ones longer than the front ones, and it emitted cries which sounded like a combined squawk and whistle. Two other men, one a police officer who fired at it, also observed the creature.

On the eighteenth a policeman at Burlington, New Jersey, spotted a flying "jabberwock" with glowing eyes, and soon residents of neighboring towns were finding mysterious tracks in the snow. It was seen at 6 o'clock the following morning in Burlington, where it prowled through an alley. The witness, Mrs. Michael Ryan, said it had long, birdlike legs, a horse's head, and short wings. A day or two later, at 4 P.M., Mrs. Davis A. White said she encountered it in her backyard in Philadelphia. This time it had alligator skin and breathed fire from its mouth. Her screams alerted her husband, who dashed outside and chased the Devil to Sixteenth Street, where shortly thereafter a trolley car nearly hit it. That evening, at Salem, New Jersey, a police officer spotted a "devil bird" with one foot like a horse's, the other like a mule's. It had a horn on its head and an ostrich's tail, and it was 11 feet long.

A Moorestown fisherman allegedly encountered it the next evening. Now it was three feet high and, except for its dog's face and devil's split hoofs, monkeylike. A Burlington motorman saw something that looked like a winged kangaroo. On the twenty-first, at 2 A.M., Nelson Evans of Glouces-

● SOURCES:

Beck, Henry Charlton. "The Jersey Devil and Other Legends of the Jersey Shore." *New York Folklore Quarterly* 3, 1 (Spring 1947): 102–06.

Bord, Janet, and Colin Bord. *Alien Animals.* Harrisburg, PA: Stackpole Books, 1981.

MacDougall, Curtis D. *Hoaxes.* New York: Dover Publications, 1958.

Martin, Douglas. "Is Jersey Devil Hunt, Still a Spirited Affair, a Wild Ghost Chase?" *Wall Street Journal* (October 31, 1979).

Sullivan, Jeremiah J., with James F. McCloy. "The Jersey Devil's Finest Hour." *New York Folklore Quarterly* 30, 3 (September 1974): 233–39.

ter City heard something on the roof of the shed in his backyard. On investigating, he found (according to the *Philadelphia Public Ledger*, January 22) the following:

It was about three feet and a half high, with a head like a collie dog and a face like a horse. It had a long neck, [and] wings about two feet long, and its back legs were like those of a crane, and it had horse's hoofs. It walked on its back legs and held up two short front legs with paws on them. It didn't use the front legs at all while we were watching. My wife and I were scared, I tell you, but I managed to open the window and say, "Shoo!" and it turned around, barked at me, and flew away.

Several hours later Daniel Flynn of Leiperville, Pennsylvania, observed the Devil as it ran along at a brisk face along the Chester Pike toward Chester. It was six feet high, he said, and had skin like an alligator's. The next morning Mary Sorbinsky of Camden, New Jersey, ran outside after she heard her dog screaming. A huge creature rose up from the ground and took flight. It had taken, Mrs. Sorbinsky reported, a chunk out of her pet.

By now business and schools had closed down in response to the mounting hysteria. But the scare reached a climax of sorts on the evening of January 21, when firemen squirted water on the Devil as it perched atop a roof in West Collingswood. Enraged, the creature swooped down on them. They fled, and the Devil flew away. Except for Mrs. Sorbinsky's, no further sightings took place until February 24, when Salem County farmer Leslie Garrison reported seeing a six-foot-long bird as it sailed over his property. Its feet were like a man's, he claimed.

In the course of this brief scare, newspapers and zoos offered rewards for the Devil's capture, though presumably with no expectation that they would ever have to pay up.

Later years would record periodic sightings, including one of a "flying lion" allegedly seen by two 10-year-old boys, and others in 1930 and 1932 of variously described monsters.

Only the 1909 events give us cause to consider the Jersey Devil anything other than a legend or a running gag, and even here the evidence, such as it is, is in no way compelling. Decades later we have no way of determining what did or did not happen during that week in January. The scare, however, was not simply an invention of a sensationalistic press. In 1974 Jeremiah J. Sullivan wrote in *New York Folklore Quarterly* that "there are many South Jerseyites still alive who remember the Devil scare of 1909." Beyond that we can only guess what witnesses saw or thought they saw. Their testimony would be more impressive if they had reported the same thing, rather than an assortment of odd and absurd apparitions. Sullivan characterized the episode as "one of the few unexplored incidents of mass hysteria connected with folklore in American history."

KANGAROOS, ERRANT ─────────────────

A strange yet comic event occurred on Chicago's Northwest Side at 3:30 in the morning of October 18, 1974. Two police officers, responding skeptically to a bizarre report from a man who claimed to have seen a kangaroo on his porch, were duly astonished to encounter the creature at the end of a dark alley. Not sure what else to do, officer Michael Byrne attempted to handcuff the animal, at which point, he would relate, it "started to scream and got vicious." An altercation then ensued, during which the five-foot-tall kangaroo landed some good swift kicks on the shins of officer Leonard Ciagi. The policemen retreated and summoned help, which was arriving as the animal departed down the street at an estimated speed of 20 miles per hour.

Over the next two or three weeks kangaroo sightings were logged not only in Chicago but in Plano, Illinois, 50 miles to the west. On the evening of November 2, two separate groups of witnesses in both of these places reported seeing a kangaroo at almost the same time. Things got no less crazy over the next couple of weeks, when sightings came out of Lansing, Illinois, and Rensselaer and Carmel, Indiana. Just after 8 A.M. on November 15, a kangaroo was seen back in Chicago, standing in a vacant lot. The witness said it was five feet tall and "black all over, except for the stomach and face, which were brown." The last known sighting took place on November 25, when Sheridan, Indiana, farmer Donald Johnson spotted a kangaroo on a deserted rural road. It was "running on all four feet down the middle of the road." When it noticed Johnson, it bounded over a barbed-wire fence and disappeared into a field.

The kangaroo or kangaroos were never killed, caught, or explained. Strange as this episode was, however, it was neither the first nor the last of its kind. Errant kangaroos have been a part of the American landscape for nearly a century.

After observing two kangaroos pass through his property in Wisconsin's Waukesha County on the morning of April 23, 1978, Lance Nero took these casts of their footprints. Their non-bovine appearance notwithstanding, they were "explained" as cow tracks. (Courtesy of Loren Coleman.)

Kangaroos in America.

In the middle of a major storm on June 12, 1899, a New Richmond, Wisconsin, woman saw a kangaroo run through her neighbor's yard. At the time a circus happened to be in town, and so some assumed the kangaroo was an escapee. In fact, the circus owned no kangaroo.

The following year, near Mays Landing, New Jersey, in the middle of Jersey devil country, a farm family heard a scream emanating from near the barn. It source was, according to one witness, "this thing that looked like a kangaroo. It wasn't such a great big animal — it was about the size of a small calf and weighed about 150 pounds. But the noise is what scared us. It sounded like a woman screaming in an awful lot of agony."

Subsequently the family often saw the animal's tracks, eight to 10 feet apart, leading to a large cedar swamp at the rear of the property.

It is not clear whether the creature that terrified rural Tennessee in January 1934 belongs in a history of anomalous kangaroos. All we know is that those who reported they had seen it said, in the words of one, "It was as fast

as lightning and looked like a giant kangaroo running and leaping across the field." But the alleged witnesses also claimed that it attacked or killed dogs, geese, and ducks. Conventional kangaroos are unaggressive and vegetarian.

These stories, which were reported in newspapers all over the country, sparked massive ridicule, but witnesses stood by their stories, and the *Chattanooga Daily Times* defended them. "There is absolutely no doubt about these facts," it editorialized. "A kangaroolike beast visited the community and killed dogs right and left, and that's all there is to it." Possibly, though no other "killer kangaroo" has ever been reported since and it is hard to resist the conclusion that this was a hoax of some sort.

One night in January 1949 the headlights of a Greyhound bus picked up a strange form crossing a highway near Grove City, Ohio. "It's about five and a half feet high, hairy, and brownish in color," said driver Louis Staub. "It has a long pointed head. It leaped a barbed-wire fence and disappeared. It resembled a kangaroo, but it appeared to jump on all fours. I'm certain it wasn't a deer."

● SOURCES:

Coleman, Loren. *Mysterious America*. Boston, MA: Faber and Faber, 1983.

Quinn, Ron. "Cryptoletters." *The ISC Newsletter* 1, 1 (Spring 1982): 10.

Shoemaker, Michael T. "Killer Kangaroo." *Fate* 38, 9 (September 1985): 60–61.

From 1957 through 1967 residents of Coon Rapids, a Minneapolis suburb, repeatedly sighted kangaroos, on occasion two of them, which apparently lived in a wooded area near the Anoka County Fairgrounds. In 1958 kangaroos were reported in the vicinity of Nebraska towns as far as 100 miles from each other. One witness, brewery owner Charles Wetzel, even gave one of his brands the name "Wetzel Kangaroo Beer."

In the 1970s and 1980s kangaroos appeared in Illinois, Wisconsin, Colorado, Delaware, California, Utah, Oklahoma, and North Carolina and in the Canadian provinces of Ontario and New Brunswick.

On April 24, 1978, two Menomonee Falls, Wisconsin, men snapped two Polaroid photographs of a huge kangaroo in the bush along a highway. Loren Coleman, the leading authority on North American kangaroo sightings, notes that the clearer of the pictures "shows a tan animal with lighter brown front limbs, hints of a lighter brown hind limb, dark brown or black patches around the eyes, inside the two upright ears, and possibly surrounding the nose and upper mouth area. The animal compares favorably with Bennett's wallaby or brush Kangaroo, a native of Tasmania, found from snowy summits to lower valleys."

Considering the quality and obvious sincerity of the witnesses — a not insignificant number of them being police officers — it seems beyond dispute that kangaroos are being seen from time to time far away from their native home. How they got here is, of course, one more question with no immediate answer.

KRAKEN

On November 30, 1861, as they sailed in the Canary Islands, the crew of the French gunboat *Alecton* encountered a gigantic sea monster. When the sailors tried to capture it, the creature swam off. Bullets and cannon fire failed to stop it. After an extended pursuit the ship got close enough so that a harpoon could be hurled into the creature's flesh. Then a noose was put around its body, but the rope slipped until it reached the dorsal fins. As the crew tried to lift it into the ship, the monster's body broke, and all but a small portion of the tail slipped back into the water.

On landing at Teneriffe, the *Alecton*'s commander contacted the French consul. He showed him the tail specimen and produced an official report which was read at the December 30 meeting of the French Academy of Sciences. One member, Arthur Mangin, expressed the consensus response. He observed that no "wise" person, "especially the man of science," would "admit into the catalogue those stories which mention extraordinary creatures like the sea-serpent and the giant squid, the existence of which would be … a contradiction of the great laws of harmony and equilibrium which have sovereign rule over living nature as well as senseless and inert matter."

In other words, the ship's crew were lying or hallucinating. There is nothing surprising about this, of course; it is the standard charge against those who claim to have witnessed unacceptably extraordinary phenomena. In this case, however, the witnesses had had the unhappy experience of encountering a strange but real animal a few years before its existence would be universally acknowledged. They had seen a giant squid — and a fairly modest example of one. It was approximately 24 feet long from the tip of its tail to the end of its eight arms. (Squids also have two tentacles, longer than the arms, but these were missing from the *Alecton* specimen, presumably because the animal had been injured or wounded. It may have been dying

In November 1861 the crew of the French steamer Alecton tried unsuccessfully to capture a giant squid and prove its existence to skeptical scientists. (Courtesy of Loren Coleman.)

when the crew came upon it.) Much larger squids are known to exist, and ones of even greater dimensions are suspected.

The Kraken, a legendary monster of the north seas, was chronicled in a classic zoological work, *The Natural History of Norway* (1752–53), written by Erik Pontoppidan, Bishop of Bergen. Pontoppidan considerably exaggerated its size ("about an English mile and a half in circumference; some say more") and claimed that its arms could pull the "largest man-of-war ... down to the bottom," but otherwise he described the giant squid with reasonable accuracy. Perhaps he did its reputation among the scientifically literate no good by arguing for its existence in the same chapter in which he defended the reality of merfolk.

One problem was that encounters with giant squids passed through folk language and imagination before they found their way to an elite educated audience, to most of which it did not occur to separate folk interpretation from folk experience. Thus an account of a stranding and slaying of a giant squid in Ireland's Dingle Bay in October 1673 attracted no particular notice when it was published in a broadsheet:

A giant squid beached in February 1980 on Plum Island, Massachusetts. (Courtesy of Loren Coleman.)

A Wonderful Fish or Beast that was lately killed, by James Steward, as it came of its own accord to Him out of the sea to the Shore, where he was alone on Horsback at the Harbour's Mouth of Dingle-Icoush, which had two heads and Ten horns, and upon Eight of the said Horns about 800 Buttons or the reassemblance of Little Coronets; and in each of them a set of Teeth, the said Body was bigger than a Horse and was 19 Foot Long Horns and all, the great Head thereof Carried only the said ten Horns and two very large Eyes. And the little Head thereof carried a wonderful strange mouth and two Tongues in it.

Squids, of course, have only one head. The "little head" is the siphon, through which water is pumped to propel the animal. The "horns" are the eight arms and two tentacles, and the "buttons" are the toothed suckers on the arms.

The first zoologist to undertake a systematic study of the Kraken was Johan Japetus Steenstrup, a nineteenth-century Dane, whose literary searches uncovered records of strandings as early as 1639 (on the Icelandic coast). He also collected physical evidence in the form of pieces of specimens and delivered a lecture on the subject to the Society of Scandinavian Naturalists in 1847. It had little impact, but six years later Steenstrup obtained the pharynx and beak of a specimen which had recently washed up on a Jutland beach; the rest of it had been cut up, as fishermen (to whom the kraken was both real and useful) habitually did, and employed as bait. Steenstrup published a description in 1857 and there gave the animal the scientific name — *Architeuthis* — by which it is still known.

His work continued to be ignored, however, and skepticism among scientists ran so deep that even the collective testimony of the *Alecton* crew could be sneered away. Zoology textbooks paid no attention to Steenstrup's new animal until the 1870s, when a series of strandings on the beaches of Newfoundland and Labrador brought some open-minded scientists, including *American Naturalist* editor A. S. Packard, to the area to investigate. A little later, in October 1873, a fisherman named Theophile Piccot and his son lopped off a tentacle of a giant squid they encountered in the water off Great Bell Island near Saint John's, Newfoundland. Piccot told Geological Commission of Canada investigator Alexander Murray that the tentacle was cut off 10 feet from the body, which meant the original could have been as long as 35 feet. Piccot claimed the animal was immense: something like 60 feet long, and from five to 10 feet across.

Giant and gargantuan.

In the decades since, controversies concerning giant squids no longer center on the answered question of their reality. Yet many questions have not been answered — little has been determined, for example, about such basic matters as their diet, habitat, and method of reproduction. Moreover, no live specimen has ever been captured for extended scientific observation — but the most intriguing remaining mystery concerns just how giant a giant squid can be.

In this context it is necessary to note that the giant squid's major enemy is the sperm whale. A rare witnessed battle between these two titans of the ocean, said to have occurred late on an evening in 1875 at the entrance to the Malacca Straits, appears in Frank T. Bullen's *The Cruise of the Cachalot* (1924):

> There was a violent commotion in the sea right where the moon's rays were concentrated.... Getting the night-glasses out of the cabin scuttle, where they always hung in readiness, [I saw a] very large sperm whale was locked in deadly conflict with a cuttle-fish, or squid, almost as large as himself, whose interminable tentacles seemed to enlace the whole of his great body. The head of the whale especially seemed a perfect network of writhing arms — naturally, I suppose, for it appeared as if the whale had the tail part of the mollusc in his jaws, and, in a business-like, methodical way, was sawing through it. By the side of the black columnar head of the whale appeared the head of the great squid, as awful an object as one could well imagine even in a fevered dream. Judging as carefully as possible, I estimated it to be at least as large as one of our pipes, which contained three hundred and fifty gallons; but it may have been, and probably was, a good deal larger. The eyes were very remarkable from their size and blackness, which, contrasted with the livid whiteness of the head, made their appearance all the more striking. They were, at least, a foot in diameter, and, seen under such conditions, looked decidedly eerie and hobgoblin-like.

Even without such remarkable eyewitness testimony, squid-whale battles could be inferred from two facts: squid remains found in whale stomachs or vomit and sucker scars on whales. Both of these relate to the issue of how large squids get.

The largest specimen documented by science was found on a New Zealand beach in 1880 and measured about 65 feet. "A significant part of this length, probably from 10 to 12 meters, consisted of the tentacles, which in a dead squid are notably elastic and easily stretched," two conservative scientific authorities wrote. "In all other squid species the length of tentacles is always regarded as an imprecise component of measurement." But even if we arbitrarily lop a number of feet off the New Zealand squid's size, we still have a handful of eyewitness reports of 80- to 90-foot specimens.

Though such direct sightings of enormous squids are rare and unimpressively documented, numerous whalers have testified to seeing some rather amazing materials vomited up by sperm whales in their death throes. Bullen, for example, saw a "massive fragment of cuttle-fish — tentacle or arm — as thick as a stout man's body, and with six or seven sucking-discs or *acetabula* on it. These were about as large as a saucer, and on their inner edge were thickly set with hooks or claws all round the rim, sharp as needles, and almost the shape and size of a tiger's."

If Bullen's story is accurate, the squid had to have been of immense size. Bernard Heuvelmans, the founder of cryptozoology, contends that the "diameter of the largest suckers is one hundredth of the length of the body and head," with a no more than 10-percent margin of variation. Surely someone, either Bullen or Heuvelmans, is in error here.

Or maybe not. Which takes us to the second controversy: sucker-scars on sperm whales. No one disputes that these marks, whose cause scientists could not satisfactorily explain until they acknowledged the kraken's reality, are made by giant squids in valiant but doomed battles with whales bent on eating them. Conflict erupts over the fact that some of these scars are as much as 18 inches in diameter, when scars of even two or three inches would be considered an occasion for the mind to boggle.

Conservative teuthologists — zoologists who specialize in the study of cephalopods: squids, cuttle-fish, and octopuses — argue that "since a scar grows as a whale grows, it is unreliable evidence for the size of a squid unless it is demonstrably recent," in the words of Clyde F. E. Roper and Kenneth J. Boss. Modern radical zoological writers, including Heuvelmans, Willy Ley, and Ivan T. Sanderson, reject this view. Heuvelmans cites whale research which indicates that "scars are rare on female whales…. A baby whale would be kept well away from such huge brutes, and, if attacked, would hardly survive." In other words, krakens are most likely to leave their marks on fully grown adult male sperm whales.

At any rate, there is no shortage of testimony concerning extraordinary squid remains in whale bellies, including one ship captain's observation of an arm or tentacle 45 feet long and 2½ inches thick and a number of others speaking of those in the 25- to 35-foot range. While these accounts come from sources ordinarily deemed reliable, the controversy will not be settled until a specimen finds its way into a laboratory.

Giant squids, which are only infrequently observed, apparently spend all but short periods of their lives in mid- to deep waters. (The strandings apparently happen when a sick squid dies and rises to the surface, to be washed to the shore.) Systematic scientific surveys of the ocean depths have only now begun — according to one estimate, only one-tenth of one percent has been studied so far — and already bizarre and heretofore unexpected animals have been observed, with the likelihood of many more waiting to be discovered. Some of the scientists involved in this research hope specifically to see a kraken. They also think it possible, even probable, that, as a *New York Times* article observes, "other creatures, perhaps even larger and stranger than the monstrous *Architeuthis*," dwell on the ocean bottom.

● SOURCES:

Bullen, Frank T. *The Cruise of the Cachalot.* New York: D. Appleton, 1924.

Goss, Michael. "Giant Squids on the Attack." *Fate* Pt. I. 38, 7 (July 1985): 34–41; Pt. II. 38, 8 (August 1985): 78–82.

Heuvelmans, Bernard. *In the Wake of the Sea-Serpents.* New York: Hill and Wang, 1968.

Ley, Willy. *Exotic Zoology.* New York: The Viking Press, 1959.

————. "Scylla Was a Squid." *Natural History* 48, 1 (June 1941): 11–13.

Rees, W. J. "The World of Science: Giant Squid: The Quest for the Kraken." *The Illustrated London News* 215, 5771 (November 26, 1949): 826.

Roper, Clyde F. E., and Kenneth J. Boss. "The Giant Squid." *Scientific American* 246, 4 (April 1982): 96–100, 104–05.

Yoon, Carol Kaesuk. "In Dark Seas, Biologists Sight a Riot of Life." *New York Times* (June 2, 1992).

LAKE MONSTERS

On July 22, 1892, as two boys trolled for bass near the south shore of Lake Geneva, they were startled to see the head of an extraordinary serpentlike creature as it rose out of the water 20 to 30 yards away. It opened its huge mouth, revealing several rows of sharp, hooked teeth, and focused its fierce eyes on the terrified onlookers. It began swimming toward them, and the boys, literally paralyzed with fear, were unable to move.

Fortunately for them, the creature executed an abrupt turn when it got within a few feet of them. As it swam toward the middle of the lake, the boys could see that it was at least 100 feet long and three feet around. "When last seen," the *Chicago Tribune* reported two days later, "the serpent was still carrying his head out of the water and slowly moving up the lake toward Keye's Park."

On February 22, 1968, at 7 P.M., farmer Stephen Coyne went to the dry bog near Lough Nahooin, one of a series of small lakes linked by streams which run through Connemara. With him were his eight-year-old son and the family dog. On reaching the bog, Coyne noticed a black object in the water and assumed that it was the dog. When he whistled for it, however, the dog came bounding up from elsewhere. The moment it saw the object in the water, it stopped and stared.

The object proved to be a strange animal with a narrow, polelike head (without visible eyes) and a neck nearly a foot in diameter. It was swimming in various directions, occasionally thrusting its head and neck underwater. Whenever this happened, two humps from its back would emerge into view as would, sometimes, a flat tail. On one occasion this tail was observed near the head, indicating that the animal was both long and flexible. The skin was black, slick, and hairless. The animal appeared to be at least 12 feet long.

Once, apparently annoyed by the dog's barking, it swam toward the group, its mouth open. Coyne stepped forward to protect the dog, and the creature retreated, to resume its casual, directionless movement through the water. Soon father and son were joined by the other five members of the Coyne family. It remained clearly in view, sometimes from as little as five or six yards away. The creature was still there when darkness fell and the Coynes decided to go home.

Between them these two stories, the first from Wisconsin, the other from Ireland, span the spectrum of lake-monster reports, from the predictably phony to the unexpectedly credible. The Lake Geneva tale is, to all appearances, a nineteenth-century newspaper hoax; though the *Chicago Tribune* account refers to "thousands of people ... flocking to the shore" of Lake Geneva in a state of intense excitement, not a single reference to the event appears in any other contemporary source. Readers of American newspapers of the last century will recognize such wondrous but undocumented tales for what they are (for other examples, see *airships, unidentified*, and *Jacko*).

The Coyne family's sighting, whatever else it may be, is no newspaper hoax. Soon after the event a team of experienced cryptozoological investigators, including University of Chicago biologist Roy P. Mackal, interviewed the adult and child witnesses and agreed that their sincerity was not open to question. A few months later, as they were engaged in an unsuccessful effort to snare the creature via a dragging operation through the tiny lake (measuring 100 yards by 80 yards), they met a local man, Thomas Connelly, who saw the same or a similar creature in September as it plunged into the water from the banks. They also heard reports from other lakes in this remote area of western Ireland.

In cases like these, misperception or misidentification seems nearly as unlikely as the creature the Coynes claimed to have seen. Reports of lake monsters abound even in the modern world, and many sightings are vague, unconvincing, and plausibly explained without recourse to the fantastic. Some of the most detailed reports (and accompanying photographs) are known or suspected fabrications. Not, however, all of them.

Monsters in the magical universe and consensus reality.
Traditions of giant freshwater "monsters" are ancient, ubiquitous, and generally unhelpful to any modern inquirer who seeks to extract zoological signals from the deafening noise of mythology and folklore. Our ancestors inhabited a magical universe in which the most fantastic and grotesque creatures were possible, and even "seen," if we are to credit contemporary accounts, which only the foolhardy would do without good cause. Lake monsters of the Middle Ages and earlier go by various names — great serpents, dragons, water horses, and innumerable others — and they share water and land with a bewildering array of supernatural entities.

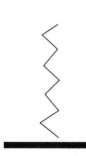

If lake monsters are seen today, presumably they were seen then, too. But unless one is willing to lapse into medieval supernaturalism, as twentieth-century Loch Ness monster hunter and chronicler F. W. Holiday eventually did (declaring before his death that these creatures are indeed dragons in the most traditional sense, a force of profound evil in the universe), one is forced to confine his or her attention to relatively recent sightings — the last two centuries, more or less.

Modern writers on the issue usually, however, cannot resist the temptation to link modern reports, especially those from the monster-haunted lochs and loughs of Scotland and Ireland, with earlier traditions of "water horses." As the argument goes, these supernatural beliefs, nonsensical if read literally, cloak the existence of real if unusual aquatic animals. But such a link is far from certain.

Lake-monster reports and water-horse traditions intersect, with rare exception (see the Loch Duvat story below), at only two points: both are associated with fresh water, and the former creatures are frequently said to have heads reminiscent of those of horses. Beyond these, the water horse (known as the "kelpie" in the Scottish Highlands) is another order of entity entirely: a dangerous shape-changer which can appear either as a shaggy man, who would leap out of the dark onto the back of a solitary traveler and frighten or — if in an especially foul humor — crush him to death, or as a young horse which after tricking an unwary soul onto its back would plunge to the bottom of the nearest lake, with predictably fatal consequences for the rider.

Though water horses are widely remarked on in folklore texts, one is hard-pressed to find "sightings" of them as opposed to rumors and folktales concerning their appearance and habits. A rare "sighting" is attributed to Mary Falconer of Achlyness, West Sutherland, Scotland. One afternoon in the summer of 1938, while walking with a companion near Loch Garget Beag, she noticed a herd of 13 ponies grazing near the water. Mrs. Falconer, who was carrying a sack full of venison, thought one of the horses, a white one, looked like a neighbor's, and decided to borrow it to carry her burden for the rest of her trip to Rhiconich.

But as she approached the animal, she found that it was too big to be her friend's horse. When she saw that it had water weeds entangled in its mane, she knew immediately that it was a water horse. At that moment it and its 12 companions bolted for the lake and disappeared below the surface. "Her companion corroborated her story in every particular," according to folklorist R. Macdonald Robertson.

Were beliefs in water horses based on "sightings" like this one? Since, as this book attests, people "see" all kinds of unlikely things, the question is not a trivial one, and not irrelevant to another question: the relationship of modern, more "scientific" (as opposed to "superstitious") images of lake monsters to current "sightings." In this regard another folklorist, Michel Meurger, writes of the cultural evolution of lake monsters, "The original mythical monster has been progressively covered over with an ideological crust of pretended facticity. This hardened layer will resist any critical investigation, because the new monsters are adapted to the European [rationalist] mind."

● SOURCES:

Benedict, W. Ritchie. "The Unknown Lake Monsters of Alberta." *Strange Magazine 5* (1990): 47–49.

Bord, Janet, and Colin Bord. *Alien Animals.* Harrisburg, PA: Stackpole Books, 1981.

Bradley, Michael. "The Pohenegamook Creature." *Pursuit 9, 3* (Summer 1976): 61–62.

Briggs, Katharine. *An Encyclopedia of Fairies: Hobgoblins, Brownies, Bogies, and Other Supernatural Creatures.* New York: Pantheon Books, 1976.

Brown, Charles E. *Sea Serpents: Wisconsin Occurrences of These Weird Water Monsters in the Four Lakes, Rock, Red Cedar, Koshkonong, Geneva, Elkhart, Michigan and Other Lakes.* Madison, WI: Wisconsin Folklore Society, 1942.

Campbell, John L., and Trevor H. Hall. *Strange Things: The Story of Fr Allan McDonald, Ada Goodrich Freer, and the Society for Psychical Research's Enquiry Into Highland Second Sight.* London: Routledge and Kegan Paul, 1968.

"Canadian 'Monster Lakes' in the News." *The*

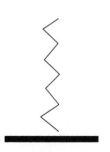

ISC Newsletter 1,2 (Summer 1982): 5.

"Canadian 'Nessies'." INFO Journal 6,3 (September/October 1977): iii.

Church, Tim. "The Flathead Lake Monster." Pursuit 8,4 (October 1975): 89–92.

Coleman, Loren. Mysterious America. Boston: Faber and Faber, 1983.

Custer, Frank. "Did a Water Beast Live Here?" Capital Times [Madison, Wisconsin] (June 21, 1977).

Haas, Joseph S., Jr. "Lake Monsters." Pursuit 12, 2 (Spring 1979): 56–57.

Haly, J. Standish. "The 'Lake Horse' of Loch Arkaig." Notes and Queries 7, 3 (January 29, 1887): 86.

Heuvelmans, Bernard. In the Wake of the Sea-Serpents. New York: Hill and Wang, 1968.

Holiday, F. W. The Dragon and the Disc: An Investigation Into the Totally Fantastic. New York: W. W. Norton and Company, 1973.

———. "Water Monsters: The Land Sighting Paradox." INFO Journal 4, 4 (March 1976): 2–4.

The scientific investigation of anomalies such as lake monsters has a short history (though sporadic efforts were mounted in the eighteenth and nineteenth centuries) and even now, as a not quite respectable enterprise, is plagued by the traditional anomalists' problem of inadequate resources. Few scientists are willing to risk reputation and career associating themselves with "monster hunts," and the funding sources on which scientific research depends are typically unavailable to heretics, however well-credentialed. Thus little about lake monsters is certain. The information that would provide certain answers is unavailable to us because the question itself is deemed illegitimate.

Thus virtually all we know about early popular beliefs concerning such creatures comes from folklorists, who had no obligation to document reports by collecting evidence and assessing their credibility. Folklorists recorded the stories, even the supposed first-person testimonies, simply as stories and, that accomplished, snapped their notebooks shut. Most also implicitly rejected supernatural, or even merely extraordinary, testimony. As David J. Hufford, a scholarly critic of such "traditions of disbelief," has written, "supernatural beliefs arise from and are supported by various kinds of error.... The research design begins with the question 'Why and how do some people manage to believe things which are so patently false?'... Such a perspective has its usefulness but ... it is ethnocentric in the most fundamental sense. It takes a body of knowledge and considers it to be simply 'the way things are' rather than a product of culture. It says over and over again: 'What I know I know, what you know you only *believe*'...."

In the account of Mrs. Falconer's alleged experience, which comes to us from a folklorist, not an investigator (either of cryptozoological animals or of anomalistic psychology), we are told only that she was accompanied by a companion, unnamed, who "corroborated her story in every particular." To someone who wants to know what, if anything, happened that afternoon, this bland statement hardly suffices. And when Robertson goes on to remark, "Mary Falconer is well known locally as a 'Seer,'" we would like to know whether that means she could lay claim to amazing paranormal insight or simply that she exhibited remarkable powers of imagination.

One would like to know more about a story collected on June 5, 1897, by Father Allan McDonald, a turn-of-the-century folklorist, from a Highlander. McDonald wrote:

> Ewen MacMillan, Bunavullin, Eriskay, of Skye descent, aged about 50 tells me that four years ago at the end of May or beginning of June he had gone to look after a mare and foal that he had at about nine or ten o'clock P.M. He went up to Loch Duvat (Eriskay) to see them. There was a foggy haze. He passed at the west end a horse belonging to John Campbell, Bunavillin, and a horse belonging to Duncan Beag MacInnes ditto. He saw an animal in front of him on the North side of the lake which he took to be his own mare and was making up to it. He got to within twenty yards of it but he could not distinguish the color on account of the haze, but in size it appeared to be no larger

than a common Eriskay pony. When he came to within twenty yards of it the creature gave a hideous or unearthly scream ... that terrified not only MacMillan but the horses that were grazing at the West end of the lake, which immediately took to flight. MacMillan ran the whole way home and the horses did not stop till they reached home. These horses were not in the habit of coming home though they might come home of their own accord occasionally.

Probably this "monster" was a wayward seal, but the tantalizing ambiguity of an unsettling image of a strange creature glimpsed darkly through nocturnal haze resonates richly in the imagination. Surely events of this sort had something to do with water-horse traditions and at least some lake-monster "sightings." MacMillan's tale is one of the relative few that lend themselves to either reading. Here water horses and lake monsters do become one, even if the true object of the sighting may have been neither.

Lake monsters in transition.

Given credible sightings and suggestive instrumented and photographic evidence, the proposition that large unknown animals may reside in freshwater bodies around the world is a defensible one. But the popular twentieth-century image of the lake monster as a long-necked, plesiosaurlike animal seems just that. The handful of nineteenth-century reports of such creatures exist only in the retrospective testimony, typically decades later, of aging witnesses. (Interestingly, in the nineteenth century some participants in the great debate about sea serpents championed plesiosaurs as the animals most likely responsible for the sightings. Bernard Heuvelmans, the leading modern historian of the subject, points, however, to significant discrepancies: the plesiosaur's neck is shorter and its tail longer than those associated with the animals described in sea-serpent reports.)

The pre-modern freshwater monster is usually a great serpent, not entirely aquatic in its habits, and often dangerous. In 1636, for example, according to a Norwegian cleric named Nicolas Gramius, "In the last flood, a great serpent from the waters came to the sea; he had lived up to that point in the Mjos and Branz rivers. From the shores of the latter river, he crossed the fields. People saw him moving like a long ship's mast, overturning all that he met on his path, even trees and huts."

Norwegians believed that monsters grew in the lakes until they were too big to live there any longer; then they migrated to the sea. It is not entirely impossible that these creatures were large eels, which have been known to migrate as much as 20 miles overland.

Aside from accounts (nearly all of them sketchy) which describe more or less biologically plausible, and even more or less recognizable, lake monsters, most of the early stories seem purely fabulous, and no more believable than tales (of which there were not a few) of dragons in the sky.

In relatively more recent times, as in sightings alleged to have taken place in central Wisconsin in the 1890s, the creature is described as 10 to 20

Hufford, David J. "Traditions of Disbelief." New York Folklore Quarterly 8, 3–4 (Winter 1982): 47–55.

"Idaho: Slimy Slim." Time (August 21, 1944): 22.

Joseph, Frank. "The Monster of Rock Lake." Fortean Times 57 (Spring 1991): 42.

"Keeping Posted: The Pink What-Is-It?" Saturday Evening Post (December 4, 1948): 10.

Mackal, Roy P. The Monsters of Loch Ness. Chicago: The Swallow Press, 1976.

Magin, Ulrich. "A Brief Survey of Lake Monsters of Continental Europe." Fortean Times 46 (Spring 1986): 52–59.

Mangiacopra, Gary S. "Water Monsters of the Midwestern Lakes." Pursuit 12, 2 (Spring 1979): 50–56.

Meurger, Michel. "The Jabberwocks of Quebec." Fortean Times 46 (Spring 1986): 40–43.

Meurger, Michel, with Claude Gagnon. Lake Monster Traditions: A Cross-Cultural Analysis. London: Fortean Tomes, 1988.

Rhys, J. "Manx Folk-Lore and Superstitions." Folk-

Lore 2, 3 (September 1891): 284–313.

Rickard, Bob. "What 'Lake Monster Traditions' Means to Me." *Fortean Times* 49 (Winter 1987): 61–67.

Robertson, R. Macdonald. Jeremy Bruce-Watt, ed. *Selected Highland Folk Tales.* North Pomfret, VT: David and Charles, 1977.

Sauer, Loie. "About That Monster You Sighted. . ." *New York Times* (April 14, 1979).

Smalley, Donald. "The Logansport *Telegraph* and the Monster of the Indiana Lakes." *Indiana Magazine of History* 42, 3 (September 1946): 249–67.

Sundberg, Jan-Ove. "The Monster of Sraheens Lough." *INFO Journal* 5, 6 (March 1977): 2–9.

Swatek, Joe. "Nebraska's Famous Lake Monster." *INFO Journal* 8, 1 (January/ February 1980):2–4.

Thomas, Nick. "'Something' (Maybe) Lurks in the Depths of a Quebec Lake." *Wall Street Journal* (November 17, 1977).

"Two Lake Monsters." *Fortean Times* 52 (Summer 1989): 21–22.

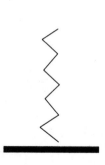

feet long, snake-shaped, but moving with an undulating motion of which snakes are incapable but which has been remarked on in many reports since then. These reports, which survive in sketchy accounts from local newspapers of the period, have a certain aura of authenticity (probably they inspired the much less believable Lake Geneva yarn that opens this entry), and are consistent with a hypothesis favored by Mackal and other scientifically trained practitioners of cryptozoology: that many lake monsters are a form of primitive, snakelike whale known as the zeuglodon.

The fabulous freshwater dragon, on the other hand, surfaced as late as October 18, 1946, in the Clearwater River near Rocky Mountain House, Alberta. Farmer Robert Forbes claimed to have seen a huge, scaly-skinned monster with fiery eyes, long, flashing teeth, and a horn dart its head out of the water long enough to swallow whole a calf which happened to be eating on the banks.

The twentieth century.
Still, on the whole Canada's lake and river monsters — the best known is Ogopogo, in British Columbia's Lake Okanagan — are strikingly uniform and amazingly like zeuglodons. The occasional scientific inquiries directed toward monster reports at specific lakes typically conclude with positive assessments of the eyewitness testimony. The evidence is soft, but it is not always easy to dismiss. Great chains of rivers ultimately linked to the oceans on the Canadian coasts provide places of entrance and egress for these hypothetical large marine mammals.

Mirages, oversized fish, big turtles, seals and sea lions, logs, and tall tales provide plausible explanations for other sightings in North America. The most documented and convincing of the United States lake monsters of our time is Lake Champlain's Champ, the subject both of a continuing serious investigation and of a relatively clear and (according to scientists who have analyzed it) possibly authentic photograph of a creature that looks rather more like a plesiosaur than a zeuglodon.

Yet Champ as plesiosaur is a distinctly twentieth-century concept. Nineteenth-century newspaper accounts, often cited as evidence that Champ is nothing new, suggest quite the opposite; many have a fabulous quality, and all describe monstrous snakelike beasts, sometimes with some mammalian features. It seems clear that Champ is some sort of fiction, in the sense either that it is wholly imaginary or that it is a misguided attempt to compress a number of different animals, some known, some unknown, into a single Loch Ness-style plesiosaur. Champlain, on the Vermont-New York border, empties into the Saint Lawrence River and thus is linked with the Atlantic Ocean. It is at least conceivable that oversized marine animals come in and out of Champlain, and this traffic has created the Champ legend.

Lake-monster reports are worldwide in scope but only spottily documented. A list of the earth's allegedly creature-haunted lakes — about 300 — appears in the Spring 1979 issue of *Pursuit.* Conceivably the real number is a little larger than that. A number of the listed lakes owe their presence solely to dubious nineteenth-century newspaper stories and frontier tall tales. Consequently the number should be viewed with suspicion.

Outside North America and the British Isles, most of the serious investigation has focused on Scandinavian lakes, especially in Norway, with inconclusive results, though some of the eyewitness reports seem credible and impressive. Where instrumented evidence is concerned, the bulk comes from the investigations that began at Loch Ness in the 1930s and continue today. Films, photographs, and sonar trackings have given Nessie a deservedly high profile and established that *something* unusual is surely going on in Scotland's most famous lake. Nonetheless, like Champ, Nessie blurs under intense focus. Some reports are utterly bizarre and zoologically senseless, more like manifestations of the Goblin Universe than of consensus reality. This is particularly true of the rare land sightings, which seem neither more nor less credible than water sightings but which sometimes involve manifestations that border on the surreal.

Fact, fantasy, and points between.

If at least a few lakes harbor real, large, and so far uncatalogued animals — mammal, reptile, amphibian, or fish — they will eventually be found. They probably would have been found by now were it not for the ridicule that surrounds the subject and discourages most qualified inquirers. In other words, the fact that no lake monster has yet been caught does not necessarily tell us that no lake monster exists to be caught. It may mean only that the proper resources have not been brought to bear, including funding for the sophisticated, expensive equipment needed to document or even capture such creatures. If a breakthrough comes, it will likely be at Loch Ness.

It is hard to believe that all eyewitnesses are mistaken and that all of their testimony is without meaning. At the same time one would be reassured if the histories of Nessie, Champ, and others could be traced more certainly past this century. Nothing in the geological and ecological histories of Ness and Champlain explains how long-necked plesiosaurs could have found their way there only in our time.

This curious issue, unremarked on or fuzzed over in the writings of even the most thoughtful cryptozoological writers, leaves an opening for both hardened skeptics and unrestrained believers. The skeptics can argue that the monsters' changing image means that it is a cultural construct, not a biological animal. The believers can speculate that it is, like the water horse of supernatural folklore, a shape-changing entity, not a biological animal. Cautious good sense compels us to favor the skeptics, of course. Still, in a world in which apparently sane and sincere persons can "see" all sorts of wildly improbable things, we cannot help wondering how far we really are from our ancestors' magical universe, in whose lakes and rivers great serpents and dragons roamed freely.

"Wisconsin Lake Monster." INFO Journal 6,1 (May 1977): 13.

X. "A Brief Survey of Canadian Lake Monsters." INFO Journal 8, 5 (March/June 1981): 2–5.

———. "A Mari Usque Ad Mare." Fortean Times 46 (Spring 1986): 44–51.

LAKE WORTH MONSTER ─────────────────

Though little known, the monster scare that rocked Lake Worth, on the northwest edge of Fort Worth, Texas, in the summer of 1969 is among the most well attested in the tangled history of hairy biped reports. It also produced one of the very few photographs ever taken of such an alleged beast.

Early on the morning of July 10, John Reichart, his wife, and two other couples showed up at a Fort Worth police station. They were so manifestly terrified that, as improbable as their story sounded, the officers had no trouble believing the six had seen something truly out of the ordinary. As the witnesses' story went, they had been parked along Lake Worth around midnight when a huge creature leaped out of a tree and landed on the Reicharts' car. It was, they said, covered with both scales and fur and looked like a cross between a man and a goat.

Four police units rushed to the scene but found nothing. They were impressed, however, by the 18-inch scratch running along the side of the witnesses' car. Swearing that it had not been there before, the Reicharts were sure it was a mark from the monster's claws.

In the previous two months other reports of a monster had come to police attention, but were attributed to pranks. The officers assumed that the Reicharts and their friends had been similarly victimized, but the frightening, aggressive nature of this latest incident made them take the matter more seriously than heretofore.

Almost exactly 24 hours after this encounter, Jack Harris, driving on the only road going into the Lake Worth Nature Center, said he spotted the creature crossing in front of him. It ran up and down a bluff and soon was being watched by 30 to 40 persons who had come to the area hoping to see it after the *Fort Worth Star Telegram* headlined a story titled "Fishy Man-goat Terrifies Couples Parked at Lake Worth." Within a short time officers from the sheriff's department were on the scene as well, observing the incredible sight. But when it appeared that some of the onlookers were going to approach it, the creature fired a spare tire, complete with rim, at them, and the witnesses jumped back into their cars. It then escaped into the underbrush.

The witnesses said it was seven feet tall, with an estimated weight of 300 pounds. It walked on two feet and had whitish-gray hair. The creature had a "pitiful cry — like something was hurting him," Harris told a reporter. "But it sure didn't sound human."

In the weeks ahead parties of searchers, many carrying guns, made nightly forays into the woods and fields along the lake. Most thought it resembled a "big white ape." It left tracks, unfortunately not preserved, that reportedly were 16 inches long and eight inches wide at the toes. On one occasion searchers fired on it and followed a trail of blood and tracks to the edge of the water. Three men claimed that one night the creature leaped on their car and got off only after the vehicle collided with a tree. Another three individuals spent a week tracking it without ever seeing it, though they heard its cry and smelled the foul odor associated with it. They also came upon dead sheep with broken necks — victims, they believed, of the creature. Allen Plaster, owner of a dress shop, took a fuzzy black and white photograph said to show the creature at close range.

Sporadic sightings would be logged for years afterwards, but the last report of the 1969 scare is attributed to Charles Buchanan. Buchanan said he had been dozing inside his sleeping bag in the back of his pickup when suddenly something lifted him up. It was the monster. Buchanan grabbed a bag with chicken in it; the creature stuffed it into its mouth, then plunged into the lake and swam to Greer Island. This event allegedly occurred on November 7.

Helmuth Naumer, a spokesman for the Fort Worth Museum of Science and History, and Park Ranger Harroll Rogers theorized that the creature was a bobcat — a preposterous explanation by any standard. Less silly, though still problematical, was a claim, never confirmed, that police caught pranksters with a costume. If a prankster was indeed responsible, he must have been both a remarkable one and, considering how many searchers were armed and trigger-happy, a remarkably brave or stupid one.

● SOURCES:

Chorvinsky, Mark. "Our Strange World: The Lake Worth Monster." *Fate 45*, 10 (October 1992): 31–35.

Clarke, Sallie Ann. *The Lake Worth Monster of Greer Island, Ft. Worth, Texas.* Fort Worth, TX: The Author, 1969.

Coleman, Loren. *Mysterious America.* Boston, MA: Faber and Faber, 1983.

Green, John. *Sasquatch: The Apes Among Us.* Seattle, WA: Hancock House, 1978.

LINDORMS

In the mid-eighteenth century Erik Pontoppidan, the bishop of Bergen, Norway, and author of *Forsog paa Norges naturalige Historie*, remarked on a belief held by residents of the Nordic coast. Sea serpents, he wrote, "are not generated in the sea, but on land, and when they are grown so big that they cannot move about on the rocks, they then go into the sea, and afterwards attain their full growth." Many farmers, he went on, had seen land snakes of "several fathoms length." They called these "the Lindormen, or great snake." Similar creatures also lived in the freshwater lakes of Scandinavia, according to popular lore.

Such creatures, or at any rate beliefs in such creatures, persisted well into the nineteenth century. They figured not only in legends but also in a body of firsthand reports. In 1885 the Swedish scientist and folklorist Gunnar Olof Hylten-Cavallius, author of (in English translation) *On the Dragon, Also Called the Lindorm*, published 48 verbatim accounts, half of them involving multiple witnesses, and offered this summary:

"In Varend [in southern Sweden] — and probably in other parts of Sweden as well — a species of giant snakes, called dragons or lindorms, continues to exist. Usually the lindorm is about 10 feet long but specimens of 18 or 20 feet have been observed. His body is as thick as a man's thigh; his color is black with a yellow-flamed belly. Old specimens wear on their necks an integument of long hair or scales, frequently likened to a horse's mane. He has a flat, round or squared head, a divided tongue, and a mouth full of white, shining teeth. His eyes are large and saucer-shaped with a frightfully wild and sparkling stare. His tail is short and stubby and the general shape of the creature is heavy and unwieldy."

Hylten-Cavallius's reports indicated that the lindorm was powerful and ill-tempered. "When alarmed," he wrote, "he gives off a loud hissing sound and contracts his body until it lies in billows; then he raises himself on his tail four or six feet up and pounces upon his prey." The creature had large, protruding, hypnotic eyes and a head variously described as catlike or horse-like, with a mane. It was most likely to be encountered in wild, unpopulated areas such as marshes, swamps, caves, and lakes. Such encounters usually traumatized witnesses, often making them physically ill or afflicting them with nightmares for years afterwards. Lindorms, which could be slain only with great difficulty, gave off an appalling stench in death.

Convinced that these were reports of real animals — the witnesses included a member of the Swedish parliament and other presumably reliable indi-viduals — Hylten-Cavallius distributed a poster which offered a reward for a lindorm's remains. From his perspective this was a perfectly reasonable approach with a good chance of success; after all, twelve of his reports con-cerned the killings of such creatures. But no takers stepped forward.

"There is no truly satisfactory explanation for these 19th-Century lindorm reports," a modern Swedish writer, Sven Rosén, observed before suggest-ing they may arise from "hallucinations such as those caused by epileptic fits." He added, "One major problem with this psychological explanation" is the multiple-witness accounts. "Many of the 31 additional cases with which I am familiar also had multiple witnesses. One can speak of 'collec-tive hallucination' without effectively explaining anything."

To folklorist Michel Meurger the nineteenth-century lindorm reports were part of the "process of the naturalization of dragons," blending "archaic and modern elements. The traditional attributes of the monster are pre-served, but the creature is now conceived more as a snake than as a super-natural creature." In his view witnesses may have been "projecting traditional fabulous creatures onto local animals [such as grass snakes] perceived as monsters under specific sighting conditions."

If such is the case, we can only conclude that Scandinavians of a century ago harbored prodigiously gifted imaginations. At the same time, Hylton-Cavallius was certainly wrong in believing the lindorms to have been real animals. As with other claims in which fabulous, folkloric elements con-verge confusingly into "real" experiences, no explanation that convinc-ingly addresses all aspects exists — or even seems possible.

● SOURCES:

Meurger, Michel. "In Jormungandra's Coils: A Cultural Archaeology of the Norse Sea-Ser-pent." *Fortean Times* 51 (Winter 1988/1989): 63–68.

Meurger, Michel, with Claude Gagnon. *Lake Monster Traditions: A Cross-Cultural Analysis.* London: Fortean Tomes, 1988.

Rosén, Sven. "The Drag-ons of Sweden." *Fate* 35, 4 (April 1982): 36–45.

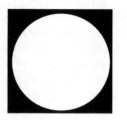

LOCH NESS MONSTERS

The story of the world's best-known lake monsters begins, according to those who hold that such animals exist, over 10,000 years ago. During the last Ice Age, glaciers carved out the largest freshwater lake (over 20 miles long, one and a half miles wide, and in places 1000 feet deep) in what one day would be called Scotland. When the thaw began, the sea moved in to fill up the fjord the glaciers had created. As the ice disappeared, the land rose slowly, and eventually the fjord became Loch Ness. Over time fresh water replaced the salt water. The descendants of the animals that had swum into the loch when it was attached to the sea lived on in their new, altered environment.

In A.D. 565 a man swimming in the River Ness (which empties toward the sea from the north end of Loch Ness), died under bizarre circumstances. St. Columba, who came on the scene soon afterwards, encountered men carrying the body. A monster had killed the man, they said. Columba sent a companion into the river, attracting the attention of the creature, which rose up from the bottom and moved menacingly toward the swimmer. As the others looked on in terror, the saint formed the sign of the cross and commanded the monster to depart in the name of God. According to a Latin text compiled by St. Adamnan a century later, the "beast, on hearing this voice of the saint, was terrified and fled backwards more rapidly than he came."

Though this account did not describe what the "beast" looked like and ascribed to it aggressive behavior of a sort not associated with the modern Loch Ness monster, most chroniclers of the mystery consider this the first known report of "Nessie."

Ambiguous references to large animals in the loch appeared in other documents over the centuries, though some authorities dispute the relevance of these to modern Nessie reports. Proponents point, too, to widespread European traditions of "water horses," known to the Scots as "kelpies." According to popular belief, kelpies found Ness a particularly pleasant abode. As evil-doing shape-changers kelpies usually took the form of horses, enticing travelers to climb onto their backs before racing toward and plunging into the nearest body of water, there to drown their victims. The link between supernatural kelpies and (presumably) biological lake monsters is a nebulous one. Aside from the obvious association of strange beasts with freshwater lakes and rivers, it rests mainly on the single fact that many modern witnesses to Nessie and other lake monsters describe their heads as horselike.

After the monster became a worldwide sensation in the 1930s, residents of the Loch area and other persons came forward with their own reports from earlier in the century and even before. For example, in 1934 D. Mackenzie wrote Rupert T. Gould, author of the first book on the Ness phenomenon (*The Loch Ness Monster and Others* [1934]), to recount a sighting in 1871 or 1872. At noon on a sunny October day he saw what looked "rather like an upturned boat ... wriggling and churning up the water." On October 20, 1933, *The Scotsman* published a letter from the Duke of Portland, who recalled that "when I became, in 1895, the tenant of the salmon angling in Loch Oich and the River Garry, the forester, the hotelkeeper and the fishing ghillies used often to talk about a horrible great beastie as they called it, which appeared in Loch Ness." In 1879 and 1880 two groups of witnesses saw, if their retrospective testimony is to be credited, a large elephant-gray animal with a small head at the end of a long neck as it "waddled" from land into the water.

Such words as upturned boat, elephant-gray color, small head, long neck, and even horrible would be applied to Nessie in numerous later reports. Ness chroniclers estimate the number of sightings to be in the thousands. Writing in the mid-1970s, biologist Roy P. Mackal asserted, "Over the years there have been at least 10,000 known *reported* sightings at Loch Ness but less [sic] than a third of these *recorded*."

The classic "monster."
The August 27, 1930, edition of the *Northern Chronicle*, published in Inverness at the loch's north end, reported that a month earlier three local men, while fishing from a boat, saw, as one put it, "a commotion about 600 yards up the loch. I saw a spray being thrown up into the air at a considerable height.... It continued until it was about 300 yards away and then whatever was causing it turned southwards in a large half circle and moved away from us. It must have been traveling at fifteen knots. My estimation of the length of the part of it we saw would be about twenty feet, and it was standing three feet or so out of the water. The wash it created caused our boat to rock violently." Though he did not describe what the source of the commotion looked like, he said it was "without doubt a living creature" and not "anything normal."

Though the account brought letters (published in the September 3 issue) from other readers attesting to their own or other people's encounters with mysterious animals in the loch, the matter attracted no wider attention.

All that would change with an incident that occurred on the afternoon of April 14, 1933, near Abriachan, a village on the northwest side of Loch Ness. A couple in a passing car spotted a mass of surging water. They stopped and over the next few minutes watched an "enormous animal rolling and plunging" out on the loch. On May 2 the *Inverness Courier* carried the story, written by Alex Campbell, who subsequently claimed his own sightings. The *Courier's* editor, Evan Barron, dubbed the animal a "monster," and the report attracted a fair amount of attention in the Scottish press. Then as other sightings came in (apparently occasioned by the expansion of an older road along the northern shore and the consequent clearing away of natural obstructions to the view), the world eventually took notice. By October, with over 20 reports noted since the April 14 incident, the "Loch Ness monster" was born.

Over the years a composite picture of the "monster" has emerged. (A few reports, however, describe something substantially different and even stranger. These will be discussed presently.) The classic Nessie has a long, vertical neck, with a head of comparable circumference. On the neck, near the end, some witnesses have said they have seen what looked like a mane of hair. The head, as already noted, may have a horselike appearance. The long, tapering body may have one, two, or three humps (Mackal suggests that multiple-hump sightings indicate the presence of more than one animal), and a long, thick tail. Persons who claim to have seen Nessie on land usually report finlike appendages which allow for clumsy forward movement outside the water and (evidently) rapid movement within it. Its color is variously said to be dark gray, dark brown, or black, though occasionally witnesses speak of a lighter color. It surfaces and descends quickly and vertically. It almost always appears when the lake is calm.

If the loch indeed harbors something unusual, common sense and biology require that more than one specimen of it exists. Early writers such as Gould naively assumed the loch harbored a single creature, but Ness proponents long ago abandoned that view and hold that a breeding population of some species of unknown animal resides in the loch. Indeed, reports of multiple Nessies, though infrequent, are made from time to time. The *Scottish Daily Press* of July 14, 1937, for example, told of eight persons who observed "three Monsters about 300 yards out in the loch. In the center were two black shiny humps, 5 ft. long and protruding 2 ft. out of the water and on either side was a smaller Monster."

If taken at face value, the varying size estimates alone indicate that not every sighting is of the same animal. Estimates of length range from as little as three feet (in rare reports of "baby monsters") to as much as 65 feet. Some Nessie investigators reject these latter kinds of estimates as exaggerated, though others contend such reports may be of an older "bull." Most estimates are between 15 and 30 feet.

Land sightings and other weirdness.
Skeptics and proponents agree that otters, diving birds, wave effects, and other conventional phenomena give rise to at least some sightings. Such

explanations do not apply to one subset of Nessie reports. Of them Henry H. Bauer, a scientist and thoughtful commentator on the Ness affair, remarks, "A considerable but unavoidable embarrassment to the most hardheaded hunters is the existence of a small number of reports of Nessies having been seen on land. In Nessiedom these events have a place that is not unlike that of the 'close encounters of the third kind' in ufology. One is brought squarely up against the phenomenon of apparently responsible and plausible individuals who insist on the reality of experiences of the most extremely improbable sort.... [A]ppearances on land have been an integral part of the affair from the start, and belief in the existence of Nessies is surely made less easy in consequence."

On the other hand, one might argue that in such "close encounters" misidentification or misperception is less likely; thus either the witnesses are lying, or they have seen something genuinely out of the ordinary. If the latter, these sightings lend credence to their aquatic counterparts and strengthen the case for anomalous, long-necked animals — in other words, classic Nessies — in the loch. Unfortunately it can also be said that at least some of the sightings only confuse the case.

The most famous of the land sightings took place on the afternoon of July 22, 1933. As they drove south down the east side of the loch between Dores and Foyers, Mr. and Mrs. F.T.G. Spicer said, they saw a bizarre animal 200 yards ahead of them. "It did not move in the usual reptilian fashion," Spicer said, "but with these arches. The body shot across the road in jerks, but because of the slope we could not see its lower parts and saw no limbs." Twenty-five to 30 feet long, it had an elephant-gray color, a bulky body, and a long neck. "We saw no tail," he recalled, "nor did I notice any mouth on what I took to be the head of the creature. We later concluded that the tail must have been curled around alongside it since there was something protruding above its shoulder which gave the impression that it was carrying something on its back." The Spicers referred to the creature, which disappeared into the bracken along the loch, as "horrible," an "abomination," a "loathsome sight."

At around 1 A.M. on January 5, 1934, a young motorcyclist and veterinary student, W. Arthur Grant, nearly collided with a creature just north of Abriachan. It lurched across the road, moving from right to left, crashed through the foliage, and splashed into the loch, disappearing immediately. Grant later related, "It had a head rather like a snake or an eel, flat at the top, with a large oval eye, longish neck and somewhat larger tail. The body was much thicker towards the tail than was the front portion. In color it was black or brown and had a skin rather like that of a whale."

The last known land sighting, said to have occurred on February 28, 1960, was of a similarly classic specimen. In mid-afternoon, through binoculars, Torquil MacLeod observed a long-necked animal with flippers. The upper half was on the shore, with the lower half tapering off into the water. He watched it for nine minutes before "it made a sort of half jump-half lurch to the left, its 'trunk' coming right round until it was facing me, then it flopped into the water and apparently went straight down."

Other land sightings, however, are bizarre beyond reason — so much so that scientifically oriented Nessie proponents usually argue that the witnesses either misobserved the classic monster or saw, as Mackal contends in one case (that of Mrs. Reid at Inverfarigaig, below), a "congenitally deformed specimen of the highland cattle common in the area." Yet, their eerie content aside, these reports — at least from the point of view of witness sincerity — seem neither more nor less credible than those with which Nessie theorists feel more comfortable.

In June 1990 *Scots Magazine* reported on a heretofore-unpublicized land sighting from April 1932. Col. L. McP. Fordyce wrote that as he and his wife were driving one morning through woods along the south side of the loch, they saw an "enormous animal" cross the road 150 yards ahead, apparently on its way to the water. "It had the gait of an elephant," he recalled, "but looked like a cross between a very large horse and a camel, with a hump on its back and a small head on a long neck. I stopped the car and followed the creature on foot for a short distance. From the rear it looked grey and shaggy. Its long, thin neck gave it the appearance of an elephant with its trunk raised." It had long, thin legs and a thin, hairy tail. Soon Fordyce lost his nerve and returned to the safety of his vehicle. Because the debut of the "Loch Ness monster" as an international media star was over a year away, the couple had no context in which to place their experience. They concluded they had seen a freak animal which had escaped from a menagerie.

Strange as it may seem, similarly unlikely beasts figure in other Ness accounts. In 1771 (or so it is alleged in a letter published in *The Scotsman*, October 20, 1933, and written by a descendant) Patrick Rose heard of a recent sighting of a monster "which was a cross between a horse and a camel." In 1912, from a distance of no more than a few yards, a group of children at Inchnacardoch Bay saw something like a long-necked camel enter the loch. A pale sandy color, it had four long legs.

But that is not the end of reports of outlandish beasts in or near the loch. Motoring along the loch's northern shore at 5 A.M. one day in April 1923, Alfred Cruickshank reportedly spotted, some 50 yards ahead of him, a "large humped body standing about six feet high with its belly trailing on the ground and about 12 feet long," with a tail of comparable length. It had four legs as thick as an elephant's and large webbed feet. "I saw the outline of what appeared to be the head," he related. It was "big and pug-nosed and was set right on the body — in other words it didn't seem to have much of a neck." Cruickshank thought that it resembled an "enormous hippo" in some (albeit hardly all) ways. It gave off a "sharp bark" before disappearing into the water. In December 1933 a Mrs. Reid allegedly saw something that looked to her like a dark, hairy hippopotamus with a large round head and thick, short legs as it rested on the slope of the loch shore.

Curiously, land sightings ceased (with one exception noted above) after the mid-1930s. Even some of the aquatic encounters, if not necessarily the best-

documented ones, are of animals other than the classic monster. A letter in the June 7, 1933, issue of the *Argus,* a Scottish newspaper, claimed that "while flying over [Ness] last week in the vicinity of Urquhart Castle we beheld in the depths a shape resembling a large alligator, the size of which would be about 25 feet long by four feet wide." A year earlier, in February 1932, a woman sighted a six- to eight-foot animal swimming up the River Ness; she described it as a "crocodile." In the early nineteenth century, according to some accounts, something resembling a "great salamander" appeared from time to time in the loch, and in 1880 diver Duncan MacDonald, while examining the wreckage of a ship which had gone down at the far south end of the loch, spotted a "very odd-looking beastie, like a huge frog." Terrified, he refused to enter the loch ever again.

Photographs.
Despite such troublingly anomalous stories, the bulk of Nessie reports are of a long-necked creature which those who know something of paleontology think resembles nothing so much as a plesiosaur, an aquatic reptile which according to conventional wisdom vanished into extinction 65 million years ago, during the Upper Jurassic Period. Where most sightings are concerned, descriptions differ notably only in size estimates.

The case for the Ness phenomenon begins, like the case for the UFO phenomenon, with a large body of eyewitness testimony from individuals whose honesty and mental health do not appear to be open to question. Such testimony deserves a respectful hearing and ought not to be dismissed out of hand. Beyond that, the evidence for Nessie includes photographs, films, and sonar traces which seem to attest to the presence of unknown animate objects at or below the loch surface.

Hugh Gray, who lived at Foyers, on the loch's southeast shore, took the first picture of Nessie on November 13, 1933, at a distance of 200 yards and from a vantage point nearly 40 feet above the water. The photograph shows an indistinct large object, evidently moving vigorously. From its left side a snake-shaped appendage extends, presumably (if one accepts the premise that Gray photographed an animal) a neck or a fin; Gray thought it was the former, with the head submerged. While generally regarded as authentic, the picture is too ambiguous to settle the matter. As J. R. Norman of the British Museum of Natural History said at the time, "I am afraid that the photo does not bring the mystery any nearer to a solution."

The following April Lt. Col. Robert Kenneth Wilson took what remains the most famous of all Nessie still pictures: the "surgeon's photograph," as it is known in the literature, though Wilson was in fact a gynecologist. The widely reproduced picture (actually the first, and far more impressive, of two) shows the head and long, curving neck of what many proponents have interpreted to be a plesiosaur. Predictably Wilson's photograph has sparked no end of controversy; even the date on which he took it is disputed. Some skeptics have claimed the date was April 1, with all that implies; the best information, however, indicates April 19. On the other hand, the lesser known second photograph, showing just the head and a small part of the neck, has led some (including proponent Mackal and skeptic Steuart Campbell) to argue that the animal is small and therefore likely to be a diving bird or otter. At this late date the matter probably will never be resolved.

Another important photograph shows an apparent fin, ostensibly attached to an unseen large animal thrashing around in the water near the surface (F. C. Adams, August 24, 1934). Some photographs show little more than unusual wakes unlike those associated with passing boats or other mundane lake traffic. Dramatic close-ups of the monster, from pictures taken by Frank Searle (a number in the early to mid-1970s) and Anthony "Doc" Shiels (1977), have appeared in many magazines and books, but serious researchers regard them as hoaxes.

To some observers pictures taken underwater in 1972 and 1975 should have settled the debate in Nessie's favor, but as it happened, they only provoked yet more controversy; eventually the most vociferous skeptics were even hurling charges of photo-tampering.

The episode started on the night of August 7, 1972, when investigators associated with the Massachusetts-based Academy of Applied Sciences and the Loch Ness Investigation Bureau were patrolling the waters near Urquhart Bay. One boat contained a sonar device; another boat held strobe and camera equipment. At 1 A.M. sonar picked up an unidentified target about 120 feet away, within range of an underwater strobe camera but apparently under or above its beam, since nothing showed up on film. Forty minutes later two large objects, 20 to 30 feet long and about 12 feet apart, were tracked, amid clear indications of salmon fleeing before them. The traces stopped after a few minutes.

Academy investigators took the film from the underwater camera to the United States to have it developed at the head office of Eastman Kodak.

Two frames showed what looked like a big flipper attached on the right to an apparent body of rough texture. (A third showed out-of-focus images of two objects. The clearer image, relatively speaking, suggests a classic Nessie: long neck, bulky body, and fins. The objects were in the spot where sonar echoes had placed them.) To improve the flipper image, which was murky because of the loch's peat-sogged water, the researchers brought them to the Jet Propulsion Laboratory (JPL), where state-of-the-art photo-analysis is routinely performed for official, military, and scientific agencies. There, through a standard computer-enhancement technique, much of the graininess of the original was removed. The pictures that would appear in *Nature* and elsewhere were the clearer enhanced ones, not the originals. "This technique has proven to be a real tool," the Academy investigators wrote. "It has been used to clarify images from space probes, in forensics to help identify fingerprints, and in medical research to classify human chromosomes." Moreover, "it cannot create patterns where there are none." According to analysts, the flipper was probably four to six feet long.

Analysts who studied the sonar records agreed that they depicted something unusual and that the something was almost certainly what had been photographed. To outside observers, including scientists and journalists who heretofore had only sneered, Nessie now looked like a credible proposition. Even *Time*, traditionally hostile to anomalous claims of any kind, conceded, "Now the skeptics may have to re-examine their doubts." To British television journalist Nicholas Witchell, author of a popular book on the monster, the "coincidence of the sonar and the photography... presented indisputable proof of the animal's presence. The one cross-checked with and corroborated the other. Here was the breakthrough."

In June 1975 the Academy team produced even more astonishing evidence. This time the evidence consisted of two dramatic pictures, taken about seven hours apart on the morning of the twentieth. The first showed, as a paper published in *Technology Review* would assert, the "upper torso, neck and head of a living creature." Again, Ness's murky water rendered this identification less than 100 percent certain; on the other hand, it took no imaginative reach whatever to detect such features. Even more startling was the second photograph — of, so it appeared, the monster's face, no more than five feet from the camera. The "head" was horselike, just as innumerable witnesses had attested, and it even exhibited the small horns some observers had reported. (One such witness was Mackal, who in 1966 watched the passage of a "convex object the size of a dinner plate, black in color, with two small protruding vertical objects about an inch or two in diameter.... It was clearly attached to a much larger mass.") According to the investigators, "Measurements indicate the 'neck' to be about one-and-one-half feet thick, the 'mouth' nine inches long and five inches wide, and the horn on the central ridge six inches long." In the Ness literature this quickly became known as the "gargoyle head" picture.

The initial response gave Nessie proponents reason to hope that the scientific mainstream was ready at last to acknowledge the presence of out-of-the-ordinary animals in the loch. On the strength of the pictures zoologists

● SOURCES:

Bauer, Henry H. *The Enigma of Loch Ness: Making Sense of a Mystery.* Urbana, IL: University of Illinois Press, 1986.

————. Letter to Jerome Clark (January 29, 1992).

————. "The Loch Ness Monster: A Guide to the Literature." *Zetetic Scholar* 7 (December 1980): 30–42.

————. *Operation Deepscan, 1987.* Blacksburg, VA: The Author, October 16, 1987.

Binns, Ronald. *The Loch Ness Mystery Solved.* Buffalo, NY: Prometheus Books, 1984.

Braithwaite, Hugh, and D. Gordon Tucker. "Sonar Picks up Stirrings in Loch Ness." *New Scientist* (December 19, 1968): 664–66.

Burton, Maurice. *The Elusive Monster.* London: Rupert Hart-Davis, 1961.

Campbell, Steuart. "The Surgeon's Monster Hoax." *British Journal of Photography* (April 20, 1984): 402–05, 410.

Corliss, William R., ed. *Strange Life: A Sourcebook on the Mysteries of Organic Nature, Vol-*

from the Smithsonian Institution, the Royal Ontario Museum, Harvard University, the New England Aquarium, and other prestigious establishments either endorsed Nessie's existence outright or declared it now to be a distinct possibility. But scientists from London's Natural History Museum sounded a skeptical note of the sort whose volume would grow in the years to come. Because a portion of the "neck" near the "head" in the first of the 1975 photographs was not visible — lost in the shadow, according to proponents — these critics concluded it did not exist. "This probably should be interpreted as two objects," they wrote; "conceivably various floating objects could assume this form."

In 1984 the popular-science magazine *Discover*, edited by Leon Jaroff, a virulent critic of all claims about unorthodox phenomena, reported and endorsed allegations by two electrical engineers who charged that someone — presumably Robert Rines, head of the Academy team — had "retouched" the 1972 flipper photographs, turning "grainy and indistinct" images into false evidence of an unknown animal. Alan Gillespie, who worked on the analysis of the photographs at JPL, rejected the charge as ludicrous; the published pictures, he said, were composites made by overlaying several different computer enhancements and the original. "The outline of the flipper is visible in the original," he said. In fact, team members had already described, years earlier, what *Discover* "discovered" (see above).

Adrian Shine of the Loch Ness and Morar Project insists that the 1975 "gargoyle head" is really a rotting tree stump. Shine brought the stump to the surface and photographed it, subsequently displaying the resulting print next to the head picture and remarking on the similarities. Most observers see no resemblance. Defenders of the Academy photo argue that the image displays bilateral symmetry, as one would expect of a living creature. The late Tim Dinsdale, the most famous of the Nessie hunters, proposed a different alternative explanation: that if rotated 90 degrees, the object would be seen as an engine block with exhaust pipe; such objects are tossed into Urquhart Bay and used as boat moorings. Nonetheless, though the uncertainty continues, the picture has this going for it: the image simply *looks* more like the head of an animal than anything else. Right or wrong, the other interpretations are undeniably counterintuitive.

Other evidence.
Malcolm Irvine of Scottish Film Productions took the first motion-picture film of Nessie on December 12, 1933, in Urquhart Bay. Two minutes long, it shows a long, dark object, just barely protruding above the water's surface 100 yards away. It is typical of other authentic Nessie films in being puzzling but inconclusive.

The whereabouts of one film of considerable potential interest are unknown — if it ever existed at all. Said to have been taken sometime in the 1930s by a London physician named McRae, it allegedly shows several minutes' footage of a three-humped creature with a slightly conical head, two horn-like projections, a stiff mane along a long neck, and — at one point, when the animal rolls over — a flipper. Supposedly McRae, fearing ridicule, decided not to release the film and showed it only to close friends, including landscape artist Alastair Dallas, who reluctantly confirmed its existence to Nessie investigator F. W. Holiday in the early 1960s.

In 1977, reviewing 22 films said to be of Nessies, Mackal said, "I classify 23% [five] of the films as positive evidence and 30% [six] as known phenomena; 40% cannot be classified in either of these categories, mainly because of insufficient or technically inadequate data, poor film quality, extreme range, etc." Among the most important was one taken by Tim Dinsdale.

On April 23, 1960, on the last day of a six-day surveillance of the loch, Dinsdale, while sitting in his car on the slope of a hill near Foyers on the eastern shore, spotted an unusual-looking, motionless object two-thirds of a mile across the water. He stepped out and observed it through binoculars, seeing a "long oval shape, a distinct mahogany color.... [I]t had fullness and girth and stood well above the water, and although I could see it from end to end there was no visible sign of a dorsal fin.... It began to move. I saw ripples break away from the further end, and I knew at once I was looking at the extraordinary humped back of some huge living creature!" He filmed it with a 16mm camera for four minutes as it swam away, partially submerged, and took a sharp left swing. Running out of film, he stopped the camera in hopes, which proved vain, that the creature would show its head and neck.

Later Dinsdale had the presence of mind to arrange for an associate to sail a boat in the same direction the creature had taken. Dinsdale filmed its passage. In 1966, when Britain's Joint Air Reconnaissance Intelligence Center (JARIC) analyzed the first film, it used the second as a basis for comparison. It estimated the boat's size to be 13.3 feet and its speed to be 6.5 mph; in fact, the boat was 15 feet long, and it was traveling at 7 mph. In other words, JARIC's estimates were generally accurate on the conservative side. According to JARIC, the object in the first film was definitely not a boat (an explanation skeptics had favored) but "probably ... an animate object." The hump was between 12 and 16 feet long and about three feet above the water. The object was moving about 10 mph.

The Dinsdale film is considered a major piece of evidence for Nessie's existence, and in the years since then no serious challenge to the JARIC analysis has been mounted.

As noted already, sonar has tracked Nessie-like targets on a number of occasions. The first known such incident took place in 1954, when a commercial vessel noted the passage of a large moving object 480 feet below it. Between 1968 and 1970 D. G. Tucker of the University of Birmingham and his associates, using sonar devices from shore and on boats, repeatedly tracked 20-foot animate objects, which swam and dived near the bottom and sides of the loch. Sometimes they were tracked in groups; in one instance the group consisted of from five to eight objects. Their behavior, speed, and size convinced Tucker that these were not fish.

ume B-1. Glen Arm, MD: The Sourcebook Project, 1976.

Dash, Mike. "Murky Waters." *Fortean Times* 46 (Spring 1986): 60–65.

———. "Cryptozoological Conference 1987." *Fortean Times* 49 (Winter 1987): 36–39.

———. "Operation Deepscan." *Fortean Times* 50 (Summer 1988): 35–38.

———. "The Camels Are Coming." *Fortean Times* 58 (July 1991): 52–53.

Dinsdale, Tim. *Loch Ness Monster.* Fourth edition. Boston, MA: Routledge and Kegan Paul, 1982.

Ellis, William S. "Loch Ness: The Lake and the Legend." *National Geographic* 151, 6 (June 1977): 759–79.

Gould, Rupert T. *The Loch Ness Monster and Others.* London: Geoffrey Bles, 1934.

Holiday, F. W. *The Great Orm of Loch Ness: A Practical Inquiry Into the Nature and Habits of Water-Monsters.* New York: W. W. Norton and Company, 1969.

———. *The Dragon and the Disc: An Investigation Into the Totally Fantastic.* New York: W. W.

229

Norton and Company, 1973.

King, James E., and J. Richard Greenwell. "Attitudes of Biological Limnologists and Oceanographers Toward Supposed Unknown Animals in Loch Ness." *Cryptozoology 2* (Winter 1983): 98–102.

Mackal, Roy P. *The Monsters of Loch Ness.* Chicago: The Swallow Press, 1976.

———. *Searching for Hidden Animals: An Inquiry Into Zoological Mysteries.* Garden City, NY: Doubleday and Company, 1980.

Meurger, Michel, with Claude Gagnon. *Lake Monster Traditions: A Cross-Cultural Analysis.* London: Fortean Tomes, 1988.

"Myth or Monster?" *Time* (November 20, 1972): 66.

"The Nessie Debate." *The ISC Newsletter 9, 2* (Summer 1990): 1–5.

Rines, Robert H., Charles W. Wyckoff, Harold E. Edgerton, and Martin Klein. "Search for the Loch Ness Monster." *Technology Review 78,5* (March/ April 1976): 25–40.

Shine, Adrian. "The Biology of Loch Ness." *New Scientist* (February

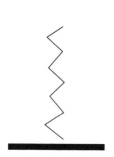

Investigators have continued to make sonar trackings of apparent unknowns in the loch. Mackal counted nine credible contacts up to the early 1970s, and the number has grown markedly since then, owing to the efforts of the Loch Ness and Morar Project and of independent projects sponsored by technology and electronics companies. In 1987 the most ambitious (and heavily publicized) of these, called Operation Deepscan, brought well over 20 vessels to the loch surface for a three-day sonar sweep between October 8 and 10. Though they covered only the southern half, 10 contacts were reported.

The nature of the beasts.

To the skeptical, Loch Ness's monsters exist only in imagination, misperception, lies, and credulity. This position is argued at greatest length in Maurice Burton's *The Elusive Monster* (1961) and Ronald Binns's *The Loch Ness Mystery Solved* (1984). While both of these have their points, they suffer from a heavily polemical tone and an unwillingness to acknowledge what by now should seem self-evident: *something* out of the ordinary is appearing in the loch. To deny that any mystery exists at all is simply to beg questions by the bagful. It is probably wiser at this stage to ask whether the phenomenon behind the mystery is merely unusual or truly extraordinary.

Explanations that posit the former range from large eels, pinnipeds (specifically elephant seals), or sirenians (Steller's sea cow). None of these, however, looks much like what witnesses report or what the photographs and films seem to show.

Of the extraordinary explanations the most popular is that the animals are surviving plesiosaurs which have adapted to Ness's cold-water temperatures, which average 42 degrees F. at the bottom on a warm summer's day. Mackal, on the other hand, first proposed a giant amphibian of a sort thought extinct for 250 million years, though to get there he had to reject as mistaken all reports of creatures over 25 feet long and to short Nessie's neck. Subsequently he changed his mind and now favors the zeuglodon, a primitive, snakelike whale, also thought long extinct, as the likely suspect in Ness and other lake-monster sightings.

The late F. W. Holiday, the most radical of the Nessie theorists, suggested that the animals are enormous prehistoric slugs. No biologist took this explanation seriously, but it did have the merit of addressing the curious feeling of fear and repulsion a number of witnesses have reported experiencing in Nessie's presence. But soon enough Holiday jettisoned even this most exotic of zoological interpretations for an explicitly occult one. His *The Dragon and the Disc* (1973) contends that the ancients had it right: Nessies and their relatives are dragons in the most literal, traditional sense; they are supernatural and evil. He goes on to link dragons with UFOs, which have a sort of symbiotic relationship (reflected in many ancient religions) with these monsters. Holiday manages even to bring the Cottingley fairy photographs into the discussion.

No single theory satisfies all the data, and observers of the Loch Ness mystery disagree even on what "the data" are. The strangest reports are the land sightings, some of which make no zoological sense whatever. Their virtual cessation six decades ago is also a puzzle. Meanwhile, however, the search continues. If large animals, unusual or extraordinary, really do reside deep in Loch Ness's waters, they are there to be found, sooner or later, one way or another.

17, 1983): 462–67.

"Skeptical Eye: The (Retouched) Loch Ness Monster." *Discover* (September 1984): 6.

Whyte, Constance. *More Than a Legend.* London: Hamish Hamilton, 1957.

Witchell, Nicholas. *The Loch Ness Story.* Baltimore, MD: Penguin Books, 1975.

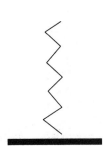

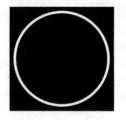

LUNAR ANOMALIES AND ARTIFACTS ———

They are called "transient lunar phenomena," or TLP. TLP are unusual, short-lasting appearances on the moon's surface, typically observed by professional or amateur astronomers through telescopes, more rarely with the naked eye. They may include dark spots, lights, or moving bodies. The first are sometimes explained as optical effects, for example shadows of nearby lunar features. Some of the lights may be no more than reflections from the sun, and the moving bodies have been dismissed as mistaken observations of earthbound objects, such as birds, seeds, or debris, mistakenly projected into space. Other such bodies are probably meteors passing between the earth and the moon.

Still, most astronomers do not contend that all TLP can be accounted for quite so easily. From an analysis of over 900 reports between 1540 and 1970, Winifred S. Cameron concluded, "Some facts indicate that some of the brightenings result from unknown atmospheric, instrumental, and geometric effects, but many puzzling aspects still remain." Other lunar anomalies include reddish patches, cloudlike manifestations, and flashes.

Extraterrestrials on the moon.
If any modern astronomers have ever speculated that some TLP are evidence of intelligent activity on the moon, they have confined such ruminations to private discourse; no such theory appears in the scientific literature. Nonetheless TLP, not to mention lunar features not ordinarily considered anomalous, have inspired much popular speculation and not a few books about alien bases on the moon.

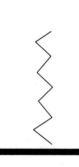

Historically the most prominent proponent of intelligent life on the moon was the great British astronomer Sir William Herschel (1738–1822). Though best remembered as the discoverer of Uranus, Herschel declared, in a paper read in 1780 to the Royal Society, that the "knowledge of the construction of the Moon leads us insensibly to several consequences ...

such as the great probability, not to say almost absolute certainty, of her being inhabited." His observations of both TLP and ordinary surface features led him to believe, at least tentatively, that he had seen cities, towns, roads, canals, forests, and even circuses. Probably Herschel's towering reputation has survived intact because he refrained from publishing these observations; they are recorded in private journals and were rediscovered only recently.

In stories published between August 25 and 31, 1835, the *New York Sun* credited Sir John Herschel, Sir William's son, with observations of, among other wonders, creatures averaging "four feet in height ... covered, except on the face, with short and glossy copper-colored hair" with "wings composed of a thin membrane, without hair, lying snugly upon their backs, from the top of the shoulders to the calves of the legs. The face, which was of a yellowish flesh color, was a slight improvement upon that of the large orang-outang, being more open and intelligent in its expression, and having a greater expansion of forehead." Sir John and his associates also saw a higher species of lunar bat-men "of infinitely greater personal beauty ... scarcely less lovely than the general representation of angels by the more imaginative school of painters."

Subsequently a *Sun* reporter, Richard Adams Locke, admitted that he had written the piece, which the *Sun* had represented as a reprint from the (nonexistent) *Edinburgh Journal of Science*. This episode, referred to as the Moon Hoax, fooled thousands of readers, especially — according to Edgar Allan Poe — the most educated ones. Poe noted, "Not one person in ten discredited it, and (strangest point of all!) the doubters were chiefly those who doubted without being able to say why — the ignorant, those uninformed in astronomy, people who *would not* believe because the thing was so novel." Historian of science Michael J. Crowe disputes the usual interpretation of Locke's motives, that he was a hoaxer, and contends that his purposes were satirical. He intended to poke fun at popular belief in life on other worlds. Instead of laughing at his account, as Locke thought they would do, his readers, to his considerable surprise, took it as gospel.

TLP, ET, and UFO.
Charles Fort, whose four classic books on anomalous phenomena were published between 1919 and 1932, had much of the satirist in him, too, but he also was seriously convinced of the reality of extraterrestrial visitation. A devoted reader of scientific journals, he collected numerous accounts of strange lights and other oddities on or near the moon. He linked these with reports of anomalous objects in the earth's atmosphere to argue that beings from other worlds had the earth under surveillance.

Fort's writings were seized upon by a small army of anomaly enthusiasts who called themselves "Forteans" and preserved and expanded upon his research in the years after his death in 1932. When "flying saucers" erupted on the world scene in the summer of 1947, the Forteans were the only people who were unsurprised; the Fortean Society and those influenced by it (such as contributors to the science-fiction magazine *Amazing*

● SOURCES:

Adamski, George. *Inside the Space Ships*. New York: Abelard-Schuman, 1955.

———. "I Photographed Space Ships." *Fate* 4, 5 (July 1951): 64–74.

Berlitz, Charles, and William L. Moore. *The Roswell Incident*. New York: Grosset and Dunlap, 1980.

Cameron, Winifred S. "Comparative Analyses of Observations of Lunar Transient Phenomena." *Icarus* 16 (1972): 339–87.

Chatelain, Maurice. *Our Ancestors Came from Outer Space: A NASA Expert Confirms Mankind's Extraterrestrial Origins*. Garden City, NY: Doubleday and Company, 1978.

Corliss, William R., ed. *Mysterious Universe: A Handbook of Astronomical Anomalies*. Glen Arm, MD: The Sourcebook Project, 1979.

———. *Strange Universe: A Sourcebook of Curious Astronomical Observations*. Glen Arm, MD: The Sourcebook Project, 1975.

———. *The Sun and Solar System Debris: A Catalog of Astronomical Anomalies*. Glen Arm,

Stories, which had taken to running articles on the evidence for space visitors) were well prepared for them.

In its July 1951 issue, *Fate*, a pulp digest devoted to "true mysteries" and co-founded by *Amazing* editor Ray Palmer, "Prof." George Adamski of Palomar Gardens, California, recounted his success in taking photographs of spaceships through his six-inch telescope. Adamski wrote, "I have taken all my pictures at night by the light of the moon because often I had noticed that a good number of the ships I saw moving through space appeared headed for the moon. Some of them seemed to land on the moon, close to the rim; while others passed over the rim and disappeared behind it.... I figure it is logical to believe that space ships might be using our moon for a base in their interplanetary travels."

On November 20, 1952, Adamski reported that he actually met a saucer pilot, a Venusian, in the desert of southern California. He then embarked on a colorful career as contactee and disciple of Space Brothers from Venus, Mars, and Saturn. In August 1954 a Venusian scoutcraft allegedly flew Adamski around the moon, showing him extraterrestrial cities and hangars as well as forests, lakes, and rivers.

To most people, including a great many ufologists, Adamski's *Inside the Space Ships* (1955), which details this lunar odyssey, read like the bad science-fiction novel it certainly was; those who believed it believed it fervently, however, and some sought to counter the scoffers with "proof" of Adamski's claims. One especially vigorous disciple, Fred Steckling, head of the George Adamski Foundation, produced a book, *We Discovered Alien Bases on the Moon* (1981), which purported to expose a vast official cover-up of both space people and an atmosphere on the moon. As evidence Steckling offered his interpretations of NASA lunar photographs. In a devastating critique astronomer Francis G. Graham remarks dryly, "Mr. Steckling shows 150 photos and drawings. One of these, of himself, we can believe."

Taking their cue from Adamski, other contactees of the 1950s and 1960s told of bases and beings on the moon. One of them, Howard Menger, even took a picture on the moon. His 1959 book *From Outer Space to You* contains a picture which, the caption informs us, "shows spacecraft landing near dome-shaped building." Ozark farmer Buck Nelson said he landed on the moon one memorable day in April 1955, in the company of Little Bucky of Venus, Little Bucky's dog Big Bo, and Buck's dog Teddy. "I was allowed to walk outside and look about a little," Nelson recalled. "I took a good look at a building so that I wouldn't get lost, as I was in strange territory, but Big Bo … went with Teddy and I [sic].... Children played with several sized dogs. They rode Big Bo like a pony and he would play with them too." Then the gang headed off for Venus.

Even conservative ufologists, however, were drawn to speculations about extraterrestrials on the moon. Though he rejected contactee testimony on such matters, Donald E. Keyhoe, a retired Marine Corps major, aviation journalist, and leading UFO proponent of the 1950s, made much of two amateur astronomers' observations, in 1953, of what they thought was a large natural bridge which had suddenly appeared near the Mare Crisium crater. Keyhoe wrote that this sudden appearance ruled out a natural explanation. Taking note of two centuries of observations of anomalous lights on the moon, he declared that the "evidence of *some* intelligent race on the moon seemed undeniable." Subsequently astronomers established that the "bridge" was an optical illusion.

Another writer of the period, M. K. Jessup, proposed an even more fantastic hypothesis. His *The Expanding Case for the UFO* (1957) defines the moon as the key to the mystery. Tens of thousands of years ago, Jessup writes, the pygmy races — much older, he says, than other human races — developed antigravity spaceships and escaped to the moon just as cataclysms wiped out other advanced civilizations such Atlantis and Mu. The pygmies continue to observe us from their present home, thus explaining both UFOs and the "little men" associated with them.

As clear photographs of the moon's surface taken during lunar explorations between 1969 and 1972 became available to the lay public, a few space enthusiasts, most prominently George H. Leonard (*Somebody Else Is on the Moon* [1976] and Don Wilson (*Our Mysterious Spaceship Moon* [1975]), professed to see evidence of extraterrestrial activities on the surface and charged that NASA was trying to suppress the most fantastic discovery of the century. Wilson held not just that spaceships are on the moon but that the moon is a spaceship — a vast hollow cosmic ark constructed thousands of years ago by an alien race.

In response to this growing popular lore, Francis Graham of the Pennsylvania Selenological Society prepared a critical review of all the claims. Though open-minded about the general topic of UFOs, Graham concluded that "there is not a single piece of unambiguous evidence for the existence of alien bases on the moon. The photography supplied by Leonard and Steckling comes in four categories: (1) Photos which show something which is readily interpreted as a natural feature by someone familiar with lunar morphology; (2) photos which are too fuzzed, out of resolution or overenlarged to tell what is there; (3) photos which appear to show something interesting and possibly artificial but which do not [appear so] when compared to other photos taken of the same area; (4) photos showing geological oddities not obviously artificial."

The Apollo aliens.
A yarn first published in a supermarket tabloid, *National Bulletin*, in September 1969 continues to circulate in fringe literature and is by now a staple of Space Age folklore. As the story goes, the Apollo 11 astronauts saw spaceships during the first landing on the moon on July 16, 1969. NASA managed to censor the radio transmissions so that the news media and therefore the rest of us were none the wiser, but someone slipped a tape of the transmission — reporting the appearance of two UFOs along a crater rim — to the *Bulletin*.

MD: The Sourcebook Project, 1986.

Crowe, Michael J. *The Extraterrestrial Life Debate 1750–1900: The Idea of a Plurality of Worlds from Kant to Lowell.* New York: Cambridge University Press, 1986.

Fort, Charles. *The Books of Charles Fort.* New York: Henry Holt and Company, 1941.

Graham, Francis G. *There Are No Alien Bases on the Moon.* Burbank, CA: William L. Moore Publications and Research, 1984.

Jessup, M. K. *The Expanding Case for the UFO.* New York: The Citadel Press, 1957.

Keyhoe, Donald E. *The Flying Saucer Conspiracy.* New York: Henry Holt and Company, 1955.

Leonard, George H. *Somebody Else Is on the Moon.* New York: David McKay Company, 1976.

Menger, Howard. *From Outer Space to You.* Clarksburg, WV: Saucerian Books, 1959.

Nelson, Buck. *My Trip to Mars, the Moon, and Venus.* Mountain View, AR: The Author, 1956.

Nixon, Stuart. "UFO Base on the Moon: Fact or Fic-

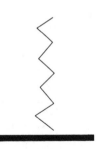

tion?" *UFO Quarterly Review* 1, 3 (July/ September 1973): 13–20.

Oberg, James E. "Myths and Mysteries of the Moon." *Fate* 33, 9 (September 1980): 38–46.

Steckling, Fred. *We Discovered Alien Bases on the Moon.* Vista, CA: George Adamski Foundation, 1981.

Wilson, Don. *Our Mysterious Spaceship Moon.* New York: Dell, 1975.

Four years later Stuart Nixon of the National Investigations Committee on Aerial Phenomena investigated the story and found, not to his surprise, that it contained not a shred of truth. The transcript of the supposed exchange between the astronauts (Neil Armstrong, Edwin Aldrin, and Michael Collins) and Mission Control contains elementary factual, terminological, and other errors. In any event, no such exchange could have been censored at the time of its transmission; the cessation of communication even for a short period would have been noticed immediately. When challenged to produce supporting evidence, the *Bulletin* could not do so; it could not even produce the reporter, identified as "Sam Pepper," who wrote the original account.

Though there seems no doubt that the story was concocted in the *Bulletin* office, it would be recycled, with elaborations, in such books as Maurice Chatelain's *Our Ancestors Came from Outer Space* (1978) and Charles Berlitz and William L. Moore's *The Roswell Incident* (1980). Chatelain claimed sources within NASA as his authority, and Berlitz and Moore referred vaguely to "additional confirmation ... from a source apparently associated with Anglia TV in London. According to this source, NASA was forced to change the originally intended landing site for the Eagle lander module because it was discovered that the first site was 'crawling' — presumably with somebody else's space hardware." Colonel Aldrin subsequently brought suit against Berlitz and Moore for reporting what he charged was a false story about him.

MAD GASSERS

In the late summer of 1944, lasting notoriety came to Mattoon, Illinois, in the person of an elusive attacker who terrorized the small east-central Illinois town (population 15,827, according to the 1940 census) for two long weeks. By the time events had run their course, the attacker would be pronounced nonexistent. The "mad gasser of Mattoon" survives as a classic example of mass hysteria. Still, intriguing questions about the episode remain.

Mattoon's phantom attacker first made his presence known on August 31, when a resident woke up feeling ill. He managed to get to the bathroom before he threw up. On returning the bedroom, he asked his wife if she had left the gas on. She said she hadn't, but when she tried to get up to check, she found she could not move. Elsewhere in town a young mother who heard her daughter coughing in another room also tried to leave her bed, with similar lack of success.

At 11 P.M. on September 1 a "sickening sweet odor in the bedroom" roused another young mother, Mrs. Bert Kearney, from sleep. As the odor quickly grew stronger, she "began to feel a paralysis of my legs and lower body," she reported. "I got frightened and screamed." An hour and a half later her husband, who was coming home from work, observed a strange man standing at the bedroom window. Kearney described him as "tall, dressed in dark clothing and wearing a tight-fitting cap." Kearney gave chase, but the prowler escaped.

These events took place before anyone had heard of a "mad gasser" or "phantom anesthetist," and whatever inspired them, it cannot have been mass hysteria. Unfortunately, at this stage the *Mattoon Journal-Gazette* picked up the story, calling Mrs. Kearney the "first victim," which not only was untrue but which also implied that more "victims" would join her. As it happened, other alleged attacks did follow, all reported in the kind of overwrought prose that frightened more than informed.

Several other residents complained to police that the sudden infusion of a "sickly sweet odor" into their homes had paralyzed them for as long as 90 minutes. No one else had seen the gasser, but late on the evening of September 5, as one couple returned home, the wife noticed a white cloth by the front door. When she picked it up, she happened to sniff it. "I had sensations similar to coming in contact with an electric current," she recounted. "The feeling raced down my body to my feet and then seemed to settle in my knees. It was a feeling of paralysis." Soon her lips and face were burning and swelling, her mouth was bleeding, and she was throwing up.

These dramatic symptoms had subsided by the time police got there, but their visit produced what seemed to be the first physical evidence: a skeleton key and an empty lipstick tube near the spot where the cloth had lain. Even as officers were interviewing the couple, however, a woman elsewhere in town was hearing a prowler outside her bedroom window. Before she could sit up, a gas seeped into the room rendering her immobile for several minutes.

Near midnight a woman called police to report that a man had tried to force his way through her door. Her screams frightened him off. According to press accounts, the man answered the gasser's general description, whatever that means. Possibly the incident had nothing to do with the phantom anesthetist (if he existed), but it was the kind of story that fueled the growing panic. In another instance, two nights later, a woman and her 11-year-old daughter said they heard someone trying to break open a window. They tried to get outside, but mysterious fumes overcame the mother and made her sick.

In a September 8 summary the *Herald*, published in nearby Decatur, noted, "Victims report that the first symptom is an electric shock which passes completely through the body. Later nausea develops, followed by partial paralysis. They also suffer burned mouths and throats and their faces become swollen."

As the days passed and the attacks continued, the community was outraged that the local police had not been able to catch the perpetrator. State authorities managed to dissuade local leaders who had planned a mass protest rally for the ninth. Meanwhile armed citizens prowled the streets at night, in defiance of the police commissioner's plea for them to get a grip on themselves. He said that a "gas maniac exists" but "many of the attacks are nothing more than hysteria. Fear of the gas man is entirely out of proportion to the menace of the relatively harmless gas he is spraying." Rumors were flying: the gasser was a lunatic, an "eccentric inventor" (the commissioner's pet theory, soon to be abandoned), or even an "apeman." The reasons for this curious last notion are lost to history.

The scare climaxed on September 10, a Sunday night, with two attacks which felled a total of five persons. By the next morning police were talking more and more skeptically, pointing to the absence of solid evidence and stipulating that all further complainants undergo examination at Mat-

An artist's imaginative drawing of Mattoon's "mad gasser" depicts him as a not-quite-human, possibly extraterrestrial being. Most authorities attribute the episode to mass hysteria. (Courtesy of Loren Coleman.)

toon Memorial Institution. A chemical analysis of the cloth from the incident five days earlier came to no particular conclusions. The next evening, when the police got calls from persons reporting attacks, the calls were dismissed as false alarms, even though in one case a physician who went to a victim's house smelled the gas himself.

At a press conference on the morning of the twelfth, the chief of police told reporters, "Local police, in cooperation with state officers, have checked and rechecked all reported cases, and we find absolutely no evidence to support stories that have been told. Hysteria must be blamed for such seemingly accurate accounts of supposed victims." Beyond that, he theorized, the odor of carbon tetrachloride from a nearby chemical plant may have been carried on the wind. He did not explain why this had not been a problem for Mattoon residents prior to August 31.

Even in the face of this official denial of his existence, the gasser made one last house call. On the evening of the thirteenth a witness saw a "woman dressed in man's clothing" spray gas through a window into Bertha Burch's bedroom. The next morning Mrs. Burch and her adult son found footprints of high-heeled shoes under the window. For reasons that will be apparent shortly, this may be the single most interesting case to come out of Mattoon.

The Botetourt gasser.

In 1945, writing in the *Journal of Abnormal and Social Psychology*, Donald M. Johnson reviewed the Mattoon scare and concluded that the local newspaper's lurid coverage was responsible for it from beginning to end. Johnson's paper proved influential in future scholarly assessments of mass panics.

Unknown to Johnson and most other commentators on the Mattoon episode then and now, a strikingly similar series of events took place in Botetourt (BOT-a-TOT) County, Virginia, in December 1933 and January 1934. Except for a brief item in the January 22, 1934, edition of the *New York Times*, the scare got only local (Virginia) coverage. It is highly unlikely that Mattoon residents were aware of it.

The first recorded attack occurred at a farm near Haymakertown late on the evening of December 22, when three separate infusions of gas into the house sickened eight members of a family and a visitor. Some of the victims thought they saw a man fleeing in the darkness. The gas caused nausea, headaches, facial swelling, and constriction of mouth and throat muscles. One victim, a 19-year-old woman, suffered convulsions for weeks afterwards. A police officer who arrived between the second and third attacks — after staying an hour, he left, and soon afterwards gas wafted through both floors of the house — found only one clue: the print of a woman's heel under the window the gas was believed to have passed through.

Over the next two weeks other persons reported similar nocturnal attacks. In one case witnesses saw a 1933 Chevrolet, with a man and woman inside, passing back and forth in front of a house around the time its occupants experienced the mysterious gas. In another instance a young mother attending to her baby said she heard a rattling window shade and mumbling voices outside. Suddenly the room filled with gas, and her body felt numb. While on his way to summon police after a gassing at his farm, F. B. Duval saw a man run toward a car parked on a rural road and drive away quickly. Duval and an officer examined the site soon afterwards and found prints of a woman's shoes.

Amid growing panic, residents of the county armed themselves and prowled back roads in search of suspicious strangers. On one occasion a searcher fired on a fleeing figure. On another, moments after a gas attack, one of the victims dashed outside in time to glimpse four men running in the direction of the nearby Blue Ridge Mountains. By the time the witness returned with a gun, he could no longer see them, but he could hear their voices. Despite skepticism in some quarters concerning the gasser's (or gassers') existence, physicians who had called on victims were certain he was (or they were) real. County Sheriff C. E. Williamson was likewise convinced.

One of the last gassings was reported near Lithia in nearby Roanoke County. Afterwards the victim found discolored snow with a sweet-smelling, oily substance in it. When analyzed, it turned out to consist of sulfur, arsenic, and mineral oil — something like the components, authorities thought, of insecticides. A trail of footprints led from the house to the barn, but none away from the barn. They were, according to press accounts, a "woman's tracks."

Michael T. Shoemaker, who investigated the episode in the 1980s, noted its many similarities to the later scare at Mattoon. "In both Mattoon and Botetourt," he wrote, "the principal physical effects were the same: a sickeningly sweet odor, nausea, paralysis, facial swelling and unconsciousness. These effects were confirmed by doctors and, moreover, in both cases doctors smelled the gas. Both gassers made repeat attacks on one family, multiple attacks in one night and assaults on unoccupied houses. The pattern of explanation was also similar, progressing from pranksters to lunatics to hysteria. Tantalizing but useless clues were found," including (Shoemaker's emphasis) *a woman's print beneath a window.*"

Horror or hysteria?

Decades later, the true causes of these strange occurrences remain no more than conjecture. Even in their time they made little sense — which is hardly evidence in itself that they were not genuinely anomalous. The hysteria explanation filled the vacuum created by the absence of any more logical explanation. It also served the purpose (especially where Mattoon was concerned) of rationalizing the civil authorities' inability to stop the attacks. Hysteria is a classic blame-the-victim strategy.

It is, however, more than that. Gas attacks in some ways reminiscent of those at Mattoon and Botetourt still are reported from time to time, typically in one building such as a school, a factory, or a theater. For example, in March 1972 workers in a Midwestern data-processing center complained of a mysterious cause that made them sick. Air, blood, and urine samples failed to detect anything out of the ordinary. Moreover, a worker —who did not speak English and was therefore socially isolated from the others — did not smell the gas even when others did. The scientists who investigated the attacks eventually told the workers a phony story — that an "atmospheric inversion" was responsible — and after that the attacks ceased. A later study by sociologists indicated that those workers most alienated from their jobs were the most susceptible.

Still, just enough aspects of the Mattoon and Botetourt incidents resist the mass-hysteria explanation and leave open the question of what really happened there.

● SOURCES:

"The Case of the Psychic Vapors." *Human Behavior* (January 1975): 13.

Coleman, Loren. *Mysterious America.* Boston, MA: Faber and Faber, 1983.

Johnson, Donald M. "The 'Phantom Anesthetist' of Mattoon: A Field Study of Mass Hysteria." *Journal of Abnormal and Social Psychology* 40 (1945): 175–86.

Shoemaker, Michael T. "The Mad Gasser of Botetourt." *Fate* 38, 6 (June 1985): 62–68.

———. "Resurrections." *Fortean Times* 49 (Winter 1987): 52–53.

Smith, Willy. "The Mattoon Gasser: A Modern Myth." *International UFO Reporter* 9, 6 (November/December 1984): 7, 9, 14.

MEN IN BLACK ———————————————

In the March 30, 1905, edition of the *Barmouth Advertiser*, a Welsh newspaper, it was reported that over a period of three nights a "man dressed in black" had appeared in the bedroom of an "exceptionally intelligent young woman of the peasant stock.... This figure has delivered a message to the girl which she is frightened to relate."

This curious incident allegedly occurred in the midst of a religious revival in which sightings of mysterious lights figured prominently. It is the first known report of a "man in black" in an arguably UFO context.

In 1953 men in black (or, as they eventually would be called, MIB) entered twentieth-century folklore permanently when Albert K. Bender of Bridgeport, Connecticut, abruptly closed down his popular International Flying Saucer Bureau (IFSB) and refused to elaborate on a cryptic statement in the last issue (October 1953) of the IFSB magazine *Space Review*. The statement indicated that Bender now knew the answer to the UFO mystery but could not publish it because of "orders from a higher source." In addition, he urged "those engaged in saucer work to please be very cautious."

Pressed by Gray Barker, who had been IFSB's chief investigator, Bender would say only that three men in black suits had visited him in September, told him what UFOs are, and threatened him with prison if he revealed what they had told him. The experience was so traumatic that Bender subsequently fell ill. He told Barker that the strangers were "members of the United States government."

The MIB's exact nature grew more ambiguous in Bender's reluctant retelling of the tale, and soon some suspected that the MIB were agents not of U.S. intelligence but of alien intelligence. Barker wrote a scary, paranoia-driven book on the episode, *They Knew Too Much About Flying Saucers* (1956), and over the next few years exploited the "Bender mystery" in various publications. Soon Bender's visitors were being identified variously as demons, agents of the International Bankers, or representatives of a civilization inside the earth.

In 1962, Bender wrote, and Barker published, *Flying Saucers and the Three Men* — a wild story which only the most impressionable readers took to be anything other than a clumsy science-fiction novel. In it Bender was taken to the South Pole by monstrous aliens, who then monitored his activities until 1960, when they returned to their home planet.

Men-in-black stories were revived in the 1960s when a New York writer, John A. Keel, recounted episodes of MIB harassment reported by UFO witnesses in New York, Ohio, West Virginia, and elsewhere. Keel even claimed some personal encounters: "I kept rendezvous with black Cadillacs on Long Island, and when I tried to pursue them they would disappear impossibly on dead-end roads.... More than once I woke up in the middle of the night to find myself unable to move, with a dark apparition standing over me." In Keel's telling, the MIB were not government agents or even human beings but paranormal entities associated with the UFO intelligences themselves. Frequently described as being vaguely Oriental in appearance, they behaved strangely, asking odd or even rude questions of those whom they confronted. They usually traveled in large black cars.

Keel warned investigators, "Do not attempt to apprehend MIB yourself. Do not attack them physically. Approach them with great caution. They frequently employ hypnotic techniques."

According to Keel, men in black had interacted with such historical figures as Julius Caesar, Thomas Jefferson, Napoleon, and Malcolm X. Moreover, "the general descriptions of the vampires... are identical to the 'men in black'." The danger of MIB visitation to those interested in UFOs — especially "the neurotic, the gullible, and the immature" — is such, Keel warned, that parents should "forbid their children from becoming involved [in UFO study]. Schoolteachers and other adults should not encourage teenagers to take an interest in the subject."

MIB reports were not confined to Keel's witnesses or even to the United States. In May 1975, two weeks after a dramatic sighting from his Piper Pa-24 — a sighting confirmed on the radar screens at the Mexico City airport — a young pilot was pursued down the freeway by four black-suited, "Scandinavian"-looking men in a black limousine. After forcing him to the side of the road, they warned him not to discuss his sighting; the pilot was on his way to do a television interview. A month later one of the strangers reappeared and threatened him again as he was on his way to a hotel to talk with J. Allen Hynek, the prominent American astronomer and UFO investigator. That was his last meeting with the MIB, whom he remembered as tall and strangely white; "I never saw them blink," he added.

By the late 1980s such tales were sufficiently numerous to warrant the attention of the *Journal of American Folklore*. The author, Peter M.

● SOURCES:

Barker, Gray. *They Knew Too Much About Flying Saucers.* New York: University Books, 1956.

Bender, Albert K. *Flying Saucers and the Three Men.* Clarksburg, WV: Saucerian Books, 1962.

Clark, Jerome. "Carlos de los Santos and the Men in Black." *Flying Saucer Review* 24, 4 (January 1979): 8–9.

———. "Men in Black." In Curtis G. Fuller, ed. *Proceedings of the First International UFO Congress*, 273–93. New York: Warner Books, 1980.

Keel, John A. *UFOs: Operation Trojan Horse.* New York: G. P. Putnam's Sons, 1970.

———. *The Mothman Prophecies.* New York: Saturday Review Press/ E. P. Dutton and Company, 1975.

———. "Investigating UFOs." *Strange Magazine* 6 (1990): 12–15.

Rojcewicz, Peter M. "The 'Men in Black' Experience and Tradition: Analogues with the Traditional Devil Hypothesis." *Journal of American Folklore* 100, 396 (April/June 1987): 148–60.

Rojcewicz, surveyed the MIB's role in flying-saucer legends and related it to earlier demonic traditions. He also told of his own MIB encounter, though giving himself the pseudonym "Michael Elliot." While doing research on UFOs in a library, he was approached by a dark-featured, dark-suited man who, speaking briefly in a slight accent about flying saucers, placed his hand on Rojcewicz's shoulder and said, "Go well in your purpose," and vanished.

Schwarz, Berthold Eric. "The Man-in-Black Syndrome." *Flying Saucer Review* Pt. I 23, 4 (1977):9–15; Pt. II. 23, 5 (1978): 22–25.

MERFOLK

"Are we to believe that all those beings equally exist, and, on the principle that there can be no smoke without a fire, are we to hold that there would be no popular conception of the banshee, the leprechaun, or the *Maighdean-mhara* (sea-maiden, mermaid), and consequently no tales told about them," the Irish historian and folklorist Douglas Hyde asked, "if such beings did not exist, and from time to time allow themselves to be seen like the wood-martin and the kingfisher?"

Hyde was venting his exasperation on a colleague, W. Y. Evans-Wentz, who had given him space in his *The Fairy-Faith in Celtic Countries* (first published in 1911) to dispute Evans-Wentz's heretical view that fairies may be real entities who dwell in a paranormal dimension of existence. Something like Hyde's question will occur to anyone who reads reports — and there is (or was) no shortage of them — of merfolk "sightings."

Consider, for example, the results of a 1723 official inquiry into the merfolk problem. A Danish Royal Commission set out to lay the issue to rest; if it found merfolk mere fantasy, then those who continued to speak of them would find themselves in trouble with the law. Free expression about such matters was preserved, however, when members of the commission themselves spotted a merman near the Faroe Islands. On the approach of their ship, it sank into the water but surfaced shortly afterwards to stare intently at them with its deep-set eyes. A few minutes of this scrutiny proved so unsettling that the ship effected a retreat. As it was doing so, the merman puffed out his cheeks and emitted a "deep roar" before diving out of sight.

Three decades later, writing in his *Natural History of Norway* (1752–1753), Bishop Erik Pontoppidan had this to say about merfolk sightings: "Here, in the diocese of Bergen, as well as in the manor of Nordland, there are several hundreds of persons of credit and reputation who affirm, with the strongest assurance, that they have seen this kind of creature."

The mythic background.

Merfolk legends or their equivalents have an ancient lineage. The earliest one known concerns the Babylonian god Oannes, human to the waist and fish-shaped from there on, who rose from the Erythrean Sea to impart knowledge and culture to the human race. (In modern times Oannes would reemerge into prominence as a prime candidate for an early extraterrestrial visitor, nominated by no less than celebrity-astronomer Carl Sagan.) Merfolklike gods and goddesses were worshipped in Syria, India, China, Greece, and Rome. In later centuries they would figure in a nearly universal folklore. We know them as merfolk, mermaids, or mermen because of the Old English word for sea: mere. Such creatures by various names were known, and allegedly sighted, all over Western Europe and just about everywhere else.

Among the early chroniclers of the phenomenon was Pliny the Elder, a first-century naturalist who accepted their existence, remarking that "it is no fabulous tale that goeth of them ... only their body is rough and scaled all over, even in those parts wherein they resemble a woman." He referred to a sighting by coastal residents who clearly saw one such creature, apparently more than once. Later they heard it dying, making a "piteous moan, crying and chattering very heavily." Bodies were found: "Many of these Nereides or Mermaids were seen cast upon the sands, and lying dead."

A variant of merfolk legends concerned the North European seal-folk or selkie, described succinctly in the classic folk ballad "The Grey Selkie of Sule Skerrie":

> I am a man upon the land
> I am a selkie [seal] in the sea.

When repairing to land to pass themselves off as people, selkies simply removed their seal skin. In many folktales merfolk do the same, enabling them to marry landbound mortals and even produce children by these unions, until at last the inevitable homesickness for the sea overtakes them, and they are gone in a splash.

Sailors usually regarded the sighting of a mermaid as a dire omen of imminent death, usually in the storm that follows such an encounter. In "The Mermaid," a traditional ballad, a ship's crew spots such a creature sitting on a rock with a comb and a glass in its hand. The captain speaks up:

> "This fishy mermaid has warned me of our doom
> And we shall sink to the bottom of the sea"....
> And three times around spun our gallant ship ...
> And she went to the bottom of the sea.

Merfolk of Scotland.

But mermaids figured in more than legend and lore. As one folklorist has remarked, "Medieval belief in the mermaid ... was widespread and substantiated." The "substantiation," as already noted, consisted of claimed sight-

ings, at least some of which were associated with individuals generally viewed as sane and sensible. Such "sightings" did not end, by any means, in the Middle Ages.

On January 12, 1809, two women standing on a beach at Sandside, Caithness, in remote northeastern Scotland, saw what looked like the face of a young woman — "round and plump and of a bright pink hue" — in the sea. It then disappeared into the water, to reappear a short time later. When they were able to observe more of the top part of its body, they could see that it had well-formed human breasts. From time to time it lifted a long, thin white arm above the waves and toss back its long green hair. ("It is interesting to note," twentieth-century Scottish folklorist R. Macdonald Robertson would write, "that whereas in all the traditional mermaid stories the maid-of-the-sea has golden hair, in eye-witness accounts it ranges in color from green to black.")

After one of the witnesses published her account, which understandably created a sensation, William Munro wrote this letter to the *London Times*, published in its September 8 edition:

> About 12 years ago, when I was Parochial Schoolmaster at Reay, in the course of my walking on the shore of Sandside Bay, being a fine warm day in summer, I was induced to extend my walk toward Sandside Head, when my attention was arrested by the appearance of a figure resembling an unclothed human female, sitting upon a rock extending into the sea, and apparently in the action of combing its hair, which flowed around its shoulders, and was of a light brown color.

> The forehead was round, the face plump, the cheeks ruddy, the eyes blue, the mouth and lips of a natural form, resembling those of a man; the teeth I could not discover, as the mouth was shut; the breasts and the abdomen, the arms and fingers of the size of a full-grown body of the human species; the fingers, from the action in which the hands were employed, did not appear to be webbed, but as to this I am not positive.

> It remained on the rock three or four minutes after I observed it, and was exercised during that period in combing its hair, which was long and thick, and of which it appeared proud; and then dropped into the sea, from whence it did not reappear to me.

> I had a distinct view of its features, being at no great distance on an eminence above the rock on which it was sitting, and the sun brightly shining.

> Immediately before its getting into its natural element it seemed to have observed me, as the eyes were directed towards the eminence on which I stood.... [P]revious to the period I beheld this object, I had heard it frequently reported by several persons, and some of them persons whose veracity I never heard disputed, that they had seen such a phenomenon as I have described, though then, like many others, I was

247

not disposed to credit their testimony on this subject. I can say of a truth, that it was only by seeing the phenomenon, I was perfectly convinced of its existence.

If the above narrative can in any degree be subservient towards establishing the existence of a phenomenon, hitherto almost incredible to naturalists, or to remove the skepticism of others, who are ready to dispute everything which they cannot fully comprehend, you are welcome to it....

Apparently such creatures were active off the coast of Scotland during this period. In a long survey of mermaid and merman sightings, the *London Mirror* of November 16, 1822, gave this account:

In 1811, a young man, named John McIsaac, of Corphine, in Kintyre, in Scotland, made oath on examination, at Campbeltown, before the sheriff-substitute of Kintyre, that he saw on the afternoon of the 13th of October, in that year, on a black rock on the seacoast, an animal of the particulars of which he gives a long and curious detail.

He states, that the upper half of it was white, and of the shape of a human body; the other half, towards the tail, of a brindled or reddish-grey color, apparently covered with scales; but the extremity of the tail itself was of a greenish-red shining color; that the head was covered with long hair; at times it would put back the hair on both sides of its head; it would also spread its tail like a fan; and, while so extended, the tail continued in tremulous motion, and, when drawn together again, it remained motionless, and appeared to the deponent to be about 12 or 14 inches broad; that the hair was very long and light brown; that the animal was between four and five feet long; that it had a head, hair, arms, and body, down to the middle, like a human being; that the arms were short in proportion to the body, which appeared to be about the thickness of that of a young lad, and tapering gradually to the point of the tail; that when stroking its head, as above mentioned, the fingers were kept close together, so that he cannot say whether they were webbed or not; that he saw it for two hours, the rock on which it lay being dry; that, after the sea had so far retired as to leave the rock dry to the height of five feet above the water, it tumbled clumsily into the sea; a minutes after[,] he observed the animal above water, and then saw every feature of its face, having all the appearance of a human being, with very hollow eyes.

The cheeks were of the same color with the rest of the face; the neck seemed short; and it was constantly, with both hands stroking and washing its breasts, which was half immersed in the water; he, therefore, cannot say whether its bosom was formed like a woman's or not. He saw no other fins or feet upon it, but as described. It continued above water for a few minutes, and then disappeared.

Three prominent citizens, the Rev. Dr. George Robertson, Campbeltown minister Norman MacLeod, and lawyer James Maxwell, who were there when McIsaac delivered his testimony, stated that "we know of no reason why his veracity should be called into question;... from the manner in which he delivered his evidence, we are satisfied that he was impressed with a perfect belief."

Five days later, on November 2, another eyewitness made sworn testimony to Kintyre's Sheriff-Substitute Duncan Campbell. Katherine Loynachan stated that on the afternoon of October 13, as she was herding cattle near the sea shore, she saw a creature sliding off one of the rocks and dropping into the water, surfacing six yards out. It had long, dark hair, white skin on its upper part, and dark brown skin on its lower, which was fishlike. In Campbell's account of her testimony, it

> turned about with the face of it towards the shore, where the declarant was standing, and having laid one hand, which was like a boy's hand, upon another rock that was near the first rock it came nearer to the shore than it was; that at this time the declarant saw the face of it distinctly which had all the appearance of the face of a child and as white, and at this time the animal was constantly rubbing or washing its breast with one hand, the fingers being close together.... [A]fter this animal continued to look towards the declarant for about half a minute, it swam about and disappeared, but in a very short time thereafter she saw the head and face of this animal appearing above water again, and swimming away south toward the farm of Corphine, but soon after disappeared, and the declarant saw it no more.

The girl was so reluctant to credit the testimony of her own senses that at first she told herself this was a boy who had fallen out of a boat and was seeking rescue. Campbell interviewed, and secured sworn testimony from, the witness's father, who recalled his daughter's running home to tell him about a strange boy who was swimming along the shore. The father, mother, and daughter all went to look but saw nothing.

A series of sightings took place off Scotland's west coast in the summer of 1814. When a frightened boy reported seeing a creature half human and half fish, he got nothing but ridicule for his efforts. A month later a group of children saw what they thought was a drowning woman, whom closer examination revealed to be something else entirely. According to a letter from a local person (*York Chronicle*, September 1):

> The upper part was exactly like a woman, the skin appeared very white, and a good deal of color in the cheeks, and very long darkish looking hair; the arms were very well proportioned above, but tapered very much towards the hands, which were no larger than a child's of eight or 10 years old, the tail was like an immense large cuddy fish ... in color and shape.

Some of the children had gone off to alert nearby farmers. By the time they arrived, the creature had swum close enough to shore so that one man, who bore a rifle, expressed his intention to shoot it, but the others dissuaded him from doing so. He contented himself with whistling at the creature. The whistle caused it to turn around and glance at him. It "remained in sight for two hours, at times making a hissing noise like a goose." It was seen on two subsequent occasions, "always early in the morning and when the sea was calm."

At Port Gordon, on August 15 of that same year, fishermen Thomas Johnstone and William Gordon were a quarter-mile from shore when they spotted, not far from them, a merman. The local schoolmaster, George McKenzie, interviewed them shortly afterwards and the next day sent an account to the editor of the *Caledonian Mercury*. The merman, he reported, was of "swarthy" countenance, with small eyes, flat nose, large mouth, and remarkably long arms. After 15 seconds it dived under water, resurfacing farther away from the boat, now accompanied by "another, whom the men assumed to be female, as they could perceive she had breasts, and her hair was not curled, but reached to a little below the shoulders; the skin of this last one too was fairer than the other's." Terrified, Johnstone and Gordon raced for the shore. The two creatures continued to gaze at them even after they made land.

Around 1830 persons at work along the shore of Benbecula, one of the islands in the Hebrides chain (off Scotland's northwest coast), spotted a small creature, half woman and half fish, in the water a few feet away. It was turning somersaults in the water as if at play. When some men tried to capture it, it evaded them. Finally a little boy hit it on the back with some stones, and it disappeared. A few days later the body washed up on shore two miles away.

According to Duncan Shaw, the district sheriff, who examined the body carefully, "the upper part of the creature was about the size of a well-fed child of three or four years of age, with an abnormally developed breast. The hair was long, dark and glossy, while the skin was white, soft and tender. The lower part of the body was like a salmon, but without scales." It was "interred in the presence of a large assemblage of the Hebridean people in the burial-ground at Nunton, where the grave is pointed out to this day," R. Macdonald Robertson stated in 1961. "I have seen it myself."

Reports of merfolk in the seas off Scotland continued through the rest of the nineteenth century and even into the twentieth. In August 1949 fishermen off Craig More claimed to have had several sightings.

New World merfolk.
Of all purported sighters of mermaids (or sighters of purported mermaids), Christopher Columbus is easily the most famous. On his voyage of discovery into the West Indies, he saw three of them "leaping a good distance out of the sea" and found them "not so fair as they are painted." In fact, this vague description, if we can draw any conclusion from it at all, is consistent with the behavior of dugongs.

A more detailed, if less plausible, story comes from the seventeenth-century explorer of America, John Smith. Smith, sailing through the West

Indies in 1614, noticed what he first took to be a young woman in the water. In Smith's appreciative but not uncritical appraisal she had "large eyes, rather too round, finely shaped nose (a little too short), well-formed ears, rather too long, and her long green hair imparted to her an original character by no means unattractive." Just as Smith began to "feel the first pains of love," she moved in such a way as to reveal that "from below the waist the woman gave way to the fish."

"One may be inclined to question the veracity of the susceptible Captain Smith," Sir Arthur Waugh, a scholarly authority on merfolk lore, observes, then adds, "It is much more difficult to doubt the detailed reports of... sober and responsible people," among whom he numbers a Capt. Whitbourne. In 1610, while sailing a small boat into harbor at St. John's, Newfoundland, Whitbourne spotted a strange creature swimming in his direction and "looking cheerfully as [if] it had been a woman, by the Face, Eyes, Nose, Mouth, Earse, Necke and Forehead." It did not get a cheerful reception. Deeply alarmed, Whitbourne backed hastily away. The creature then turned around and attempted to board a companion boat belonging to William Hawkridge, who banged it on the head. It disappeared under the water. Hawkridge later offered this laconic comment: "Whether it was a mermaid or no ... I leave it for others to judge."

The mermaid should have considered itself lucky that it did not suffer the fate of a merman who that same century tried to get into a boat in Casco Bay, off the coast of southern Maine. The boat's occupant, a Mr. Mitter, is said to have slashed off one of its arms. It sank, "dying the waters purple with its blood," in the words of a contemporary chronicler.

A second sighting, not long after that in the waters off Nova Scotia, occurred to the crews of three French vessels. This time they chased and attempted to capture a merman with ropes, but to no avail. "He brushed his mossy hair out of his eyes which seemed to cover his body as well — as much as seen above water, in some places more, in others less," the captain of one of the ships recorded. The merman dived, never to be seen again, "to the great dejection of the fishermen."

Another of Waugh's "sober and responsible people," the celebrated New World explorer Henry Hudson, noted the following in his journal:

> This evening [June 15, 1610] one of our company, looking overboard, saw a mermaid, and, calling up some of the company to see her, one more of the crew came up, and by that time she was come close to the ship's side, looking earnestly on the men. A little after a sea came and overturned her.

> From the navel upward, her back and breasts were like a woman's, as they say that saw her; her body as big as one of us, her skin very white, and long hair hanging down behind, of color black. In her going down they saw her tail, which was like the tail of a porpoise, speckled like a mackerel. Their names that saw her were Thomas Hilles and Robert Rayner.

Of this incident the eminent Victorian naturalist Philip Gosse remarked, "Seals and walruses must have been as familiar to those polar mariners as cows to a milkmaid. Unless the whole story was a concocted lie between the two men, reasonless and objectless, and the worthy old navigator doubtless knew the character of his men, they must have seen some form of being as yet unrecognized."

In 1797 a Dr. Chisholm visited the tiny island of Berbice in the Caribbean. He spent time with Governor Van Battenburgh and others who told him of repeated sightings, in the island's rivers, of strange creatures known to the Indians as mene mamma (mother of waters). In his 1801 book *Malignant Fever in the West Indies*, Chisholm wrote:

> *The upper portion resembles the human figure, the head is smaller in proportion, sometimes bare, but oftener covered with a copious quantity of long black hair. The shoulders are broad, and the breasts large and well formed. The lower portion resembles the tail portion of a fish, is of immense dimension, the tail forked, not unlike that of the dolphin.... The color of the skin is either black or tawny.... They have been generally observed in a sitting posture in the water, none of the lower extremity being discovered until they are disturbed; when by plunging, the tail appears, and agitates the water to a considerable distance round. They have been always seen employing in smoothing their hair, or stroking their faces and breasts with their hands, or something resembling hands. In this posture, and thus employed, they have been frequently taken for Indian women bathing.*

And finally, this from an 1820 issue of the *American Journal of Science:*

> *Extract from the log book of the ship Leonidas, sailing for New-York towards Havre [France], Asa Swift master; May 1817. Lat. 44 degrees, 6 degrees north. First part of the day light variable winds and cloudy; at two P.M. on the larboard quarter, at the distance of about half the ship's length, saw a strange fish. Its lower parts were like a fish; its belly was all white; the top of the back brown, and there was the appearance of short hair as far as the top of its head. From the breast upwards, it had a near resemblance to a human being and looked upon the observers very earnestly; as it was but a short distance from the ship, all the afternoon, we had a good opportunity to observe its motions and shape. No one on board ever saw the like fish, before; all believe it to be a Mermaid.*

> *The second mate Mr. Stevens, an intelligent young man, told me the face was nearly white, and exactly like that of a human person; that its arms were about half as long as his, with hands resembling his own; that it stood erect out of the water about two feet, looking at the ship and sails with great earnestness. It would remain in this attitude, close along side, ten or fifteen minutes at a time, and then dive and appear on the other side. It remained about them six hours. Mr. Stevens also stated that its hair was black on the head and exactly resembled a*

man's; that below the arms, it was a perfect fish in form, and that the whole length from the head to the tail [was] about five feet.

Explanations.

In the summer of 1978, Filipino fisherman Jacinto Fetalvero let slip the secret of his recent fishing success. One moonlit night he had met a beautiful mermaid, with "amiable bluish eyes, reddish cheeks, and green scales on her tail." She helped him "secure a bountiful catch." A torrent of ridicule ensued, and Fatalvero thereafter refused to discuss the subject.

If merfolk are still "seen," whatever that means, we may be confident that few are so naive as Fetalvero about their certain reception. Popular opinion, after all, still cannot bear even such relative commonplaces as sightings of UFOs. Even the (relatively speaking) mundane sea serpents and lake monsters — which, whether they exist or not, are in no sense zoologically out of the question — remain objects of merriment to most, and proof of mass "credulity" and susceptibility to "pseudoscience" to humorless others.

So what chance have merfolk? It is undeniably true that they appear biologically preposterous. It is also true that belief in them has given rise to numerous hoaxes, some quite amusing. Folklorist Horace Beck tells us of the eccentric Robert S. Hawker who in the mid-1820s, "before he donned the holy robes of the ministry, used to disguise himself as a mermaid, sit on a rock and sing in the moonlight — much to the awe of the villagers round about." In the mid-nineteenth century Japanese fishermen supplemented their incomes by manufacturing mermaid corpses by attaching the top halves of dead monkeys to the bottom halves of fish. P. T. Barnum and any number of sideshow hustlers since him have separated fools from their money by offering views of dead and living mermaids.

Probably very few people today are even aware that their ancestors, or some of them anyway, believed they had actually *observed* merfolk. As we have seen, published accounts in respected newspapers, magazines, and journals insisted on the credibility of witnesses, who sometimes gave sworn testimony. Modern analysts of this testimony — scientists and folklorists mostly; anomalists and paranormalists have almost universally shied away from it — take it seriously and agree that it poses questions which merit better than a mere hooting down. Among the proposed solutions have been sea cows, manatees, and dugongs, which in the words of scientist Richard Carrington "became 'transformed' into a mermaid by the expectant attention of the superstitious mariners who saw it."

Such identifications suffer from two immediate problems:

(1) According to a sighting survey by Gwen Benwell and Arthur Waugh, nearly three-quarters reportedly occurred far from areas where manatees, dugongs, and manatees are known to exist.

(2) Moreover, though plausible in cases of long-distance sightings where perceptual errors may be expected to occur, these animals (the latter

two, incidentally, found only in tropical climes) in hardly any way resemble the creatures described in the most interesting sightings, which characteristically claim not only a close view but an extended one. As Benwell and Waugh put it, "It is asking a lot of a maritime race to believe that sailors, with the trained powers of observation which their own safety, and that of their ship, so often depend, could commit such a blunder" of monumental perception.

That, however, is not quite reason to abandon such explanations in all cases. Consider the following:

In a 1927 *Illustrated London News* article naturalist W. P. Pycraft remarked on a recent mermaid sighting:

> *A journalist brought me a letter for my comment, written by a lady who, in passing quite recently down the Red Sea, had seen a "veritable mermaid." Hitherto, she averred, she had regarded such creatures as mere figments of the imagination; but now she no longer doubted, for had she not just seen one with her own eyes? It was some nine feet long, very much like a woman, but emphatically ugly. Its face was hideous; it hands looked as though they had been thrust into some fingerless glove; but it had no legs. The body terminated in a great ground, flat tail, and its skin, which was bare, was dark-grey in color. But there it was, an indubitable "mermaid"! The letter was apparently written in all seriousness.*

Pycraft rightly deduced that the woman had seen a dugong. From that he concluded, less convincingly, that it was now established that dugongs are the cause of mermaid sightings. Unfortunately, he failed to give any thought to this not-irrelevant consideration: that while the woman's identification of the animal was absurdly mistaken, her description of it was accurate, and she had not described a mermaid.

On the other hand, the people of New Ireland, an island province of Papua New Guinea, *did* describe merfolk. Called ri (and pronounced ree), these creatures were said to look like human beings down to their genitals; the legless lower trunk ended in a pair of lateral fins. Or so native informants told a visiting American anthropologist, Roy Wagner, in the late 1970s. The native witnesses claimed that the creatures reminded them of the mermaids on tuna-fish cans, though they did not regard them as intelligent beings. On one occasion Wagner himself saw a "long, dark body swimming at the surface horizontally." His companions identified it as a ri.

Though Wagner was positive these creatures were not dugongs, in fact people who lived farther north on the island considered ri just another name for dugong. A February 1985 expedition by American cryptozoologists produced underwater photographs of a ri — an unambiguous dugong — and solved at least part of the puzzle. Expedition member Thomas R. Williams pondered the remaining mystery, for which he had no answer, of "how myths of merfolk can arise and persist in the face of the obvious reality of the dugong."

● SOURCES:

Beck, Horace. *Folklore and the Sea*. Middletown, CT: The Marine Historical Association/ Wesleyan University Press, 1973.

Benwell, Gwen, and Arthur Waugh. *Sea Enchantress: The Tale of the Mermaid and Her Kin*. New York: The Citadel Press, 1965.

Berman, Ruth. "Mermaids." In Malcolm South, ed. *Mythical and Fabulous Creatures: A Source Book and Research Guide*, 133–45. New York: Greenwood Press, 1987.

Blyth, Harry. "A Mermaid." *Notes and Queries* 5, 3 (February 27, 1875): 168.

Carrington, Richard. *Mermaids and Mastodons: A Book of Natural and Unnatural History*. New York: Rinehart and Company, 1957.

Clayton, Paul. *Whaling and Sailing Songs from the Days of Moby Dick*. Tradition Records, 1956.

Costello, Peter. *The Magic Zoo: The Natural History of Fabulous Animals*. New York: St. Martin's Press, 1979.

Farish, Lucius, ed. *Omega*. Worcester,

We have no way of knowing how widely the lessons from this episode can be applied, for the simple reason that in our time no one else has ever mounted a scientific investigation of merfolk sightings as they were occurring. Nearly all commentary on the matter focuses on reports from the distant past to the nineteenth century, and therefore the theories can only be speculative.

Perhaps the most ingenious is that proposed by two *Nature* writers who tied Norse merman reports to optical effects produced by a "moderate [atmospheric] inversion," showing how the resulting distortions on the ocean surface could make killer whales, walruses, and jutting rocks look much like what the sailors reported they saw. The authors respected the witnesses' testimony, including their assertion that storms followed merfolk appearances. As behavioral scientist David J. Hufford remarks of this study, "an improved understanding of naturally occurring atmospheric optical anomalies did result from a serious consideration of an apparently fabulous medieval belief"; furthermore, the scientists "were able to document with a high degree of confidence the role of accurate observations in the development of a medieval tradition, and the accurate correlation of these observations with impending storms, apparently achieved by properly performed inductive reasoning and empirical generalization."

This sort of explanation will not necessarily enable us to unravel the enigma of the Scottish and New World sightings recounted earlier. If anything, cloudy matters only get foggier. If we assume that these sightings are not outright fictions — and few scholars of the subject believe they are — we must also assume that the observers were wildly mistaken, that what they thought they saw was only vaguely related to what they really saw. Remember, some of these sightings are supposed to have been from a distance of no more than a few feet.

If misperception under these circumstances seems inconceivable, remember the ri. But don't remember *only* the ri; remember, too, the Norse mermen which, if they did not exist as the sailors thought they did, were described precisely enough for scholars centuries later to discern their cause.

In short, to the vital question of whether we ought to trust the reports, no sure answer leaps up to satisfy us with its certainty. Some observations are precise and credible. Others are startlingly at variance with reality. Beyond this the paucity of modern investigations frustrates further understanding. It forces those who take up the question to dump a mountain's worth of theory on a mole hill's worth of solid information.

Merfolk as unknowns.

Michel Meurger, a French folklorist and authority on the lore of fabulous water beasts, derides biological explanations of merfolk sightings as naive and reductionistic. He considers them "visionary experiences," or vivid hallucinations which take their shape from images from popular superstition. He is almost certainly right in a number of cases, but such a hypothesis

MA: Controversial Phenomena Bulletin, 1965.

Heuvelmans, Bernard. "Annotated Checklist of Apparently Unknown Animals with Which Cryptozoology Is Concerned." *Cryptozoology* 5 (1986): 1–26.

Hufford, David J. *The Terror That Comes in the Night: An Experience-Centered Study of Supernatural Assault Traditions.* Philadelphia, PA: University of Pennsylvania Press, 1982.

Lehn, W. H., and I. Schroeder. "The Norse Merman as an Optical Phenomenon." *Nature* 289 (1981): 362–66.

Meurger, Michel, with Claude Gagnon. *Lake Monster Traditions: A Cross-Cultural Analysis.* London: Fortean Tomes, 1988.

Phillips, John Pavin. "A Story of a Mermaid." *Notes and Queries* 2, 9 (May 12, 1860): 360–61.

Pycraft, W. P. "The World of Science: Mermaids." *Illustrated London News* (February 19, 1927): 294.

Redpath, Jean. *Jean Redpath.* Philo Records, 1987.

Rickard, R.J.M. "Strange Tales: Mermaids." *Fort-*

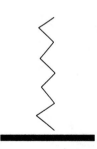

begins to look a bit labored when placed against the testimonies of multiple witnesses.

Another problem is that the merfolk of experience and the merfolk of popular superstition are manifestly different entities. The latter, intelligent beings with supernatural powers, can speak like normal human beings and even shed their fishy bottoms to live on land and romance or wed dwellers on the land. The merfolk of sightings neither speak nor communicate; for that matter they give no particular indication of possessing more than an animal's level of intelligence. (As Robertson notes, as we have already seen, even their hair color is different from that of their folkloric counterparts.)

So are they animals of some unknown type? Addressing the issue only reluctantly after dismissing it virtually out of hand in his earlier writings, Bernard Heuvelmans, the father of cryptozoology, stated in a 1986 paper, "Only a still-unrecorded species of recent Sirenia [dugongs, manatees, sea cows], or possibly — though much less likely — an unknown form of primate adapted to sea-life, could explain the abundance and persistence of merfolk reports in certain seas up to modern times." Benwell and Waugh, authors of the best modern book on merfolk lore, *Sea Enchantress* (1965), come to essentially the same conclusion.

Even if not supernatural, such an animal would be extraordinary indeed. It is hard to believe any such thing exists, not only because *a priori* it seems beyond zoological reason but also because no bodies have washed ashore and found their way into scientists' hands. These would not be, it should be emphasized, creatures living in remote depths, from which remains would not surface, but animals that cavorted frequently in shallow offshore waters. If merfolk were real, flesh-and-blood citizens of the oceanic regions of consensus reality, we would have more than sightings to document them.

Which does not explain everything, of course. One could argue that merfolk reports have as much claim to our attention as the Flatwoods monster, Mothman, flying humanoids, hairy bipeds, and reptile men, none of which makes much sense either. But someone else could retort that at least with these, there are living witnesses to interview and, sometimes, a tantalizing fragment of what may be physical evidence — a footprint, a hair, a blurry photograph — to take into account, not to mention a laboratory.

Yet it is in the nature of such things that huge claims are nearly always married to small evidence. The evidence for merfolk, consisting of the words of long-dead men and women, is even more minuscule, and it shrinks with each passing year. In the end it does not permit us — if, at any rate, we demand scrupulous intellectual honesty of ourselves, even in the face of the unthinkable — to laugh into oblivion the questions that remain. Neither, however, does it compel us to reinvent the world so that merfolk may comfortably occupy it.

ean Times 27 (Autumn 1978): 38–39.

Robertson, R. Macdonald. Jeremy Bruce-Watt, ed. *Selected Highland Folktales.* North Pomfret, VT: David and Charles, 1977.

Swift, Asa. "Mermaid." *American Journal of Science* 1, 2 (1820): 178–79.

T.G.S. "Minor Notes: Mermaids in Scotland, 1688." *Notes and Queries* 2, 149 (November 6, 1858): 371.

Wagner, Roy. "The Ri — Unidentified Aquatic Animals of New Ireland, Papua New Guinea." *Cryptozoology* 1 (1982): 33–39.

Waugh, Sir Arthur. "The Folklore of the Merfolk." *Folklore* 71 (June 1960): 73–84.

Williams, Thomas R. "Identification of the Ri Through Further Fieldwork in New Ireland, Papua New Guinea." *Cryptozoology* 4 (1985): 61–68.

Wright, A. R. "Correspondence: Mer-folk in 1814." *Folklore* 40,1 (March 1929): 87–90.

MINNESOTA ICEMAN

One day in the fall of 1968, a University of Minnesota zoology major named Terry Cullen alerted Ivan T. Sanderson to an extraordinary story: an apparently authentic Bigfoot corpse was being shown around the country as a carnival exhibit.

Sanderson, a biologist who long had been interested in unknown animals and other anomalous phenomena, was understandably intrigued. So was Sanderson's houseguest, Bernard Heuvelmans, a Belgian scientist known as the "father of cryptozoology."

The two lost no time in getting to tiny Rollingstone, Minnesota, where they met one Frank Hansen on whose farm the body, frozen in a block of ice and encased in a refrigerated coffin, reposed over the winter months during the carnival off-season. Hansen led them to a tiny trailer where the "Iceman," as it came to be called, was stored. Sanderson and Heuvelmans spent the next two days studying, sketching, and photographing the figure. Heuvelmans described it as follows:

> The specimen at first looks like a man, or, if you prefer, an adult human being of the male sex, of rather normal height (six feet) and proportions but excessively hairy. It is entirely covered with very dark brown hair three to four inches long. Its skin appears waxlike, similar in color to the cadavers of white men not tanned by the sun ... The specimen is lying on its back.... [T]he left arm is twisted behind the head with the palm of the hand upward. The arm makes a strange curve, as if it were that of a sawdust doll, but this curvature is due to an open fracture midway between the wrist and the elbow where one can distinguish the broken ulna in a gaping wound.
>
> The right arm is twisted and held tightly against the flank, with the hand spread palm down over the right side of the abdomen. Between

the ring finger and the medius the penis is visible, lying obliquely on the groin. The testicles are vaguely distinguishable at the juncture of the thighs.

The creature appeared to have been shot in the right eye. The impact apparently knocked the left eye out of its socket and blew out the back of the head.

Sanderson and Heuvelmans were soon convinced that the figure was what it purported to be: a body, not a model. They even examined what they took to be gas bubbles and odors from the creature's slowly decomposing remains.

Hansen claimed that the creature had been found floating in a 6,000-pound block of natural ice in the Sea of Okhotsk. The men who discovered it were Russian seal-hunters. (In a later version of the tale Hansen identified them as Japanese whalers.) Eventually, according to Hansen, it turned up in Hong Kong where an agent of an anonymous California multimillionaire purchased it. In due course the purchaser rented it to Hansen, who began touring the country with it in May 1967.

Heuvelmans published a paper in the February 1969 issue of the *Bulletin of the Royal Institute of Natural Sciences of Belgium*. In it he gave the Iceman the scientific name *Homo pongoides*. Meanwhile Sanderson, too, endorsed the Iceman in articles published in the scientific journal *Genus* and in the popular magazine *Argosy*. In the latter he wrote, "I defy anybody to fool Bernard Heuvelmans in a case like this. You just cannot 'make' a corpse like this."

Early in February 1969 Sanderson contacted an old friend, John Napier, curator of the primate collections at the Smithsonian Institution, in an effort to encourage the Smithsonian's participation in the investigation. Sanderson provided Napier with his report and diagrams.

As Napier would write in his *Bigfoot* (1973), "My first reaction, based on the creature's anatomy, was extreme dubiety.... On the face of it, the Iceman is some crazy sort of hybrid ... [combining] the worst features of apes and none of the best features which make these two groups extremely successful primates in their respective environments." In other words, zoologically speaking, the Iceman did not make a lot of sense.

Still, the Smithsonian tried to secure the specimen from Hansen, who said he could not provide it because the anonymous owner had taken it away. Hansen said that when he went back on tour it would be with a model that would "in many respects resemble" the original. After further investigation the Smithsonian concluded that the story and the figure were a hoax.

Over the years Hansen would tour the United States with his Iceman exhibit, neither confirming nor denying its authenticity. In his promotional material, however, he quoted the views of "scientists" (apparently Heuvelmans and Sanderson) who had declared it the genuine article.

Mystery, myth, and model.

In August 1981 C. Eugene Emery, a science reporter for the *Providence* [R.I.] *Journal-Bulletin*, wrote an article about the exhibit, which was on display at a Providence shopping mall. Soon after the story appeared, Emery learned of Howard Ball, now deceased, who made models for Disneyland. His specialty was prehistoric beasts such as the mechanical dinosaurs in the Ford exhibit at the 1964 New York World's Fair.

"He made [the Iceman] here in his studio in Torrance [California]," Ball's widow Helen told Emery. "The man who commissioned it said he was going to encase it in ice and pass it off, I think, as a prehistoric man."

Ball's son Kenneth helped his father build the figure. He says its "skin" is half-inch-thick rubber. "We modeled it after an artist's conception of Cro-Magnon man and gave it a broken arm and a bashed-in skull with one eye popped out. As I understand it, [the man who commissioned the job] took the creature to Mexico to have the hair implanted."

The Balls were much amused when they saw Sanderson's article in the May 1969 issue of *Argosy* and recognized their creation in the accompanying photographs. "I never thought it would get so carried away," Mrs. Ball said. Kenneth Ball remembered that the man who hired them "discussed with us some of the fun and some of the trials and tribulations with it."

Hansen admitted to Emery that Ball had made a figure for him but insisted that it "was discarded." When Emery pointed out that the Balls affirm that the figure and the one in *Argosy* were identical, Hansen replied lamely, "They can say whatever they want to."

Sanderson died in 1973, still convinced that the Iceman he and Heuvelmans had seen — unlike the one in subsequent circulation — was a real animal. Heuvelmans wrote a book defending it (published in French and never translated into English) it and even today contends that the original Iceman was some kind of hominid.

In a 1989 lecture at an International Society of Cryptozoology conference at Washington State University, Cullen, now a herpetologist living in Milwaukee, said that he had had many chances to examine the exhibit while it was on display at a local fair in the late 1960s. By the time Sanderson and Heuvelmans saw it, the ice had frosted over, but it was relatively clear when Cullen viewed it originally. He said he could see numerous tiny features which persuaded him this was a biological specimen, not a model, and he had gotten excited enough by it to call Sanderson at his New Jersey home. This call, of course, set in motion the whole series of events that comprise the Minnesota Iceman saga. Cullen agreed that the figure now being shown is a model.

If there ever was an authentic Minnesota Iceman, the gods seem to have done their best to ensure that virtually nobody would believe it. Reasonable human beings do not seek truth in carnival sideshows. It may, of course, reside there on some exceedingly rare occasion, but even if we choose to ignore the Balls' apparently devastating testimony and allow ourselves to imagine that Hansen managed to pull off the greatest switch in the history of zoology, we cannot escape Napier's troubling observation that the Iceman, even when scrutinized before all the excitement began, looked not at all like anything that could ever have walked the earth.

● SOURCES:

Emery, C. Eugene, Jr. "News and Comment: Sasquatchsickle: The Monster, the Model, and the Myth." *Skeptical Inquirer* 6, 2 (Winter 1981/1982): 2–4.

Hansen, Frank. "I Killed the Ape-Man Creature of Whiteface." *Saga* (July 1970): 8–11, 55–60.

Heuvelmans, Bernard. "Note Preliminaire sur un Specimen Conserve dans la Grace, d'une Forme Encore Inconnue d'Hominide Vivant: *Homo pongoides.*" *Bulletin de l'Institute Royal des Sciences Naturelles de Belgique* 45,4 (February 1969): 1–24.

Napier, John. *Bigfoot: The Yeti and Sasquatch in Myth and Reality.* New York: E. P. Dutton and Company, 1973.

"Pullman Symposium Reviews Sasquatch Evidence." *The ISC Newsletter* 8, 4 (Winter 1989): 1–5.

Sanderson, Ivan T. "Preliminary Description of the External Morphology of What Appeared to be the Fresh Corpse of a Hitherto Unknown Form of Living Hominid." *Genus* 25 (1969): 249–78.

———. "The Missing Link." *Argosy* (May 1969): 23–31.

MOKELE-MBEMBE

The strange saga of mokele-mbembe (mo-kay-lee mmmbem-bee, a Lingala word meaning "one who stops the flow of rivers") begins, in print anyway, in 1776. A book written that year by Abbe Lievain Bonaventure Proyart details the experiences of French priests as they sought to bring Catholicism to west-central Africa, in what is now Gabon, Cameroon, and the Congo. The book contains much accurate information on the animals of the region. It also remarks on a startling discovery in a forest, where priests noted tracks left by an animal "which was not seen but which must have been monstrous: the marks of the claws were noted on the ground, and these formed a print about three feet in circumference."

In the twentieth century Bernard Heuvelmans, the father of cryptozoology (the study of unknown or unexpected animals), would estimate that an animal capable of making such tracks must have been somewhere between a hippopotamus and an elephant in size. What could such an animal have been? Or, as we shall see, what could it be? A long legendary tradition — and not a few eyewitness sightings — from the tropical rain forest areas of Cameroon, Equatorial Guinea, Gabon, Congo, Northern Rhodesia, and the Central African Republic suggest an answer, albeit a fantastic one.

In the early 1870s Alfred Aloysius Smith, a young Englishman who worked for a British trading firm, was dispatched to Gabon. His labors sent him up and down the Ogooue River. Years later, with the editorial help of South African novelist Ethelreda Lewis, who recorded his story in a first-person, stream-of-consciousness style, he recounted his many adventures in a famous book, *Trader Horn* (1927). He referred in passing to two mysterious animals, or one that had two names: "The *Jago-Nini* they say is still in the swamps and rivers … Same as the *Amali* I've always taken it to be. I've seen the *Amali*'s footprints. About the size of a good frying pan in circumference and three claws instead o' five."

In 1909, while on a westward trek through the rivers of central Africa, Lt. Paul Gratz came to Lake Bangweulu in Northern Rhodesia (now Zambia). In the nearby swamp, he wrote, "lives the *nsanga*, much feared by the natives, a degenerate saurian which one might well confuse with the crocodile, were it not that its skin has no scales and its toes are armed with claws." He claimed that later, on the island of Mbawala, he was shown what were said to be strips of its skin.

The first wide discussion of these matters occurred when Carl Hagenbeck, an internationally famous animal collector, recalled a curious episode in his autobiography *Beasts and Men* (1909). He said that "some years ago" he heard from two separate sources, one an employee on a collecting expedition (Hans Schomburgh), the other an English big-game hunter, about a "huge monster, half elephant, half dragon," said to dwell in the African interior. Sometime earlier another collector, naturalist Joseph Menges, had told him of similar accounts from natives, whose descriptions fit those of the other informants: "some kind of dinosaur, seemingly akin to the brontosaurs," in Hagenback's estimation. He said he had sent an expedition to the region, consisting of enormous swamps, but disease and hostile natives kept the searchers from their destination, and Hagenbeck had been forced to abandon the effort.

Schomburgh told Hagenbeck that at Lake Bangweulu in Northern Rhodesia he had been surprised to find no hippopotamuses. His native guides explained that this was because a strange animal that lived in the lake killed hippos. Schomburgh did not record, if he heard at all, what name his informants attached to the beast, but 500 miles to the west, in the Dilolo marshes, he heard of what sounded like an identical animal, called the chimpekwe. (In 1933 J. E. Hughes, a British settler who lived along Lake Bangweulu, noted local traditions of the chimpekwe.)

These revelations generated something of a sensation. In 1910 newspapers in Europe, Africa, and the United States carried stories whose tone ranged from blistering to breathless. The furor faded after a few months, and in 1911, in a geographical journal, Northern Rhodesian colonial official Frank H. Melland felt compelled to declare, "I have never heard so much as a rumor of any animal that could be supposed to resemble a brontosaurus, or a dinosaur, which has been reputed to inhabit these swamps."

Then in 1913 the German government sent Capt. Freiherr von Stein zu Lausnitz to survey the Cameroon (which borders the Congo Republic [at that time the Belgian Congo] to the northwest), then a German colony. In his official report, which was never published though portions of it would be reprinted some years later in books and articles by German-American science writer Willy Ley, Von Stein learned that in areas of the lower Ubangi, Sanga, and Ikelemba Rivers in the Congo, many people — including experienced hunting guides who knew the local wildlife well — spoke of something called the mokele-mbembe. Von Stein wrote:

> The animal is said to be of a brownish-gray color with a smooth skin, its size approximately that of an elephant; at least that of a hippopota-

mus. It is said to have a long and very flexible neck and only one tooth but a very long one; some say it is a horn. A few spoke about a long muscular tail like that of an alligator. Canoes coming near it are said to be doomed; the animal is said to attack the vessels at once and to kill the crews but without eating the bodies. The creature is said to live in the caves that have been washed out by the river in the clay of its shores at sharp bends. It is said to climb the shore even at daytime in search of food; its diet is said to be entirely vegetable. This feature disagrees with a possible explanation as a myth. The preferred plant was shown to me, it is a kind of liana with large white blossoms, with a milky sap and applelike fruits. At the Ssombo river I was shown a path said to have been made by this animal in order to get at its food. The path was fresh and there were plants of the described type nearby. But since there were too many tracks of elephants, hippos, and other large mammals it was impossible to make out a particular spoor with any amount of certainty.

The Congo dinosaur story was revived in late 1919, when stories subsequently exposed as practical jokes were reported soberly in the *New York Times* and other newspapers. Even so, two brontosaur-hunting expeditions were announced, with suitable fanfare. In 1938 explorer Leo von Boxberger, a former colonial magistrate (Germany lost its colonies after its defeat in World War I), collected numerous mokele-mbembe reports but lost them in an attack on him and his party by unfriendly natives.

Outside the regions where the creatures allegedly lived, mokele-mbembe would have been forgotten but for the interest of pioneering cryptozoologists Ley, Ivan T. Sanderson, who wrote about them in a 1948 *Saturday Evening Post* article, and Heuvelmans, who devoted a chapter of his classic *On the Track of Unknown Animals* (1958) to "The Dragon St. George Did Not Kill."

The expeditions.
In the 1960s a young herpetologist named James H. Powell, Jr., took an interest in these reports of ostensible African sauropods after reading about them in the works of Ley, Heuvelmans, and Sanderson, with whom he subsequently conducted an extensive correspondence. Determined to probe the mystery himself, in 1972 he secured funding from the Explorer's Club to conduct field research on two species of rain-forest crocodiles in west-central Africa. While so engaged, he planned also to look into mokele-mbembe traditions and sightings. Unfortunately, because the United States and the People's Republic of the Congo then had no diplomatic relations, he was unable to get into the country.

Four years later, having despaired of resolving that problem, he set off for Gabon, and into the remote regions in which Smith ("Trader Horn") had heard tales of strange animals. These stories seemed to refer to mokele-mbembe by other names, in Powell's view.

Eventually Powell found a witness, who called the animal "n'yamala." Powell deduced that "Trader Horn and I were trying to put into English the

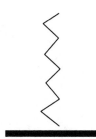

same African word," which Smith/Horn had rendered as "amali." Without being asked, the witness mentioned the plant that, according to wide report, comprises a large part of the mokele-mbembe diet. (This plant has been identified as a fruit-bearing liana which grows along the banks of rivers and lakes in tropical rain-forest regions.) Shown pictures of various animals, the witness pointed to one of a diplodocus, a long-necked sauropod dinosaur, and said it was a n'yamala. Picture tests given other native informants resulted in the same identification.

Powell returned to the area in early 1979 and secured additional testimony both from his first informant (with whom he ventured to the site of the encounter, a small lake) and from others.

A third expedition was launched in February 1980. This time Roy P. Mackal, a University of Chicago biologist with long-standing cryptozoological interests, accompanied Powell, and the two concentrated their efforts in the northern Congo, between the Sanga and Ubangi Rivers and, more specifically, between the Likouala aux Herbes River (a Ubangi tributary) and Lake Tele. Mackal thought that growing human traffic on the waterways may have caused the mokele-mbembe population to contract into the 55,000-square-mile Likoula region, mostly swamp and rain forest and still largely unmapped.

One of Mackal and Powell's major contacts, American missionary Pastor Eugene Thomas, had lived in Impfondo on the western bank of the Ubangi for many years, had often heard of mokele-mbembe, and was able to introduce them to new informants.

The two scientists trekked westward into the great swamp and in two days reached Epena on the other side. By now time was running short, and they were unable to continue on to Lake Tele. They used the remaining time seeking out witnesses, collecting strikingly similar descriptions of animals 15 to 30 feet long (most of that a snakelike head and neck, plus long, thin tail). The body was reminiscent of a hippo's, only more bulbous. The largest specimens were "the size of a small elephant. We were told that they have stubby legs, and that the hind feet have three claws. The animals are reddish brown, have no hair, but some have a comblike frill running down the back of the head and neck, a description which tallies with reports for the past 200 years." Again, informants invariably pointed to a picture of a sauropod when shown pictures of various animals to which the mokele-mbembe might be compared.

The natives said the animals, though they did not eat flesh, would upset canoes that ventured into the rivers, lakes, and streams where the creatures lived, and the local people would kill the animals. Mackal and Powell also learned of a killing of a mokele-mbembe, apparently around 1959, after pygmies trapped one in a channel going into Tele. Later, it was said, they ate its flesh, and subsequently all of them died.

In late 1981 Mackal returned to the area, this time in the company of J. Richard Greenwell, M. Justin Wilkinson, Congolese government biologist

● SOURCES:

Agnagna, Marcellin. "Results of the First Congolese Mokele-Mbembe Expedition." *Cryptozoology* 2 (Winter 1983): 103–12.

Averbuck, Philip. "The Congo Water-Dragon." *Pursuit* 14, 3 (Third Quarter 1981): 104–06.

Bright, Michael. "Meet Mokele-Mbembe." *BBC Wildlife* 2, 12 (December 1984): 596–601.

"Congo Expeditions Inconclusive." *The ISC Newsletter* 1, 1 (Spring 1982): 3–5.

"Congolese Biologist Observes Mokele-Mbembe." *The ISC Newsletter* 2, 4 (Winter 1983): 1–4.

"Dinosaur Hunt." *Fortean Times* 42 (Autumn 1984): 27.

Fuhlan [William Hichens]. "On the Trail of the Brontosaurus: Encounters with Africa's Mystery Animals." *Chambers's Journal* 7, 17 (1927): 692–95.

Greenwell, J. Richard. "Special Interview." *The ISC Newsletter* 3, 2 (Summer 1984): 7–9.

———. "Comments and Responses: Something More." *Cryptozoology* 4 (1985): 114–16.

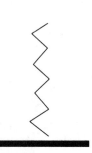

Marcellin Agnagna, and others. They interviewed more native informants and witnesses, though sometimes thwarted by a widespread belief which holds that anyone who talks about mokele-mbembe will die soon afterwards. Expedition members did not see any of the alleged creatures themselves, though on one occasion, as they were rounding a curve in the Likouala River above Epena, they heard a great "plop" sound. Then, Greenwell would write,

> A large wake (about 5") was observed originating from the east bank; under the circumstances such a wake could only be caused by the sudden submersion of a large animate object. Crocodiles do not leave such wakes, and elephants and other large mammals cannot submerge, with the exception of the hippopotamus. It is believed that hippos do not occur in the Likouala swamps, and villagers on the Likouala never see them (they are found in the Ubangi, on the edge of the Likouala swamp).

Natives had told expedition members that mokele-mbembes were often seen at sharp bends in the rivers where the water was deepest.

Subsequently they were shown a trail of broken branches through which an animal between five and seven feet high had crossed recently on its way to a pool where a mokele-mbembe was said to live. There were 12-inch round tracks leading to the pool, but nowhere were there any tracks leading out of it — which seemed to eliminate the idea that the animal responsible was a small forest elephant.

Unable to break through the thick swamp growth, the expedition did not make it to the shores of Tele, as it had hoped to do. Two subsequent expeditions claimed to do so, however, and in each case reported sightings of mokele-mbembes.

Around the time of the second Mackal expedition, Herman Regusters, an American engineer, led a group which made it, with great difficulty, to Tele. There members of the party camped for well over two weeks, during which they reportedly experienced several sightings of the creature's head and neck poking out of the water. Once they heard a "low windy roar" on the lake; it "increased to a deep-throated trumpeting growl." Regusters and his wife Kia Van Dusen said they then saw a huge creature moving through the swamp along the lake's edge. On another occasion Regusters observed it or a similar animal through binoculars in the lake. It had a slender, eight-foot neck, a small head, and 15 feet of back; its tail, assuming it had one, "would make it 30 to 35 feet long," he later estimated. Unfortunately, apparently owing to the high humidity, the cameras failed in each case, and no photographic testimony to these remarkable sights survived.

In April 1983 Agnagna led an officially sponsored, all-Congolese expedition to Tele. On the morning of May 1 he and two local villagers set out to film animal and bird species in the forest surrounding the lake. One of Agnagna's companions fell into a muddy pool and went to the lake to

"Help Us Catch a Dinosaur (on Film)!" *Fortean Times* 44 (Summer 1985): 11–12.

Heuvelmans, Bernard. *On the Track of Unknown Animals.* New York: Hill and Wang, 1958.

Ley, Willy. *The Lungfish, the Dodo, and the Unicorn.* New York: Viking Press, 1948.

———. "Congo Dragon." *Animal Life* 1, 1 (December 1953): 14–15, 48–51.

Mackal, Roy P. *Searching for Hidden Animals: An Inquiry Into Zoological Mysteries.* Garden City, NY: Doubleday and Company, 1980.

———. *A Living Dinosaur?: In Search of Mokele-Mbembe.* New York: E. J. Brill, 1987.

———. "Nessie's African Cousin." *Animal Kingdom* 83, 6 (December 1980/January 1981): 4–10.

Mackal, Roy P., J. Richard Greenwell, and M. Justin Wilkinson. "The Search for Evidence of Mokele-Mbembe in the People's Republic of the Congo." *Cryptozoology* 1 (Winter 1982): 62–72.

Melland, Frank H. "Bangweulu Swamps and the Wa-Unga."

Geographical Journal 38, 4 (October 1911): 381–95.

"Personal Glimpses: To Bring Home a Dinosaur Dead or Alive." *The Literary Digest* 64, 9 (February 28, 1920): 76–77, 80.

Powell, James H., Jr. "On the Trail of the Mokele-Mbembe." *Explorers Journal* 59, 2 (June 1981): 84–91.

Rhodes, Elizabeth. "Dinosaur: Elusion or Illusion?" *Seattle Times* (April 26, 1985).

Rickard, Bob. "Operation Congo Returns." *Fortean Times* 47 (Autumn 1986): 22–25.

Sanderson, Ivan T. "There Could Be Dinosaurs." *Saturday Evening Post* 220 (January 3, 1948): 17, 53–56.

Smith, Dwight, and Gary S. Mangiacopra. "Carl Hagenbeck and the Rhodesian Dinosaurs." *Strange Magazine* 5 (1990): 50–52.

Smith, Susan Lampert. "Search for Lost Dinosaur Lacks Money." *Wisconsin State Journal* [Madison] (November 25, 1985).

"Strange Days: Operation Congo." *Fortean Times* 45 (Winter 1985): 4.

wash himself. A short time later Agnagna heard him shouting and calling his name. When he came to the shore, the man was pointing at something out in the water. Because of the thick foliage Agnagna at first could not see what it was. He waded about 200 feet into the water until he saw a large and remarkable animal about 1,000 feet away. It fit the standard description of a mokele-mbembe.

The biologist later wrote ruefully, "The emotion and alarm at this sudden, unexpected event disrupted the author's attempt to film the animal with a Minolta XL–42 movie camera. The film had been almost totally exposed already, and the author unfortunately began filming with the lens cap on. By the time this was realized, the film had been totally exposed, as determined by subsequent processing in a French laboratory."

Agnagna carefully observed the animal for the next 20 minutes. The part of it visible above water consisted of a wide back, thin, extended neck, and small head; it stretched some 18 feet from the tip of its nose to the end of its back. If it had a tail, presumably submerged, it would, one assumes, have been a few feet longer.

"The frontal part of the animal was brown," according to Agnagna, "while the back part appeared black and shone in the sunlight." At one point it submerged slightly, leaving only its head and neck above the surface, then finally submerged completely.

(In a 1984 interview with Greenwell, who spoke with him at an International Society of Cryptozoology conference in Paris, Agnagna gave a slightly different version of events from the one above, based on his formal paper in the ISC journal *Cryptozoology*. He said he had accidently set the camera on "macro"; he had not left the lens cap on. For a time he watched the animal through the telephoto lens. Then he put that aside to take 35mm snapshots with a still camera. These photographs showed only a small, distant, ambiguous image — perhaps not surprising considering the distance. The reasons for the curious discrepancy between Agnagna's account in his formal paper and that in the later interview are not addressed in the latter.)

Other expeditions would occur. The first of the next wave, in mid-1986, went under the rubric Operation Congo and consisted of four enthusiastic but naive young Englishmen. They hired Agnagna to lead them to Tele, where they stayed for a few days without seeing mokele-mbembe. They did, however, provide this assessment of the biologist: "During the entire venture he did little more than lie, cheat and steal (our film and supplies) and turn the porters against us (telling them we were racist and out to exploit the Congolese)." They wrote that subsequently, through Pastor Thomas's contacts in the Congolese government, "Agnagna was … summoned to court and ordered to desist and hand back all the equipment loaned to him."

Agnagna accompanied two Japanese expeditions in September 1987 and the spring of 1988. The latter made it to Tele, but members saw nothing out of the ordinary, though two villagers claimed to have observed a large black object floating in the center of the lake in the early morning hours of April 5. As Operation Congo members had done before them, the Japanese were able to interview a number of individuals who claimed to have observed the animals at some point in their lives.

A not-so-impossible animal.

"We gathered more than 30 detailed descriptions of the Mokele-mbembe," Mackal wrote at the conclusion of his second expedition, "and these fit the configuration of a small sauropod so well that I find it impossible not to accept the identification, at least tentatively. Each of the reports was a first-hand, eyewitness account by informants from widely differing ethnic, cultural, religious, and geographical backgrounds."

In the absence of body, bones, or skin samples, those who have not seen mokele-mbembe for themselves must make their judgments from this sort of anecdotal testimony. That testimony, as Mackal indicates, is remarkably consistent, except for occasional references to a horn (noted, for instance, by Hagenbeck), which Mackal argues does not figure in the first-person sightings but in some of the folklore; in his A *Living Dinosaur?* (1987) he contends that the confusion stems from reports of another unknown animal of the Likouala, the emela-ntouka, the "killer of elephants" (see *Dinosaurs, living*).

Though mokele-mbembe is no doubt a startling concept, it is by no means an impossible animal. According to conventional wisdom, dinosaurs became extinct, over a several-hundred-thousand-year time span, some 65 million years ago, at the end of the Cretaceous period. For at least that long the Congo basin has remained geologically and climatically stable, and crocodiles, a close relative of the dinosaurs, have survived with little change all that time. In other words, under the circumstances, the continuance of a small population of dinosaurs in a remote, stable, and suitable environment is not *a priori* out of the question.

Still, the case is not proved and probably will not be until someone produces the flesh and bones. It is likely that even clear photographs will not persuade those who choose not to be persuaded, even if the photographer should turn out to be someone of Mackal's impeccable reputation.

For all the difficulties, the mokele-mbembe question is a potentially answerable one. But that answer will not come cheaply. In 1985 Regusters attempted to mount a follow-up expedition but failed to get the needed funding. Money promised for a third Mackal effort fell through, and by 1992, now retired from the University of Chicago, he had virtually abandoned hope for a return to the far country where one of the greatest zoological discoveries of all time may await a future explorer with courage, luck, and a substantial bankroll.

Takabayashi, Tokuharu. "The First Japanese-Congolese Mokele-Mbembe Expeditions." *Cryptozoology* 7 (1988): 66–69.

Tassy, Pascal, Glen J. Kuban, Marcellin Agnagna, and Christine M. Janis. "Comments and Responses." *Cryptozoology* 3 (1984): 136–44.

Weber, Charles W., James W. Berry, and J. Richard Greenwell. "Mokele-Mbembe: Proximate Analysis of Its Supposed Food Source." *Cryptozoology* 1 (Winter 1982): 49–53.

MOMO ————————————————————————

"Momo" got its name from the abbreviation of Missouri — Mo. — and the first two letters of monster. For a few days in the summer of 1972, it was the major story of the "silly season," the subject of tongue-in-cheek coverage in newspapers all over America.

The Momo scare was played out in and around Louisiana, a small town (pop. 4,600) in northeastern Missouri. In July 1971 two picnickers in a wooded area north of town reportedly spotted a "half-ape and half-man" with a hideous stench. Stepping out of a thicket, it walked toward them, making a "little gurgling sound," and they locked themselves inside their car. The creature ate an abandoned peanut butter sandwich and ambled back into the woods. The women reported the incident to the Missouri State Patrol but did not come forward publicly until a year later, and then only after numerous others had reported a similar sight.

Momo got its name after a series of sightings which began on the afternoon of July 11, 1972, when three children saw a creature, "six or seven feet tall, black and hairy," standing next to a tree. It was flecked with blood, apparently from the dead dog it carried under its arm. That same afternoon a neighbor heard strange growling sounds, and a farmer found that a newly acquired dog had disappeared.

Three evenings later, as the children's father Edgar Harrison and some friends stood talking outside the Harrison home, they saw a "fireball" come over nearby Marzolf Hill and apparently alight behind an abandoned schoolhouse across the street. Five minutes later another followed suit. Not long afterwards, a loud growl emanated from the hilltop and seemed to come down and toward the listeners, though its source was not visible to them. The police investigated but found nothing.

An hour or two later, as they poked around the hilltop in the darkness, Harrison and others found an old building suffused with a pungent,

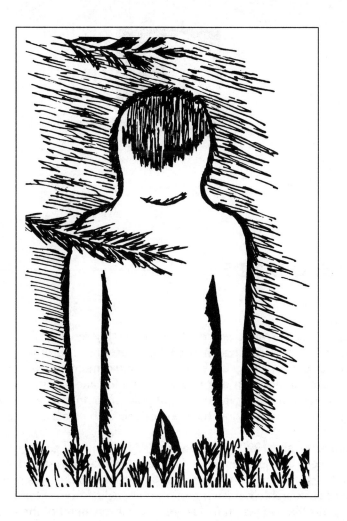

● SOURCES:

Clark, Jerome, and Loren Coleman. "Anthropoids, Monsters and UFOs." *Flying Saucer Review* 19,1 (January/February 1973): 18–24.

Coleman, Loren. *Mysterious America.* Boston, MA: Faber and Faber, 1983.

Crowe, Richard. "Missouri Monster." *Fate* 25,12 (December 1972): 58–66.

Camara, I., and G.H.H. Tate. "Letters: The 'Ape' That Wasn't an Ape." *Natural History* 60,6 (June 1951): 289.

Keith, Sir Arthur. "The Alleged Discovery of an Anthropoid Ape in South America." *Man* 29 (August 1929): 135–36.

Shoemaker, Michael T. "The Mystery of the Mono Grande." *Strange Magazine* 7 (April 1991): 2–5, 56–60.

unpleasant odor of the kind that was associated with Momo's appearances. On several occasions witnesses claimed to have seen a small glowing light which exploded and left the stench in its wake.

The scare continued for two more weeks, during which others reported seeing a hairy biped with both ape and human features. Some claimed to have heard disembodied voices. One said, "You boys stay out of these woods," and another asked for a cup of coffee. Footprints allegedly made by the creature were found on several occasions, but the only one to undergo scientific analysis was dismissed as a hoax by Lawrence Curtis, director of the Oklahoma City Zoo. A number of Louisiana residents reported fireballs and other unusual aerial objects. One, described as a UFO with lighted windows, allegedly landed for five hours on a hilltop. One family claimed to have seen a "perfect gold cross on the moon…. The road was lit up as bright as day from the cross."

MONO GRANDE

The mystery of the *mono grande* (Spanish for "big monkey") is one of primatology's most intriguing unanswered questions. The only recognized primates in the Americas are small, long-tailed monkeys; yet occasional reports from the northern end of South America attest to the presence in remote regions of larger, tailless anthropoid apes. In fact, a controversial photograph purports to show the body of one such creature.

Between 1917 and 1920 an expedition led by Swiss oil geologist Francois de Loys explored the swamps, rivers, and mountains west and southwest of Lake Maracaibo near the Colombia-Venezuela border. The participants suffered considerable hardship and a number died from disease or at the hands of hostile natives. In its last year, what remained of the expedition was camped on the banks of a branch of the Tarra River. Suddenly two creatures, male and female, stepped from out of the jungle. De Loys at first thought they were bears, but as they advanced on the camp, he could see they were apes of some sort, around five feet in height. His account omits the crucial detail of whether they were walking on two or four feet.

The creatures, giving every indication of being furious, broke off branches from nearby trees and wielded them as weapons, meanwhile crying and gesticulating vigorously. Finally they defecated into their hands and hurled the results at the party, who by now had their rifles to their shoulders. In the gunfire that followed, the female was killed, and the wounded male escaped back into the underbrush.

Though no one in the expedition was a zoologist, everyone understood that the animal was something out of the ordinary. Even the native guides swore they had never seen anything like it. Propping it up with a stick, members sat it on a gasoline crate and took a picture of it at a distance of 10 feet. According to de Loys, "Its skin was afterward removed, and its skull and jaw were cleaned and preserved." Though de Loys did not explicitly acknowledge as much, he and his starved compatriots apparently ate the animal's flesh. Later the other remains were lost. Of the original 20 members of the expedition, only four survived.

The photograph, however, was discovered by a friend of de Loys's, anthropologist George Montandon, when the latter reviewed de Loys's records and other expedition materials. Montandon was looking for information on a South American Indian tribe but considered the picture so important that he laid plans, he would write, to "go to the area in question to find the great ape of America." De Loys, he noted, had expressed no urgent interest in publishing or otherwise publicizing the photograph. Only at Montandon's insistence was it brought to the world's attention in 1929, when he reported it in papers that appeared in three French scientific journals. In these Montandon honored its discoverer by offering the formal name *Ameranthropoides loysi* for what he contended was a new animal. That same year de Loys told his story publicly for the first time in the popular magazine *Illustrated London News* (June 15).

The skeptical view.
Hardly had the ink dried on any of these than the debunkers were launching furious attacks on de Loys's credibility and Montandon's judgment. Leading the pack was the prominent British anthropologist Sir Arthur Keith, who strongly implied that de Loys had taken a picture of a smaller, tailless animal, the spider monkey, whose existence in the region no one disputed, and tried to peddle it as something more interesting. Keith wrote, "A photograph of the animal from behind would have clinched matters, but the only photograph taken was one of the front — the animal being placed in a sitting position on a box of unknown size and with no standard object in or near the body of the animal to give a clue to the dimensions of its parts."

Nonetheless other observers have, without notable difficulty, judged the figure to be approximately 5.2 or 5.3 feet tall, calculating the size from the crate on which it sat (others of its kind are 20 inches high). If this is accurate, the animal was an extraordinary spider monkey indeed; the largest known spider monkey was three feet, seven inches.

Keith also sneered at de Loys's claim that the animals had thrown feces at the party, as if the idea were too silly to be entertained, though spider monkeys and some apes do such things in confrontations with enemies. He also viewed as suspect the explorer's assertion that he had lost all evidence but the photograph. Considering the expedition's problems, however, it is hardly surprising that the maintenance of the creature's remains had no high priority; de Loys and his men were far more concerned with basic survival.

In any case, nothing in de Loys's behavior is convincingly suggestive of dishonesty in the affair, and only Montandon's interest kept the photo from being buried with the photographer. Nonetheless Keith's dismissal, however poorly advised, has remained for many the last word on the subject. In 1951, for example, *Natural History* reported that Keith had "easily demolished the 'new anthropoid'."

The nature of the beast.
In the fullest treatment of the episode yet written, anomaly researcher Michael T. Shoemaker wrote:

> Examination of the photo reveals a strange, but logical, mixture of characteristics from different genera. The flat nose, with the nostrils widely separated and flared outwards, is characteristic of New World monkeys.... Other characteristics that strongly suggest a spider-monkey are the round ridges surrounding the eye sockets, the long hair, and the extremely long fingers and toes. On the other hand, many of its characteristics contradict such an identification.... Compared to other anthropoid apes, the creature's body is like a gibbon's, but its limbs and reduced thumbs are most like those of an orangutan.... The most extraordinary characteristics lie in the shape of the head. Spider-monkeys have a distinctly triangular face, with a pronounced prognathism [jutting of the jaw beyond the upper part of the face]. The creature's face is oval, with its lower half much heavier, and with more powerful jaws, than a spider-monkey's. The creature also has little or no prognathism.... Although many New World monkeys tend to have a more prominent forehead than do Old World monkeys, none has a forehead so highly developed as this creature's forehead.

If de Loys's is the only photograph of what may be an unknown species of anthropoid ape, it is not the only report of such an animal. The first printed reference appears in a 1553 chronicle by Pedro de Cieza de Leon, who mentions native accounts and refers to a Spaniard who said "he had seen one of these monsters dead in the woods, and it was of the shape and appearance that was told." In *An Essay on the Natural History of Guiana* (1769) Edward Bancroft mentions Indian accounts of creatures "near five feet in height, maintaining an erect position, and having a human form, thinly covered with short, black hair." In 1860, in *The Romance of Natural History*, Philip Gosse pronounced as probable the existence of a "large anthropoid ape, not yet recognized by zoologists," in South America.

In 1876 Charles Barrington Brown, explorer of what was then British Guiana (now Guyana), wrote of what natives called the *Didi*, a "powerful wild man, whose body is covered with hair, and who lives in the forest." He heard it on more than one occasion and on another saw its footprints, or so they were identified to him. Sighting reports have continued into the twentieth century. In 1910 no less than the British Resident Magistrate saw two of them.

In 1968 explorer Pino Turolla, while traveling in the area of Marirupa Falls in the jungle-covered mountains of eastern Venezuela, was told of the *mono grande*. The informant, his guide, said that three of the creatures, using branches for clubs, had attacked him and killed his son several years earlier. On his return to the United States, Turolla researched the matter and came upon the de Loys photograph; on a subsequent expedition that same year he showed to his guide, who confirmed that this was what the *mono grande* looked like. Turolla persuaded the guide to take him to the canyon where the fatal attack had taken place, and there, after hearing eerie howling sounds, the explorer saw two fleeing apelike bipeds about five feet tall. He claimed a second, briefer sighting two years later while on an archaeological expedition on the eastern slope of the Andes in Ecuador.

The most recent published sighting is from Guyana in 1987. The witness, mycologist Gary Samuels, was doing field work for the New York Botanical Garden — in this instance gathering fungi from the forest floor — when he heard footsteps. When he looked up, expecting to see a Guyanese forester, he was startled to observe a five-foot-tall, bipedal ape, "bellowing an occasional 'hoo' sound."

Clearly the question of whether or not an anthropoid ape lives in South America remains an open one.

● SOURCES:

"An Alleged Anthropoid Ape Existing in America." *Nature* 123 (June 15, 1929): 924.

Camara, I., and G. H. H. Tate. "Letters: The 'Ape' That Wasn't an Ape." *Natural History* 60, 6 (June 1951): 289.

Heuvelmans, Bernard. *On the Track of Unknown Animals.* New York: Hill and Wang, 1958.

Keith, Sir Arthur. "The Alleged Discovery of an Anthropoid Ape in South America." *Man* 29 (August 1929): 135–36.

Picasso, Fabio. "More on the Mono Grande Mystery." *Strange Magazine* 9 (Spring/Summer 1992): 41, 53.

Shoemaker, Michael T. "The Mystery of the Mono Grande." *Strange Magazine* 7 (April 1991): 2–5, 56–60.

Turolla, Pino. *Beyond the Andes.* New York: Harper and Row, 1980.

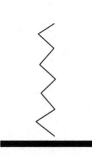

MORAG ———————————————

Loch Morar lies 70 miles to the southwest of the infinitely more famous Loch Ness. Eleven miles long and a mile and a half across at its widest point, it is separated from the sea by a quarter-mile, sits 30 feet above sea level, and averages 200 feet in depth. According to reports that go back decades and possibly centuries, it hosts a monster much like that reported at Ness and other Scottish and Irish lochs.

On April 3, 1971, Ewen Gillies, a lifelong resident of a house overlooking Loch Morar and a member of a family with centuries-old roots in the region, saw the creature for the first time. Alerted by his 12-year-old son John, who noticed it a few minutes earlier while walking down a road near the shore, Gillies stepped outside and looked out on the water. It was a clear, sunny morning, around 11 o'clock. Not quite half a mile away a huge animal lay in the water, its three- or four-foot neck pointed straight up and curving slightly at the top. The head was barely distinguishable from the neck itself. Two or three humps, moving up and down slightly, ran along its back. The skin was black and shiny. The creature was approximately 30 feet long.

Gillies went into the house to retrieve a Brownie camera. He took two pictures from an upstairs window just before the creature lowered its head, straightened its body, and sank below the water. The pictures did not turn out, but no one accused Gillies, a respected member of the community, of making up the story.

Early history.
He and his son had seen Morag. The name comes from the Gaelic *Mhorag*, traditionally believed to be the spirit of the loch and conceived of as a shape-changing mermaid whose appearance was an omen of death if glimpsed by a member of the Gillies clan. With the passage of time and the thinning of population in this wild, remote region, the older folklore faded from mem-

ory, and *Mhorag* (actually pronounced "Vorack") became Morag, a strange but not supernatural beast seen by some but seldom spoken of.

Perhaps because Morag the animal is lost to view or seen only in distorted form through the folkloric fog that hangs over the loch's history, researchers have had a hard time tracing reports beyond the late nineteenth century. In the early 1970s investigator Elizabeth Montgomery Campbell interviewed elderly residents who recalled sightings in their youth. Campbell also learned of a "persistent tradition of hideous hairy eel-like creatures that were pulled up by fishermen long ago and thrown back into the loch because they were so repulsive."

Folklorist R. Macdonald Robertson collected this story, describing an undated event from early in the century, from Alexander Macdonnell:

> Some years ago, we were proceeding one morning down the loch in the estate motor launch from Meoble to Morar pier with some school-children and other persons on board. As we were passing Bracarina Point, on the north side, some of the children excited shouted out: "Oh look! What is that big thing on the bank over there?" The beast would be about the size of a full-grown Indian elephant, and it plunged off the rocks into the water with a terrific splash.

Robertson noted that "Loch Morar's monster is said to have been seen by a number of persons of unquestionable veracity." A typical sighting is expressed in the words of one witness: "a huge, shapeless, dark mass rising out of the water like a small island."

Some who saw the shape thought it was, as they told travel writer Seton Gordon in the 1930s, a "boat without sails towing one or two smaller boats after it." These were ghost ships, they assumed. Modern witnesses at Morar, Ness, and elsewhere often say the creature's back looks like an "upturned boat."

In an unpublished memoir written in the early 1940s, Lady Brinckman, who had lived on an estate near the loch five decades earlier, recalled this incident from the summer of 1895:

> One evening, it was getting towards dinner time and I was sitting looking back, when suddenly, I saw a great shape rise up out of the loch, a good way off. I called the attention of Theodore and McLaren to it and asked if it was the launch and that it did not seem to be coming the right way. McLaren pointed a long way to the left as being where the launch would come from, and then, while we were watching, it disappeared. McLaren said, "It'll just be the monster," and he said it was a well known thing that one was seen from time to time.

In September 1931 young Sir John Hope, who as Lord Glendevon would go on to become a privy councillor and undersecretary of state for Scotland, had a curious experience which, while it involved no direct sighting, clearly suggested the presence of some huge unknown animal in the loch.

He, his brother, a friend, and a local guide had gone out on a boat to fish in a deep part of Morar. Hope, who was holding a long trout rod, felt something grab his line, dragging it "directly downwards at such a pace that it would have been madness to try and stop it with my fingers. In a very few seconds the whole line including the backing had gone and the end of the rod broke." Whatever had taken the bait, it was "something ... heavier than I have experienced before or since."

It could not have been a salmon which, even if there were one that size in the loch, would have traveled parallel to the surface rather than making a steep vertical descent. Such descents, however, are described in any number of lake monster reports. The only other conceivable candidate is a seal, but no seals are known to exist at Loch Morar. Glendevon says that when they asked their guide what the animal could have been, "he mumbled something and said he thought we had better go home." Glendevon suspected that he knew more than he was telling.

After 1933, the year the Loch Ness monster emerged into world consciousness, note was taken of Morag, and a few witnesses came forward to describe observations either of large, fast-moving humps in the water or of a long-necked creature, usually said to be 30 feet long. But as a cryptozoological mystery Morag is far less richly documented than Nessie, the focus of a nearly unending investigation spanning six decades. Photographs, sonar trackings, and a large body of eyewitness testimony have afforded Ness's monstrous denizen a credibility Morag cannot begin to claim.

In February 1970 several members of the Loch Ness Investigation Bureau formed the Loch Morar Survey to pursue the biological, operational, and historical aspects. Over the next few years they made sporadic investigations as limited time and funds permitted. On July 14, 1970, one member, marine biologist Neil Bass, spotted a "hump-shaped black object" in the water at the north end of the lake. He called to his associates, but the hump had vanished by the time they started to look for it.

"Following this, within half a minute," Bass reported, "a disturbance was witnessed by all of us ... followed by radiating water rings which traveled to form a circle, at maximum 50 yards in diameter." Bass said the apparent motion was inconsistent with an eel's; in any case it would have to be a "very, very big eel! My personal opinion is that it was an animate object, of a species with which I am not familiar in this kind of habitat."

The most dramatic Morag encounter to date took place on August 16, 1969. It is also the only sighting ever to be reported in newspapers all over the world shortly after its occurrence. It happened as two local men, Duncan McDonell and William Simpson, were on their way back from a fishing trip at the north end of the loch. It was just after 9 P.M. The sun had gone down, but there was still plenty of light.

Hearing a splash behind them, McDonell, who was at the wheel, turned to determine its cause. To his astonishment, it turned out to be a creature coming directly toward them, at a speed later estimated to be between 20 and 30 mph. Within seconds it struck the side of the boat, then stopped or slowed down. Though McDonell had the impression that the collision had been accidental, that did not allay his fear that the creature, simply by virtue of its bulk, could cause the boat to capsize. He grabbed an oar and tried to push it away. Meanwhile Simpson had rushed into the cabin to turn off the gas. He returned with a rifle and fired a single shot at the beast, with no apparent effect. It slowly moved away and sank out of sight. These events took five minutes to run their course.

When interviewed by representatives from the Loch Ness Investigation Bureau, the two agreed that the creature had been some 25 to 30 feet long, with rough, dirty brown skin. Three humps or undulations, about 18 inches high, stood out of the water, and at one point McDonell spotted the animal's snakelike head just above the surface. It was, he thought, about one foot across the top.

Theories.
Morar lies in a glacially deepened valley on Inverness-shire's west coast. Twelve thousand years ago, as the ice retreated, sea water is believed to have invaded the lake, bringing with it an abundance of marine life. Even after the sea water retreated, for a few thousand years the sea animals now in the loch may have had fairly ready access to their oceanic home, because the loch level and the low-tide level were only one-third then what they are today. The sea level at high tide would have been within a few feet of loch level.

There is no doubt that Loch Morar possesses an adequate food supply — fish, plankton, and detritus — to support a population of large animals. It is also one of nine Highland lakes with "monster" traditions and reports. (Besides Ness, the others are Oich, Canisp, Assynt, Arkaig, Shiel, Lochy, and Quoich.) Most sightings at Morar and elsewhere describe creatures bearing an undeniable resemblance to the supposedly long-extinct plesiosaur. If such animals survive, however (and there is no confirmation of this in the fossil record), they would have had to adapt to far colder water temperatures than their ancestors could handle. Roy P. Mackal, a biologist with a keen interest in lake monsters, argues that Morag, Nessie, and their relatives are zeuglodons, primitive, snakelike whales generally believed to have ceased their existence over 20 million years ago.

If the idea of relic giant prehistoric reptiles and mammals seems too fantastic to be considered, plesiosaurs and zeuglodons at least *look like* what people usually report when they recount their observations of the monsters of the Highland lochs. "Conventional" explanations pointing to sharks, seals, eels, or even mats of vegetation typically begin with the outright rejection of the witnesses' testimony and the implicit assumption that these individuals could not have seen what they said they saw; thus they saw something else, which the explainer is always willing to supply even when it defies nearly every word of the testimony. Such an approach may have its uses on occasion, but more often than not takes us only so far. Often it is easier to believe that the witnesses are lying outright than that they suffered from such massive breakdowns of their perceptual apparatus.

Meantime the mystery of Morar's Morag continues.

● SOURCES:

Campbell, Elizabeth Montgomery, and David Solomon. *The Search for Morag.* New York: Walker and Company, 1973.

Holiday, F. W. *The Dragon and the Disc: An Investigation Into the Totally Fantastic.* New York: W. W. Norton and Company, 1973.

Mackal, Roy P. *The Monsters of Loch Ness.* Chicago: The Swallow Press, 1976.

Robertson, R. Macdonald. Jeremy Bruce-Watt, ed. *Selected Highland Folktales.* North Pomfret, VT: David and Charles, 1977.

Wignall, Sydney. "Morag of Morar." *Pursuit* 15,2 (Second Quarter 1982): 50–51, 56, 63.

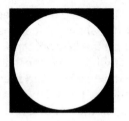

MOTHMAN

Mothman is possibly the weirdest creature ever to grace (or terrify) the UFO era. Though this winged monstrosity only rarely has been linked directly with UFOs, its most celebrated manifestations — the ones that gave it its name — coincided with a series of UFO reports and other strange events (including men-in-black visitations) in the Ohio River Valley in 1966 and 1967.

Late on the evening of November 15, 1966, as they drove past an abandoned TNT plant near Point Pleasant, West Virginia, two young married couples spotted two large eyes, two inches wide and six inches apart, attached to something that "was shaped like a man, but bigger. Maybe six or seven feet tall. And it had big wings folded against its back." The eyes were "hypnotic," the witnesses agreed. When it started to move, heading toward the plant door, the four panicked and sped away. In short order they saw the same or a similar creature on a hillside near the road. It spread its batlike wings, rose into the air, and followed the car, which by now was doing 100 mph.

"That bird kept right up with us," Roger Scarberry, one of the group, said to investigator John A. Keel. "It wasn't even flapping its wings." The witnesses told Deputy Sheriff Millard Halstead it made a sound like a "record played at high speed or the squeak of a mouse." It followed them on Highway 62 right to the Point Pleasant city limits.

The two couples were not the only persons to see the creature that night. Another group of four claimed to have seen it not once but three times. A third report is of particular interest.

At 10:30 on the evening of the fifteenth, Newell Partridge, a building contractor who lived outside Salem, West Virginia (approximate 90 miles northeast of Point Pleasant), was watching television when suddenly the screen blanked out, a "fine herringbone pattern appeared on the tube, and at the same time the set started a loud whining noise, winding up to a high pitch, peaking and breaking off, as if you were on a musical scale and you went as high as you could and came back down and repeated it.... It sounded like a generator winding up." The Partridges' dog Bandit began to howl on the porch, continuing even after they turned the set off.

Partridge stepped outside, where he saw Bandit facing toward the hay barn 150 yards away. "I shined the light in that direction," Partridge said in an interview with West Virginia writer Gray Barker, "and it picked up two red circles, or eyes, which looked like bicycle reflectors," but apparently much larger. Something about the sight deeply frightened him. They were not, he was certain, an animal's eyes.

Snarling, Bandit, an experienced hunting dog, shot off toward the figure. Partridge called to him to stop, but the dog paid no heed. At this point Partridge went inside to get a gun but then decided not to go outside again. He slept that night with the weapon by his side. By morning he realized Bandit had disappeared, and the dog had not shown up two days later when Partridge read a newspaper report of the Point Pleasant sightings.

One detail in particular struck him: Roger Scarberry's statement that as they entered Point Pleasant's city limits, the two couples had seen the body of a big dog by the side of the road. A few minutes later, on their way back out of town, the dog was gone. They and Deputy Halstead, who was following them in a separate car, had even stopped to look for the body. Partridge immediately thought of Bandit, who was never to be seen again. All that remained of him were his prints in the mud. "Those tracks were going in a circle, as if that dog had been chasing his tail — though he never did that," his master recalled. "There were no other tracks of any kind."

In another interesting point of correspondence between Partridge's experience and that of the Point Pleasant witnesses, Deputy Halstead experienced peculiar interference on his police radio when he visited the TNT area. It was loud and sounded something like a record or tape played at high speed. He finally had to turn the radio off.

The next day, after a press conference called by Sheriff George Johnson, the story hit the press wires. A reporter immediately dubbed the creature "Mothman" after a villain on the *Batman* television series.

From that time to November 1967 a number of other sightings occurred. On the evening of November 16, 1966, for example, three adults, one carrying an infant, were walking back to their car after calling on friends. Suddenly something rose slowly up from the ground. One witness, Marcella Bennett, was so frightened that she dropped her baby. A "big gray thing, bigger than a man," it had no discernible head, but it did have two large glowing red circles at the top of its trunk. As huge wings unfolded from behind it, Raymond Wamsley snatched up the child and ushered the two women inside the house they had just left. The creature apparently followed them to the porch because they could hear sounds there and,

A drawing of Mothman, the terror of the Ohio River Valley, based on eyewitness descriptions. (Courtesy of Loren Coleman.)

worse, see its eyes peering through the window. By the time the police arrived, it was gone. Mrs. Bennett was traumatized for weeks afterwards and, like other Mothman witnesses, eventually sought medical attention.

Keel, the major chronicler of the Mothman episode, wrote that at least 100 persons saw the creature; from their accounts, he compiled a composite description. According to the reports, it stood between five and seven feet tall, was broader than a man, and walked in a halting, shuffling manner on humanlike legs. It emitted a squeaky sound. The eyes, which Keel said "seemed to have been more terrifying than the tremendous size of the creature," were set near the top of the shoulders; its wings were batlike but did not flap when it flew. It typically ascended, as one observer put it, "straight up, like a helicopter." Witnesses described its skin color as gray or brown. Two observers said they heard a mechanical humming as it flew above them.

After 1967 Mothman faded back into the twilight zone — only one subsequent report, from Elma, New York, in October 1974, is known — but Keel found a West Virginia woman who said she had encountered it on a highway one evening in 1961 at the edge of Chief Cornstalk Hunting Grounds on the West Virginia side of the Ohio River. She told Keel that "it was much larger than a man. A big gray figure. It stood in the middle of the road. Then a pair of wings unfolded from its back, and they practically filled the whole road. It almost looked like a small airplane. Then it took off straight up … disappearing out of sight in seconds."

Big bird?

Whatever it may or may not have been, Mothman was no hoax, in the unanimous opinion of those who investigated the sightings. The most publicized conventional explanation came from West Virginia University biologist Robert Smith, who suggested the witnesses had seen sandhill cranes. Such cranes are not native to Ohio or West Virginia, but theoretically some could have migrated down from the plains of Canada. On November 26, 1966, a small group of people near Lowell, Ohio (70 miles north of Point Pleasant), reported seeing a group of oversized birds in some trees. When approached, the birds flew away and settled on a nearby ridge. From the descriptions (four or five feet tall, with long necks, six-inch bills, and a "reddish cast" in the head area) these are, arguably, sandhill cranes, but they bear no resemblance to what the Mothman witnesses say they observed. All of them, in fact, rejected the sandhill identification.

On the other hand, Keel suspects that in a tiny minority of cases excitable observers, spooked by the stories they had heard, may have mistaken owls encountered briefly on dark country roads for something more extraordinary. Even so, Mothman, the most improbable of beasts, resists easy accounting. Unlike some other monsters this one has much going for it, most notably an impressive number of multiple-witness sightings by individuals whom investigators and police officers deemed reliable. Any "rational" explanation for Mothman must first disregard all the testimony as wildly in error. Only a radical revision of the witnesses' descriptions can transform Mothman into a respectable inhabitant of the consensus universe.

A Mothman abroad.

Mothman's one known appearance outside Ohio and West Virginia was in England, along a rural road near Sandling Park, Hythe, Kent, on November 16, 1963. Four young people allegedly saw a "star" ascend from the night sky and disappear behind trees not far from them. Frightened, they took to their heels but stopped soon afterwards to watch a golden, oval-shaped light floating a few feet above a field 80 yards from them. The UFO moved into the wooded area and was lost to view.

Suddenly the witnesses saw a dark shape shambling toward them from across the field. It was black, human-sized, and headless, and it had wings that looked like a bat's. At this juncture the four chose not to linger further at the scene.

Other persons sighted a similar UFO over the next few nights. On the twenty-third, two men who had come to investigate found a "vast expanse of bracken that had been flattened." They also claimed to have seen three huge footprints, two feet long and nine inches wide, pressed an inch deep in the soil.

● SOURCES:

Barker, Gray. *The Silver Bridge.* Clarksburg, WV: Saucerian Books, 1970.

Bowen, Charles, ed. *The Humanoids: A Survey of Worldwide Reports of Landings of Unconventional Aerial Objects and Their Alleged Occupants.* Chicago: Henry Regnery Company, 1969.

Keel, John A. *Strange Creatures from Time and Space.* Greenwich, CT: Fawcett Gold Medal, 1970.

——. *The Mothman Prophecies.* New York: E. P. Dutton and Company, 1975.

Miller, Virginia Margaret. "Report from the Readers: The 'Mothman' Visits." *Fate* 29, 3 (March 1976): 127–29.

White, Helen M. "Do Birds Come This Big?" *Fate* 20, 8 (August 1967): 74–77.

281

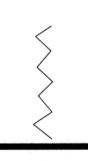

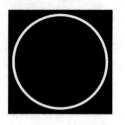

MOVING COFFINS ─────────────────────

Barbados, an island located at the easternmost edge of the West Indies, is the site of a strange story which some writers have treated as one of the great mysteries of the nineteenth century. The mysterious events in question, said to have taken place inside the Chase vault at Christ Church overlooking Oistin's Bay, allegedly occurred between 1812 and 1819 or 1820 and involved the inexplicable movement of coffins.

According to the first published account, Sir J. E. Alexander's *Transatlantic Sketches* (1833):

> *Each time that the vault was opened the coffins were replaced in their proper situations, that is, three on the ground side by side, and the others laid on them. The vault was then regularly closed; the door (a massive stone which required six or seven men to move) was cemented by masons; and though the floor was of sand, there were no marks or foot-steps or water.*

> *The last time the vault was opened was in 1819. Lord Combermere [Governor of the colony] was then present, and the coffins were found confusedly thrown about the vault, some with their heads down and others up. What could have occasioned this phenomenon? In no other vault in the island has this ever occurred.*

Over time various versions of the story saw print. Even one of the alleged witnesses, the Rev. Thomas H. Orderson, the rector of Christ Church, gave conflicting accounts to inquirers. Other accounts were published in 1844 (Sir Robert Schomburgk's *History of Barbados*) and 1860 (Mrs. D. H. Cussons's *Death's Deeds*). In the December 1907 issue of *Folk-Lore*, the noted English folklorist Andrew Lang reviewed the affair, drawing not only on printed sources but on his brother-in-law Forster M. Alleyne's investigation in Barbados. Alleyne had examined vault records but found nothing to substantiate the story, and the island's newspapers of the period had nothing to say on the subject. He did, however, come upon an unpublished description by Nathan Lucas, who witnessed the final interment of the vault in April 1820. Alleyne's father, who was on the island in 1820, alluded to the coffin disturbances in correspondence which survived from that year.

Lang's interest in the episode was fueled by another intellectual fascination of his, psychical research. He noted a report of similar events in a Lutheran cemetery on the Isle of Oesel, in the Baltic Sea, said to have taken place in 1844. The evidence for its occurrence, he conceded, consisted in its entirety of an anecdote to American diplomat Robert Dale Owen (who reported it in *Footfalls on the Boundary of Another World* [1860]); no written records were known to exist, and none have surfaced since. Lang thought it was at least possible that Owen's informants "plagiarized" the Barbados story, adding a few flourishes of their own (including the lurid detail that the hand of a suicide was found sticking out of one of the coffins).

Another moving-coffins story, however, could not have been based on the Barbados incident because it saw print before the West Indian events became known. The *European Magazine* for September 1815 related the case of "The Curious Vault at Stanton in Suffolk" in which coffins were "displaced" several times under mysterious circumstances. Nathan Lucas, one of the alleged witnesses to the final (1820) interment at the Chase Vault, mentions this English case, even quoting the article, in his privately written 1824 account.

A final tale is told by F. A. Paley in *Notes and Queries*, November 9, 1867, of an "instance which occurred within my own knowledge and recollection (some twenty years ago) in the parish of Gretford, near Stamford [England], of which my father was the rector. Twice, if not thrice, the coffins in a vault were found on re-opening it to have been disarranged. The matter excited some interest in the village at the time, and, of course, was a fertile theme for popular superstition: but I think it was hushed up out of respect to the family to whom the vault belonged." Paley quoted from an unnamed woman who claimed to remember the incident.

A Masonic hoax?
These four spottily documented nineteenth-century incidents have no twentieth-century equivalents, but they have attracted the attentions of such thoughtful latter-day writers as Lang, Rupert T. Gould, and Joe Nickell, who are responsible for the most thorough modern examinations.

Of these only Nickell comes to a firm conclusion. He argues that none of these incidents ever happened in the real world. The only one for which much information is available, the Barbados episode, is loaded with symbols and phrases which Freemasons would recognize. Nickell, who had investigated an earlier Masonic hoax involving a tale of buried treasure, contends the Barbados story was fashioned around the Masonic allegory of a "secret vault" which, according to a Masonic text, "was … in the ancient mysteries, symbolic of death, where alone Divine Truth is to be found....

● SOURCES:

Gould, Rupert T. *Oddities: A Book of Unexplained Facts.* New Hyde Park, NY: University Books, 1965.

Lang, A. "'Death's Deeds': A Bi-Located Story." *Folk-Lore* 18,4 (December 1907): 376-90.

Nickell, Joe, with John F. Fischer. *Secrets of the Supernatural: Investigating the World's Occult Mysteries.* Buffalo, NY: Prometheus Books, 1988.

Ouitanon, Frederick J. "The Ahrensburg Mystery." *Fate* 4, 4 (August 1950): 33–36.

284

We significantly speak of the place of initiation as 'the secret vault, where reign silence, secrecy and darkness.' It is in this sense of an entrance through the grave into eternal life, that the Select Master is to view the recondite but beautiful symbolism of the secret vault. Like every other myth and allegory of Masonry, the historical relation may be true or it may be false; it may be founded on fact or the invention of imagination; the lesson is still there, and the symbolism teaches it exclusive of the history."

Along with other suggestive evidence Nickell quotes these words from Lucas: "I examined the walls, the arch and every part of the vault and found every part old and similar; and a mason in my presence struck every part of the bottom with his hammer and all was solid." Nickell remarks, "In the Royal Arch degree of Masonry — to which the 'arch' above may have been in cryptic reference (just as the 'vault' suggests the 'secret vault' which, in Masonry, is said to have been 'curiously arched') — there is a reference to the 'sound of a hammer'. According to Macoy's *Illustrated History and Cyclopedia of Freemasonry*, 'The blow of the Master's hammer commands industry, silence, or the close of labour, and every brother respects or honors its sound.'" He goes on to quote from the Royal Arch decree ("We have examined the secret vault") and notes that the striking of stone — to determine its solidness — "is the means by which the secret vault is sought for and finally located!" Of course Lucas's use of the word "mason" here is also interesting.

Through his investigation Nickell learned that the men who supposedly participated in the events were Freemasons — as was Robert Dale Owen, chronicler of the alleged episode at Oesel. He also speculates that prominent Freemasons knew of the hoax. One was Sir Arthur Conan Doyle who, discussing the Barbados coffins in a December 1919 article in *The Strand*, used a word ("effluvia") whose significance only Masons would recognize. The word is "well known to Masons since it appears in the Master Mason degree," according to Nickell; "not only that, but it does so specifically in reference to 'the grave!'"

Though based entirely on circumstantial evidence, Nickell's speculations are intriguing and well argued. They are also, at this late date, unprovable. In any case, there is no compelling reason to believe any of the moving-coffin stories describe real-life occurrences.

NAZCA LINES ————————————————————

At some time before 1,000 B.C. the Nazca Valley, a desert region on Peru's southern coast, was occupied by a people whose sophisticated agricultural technology enabled them to build an irrigation system, improve their crops, and expand the area of cultivatable land. Over the next 1,500 years they also made advances in weaving, pottery, and architecture. The most celebrated of their cultural achievements, however, was the creation of a remarkable ground art whose precise function remains a mystery.

The so-called Nazca lines, of which there are thousands, consist of five kinds of markings. William H. Isbell writes:

> *Most common are the long straight lines. Thousands of these crisscross the desert in every direction.... Sometimes the lines turn back on themselves to form elaborate geometric complexes with zigzags or long parallel sets of oscillating lines. Second are the large geometric figures — elongated trapezoids or triangles — which were first noticed from the air.... Third are representational drawings of animal and plant forms accomplished with curving lines.... Frequently these three types of markings are combined in a single layout.... A fourth class of ground markings incorporates several kinds of rock piles.... The fifth class of ground art consists of figures on steep hillsides.*

The lines may be as narrow as six inches or as wide as several hundred yards. Some run for several miles. The Nazca people created them by removing the dark surface stones and placing them in the desired pattern. "Walking or sweeping the resulting figure disturbs a thin brown surface coating of material called desert varnish, which accumulates over time," William E. Shawcross writes. "This action exposes the creamy pink soil underneath." These light areas comprise the Nazca lines which, owing to the dry, stable climatic conditions of the area, have remained essentially unchanged over many centuries.

What has made these lines a curiosity that otherwise would interest only South American archaeologists is the fact that some (though not all) of the forms are visible only from the air. Within conventional archaeological circles this aspect has given rise to different interpretations: one, that the figures, which probably had some religious significance (they were not "roads," as some popular opinion had it), were not meant to be seen in their entirety, at least by human eyes, and two, that the Nazca people built balloons that enabled them to fly over the sites. This latter interpretation, though not impossible, seems devoid of supporting evidence.

Beacons of the gods?

The Nazca lines entered popular culture not long after the commencement of the UFO age, with its suggestions of extraterrestrial visitation. In the 1950s, as books and magazine articles about UFOs proliferated, some writers looked back to ancient history and mythology for evidence of early space contacts. In an article in the October 1955 issue of *Fate*, amateur archaeologist and UFO buff James W. Moseley suggested that since the markings were largely invisible from the ground, the Nazca people must have "constructed their huge markings as signals to interplanetary visitors or to some advanced earth race [presumably Atlanteans] that occasionally visited them."

Picking up on the theme, fringe archaeologist and flying-saucer contactee George Hunt Williamson devoted an entire chapter, "Beacons for the Gods," of his *Road in the Sky* (1959) to the lines. He wrote:

> [T]here were "sky gods" who came to Earth in the dim past. But why did they come and what was the necessity of immense astronomically perfect [sic] lines ...? These "gods" or heavenly messengers must have been in communication with some highly advanced civilizations on Earth: perhaps these people assisted the "gods" in the building of the lines and surfaces, or perhaps the "gods" were only the master architects and the Earth races did the actual building.

The "highly advanced civilizations" to which Williamson referred were from the lost continents of Lemuria and Atlantis, and of course the "gods" were space people. Williamson thought that archaeologically interesting sites, including the lines, had been built at "magnetic centers" at which spaceships could refuel.

In the early 1960s a French best-seller (published in England as *The Dawn of Magic* and in America as *The Morning of the Magicians* in 1963) by Louis Pauwels and Jacques Bergier offered a hodgepodge of speculations about what soon would be called "ancient astronauts" and mentioned the Nazca lines. Such speculations got their widest circulation in Erich von Däniken's *Chariots of the Gods?*, first published in West Germany in 1968 and subsequently reprinted in translated editions around the world. To von Däniken the lines represented an "airfield" on which spacecraft landed and from which they took off.

● SOURCES:

"Guardian Spirit of Nazca Lines." *New Zealand Herald* [Auckland] (November 4, 1991).

Isbell, William H. "Solving the Mystery of Nazca." *Fate* 33,10 (October 1980): 36–48.

Kozok, Paul. "The Mysterious Markings of Nazca." *Natural History* 56, 5 (May 1947): 200–07, 237–38.

Kozok, Paul, and Maria Reiche. "Ancient Drawings on the Desert of Peru." *Archaeology* 2 (1949): 206–15.

Moseley, James W. "Peruvian Desert Map for Saucers?" *Fate* 8, 10 (October 1955): 28–33.

Pauwels, Louis, and Jacques Bergier. *The Dawn of Magic*. London: Anthony Gibbs and Phillips, 1963.

Shawcross, William E. "Mystery on the Desert — The Nazca Lines." *Sky & Telescope* 68,3 (September 1984): 198–201.

Story, Ronald. *The Space-Gods Revealed: A Close Look at the Theories of Erich von Daniken*. New York: Harper and Row, 1976.

In fact, nothing in the nature of these lines sustains this interpretation. A von Däniken critic remarked indignantly, "It hardly seems reasonable that advanced extraterrestrial spacecraft would require *landing strips*"; besides, he wrote, Nazca's "soft, sandy soil … is hardly the kind of surface that would be required for an airport." Still, the notion was touted in a hugely successful documentary film based on von Däniken's book, and comparable speculations were endlessly recycled during the ancient-astronauts boom of the 1970s and wowed the ignorant and the impressionable.

Von Däniken, Erich. *Chariots of the Gods?: Unsolved Mysteries of the Past*. New York: G. P. Putnam's Sons, 1970.

Williamson, George Hunt. *Road in the Sky*. London: Neville Spearman, 1959.

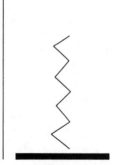

NOAH'S ARK

The Book of Genesis tells the story of Noah and his family, who escaped the Great Flood in an ark loaded with animals. At the conclusion of 40 days and 40 nights, the ark came to rest "upon the mountains of Ararat." Tradition and Bible literalists place this event in 2345 B.C. (the Genesis account was written some 1,300 years later), though geologists and archaeologists, citing the paucity of scientific evidence, doubt that any such massive flood ever took place.

If the flood did not happen, Noah and his ark did not exist, and the Bible is not inerrant. In the view of most scholars, the story should be read as one of many tales from all over the world of an immense flood and its chosen survivors. These stories do not prove that a universal deluge occurred; they seem to have arisen as responses to devastating local floods which encompassed, if not the whole world, at least the world its victims occupied.

To fundamentalists such an interpretation is unacceptable, and so for a long time hopeful seekers have searched for the remains of Noah's ark on Mount Ararat. There *is* a Mount Ararat; actually, to be more specific, there are two of them: Great Ararat (16,900 feet high) and Little Ararat (12,900). Connecting the two is a rock saddle between 7,000 and 8,000 feet high. These mountains lie in extreme eastern Turkey, along the border of Iran and Armenia.

In fact, Ararat is an ancient name for Armenia and, later, for a small northern district of that nation. The name was not attached to the mountain until around the eleventh century. Other sources, in any case, place the final resting of the ark elsewhere. The Koran mentions Mount Judi, associated with a mountain (subsequently renamed Judi after the Koran's account) to the south of Ararat. The first-century historian Flavius Josephus put the remains in what is now called Haran, a Turkish city near the Syrian border. Other ancient chroniclers had their own favored sites, most in Turkey but others in Greece, Armenia, and Iran.

Sightings and searches.

In short, historical claims for an ark on Ararat are shaky indeed. Nonetheless eventually Jews and Christians who gave thought to the subject came to believe that the ark's remains were still on Ararat. The pseudonymous travel writer Sir John Mandeville contended straight-facedly that on a clear day one could actually look up and see the ark. Around 1670 a Dutchman named Jan Struys, captured and enslaved by bandits in Armenia, met a hermit — or so he would claim later — on Ararat. Struys, believed by his captors to possess magical healing powers, treated the old man, who in gratitude handed him a "piece of hard wood of a dark color" and a sparkling stone, both of which "he told me he had taken from under the Ark."

In the nineteenth century a number of would-be discoverers climbed the mountain without finding anything — until 1876, when James Bryce of Oxford University came upon a four-foot-long stick near the peak of Great Arafat. He declared it to be a piece of the ark. On August 10, 1883, the *Chicago Tribune* published this colorful, but apparently entirely fictitious, tale:

> A paper at Constantinople announces the discovery of Noah's Ark. It appears that some Turkish commissioners appointed to investigate the avalanches on Mt. Ararat suddenly came on a gigantic structure of very dark wood, protruding from the glacier. They made inquiries of the local folk. These had seen it for six years, but had been afraid to approach it, because a spirit of fierce aspect had been seen looking out of the upper windows. The Turkish Commissioners, however, are bold men, not deterred by such trifles, and they determined to reach it.
>
> Situated as it was among the fastnesses of one of the glens of Mt. Ararat, it was a work of enormous difficulty, and it was only after incredible hardships that they succeeded. The Ark was in a good state of preservation.... They recognized it at once.
>
> There was an English-speaking man among them, who had presumably read his Bible, and he saw it was made of gopher wood, the ancient timber of the scripture, which, as everyone knows, grows only on the plains of the Euphrates. Effecting an entrance into the structure, which was painted brown, they found that the Admiralty requirements for the conveyance of horses had been carried out, and the interior was divided into partitions 15 feet high.
>
> Into only three of these could they get, the others being full of ice, and how far the Ark extended into the glacier they could not tell. If, however, on being uncovered, it turns out to be 300 cubits long [the dimensions cited in Genesis], it will go hard with disbelievers.

In 1892 Archdeacon John Joseph Nouri of the Chaldean Church reported that he had found the ark and even entered it. While there, he took the opportunity to measure it, finding — unsurprisingly — that it was 300 cubits long.

● SOURCES:

Balsiger, Dave, and Charles Sellier, Jr. *In Search of Noah's Ark*. Los Angeles: Sunn Classic Books, 1976.

Cazeau, Charles J., and Stuart D. Scott, Jr. *Exploring the Unknown: Great Mysteries Reexamined*. New York: Plenum Press, 1979.

Fasold, David. *The Discovery of Noah's Ark*. London: Sidgwick and Jackson, 1990.

Fort, Charles. *The Books of Charles Fort*. New York: Henry Holt and Company, 1941.

Hitching, Francis. *The Mysterious World: An Atlas of the Unexplained*. New York: Holt, Rinehart and Winston, 1978.

Michell, John, and Robert J. M. Rickard. *Phenomena: A Book of Wonders*. New York: Pantheon Books, 1977.

"More on 'Noah's Ark'." *INFO Journal* 2,2 (Spring 1970): 32.

Stein, Gordon. "Noah's Ark: Where Is It?" *Fate* 47, 2 (February 1988): 40–46.

Wilkins, Harold T. "Is Noah's Ark on Arafat?" *Fate* 3, 7 (November 1950): 60–66.

In the following decades a number of expeditions were launched. Most ended in disappointment, and a few others returned claiming sightings. A 1952 expedition led by wealthy French industrialist Fernand Navarra produced samples of wood which, when first tested, were dated at 5,000 years. A later, more accurate test resulted in a disappointing finding: the wood was from A.D. 800 and probably from a monks' shrine built on the side of the mountain. A 1960 *Life* photograph of a ship-shaped depression on the mountain sent an expedition racing for an on-site look — at what turned out to be a natural formation created by a recent landslide.

In the years since then, there have been other expeditions and other claims, none especially noteworthy. Most of the funding and personnel for these ventures have come from fundamentalist sources who reason that if Genesis can be shown to be accurate about Noah, its account of Creation can be trusted, too. Unfortunately the inflated pronouncements of "arkeologists," as they are called, have proven to be neither accurate nor trustworthy.

Critics have had no trouble pointing out the many flaws in arkeological thought. Scientists Charles J. Cazeau and Stuart D. Scott, Jr., remarked that "if the ark had come to rest near the summit of Ararat 5,000 years ago, it likely would have shifted by glacial movement to lower elevations long ago. To at least some extent, the ark would have broken up, the wood strewn about on the lower slopes of the mountain, easily accessible even to those who are not mountain climbers."

Charles Fort, the great anomaly collector and satirist, had this to say about Nouri's account, in words that apply to all of the arkeological quest:

I accept that anybody who is convinced that there are relics upon Mt. Ararat, has only to climb up Mt. Ararat, and he must find something that can be said to be part of Noah's Ark, petrified perhaps. If someone else should be convinced that a mistake has been made, and that the mountain is really Pike's Peak, he has only to climb Pike's Peak and prove that the most virtuous of all lands was once the Holy Land.

OGOPOGO

Around eight o'clock on a pleasant morning in mid-July 1974, a teenage girl was swimming just off the southern shore of Lake Okanagan, an 80-mile-long body of water in the southern interior of British Columbia. Her destination was a combined raft/diving platform a quarter-mile from the beach. She was only three feet from it when a huge, heavy something bumped against her legs. Startled and frightened, she lunged for the raft and climbed aboard.

From her new vantage point she looked into the clear water and saw a strange animal 15 or 20 feet away. "I could see a hump or coil which was eight feet long and four feet above the water moving in a forward motion," she told J. Richard Greenwell of the International Society of Cryptozoology over a decade later. "It was traveling north, away from me. It did not seem to be in much of a rush, and it swam very slowly.... Five to 10 feet behind the hump, about five to eight feet below the surface, I could see its tail. The tail was forked and horizontal like a whale's, and it was four to six feet wide. As the hump submerged, the tail came to the surface until its tip poked above the water about a foot."

The creature was lost to view soon afterwards. The entire incident had lasted four or five minutes.

The woman, identified at her request only as Mrs. B. Clark, told Greenwell that the animal had a "very dull dark gray" color and moved in an undulating fashion. She had the "impression that the head joined the body without a neck — like a fish or snake.... This thing looked more like a whale than a fish, but I have never seen a whale that skinny and snaky-looking before."

In fact, such a whale existed, at least at one time. Evidence of its presence can be found in the fossil record, though no trace of it has been uncovered any nearer to present time than 20 million years ago. It is known to zoolo-

Ogopogo, the monster of British Columbia's Lake Okanagan and star of "Ogopogo Days." (Courtesy of Loren Coleman.)

● SOURCES:

"Close Encounter in Lake Okanagan Revealed." *The ISC Newsletter* 6, 1 (Spring 1987): 1–3.

Conklin, Ellis E. "Ogopogo Brouhaha." *Seattle Post-Intelligencer* (March 7, 1991).

Farrow, Moira. "Encounters with 'Ogopogo'." *Vancouver Sun* (July 25, 1990). UFONS 260.

Greenwell, J. Richard. "Interview: The Lady of the Lake Talks About Ogopogo." *The ISC Newsletter* 5, 6 (Summer 1986): 1–3.

Kirk, John. "BCCC Report on Okanagan Lake, 1989." *Cryptozoology* 8 (1989): 75–79.

"Lloyds of London to Insure Ogopogo." *The ISC Newsletter* 3, 1 (Spring 1984): 3–4.

Mackal, Roy P. *Searching for Hidden Animals.* Garden City, NY: Doubleday and Company, 1980.

Moon, Mary. "Ogopogo: Canada's Loch Ness Monster." *Fate* 31, 11 (November 1978): 34–42.

292

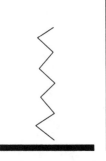

gists and paleontologists as the *Basilosaurus*, or zeuglodon, and something very much like it has been reported for decades in Okanagan. Since 1926 it has been called Ogopogo, after a parody of an English music-hall song.

Its silly name notwithstanding, Ogopogo is among the more plausible lake monsters, if for no other reason than that the reports are strikingly consistent. Moreover, they clearly do not take their inspiration from folkloric images of giant serpents or long-necked plesiosaurs. Zeuglodons are known to paleontologists and cryptozoologists and not many other people.

White settlers moved into the Lake Okanagan area around 1860 and almost immediately came to believe strange animals lived in the water. The Indians, who had long since come to that conclusion, said a serpent-like creature they called *naitaka* dwelled there, and *naitaka* figured in a cycle of supernatural legends. One of the early sightings by whites occurred in the mid-1870s, when two witnesses on opposite sides of the lake watched a long, snakelike creature swimming against the wind and current. Both had originally taken the object to be a log, and over the years many other witnesses would describe "logs that came alive."

By the 1920s hunting parties from Canada and the United States were scouring Okanagan hoping to kill a specimen, and sightings continued sporadically over the decades. Among the more impressive was one that took place on July 2, 1949, in the early evening, when a party aboard a boat just offshore saw a partially submerged animal from a distance of 100 feet. It had a "forked" horizontal tail (characteristic of whales) and moved its snakelike body in an undulating fashion (uncharacteristic of reptiles). About 30 feet of a smooth dark back was visible. The head was under water, presumably because the animal was feeding. Another witness saw the creature from land.

A 1967 sighting made by nearly 20 persons at Okanagan's southern tip makes the whale identification virtually certain: "It had a head like a bucket and was spouting water," according to one witness. On July 30, 1989, when Ogopogo appeared 1,000 feet away from an investigative team associated with the British Columbia Cryptozoology Club, John Kirk got a clear view through a telescope. "The animal's skin was whale-like," he reported.

From an analysis of over 200 reports compiled by Mary Moon, Roy P. Mackal gives this composite description of the Okanagan animals:

> The animals look most like a log, elongated, serpentine, no thickened body centrally, about 12 meters (40 feet) long, although a range of smaller sizes has been reported and a few larger, up to say 20 meters (70 feet).... The skin is described as dark green to green-black or brown to black and dark brown. Occasionally the color is given as gray to blue-black or even a golden brown. Most often the skin is smooth with no scales, although part of the body must possess a few plates, scales or similar structures observed by close-up viewers and compared to the lateral scales of sturgeon. Most of the back is smooth, although a portion is saw-toothed, ragged-edged, or serrated. Sparse hair or hair-bristle structures are reported around the head, and in a few cases a mane or comblike structure has been observed at the back of the neck.

Mackal remarks that these characteristics "fit one and only one known creature," zeuglodons, and takes note of reports of identical animals off the coast of British Columbia and in other Canadian lakes. He suggests that the Ogopogos are freshwater-adapted versions of animals which originally lived in the oceans and which also exist at Lakes Manitoba ("Manipogo"), Winnipegosis ("Winnipogo"), and Dauphin.

On the negative side, there are no convincing pictures of Ogopogo. All existing photographic evidence is inconclusive at best and suspect at worst. Possibly because Ogogopo has never received the sort of concentrated scientific attention paid to the Loch Ness monsters, there are no sonar traces or other instrumented evidence. So far the case for Ogopogo rests entirely on eyewitness testimony.

X. "A Mari Usque Ad Mare." Fortean Times 46 (Spring 1986): 44–51.

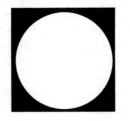

OLIVER LERCH DISAPPEARANCE

The story of a young man's tragic fate at the hands of unearthly forces has been chronicled for decades, always as a true account.

In the most common version the incident occurs on Christmas Eve 1889, 1890, or 1900 on a farm outside South Bend, Indiana. Friends and family have gathered for a holiday party. At one point during the evening Oliver Lerch (or Larch), age 20 (11 in some versions), sets out to the well to fetch water. It is a clear night, the clouds having passed earlier after dusting the ground with snow. Five minutes later horrible screams interrupt the Christmas celebration, and everyone dashes outside, where they see Oliver's tracks suddenly disappearing halfway to the well. A voice, apparently emanating from the sky though its source is not visible, screams, "It's got me! Help! Help!" The pathetic pleas fade away after a few minutes, and Oliver Lerch is never seen or heard again.

"The facts of the case," one chronicler asserted, "are clearly written down for everyone to see in the police records."

An identical tale, differing only in the name of the victim and the location of the otherworldly abduction, is told of 11-year-old Oliver Thomas of Rhayader, Wales. This version, apparently of recent vintage, first appears in "true mystery" paperbacks in the 1960s. Subsequent archival investigations in Rhayader have established conclusively that Oliver Thomas never existed.

The Lerch/Larch story is decades older. The most influential version, in the sense that retellings of it brought the story between book covers for the first time (in, for example, M. K. Jessup's *The Case for the UFO* [1955] and Frank Edwards's *Strangest of All* [1956]), appeared in the September 1950 issue of *Fate*. Twenty-seven years later another Fate writer, Joe Nickell, got the earlier contributor, Joseph Rosenberger, to confess, "There is not a single bit of truth to the 'Oliver Lerch' tale.... It was all fiction for a buck."

Though Rosenberger claimed to have made it up himself, in fact the story was known well before 1932, when Rudolf H. Horst, managing editor of the *South Bend Tribune*, responded to an inquiry from British writer Harold T. Wilkins. Horst said the story "was purely imaginary. We frequently hear of this supposed incident regarding the Lerch family, but have never been able to locate such a family."

The story's plot comes from an early science-fiction story, "Charles Ashmore's Trail," published in an 1893 collection by Ambrose Bierce, *Can Such Things Be?* Set in Quincy, Illinois, in November 1878, it tells of the title character's ill-fated trip to the well and of his family's horrified discovery of tracks that "abruptly ended, and all beyond was smooth, unbroken snow." Later family members hear his voice seeming to "come from a great distance, faintly, yet with entire distinctness of articulation." No one has been able to determine how Charles Ashmore became Oliver Lerch, however, or how a tale never intended to be anything but fantasy became a "true mystery."

● SOURCES:

Begg, Paul. *Into Thin Air: People Who Disappear.* North Pomfret, VT: David & Charles, 1979.

Edwards, Frank. *Strangest of All.* Secaucus, NJ: The Citadel Press, 1956.

Jessup, M. K. *The Case for the UFO.* New York: The Citadel Press, 1955.

Nickell, Joe. "The Oliver Lerch Disappearance: A Postmortem." *Fate* 33, 3 (March 1980): 61–65.

Nickell, Joe, and John F. Fischer. *Secrets of the Supernatural: Investigating the World's Occult Mysteries.* Buffalo, NY: Prometheus Books, 1988.

Rosenberger, Joseph. "What Happened to Oliver Lerch?" *Fate* 4, 5 (September 1950): 28–31.

Steiger, Brad. *Strangers from the Skies.* New York: Award Books, 1966.

Wilkins, Harold T. *Mysterious Disappearances of Men and Women in the U.S.A., Britain and Europe.* Girard, KS: Haldeman-Julius Publications, 1948.

ONZA

The onza is Mexico's most famous mystery feline, reported for centuries in the remote Sierra Madre Occidental Mountain range in the northwestern part of the country. Though zoologists have yet to grant it official recognition, its existence now seems nearly beyond dispute. The exact nature of the beast, however, is yet to be determined.

To the Aztecs the onza (or, as they called it, *cuitlamiztli*) was an animal distinct from the two other large cats, the puma and the jaguar, with which they shared an environment. After the Spanish conquerors arrived, they called on the emperor Montezuma, who showed them his great zoo. In it, Bernal Diaz del Castillo observed, were "tigers [jaguars] and lions [pumas] of two kinds, one of which resembled the wolf."

The later Spanish settlers of northwestern Mexico noted the presence in the wild of a wolflike cat — with long ears, a long, narrow body and long, thin legs — and gave it the name *onza*, from the Latin *uncia*, referring to the cheetah of Asia and Africa. They also remarked on its fierceness. "It is not as timid as the [puma]," Father Ignaz Pfefferkorn, a Jesuit missionary stationed in Sonora, wrote in 1757, "and he who ventures to attack it must be well on his guard." According to Father Johann Jakob Baegert, who worked with the Guaricura Indians in Baja California in the mid-eighteenth century, "One onza dared to invade my neighbor's mission while I was visiting, and attacked a 14-year-old boy in broad daylight and practically in full view of all the people; and a few years ago another killed the strongest and most respected soldier" in the area.

Yet outside its range the onza was virtually unknown. The occasional published references to it made no impression, and zoologists continued to assume that only pumas and jaguars lived there. No serious scientific field expeditions into the rugged terrain, inaccessible in many places even to horses, were ever mounted to investigate the question.

Then in the 1930s two experienced mountain hunting guides, Dale and Clell Lee, were working in the mountains of Sonora when they heard for the first time of the onza. In time they moved their operation 500 miles to the south, to Sinaloa, where they took Indiana banker Joseph H. Shirk to hunt jaguars on the wildlife-rich La Silla Mountain. There they treed and killed a strange cat which they immediately realized was something other than a puma. In fact, it looked exactly like the onzas that locals said lived in the region. After measuring and photographing it, they butchered the animal. Shirk kept the skull and skin. Their present whereabouts are unknown.

Certain they had found something of importance, the Lees described the animals to American zoologists. They were stunned when both the scientists and the newspapers ridiculed their story. Conservative and cautious by nature, unused to having their word questioned, the brothers withdrew and ceased discussing the experience — until the 1950s, when an Arizona man, Robert Marshall, befriended Dale Lee and sympathetically recorded his testimony. Marshall even went down to Mexico to conduct further investigations, the results of which he recounted in a 1961 book, *The Onza*, which, aside from a single (unfavorable) review in a scientific journal, attracted no attention whatever.

The onza in the age of cryptozoology.
In 1982, at a meeting at the Smithsonian Institution in Washington, D.C., the International Society of Cryptozoology (ISC) came into being, and for the first time biological scientists interested in unknown, unrecognized, or disputed animals had a formal structure through which research could be conducted. Cryptozoologists were among the few nonresidents of northwestern Mexico to have heard of the onza.

The ISC secretary, J. Richard Greenwell, lived in Tucson where, so he would learn, Robert Marshall also resided. So, as it happened, did Dale Lee. Marshall possessed an onza skull, and he gave Greenwell a cast of its upper tooth row. Greenwell subsequently showed it to a West German mammalogist, Helmut Hemmer, who had proposed that onzas were relics of a prehistoric species of North American cheetah *(Acinonyx trumani)*. Eventually comparison of skulls eliminated that identification from further consideration, but the very fact that the discussion had happened at all indicated that the onza was finally about to get its due.

While engaged in a unsuccessful pursuit of the long-missing Shirk skull, Greenwell and Marshall coordinated their efforts with two interested mammalogists, Troy Best and E. Lendell Cockrum, respectively of the Universities of New Mexico and Arizona. Through Cockrum they met Sinaloa, Mexico, rancher Ricardo Urquijo, Jr., who had the intact skull of an onza killed by another rancher, Jesus Vega, in the same area as the onzas associated with the other two skulls. Meanwhile Best, an authority on puma skulls, located another onza skull in the Academy of Natural Sciences in Philadelphia.

At 10:30 on the evening of January 1, 1986, two deer hunters in the San Ignacio District of Sinaloa shot and killed a large cat. It clearly was not a jaguar, and they had no idea what it was. Recalling that a few months earlier a couple of gringos (Greenwell and Marshall) had talked with a rancher friend about their interest in an unusual animal, they alerted Manuel Vega, who recognized the creature as an onza as soon as he saw it. Vega's father, in fact, had once shot an onza.

Through the help of the wealthy Urquijo family (one of whose members had supplied Cockrum with the Vega skull) the body was placed in a freezer at a commercial fishery company in Mazatlan, and Greenwell was notified. In due course Greenwell and Best photographed and dissected the creature in that city, at the Regional Diagnostic Laboratory of Animal Pathology, an agency of Mexico's Ministry of Agriculture. Greenwell wrote:

> Upon inspection, the cat, a female, appeared to be as described by the native people. It had a remarkably gracile body, with long, slender legs and a long tail. The ears also seemed very long for a puma (about 100 mm.) and small horizontal stripes were found on the inside of its forelimbs, which, as far as has been determined to date, are not found in puma. Well-developed mammae were observed, and its age was determined to be at least 4 years. It weighed about 27 kg. (in life, prior to freezing, it probably weighed a little more), compared to a range of from 36 to 60 kg. in adult female pumas. Its total length, at 186 cm., fell within the normal range of female pumas of from 150 to 233 cm. The tail, however, was 73 cm. in length, very long for a female puma of comparable size; the range in female pumas is from 53 cm. to 81 cm.

Tissue samples and organs were taken to the United States for further analysis. Unfortunately, in the intervening years Greenwell and Best would not pursue the matter with any great vigor, pleading lack of time and commitment to other projects. A preliminary comparison of tissue samples of pumas and the onza, conducted at Texas Tech University, indicates great similarities and no significant differences, but the analysts prepared no technical report. In any case, no conclusions could be drawn from a single test of this sort, since animals of different species are often quite close genetically.

The samples, still stored and frozen, will need to undergo far more study before scientists can establish whether the animal is a new species or just some local genetic oddity. The evidence to date seems to suggest the former more firmly than the latter, and it is a pity that the matter has remained stalemated as late as mid-1992.

According to one account, in 1986 ranchers trapped an onza in northern Sonora, near the Arizona border, and kept it alive for a few days while they tried to interest the authorities in looking at it. Finally, after none had expressed interest, its keepers killed the animal and disposed of its body in the dry bed of a stream.

● SOURCES:

"ICSEB III Cryptozoology Symposium." The ISC Newsletter 4, 3 (Autumn 1985): 7–8.

Marshall, Robert E. The Onza. New York: Exposition Press, 1961.

"Onza Identity Still Unresolved." The ISC Newsletter 7, 4 (Winter 1988): 5–6.

"Onza Specimen Obtained — Identity Being Studied." The ISC Newsletter 5, 1 (Spring 1986): 1–6.

"Two New Onza Skulls Found." The ISC Newsletter 4, 4 (Winter 1984): 6–7.

ORANG-PENDEK

Sumatra is a large Indonesian island which contains millions of acres of rain forest. It also hosts the gibbon, orangutan, and sun bear — the last a species of bear which, almost alone among its kind, stands on its hind feet, though it does not run on them. According to many who say they have seen them, there is another extraordinary Sumatran animal: the orang-pendek, or "little man." (Some call it the sedapa.) Those who refuse to credit the reports explain them as having arisen from misidentifications of the other animals mentioned above.

Orang-pendeks are said to stand between two and a half and five feet tall (a few reports describe slightly taller specimens) and to be covered with short dark hair, with a thick, bushy mane going halfway or farther down the back. Its arms are shorter than an anthropoid ape's, and — unlike Sumatra's other apes — it more often walks on the ground than climbs in trees. Its footprint is like that of a small human being, only broader. Its diet consists of fruits and small animals.

Witnesses frequently mention the orang-pendek's startlingly humanlike appearance, thus its name. A Dutch settler named Van Herwaarden said he encountered one in October 1923, and though he bore a rifle and was an experienced hunter, "I did not pull the trigger. I suddenly felt that I was going to commit murder." He provided this exceptionally detailed description:

> The sedapa was also hairy on the front of its body; the color there was a little lighter than on the back. The very dark hair on its head fell to just below the shoulder blades or even almost to the waist. It was fairly thick and very shaggy. The lower part of its face seemed to end in more of a point than a man's; this brown face was almost hairless, whilst its forehead seemed to be high rather than low. Its eyebrows were frankly moving; they were of the darkest color, very lively, and like human eyes. The nose was broad with fairly large nostrils, but in no way

clumsy.... Its lips were quite ordinary, but the width of its mouth was strikingly wide when open. Its canines showed clearly from time to time as its mouth twitched nervously. They seemed fairly large to me, at all events they were more developed than a man's. The incisors were regular. The color of the teeth was yellowish white. Its chin was somewhat receding. For a moment, during a quick movement, I was able to see its right ear which was exactly like a little human ear. Its hands were slightly hairy on the back. Had it been standing, its arms would have reached to a little above its knees; they were therefore long, but its legs seemed to me rather short. I did not see its feet, but I did see some toes which were shaped in a very normal manner. The specimen was of the female sex and about 5 feet high.

Because primatologists have never been shown a living or dead specimen, most have rejected the eyewitness reports as hoaxes (as was the account above, by a museum curator on the grounds that the description was "too exact") or as misidentifications of orangutans or gibbons. Some alleged orang-pendek prints have been conclusively identified as those of sun bears. Though a few others have resisted easy accounting, they have not settled the question, to which in any event few zoologists have paid any significant attention. Thus, deservedly so or no, it is usually labeled "mythical or legendary" when mentioned in print.

Recent investigations.

In the summer of 1989, British travel writer Deborah Martyr visited the montane rain forests of the Kerinci region of southwestern Sumatra. While they were camped on the slopes of Mount Kerinci, her guide informed her that to the east, in the dense forest on the other side of Mount Tujuh's crater lake, one occasionally could see orang-pendeks. When Martyr responded skeptically, the guide related his own two sightings.

Intrigued, Martyr proceeded to interview residents of the settlements in the area and collected numerous sighting reports. "All reports included the information that the animal has a large and prominent belly — something not mentioned in previous literature on the subject," she would write. Some said the mane could be dark yellow or tan in some cases, black or dark gray in others. Her suggestions that these creatures were really orangutans, sun bears, or siamangs elicited outraged reactions.

In the course of her inquiries, Martyr trekked to the south edge of the Mount Kerinci region where she was told the creatures were often seen. Though she did not have a sighting of her own, she did find tracks. Of one set she noted, "Each print was clearly delineated, the big toe and four smaller toes easily visible. The big toe was placed as it would be in a human foot. The foot had a clearly defined high, curved instep. It measured just under 6 inches (15.2 cm) in length, and fractionally under 4 inches (10.1 cm) at the widest point of the ball of the foot. The heel was narrow and well-rounded. If we had been reasonably close to a village, I might have momentarily thought the prints to be those of a healthy seven-year-old child. The ball of the foot was, however, too broad even for a people who habitually wear no shoes."

The photographs she took turned out poorly, owing to falling rain and attendant lighting conditions, but she did take a plaster cast back to Sungeipenuh and the headquarters of the Kerinci Seblat National Park, whose director had earlier dismissed orang-pendek reports because, as he told Martyr, the local people were "simple." But when he and his associates examined the cast, they agreed it was of no animal with which they were familiar.

Unfortunately, this tantalizing evidence was to fall victim to other scientists' apathy or hostility to orang-pendeks. The track was sent to the Indonesian National Parks Department and never seen again, in spite of Martyr's repeated efforts to get a statement or, failing that, a return of the sample.

Martyr, who had barely heard of the creature before her Sumatran trip, reflected ruefully, "I had mistakenly assumed that, since I myself had been able to find a number of tracks of *orang-pendek*, there would be a considerable volume of writings on the subject, and that there would also be plaster casts available. Had I realized at the time that this was not to be the case, I would have retained the surviving cast, and I also would have taken more care in photographing the actual tracks."

From her inquiries, which Martyr has said she hopes to resume, she has concluded that the orang-pendek's existence in the high rain forests of southwestern Sumatra is 80-percent probable. "If it is ground-dwelling and elusive," she says, "this could explain how it has escaped zoological notice, and is known only to the native people."

The orang-pendek's transition from cryptozoological controversy to zoological respectability will happen, it appears, only after scientists cease sneering and start investigating. To date they have done far more of the former than of the latter.

● SOURCES:

Dammerman, K. W. "The Orang Pendek or Ape-Man of Sumatra." *Proceedings, Fourth Pacific Science Congress* 3 (1930): 121–26.

Heuvelmans, Bernard. *On the Track of Unknown Animals.* New York: Hill and Wang, 1958.

Martyr, Deborah. "An Investigation of the Orang-Pendek, the 'Short Man' of Sumatra." *Cryptozoology* 9 (1990): 57–65.

Sanderson, Ivan T. *Abominable Snowmen: Legend Come to Life.* Philadelphia, PA: Chilton Book Company, 1961.

301

PALUXY TRACKS

Did dinosaurs and human beings coexist? No, according to paleontologists, who maintain that dinosaurs and people missed each other by over 60 million years. Nonetheless evidence which seemed to indicate the contrary has intrigued creationists — Christian fundamentalists who reject evolution and who believe in a literal interpretation of Genesis — and secular theorists attracted to unorthodox readings of the earth's prehistory.

In the late 1930s Roland Bird, field explorer for the American Museum of Natural History, examined some curious tracks in the limestone bed of the Paluxy River near Glen Rose, Texas, southwest of Fort Worth. Many of the tracks, believed by paleontologists to date from the Cretaceous period 100 million years ago, were clearly of dinosaurs. Others, however, were of a strange and unsettling appearance; they looked, weirdly enough, as if human beings had made them. Though these could not have been normal human beings — the tracks measured from 15 to 20 inches in length and eight in width — even Bird acknowledged they seemed to show insteps and heels in their proper places.

Though Bird rejected any notion that these tracks demanded a radical revision of conventional paleontology, others who came later were not so cautious. Some saw the tracks as a blow to a hated doctrine, evolution. By the 1960s, as the "scientific creationist" movement took shape, the conservative Christian scientists leading the assault on Darwinism and its descendants argued that the discovery "suggests that simple and complex types of life were coexistent in time past or during geologic ages," in the words of Clifford Burdick, author of *Footprints in the Sands of Time* (1975). "This does not harmonize with the hypothesis that complex types of life evolved from lower or more simple forms." Moreover, the tracks not only cast doubt on science's view that the earth is of great age, the creationists asserted, but constituted evidence for a Great Flood which creationists think occurred around 4,000 B.C. In the Flood humans and dinosaurs perished together. The tracks also showed, as the Biblical Book of Genesis indicates, that giants had once walked the earth.

As creationists vigorously promoted the Paluxy tracks as devastating disproof of evolution, evolutionary scientists, who till then had done no more than ridicule the creationist claims, launched a serious, if belated, study of the "human" prints. In the early 1980s four of them traveled to Glen Rose and two other Texas sites and examined every example cited in the antievolution literature. Some clearly had been carved and were not tracks at all, as even some creationists had conceded. Others, the scientists thought, were the product of erosion and also not tracks at all; either that, or they were dinosaur prints in which for various reasons the toe marks had not been preserved.

It would be left, however, to an amateur dinosaur investigator with a not-unsympathetic view of creationism to solve the puzzle conclusively. Since 1980 Glen J. Kuban, a computer programmer from Ohio, had been making regular pilgrimages to Paluxy to study the tracks. Four years into his investigation he made a remarkable discovery: colorations that followed the pattern of dinosaurian digits. In other words, sediments different from those in the rest of the track had filled in the toe marks and later hardened to rock.

At first other dinosaur specialists were reluctant to endorse Kuban's findings, since they violated a long-held belief that bipedal dinosaurs nearly always walked on their toes. The Paluxy tracks suggested that these dinosaurs sometimes pressed the full weight of the soles of their feet on the ground. Subsequently, after other paleontologists found the same colorations in similar tracks near Clayton, New Mexico, they accepted Kuban's interpretation as correct. Kuban and a colleague, Ronnie Hastings, invited leading creation scientists to the site and persuaded them that these were dinosaur, not human, prints. A creationist movie on Paluxy, *Footprints in Stone*, was quickly withdrawn.

Noncreationist writers on "true mysteries" also have discussed the prints, not to prove Genesis but to argue that human history is far older than generally thought. In *Worlds Before Our Own* (1978), for example, Brad Steiger wrote that advanced civilizations of giant human beings may have existed millions of years ago. "Cataclysmic changes in the Earth's crust" as well as a "prehistoric nuclear war" wiped out all nearly all evidence for their presence. Among the few surviving pieces are the Paluxy prints.

● SOURCES:

Kitcher, Philip. *Abusing Science: The Case Against Creationism.* Cambridge, MA: The MIT Press, 1982.

Patterson, John W. "Dinosaurs and Men: The Case for Coexistence." *Pursuit* 18, 3 (Third Quarter 1985): 98–102.

Schafersman, Steven. "Raiders of the Lost Tracks: The Best Little Footprints in Texas." *The Skeptical Inquirer* 7, 3 (Spring 1983): 2–6.

Steiger, Brad. *Worlds Before Our Own.* New York: Berkley-Putnam, 1978.

Wilford, John Noble. "Fossils of 'Man Tracks' Shown to Be Dinosaurian." *New York Times* (June 17, 1986).

PHANTOM ATTACKERS

The best known of the world's phantom attackers was the "mad gasser of Mattoon," a figure so elusive that eventually law-enforcement authorities in the small central Illinois town declared him nonexistent. That explanation was ratified the next year, in 1945, by a social scientist who wrote that the gasser was the creation of mass hysteria.

Though acknowledging the undeniable role of hysteria, some observers have argued that it alone is insufficient to account for every aspect of the affair. Clouded with ambiguities which are unlikely ever to be cleared up, the episode by its very nature ensures that any conclusion drawn from it can only be tentative. Particularly interesting in this regard, however, is an obscure and nearly identical series of events which occurred in Botetourt County, Virginia, between December 1933 and January 1934; according to all available evidence, Mattoonites had never heard of these incidents.

It must also be said that the irrational, even nonsensical nature of the Mattoon and Botetourt events leads us to conclude that whatever its limitations, the hysteria solution seems the only alternative to the far more extraordinary one, that the "mad gassers" stepped out of the Goblin Universe. Which is not to say there is no Goblin Universe, only that if there is one, we can reasonably demand of its residents that they provide us with more robust indications of their existence. In all but a smattering of instances, individuals believed to be responsible for the gassings were only briefly glimpsed, and even here ordinary prowlers or transients may have been mistaken for strangers from the twilight zone.

An army of apparitions.
In the summer of 1692, at Cape Ann, Massachusetts, an odd series of events began when Ebenezer Babson, returning home late one night, said he saw two men step out of his house and dash into a cornfield. When he ran inside to check on his family's welfare, his wife and children were nonplussed by his questions; no intruders had entered the house, they insisted.

Babson grabbed a gun and went outside, where he spotted the two men bolting up from behind a log. As they escaped to a nearby swamp, one was overheard saying to the other, "The man of the house is now come; else we might have taken the house."

The family repaired to a military garrison not far away, and Babson then sneaked outside, where he encountered the two men again. The following day he came upon them a third time, and they chased him into the garrison. Over the next week or two Babson, sometimes alone, sometimes in the company of others, had further encounters with mysterious strangers, suspected to be French-Canadian scouts in league with hostile Indians.

On July 14 the entire garrison watched half a dozen of the strangers. A pursuit party, with Babson in the lead, got within gunshot range. Babson fired on them, and three fell to the ground, only to rise to their feet with no apparent signs of injury. As they fled, one turned to fire on Babson; the bullet narrowly missed him and lodged in a tree, from which its intended victim subsequently retrieved it. A few minutes later the garrison group trapped one of the strangers. Babson shot him, and the man dropped. But when Babson and his companions rushed to the spot, no one was there. Several days later two scouts from the garrison observed 11 of the strange men as they performed what looked like peculiar incantations. Richard Dolliver fired on them, causing them to scatter.

Soon the entire Cape was in an uproar, and 60 armed men came from Ipswich to reinforce the garrison. As sightings continued, the strangers were accused of beating on barns, throwing stones, and other acts. Babson experienced one of the last sightings. Seeing three of the strangers, he dived behind a bush and waited in ambush — only to have his gun misfire. The strangers gave him a disdainful glance and walked on.

Soon afterwards they were gone, much to Cape residents' relief. By now, according to the famous New England clergyman, historian, and witch-hunter Cotton Mather, who wrote an account of the episode, people suspected that the strangers were something other than human beings — demons, perhaps. Four centuries later we are not likely to find out who the strangers were or were not, though one suspects that in the latter stages of the episode pranksters may have taken advantage of the hysteria.

Fears great and small.
History's most notorious phantom attack struck terror in the French provinces over a two-week period just after the outbreak of the Revolution on July 14, 1789. It began at Nantes on the twentieth, with rumors that an army was marching on the town to restore order. Between then and August 6 such hysteria erupted in other regions of France, the product of the breakdown of the legal and social order. As historian Simon Schama writes, "The effect of this prolonged sense of anxiety was to create the politics of paranoia that would eventually engulf the Revolution."

The attackers were variously thought to be Austrian, British, Spanish, or Swedish troops or "brigands," or freed galley slaves bent on vengeance.

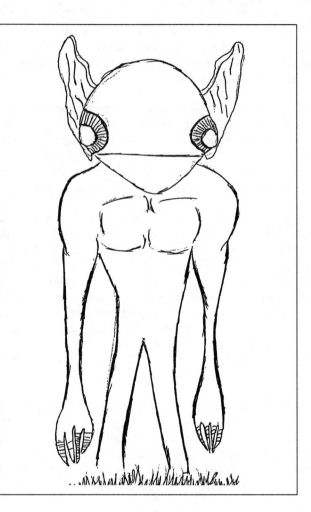

A composite drawing by investigator Budd Ledwith of witness descriptions of the Kelly humanoids. (Courtesy of Loren Coleman.)

Typically news of an attack began through the arrival in town of a frightened messenger who claimed to have witnessed the destruction of a neighboring village and the gruesome slaughter of its residents. From there the stories spread to surrounding towns, and the Fear moved in waves from, according to its leading chronicler, Georges Lefebvre, six different locations in six regions of the country.

As phantom attacks go, the Fear is among the least inexplicable. No one has tried to argue that it amounted to anything other than collective panic, and it is mentioned here only because of its notoriety and scale. In more recent times "little panics" have afflicted much more restricted regions. Sociologist Ron Westrum has described two cases which occurred in rural areas of Michigan in 1978. In both cases occupants of houses became convinced they were under nocturnal siege by mysterious figures who, with one or two exceptions, were observed only fleetingly. Westrum concluded that if these "attacks" were not purely hallucinatory — his "best guess" — they "may be the result of unusual human activity, or they may represent instances of a still unknown psychological or physical phenomenon."

Attack of the apemen.
In the early years of the twentieth century, the words "Bigfoot" and "Sasquatch" were not so instantly recognizable as they are today, though rural residents of the Pacific Northwest knew that some people believed a race of hairy giants with both ape and human features lived in the woods and mountains. According to nearly all reports then and since, these creatures are of a retiring disposition and, upon encountering a human being, opt to duck out of sight as rapidly as possible. In other words, for all their size and fierce appearance, they practically never behave aggressively.

If we are to believe Fred Beck, an exception to that pattern of behavior manifested itself one night in July 1924. The episode was reported in a local newspaper at the time; reporters who came to the site noted the presence of big footprints, and Beck swore to its truth to the end of his life decades later. In 1967 he and his son published a short book based on the elder Beck's memories of the encounter.

Beck and his four partners eked out a living prospecting for gold in the Mount Saint Helens and Lewis River region of southwestern Washington. From time to time they found giant, humanlike footprints in the sand along the water. They would also hear a peculiar "thudding, hollow thumping noise" but could never determine its source. There were also shrill whistling sounds.

By now the men would not go anywhere without their rifles. Finally, as Beck and a companion identified only as Hank were drawing water from a spring not far from their mountain cabin, they saw and shot at a seven-foot-tall apelike creature. It sprinted away, disappearing from sight for a short while, and then reappeared 200 yards down the canyon. Beck fired at it three times before it was lost to sight.

All that night, with only brief interludes of quiet, the "apes" besieged the cabin. They threw rocks at it, jumped on the roof, and tried to smash the door open even as Beck and Hank riddled it with bullets. At daybreak the attack ended, and as the sun rose, the men gingerly stepped outside. A few minutes later, spotting one of the apes standing near the edge of a canyon 80 yards away, Beck put his rifle to his shoulder, aimed, fired, and watched the creature drop 400 feet into the gorge below.

The area where these events supposedly took place is still known as Ape Canyon. Over the years several individuals have come forward to testify that Beck and his companions were victims of a prank for which they were responsible. These stories do not agree with each other, nor are they compatible with Beck's. For the hoax claims to work, we must assume that the victims helped the pranksters along by falling victim to extraordinarily vivid hallucinations. It also seems odd, when one considers the prominent role gunfire plays in the tale, that the pranksters persisted despite a clear and present danger to their very lives.

In short, it is easier to believe that Beck was the perpetrator of a hoax than that he was a victim of one. His son Ronald Beck still swears that his

father's story was "straight and true," and Peter Byrne, a noncredulous Bigfoot investigator who interviewed Beck in 1960, wrote that he "seemed to me to be honest and to be telling a true account." The other alleged witnesses were long scattered and not locatable, even if alive, by the time there was such a thing as a "Bigfoot investigator"; so except for the early newspaper accounts, we have nothing from their point of view and, at this juncture, are unlikely ever to have it.

Hairy bipeds usually compared to (and referred to as) Bigfoot have been reported outside the Pacific Northwest, in fact (or at least in allegation) in rural areas in just about every state and province of the United States and Canada. These creatures often exhibit magical or paranormal qualities — as, interestingly, did Beck's. Of them he said, "they are not entirely of this world.... I was, for one, always conscious that we were dealing with supernatural beings and I know the other members of the party felt the same."

Such creatures figure in one modern phantom-attack story related in a self-published monograph by Dennis Pilichis. Pilichis, a resident of Rome, a small town in northeastern Ohio, was for a time an active figure among UFO and monster buffs. When reports occurred in his area, he would interview witnesses. On one occasion, he would claim, he became part of the story himself.

According to his account, which names no witnesses except himself and his fellow monster hunters, in 1981 residents of the countryside around Rome began coming upon strange sights: oddly wounded or killed animals, unexplained holes in the ground, and other anomalies. Soon one farm family saw a "black form with two big red, glowing eyes" in their front yard. It was seven or eight feet tall. While one of the boys shined a light into its eyes, the father blasted it with a shotgun. It screamed and ran off into a field.

This is supposed to have happened late on the evening of June 25. This precipitated — according to Pilichis — a series of encounters, the next about two hours later, with giant gorillalike creatures with red, glowing eyes and sharp fangs. On subsequent nights these otherworldly entities, one carrying a dark blue light, were seen moving in and out of a wooded area not far from the house. The family expended a fair amount of ammunition on the creatures, which they were able to knock down but not to kill.

On July 1 Pilichis came to investigate and took casts of three-toed tracks. (All primates have five toes, but three-toed tracks are frequently associated with Midwestern hairy bipeds.) That night, staking themselves out on their roof and gazing toward the trees, they experienced some hours' worth of bizarre sights, including lights, glowing eyes, and shadowy forms. Pilichis reports:

> Everytime [sic] various family members thought they could see one of the forms, they would shoot and the forms would "scream." They would watch the woodline and start seeing red glowing eyes, standing, watching their every move. They would shoot at the red eyes,

with no effect, at the same time seeing forms running to the left and to the right of the set of "eyes."

The family members thought that for some reason, the glowing eyes were being used as some sort of diversion to draw their attention away from the forms. They shot at the forms, hitting them and hearing them scream.

On a return trip soon afterwards, Pilichis found numerous three-toed prints. Then after darkness fell he and a companion tossed rocks into the woodline, hoping to stir whatever was there. In response something fired a rock over their heads. It landed near the family members, who were standing 15 feet behind the two men. Then, Pilichis wrote, "Numerous sets of eyes could be seen throughout the night.... Sometimes three of the creatures at a time would hide behind trees ... periodically stepping out from behind them. Sets of red glowing eyes could be seen 10 to 12 feet off the ground[;] sometimes eyes could be seen only two or three feet off the ground."

Later that night Pilichis shined a high-beam flashlight directly on a 12-foot-tall creature. Family members opened fire on it, with only minimal effect. It turned sideways "with a strange sort of motion" and stepped out of the beam.

Other adventures occurred the night of August 21–22, when Pilichis and others laid a trap, using rabbits as bait, in an unsuccessful attempt to capture one of the hairy bipeds.

Pilichis's refusal to release any names, plus the dubious reputation of one of his companions (an individual associated with questionable claims in the past), assured his book a less than rapturous response even from the tiny community of UFO and monster fans. In other words, even those who thought such things *could* happen had their doubts. Such skepticism infuriated Pilichis, who subsequently dropped out of sight.

Fear of little men.
The UFO era has produced at least one classic phantom-attack story, one that attracted the attention of the Air Force's official UFO-investigative agency, Project Blue Book.

Early on the evening of August 21, 1955, Billy Ray Taylor, who lived with 10 other persons (all but two of them relatives), in a farmhouse near tiny Kelly, Kentucky, stepped outside to get drinking water in a backyard well. He dashed into the house to announce that he had seen a flying saucer drop down into a gully on the far side of a surrounding field.

No one took him seriously enough to investigate, but about an hour later, when they heard a dog's frightened barks and saw it shoot under the house with its tail between its legs, Taylor and Lucky Sutton looked out back at the strangest thing they had ever seen: a luminous, three-and-a-half-foot-tall being with an oversized head, big, floppy, pointed ears, glowing eyes,

One witness to the humanoids who allegedly laid siege to a rural house near Kelly, Kentucky, in August 1955 claimed one grabbed his hair. (Courtesy of Loren Coleman.)

and hands with talons at their ends. The figure, either made of or simply dressed in silvery metal, had its hands raised.

If this was intended as a gesture of peace, it was not so interpreted. When it got within 20 feet of the two men, they opened up on it with a shotgun and a .22 rifle. In response it flipped over and scurried into the darkness along the side of the house. A few minutes later the same or a similar being showed its face in a side window, and this time J. C. Sutton (Lucky's brother) and Taylor fired on it, in J. C.'s case at almost point-blank range.

Until 11 P.M., when all concerned packed into a car and roared at top speed to the Hopkinsville police station seven miles away, the witnesses repeatedly saw and shot at the creatures, which would roll over and escape, propelling themselves with their arms and hands. Their legs, skinny and inflexible, seemed to have no other function than to orient them vertically. If the creatures were in a tree or on the roof when hit, they would float, not fall, to the ground.

At no time did they display overt hostility. The observers had no idea how many of the creatures there were. They could be certain only that there were at least two because once they saw that number at the same time.

When they showed up at the station, the witnesses were in a state of such hysteria that police chief Russell Greenwell said it was evident something "beyond reason, not ordinary," had frightened them. On the way back to the farm, a medically trained investigator measured the pulse rate in Taylor's neck. It was twice normal. But there was additional evidence: a state police officer's sighting, made at the time of the witnesses' flight to Hopkinsville, of strange "meteors" passing overhead "with a noise like artillery fire." They were heading the opposite direction of the witnesses, in other words north in the direction of Kelly.

Though they found no direct evidence of alien visitors, Greenwell and other investigating officers found plenty of indications that shooting had been going on. Aside from that, Greenwell told ufologist Isabel Davis, "In and around the whole area, the house, the fields, that night, there was a weird feeling. It was partly uneasiness, but not entirely. Everyone had it. There were men there that I'd call brave men.... They felt it, too." They also saw an odd luminous patch along a fence where one of the beings had been shot and, in the woods beyond, a green light whose source could not be determined.

Later, on returning to the house, members of the household spotted the beings several more times, and on one occasion Lucky Sutton shot one through a window, doing more damage to the latter than to the former. The final sighting occurred at 4:45 A.M.

Investigations by police, reporters, Air Force officers, and civilian ufologists uncovered no evidence of a hoax. Even Blue Book, which usually had an explanation to suit (if not always comfortably) every occasion, confessed to being stumped. So was Davis, among the most hard-headed of UFO investigators. Inevitably, some skeptics charged that the witnesses were drunk, which Chief Greenwell testified they were not, or speculated that they had seen escaped monkeys. Of this proposed "solution" Davis wrote, "No amount of 'optical illusion' can explain a mistake of this magnitude."

Invisible rock-throwers.
One variety of phantom attack involves the tossing or dropping of stones by some seemingly invisible assailant.

An instance which attracted national attention occurred in Chico, California, in March 1922, though sporadic incidents actually dated from the previous November. Most of the rocks fell on the roof of a grain warehouse. The *Chico Record* noted, "At almost any hour one can hear the impact of rocks striking the warehouse roof and they may be seen bouncing from the eaves to the ground." Despite massive police and volunteer searches no one was ever seen tossing the stones, and the affair ended after three weeks' worth of intense activity.

Parapsychologists associate these sorts of events with poltergeists, though the late D. Scott Rogo, who investigated and wrote about such cases, said they usually were unaccompanied by more typical poltergeist antics such as rappings and tossing of housewares. These phenomena have some considerable historical lineage. As early as A.D. 530, for example, the physician to King Theodoric of the Ostrogoths was said to have fallen victim to a diabolic infestation: showers of stones fell constantly on his roof. In a 1934 West Indies case, a resident of the house at which the stones were aimed recorded, "The stones continued falling for more than a month, day and night. Sometimes stones would fall inside the house even when it was closed."

In many cases the stones are reported to fall with a slowness which seems to defy the law of gravity, and they feel warm to the touch if retrieved soon after their fall. They may have other peculiar characteristics as well. Around the turn of the century W. G. Grottendieck, a Dutch traveler in Sumatra, recorded this experience:

> I put on my bullsack and mosquito netting on the wooden floor and soon fell asleep. At about one o'clock at night I half awoke, hearing something fall near my head outside the mosquito curtain on the floor. After a couple of minutes I completely awoke and turned my head half around to see what was falling on the floor. They were black stones from ⅛ to ⅔ of an inch long. I got out of the curtain and turned up the kerosene lamp that was standing on the floor at the foot of the bed. I saw then that the stones were falling through the roof in a parabolic line. They fell on the floor close to my head-pillow. I went out and awoke the boy (a Malay-Pelambang coolie) who was sleeping on the floor in the next room. I told him to go outside and examine the jungle up to a certain distance. He did so whilst I lighted up the jungle a little by means of a small "ever-ready" electric lantern. At the same time that my boy was outside the stones did not stop falling. My boy came in again, and I told him to search the kitchen to see if anybody could be there. He went to the kitchen and I went inside the room again to watch the stones falling down. I knelt down near the head of my bed and tried to catch the stones while they were falling through the air towards me, but I could never catch them; it seemed to me that they changed their direction in the air as soon as I tried to get hold of them. I could not catch any of them before they fell to the floor. Then I climbed up the partition-wall between my room and the boy's and examined the roof just above it from which the stones were flying. They came right through the "kadjang" but there were no holes in the Kadjang. When I tried to catch them there at the very spot of coming out, I also failed.

Grottendieck reported that the stones fell with abnormal slowness, yet hit the ground with a loud bang as if they had descended swiftly.

In December 1983 Rogo investigated an in-progress stone-throwing episode in Arizona. The target was a house being built on the far reaches

● SOURCES:

Beck, Fred, and R. A. Beck. *I Fought the Apemen of Mt. St. Helens.* Kelso, WA: The Authors, 1967.

Beck, Ronald A. "Cryptoletters." *The ISC Newsletter* 1, 3 (Autumn 1982): 10.

Bessor, John P. "Phantom Guerillas Invaded Cape Ann." *Fate* 32,6 (June 1979): 63–65.

Byrne, Peter. *The Search for Big Foot: Monster, Myth or Man?* Washington, DC: Acropolis Books, 1975.

Davis, Isabel, and Ted Bloecher. *Close Encounter at Kelly and Others of 1955.* Evanston, IL: Center for UFO Studies, 1978.

Mather, Cotton. *Magnalia Christi Americana.* Hartford, CT: Silas Andrus and Son, 1853.

Pilichis, Dennis. *Night Siege: The Northern Ohio UFO-Creature Invasion.* Rome, Ohio: The Author, 1982.

Quast, Thelma Hall. "Rocks Rain on Chico, California." *Fate* 29, 1 (January 1976): 73–81.

Rickard, Bob. "More Phantom Sieges." *Fortean Times* 45 (Winter 1985): 58–61.

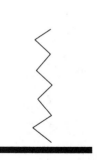

of Tucson's northeast side, in an essentially rural area. Events had begun the previous September and in time became daily occurrences. In the early stages the rocks landed on the rooftop, but soon they escalated in frightening ways. According to Rogo:

> The missiles would start striking the house in brief flurries; five or so rocks would strike the front of the house or [the family's] van at two- or three-second intervals. There would then be a brief hiatus of about five to fifteen minutes, and then another flurry would begin. Sometimes these rocky barrages would be somewhat sporadic and brief, but on other occasions the attacks would go on for two or three hours.

In early November the family contacted the sheriff's office, and in the next month police agencies conducted surveillance of several kinds, including covert; not even the affected family members were aware of the observers. There also were repeated aerial searches. Nothing could stop the bombardment, however, and law-enforcement officers, reporters, professional trackers, and curiosity-seekers and their vehicles were struck with uncanny accuracy even in the deep darkness. The stones appeared to be coming from the brush that surrounded three sides of the house, but as Rogo found when he experimented, the stone thrower could not have thrown projectiles through the brush itself, which was too thick; he would have had to stand and throw over it. Yet even when flashlight and searchlight beams bathed the brushy area as the stones sailed toward their targets, no one was seen.

After December 7 the stone-throwing stopped. The police were stumped, but the family was merely relieved.

Rogo, D. Scott. *The Poltergeist Experience.* New York: Penguin Books, 1979.

———. *On the Track of the Poltergeist.* Englewood Cliffs, NJ: Prentice-Hall, 1986.

Rothovius, Andrew E. "The Great Fear." *Fate* 34, 11 (November 1981): 70–75.

Schama, Simon. *Citizens: A Chronicle of the French Revolution.* New York: Alfred A. Knopf, 1989.

Westrum, Ron. "Phantom Attackers." *Fortean Times* 45 (Winter 1985): 54–58.

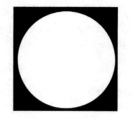

PTEROSAUR SIGHTINGS

The flying reptiles known as pterosaurs, including pterodactyls and their cousins the pteranodons, lived from the lower Jurassic to nearly the end of the Cretaceous period – in other words, from approximately 160 to 60 million years ago.

About 60 million years later, on January 11, 1976, two ranch hands near Poteet, just south of San Antonio, Texas, sighted a five-foot-tall birdlike creature standing in the water of a stock tank. "He started flying," Jessie Garcia reported, "but I never saw him flap his wings. He made no noise at all."

Around the same time two sisters, Libby and Deany Ford, observed a "big black bird" near a pond northeast of Brownsville, which lies along the Texas-Mexico border. "It was as big as me," Libby said, "and it had a face like a bat." Later, as the two girls looked through a book in an effort to identify the creature, they found out what it was.

Driving to work on an isolated rural road southwest of San Antonio, Texas, on the morning of February 24, three elementary school teachers saw a shadow cast cover the entire road. The object responsible for it, passing low overhead, looked like an enormous bird with a 15- to 20-foot wingspan. "I could see the skeleton of this bird through the skin or feathers or whatever, and it stood out black against the background of the gray feathers," one of the witnesses, Patricia Bryant, said. According to David Rendon, "It just glided. It didn't fly. It was no higher than the telephone line. It had a huge breast. It had different legs, and it had huge wings, but the wings were very peculiar like. It had a bony structure, you know, like when you hold a bat by the wing tips, like it has bones at the top and in-between."

Never having seen anything remotely like it, the three witnesses went to the encyclopedia as soon as they got to school. After some searching they found what they were looking for. They learned that the animal they had observed was not unknown after all.

At 3:55 A.M. on September 14, 1982, James Thompson, an ambulance technician, was driving along Highway 100 four miles east of Los Fresnos, Texas, midway between Harlingen and Brownsville, on his way back from an inspection on South Padre Island. He suddenly spotted a "large birdlike object" pass low over the highway 150 feet in front of him. Its strange-looking tail almost literally stopped him in his tracks. He hit the brakes, pulled the vehicle to the side of the road, and stared intently at the peculiar object, which at first he had a hard time believing was a living creature.

"I expected him to land like a model airplane," Thompson said. Then "he flapped his wings enough to get above the grass.... It had a black, or grayish, rough texture. It wasn't feathers. I'm quite sure it was a hide-type covering." Its thin body, which ended with a "fin," stretched over eight feet; its wingspan was five to six feet. The wings had "indentations" on their tops and possibly their bottoms as well. At the back of the head it had a hump like a Brahma bull's. There was "almost no neck at all."

Later he consulted books in an effort to identify the "bird." Like the Ford sisters and the San Antonio teachers over six years earlier, he had no particular trouble finding out what he had seen. The trouble was, however, that the books told him he had seen a pterosaur.

Out of Africa.
In the early twentieth century a traveler and writer named Frank Melland worked for the British colonial service in Northern Rhodesia (now Zambia). While there he learned of a flying creature which lived along certain rivers. Called *kongamato* ("breaker of boats"), it was considered extremely dangerous. Native informants described it as "like a lizard with membranous wings like a bat." Melland wrote in his 1923 book In *Witchbound Africa*:

> Further enquiries disclosed the "facts" that the wing-spread was from 4 to 7 feet across, that the general color was red. It was believed to have no feathers but only skin on its body, and was believed to have teeth in its beak: these last two points no one could be sure of, as no one ever saw a kongamato *close and lived to tell the tale. I sent for two books which I had at my house, containing pictures of pterodactyls, and every native present immediately and unhesitatingly picked it out and identified it as a* kongamato. *Among the natives who did so was a headman (Kanyinga) from the Jiundu country, where the* kongamato *is supposed to be active....*
>
> The natives assert that this flying reptile still exists, and whether this be so or not it seems to me that there is presumptive evidence that it has existed within the memory of man, within comparatively recent days. Whether it is scientifically possible that a reptile that existed in the mesozoic age could exist in the climatic conditions of to-day I have not the necessary knowledge to decide.

In 1942 Col. R. S. Pitman looked back on his African days in a memoir, *A Game Warden Takes Stock:*

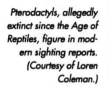

Pterodactyls, allegedly extinct since the Age of Reptiles, figure in modern sighting reports. (Courtesy of Loren Coleman.)

When in Northern Rhodesia I heard of a mythical beast, alleged to have a similar death-dealing attribute, which intrigued me considerably. It was said to haunt formerly, and perhaps still to haunt, a dense, swampy forest region in the neighborhood of the Angola and Congo borders. To look upon it too is death. But the most amazing feature of this mystery beast is its suggested identity with a creature bat- and birdlike in form on a gigantic scale strangely reminiscent of the prehistoric pterodactyl. Where the devil does the primitive African derive such a fanciful idea?

A 1947 book, Frederick Kaigh's *Witchcraft and Magic in Africa*, refers to a spot on the "Rhodesian-Congo border near the north-eastern border of the Jiundu Swamp, a foetid, eerie place in which the pterodactyl is locally supposed to survive with spiritual powers of great evil."

Flying snakes and other terrors.
In the late 1930s J.L.B. Smith, a South African chemist with a keen interest in ichthyology (the study of fish), and an associate, Marjorie Courtenay-Latimer, entered zoological history as co-discoverers of the coelacanth, a large fish heretofore known only from the fossil record and assumed to have been extinct for some 60 million years.

Smith was also fascinated with other reports of animals generally assumed no longer to exist, and at one point he had correspondence (since lost but referred to in his memoir of the coelacanth episode, *Old Fourlegs* [1956]) with members of a German missionary family. They told him that while living near Mount Kilimanjaro (in northeast Tanzania near the Kenya border), one member had had a close sighting of a "flying dragon." This flying dragon was known prior to the incident through numerous reports native witnesses had given them.

For her part Courtenay-Latimer once investigated reports of similar creatures in southern Namibia (then South-West Africa). In one instance native shepherds had walked off their job after complaining that their employer, the white owner of a large ranch, did not take seriously their insistence that a large flying snake lived in the mountains nearby. With no one else to watch the livestock, the farmer dispatched his 16-year-old son to the site. When he failed to return that evening, a search party set out to the mountains to look for him. He was found unconscious.

Even after regaining consciousness, for three days the young man could not speak — owing, his attending physician said, to shock. Finally the son related that he had been relaxing beneath a tree when a sudden roaring noise, like a powerful wind current, startled him. As he looked up, he saw a huge "snake" flying down from a ridge. The closer it got, the louder was the roaring sound. All around the sheep were scattering. The creature landed in a cloud of dust. The boy noticed a strong odor reminiscent of burned brass. At this point he passed out.

Courtenay-Latimer, who arrived on the scene soon afterwards, interviewed witnesses, including other farmers and local police officers, and examined marks on the ground reportedly left by the creature. She was told that a police party had seen the creature disappear into a crevice in the mountain. Sticks of dynamite were heaved into the opening, from which a low moaning sound subsequently emanated, followed by silence. The creature was seen no more.

Cryptozoologist Roy P. Mackal corresponded years later with Courtenay-Latimer about the episode. Reflecting on the strange episode, he wrote, "A snake, even a very large one, hurtling or falling over a ledge or mountain precipice hardly would disturb the air as described. In fact, it is hard to attribute such a disturbance even to a large gliding creature, suggesting instead that some kind of wing action must have been involved." Mackal asks, "Could some species of pterodactyl with elongated body and tail still survive?"

(In a dispatch out of Columbia, South Carolina, on May 30, 1888, the *New York Times* reported that three evenings earlier, at dusk, three women on a stroll through the woods of Darlington County "were suddenly startled by the appearance of a huge serpent moving through the air above them. The serpent was distant only two or three rods when they first beheld it, and was sailing through the air with a speed equal to that of a hawk or buzzard but without any visible means of propulsion. Its movements in its flight resembled those of a snake, and it looked a formidable object as it wound its way along, being apparently about 15 feet in length.... The flying serpent was also seen by a number of people in other parts of the county early in the afternoon of the same day, and by those it is represented as emitting a hissing noise which could be distinctly heard.")

According to Carl Pleijel of the Swedish Museum of Natural History, a sighting of such a pterodactyl-like creature occurred in Kenya in 1974. The witnesses were members of an British expedition, Pleijel told journalist Jan-Ove Sundberg, citing as his source an unnamed person he deemed

● SOURCES:

Clark, Jerome, and Loren Coleman. *Creatures of the Outer Edge.* New York: Warner Books, 1978.

Coleman, Loren. *Curious Encounters: Phantom Trains, Spooky Spots, and Other Mysterious Wonders.* Boston, MA: Faber and Faber, 1985.

"A Flying Serpent." *New York Times* (May 30, 1888).

Heuvelmans, Bernard. *On the Track of Unknown Animals.* New York: Hill and Wang, 1958.

————. "Of Lingering Pterodactyls." *Strange Magazine* 6 (1990): 8–11, 58–60.

"Highlights of Galveston Meeting." *The ISC Newsletter* 10, 2 (Summer 1991): 4–6.

Lloyd, Lorna. "Cryptoletters." *The ISC Newsletter* 7, 4 (Winter 1988): 11.

Mackal, Roy P. *Searching for Hidden Animals.* Garden City, NY: Doubleday and Company, 1980.

"News & Notes." *The ISC Newsletter* 2, 4 (Winter 1983): 8–9.

317

credible. Sundberg interviewed a "museum superintendent here in Sweden ... whose name I don't want to mention" and from him heard of an American expedition's sighting over a swamp in Namibia in late 1975. No further details have ever been forthcoming.

If the rumors out of Sweden are vague and undocumented, continuing reports from Namibia seem more substantial. In the summer of 1988, Mackal traveled to that nation with a small group of associates. From an isolated private desert area owned by Nambibians of German descent, he said, come continuing reports of "flying snakes." Witnesses whom Mackal interviewed said the animals indeed had wings — of 30 feet, no less — but no feathers. The creatures apparently live in caves and crevices in the many kopjes (small veld hills) that dot the landscape. Expedition members found ostrich bones in almost inaccessible spots atop kopjes, possibly evidence that the kills had been carried there by flying creatures. One expedition member who stayed on after Mackal had left to return to the United States reported seeing one from a thousand feet away. It was, he said, black with white markings and had enormous wings which it used to glide through the air.

Though the idea that pterosaurs may have survived tens of millions of years past their time is a fantastic and unlikely one, it is not entirely impossible. Whatever else they may be, the occasional sightings of huge winged reptiles by seemingly sane and sober individuals surely comprise the stuff of one of cryptozoology's most intriguing mysteries.

Smith, J. L. B. Old Fourlegs: The Story of the Coelacanth. London: Longmans, Green and Company, 1956.

Sundberg, Jan-Ove. "The Monster of Sraheens Lough." INFO Journal 5, 6 (March 1977): 2–9.

Sutherly, Curt. "Pterodactyls and T-Birds." Pursuit 9, 2 (April 1976): 35–36.

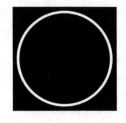

PWDRE SER

For centuries the phenomenon of *pwdre ser* (a Welsh phrase meaning "rot from the stars") was known to everyone, from peasants in the field to scientists in the universities, and it figured in everything from folklore to academic discourse. Today only a handful of anomalists and historians of science remember it. Yet instances of what give every appearance of being classic *pwdre ser* (also known as "star jelly") continue to occur.

In 1541 the poet Sir John Suckling wrote:

> *As he whose quick eye doth trace*
> *A false star shot to a mark't place*
> *Do's run apace*
> *And, thinking it to catch,*
> *A jelly up do snatch.*

Or in John Dryden's words in 1679:

> *When I had taken up what I supposed a fallen star*
> *I found I had been cozened with a jelly.*

What Suckling and Dryden had in mind were the sorts of stories that follow.

At 4 P.M. on May 16, 1808, on a warm, cloudless day, the sun dimmed for an unknown reason, and as soon as that happened, a correspondent wrote in the *Transactions of the Swedish Academy of Sciences* (1808), "there appeared on the western horizon, from where the wind blew, to arise gradually, and in quick succession, a great number of balls, or spherical bodies, to the naked eye of a size of the crown of a hat, and of a dark brown color." As these curious objects approached the sun, they grew darker until they became "entirely black." For a brief period they ceased their flight and hovered in the air. When they resumed their motion, they picked up speed, traveling in a nearly straight line until they disappeared in the eastern horizon. The correspondent recorded:

> *During this course, some disappeared, others fell down.... The phenomenon lasted uninterruptedly, upwards of two hours, during which time millions of similar bodies continually rose in the west, one after the other irregularly, and continued their career in exactly the same manner. No report, noise, nor any whistling or buzzing in the air was perceived. As these balls slackened their course on passing by the Sun, several were linked together, three, six, or eight of them in a line, joined like a chain-shot by a thin and straight bar; but on continuing again a more rapid course, they separated, and each having a tail after it, apparently of three or four fathoms length, wider at its base where it adhered to the ball, and gradually decreasing, till it terminated in a fine point. During the course, these tails, which had been the same black color as the balls, disappeared by degrees.*

Some of the balls fell to the earth not far from an observer who happened to be an official of the Swedish Academy, K. G. Wettermark. Wettermark noticed that as the objects came downward, they lost their dark color, then were lost to view briefly, then became visible again but now with changing colors, "in this particular exactly resembling those air-bubbles which children use to produce from soapsuds by means of a reed. When the spot, where such a ball had fallen, was immediately after examined, nothing was to be seen, but a scarcely perceptible film or pellicle, as thin and fine as a cobweb, which was still changing colors, but soon entirely dried up and vanished."

In 1819 the *American Journal of Science* reported an extraordinary incident which had taken place on August 13 of that year. According to Prof. Rufus Graves, between 8 P.M. and 9 P.M. a fireball "of a brilliant white light resembling burnished silver" descended slowly from the sky and onto the front yard of an Amherst, Massachusetts, man, Erastus Dewey. Two women had seen its light reflected on the wall just before it settled on the ground. In the morning, 20 feet from his front door, Dewey found, according to Graves, who soon examined the material, a

> *circular form, resembling a sauce or salad dish bottom upwards, about eight inches in diameter and one in thickness, of a bright buff color, with a fine nap upon it similar to that on milled cloth.... On removing the villous coat, a buff colored pulpy substance of the consistence of good soft soap, of an offensive, suffocating smell appeared; and on a near approach to it, or when immediately over it, the smell became almost insupportable, producing nausea and dizziness. A few minutes exposure to the atmosphere changed the buff into a livid color resembling venous blood. It was observed to attract moisture very rapidly from the air. A half-pint tumbler was nearly half filled with the substance. It soon began to liquefy and form a mucilaginous substance of the consistence, color, and feeling of starch when prepared for domestic use.*

Within two or three days the substance had vanished from the tumbler. All that remained was a dark-colored residue on the sides and bottom of the glass. When this material was rubbed between the fingers, it became a fine, odorless ash. (In 1712, when the Rev. John Morton of Emmanuel College burned some *pwdre ser*, he noted that "there was left a film like isinglass, and something like the skins and vessels of animal bodies.")

Late on the evening of October 8, 1844, two men walking in a plowed field near Coblentz, Germany, were startled to observe the fall of a luminous object that crashed to earth not 20 yards from them. Because it was too dark to investigate, they marked the spot and returned early the next morning. Where the presumed meteorite had come down, however, there was now a gray, gelatinous mass which shook when they poked it with a stick. They did not try to preserve it, according to the *Reports of the British Association*.

The rise of skepticism.
By the 1860s most scientists discounted such reports, in part because new understanding of the nature of meteors and meteorites seemed to eliminate any possibility that they could contain, or be, organic matter. Moreover, some botanists were certain that the material was *nostoc*, a blue-green algae, or — if not that — perhaps bird vomit. Edward Hitchcock, an Amherst College chemistry professor, was convinced, for example, that he recognized the Amherst material as a "species of gelatinous fungus, which I had sometimes met with on rotten wood in damp places, during dog days." He declared that it was an "entire mistake" that had caused observers to connect it with the falling object, though his colleague Prof. Graves adamantly insisted that there could be "no reasonable doubt that the substance found was the residuum of the meteoric body."

There was a time, ironically, when scientists rejected the existence even of conventional meteorites. They deemed it an "entire mistake" for observers to connect stones and rocks with the glowing "falling stars" that they were positive had fallen at the exact spot. Now, of course, no one disputes the correctness of the witnesses' observations or defends the rationalizations of the putative experts.

Still, one can hardly blame scientists for being reluctant to embrace so incredible a phenomenon as *pwdre ser*, which makes no sense in terms of anything we know about meteorites — unless, of course, this phenomenon is wholly separate from meteorites and should not be classed with them at all. The Swedish case above certainly indicates as much.

A modern case.
Twentieth-century reports of falls of gelatinous materials are infrequent but probably no rarer than in earlier centuries. If not ignored altogether, they are subjected to quick dismissal via contrived explanations.

The most publicized recent case took place in August 1979 in Frisco, Texas, a Dallas suburb. On the night of August 10, a bright light was seen to descend in the neighborhood where Martin and Sybil Christian lived. The next morning Mrs. Christian found three purple blobs in her front lawn. One of the blobs dissolved; the other two were frozen and sent for analysis. The result was an "identification" as industrial waste from a nearby battery-reprocessing plant. In fact, the factory denied any responsibility; chemical analysis showed significant differences between the two substances, and they did not even look alike to the eye.

● SOURCES:

Burke, John G. *Cosmic Debris: Meteorites in History*. Berkeley, CA: University of California Press, 1986.

Corliss, William R., ed. *Handbook of Unusual Natural Phenomena*. Glen Arm, MD: The Sourcebook Project, 1977.

Fort, Charles. *The Books of Charles Fort*. New York: Henry Holt and Company, 1941.

Schultz, Ted. "Blobs from Space?" *Fate* 34, 12 (December 1981): 85–90, 92.

RAIN, ANOMALOUS

Every day for three weeks, between mid- and late afternoon, whether the sky was cloudy or clear, water fell on a patch of land between two trees in Charlotte, North Carolina, according to the *Charlotte Chronicle* of October 21, 1886. The day of publication an observer for the U.S. Signal Corps went to the site and there saw, he reported to *Monthly Weather Review* (October issue), "precipitation in the form of rain drops at 4:47 P.M. and 4:55 P.M., while the sun was shining brightly."

He was back the following afternoon. Between 4:05 P.M. and 4:25 P.M., he wrote, "a light shower of rain fell from a cloudless sky.... Sometimes the precipitation falls over an area of half an acre, but always appears to center at these two trees, and when lightest occurs there only." Not long afterwards the phenomenon ceased as quickly, and as mysteriously, as it had begun.

Meantime something of the same was occurring in Aiken, South Carolina. Late in October rain fell from morning till late at night on two graves in the town cemetery — and nowhere else — and was seen by hundreds of locals. Not a cloud filled the sky.

Falls of water from clear skies are an odd meteorological phenomenon usually explained (or explained away) as an effect resulting from wind-blown precipitation from elsewhere. Other explanations suggested by William R. Corliss, compiler of the *Sourcebook Project,* a multivolume catalog of natural anomalies, include "transient atmospheric disturbances, such as gravity waves and the sudden expansion and cooling of wind blowing across mountain ranges. Large influxes of meteoritic dust may also stimulate precipitation." None of these explains instances like those recorded above, in which the fall remains oddly and precisely localized. Such cases, however, are rare.

Blood-red rains.

A more common precipitation anomaly is colored rain, of which hundreds, perhaps thousands, of examples exist. The most dramatic concern "rains of blood." Corliss expresses the conventional view when he writes, "The coloring matter in blood rains inevitably turns out to be reddish dust and organic matter," and attributes contrary views to "the superstitious." In fact, the adverb "inevitably" overstates the case, and the characterization of the intellectual deficiencies of witnesses and informants is untrue and unwarranted. Still, one sympathizes; blood rains are not only wildly incredible but profoundly alarming, and every intellectual and emotional impulse commands us to put them out of their existence as quickly as possible.

In July 1841 slaves in a field in Wilson County, Tennessee, reported that just before noon a small red cloud suddenly appeared in an otherwise clear sky; from the cloud fell a shower of "blood, muscular fibre, adipose matter," in the words of a local physician, W. P. Sayle, who examined it at the site. Enclosing some samples, Sayle wrote to a professor of chemistry at the University of Nashville:

> The particles I send you I gathered with my own hands. The extent of surface over which it spread and the regular manner it exhibited on some green tobacco leaves, leave very little or no doubt of its having fallen like a shower of rain.... I have sent what I think to be a drop of blood, the other particles composed of muscle and fat, although the proportion of the shower appeared to be a much larger quantity of blood than of other properties.

Another physician, G. W. Bassett of Virginia, recounted this event in the spring of 1850 in a letter to a colleague:

> About four P.M. yesterday, being Good Friday, a small cloud passed over Mr. Chas. H. Clarke and several of my servants, a few paces from the south bank of the Pamunkey River in the lower end of Hanover County, Virginia, on the estate called Farmington, and discharged around the parties, over a surface of something less than a rood of ground, various pieces of flesh and liver, too well defined in each sort to allow any mistake in their character. I gathered this morning from the spot, from four to six ounces, distributed over the above-mentioned surface. The pieces picked up at the remotest points, in a line from N.W. to S.E., were about 25 paces from each other. One would weigh near an ounce. The direction of the cloud was from N.E. to S.W., as described by Mr. Clarke, who is a gentleman of intelligence and established credibility. Mr. Brown, with myself, visited the spot this morning and all aided in picking up 15 to 20 pieces which I have by me at this moment and from which I send you a sample and desire it may be passed over to Dr. Gibson, that he may ascertain what sort of flesh it is. The flesh and liver are in a perfect state at this moment and the latter part I shall put in alcohol for the future inspection of the curious.

A similarly grisly rain is said to have taken place the previous February 15 in Simpson County, North Carolina, where pieces of flesh, liver, brains, and blood, all looking fresh, fell out of a red cloud and splattered over an area 30 feet wide and 250 to 300 yards long. According to the *San Francisco Herald* of July 24, 1851, blood and flesh, with pieces ranging in size from a pigeon's egg to a small orange, descended in a two- to three-minute shower on an Army station at Benicia, California, covering a spot of ground 30 yards wide and 300 yards long.

One Sunday in July 1869 blood reportedly fell out of a clear sky and landed on two acres of a corn field near Los Angeles. Those who saw it — a funeral party that included members of the clergy — had no doubt that the substance was blood. Not only was it a thick, vivid red, but it contained hairs and portions of organs.

It is easier to believe that stories like these are wholly fictitious than it is to credit complacent assertions that the fallen material was really water colored from dust or plant matter. Here, after all, we have rational, educated witnesses. These, moreover, are not the only such stories. A vividly red and bloodlike rain during a storm on October 16 and 17, 1846, caused widespread terror among French witnesses. A chemist who studied the material under a microscope noted a "great quantity of corpuscles." Rather more specifically, after a red stuff rained on Messignadi, Calabria, the Italian Meteorological Bureau identified it as bird's blood.

On March 8, 1876, "flakes of meat" came down out of the sky to land on a Bath County, Kentucky, field, and one brave witness tasted a "perfectly fresh" sample. It reminded him, according to *Scientific American* (March 1876), of "mutton or venison." This widely reported event sparked some considerable controversy and soon fell victim to two conventional, contradictory, and unconvincing explanations. One was that the material was nostoc (blue-green algae) which had been there on the ground all along but sprouted in the wake of a rain; in fact, the sky was clear during the fall. The second averred the material to be buzzard vomit, even though it fell in thick volume, consisted of numerous flakes from one to four inches square, and covered ground, trees, and fences on a strip of land 100 yards long and 50 yards wide.

In 1888, after a red rain fell on the Mediterranean region on two occasions 12 days apart, samples were burned, leaving a strong and persistent "odor of animal matter," according to the French scientific journal *L'Astronomie*.

If we cannot properly explain these sorts of stories, we can, at least, be relieved that after the nineteenth century they become exceedingly rare. Whether that is because they occur less frequently, or simply because owing to their outlandish character they see print less often than they did in what Charles Fort called the "days of less efficient strangulation," we can only speculate. A rare twentieth-century instance was recorded in Sao Paulo, Brazil, newspapers on August 30, 1968, describing a meat and blood shower on two small towns between Sao Paulo and Rio de Janeiro. According to a terse statement from a law-enforcement officer:

● SOURCES:

Aldrich, Hal R. "Rainbows Keep Falling on My Head." INFO Journal 6, 2 (July/August 1977): 2–6.

Constance, Arthur. *The Inexplicable Sky.* New York: The Citadel Press, 1957.

Corliss, William R., ed. *Handbook of Unusual Natural Phenomena.* Glen Arm, MD: The Sourcebook Project, 1977.

———. *Tornados, Dark Days, Anomalous Precipitation, and Related Weather Phenomena: A Catalog of Geophysical Anomalies.* Glen Arm, MD: The Sourcebook Project, 1983.

D'Ercole, Tom, as told to Rene Decker. "True Mystic Experiences: My Own Little Cloud." *Fate* 32, 2 (February 1979): 54–55.

Fort, Charles. *The Books of Charles Fort.* New York: Henry Holt and Company, 1941.

Knight, Damon. *Charles Fort: Prophet of the Unexplained.* Garden City, NY: Doubleday and Company, 1970.

Splitter, Henry Winfred. "Wonders from the Sky." *Fate* 6, 10 (October 1953): 33–40.

"World Round-up: 'Fortean' Fall of Flesh and Blood." *Flying Saucer Review* 14, 6 (November/December 1968): iv.

X. "The Charlotte Phenomenon." *INFO Journal* 13, 3 (March 1990): 15–17.

The pieces of flesh were found lying at distances of half a meter apart, their size varying between lengths of 5 cm. and 20 cm. The meat was of a spongy texture and violet in color, and was accompanied by drops of blood. The sky at the time was quite clear. No aircraft had been seen just prior to, during, or after the event, nor were there any birds in the sky.

REPTILE MEN

In 1954 archaeologists on an expedition along the Amazon River encountered a bizarre aquatic biped with gills and scales. In November 1958 a Riverside, California, man driving in a car near the Santa Ana River was attacked by a similar creature, with a "round, scarecrowish head," shiny eyes, and scales. It left long scratches on his windshield, and as he accelerated, he hit it and drove over it.

The first story is from a classic science-fiction film, Universal's *The Creature from the Black Lagoon* (1954). The second is supposed to have happened in real life to an alleged witness named Charles Wetzel. The following evening another motorist claimed that the same kind of monster jumped out of the bushes at his car.

Though fairly rare, accounts of reptilian bipeds crop up from time to time, usually in brief sighting reports. But the idea of such creatures was current at least as early as 1878, when Louisville's Metropolitan Theater exhibited the "Wild Man of the Woods," described as six feet, five inches tall and covered with "fish scales." Presumably this reptile man was an ordinary man garbed for the occasion, which was the culling of cash from the credulous, but nearly a century later, in October 1975, residents of tiny Milton, Kentucky, north of Louisville, reported seeing a bipedal "giant lizard."

Both Milton and Louisville border the Ohio River. So does Evansville, Indiana, where on August 21, 1955, Mrs. Darwin Johnson was swimming when a clawlike hand gripped her knee from below the water and pulled her under. She struggled with the unseen grabber and managed to free herself, but no sooner had she come to the surface than she was dragged down again. She was able to lunge at a friend's inner tube, and the *thump* she made on contact with it apparently scared the attacker away. Though never observed, the creature left a green palm stain on Mrs. Johnson's knee and scratches and marks for which she sought medical attention.

In March 1972 several badly frightened Loveland, Ohio residents, including two police officers, told of seeing a bizarre frog-faced biped in the early-morning darkness. (Courtesy of Loren Coleman.)

Loveland Frog

Northeast of Cincinnati, in Loveland, Ohio, along the Miami River, reports of more or less reptilian bipeds have been made since at least 1955, when a driver returning home from work at 3:30 A.M. on May 25, reported that he had spotted three grotesque-looking creatures with lopsided chests, wide, lipless, froglike mouths, and wrinkles rather than hair on their heads. One held a spark-generating, bar-shaped device above itself. He watched them from his parked car for three minutes before leaving to alert Loveland Police Chief John Fritz. As he did so, he smelled a strong odor reminiscent of "fresh-cut alfalfa, with a slight trace of almonds." Fritz found nothing but was nonetheless convinced of the witness's sincerity.

Nearly 17 years later, on March 3, 1972, at 1 A.M., two Loveland police officers encountered something comparable: a four-foot-tall, frog-faced biped with textured leathery skin. They saw it jump over a guard rail and descend an embankment leading to the Little Miami River. About two weeks later one of the officers saw the thing again, first lying in the road, then getting up to go over a guard rail. He took a shot at it but apparently missed. A local farmer also reported seeing such a creature.

In the summer of 1972, at Thetis Lake, British Columbia, there were two reports of a silver-colored creature which emerged from the water, in the first instance (on August 19) to chase a couple of young men from the beach. One supposedly suffered lacerations in the hand from six sharp points atop the thing's head. A witness to the second incident, on August 23, said it was "shaped like an ordinary body, like a human being body, but it had a monster face, and it was all scaly." It had a sharp point on its head and "great big ears."

The following summer, people in the Newton-Lafayette area of New Jersey told of encounters with a giant creature that looked like a cross between a man and an alligator.

● SOURCES:

Coleman, Loren. *Curious Encounters: Phantom Trains, Spooky Spots, and Other Mysterious Wonders.* Boston, MA: Faber and Faber, 1985.

———. "On the Trail: The Strange Case of the Two Charlie Wetzels." *Fortean Times* 39 (Spring 1983): 44–46.

———. "Other Lizard People Revisited." *Strange Magazine* 3 (1988): 34, 36.

Coleman, Loren, and Mark Chorvinsky. "'Lizard People' of the Movies." *Strange Magazine* 4 (1989): 34–35.

Davis, Isabel, and Ted Bloecher. *Close Encounter at Kelly and Others of 1955.* Evanston, IL: Center for UFO Studies, 1978.

Keel, John A. *Strange Creatures from Time and Space.* Greenwich, CT: Fawcett Books, 1970.

Picasso, Fabio. "Infrequent Types of South American Humanoids." *Strange Magazine* 8 (Fall 1991): 21–23, 44.

RI

While doing field work in New Ireland, an island province of Papua New Guinea, University of Virginia cultural anthropologist Roy Wagner heard strange stories of creatures which even his best-educated informants assured him "really exist." In fact, they appeared regularly in the ocean just off New Ireland's central and southern coasts. Called "ri" (pronounced *ree*), the creatures had generally human features down to their genital area; the lower truck had no legs and ended in a pair of lateral fins. Natives compared the creatures, which they said were air-breathing mammals, to the mermaids on tuna-fish cans.

In November 1979, from the central coastal village of Ramat, Wagner saw what a native told him was a ri in Pamat Bay. Several hundred yards away, he wrote, "something large [was] swimming at the surface in a broad arc toward the shore. We watched as it came closer, and the best view I got was of a long, dark body swimming at the surface horizontally. Suddenly, a sawfish jumped immediately in front of it (the range was close enough that I could identify the facial projection), and the dark object submerged and did not reappear."

Wagner interviewed a number of Barok-speaking islanders who said they had eaten ri flesh. They did not consider ri to be intelligent beings like humans. The ri communicated by whistling and fed on fish. Wagner was certain that his informants were not confusing ri with dugongs ("sea cows"). "For a Barok man to identify the corpse of a *ri* washed up on a beach or caught in a net as that of a dugong," he wrote, "would be as unlikely as for an American hunter to bring home a deer on his front bumper and try to convince his neighbors it is a bear." He added that New Ireland's people were equally familiar with dolphins.

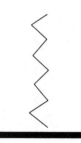

His formal report, published in the first issue of *Cryptozoology*, the journal of the newly formed International Society of Cryptozoology (ISC), created something of a sensation. In the summer of 1983, Wagner, ISC secretary J. Richard Greenwell, and two other men traveled to New Ireland, interviewed witnesses, and saw a ri themselves. It happened on the afternoon of July 5, from the village of Nokon on Elizabeth Bay some 40 miles south of Ramat. At 10-minute intervals the creature, clearly feeding, would surface for a few seconds, making good sightings, much less decent photographs, virtually impossible. It appeared to be five to seven feet long, skinny, and possessed of a mammalian tail. Attempts to capture a specimen using a net met with technical problems and had to be abandoned. Expedition members had other, though briefer, sightings of what appeared to be the same animal.

They returned convinced that the ri was some kind of unusual animal, not a known animal to which the local imagination had assigned fantastic properties. Still, they noted that "villages further north in central New Ireland regard the dugong and the Ri as the same animal." Other islanders, however, insisted that they were different. The investigators were inclined to agree. The ri stayed underwater for as long as 10 minutes, while the zoological literature indicated that a submerged dugong comes up for air every one or two minutes. Marine biologist Paul Anderson, a specialist in dugongs, provided Greenwell with a film of surfacing dugongs, but Greenwell thought that neither the creature's shapes nor its actions resembled those of the animal he and his associates had seen.

A second expedition in February 1985 solved the mystery. A well-equipped group sponsored by the Ecosophical Research Association saw a ri in Nokon Bay from the deck of the diving ship *Reef Explorer*. When it dived, the captain, Kerry Piesch, followed it underwater and took three photographs. Slightly over five feet long, the animal was greenish-gray in color, with a distinct neckless head, and short, paddle-shaped limbs. It was a dugong.

Expedition member Tom Williams later remarked, "One of the lingering questions which remain is how myths of merfolk can arise and persist in the face of the obvious reality of the dugong. There is apparently a kind of belief system at work whose nature transcends the strict discipline of zoology and spills over into the realm of anthropology and psychology." Greenwell concluded, "Although we have not found a new species, we have uncovered new data on dugong behavior in deeper water."

● SOURCES:

"New Expedition Identifies Ri as Dugong." *The ISC Newsletter* 4, 1 (Spring 1985): 1–3.

"New Guinea Expedition Observes Ri." *The ISC Newsletter* 2, 2 (Summer 1983): 1–2.

Wagner, Roy. "The *Ri*—Unidentified Aquatic Animals of New Ireland, Papua New Guinea." *Cryptozoology* 1 (1982): 33–39.

Wagner, Roy, J. Richard Greenwell, Gale J. Raymond, and Kurt Von Nieda. "Further Investigations into the Biological and Cultural Affinities of the Ri." *Cryptozoology* 2 (Winter 1983): 113–25.

Williams, Thomas R. "Identification of the Ri Through Further Fieldwork in New Ireland, Papua New Guinea." *Cryptozoology* 4 (1985): 61–68.

RINGING ROCKS

Southeastern Pennsylvania is dotted with sites where rocks ring when struck by a hammer. These include the Stony Garden (Haycock, Bucks County), the Devil's Race Course (Franklin County), and others in the South Mountain region and at Pottsdown. By far the most famous site, and the most studied, is in Upper Black Eddy in Bucks County. It is located a mile west of the Delaware River near the New Jersey state line.

Set in a forested area, the Ringing Rocks appear in a field which has no vegetation except lichens. Ten feet thick and seven acres around, the rocks are composed of diabase, in other words part of the earth's basic crustal structure. There is nothing unusual about them except that when struck hard, they ring. In June 1890 Dr. J. J. Ott, backed by a brass band, played a few selections on the rocks for an appreciative Buckwampum Historical Society gathering. Ott, in short, had learned what other investigators have since confirmed: that the rocks don't have to be in their natural location to ring. They do not even have to be intact.

Curiously, though made up of the same materials, not all of the Ringing Rocks ring — only about 30 percent of them, according to those who have experimented with them.

Though this is undoubtedly a natural phenomenon, it is an odd one for which no fully satisfactory explanation has ever been proposed. In 1965 geologist Richard Faas of Lafayette College, Easton, Pennsylvania, conducted laboratory experiments using sensitive equipment. He learned that when he struck a ringing rock, a series of subaudible frequencies were produced, and these added up to a tone that could be heard by the human ear. He could not, however, determine a specific physical cause.

Some writers have made remarkable — almost occult — claims for the ringing rocks, asserting that something about the rock field spooks animals, even insects, which make a point of keeping their distance. There is nothing especially mysterious about this, according to investigator Michael A. Frizzell, since the area is barren, open, and hotter than the surrounding forest during the summer, thus generally inhospitable to living creatures.

More interesting is a claim made by the late Ivan T. Sanderson, though since then there has been no published replication: "[T]here are some larger rocks which, when hit appropriately, give rise to a whole scale; ... two different ringers when knocked together while suspended on wires produce (invariably, it seems) but one tone, however many different combinations are used."

Ringing rocks have been noted all over the world. Curiously, the kinds of rock possessing such talents vary. The absence of clear patterns in the creation of such odd geological phenomena continues to frustrate theorists.

● SOURCES:

Corliss, William R., ed. *Strange Planet: A Sourcebook of Unusual Geological Facts, Volume E-1*. Glen Arm, MD: The Sourcebook Project, 1975.

———. *Unknown Earth: A Handbook of Geological Enigmas*. Glen Arm, MD: The Sourcebook Project, 1980.

Frizzell, Michael A. "The Riddle of the Ringing Rocks." *Fate* 36, 10 (October 1983): 70–76.

Gibbons, John, and Steven Schlossman. "Rock Music." *Natural History* 79 (December 1970): 36–41.

Sanderson, Ivan T. *"Things."* New York: Pyramid Books, 1967.

"Why the Rocks Ring." *Pursuit* 4 (April 1971): 38–41.

SEA SERPENTS

The American ship *Silas Richards* was sailing off St. George's Bank south of Nova Scotia at 6:30 P.M. on June 16, 1826, when its captain, Henry Holdredge, and a passenger, Englishman William Warburton, saw a most peculiar sight: an enormous, many-humped snakelike creature slowly approaching the vessel. Warburton raced to inform the other passengers, who were below deck, but only a handful responded. Warburton recalled, "The remainder refused to come up, saying there had been too many hoaxes of that kind already."

Even in the early years of the nineteenth century, the sea serpent had a reputation as, in Bernard Heuvelmans's words, the "very symbol of a hoax." That reputation would withstand a battering in the later years of the century, with the publication of a number of reports which could not reasonably be ascribed to mistakes, delusions, or lies, and emerge intact in our time to figure in inane cliches about the "silly season."

That the sea serpent has such a reputation says far more about the capacity of human beings for blind incredulity than it does about the quality of the evidence for the creature once called the "great unknown." Perhaps the sea serpent is due for a revival. With the initiation of systematic deep-sea research in recent years, marine biologists have discovered a bewildering variety of life forms, some never suspected, others thought extinct for millions of years. An article in the June 2, 1992, issue of the *New York Times* remarks, "Scientists concede that other creatures, perhaps even larger and stranger than the monstrous *Architeuthis* [giant squid], may continue to defy discovery in their vast watery refuges."

Early history.
Though sea serpents are ubiquitous in myths and legends, the first attempt to describe them as figures in natural history appears in a 1555 work by Olaus Magnus, the exiled Catholic archbishop of Uppsala, Sweden. The

archbishop wrote that sailors off the coast of Norway had often seen a "Serpent... of vast magnitude, namely 200 feet long, and moreover 20 foot thick." A dangerous beast, it lived in caves along the shore and devoured both land and ocean creatures, including an occasional seaman. "This Snake disquiets the shippers," Olaus Magnus wrote, "and he puts up his head on high like a pillar."

Except for this last detail, Magnus's is an exaggerated and unbelievable account, but we know from chroniclers who came after him that "serpents" were reported regularly in the North Sea, though not everyone regarded them as dangerous. In 1666 Adam Olschlager wrote of a sighting of a "large serpent, which seen from afar, had the thickness of a wine barrel, and 25 windings. These serpents are said to appear on the surface of the water only in calm weather and at certain times."

In 1734 a Protestant priest, Hans Egede, saw a "monster," estimated to be 100 feet long, rise from the water off the coast of Greenland. He recorded the experience in a book published in 1741. A little over a decade later, the most influential of the early treatments appeared: *The Natural History of Norway* (1752–1753) by Bishop Erik Pontoppidan.

In one chapter, destined to be cited frequently in the controversies of the next two centuries, the bishop addressed the question of merfolk, the kraken (known to us as the giant squid and, though once deemed mythical, recognized by science since the late 1800s), and the sea serpent, all of which he believed, on the testimonies of individuals of good reputation, to exist. The reports indicated, Pontoppidan wrote, that more than one kind of animal was involved. Egede's monster, for example, was distinctly different from those seen off the Scandinavian coasts. For example: "The head in all the kinds has a high and broad forehead, but in some [as in Egede's] a pointed snout, though in others that is flat, like that of a cow or horse, with large nostrils, and several stiff hairs standing out on each side like whiskers."

In the New World.
In An Account of *Two Voyages to New England*, published in 1674, John Josselyn recalled a 1639 conversation with residents of the Massachusetts colony: "They told me of a *sea-serpent* or snake, that lay coiled upon a rock at Cape Ann." This is the first known printed reference to an American sea serpent. In the next century and a half thousands of residents of New England and Canada's maritime provinces would observe comparable creatures.

One of the better of these early reports comes from Capt. George Little of the frigate *Boston:*

> In May, 1780, I was lying in Round Pond, in Broad Bay [off the Maine coast], in a public armed ship. At sunrise, I discovered a huge Serpent, or monster, coming down the Bay, on the surface of the water. The cutter was manned and armed. I went myself in the boat, and proceeded after the Serpent. When within a hundred feet, the mariners

*were ordered to fire on him, but before they could make ready, the
Serpent dove. He was not less than from 45 to 50 feet in length; the
largest diameter of his body, I should judge, 15 inches; his head nearly
the size of that of a man, which he carried four or five feet above the
water. He wore every appearance of a common black snake.*

A year earlier the crew of the American gunship Protector had an extraordinary encounter in Penobscot Bay. One of the witnesses was an 18-year-
old ensign, Edward Preble, who would go on to become a commodore
and a notable figure in U.S. naval history. In his biography of Preble, James
Fenimore Cooper recounts this event:

*The day was clear and calm, when a large serpent was discovered out-
side the ship. The animal was lying on the water quite motionless.
After inspecting it with the glasses for some time, Capt. [John Foster]
Williams ordered Preble to man and arm a large boat, and endeavor to
destroy the creature; or at least to go as near to it as he could.... The
boat thus employed pulled twelve oars, and carried a swivel in its
bows, besides having its crew armed as boarders. Preble shoved off,
and pulled directly towards the monster. As the boat neared it, the serpent raised its head about ten feet above the surface of the water, looking about it. It then began to move slowly away from the boat. Preble
pushed on, his men pulling with all their force, and the animal being
at no great distance, the swivel was discharged loaded with bullets.
The discharge produced no other effect than to quicken the speed of
the monster, which soon ran the boat out of sight.*

There were sporadic sightings in the following decades, but the New England sea serpent did not become an international cause célèbre until the
second decade of the nineteenth century. Over a period of several years,
from Boston up to Cape Ann at the northeastern tip of Massachusetts,
numerous witnesses on both ship and shore saw the animal. Some representative reports:

Hawkins Wheeler, June 6, 1819: *I had a fair and distinct view of the
creature, and from his appearance am satisfied that it was of the serpent kind. The creature was entirely black; the head, which perfectly
resembled a snake's, was elevated from four to seven feet above the
surface of the water, and his back appeared to be composed of
bunches or humps, apparently about as large as, or a little larger than,
a half barrel; I think I saw as many as ten or twelve.... I considered
them to be caused by the undulatory motion of the animal — the tail
was not visible, but from the head to the last hump that could be seen,
was, I should judge, 50 feet.*

Solomon Allen III, August 12, 13, and 14, 1817: *I have seen a strange
marine animal, that I believe to be a serpent, in the harbor in ...
Gloucester. I should judge him to be between eighty and ninety feet in
length, and about the size of a half barrel.... I was about 150 yards
from him.... His head formed something like the head of a rattlesnake,*

but nearly as large as the head of a horse. When he moved on the surface of the water, his motion was slow, at times playing about in circles, and sometimes moving nearly straight forward. When he disappeared, he sunk [sic] apparently down.

Samuel Cabot, August 14, 1819: [M]y attention was suddenly arrested by an object emerging from the water at the distance of about one hundred or one hundred and fifty yards, which gave to my mind at the first glance the idea of a horse's head.... I perceived at a short distance eight or ten regular bunches or protuberances, and at a short interval three or four more.... The Head ... was serpent shaped[;] it was elevated about two feet from the water.... [H]e could not be less than eighty feet long.

On August 19, 1817, the Linnean Society of New England met in Boston and selected three men — a judge, a physician, and a naturalist — to conduct inquiries. They were to interview witnesses and secure affidavits from them. The sightings went on almost daily through the end of the month. From all this testimony, and from that of other witnesses in 1818 and 1819, a composite description of the sea serpent emerged: a huge snakelike creature, dark on top, lighter on its underside, moving with vertical undulations.

The animal, whatever else it may have been, was not a serpent. Reptiles move laterally, not vertically. Nonetheless the Society investigators concluded that the animal, an enormous reptile, was appearing close to shore because it had laid its eggs there. No such eggs were found, despite repeated searches, but when a farmer killed a three-foot black snake in a field just off Cape Ann, he noticed it had a series of bumps along its back — just as the sea serpent was reported to have.

The Society foolishly endorsed the farmer's suggestion that this was a recently hatched baby sea serpent. Subsequently another scientist, Alexandre Lesuerur, showed that the specimen was no more than a deformed version of the common black snake. Though Lesuerur did not intend to debunk the sightings of the much larger New England sea serpents, his analysis was seized upon by skeptics and their journalistic allies, and the entire affair ended in derision.

The "great unknown."

No amount of laughter, however, could stop the sightings, which kept coming in from all over the world, though it could stop some people from reporting them. When the great American statesman Daniel Webster saw a sea serpent while on a fishing trip off the Massachusetts coast, he pleaded with his companion, according to Henry David Thoreau, "For God's sake never say a word about this to anyone, for if it should be known that I have seen the sea serpent, I should never heard the last of it."

For all the attempts to explain them conventionally — one scoffer averred that every sighting arose from "defective observation connected with an extravagant degree of fear" —the sea serpent did not lose all its supporters in the ranks of the rational and the learned. Sightings saw print mostly in newspapers but also occasionally in scientific periodicals. In 1835 the *American Journal of Science*, after reporting one clear observation, remarked, "We must therefore consider this case as settling the question of the real existence of a Sea Serpent. The absence of paddles or arms forbids us from supposing that this was a swimming saurian."

Of course this did not settle the issue at all, and in 1837 a German zoologist, Hermann Schlegel, "proved" that sea-serpent sightings were caused by observations of rows of porpoises. The sea serpent was fortunate enough, however, to attract the attention of *Zoologist* editor Edward Newman, who in 1847 opened the pages of his journal to open-minded discussion of the subject. He was well aware, of course, that he was defying convention. In an editorial he noted, "It has been the fashion for ... many years to deride all records of this very celebrated monster." He went on to chide critics for *a priori* approaches which ignored "fact and observation" on the grounds that the sea serpent "ought not to be." "Fact-naturalists," on the other hand, "take a different road to knowledge, they enquire whether such things are, and whether such things *are not*."

The following year the most famous sea-serpent report of all time took place. It occurred on the late afternoon of August 6, 1848, and the witnesses were the captain and crew of the frigate *Daedalus*, on their way back to England from the Cape of Good Hope. Soon after its arrival at Plymouth on October 4, several newspapers reported rumors of a spectacular 20-minute sea-serpent sighting, and the Admiralty asked Peter M'Quhae, the captain, to supply a report either denying or detailing the incident. On the eleventh M'Quhae wrote Adm. Sir W. H. Gage a letter which the *Times* of London reprinted two days later. It reads in part:

> [T]he object ... was discovered to be an enormous serpent, with head and shoulders kept about four feet constantly above the surface of the

sea, and as nearly as we could approximate by comparing it with the length of what our main-topsail yard would show in the water, there was at the very least 60 feet of the animal [above water], no portion of which was, to our perception, used in propelling it through the water, either by vertical or horizontal undulation. It passed rapidly, but so close under our lee quarter, that had it been a man of my acquaintance, I should easily have recognized his features with the naked eye; and it did not, either in approaching the ship or after it passed our wake, deviate in the slightest degree from its course to the S.W., which it held on at the pace of from 12 to 15 miles per hour, apparently on some determined purpose.

The diameter of the serpent was about 15 or 16 inches behind the head, which was, without any doubt, that of a snake, and it was never, during the 20 minutes that it continued in sight of our glasses, once below the surface of the water; its color a dark brown, with yellowish white about the throat. It had no fins, but something like the mane of a horse, or rather a bunch of seaweed, washed about its back. It was seen by the quartermaster, the boatswain's mate, and the man at the wheel, in addition to myself and officers above mentioned.

The *Zoologist* soon afterwards published the private notes of another witness, Lt. Edgar Drummond, who confirmed M'Quhae's account in all particulars but one. What M'Quhae had called a mane Drummond deemed a dorsal fin. Ten years later another officer recalled the incident in a letter to the *Times*. "My impression," he wrote, "was that it was rather of a lizard than a serpentine character, as its movement was steady and uniform, as if propelled by fins, not by any undulatory power."

These accounts sparked an uproar. Those who could not credit the sea serpent, even when reported by sane, sober, and experienced British officers, scrambled to concoct alternative explanations. One held that M'Quhae and the others had seen a patch of seaweed. Slightly less preposterous was a notion advanced by Sir Richard Owen, the great anatomist best remembered for his role, a few years in the future, as one of the most implacable foes of Charles Darwin's theory of evolution. Owen declared that the animal M'Quhae saw could not have been a reptile — here he was certainly correct — and so it must be a giant seal, with the witnesses' excitement and overwrought imagination supplying the unseal-like details.

Writing in the November 28 issue of the *Times*, M'Quhae boldly took on the esteemed professor, who happened to be the Admiralty's consultant on sea serpents, whose existence he had pronounced less likely than ghosts'. The captain flatly rejected Owen's speculations, citing the quotations out of context and false conclusions the scientist had used to buttress his argument. "Finally, I deny the existence of excitement, or the possibility of optical illusion," he stated. "I adhere to the statement, as to form, color, and dimensions, contained in my official report to the Admiralty; and I leave them as data whereupon the learned and scientific may exercise the 'pleasures of imagination' until some more fortunate opportunity shall occur of making a closer acquaintance with the 'great unknown' — in the present instance assuredly no ghost."

Though their contemporaries thought M'Quhae got the better of the argument and the sea serpent still had a few prominent champions (such as the famous naturalist Philip Gosse), the weight of scientific opinion continued its slide into negativism. Despite a multitude of reports by men and women of responsible position and impeccable reputation, despite sightings by whole ship crews, notwithstanding statements under oath, the creature was more and more viewed as an impossibility. The world was now too well explored for it to harbor unknown beasts of great size, the reasoning went. Moreover, if they existed, why did such creatures never get stranded on beaches, leaving carcasses which would settle the question for once and always? Of course the latter was something of a self-fulfilling prophecy, because prejudice against sea serpents had become so entrenched that when unusual carcasses were found, often scientists refused to examine them. On the other hand, when examinations were accomplished, the carcasses typically proved to be from known sea animals, notably the basking shark.

Final solutions to the sea-serpent mystery were regularly declared. One caustic observer of these attempts to bury the monster, Richard A. Proctor, wrote in 1885:

> *Because one captain has mistaken a lot of floating sea-wreck half a mile away for a sea monster, therefore the story of a sea creature seen swiftly advancing against wind and sea, at a distance of less than 200 yards, meant nothing more than misunderstood sea-weed. Another mistakes a flight of birds in the distance, or a shoal of porpoises, and even a range of hills beyond the horizon, for some sea-serpentine monster, and forthwith other accounts, however manifestly inconsistent with such explanations, are regarded as explained away. Then, worst of all, some idiot invents a sea-serpent to beguile his time and find occupation for his shallow pate, and so soon as the story is shown to be only a story, men of sense and standing, as incapable of the idiocy of inventing sea-monsters as I am of inventing a planet, are supposed to have amused their leisure by sending grave reports of non-existent sea-monsters to men under whom they (the seamen, not the monsters) held office, or by taking oath before the magistrates that they had seen sea creatures which they had invented, and by parallel absurdities.*

In 1892 A. C. Oudemans revived the question in a classic work, *The Great Sea Serpent*, which as a summary and analysis of the evidence would be unmatched until the publication in 1968 of Bernard Heuvelmans's *In the Wake of the Sea-Serpents*. In 591 pages Oudemans, a respected Dutch zoologist, reviewed 187 cases and from them concluded that all sea-serpent sightings were of a single species of animal, a gigantic long-necked seal.

The twentieth-century serpent.
In 1933 reports of strange animals in a Scottish lake caused a sensation, and the legend of the Loch Ness monster entered international popular

culture. Though within fairly short order Ness's alleged inhabitants would acquire a reputation, at least among those who had not bothered to pay attention to the evidence, as creatures in an absurd tall tale, for a period of time the Ness story reminded scientists and others of the still-unsolved mystery of the sea serpent. Oudemans for one assumed that one of the Ness animals would soon be caught or killed and the identity of the sea serpent would be known with certainty.

In 1933 there was a rash of reports of a sea serpent off the coast of British Columbia. Occasional sightings had occurred in the past, going back to at least 1897, but the Loch Ness uproar gave water monsters generally a new cachet. Soon the Canadian animal was given the name Cadborosaurus, which combined Cadboro Bay, on Victoria Island's southeast coast, and saurus. Cadborosaurus soon became "Caddy."

The first widely publicized sighting took place on October 8, 1933, and involved a witness of high repute: Maj. W. H. Langley, a barrister and clerk of the British Columbia legislature. Sailing his sloop past Chatham Island early in the afternoon, he spotted a greenish-brown-colored serpent with serrated body, "every bit as big as a whale but entirely different from a whale in many respects." He estimated its length at 80 feet.

In 1937, according to an account told to investigators years later, whalers killed a sperm whale off the Queen Charlotte Islands in northern British Columbia. When they cut its stomach open, they found inside the semidigested remains of a 10-foot-long, snakelike creature with a horselike head and humped back. This remarkable specimen was returned to the ocean.

Two scientists, University of British Columbia oceanographer Paul LeBlond and Royal British Columbia Museum marine biologist Edward Bousfield, have spent some years investigating reports like these. By 1992 they were willing to endorse the reality of the animals in a formal lecture to a conference of the American Society of Zoologists.

Another much-publicized sea serpent is Chessie, the Chesapeake Bay monster. It got its name in 1982, following a number of sightings in the spring and summer. As with Caddy, these have attracted the attention of scientists with cryptozoological interests. Sightings include one made by Robert and Karen Frew on May 31, 1982. At 7 P.M., while entertaining guests outside their home overlooking the bay at Love Point on the northern tip of Kent Island, at the mouth of the Chester River, they saw a strange creature 200 feet from shore in calm water only five feet deep.

Robert Frew watched it through binoculars for a few minutes before securing his video camera and focusing on the enigmatic animal, which submerged and reappeared several times during the sighting. The closest the creature came was within 100 feet of shore and within 50 feet of some boys who were playing on a pile of submerged rocks. Though the Frews and their friends shouted to alert the boys (their cries and all other com-

● SOURCES:

Aldrich, Hal B. "Was It a Plesiosaur?" INFO Journal 6, 3 (September/October 1977): 13–14.

Bandini, Ralph. "I Saw a Sea Monster." Esquire (June 1934): 90, 92.

Bayanov, Dmitri. "Black Sea Serpents." Fortean Times 51 (Winter 1988/1989): 59.

Bradford, Gershom. "Sea Serpents? No or Maybe." The American Neptune 13, 4 (October 1953): 268–76.

Burr, Malcolm. "Sea Serpents and Monsters." The Nineteenth Century and After 115 (February 1934): 220–30.

Chorvinsky, Mark. "The 'Mary F.' Morgawr Photographs Investigation." Strange Magazine 8 (Fall 1991): 8–9, 11, 46–48.

Chorvinsky, Mark, and Mark Opsasnick. "A Field Guide to the Monsters and Mystery Animals of Maryland." Strange Magazine 5 (1990): 41–46.

Clark, Jerome. "America's Water Monsters: The New Evidence." Fate 36, 4 (April 1983): 62–65, 68–70.

Colombo, John Robert. Mysterious Canada: Strange Sights, Extraor-

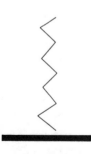

ments made during the event are recorded on the videotape), the boys never heard them and so apparently never saw the animal.

The witnesses estimated the animal to be 30 to 35 feet long but slightly less than a foot in diameter. Much of it remained under water, but as it surfaced repeatedly, more and more of it became visible. Frew said, "The first time up, we saw its head and about four feet [of back]. The next time about 12 feet, the next time about 20." The visible part of the back seemed to have humps. Its head was shaped like a football, only "a little more round." Observers could not discern eyes, ears, or mouth. It was the odd shape of the head more than anything else that led Frew to reject the idea that the animal was some kind of snake. The Frews, familiar with a wide variety of sea life, rejected theories that they had misperceived a conventional animal.

On August 20 seven scientists from the Smithsonian Institution, along with representatives of the National Aquarium and Maryland's Department of Natural Resources, met at the Smithsonian to view and discuss the Frew videotape. In a subsequent report recounting the group's conclusions, George Zug of the Smithsonian's National Museum of Natural History wrote, "All the viewers of the tape came away with a strong impression of an animate object.... We could not identify the object.... These sightings are not isolated phenomena, for they have been reported regularly for the past several years."

The twentieth century has seen no let-up in sea-serpent reports in the world's oceans. The presence of an organization like the International Society of Cryptozoology, whose board of directors and general membership include a surprising number of well-credentialed and impressively affiliated biologists, makes serious research both possible and at least quasi-respectable. Along with other books on a wide range of cryptozoological questions, the ISC's president, Bernard Heuvelmans, can claim credit for producing the most comprehensive volume ever written on the sea serpent. It is not likely that we will see anything to compare to *In the Wake of the Sea-Serpents* in our time.

The varieties of sea-serpent experience.

In the last chapter of his book, at the end of a detailed recitation and searching analysis of every sea-serpent report, credible or otherwise, known through 1966 (587 in all, of which he judged 358 authentic observations of unknown animals), Heuvelmans parted company with nearly all of his predecessors: he bluntly acknowledged the futility of trying to force-fit from these sightings a description of a single species of animal. Virtually every other commentator, including Oudemans and Rupert T. Gould (author of the important *The Case for the Sea Serpent* [1930]), had dismissed or rationalized away all discordant detail as due to error or invention. Heuvelmans found, however, that these supposedly anomalous features reappeared so often that they had to be taken into consideration. And if they were, they suggested that "sea serpent" is a generic term covering several unrecognized marine animals. Among them:

dinary Events, and Peculiar Places. Toronto: Doubleday Canada Limited, 1988.

Corliss, William R., ed. *Strange Life: A Sourcebook on the Mysteries of Organic Nature, Volume B-1.* Glen Arm, MD: The Sourcebook Project, 1976.

Costello, Peter. *In Search of Lake Monsters.* New York: Coward, McCann and Geoghegan, 1974.

Geller, L. D. "Notes on Sea Serpents of Coastal New England." *New York Folklore Quarterly* 26, 2 (June 1970): 153–60.

Gould, Rupert T. *The Case for the Sea Serpent.* London: Philip Allan, 1930.

Heuvelmans, Bernard. *In the Wake of the Sea-Serpents.* New York: Hill and Wang, 1968.

———. "How I Conquered the Sea-Serpent Some Twenty-Five Years Ago." *Strange Magazine* 3 (1988): 10–13, 56–57.

LeBlond, Paul H. "A Previously Unreported 'Sea Serpent' Sighting in the South Atlantic." *Cryptozoology* 2 (1983): 82–84.

Lester, Paul. *The Great Sea Serpent Controversy: A Cultural Study.*

Long-necked (48 sightings). Description: A long neck, angled toward the head; hump or humps on the back; no tail; two horns, sometimes described as ears. Sample report: In the summer of 1950, John Handley, bathing in the surf on the Kent coast, saw a long-necked creature rise out of the water less than 100 yards away. It had ears and a horselike head more than two feet across. A woman also observed the creature. Classification: Almost certainly a pinniped. Range: Cosmopolitan.

Merhorse (37 sightings). Description: Floating mane, medium to long neck, big eyes, hair or whiskers on the face. Sample report: In November 1947 Vancouver Island fisherman George W. Saggers encountered a strange serpentlike animal in Ucluelet Harbor, at a distance of 150 feet. Its head and neck were four feet above the water; it had "two jet black eyes about three inches across and protruding from the head.... It appeared to have some sort of mane.... The color of the mane was dark brown," he wrote. Classification: Probably a pinniped. Range: Cosmopolitan.

Many-humped (33 sightings). Description: String of dorsal humps, slender neck of medium length, small but prominent eyes, striped dark on top of the body, white on underside, white stripes on neck. Sample report: On June 20, 1815, Capt. Elkanah Finney focused a telescope on a sea serpent in Cape Cod Bay: "I then had a good view of him through my glass, at the distance of a quarter of a mile. His appearance in this situation was like a string of buoys. I saw perhaps thirty or forty of these protuberances or bunches, which were about the size of a barrel. The head [front part visible above water] appeared to be about six or eight feet long, and where it was connected with the body was a little larger than the body. His head tapered off to the size of a horse's head.... [W]hat I supposed to be his under jaw had a white stripe extending the whole length of the head, just above the water. While he lay in this situation, he appeared to be about a hundred or a hundred and twenty feet long." Classification: Cetacean. Range: North Atlantic.

Many-finned (20 sightings). Description: Triangular fins looking like a huge crest, short, slender neck. Sample report: In December 1878 an Englishwoman named Mrs. Turner was aboard the liner *Poonah* anchored off Suez or Aden; she could not remember which when she related her experience to Robert P. Greg, who subsequently wrote a letter to Oudemans. She observed an extraordinary animal motionless on the surface 150 feet away. Greg wrote, "She saw both the head and 7 or 8 fins of the back, all at the same time in a line. She cannot remember exactly how many dorsal fins there were, but they were large, slightly curved back and not all the same size.... The head looked 4–6 feet diameter, like a large tree trunk.... The color was nearly black like a whale. The whole length appeared considerable, perhaps as long as an ordinary tree, or moderate sized ship!" Classification: Cetacean. Range: Tropical waters.

Super-Otter (13 sightings). Description: Slender, medium-length neck and long, tapering tail, several vertical bends in the body. Sample report: Hans Egede, a Protestant missionary known as the Apostle of Greenland,

Birmingham, England: Protean Publications, 1984.

Ley, Willy. *Exotic Zoology.* New York: The Viking Press, 1959.

McLellan, Wendy. "A Serpent Lurking in the Deep?" *Vancouver* [British Columbia] *Province* (August 2, 1992).

Mangiacopra, Gary S. "The Great Unknowns of the 19th Century." *Of Sea and Shore* (Winter 1976–77): 201–05, 228.

Mawnan-Peller, A. *Morgawr: The Monster of Falmouth Bay: A Short History.* Falmouth, Cornwall, England: Morgawr Productions, 1976.

Meurger, Michel. "In Jormungandra's Coils: A Cultural Archaeology of the Norse Sea-Serpent." *Fortean Times* 51 (Winter 1988/1989): 63–68.

Moore, Gary. "The Gloucester Moncester." *Boston Herald American Beacon* (January 9, 1977): 20–22, 26–27.

Oudemans, A. C. *The Great Sea Serpent.* Leiden, Netherlands: E. J. Brill, 1892.

Proctor, Richard A. "Monster Sea-Serpents." *Knowledge* 7 (1885): 273–74.

Saggers, George W.

"Sea Serpent off Vancouver." *Fate* 1, 2 (Summer 1948): 124–25.

Sansom, John H. "Fabulous Lunkers." *Fate* 41,3 (March 1988): 62–69.

"Sea Serpent." *American Journal of Science* 1, 11 (1826): 196.

"'Sea Serpents' Seen off California Coast." *The ISC Newsletter* 2, 4 (Winter 1983): 9–10.

W. "On the History of the Great Sea Serpent." *Blackwood's Edinburgh Magazine* 13, 3 (April 1818): 32–42.

Westrum, Ronald. "A Note on Monsters." *Journal of Popular Culture* 8, 4 (Spring 1975): 862–70.

———. "Sea-Serpent Reporting Dynamics." *Pursuit* 8, 4 (October 1975): 86–88.

———. "Knowledge About Sea Serpents." In Roy Wallis, ed. *The Sociological Review Monograph No. 27: On the Margins of Science: The Social Construction of Rejected Knowledge*, 293–314. Great Britain: University of Keele, March 1979.

Wood, J. G. "The Trail of the Sea-Serpent." *The Atlantic Monthly* 53, 320 (June 1884): 799–814.

recorded this 1734 manifestation, witnessed while he was on his second voyage to Greenland: "This Monster was of so huge a Size, that coming out of the Water, its Head reached as high as the Mast-Head; its Body was bulky as the Ship, and three or four times as long. It had a long pointed Snout, and spouted like a Whale-Fish; great broad Paws, and the Body seemed covered with shell-work, its skin very rugged and uneven. The under Part of its Body was shaped like an enormous huge Serpent, and when it dived again under Water, it plunged backwards into the Sea, and so raised its Tail aloft, which seemed a whole Ship's Length distant from the bulkiest part of its Body." Classification: Uncertain, but possibly a surviving form of primitive cetacean. Range: North Atlantic (possibly extinct; last known sighting in 1848).

Super-Eel (12 sightings). Description: Serpentine body, long tapering tail. Sample report: Two British naturalists aboard the yacht *Valhalla*, on a scientific cruise 15 miles off the mouth of the Parahiba in Brazil, spotted a strange animal in the water at mid-morning on December 7, 1905. E.G.B. Meade-Waldo wrote: "I … saw a large fin or frill sticking out of the water, dark seaweed-brown in color, somewhat crinkled at the edge. It was apparently about 6 feet in length, and projected from 18 inches to 2 feet from the water." After securing field glasses, he watched a "great head and neck [rise] out of the water in front of the frill; the neck did not touch the frill in the water, but came out of the water *in front* of it, at a distance of certainly not less than 18 inches, and from 7 to 8 feet was out of the water; head and neck were all about the same thickness. The head had a very turtle-like appearance, as had also the eye…. It moved its head and side in a peculiar manner; the color of the head and neck was dark brown above, and whitish below — almost white, I think." Classification: Fish. Range: Cosmopolitan.

Heuvelmans acknowledged, "I cannot claim to have entirely solved the problem of the great sea-serpent, but I have cleared up a good deal of it. To solve the whole complex problem, without being able to examine the remains of the animals in question, we need many more detailed and exact reports." He noted that hoaxes and misidentifications of known marine animals have added no small measure of confusion. Aside from reports that had to be eliminated from the analysis because of lack of detail, Heuvelmans counted 49 hoaxes and 52 mistakes among the reports he collected.

(Some of the most spectacular hoaxes would be perpetrated in the decade after *In the Wake* saw print. They involved widely published photographs, allegedly taken by an untraceable "Mary F.," allegedly of the Cornish sea serpent Morgawr off Falmouth Bay. An account in *Strange Magazine*, the result of extensive inquiries conducted by Mark Chorvinsky, identifies the hoaxer as professional prankster Tony "Doc" Shiels. So far, however, Shiels admits nothing. Whoever the perpetrator may be, there is no doubt that the photographs are bogus. Shiels also has taken dubious-looking pictures of what he maintains is the Loch Ness monster.)

In common with every other twentieth-century commentator, Heuvelmans rejects the idea that sea serpents are serpents as such. All but one of the proposed candidates above are mammals. But he does leave the door open slightly for the possibility that an unknown reptile may have been observed on rare occasion. His collection includes a scant four reports of what he calls a "marine saurian," a huge lizard- or crocodile-shaped creature encountered in tropical waters. If it exists, it may be, in Heuvelmans's view, "a surviving thalattosuchian, in other words a true crocodile of an ancient group, a specifically and exclusively oceanic one, which flourished from the Jurassic to the Cretaceous periods. But it could also be a surviving mosasaur, a sea cousin of the monitors of today. It would not be surprising if it had survived for so long in the sea, since it is well designed to dive deep and remain unseen."

Interestingly enough, though Heuvelmans does not mention the fact, some witnesses claim to have sighted giant "crocodiles," "alligators," or "salamanders" in Loch Ness, though writers and investigators obsessed with the notion of the classic long-necked, plesiosaurlike Nessie have consistently ignored or downplayed such sightings.

To the most frequently stated objection to sea serpents — the absence of stranded carcasses — Heuvelmans writes that the kinds of beasts responsible for such sightings "all belong by nature to the category of animals least likely to be stranded, and quite capable of getting off the shore again, if by misfortune they are." Apparently they die far out at sea.

From all indications the sea-serpent question is being resurrected. No doubt, however, it will take an actual specimen to silence all skeptics. Nonetheless, as the dimensions of our ignorance about the fauna and flora of the ocean depths become ever more apparent, *a priori* objections to the existence of gigantic unknown sea animals have fallen by the wayside. The sea serpent's time may at last have arrived.

Yoon, Carol Kaesuk. "In Dark Seas, Biologists Sight a Riot of Life." *New York Times* (June 2, 1992).

345

SIRIUS MYSTERY————————————————————

If the "ancient astronaut" fad of the 1970s produced one book of substance, many agree it is Robert K. G. Temple's *The Sirius Mystery* (1977). Learned, extensively researched, and unlike anything by Erich von Däniken or other pop theorists of the gods-from-outer-space school, it presents a complex, many-sided argument for an early extraterrestrial presence in West Africa. The core of Temple's case is this:

The Dogon are a tribe believed to be of Egyptian descent. After leaving Libya centuries ago, they settled in Mali, West Africa, bringing with them astronomical lore traceable to pre-dynastic Egypt before 3200 B.C. In the late 1940s four of their priests told two French anthropologists of a secret Dogon oral tradition concerning the star Sirius (8.6 light years from earth). The priests said Sirius has a companion star which is invisible to the human eye; this star takes a 50-year elliptical orbit around Sirius A, is small and incredibly heavy, and rotates on its axis.

All of these things happen to be true. What makes them so remarkable is that Sirius's white-dwarf companion, called Sirius B, was first photographed in 1970. Its existence was suspected as early as 1844, but it was not seen through a telescope until 1862 and was not understood to be densely packed until the early decades of the twentieth century. The Dogon beliefs, on the other hand, are supposedly thousands of years old. Even if these people had access to modern Western astronomy textbooks, they could not have known about Sirius B, or for that matter about the rotations and orbits of planets in our solar system, or about the four major moons of Jupiter and the rings of Saturn — unless, perhaps, they learned of it, as their mythology indicates, from unearthly sources.

The unearthly sources were Nommos, amphibious, repulsive-looking beings who arrived in an ark in the company of fire and thunder. The Nommos, who lived mostly in the sea, are depicted as partly fishlike and, at least in a general way, reminiscent of merfolk. Nommo (whom the Dogon refer to interchangeably in both the singular and the plural) apparently is the same creature the Babylonians call Oannes, the Accadians Ea, and the Sumerians Enki; the Egyptian goddess Isis, depicted as what later would be termed a mermaid, is also related to the worship of Sirius.

The Dogon say a third star exists in the Sirius system. Larger and lighter than Sirius B, Sirius C also revolves around Sirius A. Around this third star orbits a planet from which the Nommos came.

Alternative explanations.

Though Temple's book got generally more favorable reviews than did other works in the ancient-astronaut genre, criticisms of it by popular-science writer Ian Ridpath and celebrity-astronomer Carl Sagan had a marked negative influence on the seriousness with which elite opinion would come to view *The Sirius Mystery*. Temple would complain that magazines ranging from *Omni* to *Nature* refused to publish his rejoinders to criticisms made in their pages.

Ridpath devised (and subsequently passed on to Sagan) a simple explanation: the Dogon got their supposedly ancient astronomical knowledge from modern astronomically knowledgeable informants — presumably Westerners who discussed astronomy with Dogon priests, who quickly incorporated this new information about Sirius into the body of older lore concerning the star. French anthropologist Germaine Dieterlen, who had lived among the Dogon for most of her life and whose paper on their astronomical mythology first caught Temple's attention, characterized this claim as "absurd" when asked about it by a reporter for BBC-TV's *Horizon* program. As she uttered the word, she held up a 400-year-old Dogon artifact depicting the Sirius configuration.

Temple also pointed out that some of the information, for example that concerning the superdensity of Sirius B, was only a few years old when anthropologists collected it from the Dogon in 1931. The anthropologists, Temple wrote, "would have known if some group of Western amateur astronomers had rushed out to the desolate hinterland of Mali to implant this knowledge in the presumably pliant minds of the Dogon priests in that narrow period of two or three years before their own arrival. How all of this was then supposed to have filtered down through the entire Dogon and surrounding cultures of over two million people and been embodied in the hundreds of thousands of objects, symbols, woven blankets, carved statues, etc., etc., which exist in those cultures relating to the 'Sirius Mystery' in only two or three years baffles me." These and other remarks, published as an "Open Letter to Carl Sagan" in *Zetetic Scholar*, elicited no response whatever from the man to whom they were addressed.

Ridpath, Sagan, and a later critic, James E. Oberg, treated Temple's point-by-point refutations as if they did not exist. Oberg, for example, used the modern-informant claim in a Fate article, to which Temple responded with a detailed critique in a subsequent issue. Nonetheless Oberg incorporated

● SOURCES:

Kaler, James B. "White Sirian Stars: Class A." *Sky & Telescope* 73, 5 (May 1987): 491–94.

Oberg, James E. *UFOs and Outer Space Mysteries: A Sympathetic Skeptic's Report.* Norfolk, VA: The Donning Company, 1981.

———. "Ancient Astronauts in West Africa?" *Fate* 31, 11 (November 1978): 76–81.

Ridpath, Ian. *Messages from the Stars.* New York: Harper and Row, 1978.

———. "Investigating the Sirius 'Mystery'." *Skeptical Inquirer* 3, 1 (Fall 1978): 56–62.

Sagan, Carl. *Broca's Brain: Reflections on the Romance of Science.* New York: Random House, 1979.

Story, Ronald. *Guardians of the Universe?* New York: New English Library, 1980.

Temple, Robert K. G. *The Sirius Mystery.* New York: St. Martin's Press, 1977.

———. "In Defense of *The Sirius Mystery*." *Fate* 33, 10 (October 1980): 83–88.

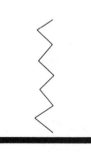

———. "On the Sirius Mystery: An Open Letter to Carl Sagan." *Zetetic Scholar* 8 (July 1981): 29–33.

his article, word for word, into a later book which neglected not only to answer Temple but even to acknowledge the response's existence. Ronald Story's *Guardians of the Universe?* (1980), an attack on ancient-astronaut theories, recycles the by-now-unkillable canard that the Dogon Sirius beliefs are of recent origin. Story sneers that the "deeper one looks into the 'Sirius mystery,' the less mysterious it becomes.... [C]ertain key information has been withheld, or missed, by the author writing the story" — a criticism that more fairly could be leveled against Story, Sagan, Ridpath, and Oberg.

More serious criticism focuses on the unlikelihood of there being a third star in the Sirius system or of intelligent life's having developed there. Sirius figures in no exobiologist's list of places to look for evidence of extraterrestrial civilizations.

Still, it seems hard to deny that Temple raised serious questions which deserved better than the superficial answers they received. Two decades after publication of *The Sirius Mystery*, the book has been all but forgotten. The mystery of the Dogon's curious astronomical knowledge, however, remains.

SKY SERPENTS

From antiquity through the nineteenth century, reports of sightings of enormous aerial dragons or snakes occasionally saw print.

Such stories first appear in medieval sources. According, for example, to the *Anglo-Saxon Chronicle*, in A.D. 793 "terrible portents appeared.... These were exceptional flashes of lightning, and fiery dragons were seen flying in the air, and soon followed a great famine." Nineteen years earlier, in 774, "red signs appeared in the sky after sunset, and horrid serpents were seen in Sudsexe, with great amazement," wrote Henry, Archdeacon of Huntington, in *Historia Anglorum*.

In April 1388 a "flying dragon was seen ... in many places" (*Knighton's Continuator*). On December 5, 1762, a "twisting serpent" lit up the sky as it slowly descended and vanished over Bideford, Devonshire, England. It was visible for six minutes.

Though we expect to read of such unbelievable magical phenomena in the chronicles of the Middle Ages, it is a little disconcerting to encounter them in relatively recent times. In the mid-1800s Nebraska settlers claimed to have witnessed comparably bizarre sights. Western historian Mari Sandoz noted, "Back in the hard times of 1857–58 there were stories of a flying serpent that hovered over a Missouri River steamboat slowing for a landing. In the late dusk it was like a great undulating serpent, in and out of the lowering clouds, breathing fire, it seemed, with lighted streaks along the sides." A frontier folk ballad from the period refers to a "flyin' engine/ Without no wing or wheel/ It came a-roarin' in the sky/ With lights along the side/ And scales like a serpent's hide."

The reference to a "flyin' engine" may suggest that the object was some sort of unearthly machine rather than a living creature, but other tales indicate otherwise. In June 1873 farmers near Bonham, Texas, sighted an "enormous serpent" in a cloud, the *Bonham Enterprise* asserted, and were — no surprise —"seriously frightened." The account goes on:

> It seemed to be as large and as long as a telegraph pole, was of a yellow striped color, and seemed to float along without any effort. They could see it coil itself up, turn over, and thrust forward its huge head as if striking at something, displaying the maneuvers of a genuine snake. The cloud and serpent moved in an easterly direction, and were seen by persons a few miles this side of Honey Grove.

A few days later, in its July 6 edition, the New York Times declared this the "very worst case of delirium tremens on record." It had nothing to say, however, about another manifestation, chronicled in a Kansas newspaper, the *Fort Scott Monitor*, a few days earlier, on June 27:

> A strange and remarkable phenomenon was observed at sunrise yesterday morning.... When the disc of the sun was about halfway above the horizon, the form of a huge serpent, apparently perfect in form, was plainly seen encircling it and was visible for some moments.

If the Fort Scott apparition existed outside the imagination of the individual who wrote these words, it was probably an unusual auroral phenomenon. The Bonham serpent cannot be so easily explained, if we credit the account, which — since frontier newspapers were full of practical jokes and tall tales — we are not compelled to do.

A final nineteenth-century sky-serpent story comes from a man who signed himself "R. B." in a letter to the editor of the *Frederick News*, a Maryland paper, on November 29, 1883. At 6:30 one morning, he averred, he had been standing on a hilltop when he saw, over Catoctin Mountain, a "monstrous dragon with glaring eye-balls, and mouth wide open displaying a tongue, which hung like a flame of fire from its jaws, reared and plunged."

● SOURCES:

Bullard, Thomas E., ed. *The Airship File: A Collection of Texts Concerning Phantom Airships and Other UFOs, Gathered from Newspapers and Periodicals Mostly During the Hundred Years Prior to Kenneth Arnold's Sighting.* Bloomington, IN: The Author, 1982.

Chorvinsky, Mark, and Mark Opsasnick. "A Field Guide to the Monsters and Mystery Animals of Maryland." *Strange Magazine* 5 (1990): 41–46.

Evans, Jonathan D. "The Dragon." In Malcolm South, ed. *Mythical and Fabulous Creatures: A Source Book and Research Guide,* 27–58. New York: Greenwood Press, 1987.

Gaddis, Vincent H. "Visitors from the Void." *Amazing Stories* 21,6 (June 1947): 159–61.

Reid, Frank. "A Rare UFO — The `Flying Serpent'." *Saucer News* 3,6 (October/November 1956): 4–5.

Sandoz, Mari. *Love Song to the Plains.* Lincoln, NE: University of Nebraska Press, 1966.

Wilkins, Harold T. *Flying Saucers on the Attack.* New York: The Citadel Press, 1954.

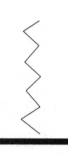

SKYQUAKES

On July 4, 1808, while exploring the Rocky Mountains, the Lewis and Clark Expedition had an odd experience. They recorded it in their journal thus:

> Since our arrival at the Falls we have repeatedly heard a strange noise coming from the mountains in a direction a little to the north of west. It is heard at different periods of the day and night, sometimes when the air is perfectly still and without a cloud, and consists of one stroke only, or five or six discharges in quick succession. It is loud, and resembles precisely the sound of a six pound piece of ordnance at the distance of three miles.

Such phenomena, sometimes described as sounding like muffled thunder or cannon fire, have long been noted. They figure in American Indian and other legends, and in our time they have been incorporated into our own reigning folklore; some writers have linked them to UFOs and to parallel universes. The best known of these "skyquakes" are the Barisal Guns of India and the Moodus Noises of Connecticut, but comparable sounds have been heard all over the world.

For example, members of an exploration party along the Darling River, near what is now Bourke, New South Wales, Australia, were startled by mysterious sounds which erupted one afternoon in February 1829. The leader's diary recorded the event:

> About 3 P.M. on the 7th Mr. Hume and I were occupied tracing the chart upon the ground. The day had been remarkably fine, not a cloud was there in the heavens, nor a breath of air to be felt. On a sudden we heard what seemed to be the report of a gun fired at the distance of between five and six miles. It was not the hollow sound of an earthly explosion, or the sharp cracking noise of falling timber, but in every

way resembled a discharge of a heavy piece of ordnance. On this all were agreed, but no one was certain where the sound proceeded. Both Mr. Hume and myself [sic] had been too attentive to our occupation to form a satisfactory opinion; but we both thought it came from the N.W. I sent one of the men immediately up a tree, but he could observe nothing unusual.

The confusion about the location of the source is typical. It explains why the sounds are known as skyquakes; to many who hear them, they seem to be coming out of the air. In truth, as a natural, if unusual, phenomenon linked to earthquakes and seismic activity, the sounds actually emanate from underground. Scientists do not know why earthquake activity (sometimes so slight as to be measurable only with instruments) generates these peculiar noises in some places and not in others. Since 1981, however, the Weston Observatory of Boston College has been monitoring earthquake activity in New England and has amassed considerable data on the Moodus phenomena. Possibly answers to the physical mechanisms behind skyquakes will emerge from this research.

● SOURCES:

Brooke, Harrison V. "Thunder of the Mackimoodus." *Fate* 28, 10 (October 1975): 70–79.

Cleland, J. Burton. "Barisal Guns in Australia." *Nature* 81 (1909): 127.

Corliss, William R., ed. *Strange Phenomena: A Sourcebook of Unusual Natural Phenomena.* Glen Arm, MD: The Author, 1974.

———. *Handbook of Unusual Natural Phenomena.* Glen Arm, MD: The Sourcebook Project, 1977.

Fort, Charles. *The Books of Charles Fort.* New York: Henry Holt and Company, 1941.

Gould, Rupert T. *Enigmas: Another Book of Unexplained Facts.* London: Philip Allan, 1929.

Rierden, Andi. "A Steady Observer for Trembling Moodus." *New York Times* (August 6, 1989).

Robinson, Charles H. "Barisal Guns." *Nature* 53 (1896): 487.

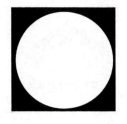

SPACE BROTHERS

On the afternoon of November 20, 1952, George Adamski, a lifelong occult teacher, met a Venusian named Orthon in the desert of southern California. This initiated a series of events which would involve further contacts with Venusians as well as Martians and Saturnians. Adamski would also travel into space and on one occasion attend a conference on Saturn.

These claims, chronicled in three books published between 1953 and 1961, electrified many in the movement which emerged in the wake of Kenneth Arnold's June 24, 1947, sighting of what newspapers quickly called "flying saucers." A movement based on such stories spread from California to much of the rest of the world. Other prominent claimants included Orfeo Angelucci, Truman Bethurum, Daniel Fry, Howard Menger, George Van Tassel, and George Hunt Williamson, all of whom published books in the 1950s and who were popular figures on the occult circuit.

According to these "contactees," friendly, good-looking, humanlike space people pilot the saucers. They are here on a benevolent mission for the Galactic Federation. In the universe the earth is viewed as something of a backwater, its occupants primitive and violent; earthlings threaten to upset the "balance of the universe" with their atomic weapons and warlike ways. If earthlings will heed the space people's gentle message, they will enter a New Age of peace and prosperity and claim their place in the larger order. In some variants of this theme, the earth is about to undergo massive geological changes which will destroy a significant portion of the planet's population; those who follow the space people's direction will be saved, either by relocating to places which will remain stable during the upheaval or by entering spaceships which will pick them up at the appropriate time.

Early on, contactees and their followers attached the affectionate nickname "Space Brothers" to the extraterrestrials, apparently in recognition of the latter's charitable nature and essentially religious outlook. Contactee

● SOURCES:

Adamski, George.
Inside the Space Ships.
New York: Abelard-
Schuman, 1955.

Clark, Jerome. UFOs in
the 1980s: The UFO
Encyclopedia, Volume
1. Detroit, MI: Apogee
Books, 1990.

———. The Emergence
of a Phenomenon: UFOs
from the Beginning
Through 1959 — The
UFO Encyclopedia, Vol-
ume 2. Detroit, MI:
Omnigraphics, 1992.

Curran, Douglas. In
Advance of the Landing:
Folk Concepts of Outer
Space. New York:
Abbeville Press, 1985.

Evans, Hilary. Gods,
Spirits, Cosmic Guard-
ians: A Comparative
Study of the Encounter
Experience. Wellingbor-
ough, Northampton-
shire, England: The
Aquarian Press, 1987.

Stupple, David. "Mahat-
mas and Space Broth-
ers." Journal of American
Culture 7 (1984): 131–
39.

theology is based in the doctrines of Theosophy, an occult system developed by Helene Petrova Blavatsky in the latter nineteenth century. In an
early-twentieth-century refinement of Blavatsky, Charles Leadbeater wrote
that Venus, which operates on a higher evolutionary plane than earth, is
inhabited by advanced beings called "Lords of the Flame," who occupy
the highest rank in the "Great White Brotherhood" — spirit Masters who
guide the development of the human race. Possibly the term "Space Brothers" has its origins in the earlier "Brotherhood."

Though the physical contactees, who often produced dubious photographs and other "evidence" supposed to validate their claims, dominated the scene in the first years of the UFO era, there were also psychic
contactees who channeled space messages or received them in dreams or
through automatic writings. By the early 1960s even some of Adamski's
most committed disciples had begun to entertain doubts about his sincerity as his tales grew ever taller. But most psychic contactees were manifestly sincere, even if to unsympathetic observers — including most
mainstream ufologists — their message was inherently incredible, and they
began to define the movement.

Only one physical contactee, Eduard (Billy) Meier of Switzerland, has had
any impact on the New Age scene. Meier produces photographs both of
purported "beamships" from the Pleiades and of their beautiful occupants.
In one instance a lovely Pleiades woman turned out to be a model in an
advertisement which had appeared in a European fashion magazine. More
typical of modern devotees of Space Brothers are those who flock to
Laramie, Wyoming, every summer to attend the Rocky Mountain Conference on UFO Investigation; the conference caters mostly to contactees
who live in small western towns or on farms or ranches and who believe
themselves to be recipients of mental messages from kindly off-worlders.

SPONTANEOUS HUMAN COMBUSTION ——

Spontaneous human combustion (SHC) is an alleged phenomenon in which an internally generated flame suddenly consumes the victim's flesh and bone. If it is what it purports to be, it is one of nature's most extraordinary mysteries, utterly inexplicable to modern science.

What is usually called the best-documented case of SHC took place in 1951 in St. Petersburg, Florida, when a 67-year-old woman named Mary Reeser perished under unusual circumstances. Her body was discovered at 8 A.M. on July 2 when her landlady tried to enter Mrs. Reeser's small apartment to deliver a message. When the handle turned out to be too hot to handle, the landlady summoned two painters from across the street. They pushed through the door and found, amid a great deal of smoke, Mrs. Reeser's charred remains, reduced to ash except for a foot and what some accounts later asserted was a "shrunken skull" (unconfirmed in the official report; a skull exposed to great heat will explode, not contract). The overstuffed chair in which she had been sitting had been reduced to ashes and a few coiled springs.

This incident, which attracted national attention at the time of its occurrence, has been cited repeatedly in the literature of SHC. But beliefs and controversies concerning such deaths go back at least several centuries and figured in eighteenth- and nineteenth-century medical debates. In 1833, in a paper read to the French Academy of Sciences, M. J. Fontelle reviewed a number of cases and remarked that victims tended to be old women fond of liquor and that the fire damage did not extend to flammable materials on or near the body. This latter feature, while repeated in much subsequent writing on SHC, in fact figures in only a relatively few cases. Mrs. Reeser's nightgown, for example, was consumed, as was her chair.

An objective reading of the "evidence" leads one to the conclusion that either it is a true anomaly which suffers from inadequate documentation or

● SOURCES:

Arnold, Larry E. "The Flaming Fate of Dr. Bentley." *Fate* 30, 4 (April 1977): 66–72.

———. "The Man Who Survived Spontaneous Combustion." *Fate* 35, 9 (September 1982): 60–65.

Christie, Peter. "The Grace Pett SHC: A Re-examination." *Fortean Times* 35 (Summer 1981): 6–9.

Eckert, Allan W. "The Baffling Burning Death." *True* (May 1964): 33, 104–12.

Farish, Lucius, ed. *Omega*. Worcester, MA: Controversial Phenomena Bulletin, 1965.

Gaddis, Vincent H. *Mysterious Fires and Lights*.

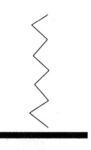

it is simply a manufactured mystery generated out of imaginative interpretations of fire deaths which may have been unusual but which had conventional causes. For all the claims made for it, the Mary Reeser death seems a mundane sort of tragedy. When her son, a physician, last saw her on the previous evening, Mrs. Reeser informed him that she had taken two sleeping pills. The official conclusion, that she fell asleep while smoking and burned up along with her flammable nightgown, is entirely reasonable. Her own body fat — Mrs. Reeser was overweight — further fueled the flames.

One popular pre-twentieth-century theory about SHC held that drunkards were particularly susceptible because the liquor in their bodies made them combustible. (The most famous literary victim of SHC, Mr. Krook in Charles Dickens's *Bleak House*, was intoxicated at the time of his extraordinary demise.) This hypothesis is without scientific basis, though it was beloved of temperance advocates. Still, there is a relationship between drunkenness and fire deaths. "Drunken persons," Joe Nickell and John F. Fischer remark, are "more careless with fire and less able to properly respond to an accident."

In several critical articles on SHC claims, Nickell and Fischer note the suggestive circumstances in which victims typically are found: "a broken oil lamp on the floor, a victim's pipe, a candlestick lying near the remains. But in addition there was often a large quantity of combustible material under the body to aid in its destruction: bedding, for example, or a chair's stuffing — even wooden flooring possibly impregnated with oils or waxes. Interestingly enough, there was evidence that melted human fat had increased the destruction in a number of instances."

If SHC, like the Bermuda Triangle, has the appearance more of a manufactured mystery than of an authentic enigma, it has nonetheless inspired no end of theories, from those claiming to explain it "scientifically" (as the consequence, in one speculation complete with charts, of "geomagnetic fluctuations") to those positing frankly occult causes (the internalization of destructive psychokinetic impulses). The leading proponent of SHC is a Pennsylvania man of New Age sympathies, Larry E. Arnold, who links such events with a variety of paranormal phenomena. Elsewhere SHC has little support today even among maverick scientists. If it is a real phenomenon, a convincingly documented case of it has yet to be recorded.

New York: David McKay Company, 1967.

Harrison, Michael. *Fire from Heaven: A Study of Spontaneous Combustion in Human Beings.* London: Sidgwick and Jackson, 1976.

Hough, Peter A., and Jenny Randles. "The Creation of a Myth?: Postmortem on the Jacqueline Fitzsimon 'SHC' Inquest." *Fortean Times* 47 (Autumn 1986): 60–64.

Nickell, Joe, with John F. Fischer. *Secrets of the Supernatural: Investigating the World's Occult Mysteries.* Buffalo, NY: Prometheus Books, 1988.

Nickell, Joe, and John F. Fischer. "Spontaneous Human Combustion." *Fire and Arson Investigator* Pt. I. 34,3 (March 1984): 4–11; Pt. II. 34,4 (June 1984): 3–8.

———. "Reeser's Spontaneous Human Combustion Reconsidered." *Fate* 38, 4 (April 1985): 64–68.

———. "Did Jack Angel Survive Spontaneous Combustion?" *Fate* 42, 5 (May 1989): 80–84.

Wolf, R. Martin. "Another Case of SHC?" *Pursuit* 9, 1 (January 1976): 16–17.

SPRINGHEEL JACK

Victorian England played host to periodic reports of a strange man or being to whom the press referred variously as "Springald," "Spring Heeled Jack," or "Springheel Jack." The figure's presence was first noted in September 1837, when he assaulted four separate persons, three of them women, at locations in and around London. In one instance he ripped off the top of victim Polly Adams's dress, scratching her belly with fingers that felt as if they were made of iron.

What made these incidents different from conventional sexual crimes was the attacker's appearance. He was tall, thin, and powerful, wore a cloak, and had pointed ears, glowing eyes, and a mouth that spat blue flames into victims' faces. He also could effect enormous leaps which enabled him to move with such rapidity that it was impossible to escape or catch him.

By January 1838 London's Lord Mayor, Sir John Cowan, had declared Springheel Jack a public menace and formed a vigilance committee to bring the bizarre criminal to justice. But the attacks went on regardless. On the evening of February 20, for example, a stranger appeared at the gate of a London residence and called out, "For God's sake, bring me a light, for we have caught Spring-heeled Jack in the lane!" When 18-year-old Jane Alsop brought a candle, she saw a figure, according to the *London Times* (February 22), "who appeared to be enveloped in a large cloak.... [H]e threw off his outer garment, and applying the lighted candle to his breast, presented a most hideous and frightful appearance, and vomited forth a quantity of blue and white flame from his mouth, and his eyes resembled red balls of fire.... [H]e wore a large helmet, and his address, which appeared to fit him very tight, seemed to her to resemble white oil skin."

He lunged for her, his clawlike hands ripping her dress. The young woman struggled with him and was soon rescued by a sister, who with great diffi-culty pulled her into the house and slammed the door. Undeterred, Jack

knocked two or three times on the door and left only when family members looking out from an upstairs window shouted for the police. Jack dashed across a field, dropping his cloak in his haste. When it was quickly picked up by someone else, the Alsops and later the police concluded that Jack had an accomplice.

Sporadic attacks continued through 1839, and a few were recorded in 1843. In 1845, in daylight and in view of numerous witnesses, Jack bounded toward a young prostitute who was crossing a bridge in a London slum. Grabbing her by the shoulders, he breathed fire into her face, tossed her into the open sewer below, and watched her drown. It was the only murder with which his name would be linked.

However bizarre his appearance and behavior, Springheel Jack was assumed by investigating authorities to be a real person. Rumors spread that he was Henry, the Marquis of Waterford, a young Irish nobleman of rowdy habits and cruel humor, but it was not possible, nor is it now, to effect huge leaps with springs concealed in boot heels. When German soldiers tried this during World War II, 85 percent of them reportedly suffered broken ankles.

In any case, Waterford died in 1859, and in 1877 Jack merrily bounded from rooftop to rooftop in Caistor, Norfolk, nearly all of whose citizenry witnessed the spectacle. Observers said he had huge ears and was dressed in something resembling sheepskin. In August of the same year Jack, clad in an oilskin suit and wearing a "shining helmet," appeared before soldiers at Aldershot's North Camp. A sentry who fired on the figure claimed that his bullet passed through it without effect. Jack's last known return to England was in Liverpool in September 1904.

Half a century later and an ocean away, at 2:30 A.M. on June 18, 1953, three Houston residents seeking relief from the heat by sitting in front of their apartment building said they saw a "huge shadow" cross the lawn in front of them, then "bounce upward into a pecan tree." A dim gray light illuminated the figure in the tree. It was a tall man with a "black cape, skin-tight pants, and quarter-length boots." He was dressed in "gray or black tight-fitting clothes." One witness thought she saw wings on the figure, but possibly this was an optical illusion caused by the cape. After a few minutes the figure "just melted away," his disappearance followed by a "loud swoosh" across the street and the rapid ascent of a rocket-shaped object.

Investigating police officers judged the witnesses sincere and clearly frightened. If this was Jack, it is the only time he has ever been reported in the company of a UFO.

● SOURCES:

Gross, Loren E. *UFOs: A History, 1953: March–July.* Fremont, CA: The Author, 1989.

Haining, Peter. *The Legend and Bizarre Crimes of Spring Heeled Jack.* London: Frederick Muller, 1977.

"Outrage on a Young Lady." *London Times* (February 22, 1838).

Stein, Gordon. "The Strange Crimes of Spring Heeled Jack." *Fate* 41, 11 (November 1988): 48–54.

Vyner, J. "The Mystery of Springheel Jack." *Flying Saucer Review* 7, 3 (May/June 1961): 3–6.

TATZELWURM

Though zoologists do not recognize its existence, the tatzelwurm (German for "worm with claws") has been reported for at least two centuries and possibly longer, mostly though not entirely in the Swiss and Austrian Alps.

Aside from vague folk traditions of a mountain-dwelling dragon with a cat-like head and spiked ridges along its back, the first known "sighting" is associated with one Hans Fuchs, who in 1779 saw two tatzelwurms suddenly appear in front of him. Badly frightened, he suffered a heart attack from which he subsequently died, though not before telling family members of his encounter. A relative did a painting to commemorate his death, and in it are the images of two large, lizardlike creatures. German crypto-zoologist Ulrich Magin remarks, "This depiction of the two monsters is still the best we have of the creature." A 1934 photograph said to show a tatzelwurm is almost certainly a hoax.

In the later nineteenth century, sightings grew more frequent, with witnesses characteristically describing a thick, light-colored cylindrical body, four legs with three toes, and wide mouth with sharp teeth. The creature was said to have either a short neck or no neck at all and to be about seven feet long. Most observers thought it had smooth skin, but a significant plurality believed they had seen small scales. Nearly all agreed it had a short, blunt unlizardlike tail.

Nor was there any disagreement about the tatzelwurm's behavior. If it did not flee as soon as it realized it was being seen, it attacked the witness, sometimes taking huge leaps (accounting for its alternate name, spring-wurm, or "jumping worm") and making a snorting or whistling sound while in flight. If the witness did not get away fast enough, the creature would bite him.

The tatzelwurm reportedly hibernates during the winter, sleeping in crevices on mountainsides (thus its third name, stollenwurm, German for "worm that lives in holes"); occasionally, however, farmers find them sleeping in the hay. One farmer who said he killed a hibernating tatzelwurm saw a green liquid drain out of its mouth. In 1924 the five-foot-long skeleton allegedly was found by two men, who said it resembled a lizard's.

Reports have been infrequent in recent years, and the tatzelwurm has been relegated to the status of minor popular superstition (perhaps a dim echo of the once-ubiquitous dragon legend), from the skeptic's point of view, or to cryptozoological footnote, from the point of view of those who think the stories may describe a genuine unknown animal. Among the latter, the tatzelwurm is theorized to be an unrecognized variety of otter, a European form of the Asian giant salamander, and a relative of the American Gila monster.

● SOURCES:

Heuvelmans, Bernard. *On the Track of Unknown Animals.* New York: Hill and Wang, 1958.

Magin, Ulrich. "European Dragons: The Tatzelwurm." *Pursuit* 19, 1 (First Quarter 1986): 16–22.

Meurger, Michel, with Claude Gagnon. *Lake Monster Traditions: A Cross-Cultural Analysis.* London: Fortean Tomes, 1988.

TELEPORTATION

Teleportation — a word coined by Charles Fort to describe the instantaneous transport of a person or object from one place to another — is best known to readers of science fiction. Less known is the fact, or allegation, that it takes place in real life. Though there is no shortage of stories attesting to these occurrences, convincing reports are rare. There are, moreover, a number of unambiguously fraudulent claims of teleportation.

The last of these appear not infrequently in accounts from nineteenth-century Spiritualist circles. There physical mediums of dubious reputation plied their trade to mostly credulous sitters and from time to time persuaded them that they had moved through space in some inexplicable manner. Because psychic claims are outside the scope of this book, these episodes will not be reviewed here. (A comprehensive overview appears in the "teleportation" entry of Volume Two of Leslie A. Shepard's *Encyclopedia of Occultism and Parapsychology*, third edition, Gale Research, 1991, pages 1675–79.) Our discussion will concentrate on those incidents said to have occurred spontaneously in a natural setting.

Into the fourth dimension.
Of all teleportation tales perhaps none has been so widely told as that of Tennessee farmer David Lang, who one afternoon in 1880, while crossing a field, vanished in full view of full witnesses, including three members of his family. Most chroniclers have speculated that Lang, in common with other persons who have disappeared mysteriously, fell into the "fourth dimension." (Or, as Charles Fort remarked in *Lo!* [1931], "Oh, yes, I have heard of 'the fourth dimension,' but I am going to do myself some credit for not lugging in that particular way of showing that I don't know what I'm writing about.") In the 1970s an investigation by writer Robert Schadewald determined that neither David Lang nor any of the "witnesses" had ever existed and that the narrative bore a suspicious resemblance to the

plot of Ambrose Bierce's late-nineteenth-century short story "The Difficulty of Crossing a Field." (See *David Lang disappearance*.)

A more credible-sounding story, this one about a presumed near-disappearance into another dimension, figures in several December 1873 articles in the *Bristol Daily Post* and the *London Times*, where it is treated more as an unusual court case than as a brush with the unknown. On December 8 Mr. and Mrs. Thomas B. Cumpston, two elderly, respectable residents of Leeds, arrived in Bristol, signed themselves into the Victoria Hotel, and some hours later found themselves under arrest for disorderly conduct. At the railway station where they were arrested, a terrified Cumpston told the night superintendent, "My wife and I have escaped from a den of thieves and rogues. We had to defend ourselves with a pistol." Cumpston had fired twice, once into the roof and later into the street. Suspecting them of insanity, the superintendent notified police.

In police court the couple said that early in the evening they had heard strange, loud sounds in or near their room. They complained to the landlady, who also heard them but shrugged them off. The sounds ceased, and the Cumpstons went to bed. At three or four o'clock in the morning the sounds resumed, this time accompanied by an alarming sensation that the floor was giving out. The couple's shouted words echoed weirdly or else were repeated by unseen presences. The floor "opened," and Mr. Cumpston felt as if he were being dragged into it. His wife pulled him out, and the two jumped out a window. In their panic and confusion they thought criminals had attempted to kidnap them and were following them as they ran to the station.

The landlady testified that she had indeed heard unusual sounds, though she proved unable to provide any meaningful description of them. The police said they had checked out the room and seen nothing out of the ordinary. The court concluded that the Cumpstons had suffered a "collective hallucination" and discharged them into the company of someone from Leeds.

Though the true nature of the couple's experience will never be known, the event, unlike the David Lang disappearance, undoubtedly happened. Those unsatisfied with the hallucination solution prefer another, more fantastic answer. Eighty years later Harold T. Wilkins would suggest:

> The strange noises and the hole in the floor described by the Cumpstons are impossible to explain unless one assumes that under certain conditions an unknown force operates which is able to create a vortex in solid matter.... [M]atter is "solid" only relative to human perceptions; on the atomic level it may be described as mostly empty space. A human being drawn into such a vortex, or whirlpool, in matter may be deposited in some spot dozens and even thousands of miles from his starting point. On occasion, in fact, it seems that a vortex could operate over astronomical distances so as to teleport a being from one planet to another.

Teleported people.

Teleportations of human beings are not hard to find in folkloric and religious contexts. One early example of the former, recorded by the Rev. Robert Kirk in his classic work on seventeenth-century Scottish fairy traditions, *The Secret Common-Wealth* (1692), remarks on one unfortunate man's plight:

> *His neibours often perceaved this man to disappear at a certane Place, and about one Hour after to become visible, and discover himselfe near a Bow-shot from the first Place. It was in that Place where he became invisible, said he, that the Subterraneans [fairies] did encounter and combate with him.*

Another seventeenth-century story, known to us through an affidavit signed by Swedish clergyman Peter Rahm, recounts a troll's appearance at the Rahms' doorstep late one evening in 1660. After repeated entreaties Mrs. Rahm agreed to accompany the little man to his residence where his wife was giving birth. On her return Mrs. Rahm told her husband, according to his account, "it seemed to her as if she was carried along in the wind" on her way both to and from the fairy realm.

Mrs. Rahm's description of the physical sensation associated with teleportation is echoed in the Old Testament, wherein the prophet "Elijah went up by a whirlwind into heaven" (II Kings 2:1).

The great first-century pagan philosopher and physician Apollonius of Tyana, for example, was said to have transported himself instantaneously to Ephesus to treat sufferers from a plague. Many Christian saints, according to legend, removed themselves, often carried by angels, from one location to another with similar swiftness. Early in his career, though for some reason no longer, Sathya Sai Baba, a modern Indian religious teacher said to have miraculous supernatural powers, teleported himself in full view of others. "As we were approaching the river and passing a hill on our right-hand side," one witness told Icelandic psychologist Erlendur Haraldsson, Baba "would sometimes suddenly disappear. He would, for example, snap his fingers and ask those around him to do the same. And hardly had we snapped our fingers when he had vanished from amongst us and we could see him on the top of the hill waiting for us." Haraldsson devotes an entire chapter of his book-length investigative report on Baba, *Modern Miracles* (1987), to similar accounts.

In 1901, shortly after the Pansini family moved into a large house in Ruvo, Italy, poltergeist phenomena of various kinds erupted. Seven-year-old Alfredo Pansini fell into trances, during which "angels" spoke through him and he had clairvoyant visions. He also took to vanishing suddenly from the house and reappearing in a dazed state elsewhere in town or in nearby towns. These alleged teleportations occurred frequently for three years, ending when he reached puberty in 1904. Just before then, however, Alfredo's younger brother Paolo began teleporting as well, and on one occasion both disappeared from their house and appeared aboard a fishing boat a few miles out at sea from the port of Baletta.

Joseph Lapponi, a medical advisor to Popes Leo XIII and Pius X, interviewed witnesses and wrote a book on the case. Once, according to Lapponi, Bishop Bernardi Pasquale locked the two boys in their room, sealing all doors and windows; yet within a few minutes the youths disappeared. Even so, one cannot help suspecting that a couple of clever boys were having fun at their elders' expense.

Teleported objects.

The noted psychical researcher Hereward Carrington, who was interested in the common human experience of misplaced objects, thought that something other than absent-mindedness and inattention may underlie some such episodes. Carrington wrote of one incident:

> *Miss K., a nurse and a most methodical person, had the habit of invariably placing her bunch of keys on the dining room table the moment she entered her flat. One day she did this as usual (so she declares) and, a short time afterwards, looked for them as she was about to leave the apartment, on another "case." Her keys had disappeared. She looked for them everywhere; they were not to be found. She finally had to have other keys made for the front door, etc. Several days later, she wished to get a cork for a medicine bottle, having broken the old one. These corks were kept in a tin box, in the bottom partition of a trunk, standing in the hall. She does not (she says) have occasion to open this drawer on the day in question, nor subsequently until she looked for the cork. Nevertheless, her keys were there, peacefully reposing in the tin box.*

Raymond Bayless, a Los Angeles artist with parapsychological interests, has reported a 1957 experience which took place while he was holding a long-handled brush and speaking with a student. The room was empty except for two stools and an easel, and there was no rug or carpet on the floor. A large northern window brought in abundant sunlight. Suddenly the brush slipped from his hand. Both he and the student heard a clicking sound as it hit the floor. When Bayless reached down to retrieve it, he was astonished to find it nowhere to be found. A thorough search of the stark room uncovered no sign of it. "It had just vanished into thin air," Bayless concluded.

Where an instance like the first is concerned, one is free to speculate that the woman suffered a brief spasm of amnesia and herself placed her keys in the bottom of a trunk. Of course no evidence supporting such speculation exists, but such off-the-cuff explanations appeal to us for the simple reason that it is easier to believe in memory lapses than in teleportation. Nonetheless Bayless's experience does not seem to lend itself to easy accounting.

Besides Carrington, the late D. Scott Rogo was the only serious anomalist to collect cases of "spontaneous dematerialization" in any systematic way. Rogo believed he had experienced it on a number of occasions in his own life. After he wrote about his and other people's possibly paranormal thefts in *Fate*, he was inundated with mail from readers with their own stories.

● SOURCES:

Carrington, Hereward. "Mysterious Disappearances." *Psychic Research* 24 (1930): 554–55.

Creighton, Gordon. "Teleportations." *Flying Saucer Review* 11, 2 (March/April 1965): 14–16.

Fodor, Nandor. *Mind Over Space.* New York: The Citadel Press, 1962.

Fort, Charles. *The Books of Charles Fort.* New York: Henry Holt and Company, 1941.

Haraldsson, Erlendur. *Modern Miracles: An Investigative Report on Psychic Phenomena Associated with Sathya Sai Baba.* New York: Fawcett Columbine, 1987.

Keightley, Thomas. *The Fairy Mythology.* London: G. Bell, 1878.

Knight, Damon. *Charles Fort: Prophet of the Unexplained.* Garden City, NY: Doubleday and Company, 1970.

Michell, John, and Robert J. M. Rickard. *Phenomena: A Book of Wonders.* New York: Pantheon Books, 1977.

Palmer, Stuart. "How Lost Was My Father?" *Fate* 6, 7 (July 1953): 75–85.

As random events subject to other interpretations (valid or invalid), incidents like these do not constitute serious evidence for extraordinary claims about teleportation and other dimensions — though one cannot help being attracted to the implicit argument that such phenomena are part of the common experience of all of us.

Some theorists have suggested that teleportation is responsible for falls from the sky and for appearances of animals far from their native habitats (see *kangaroos, errant*). Ivan T. Sanderson, a trained zoologist and an imaginative anomalist, even wrote that it is "reasonable to suspect" that ants have "developed teleportation as a system of moving precious stuff around in an emergency."

Rogo, D. Scott. *The Haunted Universe: A Psychic Look at Miracles, UFOs and Mysteries of Nature.* New York: New American Library, 1977.

———. *Miracles: A Parascientific Inquiry Into Wondrous Phenomena.* New York: The Dial Press, 1982.

———. *Beyond Reality: The Role Unseen Dimensions Play in Our Lives.* Wellingborough, Northamptonshire, England: The Aquarian Press, 1990.

Sanderson, Ivan T. *"Things".* New York: Pyramid Books, 1967.

Sanderson, Stewart, ed. *The Secret Common-Wealth and A Short Treatise of Charms and Spels by Robert Kirk.* Totowa, NJ: Rowman and Littlefield, 1976.

Schadewald, Robert. "David Lang Vanishes… Forever." *Fate* 30, 12 (December 1977): 54–60.

Wilkins, Harold T. "They Fly Through the Air." *Fate* 6, 11 (November 1953): 88–92.

THUNDERBIRD PHOTOGRAPH

In April 1890 two riders sighted an enormous flying creature — which Indians would have recognized immediately as a thunderbird — alighting on the Arizona desert. The beast had the body of a serpent, immense wings, two clawed feet, and an alligatorlike face with saucer-sized eyes. The men got as close to it as their terrified horses would allow. They proceeded on foot, rifles in hand, but the creature saw them and flew away, only to land again not far away. This time it came down on one of its wings and so was unable to escape as the men pumped bullets into it.

When measured, the wings were found to span an incredible 160 feet. The body, 92 ½ feet long, was smooth and featherless, more like a bat's than a bird's. The men cut off a portion of the wing and brought it with them to Tombstone.

That at least is how the *Tombstone Epitaph* told the story in its April 26, 1890, issue. That was the extent of its coverage; there was no follow-up article. To all appearances this is simply yet another of the tall tales with which newspapers on the American frontier regularly regaled readers. What distinguishes it from many others, however, is that it gave rise to an odd modern legend.

The story was revived in a 1930 book, Horace Bell's On the *Old West Coast*. Thirty-three years later, in a sensationalistic article in the men's action magazine Saga, Jack Pearl wrote that in 1886 the *Epitaph* "published a photograph of a huge bird nailed to a wall. The newspaper said it had been shot by two prospectors and hauled into town by wagon. Lined up in front of the bird were six grown men with their arms outstretched, fingertip to fingertip. The creature measured about 36 feet from wingtip to wingtip."

Pearl further claimed that in 1889, after being ridiculed in a Tombstone saloon, one of the prospectors challenged his harassers to go after the bird themselves. "There's plenty more of 'em nesting in the tops of them mountains," he is supposed to have said. The drunks set out into the desert, but when one went into the bushes to relieve himself, his companions heard him screaming, "It's got me!" They ran to investigate and found his footsteps had vanished in the middle of a clearing. All they could hear was his anguished voice coming from above them and finally fading out.

(The second half of this story is clearly patterned after another nineteenth-century yarn [sometimes set in 1889], the Oliver Lerch disappearance, in which a young man is snatched up by an unseen something, his footsteps suddenly ending and his screaming voice exclaiming, "It's got me!")

In any case, in a letter published in the September 1963 issue of *Fate*, H. M. Cranmer of Renova, Pennsylvania, mentioned the photograph, which he said was taken "about the year 1900." The creature's 36-foot wings were "nailed against the wall of the *Tombstone Epitaph....* A picture showed six men, with outstretched arms touching, standing under the bird. Later, a group of actors dressed as professors were photographed under the bird, with one of them saying, 'Shucks, there is no such bird, never was, and never will be.'" In another letter in the March 1966 issue, Cranmer indicated he had received his "splendid account" from a "lady in Tombstone." In neither this nor the previous letter does Cranmer indicate that he had actually *seen* the photograph, though now he declared, "This picture was circulated in papers all over the United States."

Ivan T. Sanderson, a biologist and writer on natural anomalies, now claimed that he once possessed a photocopy of the picture but had lent it to two associates, who lost it. Soon others began to "remember" that they, too, had seen it somewhere. The editors of *Fate* thought they may have published the picture in an early issue (the magazine started in 1948), but a search through all existing issues indicated otherwise. Meanwhile, after the original *Epitaph* story (which mentions no photograph) was revived in a 1969 issue of *Old West*, reader Harry F. McClure wrote in to say he had personally known the men who killed the thunderbird.

Responding to numerous letters from inquirers, the *Epitaph* conducted a thorough search which uncovered no such photograph in any issue of the newspaper. An extended survey of other Arizona and California papers of the period came to similarly negative results.

Still, as late as 1990 writer John A. Keel insisted, "I *know* I saw it. And not only that — I compared notes with a lot of other people who also saw it.... It was either in one of the tabloids or one of the men's magazines.... It looked like a pterodactyl or something.... The guys were all wearing cowboy boots and cowboy hats and they were all kind of scrungy, like they had been out riding the range." That same year W. Ritchie Benedict swore that he had seen Sanderson displaying the photograph on a Canadian television show. "As I recall," he wrote, "the creature had a very pointed head and its eyes were closed."

● SOURCES:

Bell, Horace. *On the Old West Coast.* New York: William Morrow and Company, 1930.

"Benedict Hot on Thunderbird Photo Trail." *Strange Magazine* 6 (1990): 44.

Chorvinsky, Mark. "Cryptozoo Conversation with John A. Keel." *Strange Magazine* 5 (1990): 35–40.

Cranmer, H. M. "Report from the Readers: Thunderbird Sightings." *Fate* 16, 9 (September 1963): 116–17.

———. "Report from the Readers: Bird Call." *Fate* 19, 3 (March 1966): 131–32.

Hall, Mark A. *Thunderbirds!: The Living Legend of Giant Birds.* Bloomington, MN: Mark A. Hall Publications and Research, 1988.

McClure, Harry F. "Monster Bird." *Old West* (Summer 1970): 84.

Parrish, J. K. "Our Country's Mysterious Monsters." *Old West* (Fall 1969): 25, 37–38.

Pearl, Jack. "Monster Bird That Carries off Human Beings!" *Saga* (May 1963): 28, 30–31, 83–85.

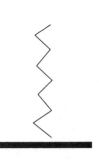

In a review of the episode, Mark A. Hall wrote, "The simple description of the photo — the six men posed to show the size of the dead bird — seems to create a vivid mental image in the minds of many, causing people who have always been particularly curious and eclectic in their knowledge to think it somehow familiar, even when they are unlikely to have ever seen it. Enough people have independently confessed to this reaction that I suspect it has contributed to the mistaken ideas about this photograph. People may think they have seen it when they truly have not."

Those disinclined to take such a prosaic view could take heart from an alternative interpretation offered by Charles Wiedemann: "If we consider the concept of parallel universes or separate realities, it is conceivable that a shift or switch has occurred between two realities. Where, previously, certain publications in 'our' reality portrayed the thunderbird (whereas publications in the parallel reality excluded it), *now* the situation has become reversed. In 'our' universe all thunderbird pictures have gone out of existence, and the situation is exactly as if they had never existed in the first place."

Wiedemann, Charles. "Jumping Carefully to Conclusions." *Pursuit* 9, 2 (April 1976): 44–45.

Winters, Wayne. "Report from the Readers: Situation Normal: All Fowled up." *Fate* 19, 8 (August 1966): 128–29.

THUNDERBIRDS ————————————————

A belief once widespread among North American Indian tribes held that giant supernatural flying creatures, known as Thunderbirds, cause thunder and lightning. They accomplish the former by the flapping of wings, the latter by the closing of eyes. Thunderbirds also war with other supernatural entities and sometimes grant favors to human beings. They are frequently depicted on totem poles.

The link between these mythological beasts and the "real" giant birds of modern reports is problematical, but there is no doubt that if it means nothing else for anomalists, the tradition has provided a name for what people long have claimed to see in the heavily forested Allegheny Plateau of north-central Pennsylvania.

"Thunderbirds are not a thing of the past," Pennsylvania writer Robert R. Lyman declared in 1973. "They are with us today, but few will believe it except those who see them. Their present home is in the southern edge of the Black Forest, north of the Susquehanna River, between Pine Creek at the east and Kettle Creek at the west. All reports for the past 20 years have come from that area."

Lyman himself claimed to have seen one of the birds in the early 1940s. When first observed, it was sitting on a road north of Coudersport. It then rose a few feet into the air, spreading wings which measured at least 20 feet, then flew into — not above — the dense woods lining the highway. It negotiated the dense second-growth timber with "no trouble," according to Lyman. In common with nearly everyone who reports seeing a thunderbird, Lyman thought it looked like a "very large vulture," brown, with short neck and eyes and with "very narrow" wings.

The witness had the impression that this specimen was a young representative of the species. In 1969 the wife of Clinton County sheriff John Boyle, while sitting in front of the couple's cabin in remote Little Pine Creek, saw an enormous gray-colored bird land in the middle of the creek. A few moments later it rose to fly away, and "its wingspread," she said, "appeared to be as wide as the streambed, which I would say was about 75 feet" — making the creature truly otherworldly. That same summer three men claimed to have seen a thunderbird snatch up a 15-pound fawn near Kettle Creek.

Over in the Jersey Shore, Pennsylvania, area, just east of Clinton County, numerous reports of thunderbirds have been logged over the years. On October 28, 1970, several persons driving west of town saw what one of them, Judith Dingler, described as a "gigantic winged creature soaring towards Jersey Shore. It was dark colored, and its wingspread was almost like [that of] an airplane."

Pennsylvania's thunderbird stories have been traced well into the nineteenth century. Unfortunately no comprehensive account of their history has been published, and so far printed material on what should be a tradition of much interest to both folklorists and anomalists is spotty, confined mostly to short (and usually unsatisfactory) accounts in local newspapers.

Yet reports of thunderbirds, sometimes described as giant vultures or eagles, are a nationwide phenomenon, and the descriptions are so similar that Mark A. Hall, the leading authority on the question, offers this general description based on eyewitness testimony:

> The bird is distinguished by its size and lifting capabilities exceeding those of any known bird living today anywhere in the world. Wingspan estimates are necessarily all guesswork. But observers sometimes have had the benefit of a measurable object for comparison or the benefit of time to observe a resting bird. The results most often provide sizes of 15 to 20 feet.... The bird at rest or on the ground appears to be four to eight feet ... tall.... Typically the coloring of the birds overall is dark: a brown, a gray, or black.

Attack of the giant vultures.
In July 1925 two visitors to Consolation Valley in the Canadian Rockies of Alberta spotted what they thought was at an eagle at some considerable altitude. As it approached the Tower of Babel, a 7500-foot-high peak within the range, they noticed that it was huge and brown and, even more startlingly, carried a large animal in its talons. Shouts from the observers caused it to drop the animal, which turned out to be a 15-pound mule-deer fawn.

All conventional ornithological knowledge tells us that such reports — the two we have seen are only two of many and not, as we shall see, even the most fantastic — describe the impossible. The largest predatory birds such as the eagle attack only "small mammals, reptiles, fish, and, perhaps, some other birds," according to wildlife authority Roger A. Caras. The largest American birds, the rare and endangered California condors, have a wingspan of slightly over 10 feet, though one captured specimen early in the century was measured at 11 feet, four inches. Even so, their weak feet do not permit them to carry their prey; instead they feed on carrion.

Here are some representative sightings of the vulture variety of thunderbird:

Kentucky, 1870: A "monster bird, something like the condor of Sinbad the Sailor," landed on a barn owned by James Pepples in rural Stanford. Pepples fired on the creature, wounding it, and took it into captivity. A contemporary press account says, "On measurement, the bird proved to be seven feet from tip to tip. It was of a black color, and both similar and dissimilar in many ways, to an eagle." Nothing is known of its fate. Illinois–Missouri border, 1948: A number of persons told of seeing an immense bird said to be the size of a Piper Cub airplane and to look like a condor. Puerto Rico, 1975: During a spate of unexplained nocturnal killings of farm and domestic animals, owners sometimes reported being awakened by a "loud screech" and hearing the flapping of enormous wings. Several witnesses claimed daylight sightings of what one called a "whitish-colored gigantic condor or vulture." Northern California, October 1975: Residents of a Walnut Creek neighborhood saw an immense bird, over five feet tall with a "head like a vulture" and gray wings, dwarfing a nearby eucalyptus tree. Five minutes later it flew away, revealing a 15-foot wingspan. Around the same time, in nearby East Bay, a number of persons observed the same or a similar bird sitting on a rooftop.

A remarkable series of events which took place in 1977 attracted wide publicity. They began on the evening of July 25 in Lawndale in central Illinois. Three boys, one of them 10-year-old Marlon Lowe, were playing when they saw two large birds come out of the south. They swooped out of the sky toward one boy, who jumped into a swimming pool to escape. They then turned their attention to Marlon, who was grabbed by the straps of his sleeveless shirt and lifted two feet above the ground. As Marlon screamed, his parents Jake and Ruth Lowe and two friends, Jim and Betty Daniels, heard him and witnessed the bizarre sight of the boy held in the talons of a flying bird. Marlon was beating at it with his fists until finally, after carrying him for about 40 feet, it dropped him. By this time Mrs. Lowe, who had headed off in pursuit, was so close to the birds that she had to back up. Then, she said, "the birds just cleared the top of the camper, went beneath some telephone wires and flapped their wings — very gracefully — one more time." They flew off toward the north and in the direction of the tall trees along Kickapoo Creek.

According to the witnesses, the birds were black, with white rings on their long necks. They had curved beaks and eight- to 10-foot wingspreads. They looked, the Lowes decided after consulting books in a library, like condors.

The authorities wasted no time or tact in declaring that all concerned were liars, and the Lowes found themselves at the receiving end of withering ridicule. Marlon himself suffered from nightmares for weeks afterwards, though there were no physical injuries.

The Lowes and their friends were not the only people who reported seeing strange birds in the area. On July 28 a woman driving near Armington, not far from Lawndale, at 5:30 P.M. briefly glimpsed a huge bird flying at rooftop level and larger than the hood of her car. She noticed that it had a ring of white around its neck. Two and a half hours later, at a farm in McLean County, six persons flying model airplanes suddenly noticed an enormous bird about to land atop the barn. Their shouts apparently caused it to change its mind, but it circled them and stayed in sight for some minutes before heading north in the direction of Bloomington. Its wingspan was estimated to be 10 feet, its body six feet long. The wings had white tips at the ends, and the body was brown.

At 5:30 the following morning, between Armington and Delavan, mail carrier James Majors stopped to watch two large birds in the sky. As one remained behind, another descended until it was just above a corn field. Extending its claws two feet, it closed in on a nearby pig farm. It snatched what Majors thought was a 40- or 50-pound baby pig, passed across the road in front of him within 30 or 40 feet, and joined up with its companion. At this point Majors could hear the flapping of their wings, which made a noise like that of a "jet taking off." These were, in other words, thunderbirds in an almost literal sense. Majors thought they looked like condors, only larger. They had eight-foot wingspans.

Other sightings followed. One of the more interesting ones was also one of the last. It occurred on August 11, on a farm south of Odin, Illinois. At 7 A.M. a large gray-black bird flew out of the northeast and in a circle about 300 feet away, as if looking for a tree big enough to hold it. Finally it landed on one near a small pond close to the house. John and Wanda Chappell were able to watch it closely for five minutes — making theirs the most detailed report of all.

"It looked like a prehistoric bird," Mrs. Chappell said. "It was really fantastic. The head didn't have any feathers, and it had a long neck, crooked, kind of 'S' shaped. The body was covered with feathers.... We couldn't tell much about the feet, but it had long legs." Her husband estimated its wingspan at 10 to 12 feet, she at 14. They agreed, however, that it was four feet high; the distance from the tip of the beak to the back of the neck was eight inches.

After a few minutes the bird left in a southwest direction.

Monster eagles.
"The stories about eagles carrying off human babies, and even small children, are absolutely endless," Roger Caras writes in *Dangerous to Man*. "It is pure myth; yet the stories persist."

Still, scientists who have investigated such reports have not always dismissed them as readily as Caras does, though it is certainly true that the capacity of any conventionally sized eagle (which never weighs much over seven pounds) to carry anything but the smallest animals has never been demonstrated. Yet at least one such abduction, however "impossible," is impressively documented.

On June 5, 1932, Svanhild Hansen, a 42-pound five-year-old girl, was taken from her parents' Leka, Norway, farm by a huge eagle; the bird transported her more than a mile until it dropped her on a high ledge and continued to circle overhead. When rescuers reached the ledge, the child was asleep and, aside from a few small scratches, unharmed. Zoologist Hartvig Huitfeldt-Kaas, who spent a month investigating the story, pronounced it "completely reliable." The eagle, if that is what it was, was seen on several subsequent occasions.

Other cases, though less richly documented, are just as interesting. All of them do not have happy endings. A nineteenth-century nature encyclopedia (Felix A. Pouchet's *The Universe* [1868]) tells this sad story from the French Alps, 1838:

> *A little girl, five years old, called Marie Delex, was playing with one of her companions on a mossy slope of the mountain, when all at once an eagle swooped down upon her and carried her away in spite of the cries and presence of her young friend. Some peasants, hearing the screams, hastened to the spot but sought in vain for the child, for they found nothing but one of her shoes on the edge of a precipice. The child was not carried to the eagle's nest, where only two eaglets were seen surrounded by heaps of goat and sheep bones. It was not until two months later that a shepherd discovered the corpse of Marie Delex, frightfully mutilated, and lying upon a rock half a league from where she had been borne off.*

A Tippah County, Mississippi, school teacher recorded the following in the fall of 1868:

> *A sad casualty occurred at my school a few days ago. The eagles have been very troublesome in the neighborhood for some time past, carrying off pigs, lambs, &c. No one thought that they would attempt to prey upon children; but on Thursday, at recess, the little boys were out some distance from the house, playing marbles, when their sport was interrupted by a large eagle sweeping down and picking up little Jemmie Kenney, a boy of eight years, and when I got out of the house, the eagle was so high that I could just hear the child screaming. The eagle was induced to drop his victim; but his talons had been buried in him so deeply, and the fall was so great, that he was killed — or either would have been fatal.*

A tale with a less tragic conclusion goes back to July 12, 1763, and the mountains of Germany, where a peasant couple left their three-year-old daughter lying asleep by a stream as they cut grass a short distance away. When they went to check on her, they were horrified to find her missing. A frantic search proved fruitless until a man passing by on the other side of the hill heard a child crying. As he went to investigate, he was startled at

● SOURCES:

Bord, Janet, and Colin Bord. *Alien Animals.* Harrisburg, PA: Stackpole Books, 1981.

Capparella, Angelo P. Review of Mark A. Hall's *Thunderbirds!: The Living Legend of Giant Birds.* Cryptozoology 9 (1990): 94–96.

Caras, Roger A. *Dangerous to Man: The Definitive Story of Wildlife's Reputed Dangers.* Revised edition. South Hackensack, NJ: Stoeger Publishing Company, 1977.

Clark, Jerome, and Loren Coleman. *Creatures of the Outer Edge.* New York: Warner Books, 1978.

Coleman, Loren. *Curious Encounters: Phantom Trains, Spooky Spots, and Other Mysterious Wonders.* Boston, MA: Faber and Faber, 1985.

Hall, Mark A. *Thunderbirds!: The Living Legend of Giant Birds.* Bloomington, MN: Mark A. Hall Publications and Research, 1988.

Michell, John, and Robert J. M. Rickard. *Living Wonders: Mysteries and Curiosities of the Animal World.* New York: Thames and Hudson, 1982.

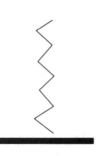

the sight of a huge eagle flying up before him. At the spot from which it had ascended, he found the little girl, her arm torn and bruised. When the child was reunited with her parents, they and her rescuer estimated that the bird had carried her well over 1,400 feet.

Twentieth-century zoologist C. H. Keeling characterizes this as the only eagle-abduction story he finds "even remotely convincing" — notwithstanding the "simple and unalterable fact … that no eagle on earth can carry off more than its own weight."

The problem of explanation.

No trained ornithologists have ever concerned themselves with the thunderbird phenomenon in its entirety, and few have ever had any participation even in specific reports beyond the rejection of them out of hand. The skepticism is not difficult to understand.

Illinois State University ornithologist Angelo P. Capparella, who harbors a sympathetic interest in cryptozoology, remarks, "The lack of interest of most ornithologists in Thunderbirds is probably due to two factors. First, there is the lack of sightings from the legions of competent amateur birdwatchers.... [T]he number of good birdwatchers scanning the skies of the U.S. and Canada is impressive. Every year, surprising observations of birds far from their normal range are documented, often photographically. How have Thunderbirds escaped their roving eyes?" A second reason, Capparella writes, is that such creatures lack an adequate food source in the areas where they have been reported.

In some instances — if not the ones cited here — witnesses have mistaken cranes, blue herons, and turkey buzzards for more extraordinary and mysterious birds. In other cases — the ones here, for example — it is easier to believe in pure invention than in honest misidentification. And indeed hoax is about the only option left to those who believe that if an event is impossible, it cannot happen. Those who believe otherwise are those who believe in a Goblin Universe, which may be the true home of the thunderbird.

Robiou Lamarche, Sebastion. "UFOs and Mysterious Deaths of Animals." *Flying Saucer Review* 22, 5 (1976): 15–18.

Stein, Gordon. "Unidentified Flapping Objects." *Fate* 41, 5 (May 1988): 66–71.

THUNDERSTONES ————————————————————————

This account appeared in the March 14, 1912, issue of the august British scientific journal *Nature:*

> *During a heavy thunderstorm which ensued on Monday, March 4, between 2.30 P.M. and 4.15 P.M., an aerolite was observed to fall at Colney Heath, near St. Albans [Hertfordshire]. The observer [H.L.G. Andrews], who has placed the specimen in my hands for examination, stated that the stone fell within a few feet from where he was standing, and that it entered the ground for a distance of about 3 ft. Its fall was accompanied by an unusually heavy clap of thunder. The example weighs 5 lb. 14-½ oz., and measures 6-¾ in. x 5-⅝ in. at its great length and breadth respectively. The mass is irregularly ovate on the one side, and broken in outline on the other. The actual surface throughout is fairly deeply pitted, and under magnification exhibits the usual chondritic structure of the crystalline matter with interspersed particles of what appears to be nickeliferous iron.*

The following week, in the March 21 issue, the correspondent, G. E. Bullen, wrote, "I have now submitted the stone for examination by Dr. George T. Prior, of the British Museum (Natural History), who informs me that it is not of meteoritic origin."

If this is an authentic case, it is indeed a remarkable one: a rare modern, Western report of a thunderstone. Rejected by nearly all learned commentators as a misperception or absurd superstition, thunderstones are the subject of many folk traditions and fewer documented, firsthand sightings. They are said to be aerial objects which crash to earth during intense storms, usually in the wake of lightning and a heavy peal of thunder. Often, though not always, they are alleged to be shaped like manufactured artifacts.

The thunderstone tradition is part of the history of meteorites. Charles Fort, the great anomaly collector, summarized that history thus: "Peasants believed in meteorites. Scientists excluded meteorites. Peasants believe in 'thunderstones.' Scientists exclude 'thunderstones.'" Until the early nineteenth century most scientists denied that such things as meteorites could exist — no prevailing theory concerning the causes of atmospheric phenomena could accommodate the notion of stones falling from the sky — and they "explained" meteorite falls as an illusion. They held that lightning had merely struck stones already on the ground, and observers mistakenly deduced that the stones had arrived with the lightning.

Meteorites, we know now, are not associated with lightning, though there is nothing to stop a fall of one, coincidentally, with an electric storm. In any event, it looks very much as if what eighteenth-century scientists were explaining were thunderstone, not meteorite, manifestations. Moreover, lightning *was* hitting ground objects. As historian of science John G. Burke notes, thunderstone traditions worked to hinder scholarly recognition of the reality of meteorites. He remarks that the "studies of early paleontologists, archaeologists, and mineralogists ... tended to prove that the stones alleged to have fallen during thunderstorms were either fossils, ancient stone implements, or crystal masses of a common mineral."

Nonetheless, according to widespread and often credible reports, non-meteoritic stones do fall anomalously out of the sky (see *Falls from the sky [inorganic matter]*). If thunderstones are seen in this context, a generous interpretation of an admittedly thin body of evidence permits us to declare them one variety of enigmatic, so far unexplained — but probably not extraordinary to the point of paranormality — occurrence.

The thinness of the evidence, incidentally, does not necessarily mean the absence of any *potential* abundance of evidence. All it tells us is that resistance to the idea of thunderstones has discouraged serious investigators from seeking such evidence. One need only read nineteenth-century scientific journals for examples of the intense ridicule attached to the subject.

The hostility was so extreme that an 1884 writer for the *American Journal of Science*, referring to an article just published in *Cornhill Magazine*, expressed astonishment that "any man of ordinary reasoning powers should write a paper to prove that thunderstones do not exist" (emphasis added). Even so, the *Cornhill* contributor could not have been more contemptuous of the subject, deriding the testimony of native peoples in a way that today would be considered racist; moreover, as William R. Corliss would observe nearly a century later, "it seems to be the writer's intent to assert that all who did not subscribe to the science of 1884 were also savages."

Where thunderstones — as well as many other of the phenomena this book describes — are concerned, perhaps we would all do well to remember that a century from now the science of the 1990s will seem as antique as that of the 1880s. Thunderstones may or may not exist. What is more certain is that we do not know everything, and it ill behooves us to pretend otherwise.

● SOURCES:

Burke, John G. *Cosmic Debris: Meteorites in History.* Berkeley, CA: University of California Press, 1986.

Corliss, William R., ed. *Strange Phenomena: A Sourcebook of Unusual Natural Phenomena, Volume G-1.* Glen Arm, MD: The Sourcebook Project, 1974.

——. *Strange Phenomena: A Sourcebook of Unusual Natural Phenomena, Volume G-2.* Glen Arm, MD: The Sourcebook Project, 1974.

——. *Handbook of Unusual Natural Phenomena.* Glen Arm, MD: The Sourcebook Project, 1977.

Fort, Charles. *The Books of Charles Fort.* New York: Henry Holt and Company, 1941.

Jessup, M. K. *The Case for the UFO.* New York: The Citadel Press, 1955.

Moore, Alvin E. *Mystery of the Skymen.* Clarksburg, WV: Saucerian Press, 1979.

X, Mr. "Tasaday, Tau't Batu and Thunderstones." *Fortean Times* 49 (Winter 1987): 48–49.

377

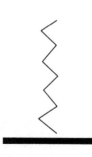

THYLACINE

One of the liveliest ongoing cryptozoological controversies concerns an Australian animal which, though officially judged extinct, may yet be alive. What makes the matter particularly fascinating is that it is a mystery on two levels, the first relatively moderate, the second decidedly extraordinary.

History and prehistory.
The thylacine, a carnivorous marsupial, came into existence on the Australian mainland late in the age of mammals. Though it looked something like a cross between a fox, a wolf, a tiger, and a hyena, it was in fact related to the opossum, with which zoologists believe it shared a common ancestor.

The male thylacine, which measured over six feet long between head and tail, was the size of a large dog. Its head looked much like a fox's or a dog's, but beginning mid-back and extending all the way to the tail, it had tigerlike stripes (thus its popular nickname "Tasmanian tiger"). Its bunched and extended rear, reminiscent of a hyena's, ended in a stiff, unwagging tail. Its fur was coarse and sandy-brown. Females were slightly smaller, but with twice the number of stripes, and these starting just behind the neck. Females also had a pouch, as all marsupials do, but it faced the rear, presumably so as to protect its young as it moved through undergrowth.

Approximately 12,000 years ago thylacines were driven off the mainland, probably as a result of competition from dingoes which, brought over by Indonesian mariners, quickly proved to be more efficient predators. Or so zoologists conclude from the absence of any fossil record of a mainland thylacine since then. It is surmised that the animals retreated to Tasmania, now an island state off Australia's southeast coast but then connected to the continent by land bridge. The first published mention of a thylacine is an 1805 Tasmanian newspaper, where the animal is called "destructive." The thylacine's days were numbered.

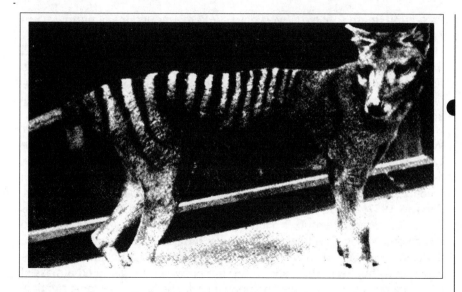

The last officially recognized thylacine, sometimes called the "Tasmanian tiger," died in captivity at the Hobart Zoo in the 1930s, but reports of the animal in the wild persist. (Courtesy of Loren Coleman.)

Convinced that they were responsible for the mass slaughter of sheep, which had been brought to Australia in 1803, authorities commenced a campaign to wipe out the "tigers." (In fact, according to modern experts, feral dogs and "duffers" [rustlers] were a far greater threat to livestock than the hated thylacines ever were.) Both private companies and government agencies offered rewards for thylacine scalps, and the killing began. By the early twentieth century thylacines had become a rare sight. Bounty-hunters were not their only enemy, however; a distemper epidemic decimated much of the population, and settlers were claiming more and more of their habitat. But it was the relentless hostility of armed human beings that ensured the thylacines' extinction. "Farmers continued to see the creature as a menace," two historians of the thylacine write, "long after it was capable of reproducing itself in any numbers."

According to the standard histories, the last specimen for which a bounty was paid was shot in 1909. The final one shot was gunned down in 1930. Captured in 1933, the last one on earth died on September 7, 1936, in Tasmania's Hobart Domain Zoo, just two months after Tasmania passed a law declaring the thylacine a protected species. "Benjamin," as the one remaining thylacine was named, "was tame and could be patted," its keeper, Frank Darby, recalled, but "it was frequently morose and showed no affection."

The first mystery.
Only after the thylacine was gone for good did most Tasmanians begin to regret what they had done. In time the Tasmanian coat of arms would depict two thylacines, and Australians would informally adopt it as their most beloved lost animal, its disappearance nothing less than a national tragedy.

Yet as little as a year after Benjamin's death and the thylacine's official passing from the domain of living species, Australia's Animals and Birds

Protection Board sent two investigators into the mountains of northwestern Tasmania to look into the possibility that a few thylacines might have survived. They returned with a handful of intriguing sighting reports collected from residents of the area. Though hardly conclusive, they encouraged the board to sponsor further searches. A 1938 expedition found the first physical evidence: footprints with the thylacine's distinctive five-toed front legs and four-toed hind legs.

World War II got in the way of further investigation, but in late 1945 a private expedition viewed a set of tracks and heard some sighting reports, though none of its members saw anything themselves. After that Australian wildlife specialists essentially abandoned the question for a number of years. Then in 1957 zoologist Eric R. Guiler, chairman of the Animals and Birds Protection Board, went to Broadmarsh, where a mysterious marauder had killed some sheep. The tracks were, Guiler thought, unmistakably those of a thylacine. Converted to belief in living thylacines, Guiler mounted nine expeditions between 1957 and 1966, during which he gathered a mass of evidence but, again, produced no body; nor did he have a personal sighting.

In 1968 other researchers established a Tiger Center, to which witnesses could report sightings. Search parties continued to prowl the bush. A late-1970s project sponsored by the World Wildlife Fund (Australia) involved the setting-up of a number of automatic-camera units at locations where witnesses said they had seen thylacines. Bait was placed to lure the animals across an infra-red beam which would trigger a camera. The cameras caught nine different species, most prominently the Tasmanian devil (which on occasion has been mistaken for the thylacine), and in his official report in 1980, project leader Steven J. Smith of the National Parks and Wildlife Service (NPWS) expressed the view that thylacines are indeed extinct.

In 1982, however, in a published survey of 104 sightings reported to the NPWS between 1970 and 1980, he moderated his conclusion. Writing with D. E. Rounsevell, he observed, "If thylacines still exist in Tasmania, they are few, and the difficult task of rediscovering them may be facilitated by careful analysis of the growing collection of reported sightings" — the majority clustered in the northern regions of the state, where in earlier decades most of the bounties had been collected.

Guiler also conducted a hidden-camera operation, with similarly disappointing results, but remained convinced that the animals still existed because of sightings and tracks which he thought otherwise inexplicable.

Events in the affair took a new turn one rainy night in March 1982. An NPWS park ranger in a forested area of northwestern Tasmania woke from a nap in the back seat of his car. He turned on his spotlight, and shined it on an animal 20 feet away. He said it was a thylacine, "an adult male in excellent condition, with 12 black stripes on a sandy coat." Unfortunately the rain wiped out any tracks it may have made.

The NPWS held up announcement of the encounter until January 1984, in an effort to discourage curiosity-seekers who might threaten the animal and whatever companions might live in the same area. Yet the NPWS statement did not amount to an official certification of the thylacine's return from the dead. There was still, after all, no body. But more important than scientific concerns were the potential economic and political problems. What financial hardship would befall a mining or timber company on whose property thylacines were found to be living? The animals, after all, would be endangered and in need of protection; would mineral or lumber rights — along, of course, with the tax revenues associated with them — have to be surrendered? And who would pay the compensation?

Since then other expeditions have been launched, but Tasmania's thylacine remains elusive, and skeptics, of whom there still are some, dismiss the reports as the consequence of wishful thinking or misperceptions of other animals, in particular feral dogs (which in the past undeniably have been mistaken for thylacines). In any case, sightings continue. In 1991 as many as 13 reports were logged, and the Tasmanian Parks Wildlife and Heritage Authority deemed three of them "very good." Zoologist Bob Green remarked of thylacines, "They are extremely cunning animals. For every one that's seen, I believe they see a thousand humans. I have received samples of dung and footprints sent in by experienced bushmen who know what they have seen. I believe that the thylacine not only exists but is coming back strongly."

The second mystery.
In 1981, following a number of sightings of an unusual animal in an area of southwestern Western Australia, the state's Agricultural Protection Board hired Kevin Cameron, a tracker of aboriginal descent, to investigate. In due course Cameron would claim to have seen the animal himself and to have identified it: as a thylacine.

Even those inclined to take seriously the notion of surviving thylacines in Tasmania blanch at reports like these. Not only is there no fossil evidence of a mainland thylacine in the past 12,000 years, but there is no indication that the animal was known either to Australia's aborigines or to the Europeans who settled the country in the nineteenth century.

In 1951 a man from Dwellingup came to the Western Australian Museum in Perth, where he showed photographs and casts of tracks of what he insisted was a thylacine — which he said he had seen with his own eyes. But the staff zoologist with whom he spoke rejected the report and the supporting evidence out of hand. Some years later other reports of a strange sheep-killing animal led that same zoologist, Athol M. Douglas, into the bush, where he tracked and killed the culprit, a feral Afghan hound with long, matted hair. The experience only reinforced his skepticism about thylacine reports. Even so, over the years he occasionally examined carcasses of kangaroos and sheep and noted uneasily that the animals had been slain in exactly the way thylacines — and not dogs or dingoes — slay their prey.

In February 1985 all of Douglas's doubts evaporated when Cameron handed him five color photographs. They showed the profile of an animal burrowing at the base of a tree. Though its face was hidden in the brush, its striped back and long, stiff tail belonged to no creature but the thylacine. Cameron would not tell Douglas where he had taken the pictures, but he did produce casts of its prints. Douglas thought Cameron's account of its behavior rang true to reports in the scientific literature — all the more impressive evidence of the witness' credibility, in his view, since Cameron was barely literate.

Still, Cameron's odd, secretive behavior warned Douglas that something was amiss. Cameron gave, retracted, then granted permission to Douglas to use the photographs with an article to appear in *New Scientist*, a British popular-science weekly. Just before the manuscript was submitted to the magazine, Douglas would later recall in *Cryptozoology:*

> Cameron ... accompanied me to the photographic laboratory to have the enlargements made. This was the first time I saw the negatives with full-frame, good-quality enlargements. When I saw the negatives, I realized Cameron's account with regard to the photographs was inaccurate. The film had been cut, frames were missing, and the photos were taken from different angles — making it impossible for the series to have been taken in 20 or 30 seconds, as Cameron had stated. There were no photographs of the animal bounding away. Furthermore, in one negative, there was the shadow of another person pointing what could be an over-under .12 shotgun. Cameron had told me he had been alone. It would have been practically impossible for an animal as alert as a thylacine to remain stationary for so long while human activity was going on in its vicinity. In addition, it is significant that the animal's head does not appear in any of the photographs.

Some *New Scientist* readers noticed a couple of glaring discrepancies: one, the animal did not seem to have moved at all from photograph to photograph, and two, markedly varying shadow patterns suggested that a difference of at least an hour, possibly more, separated some pictures from the rest. To the critics this could only mean that Cameron had photographed, in fairly leisurely fashion, a stuffed model of a thylacine.

But Douglas thought it more likely that one of the pictures, evidently the first taken, showed a living thylacine. "The full frame of this negative is the one which shows the shadow of the man with a rigid gun-like object pointing in the direction of the thylacine at the base of the tree," he wrote. "This shadow was deliberately excluded in the photo published in *New Scientist*. If I am correct in this supposition, the thylacine was alive when the first photo was taken, but had been dead [and frozen in *rigor mortis*] for several hours by the time the second photograph was taken."

Douglas hoped that someone would find the carcass, "presumably shot by 'persons unknown,'" but none has ever surfaced. Presumably the reason is that Australian law decrees that anyone convicted of killing the (officially extinct) thylacine is subject to a $5,000 fine.

In 1966 a Western Australia Museum team recovered a thylacine carcass in a cave near Mundrabilla Station. Carbon dating placed its age at 4,500 years, which cut in more than half the standard date of the animal's disappearance from the mainland. In fact, according to Douglas, the carcass may be more recent — much more recent — than that. The condition of the body suggested it had died no more than a year ago, and probably less. "During my 1986 visit to the cave," he wrote, "I found a dingo carcass; it was hairless, dry and odorless, and its skin was like parchment. The thylacine carcass had been — and is — in a far superior state of preservation than this dingo carcass, yet the dingo carcass could not have been in the cave for more than 20 years." The "inaccurate dating could have resulted from contamination from the groundwater which saturated the carcass," he suggested.

Western Australia (which covers one-third of Australia's continental land mass) is not the only mainland state to claim to thylacine sightings.

According to cryptozoological investigator Rex Gilroy, numerous "reports of large striped dog-like animals, possibly thylacines," have been made from "over a wide area of the rugged eastern Australian mountain ranges, from far north Queensland through New South Wales to eastern Victoria." Moreover, "plaster casts have been made of tracks found on the mainland"; these "compare with others from Tasmania, leaving little doubt as to the animal's identity."

Gilroy says he once saw the animal himself. As he and a friend drove toward the Blue Mountains west of Sydney, New South Wales, something dashed out of the scrub along the highway and ran in front of them. It was "almost the size of a full-grown Alsatian dog, with fawn-colored fur and a row of blackish stripes. For a few seconds it stood there in the glare of the headlights before running off into the scrub, towards the Grose Valley nearby. I have no doubt that it was a thylacine; its appearance matched that of stuffed specimens preserved in Government museums."

Among those who say they have seen thylacines in the mountainous wilderness of the Namadgi-Kosciusco National Park along the New South Wales-Victoria border is ranger Peter Simon, who saw one for several seconds in broad daylight from a distance of 100 feet. In 1990, after writing an article about the thylacine mystery in *The Age*, Melbourne's leading newspaper, Graeme O'Neill received cards and letters from Victoria residents who reported their own sightings. "The way they told their stories, and the internal consistency of each account, left me in no doubt," he remarked, "that each had seen something unusual [and] … broadly consistent with the appearance of a thylacine."

And beyond.
To Australian writer Tony Healy there is something downright paranormal about mainland thylacines. He notes that the night before Ranger Simon's sighting, his dogs, participants in the slayings of over 300 wild pigs, refused to get out of the truck after they and their master heard harsh, thy-

● SOURCES:

Beresford, Quentin, and Garry Bailey. *Search for the Tasmanian Tiger.* Sandy Bay, Tasmania, Australia: Blubber Head Press, 1981.

Dash, Mike, and Rex Gilroy. "The Lost Australians." *Fortean Times* 62 (April 1992): 54–56.

Douglas, Athol M. "Tigers in Western Australia?" *New Scientist* 110, 1505 (April 24, 1986): 44–47.

———. "The Thylacine: A Case for Current Existence on Mainland Australia." *Cryptozoology* 9 (1990): 13–25.

Earley, George W. "Tasmanian Tiger Update." *INFO Journal* 64 (October 1991): 13–14.

Gilroy, Rex. "On the Trail of a 'Tiger'." *Fortean Times* 49 (Winter 1987): 46–47.

Goss, Michael. "Tracking Tasmania's Mystery Beast." *Fate* 36, 7 (July 1983): 34–43.

Guilder, Eric R. *Thylacine: The Tragedy of the Tasmanian Tiger.* Oxford, England: Oxford University Press, 1985.

Healy, Tony. "The Riddles of Oz." *Fortean*

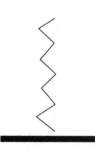

lacine-like panting sounds in the bush. In 1982 a Western Australia farm couple who claimed to have lost livestock to thylacines told a Perth newspaper that a "prickly feeling" at the back of their necks was invariably their first warning of the animals' presence.

If these are tiny threads on which to frame a fantastic hypothesis, or if even flesh-and-blood mainland thylacines strain credulity, consider this 1974 report:

On April 7, 1974, at 3:30 A.M., Joan Gilbert spotted a "strange striped creature, half cat and half dog," as it passed in front of her car's headlights. "It was," she recalled, "the most peculiar animal I have ever seen. It had stripes, a long thin tail, and seemed to be all gray, though it might have had some yellow on it. Its ears were set back like a member of the cat family, and it was as big as a medium-sized dog. It was thin, and it definitely was not a fox."

It was, she discovered when she looked through reference books at the library, an animal she had never heard of: a thylacine. The sighting did not take place in Tasmania. It did not take place in Western Australia or Victoria or New South Wales. It happened on the outskirts of Bournemouth. In England.

Times 49 (Winter 1987): 42–45.

"Out of Place." The News 9 (April 1975): 15–20.

Rickard, Bob. "The Return of the Tiger?" Fortean Times 49 (Winter 1987): 5–7.

"Thylacine Reports Persist After 50 Years." The ISC Newsletter 4, 4 (Winter 1985): 1–5.

Wilford, John Noble. "Automatic Cameras Stalk Tasmania's Rare Tiger." New York Times (May 27, 1980).

TUNGUSKA EVENT

A strange event that occurred in a remote swampy area of Siberia in 1908 even now, nearly a century later, continues to spark wonder, controversy, and theories of widely varying plausibility.

At 7:15 on the morning of June 30, a blazing white light was seen descending over the forests northwest of Lake Baykal near the Stony Tunguska River. It was so bright that it cast shadows on the earth beneath it. As it plummeted, it leveled trees and smashed houses, finally detonating with such explosive force that seismic shocks were registered around the world. An enormous "pillar of fire" rose straight up and was seen hundreds of miles away. As huge thunderclaps sounded through the air, a searing thermal current tore through the area, igniting fires in forests and towns. At least three shock waves followed the thermal wave. The destruction was massive, extending as far as 375 miles. Thick, dark clouds rose above the detonation site, and a black rain composed of dirt and particles fell on central Russia. That night the sky remained eerily bright all through northern Europe.

Presumably the mysteries surrounding this astonishing manifestation could have been solved had scientists been able to go to the site immediately. But Russia's unstable political situation, a few years later to explode in war and revolution, kept scientists' attention focused on more immediate matters. The first expedition, led by Leonid Kulik of the Russian Meteorological Institute, did not reach the area until 13 years later.

Expedition members expected to find a meteorite crater but were surprised to discover nothing of the sort. Instead they found that the trees had been damaged from above. Moreover, those closest to the impact site were still standing, though devoid of bark and branches. Trees farther away were flattened and pointing away from the site. Kulik and his companions searched diligently but unsuccessfully for meteorite fragments.

● **SOURCES:**

Baxter, John, and Thomas Atkins. *The Fire Came by: The Riddle of the Great Siberian Explosion.* Garden City, NY: Doubleday and Company, 1976.

Carlson, John B. "The Tunguska Event... and Another Far-Out Theory." *INFO Journal* 3, 4 (February 1974): 18–19.

Frazier, Kendrick. "Egregiously Yours: Lithium Meteor?" *Skeptical Inquirer* 3, 2 (Winter 1978): 54–55.

Ganapathy, Ramachandran. "The Tunguska Explosion of 1908: Discovery of Meteoritic Debris Near the Explosion Site and at the South Pole." *Science* 220,

Nonetheless Kulik, whose work continued until the outbreak of World War II (in which he would be killed), remained convinced that a meteorite was responsible. A colleague, Vasili Sytin, disagreed; in the absence of evidence for extraterrestrial causation, he argued, logic required an earthly explanation: an unusually violent windstorm.

Extraterrestrial hypotheses.

In the wake of the atom-bomb attacks on Hiroshima and Nagasaki the year before, Soviet science-fiction writer A. Kasantsev published a story in the January 1946 issue of *Vokrug Sveta*. In the story a Martian spaceship is vaporized in an atomic explosion over Tunguska.

Though the story was fantasy, Kasantsev was attacked by Soviet scientists for proposing what they believed to be an absurd explanation. Nonetheless the suggestion of a spaceship crash would have a lasting impact on the popular imagination, first of the Soviet people and later of the world. Two maverick Soviet scientists, Felix Zigel and Aleksey Zolotov, championed it in later decades, with the latter even claiming to have detected "abnormal radioactivity" at the site. Tests by other scientists, however, provided only ambiguous confirmation. In 1976 a popular book, *The Fire Came by*, championed the spaceship hypothesis, but the idea has little if any support from Western — or Russian — scientists.

Today most speculation focuses on meteorites, comets, and asteroids. It is almost universally agreed that the object, possibly as large as 200 yards in diameter, never struck the earth but exploded in midair owing to the air pressure piled in front of it as it descended.

"Had the Tunguska object been a comet," Stephen P. Maran writes in *Natural History*, "the failure to find fragments of rock or iron from the explosion would be understandable. Any cometary ice that reached the ground probably would have melted before the first scientific expedition reached the site.... [I]f the Tunguska object was an asteroid or meteoroid and thus made of stone and iron ... either there are fragments, which have been overlooked by repeated Soviet scientific expeditions, or ... the incoming object ... shattered totally into dust in the explosion."

4602 (June 10, 1983): 1158–61.

Hobana, Ion, and Julien Weverbergh. *UFOs from Behind the Iron Curtain.* New York: Bantam Books, 1975.

Maran, Stephen P. "What Struck Tunguska?" *Natural History* 93, 2 (February 1984): 36–37.

Oberg, James. "Tunguska Echoes." *Skeptical Inquirer* 3, 2 (Winter 1978): 49–57.

Schadewald, Robert. "The Tungus Event Once More." *INFO Journal* 6, 1 (May 1977): 6–8.

"Tunguska: Comet or Asteroid?" *Sky & Telescope* 72,6 (December 1986): 577–78.

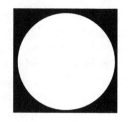

UMMO

There is no stranger, more complex UFO hoax than the Ummo affair. It is supposed to have begun in 1965, when Fernando Sesma, a contactee who directed the Society of Space Visitors, allegedly received a phone call from a man who spoke in Spanish with a foreign accent. The caller said he represented an "extraterrestrial order" and declined the offer to meet personally but promised further communications.

Soon documents said to have been written by residents of Ummo, identified as a planet revolving around the star Iumma 14.6 light years from the sun, were arriving in the mail for Sesma and his associates. Each document bore an unusual symbol which resembled a closed parenthesis and an open parenthesis joined by a plus sign:)+(. Though conventional astronomy recognizes neither Ummo nor Iumma, in time their existence became an article of faith to devoted disciples in Europe and the Americas.

On February 6, 1966, several soldiers and two civilian witnesses saw a large circular object touch down briefly in a Madrid suburb. One observer who caught a glimpse of the UFO's underside saw a curious symbol which those privy to Ummo's secrets immediately recognized.

An advertisement in the May 20, 1967, issue of the Spanish newspaper *Informaciones* announced that on June 1 an Ummo craft would land outside Madrid and carry some of the faithful to the home planet. On that date, in San Jose de Valderas, a Madrid suburb, a flying object with the Ummo symbol on it was seen by a number of witnesses. Two sets of photographs of this UFO turned out to be fakes. In spite of the photographer's effort to hide the fact, it was determined that they were taken by the same man, an untraceable "Antonio Pardo." The image, in which the symbol is clearly visible, is no more than 8.5 inches in diameter, a simple model made of plastic plates. The symbol apparently was scrawled on the bottom of the model with a marker pencil.

Later that evening, in yet another Madrid suburb, Santa Monica, witnesses reportedly saw a UFO descending toward the ground, then taking off and disappearing in the darkness. The next morning apparent landing traces were found at the site. So were metallic cylinders, each with a disc at its center. When opened, the inside of the cylinders contained the Ummo symbol. Shortly thereafter, local shopkeepers received a letter signed by "Henri Dagousset," who asked that the capsules be sent to one "Antoine Nancey." Neither "Dagousset" nor "Nancey," it turned out, existed. When studied in a scientific laboratory, moreover, the ostensibly extraterrestrial artifacts were proven to consist of conventional earthly materials. One investigator speculates the "UFO" seen in these two incidents was a radio-controlled model. Perhaps significantly, both sightings occurred near an airport and the Aerotechnical School, "both of which would have been convenient places to build, control, and hide a disk-shaped model."

Meanwhile growing numbers of Spanish ufologists were getting Ummo documents. By the end of the decade, at least 600 pages of ruminations on Ummo science, philosophy, politics, and civilization had been collected. The documents arrived via conventional mail; most had a Madrid postmark, but others were sent from Australia, New Zealand, England, Argentina, France, Czechoslakavia, Yugoslavia, and the United States.

The science described in these communications suggested that the author or authors had a university education and a familiarity with current physical and biological knowledge and theory. But few sophisticated readers believed that these were the thoughts of a true advanced extraterrestrial race. In fact, as Jacques Vallee, a ufologist trained in astrophysics and computer sciences, wrote, "The Ummo technology is without major surprises, and it matches the kind of clever extrapolations one finds in any good science-fiction novel.... The computers of Ummo... may have seemed advanced by the standards of the equipment available in Spain in the Sixties, but they are downright primitive by state-of-the-art Silicon Valley standards."

The Ummites, who look much like us, reportedly arrived on earth on April 24, 1950, when they landed in the French Alps. Since then they have been observing terrestrial affairs though without interfering in them. They communicate by telepathy because when they turn 14 their vocal cords close up. Apparently, however, they are able to speak over the phone, if the testimony of those who say they have received calls from them is to be credited. According to Hilary Evans, "Most of the letters were written in Spanish and the rest were in French, although it looks as though they were written by a Spaniard — occasionally the Spanish spelling of a word is used instead of the French."

What amounts to an Ummo cult claims followers around the world. Compilations of the documents have been published in Spanish and English, and Ummo-composed letters continue to be produced. According to Spanish ufologists Carlos Berche Cruz and Ignacio Cabria Garcia, the most likely instigators of the hoax are Sesma and individuals within his organization, though the investigators concede the charge cannot be proven.

They point out, however, that in the 1950s Sesma invented a cabalistic language and circulated writings about his pre-Ummo space contacts in which Ummo-like concepts and ideas were featured.

Other writers have speculated, though without evidence, that Ummo is a sociological experiment engineered by an intelligence agency.

● SOURCES:

Evans, Hilary. "Ummo: A Perfect Case?" *The Unexplained* 12, 134 (1983): 2661–65.

————. "The Ummites Tell All." *The Unexplained* 12, 135 (1983): 2686–89.

————. "Ummo — Red Alert." *The Unexplained* 12, 137 (1983): 2738–40.

Vallee, Jacques. *The Invisible College: What a Group of Scientists Has Discovered About UFO Influences on the Human Race.* New York: E. P. Dutton and Company, 1975.

————. *Revelations: Alien Contact and Human Deception.* New York: Ballantine Books, 1991.

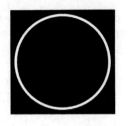

UNIDENTIFIED FLYING OBJECTS —————

One January evening, as he was hunting six miles south of Denison, Texas, John Martin saw a fast-moving object in the southern sky. When it passed overhead, he noted its resemblance to a "large saucer." What distinguished Martin's sighting from many thousands of others is that it took place in 1878.

"Flying saucers" as a phenomenon did not enter popular culture until late June 1947, after a flurry of sightings of mysterious aerial discs excited speculation focusing on, as some thought, secret American or Soviet aircraft and, as others suspected, extraterrestrial visitors. On the twenty-fourth, private pilot Kenneth Arnold spotted nine disc-shaped objects flying in formation and at an estimated 1,200 mph over Mount Rainier, Washington. In a newspaper interview he compared their motion to that of saucers skipping across water. Soon afterwards an anonymous headline writer in the Pacific Northwest coined the phrase "flying saucer," and the UFO age began, though "unidentified flying objects" — the more sober and literally descriptive phrase thought up by an equally anonymous U.S. Air Force functionary — would not become a part of the public vocabulary until the mid-1950s.

Yet, as the Martin report indicates, flying saucers and UFOs were around before 1947. In fact, from November 1896 until May 1897 newspapers all across America were filled with stories about mysterious "airships" — cigar-shaped objects often said to flash brilliant searchlights — which at least some theorists, not to mention more than a few hoaxers, linked to visitors from Mars. Reports of what could reasonably be called UFOs appear sporadically in scientific journals and newspapers in the earlier decades of the nineteenth century but are rare or nonexistent before that. Pre-1800 reports of anomalous aerial phenomena, sometimes cited as evidence of the UFO phenomenon's long history, are more credibly explained as manifestations of nature or psyche. UFOs seem a relatively recent presence.

Kenneth Arnold's sighting of nine "flying saucers" over Mount Rainier, Washington, on June 24, 1947, brought the UFO phenomenon into popular consciousness. Arnold reported that the lead object resembled a crescent, while the other eight were flat and disc-shaped.

"Airship" scares continued into the twentieth century, though soon extraterrestrial theories were eclipsed by fears of hostile (usually German) aeronauts or by expectations that a secret inventor was flight-testing his breakthrough in aviation technology. History attests that neither Germans nor reclusive geniuses were responsible.

Other kinds of UFOs also were being seen with growing frequency. Some witnesses even spoke of landed ships and strange-looking occupants — the kinds of reports that decades later would be called "close encounters of the third kind." More often, objects of the various shapes destined in our time to become familiar, if unsettling, sights were observed in the air. Even so, only Charles Fort (1874–1932), who chronicled such manifestations in three books published between 1919 and 1931, kept interplanetary theories alive. During World War II Allied pilots in both the European and Pacific theaters called them "foo fighters" and assumed they were Axis devices. The Soviets were thought (wrongly) to be behind the "ghost rockets" that inundated northern Europe during much of 1946.

The official history.
The role of official agencies in UFO investigation is a subject of continuing dispute. There is, indisputably, a public history, and there is also evidence of a history concealed by official secrecy.

In the public history, the first U.S. Air Force effort to study UFO reports was conducted under the code name Project Sign, set up under the Air Materiel Command at Wright Field, Dayton, Ohio (later Wright-Patterson Air Force Base), on December 30, 1947. Sign investigated sighting reports considered significant (routine sightings were handled by intelligence officers at local air bases). The first of these was a January 7, 1948, incident in which a Kentucky Air National Guard pilot, Capt. Thomas F. Mantell, Jr., died in a plane crash while trying to intercept something he described, in

After initial press reports in July 1947 that the Air Force had recovered wreckage from a "flying disc" in Lincoln County, New Mexico, authorities subsequently claimed that the material was from a downed balloon — a story now known to be false.

Army Finds Air Saucer On Ranch in New Mexico

Disk Goes To High Officers

Picked Up Last Week

ROSWELL, N.M.—(AP)— The Army Air Forces have today announced a flying disk had been found on a ranch near Roswell and is in Army possession.

Lt. Warren Haught, public information officer at the Roswell Army Air Field, announced that first had been located last week, and had been turned over to the authorities. Some of the speculation at the sheriff's office.

"It was immersed at the Roswell Army Air Field and subsequently loaned" by Maj. Jesse A. Marcel of the 509th bomb group intelligence office at Roswell, "to higher headquarters."

The Army gave no other details.

'Flying disc' turns up as just hot air

Fort Worth, Tex., July 9 (AP).—An examination by the Army revealed last night a mysterious object found on a lonely New Mexico ranch was a harmless high-altitude weather balloon — not a grounded flying disc.

Army Knocks Down Disk—

IT'S A WEATHER BALLOON

Device Is Only A Wind Target

Object Found in N. Mexico Identified at Fort Worth

(Map on Page 5.)

FORT WORTH, Tex., July 8.—(P)—A "flying disc" reported by the Army Air Forces to have been found near Roswell, N.M. was rudely stripped of its glamor tonight by a Fort Worth Army airfield weather officer. He identified the object as a weather balloon.

Warrant Officer Irving Newton, a forecaster at the base weather station, said the object was a ray wind target used to determine the direction and velocity of winds at high altitudes.

80 Stations Use Same Type Balloon

Newton said there were some 80 weather stations in the United States using this type of balloon and that it could have come from any one of them.

The balloon was shipped to the 8th Air Force headquarters here from Roswell and on orders from Washington was to have been forwarded to Wright Field, near Dayton.

Lt. Warren Haught, public information officer at Roswell announced earlier today that "the main rumors regarding the flying disk became a reality yesterday when the intelligence office of the 509th Atomic Bomb Group of the 8th Air Force Roswell Army Airfield was fortunate enough to gain possession of a disc through the cooperation of one of the local ranchers and the sheriff's office."

A Historical Perspective   143

one of his last radio transmissions, as a "metallic object … of tremendous size." Though the Air Force first contended, implausibly, that this "object" was the planet Venus, it eventually would be identified as a balloon launched in connection with the Navy's then-classified Skyhook project.

A more impressive report came later in 1948 from two Eastern Air Lines pilots, Clarence S. Chiles and John B. Whitted. As their DC-3 flew over Alabama at 2:45 A.M. on July 24, Chiles and Whitted sighted a wingless, torpedo-shaped object as it streaked past them. It had two rows of square windows from which, Chiles reported, "a very bright light was glowing. Underneath the ship there was a blue glow of light." A flame extended 50 feet from the rear. The UFO, in view for no more than 10 seconds, was also seen by a passenger. Sign investigators learned that an hour earlier, a ground-maintenance crewman at Robins Air Force Base, Georgia, had observed an identical UFO. Moreover, four days before that, a rocket-shaped object with two rows of windows had been seen over The Hague, Netherlands.

By the time of the Chiles-Whitted sighting, Sign had split into factions with differing views of the flying-disc mystery. One held that the objects were interplanetary spacecraft, another that they were Soviet secret weapons, yet another that they were mundane phenomena which had been misinterpreted. Because it seemed clear that the Chiles-Whitted object was neither terrestrial nor conventional, the first faction boldly prepared an "estimate of the situation" which argued that the UFO evidence pointed unmistakably to otherworldly visitation. The estimate, classified Top Secret, was sent through channels all the way to the Air Force Chief of Staff, Gen. Hoyt S. Vandenberg, who rejected it and ordered all copies burned. The document remained secret until 1956, when a book by a retired Air Force UFO-project officer, Edward J. Ruppelt, reported the story behind it. Though other sources backed Ruppelt's account, for years the Air Force insisted the document was a fiction created by, as a Pentagon UFO spokesman put it in 1960, "avid saucer believers."

In fact, Vandenberg's rejection of the estimate's conclusion led to the dissolution of the ET faction, whose members left the Air Force or were reassigned. The anti-UFO faction now came into prominence, and on February 11, 1949, the aptly named Project Grudge was created to replace the demoralized Sign. Grudge devoted itself to minimal investigating and maximum debunking, and by the end of the year, its files had been put into storage. By the summer of 1950, it was down to a single investigator, Lt. Jerry Cummings.

After a series of radar/visual sightings of fast-moving UFOs over Fort Monmouth, New Jersey, in September 1951, complaints about the quality of Grudge's work by the head of Air Force Intelligence, Maj. Gen. C. P. Cabell, and other high-ranking officers and officials led to the reorganization of the project. Lt. Ed Ruppelt, an intelligence officer assigned to the Air Technical Intelligence Center (ATIC) at Wright-Patterson AFB, became its head. Ruppelt insisted that investigations be conducted without prior judgments about the reality or unreality of UFOs, and under his leadership Grudge — and, as it became known in March 1952, Project Blue Book — did just that. By the time he left the project in early 1954, Ruppelt was essentially convinced of the reality of space visitors, and memoir of his experiences, *The Report on Unidentified Flying Objects* (1956), would become one of the literature's most important works.

Blue Book, however, would revert before long to the pattern Grudge had set. The summer 1952 sighting wave instigated this renewed skepticism, culminating in a spectacular series of radar and eyewitness observations over Washington, D.C., on the weekends of July 19–20 and 26–27. Intelligence channels were clogged with UFO-related traffic, leading to high-level concerns about the Soviet Union's ability to exploit this communications logjam and also to use UFO stories for psychological-warfare purposes.

Because of this concern, in January 1953 a panel of five scientists, all UFO skeptics, was secretly convened to examine Blue Book's data. Over the next four days they spent a total of 12 hours considering various sighting reports as well as two UFO films (one taken in Montana, the other in Utah) before declaring further official study a "great waste of effort." The Robertson panel (named after its head, physicist and CIA employee H. P. Robertson) recommended a public "debunking" campaign which "would result in the reduction in public interest of 'flying saucers'." It also urged that civilian UFO groups "be watched because of their potentially great influence on mass thinking.... The apparent irresponsibility and the possible use of such groups for subversive purposes should be kept in mind."

Though the Robertson panel and its recommendations remained classified for years, they would exert an enormous impact on the course of UFO history. The Air Force began immediately to reduce Blue Book's status and resources, and after Ruppelt's departure the project became mostly a public-relations exercise devoted to explaining sightings by whatever means necessary and downplaying their significance. Even the Air Force's chief scientific advisor, astronomer J. Allen Hynek, who had attended the meetings (though not as a panel member), would complain, "The Robertson panel ... made the subject of UFOs scientifically unrespectable, and for nearly 20 years not enough attention was paid to the subject to acquire the kind of data needed even to decide the nature of the UFO phenomenon."

The Air Force botched an opportunity to do just that when it prepared *Project Blue Book Special Report 14*, released in October 1955. The report had its genesis in a January 1952 agreement between Grudge and the Battelle Memorial Institute, a think tank based in Columbus, Ohio. Battelle was to analyze UFO reports and in other ways to assist the Air Force in dealing with the problem. Project Stork, as the classified Battelle project was code-named, officially commenced work on March 31 and continued into the spring of 1955. Its findings were incorporated into *Report 14*.

The Stork study found that from a number of points of view, the best UFO sightings were puzzling indeed. A chi-square test, used in statistics to determine whether one thing is truly different from another, showed that there was virtually no possibility that "unknown" (unexplained) sightings were the same as "knowns" (explained) — thus falsifying the hypothesis that unknowns are simply knowns for which there is insufficient information for a proper identification. As Stork learned, the unknowns were the cases for which the *greatest* amount of information was available.

This was not what the Air Force wanted to hear, and even Stork's scientists blanched at endorsing what looked like incontrovertible evidence for the extraordinary nature of the UFO phenomenon. A manipulation of data which would be criticized by virtually every independent scientist who studied *Report 14* (Hynek would call it "utterly incredible") allowed Secretary of the Air Force Donald A. Quarles to declare, "On the basis of this study we believe that no objects such as those popularly described as flying saucers have overflown the United States."

The Air Force's consistently negative stance toward UFOs and its often contrived solutions of sightings fed widespread suspicion that the debunking was a cover for real concern about the phenomenon's implications. Perhaps, critics such as retired Marine Corps Maj. Donald E. Keyhoe argued, the Air Force was well aware of the reality of extraterrestrial visitation but feared a worldwide panic if it acknowledged as much.

In March 1966, after much-publicized sightings in Michigan and Air Force representative Hynek's dismissal of some of them as inspired by swamp gas, Blue Book became the object of withering press ridicule and Congressional criticism. Testifying before the House Armed Services Committee on April 5, Hynek urged that a "civilian panel of physical and social scientists ... examine the UFO problem critically for the express purpose of determining whether a major problem really exists." This was a public expression of a view Hynek had stated through official channels the year before.

By now UFOs had become a major public-relations headache to the Air Force which, hoping someone would take the problem off its hands, was only too happy to follow Hynek's advice. After an Ad Hoc Committee to Review Project Blue Book, consisting of six scientists, made the same suggestion, the Air Force entered into a contract with the University of Colorado for what was touted as an independent scientific study of UFOs.

Hynek said later that the Condon Committee — as it was called informally, after its director, physicist Edward U. Condon — was essentially a setup. Its purpose, knowledgeable Air Force sources told him, was to rid the service of its UFO albatross. Condon made little secret of his antipathy to the subject, and soon the operation was embroiled in controversy. Two investigators who disagreed with Condon's views were fired, and a book (co-authored by the ousted David R. Saunders, a psychologist) and a *Look* magazine article exposed what they characterized as hypocrisy and incompetence within the project.

The Condon report, formally titled *Scientific Study of Unidentified Flying Objects* and released in early 1969, came to predictably negative conclusions ("further scientific study of UFOs probably cannot be justified in the expectation that science will be advanced thereby," according to Condon's introduction). Yet by its own admission fully one-third of its cases were unexplained even after in-depth scrutiny. Critics such as James E. McDonald, a University of Arizona atmospheric physicist, charged that even some of the supposedly explained cases were actually unknowns. Once again, as with *Project Blue Book Special Report 14*, an official report's conclusions did not follow from its data.

Nonetheless the Air Force had what it wanted: an excuse to close down Project Blue Book. On December 17, 1969, Secretary of the Air Force Robert C. Seamans, Jr., announced Blue Book's end and said, in words that echoed Condon's, that the project's continuance "cannot be justified either on the ground of national security or in the interest of science."

The phenomenon after 1947.
UFO sightings are worldwide in scope and vary little if at all from one nation to another. The most commonly reported UFO shapes are discs and cigars; recent years have seen growing numbers of reports of boomerangs

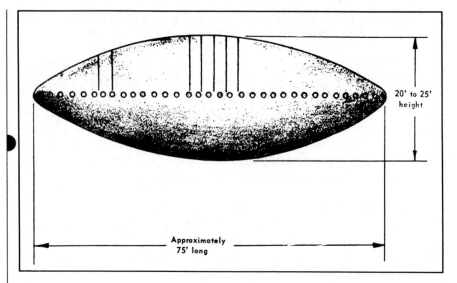

20' to 25'
height

Approximately
75' long

and triangles. A significant number of sightings are simply of points of light in the night sky. Such sightings often have conventional explanations — Venus, meteors, passing aircraft — but in some instances the behavior of the lights defies such mundane accounting.

In his 1972 book *The UFO Experience*, Hynek broke reports into these general categories: nocturnal lights; daylight discs; radar/visual cases; close encounters of the first kind (CE1s — a UFO is seen at less than 500 feet from the witness); close encounters of the second kind (CE2s — a UFO physically affects its environment); and close encounters of the third kind (CE3s — occupants are observed in connection with a UFO sighting).

The best evidence for UFOs as extraordinary physical phenomena comes from radar/visual cases and CE2s. Among the former is a remarkable incident that occurred over several hours between August 13 and 14, 1956, at two English bases run jointly by the Royal Air Force and the U.S. Air Force. Unidentified targets traveling at high speed were tracked on air and ground radar and seen visually by earthbound observers and pilots in flight. The Condon Committee's investigator, physicist Gordon David Thayer, would conclude, "The apparently rational, intelligent behavior of the UFO suggests a mechanical device of unknown origin as the most probable explanation of this sighting."

The best-documented CE2 of the landing-trace variety took place late on the afternoon of January 8, 1981, when an old man working in his garden in Trans-en-Provence, France, reported that he had witnessed the landing of a "ship ... in the form of two saucers upside down, one against the other." The object rested on the ground for a short period of time before flying away. In its wake it left traces, impressions, and other evidence of the presence of a large vehicle. An intensive investigation of the report was mounted by France's official UFO-monitoring agency, Group d'Etude des

This "flying cup" photograph, taken in the 1950s, is one of the many hundreds of fake UFO pictures taken since 1947. Phony photographs are the most common type of UFO hoax because they are the easiest to perpetrate and usually the hardest to disprove.

Phenomenes Aerospatiaux Non-Identifies (GEPAN), which took soil, leaf, and plant samples to France's leading botanical laboratory, headed by Michel Bounias. In 1983, in a 66-page scientific monograph on the case, GEPAN noted that the leaves had inexplicably lost 30 to 50 percent of their chlorophyll and had aged abruptly in ways that could not be duplicated in the laboratory. There was evidence of an "occurrence of an important event which brought with it deformations of the terrain caused by mass, mechanics, a heating effect, and perhaps certain transformations and deposits of trace minerals [phosphate and zinc].... For the first time we have found a combination of factors which conduce us to accept that something similar to what the eyewitness has described did take place there."

By their nature CE3s are the most bizarre UFO claims and the ones most likely to inspire sensationalistic publicity. For some early ufologists they were the most difficult to accept. Yet even on those rare occasions when it investigated such reports, the Air Force confessed it could not explain them. In most cases the witnesses — both multiple or independent witnesses — seem credible, and psychological inventories of such claimants have indicated they are not mentally ill. CE3s range in variety from brief sightings of humanoids (nearly all CE3s describe humanoids) to abductions into UFOs and interaction with their occupants.

One of the best-attested CE3s happened at Boianai, Papua New Guinea, on the evenings of June 26 and 27, 1959. An Anglican missionary from Australia, the Rev. W. B. Gill, and three dozen other witnesses saw, through the dome of a hovering UFO, illuminated humanlike figures. Gill thought they were "busy at some unknown task." During the second sighting Gill and others waved at the figures, who waved back.

Cons and contacts.
Though popular belief holds that many UFO reporters are conscious hoaxers, hoaxes — as opposed to honest misidentifications, which underlie a large number of ostensible UFO sightings — are relatively uncommon. Even the Air Force found that hoaxes comprised only about one percent of the reports it received, and a significant percentage of these were of alleged UFO photos, notoriously easy to fake. Still, spectacular hoaxes have been recorded.

The Arnold sighting in 1947 was only days old when the first major hoax was perpetrated by two Tacoma, Washington, men who produced what they asserted was a slaglike substance dropped from a "flying doughnut" which had hovered over nearby Maury Island. In the course of an official investigation, two Army Air Force officers were killed in a plane crash, fueling rumors that they had been murdered for knowing too much. The men's story, however, was nothing more than a practical joke which had gotten out of hand.

From the early 1950s on, flamboyant figures, based mostly though not exclusively in southern California, claimed ongoing contact with benevolent visitors from Venus, Mars, Saturn, and other planets. Many of these "contactees," as they were called, also told of interplanetary travels and meetings with extraterrestrials ("Space Brothers") in deep space or on other worlds. As proof they produced suspiciously clear close-up photographs of spaceships and conveniently blurred photographs of their Space Brother friends.

The most prominent figure in the movement was George Adamski, whose adventures began on November 20, 1952, when he allegedly encountered Orthon, a Venusian, in the California desert. Truman Bethurum, Daniel Fry, George Van Tassel, Howard Menger, and others also wrote books, lectured widely, and attracted followings among occult-oriented saucer enthusiasts. By the 1970s most of the original contactees were dead or relatively inactive, but a Swiss farmer, Billy Meier, filled the vacuum with photographs of "beamships" and tales of contacts with "cosmonauts" from the Pleiades. Though Adamski, Meier, and the rest were subjected to printed reports which exposed embarrassing information — in Meier's case, a photograph said to be of a cosmonaut was shown to be of a fashion model and clipped from a popular European magazine — their disciples remained unfazed, and even now Adamski, who died in 1965, is a hero of the movement.

Not all, or even many, contactees were charlatans of this sort. Most believed they were in psychic, not physical, contact with space people; thus they did not feel obligated to produce manifestly dubious "evidence" to support stories of face-to-face meetings. Some psychic contactees demonstrated their sincerity in unmistakable, even shocking ways. Gloria Lee, for example, fasted to death at the direction of a friend from Jupiter. Through automatic writing Dorothy Martin of Oak Park, Illinois, received messages from the spaceman Sananda, who warned her of devastating geological upheavals to occur on December 20, 1954. She and her followers alerted the press and quit jobs in anticipation of deliverance by spaceship on the appointed date. When the saucer failed to show, worldwide ridicule followed.

The contactee movement continues today, though in different form. The superstars are gone, and there are few professional contactees. The typical modern contactee is outwardly indistinguishable from his or her neighbor; the individual's communications with extraterrestrials (through visions, voices, automatic writing, or channeling) are kept secret from all but a few family members and trusted associates. Every year some of these "folk" contactees meet on the University of Wyoming campus in Laramie, where psychologist and contactee R. Leo Sprinkle hosts the Rocky Mountain Conference on UFO Investigation.

In the 1980s a new kind of hoaxer appeared on the scene. As old suspicions of an official UFO cover-up of significant UFO findings were revived among ufologists, several individuals busily marketed their alleged knowledge of sinister UFO secrets. Through high-priced books, videos, and tapes they spread a message of fear and paranoia which combined tales of secret U.S. government pacts with cannibalistic aliens with right-wing, sometimes openly anti-Semitic, conspiracy theories.

Theories about UFOs.
Until the mid-1960s two interpretations of the phenomenon dominated the controversy about UFOs. (Early speculations about secret weapons largely died out in the 1950s.) One was that UFOs were nonsense — in other words, all explainable as hoaxes, misinterpretations, or delusions — and the other was that they were extraterrestrial spacecraft. The champion of the former school was Donald H. Menzel, a Harvard University astronomer; the latter's champion was Donald E. Keyhoe, an aviation journalist. Both wrote influential books and articles arguing their positions and claimed powerful allies in science, government, and the military.

In the latter 1960s some ufologists began considering new approaches to the UFO puzzle. John A. Keel, a New York writer, and Jacques Vallee, a French-American theorist trained in astronomy and computer science, suggested that UFO reports, particularly those of the "high-strangeness" variety, were more indicative of paranormal phenomena than of nuts-and-bolts/flesh-and-blood visitors from other planets. In *UFOs: Operation Trojan Horse* (1970) Keel called the UFO intelligences "ultraterrestrials" and characterized them as ill-intentioned beings from other dimensions of exis-

In the 1980s a document supposedly prepared for supersecret UFO project "Majestic-12" surfaced. It purports to be a November 18, 1952, briefing for President-elect Eisenhower on recovered UFO wreckage and alien bodies. It is almost certainly a hoax, but identity and motives of hoaxers remain a mystery.

tence. Vallee's *Passport to Magonia* (1969) linked modern flying saucers to earlier traditions of fairies and other supernatural entities. In later books such as *The Invisible College* (1975), *Messengers of Deception* (1979), and *Revelations* (1991), he added conspiracy themes to the mix, hinting that secret groups were manipulating the phenomenon for their own purposes.

Other ufologists considered the occult school too speculative for their tastes but agreed with Keel and Vallee that the key to the mystery lay in the most bizarre reports, which traditional ufologists, obsessed with credibility, documentation, and evidence, had ignored or belittled. Contact claims suddenly became respectable — not as literally believed accounts of interplanetary encounters but as visionary experiences shaped by the personalities and cultural environments of the visionaries. Thus those UFO encounters not otherwise explainable (as misidentifications, hoaxes, or poorly understood natural phenomena such as earthquake lights and ball lightning) were seen as no more than unusually vivid dreams; abductions by extraterrestrials, for example, were just a Space Age variant of what earlier ages would have experienced as kidnappings by fairies.

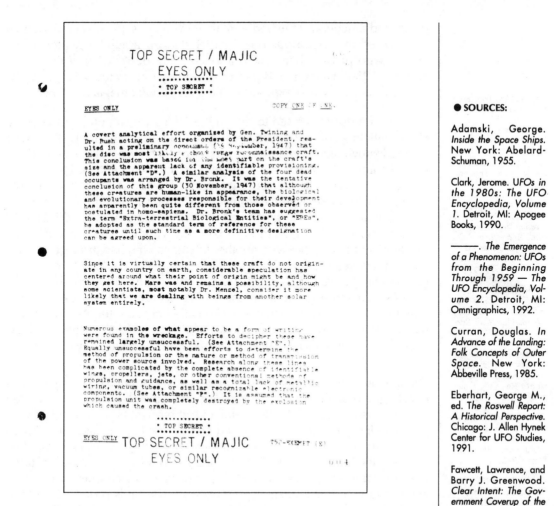

TOP SECRET / MAJIC
EYES ONLY
••••••••••••
• TOP SECRET •
••••••••••••

EYES ONLY   COPY ONE OF ONE.

A covert analytical effort organized by Gen. Twining and
Dr. Bush acting on the direct orders of the President, resulted in a preliminary consensus (19 September, 1947) that
the disc was most likely a short range reconnaissance craft.
This conclusion was based for the most part on the craft's
size and the apparent lack of any identifiable provisioning.
(See Attachment "D".) A similar analysis of the four dead
occupants was arranged by Dr. Bronk. It was the tentative
conclusion of this group (30 November, 1947) that although
these creatures are human-like in appearance, the biological
and evolutionary processes responsible for their development
has apparently been quite different from those observed or
postulated in homo-sapiens. Dr. Bronk's team has suggested
the term "Extra-terrestrial Biological Entities", or "EBEs",
be adopted as the standard term of reference for these
creatures until such time as a more definitive designation
can be agreed upon.

Since it is virtually certain that these craft do not originate in any country on earth, considerable speculation has
centered around what their point of origin might be and how
they get here. Mars was and remains a possibility, although
some scientists, most notably Dr. Menzel, consider it more
likely that we are dealing with beings from another solar
system entirely.

Numerous examples of what appear to be a form of writing
were found in the wreckage. Efforts to decipher these have
remained largely unsuccessful. (See Attachment "E".)
Equally unsuccessful have been efforts to determine the
method of propulsion or the nature or method of transmission
of the power source involved. Research along these lines
has been complicated by the complete absence of identifiable
wings, propellers, jets, or other conventional methods of
propulsion and guidance, as well as a total lack of metallic
wiring, vacuum tubes, or similar recognizable electronic
components. (See Attachment "F".) It is assumed that the
propulsion unit was completely destroyed by the explosion
which caused the crash.

••••••••••••
• TOP SECRET •
••••••••••••
EYES ONLY TOP SECRET / MAJIC   TSC-EXEMPT (E)
EYES ONLY

● SOURCES:

Adamski, George. *Inside the Space Ships.* New York: Abelard-Schuman, 1955.

Clark, Jerome. *UFOs in the 1980s: The UFO Encyclopedia, Volume 1.* Detroit, MI: Apogee Books, 1990.

————. *The Emergence of a Phenomenon: UFOs from the Beginning Through 1959 — The UFO Encyclopedia, Volume 2.* Detroit, MI: Omnigraphics, 1992.

Curran, Douglas. *In Advance of the Landing: Folk Concepts of Outer Space.* New York: Abbeville Press, 1985.

Eberhart, George M., ed. *The Roswell Report: A Historical Perspective.* Chicago: J. Allen Hynek Center for UFO Studies, 1991.

Fawcett, Lawrence, and Barry J. Greenwood. *Clear Intent: The Government Coverup of the UFO Experience.* Englewood Cliffs, NJ: Prentice-Hall, 1984.

Fort, Charles. *The Books of Charles Fort.* New York: Henry Holt and Company, 1941.

Gillmor, Daniel S., ed. *Scientific Study of Unidentified Flying*

401

Jerome Clark and Loren Coleman's *The Unidentified* (1975) was the first book to argue this position; later books by French authors Michel Monnerie, Gerard Barthel and Jacques Brucker, and — most influentially — England's Hilary Evans would make the "psychosocial hypothesis," as it came to be called, a major force in world ufology, especially in Europe.

Crashes, cover-ups, and controversies.

In the United States, however, the enthusiasm for occult and psychosocial approaches had mostly passed by the late 1970s. One reason was that the release of many heretofore classified UFO reports, retrieved through the Freedom of Information Act, reminded ufologists of the radar/visual cases and other impressive sightings that had excited their interest in the subject to start with. Related to this was revived speculation about an official cover-up.

Keyhoe and other early critics of the cover-up suspected the Air Force of hiding dramatic sightings by interceptor pilots as well as films and radar trackings of UFOs. Few credited widespread rumors that the Air Force possessed more positive proof of extraterrestrial visitation, such as the remains of crashed saucers and the bodies of their occupants. Reports of this nature had figured in a notorious hoax perpetrated on a gullible writer, Frank Scully, who passed them on in a best-selling book, *Behind the Flying Saucers* (1950). Launched as part of a scam by two confidence artists, the hoax subsequently was exposed in the then-popular magazine *True*.

Even so, the stories refused to die. In the 1970s veteran ufologist Leonard H. Stringfield started collecting reports and interviewing individuals who claimed knowledge, sometimes firsthand, of such events. Two other ufologists, Stanton T. Friedman and William L. Moore, concentrated their attention on one particular episode, the alleged crash of a UFO in Lincoln County, New Mexico, in early July 1947, and pursued the first in-depth investigation of what Stringfield had dubbed a "retrieval of the third kind." They interviewed nearly three dozen individuals who were directly involved and also spoke with another fifty or so who had indirect involvement. A few years later a Chicago organization, the J. Allen Hynek Center for UFO Studies (CUFOS), conducted its own inquiry, bringing the total of sources, ranging from area ranchers to Air Force generals, to over four hundred. The "Roswell incident" — so called because the Air Force's initial investigation was conducted out of Roswell Field in Roswell, New Mexico — emerged as a central concern of American ufology.

Though the Roswell incident itself seemed well documented and genuinely puzzling, it brought with it a host of less verifiable claims. Moore reported that his investigation of the Roswell incident brought him into contact with cover-up insiders within military and civilian intelligence agencies. These individuals, to whom he assigned various avian pseudonyms and whom he dubbed "the birds" (Falcon, Condor, Sparrow, and so on), related fantastic tales not only of spaceship crashes but of face-to-face contact between aliens and U.S. government representatives. The birds promised, in their words, a "truckload of documents" to support these incredible allegations but produced only a handful of pieces of paper, including pages from a briefing book supposedly prepared for President Carter.

The most notorious document arrived one day in December 1984 in an envelope, postmarked Albuquerque and sent to Moore associate Jaime Shandera with no return address. Inside the envelope was a roll of 35mm film which, when developed, was found to contain a portion of a Presidential briefing document dated November 18, 1952. Allegedly written by Vice Adm. Roscoe H. Hillenkoetter, it purported to inform President-elect Dwight D. Eisenhower of two UFO crashes — one in Roswell in 1947, the other along the Texas-Mexico border in 1950 — and of the existence of an "Operation Majestic-12" (MJ-12 for short), consisting of prominent figures in intelligence, science, and the military, who oversaw the study of the wreckage and the corpses of "extraterrestrial biological entities" (EBEs).

When a copy of the briefing paper came into the hands of British ufologist Timothy Good (who claimed an unnamed intelligence source had given it to him), Good announced as much to the British press. Moore and Shan-

Objects. New York: Bantam Books, 1969.

Hall, Richard H., ed. *The UFO Evidence.* Washington, DC: National Investigations Committee on Aerial Phenomena, 1964.

Hendry, Allan. *The UFO Handbook: A Guide to Investigating, Evaluating and Reporting UFO Sightings.* Garden City, NY: Doubleday and Company, 1979.

Hopkins, Budd. *Intruders: The Incredible Visitations at Copley Woods.* New York: Random House, 1987.

Hynek, J. Allen. *The UFO Experience: A Scientific Inquiry.* Chicago: Henry Regnery Company, 1972.

Jacobs, David Michael. *The UFO Controversy in America.* Bloomington, IN: Indiana University Press, 1975.

———. *Secret Life: Firsthand Accounts of UFO Abductions.* New York: Simon and Schuster, 1992.

Keel, John A. *UFOs: Operation Trojan Horse.* New York: G. P. Putnam's Sons, 1970.

Keyhoe, Donald E. *Flying Saucers from Outer Space.* New York: Henry Holt and Company, 1953.

402

dera released their copy at the same time — May 1987 — and the result was furious controversy and massive publicity, including coverage in the *New York Times* and on ABC television's *Nightline*. The FBI launched a probe out of its offices in New York City and Los Angeles but was as unsuccessful as ufologists were in getting to the bottom of the matter. For technical reasons having to do with a suspicious signature and format problems, the document is believed to be a forgery by all but a few diehard defenders. The forger's motives and identity, however, remain as mysterious as do those of Moore's "birds."

The future of ufology.

Recent years have seen the growing professionalization of UFO study. This is partly the result of a natural maturation process, but it also has to do with the influx into ufology's ranks of social scientists and mental-health professionals intrigued by UFO-abduction experiences reported by apparently sane and sincere persons. In the early 1990s systematic work on the phenomenon commenced as efforts were made to determine whether such experiences were internally or externally generated.

The psychosocial hypothesis still holds sway in Europe, though it has been challenged by a series of spectacular radar/visual cases in Belgium between 1989 and 1990. In America, interest in cover-ups, crashes, and the extraterrestrial hypothesis continues, with new discoveries, documents, rumors, and stories surfacing regularly. Whether or not it succeeds in making its case or in settling its disagreements, ufology has unquestionably entered what may be its liveliest period.

Menzel, Donald H., and Ernest H. Taves. *The UFO Enigma: The Definitive Explanation of the UFO Phenomenon*. Garden City, NY: Doubleday and Company, 1977.

Randle, Kevin D., and Donald R. Schmitt. *UFO Crash at Roswell*. New York: Avon Books, 1991.

Ruppelt, Edward J. *The Report on Unidentified Flying Objects*. Garden City, NY: Doubleday and Company, 1956.

Sagan, Carl, and Thornton Page, eds. *UFOs — A Scientific Debate*. Ithaca, NY: Cornell University Press, 1972.

Saunders, David R., and R. Roger Harkins. *UFOs? Yes!: Where the Condon Committee Went Wrong*. New York: World Publishing Company, 1968.

Vallee, Jacques. *Passport to Magonia: From Folklore to Flying Saucers*. Chicago: Henry Regnery Company, 1969.

403

UNIDENTIFIED SUBMARINE OBJECTS ————

While sailing in the equatorial Atlantic Ocean in the early morning hours of October 28, 1902, the *Fort Salisbury* came upon an incredible sight. As second officer A. H. Raymer noted in the ship's log:

Dark object, with long, luminous trailing wake, thrown in relief by a phosphorescent sea, seen ahead, a little on starboard bow. Look-out reported two masthead lights ahead. These two lights, almost as bright as a steamer's lights, appeared to shine from two points in line on the upper surface of the dark mass.

Concluded dark mass was a whale and lights phosphorescent. On drawing nearer dark mass and lights sank below the surface. Prepared to examine the wake in passing with binoculars.

Passed about forty to fifty yards on port side of wake, and discovered it was the scaled back of some huge monster slowly disappearing below the surface. Darkness of the night prevented determining its exact nature, but scales of apparently 1 ft. diameter and dotted in places with barnacle growth were plainly discernible. The breadth of the body showing above water tapered from about 30 ft. close abaft where the dark mass had appeared to be about 5 ft. at the extreme end visible. Length roughly about 500 ft. to 600 ft.

Concluded that the dark mass first seen must have been the creature's head. The swirl caused by the monster's progress could be distinctly heard, and a strong odor like that of a low-tide beach on a summer day pervaded the air. Twice along its length the disturbance of the water and a broadening of the surrounding belt of phosphorus indicated the presence of huge fins in motion below the surface.

The wet, shiny back of the monster was dotted with twinkling phosphorescent lights, and was encircled with a band of white phosphorescent sea.

Such are the bare facts of the passing of the sea serpent in latitude 5 deg. 31 min. S., longitude 4 deg. 42 min. W., as seen by myself, being officer of the watch, and by the helmsman and look-out man.

The account's laconic tone notwithstanding, this incredible but supposedly true story challenges the reader's boggle threshold. To Bernard Heuvelmans, the father of cryptozoology and the greatest living authority on sea-serpent reports, it can only be "all nonsense." As Charles Fort wryly observed, "So doubly damned is this datum that the attempt to explain it was in terms of the accursed Sea Serpent."

If we are to believe this story, of course, we have no choice but to assume that the object was a machine masquerading as a sea serpent. If that notion sounds familiar, it is probably because you have read Jules Verne's *Twenty Thousand Leagues Under the Sea.* First published in 1870, still in print, and one of the most popular science-fiction novels of all time, it concerns the marvelous invention of Capt. Nemo, who designed his submarine *Nautilus* so that those who saw it would think it was a sea serpent.

But are we to believe the story? It was reported as true in the *London Daily Mail* (November 19, 1902), and when interviewed, the ship's captain, not himself a witness, remarked of his second officer, "I can only say that he is very earnest on the subject and has, together with the lookout and the helmsman, seen something in the water, of a huge nature, as specified."

An even more fantastic story, if that is possible, was published in a Washington newspaper, the *Tacoma Daily Ledger*, on July 3, 1893. The witnesses, most of them named, were identified as members of a fishing party which left Tacoma on the afternoon of the first and camped that evening on Henderson Island, not far from a large band of surveyors. The narrative that follows is attributed to one of the fishermen:

It was, I guess, about midnight before I fell asleep, but exactly how long I slept I cannot say, for when I woke it was with such startling suddenness that it never entered my mind to look at my watch, and when after a while I did look at my watch, as well as every watch belonging to the party, it was stopped.

I am afraid that you will fail to comprehend how suddenly that camp was awake.

Since the creation of the world I doubt if sounds and sights more horrible were ever seen or heard by mortal man. I was in the midst of a pleasant dream, when in an instant a most horrible noise rang out in the clear morning air, and instantly the whole air was filled with a strong current of electricity that caused every nerve in the body to sting

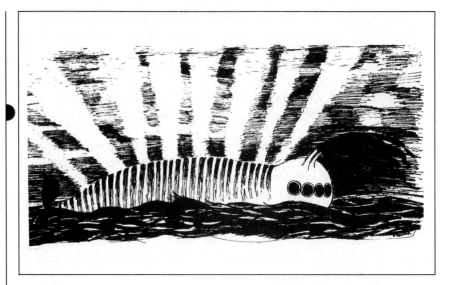

A fantastic account of a fishing party's encounter with a monstrosity combining the features of a sea serpent and a futuristic submarine was published as a true story in the Tacoma Daily Ledger, *July 3, 1893. (Courtesy of Loren Coleman.)*

with pain, and a light as bright as that created by the concentration of many arc lights kept constantly flashing. At first I thought it was a thunderstorm, but as no rain accompanied it, and as both light and sound came from off the bay, I turned my head in that direction, and if it is possible for fright to turn one's hair white, then mine ought to be snow white, for right before my eyes was a most horrible-looking monster.

By this time every man in our camp, as well as the men from the camp of the surveyors, was gathered on the bank of the stream; and as soon as we could gather our wits together we began to question if what we were looking at was not the creation of the mind. But we were soon disburdened of this idea, for the monster slowly drew in toward the shore, and as it approached, from its head poured out a stream of water that looked like blue fire. All the while the air seemed to be filled with electricity, and the sensation experienced was as if each man had on a suit of clothes formed of the fine points of needles.

One of the men from the surveyors' camp incautiously took a few steps in the direction of the water, which reached the man. He instantly fell to the ground and layt as though dead.

Mr. [W. L.] McDonald attempted to reach the man's body to pull it back into a place of safety, but he was struck with some of the water that the monster was throwing and fell senseless to the earth. By this time every man in both parties was panic-stricken, and we rushed to the woods for a place of safety, leaving the fallen men lying on the beach.

As we reached the woods the "demon of the deep" sent out flashes of light that illuminated the surrounding country for miles, and his roar — which sounded like the roar of thunder — became terrific. When we reached the woods we looked around and saw the monster making off in the direction of the sound, and in an instant it disappeared off in the direction of the sound, and in an instant it disappeared beneath the waters of the bay, but for some time we were able to trace its course by a bright luminous light that was on the surface of the water. As the fish disappeared, total darkness surrounded us, and it took us some time to find our way back to the beach where our comrades lay. We were unable to tell the time, as the powerful electric force had stopped our watches. We eventually found McDonald and the other man and were greatly relieved to find that they were alive, though unconscious. So we sat down to wait the coming of daylight. It came, I should judge, in about half an hour, and by this time, by constant work on the two men, both were able to stand.

This monster fish, or whatever you may call it, was fully 150 feet long, and at its thickest part I should judge about 30 feet in circumference. Its shape was somewhat out of the ordinary insofar that the body was neither round nor flat but oval, and from what we could see the upper part of the body was covered with a very coarse hair. The head was shaped very much like the head of a walrus, though, of course, very much larger. Its eyes, of which it apparently had six, were as large around as a dinner plate and were exceedingly dull, and it was about the only spot on the monster that at one time or another was not illuminated. At intervals of about every eight feet from its head to its tail a substance that had the appearance of a copper band encircled its body, and it was from these many bands that the powerful electric current appeared to come. The bands nearest the head seemed to have the strongest electric force, and it was from these first six bands that the most brilliant lights were emitted. Near the center of its head were two large hornlike substances, though they could not have been horns for it was through them that the electrically charged water was thrown.

Its tail from what I could see of it was shaped like a propeller and seemed to revolve, and it may be possible that the strange monster pushes himself through the water by means of this propellerlike tail. At will this strange monstrosity seemed to be able to emit strong waves of electric current, giving off electro-motive forces, which causes any person coming within the radius of this force to receive an electric shock.

Amusingly, like Raymer, the narrator of the above tale, a tall one by any standard, insists on characterizing the "monstrosity" as a sea serpent rather than an extraordinary technological device. Though we probably will never know for sure, one suspects that this is just one of the many outrageous, and less than strictly factual, yarns with which nineteenth-century American newspapers regaled their readers.

Other USOs.

If reports like the two above compel wonder more than belief, they do not necessarily relegate reports of unidentified submarines objects (USOs) to the realm of popular fantasy. Even in the nineteenth century some surprisingly credible reports of such phenomena were recorded. One of the more impressive occurred on June 18, 1845, in the eastern Mediterranean Sea. The crew of the brig *Victoria* saw three bright, luminous objects emerge from the sea and shoot into the sky, where they were visible for 10 minutes.

Prof. Baden-Powell collected reports from these and other witnesses and published their testimony in an 1861 issue of *Report of the British Association.* One man who observed the sight independently from land said the objects were five times the size of the moon, with "sail-like or streamerlike" appendages. He and other witnesses, who had the objects in view for between 20 minutes and an hour, said they appeared to be joined together.

On November 12, 1887, near Cape Race, a "large ball of fire" — one account describes it as "enormous" — rose from the sea, ascended 50 feet, then approached a nearby ship, the British steamer *Siberian*, moving against the wind as it did so. It then retreated and flew away. The incident was reported and discussed in *Nature, L'Astronomie,* and *Meteorological Journal.*

Modern UFO literature records a number of supposed USO incidents, but many seem explainable as sightings of terrestrial submarines in unexpected places. During the 1960s and 1970s, for example, Scandinavia was plagued with submarines in its territorial waters, and some writers have claimed these were extraordinary unknowns; they were, however, Soviet craft on spy missions.

Here is a sampling of the more puzzling reports:

Off the Alaska coast, summer 1945: Around sunset a large round object, something like 200 feet in diameter, emerged from the sea about a mile from the U.S. Army transport *Delarof*. After ascending a short distance, it turned toward the ship, approached it, and circled it silently two or three times before it flew off and disappeared in the southwest.

North Atlantic, late summer 1954: The crew of the *Groote Beer*, a ship owned by the Dutch government, observed a flat, moon-shaped object rise out of the ocean. Watching it through binoculars, Capt. Jan P. Boshoff noted its gray color and bright lights around the edges. It flew off at a 60-degree angle, covering 32 minutes of arc in one and a half minute's time. It or another unknown object was also seen by the Honduran freighter *Aliki P.*, sailing in the same general area. It radioed the Long Island Coast Guard: "Observed ball of fire moving in and out of water without being extinguished. Trailing white smoke. Moving in erratic course, finally disappeared."

Westchester County, New York, September 17, 1955: Around 1:30 A.M. a couple named Bordes, fishing enthusiasts, were rowing out onto a lake on Titicus Reservoir when they saw an object come out of the water a few feet from their boat and toward the shore. Rose-colored and luminous, it was the size and shape of a basketball. After rising a foot into the air, it fell back into the water with a loud splash and disappeared. Unnerved, the Bordeses headed for shore. On their way they saw, 200 yards to the southeast and at the center of the lake, two parallel lights, wavy in shape but rigid,

● SOURCES:

Coleman, Loren. *Curious Encounters: Phantom Trains, Spooky Spots, and Other Mysterious Wonders.* Boston, MA: Faber and Faber, 1985.

Corliss, William R., ed. *Strange Phenomena: A Sourcebook of Unusual Natural Phenomena, Volume G-1.* Glen Arm, MD: The Author, 1974.

Dash, Mike. "Swedish Mystery Subs Mystery." *Fortean Times* 51 (Winter 1988/1989): 26–30.

Fort, Charles. *The Books of Charles Fort.* New York: Henry Holt and Company, 1941.

Hall, Richard. "Aerial Anomalies at Sea." *INFO Journal* 4, 3 (May 1975): 6–9.

Heuvelmans, Bernard. *In the Wake of the Sea-Serpents.* New York: Hill and Wang, 1968.

Lorenzen, Jim, and Coral Lorenzen. *UFOs Over the Americas.* New York: Signet, 1968.

"More Lake Mysteries." *INFO Journal* 6, 3 (September/October 1977): 5.

Ribera, Antonio. "UFOs and the Sea." *Flying*

30 feet in length, along or just under the surface. "Above these 'serpents' was a round light of lesser brilliance, more yellowish-white in hue," an investigator reported. "Considerably smaller than a full moon, and dimmer than a car headlight, it appeared the size of a basketball ... at a distance of a few hundred feet. It was not hovering in midair, but was apparently fixed to a solid body, which was only intermittently visible as a dim gray shape against the blackness." It appeared to be a rotating spotlight. The couple watched the object for a time and even tried to approach it. When they left, considerably shaken, it was still there. The couple emphatically rejected any suggestion that they had seen another boat.

Shag Harbor, Nova Scotia, October 4, 1967: Just before midnight two men driving in a car saw a row of bright reddish-orange lights. They "came off and on one at a time," according to the *Yarmouth* [Nova Scotia] *Light Herald* (October 12). "The lights were at an angle of 45 degrees, dipping to the right, and the lights came on in order from bottom to top." Five other persons in a car stopped and watched the lights fly off to the water half a mile from shore, where they changed into a single bright white light which bobbed on the waves. Numerous other people, including a Royal Canadian Mounted Police constable, also saw it, and a number of boats set out to find it. "Within an hour," the paper related, "the boats had arrived in the area where the object had disappeared, and reported finding a very large patch of bubbling water and foam. One fisherman described the froth as 80 feet wide and yellowish in color and said that he had never seen anything like it before in the area."

Underwater civilization?
Taking reports such as these and combining it with Bermuda Triangle lore, Ivan T. Sanderson wrote a book, *Invisible Residents* (1970), which treated these as evidence that underwater OINTs (Other Intelligences) evolved on the earth and developed a sophisticated technological civilization.

"If a superior technological type of intelligent civilization(s) developed on this planet under water," he wrote, "they [sic] would very likely have gotten much farther ahead than we have, having had several millions, and possibly up to a billion years' headstart on us, life as we know it having started in the sea."

Such sweeping speculations are unsustained by any real evidence, and no significant writers on anomalous phenomena have shown any interest in endorsing them. There are, however, occasional suggestions either that extraterrestrial UFOs maintain bases in oceans and lakes or that such craft are exploring the watery regions along with the earth's land areas.

Saucer Review 10, 6 (November/December 1964): 8–10.

Sanderson, Ivan T. *Invisible Residents: A Disquisition upon Certain Matters Maritime, and the Possibility of Intelligent Life Under the Waters of This Earth.* New York: World Publishing Company, 1970.

"USO Update." *INFO Journal* 4, 1 (May 1974): 30–33.

VILE VORTICES ———————————————————————

Ivan T. Sanderson, a zoologist with a wide-ranging curiosity about anomalous phenomena and a creative imagination which often outraced available evidence, subscribed to the view that an intelligent civilization lives, undetected by the rest of us, in the oceans of the earth. (It may also be, he said, that "there are intelligent entities who have been coming here from elsewhere" and who base themselves in the oceans to avoid detection.) At least some UFOs are their aircraft, which double as submarines.

Taking note of what he characterized as mysterious plane and ship disappearances, he went on to suggest that these marine "OINTs" (Other Intelligences) may be snatching people as they traverse the oceans. These disappearances take place in disproportionate numbers in 10 "vile vortices" — lozenge-shaped areas which stretch in parallel bands at equal distances above and below the equator, exactly 72 degrees apart. Besides these 10, Sanderson added the two polar regions to make a total of a dozen vile vortices.

"And do not for a moment think that the disappearance of planes, ships, and subs is the *only* odd occurrence reported," he wrote. "Other oddities include wild reports of all sorts of UAOs [unidentified aerial objects] therefrom."

The vortices, of which the most famous is the — to Sanderson misnamed — Bermuda Triangle, are areas where OINTs operate. They are also areas where erratic natural phenomena (sudden high winds, storms, rough water) cause disturbances in space and time. In this milieu, where the OINTs are most likely to be detected, they are on occasion forced to take dramatic action to keep their presence a secret. Not wanting us to "know about their presence and activities," the OINTs may kidnap a "whole ship and everything in and on it."

There is no reason to believe that vile vortices exist in the first place, much less that they are related to aquatic, extraterrestrial, or interdimensional intelligences. Sanderson's evidence ranged between thin and incorporeal. In some cases it consisted of little more than vague rumors of unexplained events in the proposed areas. Even in the case of the most famous, most documented "vortice," the Bermuda Triangle, dispassionate analysis by Larry Kusche and others has shown a lot less mystery than met the eyes of Sanderson and other uncritical chroniclers. Vile vortices, in short, never existed outside Sanderson's musing.

● SOURCES:

Kusche, Larry. *The Bermuda Triangle Mystery Solved.* Buffalo, NY: Prometheus Books, 1986.

Sanderson, Ivan T. *More "Things."* New York: Pyramid Books, 1969.

———. *Invisible Residents: A Disquisition Upon Certain Matters Maritime, and the Possibility of Intelligent Life Under the Waters of the Earth.* New York: World Publishing Company, 1970.

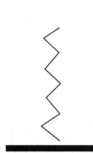

VULCAN

In 1846 Urbain Leverrier of the Paris Observatory was one of two astronomers to predict where an eighth planet would be discovered. When seen (or at least recognized for what it was) soon afterwards, Levierrier's calculations proved substantially correct. The planet was less than one degree of arc from the position Leverrier had assigned it. The French astronomer had inferred Neptune's existence from disturbances in the orbit of Uranus.

Leverrier, whose egotism was both gigantic and legendary, wanted the new planet named after him and fought to diminish recognition for the British astronomer John Adams, who many thought deserved to be named co-discoverer.

Leverrier's sense of tarnished honor, coupled with a desire for unambiguous acclaim, undoubtedly had much to do with a peculiar episode which began a few years later. Leverrier now focused his attention on the opposite end of the solar system, toward Mercury, which like Uranus had its own orbital irregularities. Though relativity theory would eventually provide a satisfactory explanation for the problem, in his time the only cause Leverrier could imagine was an intra-Mercurial plant — in other words, a world in orbit between Mercury and the sun.

On December 22, 1859, Leverrier received a letter from a country doctor and astronomy buff named Lescarbault. Lescarbault made an extraordinary claim: that on March 26, 1859, he had seen a round black spot — a planet in transit — cross the upper part of the sun's face, moving along an upward-slanting path. Over the hour and a quarter it was in view, it crossed less than one-fourth of the sun's diameter.

Leverrier immediately enlisted an associate to serve as witness, then headed straight to the village of Orgeres, where Lescarbault lived. Once there, Leverrier knocked on his door, refused to identify himself, and spoke rudely to the physician, calling him "the man who pretends to have seen an intra-Mercurial planet." He demanded to know how Lescarbault could have come to such an absurd conclusion. Thoroughly intimidated by this belligerent stranger, the physician recounted his observations in detail. At the end Leverrier revealed who he was, congratulated him warmly, and on his return to Paris saw to it that Lescarbault would be decorated with the Legion of Honor.

Within days the new discovery had the astronomical world abuzz. Leverrier, perhaps having achieved a degree of modesty after the unpleasant events surrounding Neptune's detection, suggested the planet be named Vulcan. By January, excited discussions about the discovery were appearing in the astronomical journals. Leverrier calculated its size (about 1/17th that of Mercury, he thought) and suggested that it transited the sun's face in early April and early October. He also cited twenty earlier observations of what he could now confidently identify as Vulcan.

From the beginning, however, there were skeptics. One was a Brazilian astronomer who reported that at the same time Lescarbault was observing the sun's face, he too had been doing so, only with a far more powerful telescope. He had seen nothing out of the ordinary.

Over the next few decades astronomers watched for Vulcan during the periods Leverrier believed it would be in sight. The results were mostly disappointment, erroneous observations (usually of sunspots), and some sightings of anomalous objects which, whatever they may have been, clearly were not Vulcan. By the end of the century, skepticism was nearly total. In 1899 Asaph Hall, discoverer of the moons of Mars, remarked that the planet no longer figured in the discourse of "rational astronomy."

Still, some of the sightings that played a role in the controversy were and are puzzling. A few would be called UFO reports were they to be made today. Among the more interesting were those that indicated that the objects being seen were much closer to the witnesses than they thought. If so, this would explain why — as in the case of Lescarbault's sighting — astronomers elsewhere did not see the same things.

Aside from Lescarbault's, the most publicized such instance concerned independent observations by a Wyoming astronomer and another in Colorado — but no one else — of two shining objects seen some distance from the sun during a total eclipse on July 29, 1878. A furious exchange erupted in the astronomical press, and the two were accused of having made the most elementary of errors: they had mistaken two well-known stars for two unknown objects. The two observers would have none of it. "I have never made a more valid observation," one of them, Lewis Swift, wrote in *Nature*, "nor one more free from doubt."

● SOURCES:

Campbell, W. W. "The Closing of a Famous Astronomical Problem." *Popular Science Monthly* 74 (1909): 494–503.

Corliss, William R., ed. *Mysterious Universe: A Handbook of Astronomical Anomalies.* Glen Arm, MD: The Sourcebook Project, 1979.

———. *The Sun and Solar System Debris: A Catalog of Astronomical Anomalies.* Glen Arm, MD: The Sourcebook Project, 1986.

Fort, Charles. *The Books of Charles Fort.* New York: Henry Holt and Company, 1941.

Gould, Rupert T. *Oddities: A Book of Unexplained Facts.* London: Philip Allan, 1928.

Grossinger, Richard. *The Night Sky.* Los Angeles: Jeremy P. Tarcher, 1981.

Hall, Asaph. "Plus Probans Quam Necesse Est." *Popular Astronomy* 7 (1899): 13.

Hricenak, David. "Phantom Planets and Free-Worlds." *INFO Journal* 8, 5 (March/June 1981): 5–6.

Swift, Lewis. "The Intra-Mercurial Planet Question." *Nature* 21 (1880): 299.

WEREWOLVES

In the early spring of 1971, residents of a Mobile, Alabama, neighborhood claimed to have had nocturnal encounters with an extraordinary creature. "The top half was a woman," one witness said, "and the bottom was a wolf." The witness added, unnecessarily, "It didn't seem natural."

Such reports, which the Mobile police investigated with inconclusive results, are modern echoes of ancient beliefs about werewolves — human beings apparently able to transform themselves partially or wholly into wolves. The first half of the name comes from the Teutonic *wer*, meaning "man"; thus a werewolf is a man-wolf.

Though known to most of us simply as a scary monster in horror movies and novels, the werewolf once was feared as a real-life menace. The first known use of the word in print goes back to the eleventh century, but a werewolf story survives from the first-century *Satyricon*. Beyond that, lycanthropy figures in Greek mythology, where Zeus, furious when he learns that Lykaon has served him and other gods human flesh, turns Lykaon into a wolf. Inspired by this myth, a cult took root in Arcadia. An initiate committed human sacrifice, an act that made him a "wolf" for nine years. Other scattered references in ancient writings testify to early fascination with man-wolves.

Origins.
Historians, folklorists, and psychiatrists have offered various theories about the origin of the nearly universal belief in lycanthropy, the human-animal transformation that includes not only wolves but bears, big cats, hyenas, and other fierce creatures.

Of all of these the werewolf is best known, at least in the West, no doubt because the wolf was the predator most feared by Europeans. Medieval and later chronicles tell of attacks by wolves on human beings (see *Beast*

of Gevaudan), usually during wars and hard winters. Though zoologists today attest to the wolf's harmlessness to humanity (the harm, in fact, is entirely in the other direction), folklorists W.M.S. Russell and Claire Russell argue that "it is difficult to believe that all the past accounts, often highly circumstantial, are legendary." Moreover, "modern wolves have had many generations' experience of fire-arms, and are likely to be more cautious than their ancestors." The relationship between werewolf lore and rapacious wolves is made explicit in fifteenth- to eighteenth-century books on hunting; here a wolf that has developed a taste for human flesh is called a werewolf or (in French) *loup-garou*.

In northern Europe, wolfmen or berserkers — warriors clad in suits made of wolf skin — were notoriously murderous and deeply feared. At the same time, however, in Germany it was believed that after death, honored ancestors became wolves. Their descendants were sometimes given names such as Wolfhard, Wolfbrand, and Wolfgang on the theory that thereby wolf spirits would enter them and afford them strength and courage. In the Baltic and Slavic regions of Europe, people worshipped a wolf deity of uncertain temperament; it could protect, but it could also turn on the faithful without warning. As Christianity rose to power, the priesthood condemned such pagan beliefs as Satanic.

As a consequence werewolves came to be seen as the devil's agents. Theological writers debated whether humans literally turned into wolves or simply were perceived as wolves by those whom Satan had deluded. Consensus held forth for the latter, on the grounds that only God, whose powers are greater than the devil's, could effect a physical change of species. In the words of St. Augustine:

> *It is very generally believed that by certain witches' spells and the power of the Devil men may be changed into wolves … but they do not lose their human reason and understanding, nor are their minds made the intelligence of a mere beast. Now this must be understood in this way: namely, that the Devil creates no new nature, but that he is able to make something appear to be which in reality is not. For by no spell nor evil power can the mind, nay, not even the body corporeally, be changed into the material limbs and features of any animal … but a man is fantastically and by illusion metamorphosed into an animal, albeit he to himself seems to be a quadruped.*

Persons who believed themselves to be werewolves testified, both under torture and otherwise, that they rubbed themselves with a salve before undergoing the transformation. The salve contained hallucination-inducing plants such as henbane and deadly nightshade. An interesting though in some ways unbelievable mid-eighteenth-century French account tells of a woman on trial as a suspected werewolf. Promised leniency if she would reveal her secrets, she had a pot of salve delivered from her house. After rubbing the substance on her head, neck, and shoulders, she lapsed into a three-hour coma. When she revived, she said she had turned into a wolf and in that condition killed a cow and a sheep. Investigators dispatched to the site found the animals' remains in the designated place.

The salve here is the "witches' salve," which they used to cover themselves before flying off to Sabbats. During the witch trials of the Renaissance period many writers, noting the salve's hallucinogenic effects, concluded that both Sabbats and human-wolf transformations occurred only in drug-inflamed imaginations. Others noted the role of mental illness ("melancholy"), sometimes aided and abetted by the devil's ability to confuse perception, in causing deluded individuals to believe they could turn into wolves or to think they had seen others doing so.

Werewolfery also was associated with persons we today would deem murderously mentally ill. Among the most notorious of these serial killers was Stubbe Peeter, who was tried in Germany in 1589 for 25 years of hideous crimes, including murder of adults and children (including his own son), cannibalism, incest, and attacks on animals. Peeter claimed to have made a pact with Satan, who provided him with a girdle which turned him into a wolf. Nine years later French authorities arrested Jacques Roulet, a beggar, after they found him crouched in a bush and covered with blood from the badly mutilated nearby body of a 15-year-old boy. In his confession Roulet said he had slain the youth while a werewolf, a state he entered via the application of ointment.

Modern psychiatric literature documents the survival of lycanthropy as a serious mental disorder. At least one case (described in the November 1975 issue of the *Canadian Psychiatric Association Journal*) had its origins in an LSD trip that an American soldier took in a European forest — a psychic and geographic echo of hallucinogens and werewolves past. Generally, according to psychiatrists Frida G. Surawicz and Richard Banta, lycanthropy is a "severe type of depersonalization" which may be triggered by drug abuse, paranoid schizophrenia, brain damage, or other causes. Psychoanalyst Nandor Fodor wrote that the "origin of 'lycanthropy' cannot be traced to a point in historic time or to particular civilizations. It is in the human psyche, in human experience, that the 'lycanthropic' fantasy is born.... In our dream life, the old, savage, lycanthropic beliefs are active conditions. They can be exploited, functionally, for criminal motives, while symbolically, the transformation represents self-denunciation for secret deeds or desires." Jungian psychologist Robert Eisler theorized that an archetype of the wolf, representing nature at its animal fiercest, lies deep in the collective unconscious, surviving as a kind of racial memory from a time when early human beings were hunter-killers. Under some circumstances such archetypal material may rise up to overwhelm consciousness and plunge the individual into a pathological identification with the wolf.

Sightings.
Werewolves are found not only in mythology, folklore, and popular culture but in sighting reports as well. There are, however, relatively few of these. Of course, this is exactly what we would expect if werewolves — that is, man-wolves — do not exist, as every sensible person assumes. On the other hand, most of what we know about the werewolf tradition is filtered through the writings of anthropologists and folklorists; they, being sensible people, ignored sighting reports from native informants or perhaps

● SOURCES:

Andrade, J. M. "The Wolfman of Aveloso." *Fate* 33, 9 (September 1980): 47–50.

Burton, Brigadier-General R. G. "Wolf-Children and Werewolves." *Chambers's Journal 7*, 14 (1924): 306–10.

Cheilik, Michael. "The Werewolf." In Malcolm South, ed. *Mythical and Fabulous Creatures: A Source Book and Research Guide*, 265– 89. New York: Greenwood Press, 1987.

Clark, Jerome, and Loren Coleman. *Creatures of the Outer Edge*. New York: Warner Books, 1978.

Coleman, Loren. "The Cryptozoo News." *Strange Magazine 7* (April 1991): 38–41.

Fodor, Nandor. *The Haunted Mind: A Psychoanalyst Looks at the Supernatural*. New York: Garrett Publications, 1959.

Gordon, Stan. "UFOs, in Relation to Creature Sightings in Pennsylvania." In Walter H. Andrus, Jr., ed. *MUFON 1974 UFO Symposium Proceedings*, 132–49. Seguin, TX: Mutual UFO Network, 1974.

416

never thought to ask about them, on the assumption that since werewolves do not exist, no one could have seen one.

Still, werewolves are only marginally less improbable than other things people see or think they see, as many other entries in this book attest. In short, we ought not to be too surprised at sighting reports, which are real enough even if werewolves are not. Yet most of the sightings are poorly documented, and those that come from apparently credible witnesses may be subject to other interpretations, albeit perhaps not in every instance one that will please those determined to link each oddity of human testimony to a comfortingly conventional stimulus. In any case, if the stories that follow do not amount to a case for real-life man-wolves, they are nonetheless worth noting, and they are undeniably interesting.

In a 1960 issue of Fate, Mrs. Delburt Gregg of Greggton, Texas, told of an encounter with a shapeshifting creature. Such reports are exceedingly rare in modern times. The other sightings surveyed below are simply of creatures that *looked* like man-wolves; nobody claims to have seen one becoming another. Mrs. Gregg does not make such a claim either, but she comes closer than anyone else in a tale that sounds more like an early chapter from a werewolf novel than a real-life experience.

As her story goes, one night in July 1958 while her husband was away on business, Mrs. Gregg moved her bed close to a screened window hoping to catch the cool breeze from a thunderstorm brewing on the southwestern horizon. She had dozed off only a short time before she heard a scratching sound on the screen. In a flash of lightning she saw a "huge, shaggy, wolflike creature... clawing at the screen and glaring at me with baleful, glowing, slitted eyes. I could see its bared white fangs."

She leaped from bed and grabbed a flashlight as the creature fled through the yard and into a clump of bushes. "I watched for the animal to come out of the bushes," she wrote, "but, after a short time, instead of a great shaggy wolf running out, the figure of an extremely tall man suddenly parted the thick foliage and walked hurriedly down the road, disappearing into the darkness."

More characteristic of modern American werewolf stories are those told between July and October 1972 by a number of residents of Ohio. They reported seeing a six- to eight-foot-tall creature which one witness described as "human, with an oversized, wolflike head, and an elongated nose." Another said it "had huge, hairy feet, fangs, and it ran from side to side, like a caveman in the movies." It also had glowing red eyes. During the early morning hours it allegedly sneaked up behind a trainman working along the tracks in downtown Defiance and whacked him with a two-by-four. Presumably we have here a prankster or a madman dressed to scare.

Four Gallup, New Mexico, youths allegedly encountered what they called a "werewolf" along the side of a road near Whitewater one day in January 1970. It managed to pace with their car, which was traveling at 45 miles

Grof, Stanislav. *The Adventure of Self-Discovery.* Albany, NY: State University of New York Press, 1988.

Gregg, Mrs. Delburt. "True Mystic Experiences: Werewolf?" *Fate* 13, 3 (March 1960): 60–61.

"Is 'Wolf Woman' Sulking Around the City? Various Area Persons Claim Seeing Creature." *Mobile* [Alabama] *Register* (April 8, 1971).

James, Farley. "The Home of the Loup-Garou." *Fate* 16, 10 (October 1963): 42–47.

Lidman, Mark J. "Wild Men and Werewolves: An Investigation of the Iconography of Lycanthropy." *Journal of Popular Culture* 10, 2 (Fall 1976): 388–97.

Otten, Charlotte F., ed. *A Lycanthropy Reader: Werewolves in Western Culture.* New York: Dorset Press, 1986.

Russell, W.M.S., and Claire Russell. "The Social Biology of Werewolves." In J. R. Porter and W.M.S. Russell, eds. *Animals in Folklore,* 143–82. Totowa, NJ: Rowman and Littlefield, 1978.

Schwarz, Berthold Eric. "Berserk: A UFO-Crea-

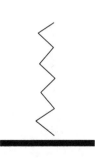

ture Encounter." *Flying Saucer Review* 20, 1 (July 1974): 3–11.

"Search for 'Wolf Girl' Unsuccessful." *Kansas City Times* (July 29, 1974).

Stein, Gordon. "Werewolves." *Fate* 41, 1 (January 1988): 30–40.

Woods, Barbara Allen. "The Devil in Dog Form." *Western Folklore* 13, 4 (October 1954): 229–35.

per hour. One witness reported, "It was about five feet seven, and I was surprised it could go so fast. At first I thought my friends were playing a joke on me, but when I found out they weren't, I was scared! We rolled up the windows real fast and locked the doors of the car. I started driving faster, about 60, but it was hard because that highway has a lot of sharp turns. Someone finally got a gun out and shot it. I know it got hit and it fell down, but there was no blood. I know it couldn't be a person because people cannot move that fast."

This sounds like a "skin-walker," the name the Navahos of the Southwest give to the werewolf. In 1936, in *Yale Publications in Anthropology*, anthropologist William Morgan recounted an interview with a Navaho identified only as Hahago. Hahago said of skin-walkers, "They go very fast.... They can go to Albuquerque in an hour and a half" — a four-hour trip by automobile, according to Morgan.

In the fall of 1973 western Pennsylvania played host to dozens of reports of strange apelike creatures, sometimes seen in association with UFOs, said to have (in one witness's words) "fire red eyes that glowed in total darkness," to be seven to eight feet tall, and to give off a strong, unpleasant odor. "Another type of creature," investigator Stan Gordon noted, "was said to be between five and six feet tall. It was described as looking just like an extremely muscular man with a covering of thick dark hair. Again in these reports, the arms were very long and hung down past the knees. This creature appeared to have superior agility exceeding that of a deer. From footprints discovered, the stride of the creatures varies between 52 and 57 inches. In these reports there was no indication of odors." Two sketches published in *Flying Saucer Review* (January 1974, page 5) show these creatures to bear a striking resemblance to the traditional werewolf, though neither witnesses nor investigators remarked on the fact.

If these stories are not outright hoaxes, they clearly indicate the presence of extraordinary, otherworldly creatures which challenge consensus views of reality. On the other hand, in some cases it is possible both to believe the witnesses and to keep one's ties to reality intact. In the Delphos, Kansas, area during July 1974, for example, several persons encountered what a newspaper described as a "young child about 10 or 12 years old, with blood, matted hair, dressed in tattered clothing[,] running through vines and brush in a wooded area in the northwest edge of Delphos." She was dubbed the "wolf girl." Though local authorities never found her, she may well have existed, probably as a mentally retarded runaway or abandoned child.

Some medically educated theorists have suggested that sightings of werewolves really were of individuals afflicted with a rare genetic disease called porphyria. Porphyria sufferers experience tissue destruction in the face and fingers, skin lesions, and severe photosensitivity. Their facial skin may take on a brown pigmentation, and they may fall victim to personality disorders. The aversion to light, plus the physical disfigurement, may lead the victim to wander about only at night. "These features," British neurologist L. Illis wrote in a 1964 issue of *Proceedings of the Royal Society of Medicine*, "fit well with the description, in older literature, of werewolves."

WHEELS OF LIGHT ——————————————

Passing between Oyster Reed and Pigeon Island in the Indian Ocean late on a calm, starlit January evening in 1880, Cmdr. R. E. Harris and other crew members of the steamship *Shahihehan* saw an incredible sight. Harris's account was published in the *Calcutta Englishman* on January 21:

> *I ... observed a streak of white matter on the horizing bearing south-south-west. I then went to the bridge and drew the third officer's attention to it. In a few minutes it had assumed the shape of a segment of a circle measuring about 45 degrees in length and several degrees in altitude about its center. At this time it shone with a peculiar but beautiful milky whiteness, and resembled (only in a huge mass, and greater luminous intensity) the nebulae sometimes seen in the heavens. We were steaming to the southward, and as the bank of light extended, one of its arms crossed our path. The whole thing appeared so foreign to anything I had ever seen, and so wonderful, that I stopped the ship just on its outskirts, so that I might try to form a true and just conception of what it really was. By this time all the officers and engineers had assembled on deck to witness the scene, and were all equally astonished and interested. Some little time before the first body of light reached the ship I was enabled, with my night glasses, to resolve in a measure what appeared, to the unassisted eye, a huge mass of nebulous matter. I distinctly saw spaces between what again appeared to be waves of light of great luster. These came rolling on with ever-increasing rapidity till they reached the ship, and in a short time the ship was completely surrounded with one great body of undulating light, which soon extended to the horizon on all sides. On looking into the water it was seen to be studded with patches of faint, luminous, inanimate matter, measuring about two feet in diameter. Although these emitted a certain amount of light, it was most insignificant when compared with the great waves of light that were floating on the surface of the water, and which were at this time converging*

upon the ship. The waves stood many degrees above the water, like a highly luminous mist, and obscured by their intensity the distant horizon; and as wave succeeded wave in rapid succession, one of the most grand and brilliant, yet solemn, spectacles that one could ever think of was here witnessed. In speaking of waves of light I do not wish to convey the idea that they were mere ripplings, which are sometimes caused by fish passing through a phosphorescent sea, but waves of great length and breadth, or in other words, great bodies of light. If the sea could be converted into a huge mirror and thousands of powerful electric lights were made to throw their rays across it, it would convey no adequate idea of this strange yet grand phenomenon.

As the waves of light converged upon the ship from all sides they appeared higher than her hull, and looked as if they were about to envelop her, and as they impinged upon her, her sides seemed to collapse and expand.

Whilst this was going on the ship was perfectly at rest, and the water was like a millpond.

After about half an hour had elapsed the brilliance of the light somewhat abated, and there was a great paucity of faint lustrous patches which I have before referred to, but still the body of light was gone, and, if emanating from these patches, was out of all proportion to their number.

This light I do not think could have been produced without the agency of electro-magnetic currents exercising their exciting influence upon some organic animal or vegetable substance; and one thing I wish to point out is, that whilst the ship was stopped and the light yet some distance away, nothing was discernible in the water, but so soon as the light reached the ship a number of luminous patches presented themselves, and as these were equally as motionless as the ship at the time, it is only natural to assume that they existed and were actually in our vicinity before the light reached us, only they were not made visible till they became the transmitting media for the electro-magnetic currents. This hypothesis is borne out by the fact that each wave of light in its passage was distinctly seen to pass over them in succession, and as the light became gradually less brilliant, they also became less distinct, and had actually disappeared so soon as the waves of light ceased to exist.

On May 15, 1879, on a clear night, the captain of the H.M.S. *Vulture* recorded a similarly extraordinary phenomenon, observed in the Persian Gulf:

I noticed luminous waves or pulsations in the water, moving at great speed and passing under the ship from the south-south-west. On looking towards the east, the appearance was that of a revolving wheel with center on that bearing, and whose spokes were illuminated, and

looking towards the west a similar wheel appeared to be revolving, but in the opposite direction. I then went to the mizen top (fifty feet above water) with the first lieutenant, and saw that the luminous waves or pulsations were really travelling parallel to each other, and that their apparently rotatory motion, as seen from the deck, was caused by their high speed and the greater angular motion of the nearer than the more remote part of the waves. The light of these waves looked homogeneous, and lighter, but not so sparkling, as phosphorescent appearances at sea usually are, and extended from the surface well under water; they lit up the white bottoms of the quarter-boats in passing. I judged them to be twenty-five feet broad, with dark intervals of about seventy-five between each, or 100 from crest to crest, and their period was seventy-four to seventy-five per minute, giving a speed roughly of eighty-four English miles an hour.

From this height of fifty feet, looking with or against their direction, I could only distinguish six or seven waves; but, looking along them as they passed under the ship, the luminosity showed much further.

The phenomenon was beautiful and striking, commencing at about 6h. 3m. Greenwich mean time [9:40 P.M.], and lasting some thirty-five minutes. The direction from which the luminous waves travelled changed from south-south-west by degrees to south-east and to east. During the last five minutes concentric waves appeared to emanate from a spot about 200 yards east, and these meeting the parallel waves from south-east did not cross, but appeared to obliterate each other at the moving point of contact, and approached the ship, inclosing an angle about 90 degrees.

Such strange phenomena continue to be seen to the present day, mostly (though not exclusively) in the Indian Ocean. Sometimes they appear in association with luminous parallel bars, as in this September 27, 1959, incident from the East Indian Archipelago. This account appeared in the journal *Marine Observer* in 1960:

The first indication of anything unusual was the appearance of white caps on the sea here and there, which made me think that the wind had freshened, but I could feel that this was not so. Then flashing beams appeared over the water, which made the Officer on watch think that the fishing boats were using powerful flashlights. These beams of light became more intense and appeared absolutely parallel, about 8 ft wide, and could be seen coming from right ahead at about 1/2 sec intervals. At this time, I thought I could hear a swish as they passed, but decided that this was imagination. They did not appear like rings or arcs of a circle, unless it was a circle so big as to make them appear as straight lines. It was like the pedestrian's angle of a huge zebra crossing passing under him whilst he is standing still. While this part of the phenomenon was at its height it looked as if huge seas were dashing towards the vessel, and the sea surface appeared to be boiling, but it was more or less normal around a fish-

421

● SOURCES:

Corliss, William R., ed. *Strange Phenomena: A Sourcebook of Unusual Natural Phenomena.* Glen Arm, MD: The Author, 1974.

———. *Handbook of Unusual Natural Phenomena.* Glen Arm, MD: The Sourcebook Project, 1977.

———. *Lightning, Auroras, Nocturnal Lights, and Related Luminous Phenomena: A Catalog of Geophysical Anomalies.* Glen Arm, MD: The Sourcebook Project, 1982.

Cramp, Leonard G. *Piece for a Jig-Saw.* Cowes, Isle of Wight: Somerton Publishing Company, 1966.

Durant, Robert J. "Submarine Lightwheels." *Pursuit* 7, 3 (July 1974): 58–59.

Fort, Charles. *The Books of Charles Fort.* New York: Henry Holt and Company, 1941.

Hall, Richard. "Aerial Anomalies at Sea." *INFO Journal* 4, 3 (May 1975): 6–9.

ing vessel which we passed fairly close. The lights of various fishing vessels were visible through the beams of light, though dimmed by the brightness of the latter. The character of the flashes changed and took on the appearance of beams from a lighthouse situated about two miles on the starboard bow, or as if the center of a giant wheel was somewhere on the starboard bow with the beams as its spokes. As the beams from the vessel on the starboard bow weakened, the same pattern appeared on the port bow at the same distance and regularity. The wheel on the starboard bow revolved anticlockwise and the one on the port bow revolved clockwise, i.e. both wheels were revolving towards the ship. The wheel on the starboard bow diminished as the one on the port bow increased; when the latter was at its peak the one on the starboard bow had disappeared. The next change was that the beams appeared to be travelling in the exact course of the ship, i.e., the beams now seen were a reversal of those seen at first.

More than a hundred well-attested sightings like these have been recorded in the last century and a half. To the extent that scientists have paid attention, they have been forced to acknowledge that these phenomena seem to defy explanation. Nearly all witnesses and commentators agree that the glow comes from bioluminescent organisms in the sea. The problem is explaining what triggers the luminescence and what causes the organisms to manifest in long-lasting, fast-moving, stable, complex geometric patterns.

Not surprisingly these marine apparitions have inspired speculation about "vast wheel-like super-constructions," in the words of Charles Fort. Fort's disciple Ivan T. Sanderson theorized that "some source of energy starts broadcasting some invisible 'waves' on the electromagnetic (or other) spectrum which stimulate or activate the light-producing mechanisms of the *Noctiluca* [single-celled bioluminescent sea creatures].... [This] energy is broadcast in the form of a series of radiating bands whose source of origin is revolving; we would then have a progressive and, to our eyes, instantaneous turning on and off of the *Noctiluca* as the beams swept by them."

Such speculations would be more compelling if, for one thing, witnesses reported the kind of water displacement one would expect from the rapid passage, not far under the surface, of a vast structure. Instead witnesses insist on the sea's placidity during the sighting.

We would also expect sightings of airborne structures of comparable description. Even Fort, who thought the wheels to be of extraterrestrial origin, found only one — a December 20, 1893, report of an "enormous wheel" over three Southeastern states — and its relevance is by no means certain. As Sanderson points out, the "'wheels of light' are not wheels at all but might better be called 'sunbursts,' like the old Japanese flag."

Nonetheless one intriguing report leaves the question of a UFO/light-wheel link open at least a crack. It is said to have taken place in September 1961, near Leba, Poland, a resort on the Baltic Sea coast. Late one evening a vacationer, Czeslaw Kawecki, on a walk through the sand dunes that

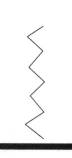

separate the sea from an inland lake, stopped to look out on the Baltic. After a short time he turned to go, only to hear a sound of rushing waters. He whirled around in time to see something rising out of the water 100 yards away. "It looked like a round hill — pushed up from beneath," he said. "Then splashes of water gushed from the top and like fountain jets fell around the 'hole' in the waves. From this opening in the water emerged an object which at first I took to be an elongated triangle.... [T]he object rose a few meters and hovered above the same spot, and there was now a whirlpool of water rushing inwards with a loud sucking and gurgling noise. The object itself was black and silent."

Sanderson, Ivan T. *Invisible Residents: A Disquisition upon Certain Matters Maritime, and the Possibility of Intelligent Life Under the Earth.* New York: The World Publishing Company, 1970.

Leonard G. Cramp gives this account in his *Piece for a Jig-Saw* (1966):

> Suddenly there appeared a belt of steady white light segmented by a number of convex dark streaks. This light made glowing reflections on the lower rim of the object. It also lighted considerably the upper rim and all the rest. Now it became apparent that "the thing" had the shape of a huge funnel with two rims, separated by a belt of segmented light. About half way up the upper part was a thin strip of something whiter than the rest, of a rather dark body. The slim end of this "funnel" had a rounded top, from which protruded a stump, thinning upwards, and bent in the middle on one side.
>
> The stillness of this object lasted about a minute[;] then, there appeared the glow of a second light under the object. Also a white one, but much stronger and sharper than that emitted by the segmented belt and almost immediately the "funnel" tilted slowly northwards revealing the bottom. After remaining in this position for about half a minute without changing, it glided about 50 meters eastwards, stopped but soon glided back and stopped again. All the time the bottom of the object was visible and consisted of a dark circular perimeter corresponding to the lower (and wider) rim of the "funnel." Towards the center was a wide ring of strong white light, with a number of dark, hook-shaped streaks upon it. Next was a dark ring with three evenly spaced triangular spokes, which protruded over half the width of the lit, streaky ring. Finally, there was a central disc which looked as if it was made of highly polished silver or crystal. It reflected the light with great brilliance.

"There was some rotating movement involved," Kawecki reported. "I could not make out whether the spikes were moving or the dark streaks gyrated under them. But I had no doubt that one or the other rotated. The light now became bluish and more intense. Then the object moved towards the north and upwards at an angle of about 45 degrees, with a speed not exceeding that of a jet. It became just a diminishing spot of light until it finally disappeared. There was no sound. The entire observation lasted not more than four to five minutes."

The object was about 18 feet wide and 20 feet high. After the UFO's departure he noticed several other persons who had also witnessed the bizarre sight.

423

WHITE RIVER MONSTER —————————————————

From about 1915 through the early 1970s, residents of Newport in north-eastern Arkansas occasionally reported seeing a "monster" in the White River, which flows through the town. Sightings were not continuous but tended to occur in spates. In July 1937, for example, a number of local people either saw strange disturbances in the water or caught a glimpse of the cause.

One witness was Bramblett Bateman, who in an affidavit swore he had seen, on or around July 1, "something appear on the surface of the water. From the best I could tell, from the distance [375 feet], it would be 12 feet long and four or five feet wide. I did not see either head nor [sic] tail, but it slowly rose to the surface and stayed in this position for some five minutes. It did not move up or down the river at this particular time, but afterward on different occasions I have seen it move up and down the river, but I never have, at any time, been able to determine the full length or size of said monster."

Jackson County Deputy Sheriff Z. B. Reid was with Bateman when the creature appeared later that July 1. They saw, Reid testified, "a lot of foam and bubbles coming up in a circle about 30 feet in diameter some 300 feet from where we were standing. It did not come up there but appeared about 300 feet upstream. It looked like a large sturgeon or cat fish. It went down in about two minutes."

The next publicized sightings occurred in June and July 1971. One witness reported seeing a "creature the size of a boxcar thrashing ... the length of three or four pickup trucks" and two yards across. "It looked as if the thing was peeling all over, but it was a smooth type of skin or flesh," he said. Other sighters, one of whom took a blurry photograph of a large surfacing form on June 28, described (as had witnesses in previous decades) a roar associated with the creature's appearance, a combination of a cow's moo and a horse's neigh. On those rare occasion its face was seen, if only briefly, it was said to have a protruding "bone" on its forehead.

In the most frightening encounter, Ollie Ritcherson and Joey Dupree were cruising near Towhead Island looking for the monster when their boat collided with something. The boat rose into the air on the back of some huge animal which they were not able to see clearly. The two had come to the site because two weeks earlier huge tracks leading to and from the river had been found on the island. Each of the three-toed tracks was 14 inches long and eight inches wide, with a large pad and another toe with a spur extending at an angle. There was evidence, in the form of bent trees and crushed vegetation, that a large animal had walked on the island and even lain down at one point.

According to biologist Roy P. Mackal, "The White River case is a clear-cut instance of a known aquatic animal outside its normal habitat or range and therefore unidentified by the observers unfamiliar with the type. The animal in question clearly was a large male elephant seal, either *Mirounga leonina* (southern species) or *Mirounga angustirostris* (northern species)." Mackal suggests that the creature wandered up through the mouth of the Mississippi River to the White River, which branches off from the Mississippi in east-central Arkansas.

A more startling hypothesis was suggested by another maverick biologist, Ivan T. Sanderson, who labeled it "a truly gigantic penguin."

● SOURCES:

"Arkansas Has a Problem." *Pursuit* 4 (October 1971): 89–95.

Mackal, Roy P. *Searching for Hidden Animals: An Inquiry Into Zoological Mysteries.* Garden City, NY: Doubleday and Company, 1980.

WILDMAN

For centuries, in remote regions of central and southern China, residents and travelers have spoken of something called the "wildman," or yeren. Early literary references to what seems to be the same creature also refer to it as a "hill ghost," "mountain monster," "man bear," or "monkeylike, but not a monkey." A seventeenth-century account from Hubei province notes, "In the remote mountains of Fangxian County, there are rock caves, in which live hairy men as tall as three meters. They often come down to hunt dogs and chickens in the villages. They fight with whoever resists."

Though in the late 1950s some Chinese scientists took an active interest in the yeti, the "abominable snowman" of the Himalayas, China's native hairy giants attracted neither notice nor respect. Except to those who claimed direct encounters — mostly peasants and soldiers in the provinces but also at least two scientists — conventional wisdom relegated the yeren to the realm of popular superstition. Yet had anyone had been paying attention, he or she would have heard some interesting stories.

For example, biologist Wang Tselin reportedly saw a yeren killed in 1940 in the Gansu area. It was, he said, a female about six and a half feet tall and covered with grayish-brown hair, with a face that combined human and ape features in a way that reminded him of the prehistoric Beijing Man. In 1950 geologist Fan Jingquan said he observed two wildmen, apparently mother and son, in a mountain forest on two occasions.

The first official inquiry was launched in 1961, following the reported slaying of a female yeren by road builders in a thick forest in the Xishuang Banna area. By the time representatives of the Chinese Academy of Sciences came to the region, the body was no longer available, and the scientists concluded that the animal had been nothing more than a gibbon. This skeptical analysis killed government interest in the question for the next fifteen years, though two decades later Zhou Guoxing, an anthropologist with the Beijing Natural History Museum, would interview a local journalist who participated in the investigation. According to Zhou, "He stated that the animal which had been killed was not a gibbon, but an unknown animal of human shape."

A multiple-witness 1976 encounter revived interest in the yeren and brought it international attention for the first time. Early in the morning of May 14, six local bureaucrats on their way home from a meeting spotted a "strange, tailless creature with reddish fur" on a rural highway near Chunshuya, Hubei province. Switching the headlights on high, the driver followed the creature as it tried to escape up an embankment along the roadside. It slipped and landed right in front of the jeep, which nearly hit it. The five passengers jumped out and surrounded the beast, now positioned on all fours and staring directly into the headlights.

Afraid to approach it too closely, the witnesses, who were not armed, got no closer than six feet. One of them, Zhou Zhongyi, tossed a rock at the yeren's buttocks, causing it to stand briefly. At this the group retreated, and the animal lumbered away and this time executed a successful climb up the slope.

The party described the creature as over six feet tall, covered in thick brown- and purpled-red wavy hair, with a fat belly and pronounced buttocks. The eyes struck them as humanlike, but the face was clearly apelike, with large ears and a protruding monkeylike snout.

Investigations and evidence.
This sighting caused something of a stir at the Chinese Academy of Sciences, which the next year sent 110 investigators into the field. They concentrated their efforts on the forests of Fang County and the Shennongjia area of Hubei, a massive forest preserve of steep mountains and deep valleys where a wide variety of rare and exotic animals, including the giant panda (discovered only in 1869), live. None of the participants had a personal sighting, but witnesses were interviewed and alleged yeren footprints, hair, and feces were collected.

Zhou Guoxing, one of the expedition leaders, later noted that there seemed to be two types of yeren: "a larger one of about two meters in height, and a smaller one, about one meter in height." There were also two types of footprints: "One is large, 30–40 cm, remarkably similar to that of man, with the four small toes held together and the largest one pointing slightly outwards. The other type is smaller, about 20 cm, and more similar to the footprint of an ape or monkey, with the largest toe evidently pointing outwards."

The second, smaller type of yeren seems beyond dispute, and in fact it is possible, according to Zhou, that both living and dead specimens are already in scientists' hands. One was killed on May 23, 1957, near the village of Zhuanxian in Zhejiang province. A biology teacher had the presence of mind to preserve the hands and feet. When Zhou learned of this in

● SOURCES:

Bord, Janet, and Colin Bord. *The Evidence for Bigfoot and Other Man-Beasts.* Wellingborough, Northamptonshire, England: The Aquarian Press, 1984.

Coleman, Loren. *The Yeti and the Yeren.* Portland, ME: The Author, 1992.

Coleman, Loren, and Peter Rodman. "Abominable Wild Man Roams China." *Fate* 34, 6 (June 1981): 58–62.

Greenwell, J. Richard, and Frank E. Poirier. "Further Investigations Into the Reported Yeren — The Wildman of China." *Cryptozoology* 8 (1989): 47–57.

Lapseritis, Jack, and Frank E. Poirier. "Comments and Responses." *Cryptozoology* 3 (1984): 122–25.

"New Chinese Wildman Investigation." *The ISC Newsletter* 9, 2 (Summer 1990): 8–9.

Poirier, Frank E. "Comments and Responses: More on China's Wildman." *Cryptozoology* 6 (1987): 141.

Poirier, Frank E., Hu Hongxing, and Chung-Min Chen. "The Evidence for Wildman in Hubei Province, People's

Republic of China." *Cryptozoology* 2 (Winter 1983): 25–39.

Poirier, Frank E., and Michael K. Diamond. "Comments and Responses." *Cryptozoology* 4 (1985): 112–14.

Sanderson, Ivan T. *Abominable Snowmen: Legend Come to Life.* Philadelphia: Chilton Book Company, 1961.

Topping, Audrey. "Hairy Wild Men of China." *Science Digest* 89, 7 (August 1981): 64–67, 113.

"Wild Man." *Fortean Times* 42 (Autumn 1984): 23.

Wren, Christopher S. "On the Trail of the 'Wild Man' of China." *New York Times* (June 5, 1984).

Yuan Zhenxzin and Huang Wanpo. *Wildman.* London: Fortean Times, 1981.

———. "Wildman: Fact or Fiction." *Fortean Times* 31 (Spring 1980): 2–5.

Zhou Guoxing. "The Status of Wildman Research in China." *Cryptozoology* 1 (Winter 1982): 13–23.

———. "Morphological Analysis of the Jiulong Mountain 'Manbear' (Wildman) Hand and

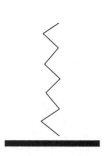

1981, he went to the site and collected the specimens. After some considerable study he concluded that they "belonged to a kind of large stump-tailed monkey unknown to science." Subsequently he identified the animal as a stump-tailed macaque. Not long afterwards just such an animal was captured in the Huang Mountain region and taken to the Hefei Zoo. Zhou wrote that this specimen

> *is mainly ground-dwelling.... The body is large, about 70–90 cm in standing height. A tall individual could reach one meter. Its extremities are strongly built. It weighs more than 20 kilograms. A large male could weigh over 33 kilograms, while females would be smaller. The back hair is brown in color. The adult male has whiskers, and has a reddish color on the face.*

Ohio State University anthropologist Frank E. Poirier suggested that many yeren reports — he made no distinction between the taller and shorter varieties — were probably sightings of a rare, endangered animal which inhabits the region but which is seldom seen: the golden monkey. After a 1989 expedition, however, Poirier moderated his earlier conviction that the yeren does not exist, at least as an unknown animal, notwithstanding the fact that, as he and colleague J. Richard Greenwell acknowledged, "the umbrella-term *yeren* (Wildman) has encompassed a wide variety of known animals, such as bears, gibbon apes, and macaque and golden monkeys." Poirier himself was once mistaken for a yeren, after villagers who had never seen a Westerner encountered a near-nude Poirier napping by a river.

Poirier and Greenwell speculate that the smaller, quadrupedal yeren may be "orang-utans (*Pongo*), either the known species or, more likely, a related species — perhaps even a fossil form — populations of which may survive in rugged and isolated pockets of the country."

The smaller yeren, in short, is a question largely of interest to primatologists. But the other yeren, if accurately described, is something else: a Chinese cousin of North America's Bigfoot/Sasquatch. Entirely bipedal, it stands between six and eight feet tall and has a strikingly humanlike face. A witness gave this description to Academy of Sciences researchers:

> *He was about seven feet tall, with shoulders wider than a man's, a sloping forehead, deep-set eyes and a bulbous nose with slightly upturned nostrils. He had sunken cheeks, ears like a man's but bigger, and round eyes, also bigger than a man's. His jaw jutted out and he had protruding lips. His front teeth were as broad as a horse's. His eyes were black. His hair was dark brown, more than a foot long and hung loosely over his shoulders. His whole face, except for the nose and ears, was covered with short hairs. His arms hung below his knees. He had big hands with fingers about six inches long and thumbs only slightly separated from the fingers. He didn't have a tail, and the hair on his body was short. He had thick thighs, shorter than the lower part of his leg. He walked upright with his legs apart. His feet were each about 12 inches long and half that broad — broader in*

front and narrow behind, with splayed toes. He was a male. That much I saw clearly.

Investigators have collected dozens of alleged yeren hairs and examined them in laboratories. Li Jian, a historian of science and secretary general of the Society for the Survey and Research of the Chinese Wildman, told the *New York Times* that microscopic comparison of eight such hairs with samples from human beings, apes, goats, and pigs had indicated the "wild man is in the middle between bears or apes and human beings." Studying samples from various regions of China, physicists at Fudan University determined that the proportion of iron to zinc was 50 times that found in human hair and seven times that in the hair of recognized primates. As Poirier and Greenwell observe, this appears to suggest that "some specific Wildman hairs derive from a higher primate not yet known to zoology." An independent analysis produced an identical finding.

Biologists at East China Normal University used a scanning electron microscope to examine yeren hairs which they compared to samples of human and primate hairs. Their conclusion: the former were neither human nor known primate hair but from an unrecognized primate with a morphological affinity to humans. This discovery, of course, is consistent with what one would expect from eyewitness descriptions of the large yeren.

Among zoologists prepared to accept the possibility of the large yeren's existence, a favorite speculation, shared by Bigfoot researchers, is that the creature is a surviving *Gigantopithecus*, a giant, apparently biped primate believed to have gone extinct in China some 300,000 years ago after a 8 million-year evolutionary history. "It takes only a little 'push' to propose its survival another half-million years to the present time," Poirier and Greenwell write, pointing out that the giant panda, which is just as old, shares the same habitat.

Foot Specimens." *Cryptozoology* 3 (1984): 58–70.

———. "Comments and Responses: On Wildman Reports and Chinese Macaques." *Cryptozoology* 5 (1986): 109–11.

YETI

In 1832, writing in the *Journal of the Asiatic Society of Bengal*, B. H. Hodgson, British Resident of the court of Nepal, made what may be the first reference in English to a strange biped in the Himalayas. He related that as they were collecting specimens in a northern Nepal province, his native hunters encountered an erect, tailless creature with long, dark hair all over its body. Taking it to be a demon, they fled in terror. Hodgson took it to be an orangutan.

In 1889 Maj. L. A. Waddell became the first Westerner to come upon a mysterious humanlike footprint in the Himalayan snows. His Sherpa guides told him that the track, found at 17,000 feet, was from a hairy wild man of a sort long known to them. "The belief in these creatures is universal among Tibetans," Waddell wrote in *Among the Himalayas* (1899), but none with whom he spoke "could ever give me an authentic case. On the most superficial investigation it always resolved into something that somebody had heard tell of." He was sure these creatures were in fact "great yellow snow-bears."

The first Westerner actually to see what may have been such creatures (though there are other, unsubstantiated claims for that distinction) was Lt. Col. C. K. Howard-Bury, who led a reconnaissance expedition up Mount Everest in September 1921. At 20,000 feet on the side of the mountain that faces northern Tibet, the group found a large number of footprints three times the size human beings would make. The Sherpas attributed them to what Howard-Bury, apparently incorrectly, transcribed as *metoh-kangmi*. A Calcutta Statesman columnist who was shown the colonial officer's official report mistranslated the word as "abominable snowman." Apparently Howard-Bury had misunderstood the Sherpa term meh-teh, which means, approximately, "manlike thing that is not a man."

In any case, "abominable snowman" entered the English language and popular culture soon afterwards, as a consequence of the massive newspa-

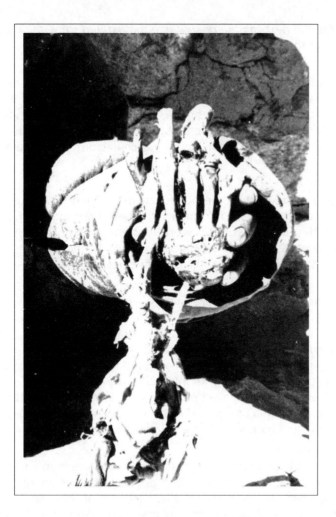

431

per coverage accorded Howard-Bury's testimony, notwithstanding his belief that the tracks "were probably caused by a large 'loping' grey wolf, which in the soft snow formed double tracks rather like those of a bare-footed man." This explanation is hard to square with what Howard-Bury describes of the prints.

Four years later N. A. Tombazi, a British photographer and member of the Royal Geographical Society, saw a strange creature in the Himalaya range. The incident occurred near the Zemu Glacier, at 15,000 feet altitude. He recorded this account:

> The intense glare and brightness of the snow prevented me from seeing anything for the first few seconds; but I soon spotted the "object" referred to, about two to three hundred yards away down the valley to the east of our camp. Unquestionably, the figure in outline was exactly like a human being, walking upright and stopping occasionally to uproot or pull at some dwarf rhododendron bushes. It showed up dark against the snow and, as far as I could make out, wore no clothes.

Within the next minute or so it had moved into some thick scrub and was lost to view.

Two hours later, as the party descended, Tombazi went to check the area where he had seen the creature. There he examined 16 footprints "similar in shape to those of a man, but only six to seven inches long by four inches wide at the broadest part of the foot....The prints were undoubtedly of a biped, the order of the spoor having no characteristics whatever of any imaginable quadruped."

From these somewhat vague accounts, plus much more specific and detailed ones from native informants, the yeti (from the Sherpa *yeh-teh*, meaning "that thing") entered world consciousness. Since then it has inspired countless expeditions, speculations, and debates, with no resolution in sight and the quality of the evidence not significantly improved.

Probably the most interesting sighting by a Westerner took place on Mount Annapurna in 1970. The witness, prominent British mountaineer Don Whillans, was looking for a campsite one evening when odd cries sounded. His Sherpa companion said they were a yeti's call, and Whillans caught a glimpse of a dark figure on a distant ridge. The next day he found humanlike tracks sunk 18 inches into the snow, and that night, sensing the creature's presence, he looked out of his tent and saw, in the moonlight, an ape-shaped animal as it plucked at tree branches. He watched it for 20 minutes through binoculars before it wandered away.

This far from adequate description is the best we have from any other than native sources. Many Western writers are suspicious of Sherpa accounts, as primatologist John Napier remarks, "because of their vagueness as to time and place, the obvious garnish of common folklore themes, and motivation derived from the animistic philosophy of Tibetan Buddhism." There are also other problems, as we shall see, associated with some demonstrably dubious claims of physical evidence of yetis.

Still, if yetis exist, the people most likely to encounter them are the people who share the neighborhood, and that the hardy Sherpas surely do. Investigators who take their testimony seriously have recorded their conviction that at least two yetis exist: the *dzu-teh* ("big thing"), seven to eight feet tall, and the meh-teh, in the five- to six-foot range. Far more frequently reported than the *dzu-teh*, the *meh-teh* is what most people think of as the "abominable snowman." Edward W. Cronin, Jr., gives this composite description:

Its body is stocky, apelike in shape, with a distinctly human quality to it, in contrast to that of a bear. It stands five and a half to six feet tall and is covered with short, coarse hair, reddish-brown to black in color, sometimes with white patches on the chest. The hair is longest on the shoulders. The face is robust, the teeth are quite large, though fangs are not present, and the mouth is wide. The shape of the head is conical, with a pointed crown. The arms are long, reaching almost to the knees. The shoulders are heavy and hunched. There is no tail.

Physical evidence?

In the scientific and serious popular literature most of the debate has centered on the tracks which, whatever one makes of the sightings or the credibility of witnesses to the animal itself, undeniably exist. Skeptics usually explain these as the spoor of conventional animals such as snow leopards, foxes, bears — or even wandering Tibetan lamas (who evidently do not mind freezing their feet) — and sometimes claim that melting has distorted their shapes into "yeti" prints. Though by now a virtual article of faith among skeptics, this last notion is a dubious one. Napier, no yeti believer, writes that "there is no real experimental basis for the belief that single footprints can become enlarged and still retain their shapes, or that discrete prints can run (or melt) together to form single large tracks."

In any case, some of the tracks are found fresh — in other words, before the elements have had a chance to act on them. Among the more impressive incidents involving tracks is one that happened in 1972 to members of the Arun Valley Wildlife Expedition, a multidisciplinary ecological survey of a deep river valley in far-eastern Nepal where many rare animals and plants live isolated and undisturbed. Its participants, including leader Edward Cronin, a zoologist, were open-minded about the yeti's possible existence and even looked for evidence in the course of their two-year effort, but this was not the main purpose of their endeavor.

On the night of December 17, Cronin and expedition physician Howard Emery, along with their Sherpa guides, camped on a depression at 12,000 feet in the ridge of Kongmaa La mountain. The next morning, when Emery awoke and stepped outside, he was startled to find footprints of a bipedal creature which had walked between the two tents sometime in the night. Nine inches long and four and three-quarters wide, perfectly preserved, the tracks showed, Cronin recorded, a "short, broad, opposable hallux, an asymmetrical arrangement of the four remaining toes, and a wide, rounded heel." They looked very much like a yeti print photographed by mountaineer Eric Shipton in 1951.

Expedition members followed the prints for some distance. The creature had come up and down the slope to the north, crossed through the camp, and proceeded over the south slope. Then it returned to the top of the ridge. Its tracks disappeared down the south slope in scrub and rock. "The slope was extremely steep," Cronin wrote, "and searching for the prints was arduous and dangerous. We realized that whatever creature had made them was far stronger than any of us."

If prints associated with the yeti continue to resist conventional explanation, other kinds of evidence have proven disappointing or, at best, ambiguous. The 1954 *London Daily Mail* expedition examined a "yeti scalp," said to be 350 years old, preserved as a kind of sacred object in a Tibetan lamasery. Four years later members of an expedition led by Texas

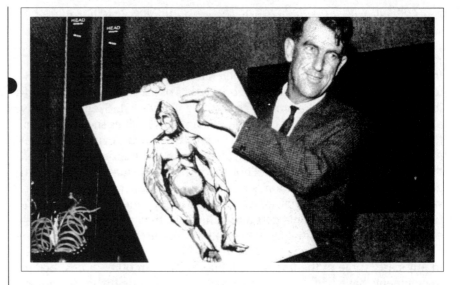

Sir Edmund Hillary's debunking of yeti did much to discourage later scientific research into the Himalayas' fabled "abominable snowman." (Courtesy of Loren Coleman.)

● SOURCES:

Bishop, Barry C. "Wintering on the Roof of the World." *The National Geographic* 122, 4 (October 1962): 502–47.

Bord, Janet, and Colin Bord. *The Evidence for Bigfoot and Other Man-Beasts.* Wellingborough, Northamptonshire, England: The Aquarian Press, 1984.

Burton, Maurice. "The World of Science: The Snowman." *The Illustrated London News* 229, 6126 (November 3, 1956): 756–59.

Coleman, Loren. *Tom Slick and the Search for the Yeti.* Boston, MA: Faber and Faber, 1989.

———. *The Yeti and the Yeren.* Portland, ME: The Author, 1992.

Cronin, Edward W., Jr. "The Yeti." *The Atlantic Monthly* 236, 5 (November 1975): 47–53.

———. "Tracking the Yeti in the Snowfields of the Himalayas." *Pursuit*

oilman Tom Slick looked at it and another specimen. Two years later, in the course of a much-publicized expedition sponsored by the publishers of *World Book Encyclopedia*, Sir Edmund Hillary, whose blunt derision did much to dampen subsequent scientific interest in the yeti question, was able to secure yet a third specimen. It turned out, analysts — with the notable exception of British Museum authority John Hill — agreed, to be from a serow (goat antelope).

The 1958 Slick expedition also collected two examples of alleged yeti hands. One, at a lamasery at Makulu, proved to be the paw and forearm of a snow leopard. The other, a far more interesting matter, may be the single best piece of evidence for yeti's existence; ironically, owing to confusion and misunderstanding, it is usually treated as devastating disproof.

In early 1959 expedition member Peter Byrne was permitted into a lamasery at Pangboche, Nepal, where he had learned that a purported yeti hand was kept. The monks had specified that the hand was not to leave the premises, but Byrne, who had carefully worked out a plan of action, managed to persuade the lamas to let him examine it privately. They had no idea what Byrne had brought with him: human hand parts, secured from British primatologist W. C. Osman Hill, a scientific consultant to the expedition. Byrne reported to Slick in a February 3 letter:

> I shall not go into detail here of how we got the thumb and the phalanx of the Pangboche hand. The main thing is that we have them, and that the lamas of the monastery do not know *that we have them.* Because they do not know it is of the utmost importance that there is [sic] no news releases on this or any publicity for some time.... The Pangboche hand is still complete, as far as the lamas are concerned. It still has a thumb and an index procimal phalanx. What they do not know, and what they must never know, *is that the thumb and the p. phalanx at present on the hand are human ones, which we switched.*

15, 3 (Third Quarter 1982): 100–05, 128–30.

Heuvelmans, Bernard. *On the Track of Unknown Animals.* New York: Hill and Wang, 1958.

Hillary, Sir Edmund. "Epitaph to the Elusive Abominable Snowman." *Life* 50, 2 (January 13, 1961): 72–74.

Hunt, John. "Unseen Yeti." *Geographical Magazine* 51, 9 (June 1979): 629–34.

Kirtley, Bacil F. "Notes Upon a Central Asian Legend." *Folklore 74* (Spring 1963): 318–20.

Ley, Willy. *Exotic Zoology.* New York: The Viking Press, 1959.

Markotic, Vladimir, ed. Grover Krantz, associated ed. *Sasquatch and Other Unknown Hominoids.* Calgary, Alberta: Western Publishers, 1984.

Masters, John. "The Abominable Snowman." *Harper's Magazine* 218, 1304 (January 1959): 30–34.

The stolen samples, which included a piece of skin, were placed in a pack and taken undetected across the Nepalese border. But getting them out of India, where customs were stricter, was a more complicated matter. As it happened, however, two close friends of expedition cosponsor Kirk Johnson were staying at a Calcutta hotel, and Byrne sought their assistance. The friends, film actor James Stewart and his wife Gloria, wrapped the samples in underwear, buried them deep in their luggage, and brought them undetected to London, where they were given to Johnson. Johnson brought them to Hill on February 20.

Hill concluded, disappointed, that the thumb and phalanx were "human." Later, however, he would change his mind, declare them less than fully human — possibly even the remains, unlikely as it seemed, of a Neanderthal man. Two other scientists who examined the samples at the time confessed to puzzlement. Zoologist Charles A. Leone regretted his "inability to make a positive identification," and anthropologist George Agogino later told writer Gardner Soule, "Many people who have examined this hand feel that it is a human hand with very primitive characteristics.... I do

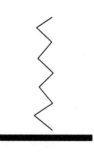

not feel that this hand is a normal human hand at all…. It is highly characteristic, however, of all the giant anthropoids." Blood tests of the skin sample indicated it was from no known human or primate.

Because of the circumstances under which the samples were collected — the technical term is thievery — none of this was known when Hillary, who deemed the yeti something of a joke (intimating, for example, that Sherpa sightings and Sherpa drinking habits are not unconnected), declared with much amusement that the Pangboche hand is "essentially a human hand, strung together with wire, with the possible inclusion of several animal bones." This, of course, is precisely what it was after Byrne got through with it. Had Hillary directed his attention to the "animal" (nonhuman) bones instead of the irrelevant planted human bones, he and his associates would likely have been as astonished and puzzled as Hill and his colleagues were.

Unfortunately, the present whereabouts of the samples are unknown.

State of the controversy.
After the heyday of expeditions in the 1950s, culminating in the debunking that followed Hillary's venture in 1960, scientific and popular interest in the "abominable snowman" peaked, though a few books, magazine articles, and infrequent forays into the Himalayas (such as Cronin's in 1972-74) occasionally have revived the issue. In 1986, in a farcical episode, an English traveler took what he sincerely believed to be a yeti photograph; subsequent investigation conclusively proved that the "yeti" was a mountain rock. In February and March of the same year, the New World Explorers Society collected reports, some relatively recent, from native informants and returned with alleged yeti hair, described only as "long, black, and coarse." The fibers were handed over to the International Society of Cryptozoology for analysis, but the results, if any, had not been published as of late 1992.

Fecal droppings associated with yetis comprise another kind of evidence. Eggs found in samples collected by Slick's 1959 expedition were determined to be from a previously unknown parasitic worm. Bernard Heuvelmans has remarked of this fact, "Since each species of mammal has its own parasites, this indicated that the host animal is also equally an unknown animal."

Most students of the yeti believe the *dzu-teh*, supposedly the larger version of the beast, is in fact a blue bear. If there is a yeti, it is the *meh-teh*. Those who think it is a real unknown animal agree that it does not live in the high mountain snows but in the surrounding mountain forests. But what kind of animal is it?

Nicholas Warren offers a conservative positive interpretation. "The concept of a vegetarian ape, occasionally straying from the forests into the high snowfields, is not only logical, but also plausible, as an explanation of the small yeti," he says. More often, however, yeti students from Willy Ley

Miller, Marc E., and William Cacciolfi. "Results of the New World Explorers Society Himalayan Yeti Expedition." *Cryptozoology* 5 (1986): 81–84.

Murray, W. H. "Is There an Abominable Snowman?" *The Scots Magazine* n.s. 59, 2 (May 1953): 91–97.

Napier, John. *Bigfoot: The Yeti and Sasquatch in Myth and Reality.* New York: E. P. Dutton and Company, 1973.

"People: Looking for a Legend." *Newsweek* (February 18, 1957): 29–30.

Sanderson, Ivan T. *Abominable Snowmen: Legend Come to Life.* Philadelphia, PA: Chilton Books, 1961.

Smythe, F. S. "'Abominable Snowmen'! Mysterious Himalayan Tracks Explained." *The Illustrated London News* 191, 5143 (November 13, 1937): 818.

Soule, Gardner. *Trail of the Abominable Snowman.* New York: G. P. Putnam's Sons, 1966.

Topley, Marjorie. "Correspondence: Literary Evidence for the Existence of the 'Snow Man'." *Man* 60 (February 1960): 27.

to Edward Cronin to Loren Coleman have been drawn to another, rather more extraordinary interpretation of a sort that has been applied to other kinds of reported, though unrecognized, anthropoids such as Bigfoot and the Chinese wildman: *Gigantopithecus*, a large prehistoric ape, fossil remains of which have been uncovered in, among other places, the Himalayan foothills.

When Slick showed native witnesses photographs of various animals and asked them which one the yeti most looked like, there was, he said, "a unanimous selection, in the same order, with the first choice being the gorilla standing up, the second choice being an artist's drawing of a prehistoric ape-man, *Australopithecus*, and the third choice being an orangutan standing up, which they liked particularly for the long hair."

Vlcek, Emanuel. "Old Literary Evidence for the Existence of the 'Snow Man' in Tibet and Mongolia." *Man* 59 (August 1959): 133–34.

Vlcek, Emanuel, with Josef Kolmas and Pavel Poucha. "Shorter Notes: Diagnosis of the 'Wild Man' According to Buddhist Literary Sources from Tibet, Mongolia and China." *Man* 60 (October 1960): 153–55.

Wilkins, Harold T. "The Abominable Snowmen." *Fate* 4, 2 (March 1951): 36–43.

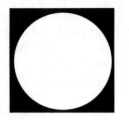

YETI PHOTOGRAPH ───────────────────────────

On March 6, 1986, while traveling alone and on foot through the Garhwal Himalaya of North India, Englishman Tony Wooldridge saw something unusual. "Strange tracks came up a steep gully on the right and then went from bush to bush in the wood," he recalled. Puzzled, he wondered "what creature could be sharing the wood with me but could think of no satisfactory explanation."

A little over two hours later, at 12:30 P.M., Wooldridge stopped his ascent out of concern about the stability of an exposed steep snow slope, where evidence indicated a recent avalanche. As he delicately surveyed the area to check out the prospects of a sudden new avalanche, he said, "I noticed a large smooth groove in the loose snow which might have been caused by a large rock sliding down. But the groove came to an abrupt halt just at the point where a set of tracks led off across the slope, behind and beyond a spindly shrub. Standing behind the shrub was a large, erect shape, perhaps up to two meters tall. Convinced that whatever it was it would disappear quickly, I took several photographs rapidly and then moved up about 50 meters nearer to a rocky outcrop, which was as close as I could get without venturing onto the broad, open snow slope which had just avalanched.

"It was difficult to restrain my excitement as I came to the realization that the only animal I could think of, which remotely resembled this one in front of me, was the yeti."

Wooldridge stared intently at "this all-too-real creature, standing with its legs apart, apparently looking down the slope with its right shoulder towards me. Its head was large and squarish, and the whole body appeared to be covered in dark hair, although the upper arm was a slightly lighter color. The creature was amazingly good at remaining motionless."

He took a number of pictures from a range of about 500 feet. By now 45 minutes had passed. In all that time the figure had not moved. Finally, with the weather deteriorating, Wooldridge left the scene. On the way down the slope he noticed many tracks comparable to those he had seen earlier.

On his return to England on March 15, Wooldridge took the pictures to wildlife authorities, whose responses ranged from guarded to enthusiastic. The photographs made their first public appearance on BBC's Wild Britain on July 13. To all appearances scientists now had significant evidence of yeti's existence. One major dissenter, however, was American anthropologist Grover S. Krantz, one of a handful of scientists who admit to being "absolutely convinced" that a North American Bigfoot exists. "Those pictures are definitely not of a yeti," he told the New York Times. Besides the fact that Wooldridge had never seen the figure move, Krantz said, "There are other details that look wrong, too. The head, for instance, doesn't appear to join the spine at an angle one would find in a primate, if that's what it is."

A year later Wooldridge returned to the mountain site and took stereo photographs of the location. In turn he gave these to two photoanalysts, David Stevens and Ernest Wickens of University College, London. Comparing the earlier and later photographs, Stevens and Wickens concluded that the "object, believed animate, was an outcrop of rock partially covered in snow and resembling an animate form." A color photograph taken by a local resident in the summer, with the snow gone, showed a conspicuous rock formation in the place where the "yeti" had stood.

Acknowledging his error, Wooldridge described the results as "obviously very disappointing. I appear to have jumped to a false conclusion which has taken nearly two years to sort out."

● SOURCES:

Browne, Malcolm W. "Abominable Snowman Wins Another Believer." New York Times (November 3, 1987).

Rickard, Bob. "The Yeti: Photographed, at Last!" Fortean Times 48 (Spring 1987): 38–43.

Rickard, Bob. "Yeti Was a Rock After All." Fortean Times 50 (Summer 1988): 8.

Bayanov, Dmitri. "The Case for the Australian Hominoids." In Vladimir Markotic, ed. Grover Krantz, associated ed. The Sasquatch and Other Unknown Hominoids, 101–26. Calgary, Alberta: Western Publishers, 1984.

Bord, Janet, and Colin Bord. Alien Animals. Harrisburg, PA: Stackpole Books, 1981.

Healy, Tony. "The Riddles of Oz." Fortean Times 49 (Winter 1987): 42–45.

439

YOWIE

Yowie, the Australian version of Bigfoot, has long been a feature of the cryptozoological landscape down under. Virtually no modern Australian zoologist acknowledges its existence, which indeed seems an incredible proposition. Australia has been separated from the Asian continent for some 70 million years — far too long ago for anthropoid apes to have crossed over and evolved into the kind of creature Australians, both native and European immigrant, have been reporting for many years.

The first known printed reference appears in 1835, in J. Holman's *Travels*, where it is said, "The natives are greatly terrified by the sight of a person in a mask calling him 'devil' or *Yah-hoo*, which signifies evil spirit." In an 1842 issue of *Australian and New Zealand Monthly Magazine*, an article titled "Superstitions of the Australian Aborigines: The Yahoo" notes:

> The natives of Australia have, properly speaking, no idea of any super-natural being; at the same time, they believe in the imaginary exis-tence of a class which, in the singular number, they call Yahoo, or, when they wish to be anglified, Devil-Devil…. On the other hand, a contested point has long existed among Australian naturalists whether or not such an animal as the Yahoo existed, one party contending that it does, and that from its scarceness, slyness, and solitary habits, man has not succeeded in obtaining a specimen, and that it is most likely to be one of the monkey tribe.

Two years later Mrs. Charles Meredith, in her *Notes and Sketches of New South Wales During a Residence in the Colony from 1839 to 1844*, wrote of the terror the yahoo inspired in the aborigines. The yahoo, she reported, "lives in the tops of the steepest and rockiest mountains, which are totally inaccessible to all human beings."

(No one knows how the word "yahoo" — usually associated with Jonathan Swift, in whose famous satire *Gulliver's Travels* [1726] Yahoos are a race of degraded people — was absorbed into the aboriginal vocabulary. The expression entered common usage as a word denoting uncouth or ignorant individuals. In the eighteenth and nineteenth centuries English speakers sometimes applied it to orangutans. Coincidentally or otherwise, native inhabitants of the Bahamas call their local apeman the "yahoo.")

Australian settlers began seeing the yahoo, too. An 1881 newspaper article mentions the "first appearance for some considerable time past." Two or three local men allegedly had seen a creature which looked like a "huge monkey or baboon ... somewhat larger than a man." On October 3, 1894, while riding in the New South Wales bush in the middle of the afternoon, Johnnie McWilliams said he spotted a "wild man or gorilla" which stepped out from behind a tree, looked at him briefly, and dashed for a wooded hillside a mile away. The *Queanbeyan Observer* (November 30), calling the witness a "truthful and manly fellow," added, "For many years there have been tales of trappers coming across enormous tracks of some unknown animals in the mountain wilds around Snowball."

Around the turn of the century Joseph and William Webb, camped in the range in New South Wales, reportedly fired on a "formidable-looking" apelike creature which left "footprints, long, like a man's, but with longer, spreading toes; there were its strides, also much longer than those of a man." They found "no blood or other evidence of their shot['s] having taken effect," according to John Gale (*An Alpine Excursion* [1903]). On August 7, 1903, the *Queanbeyan Observer* printed a letter from a man who claimed to have witnessed a killing of a yahoo by aborigines. "It was like a black man," he said, "but covered all over with gray hair."

Cattleman and poet Sydney Wheeler Jephcott contributed this remarkable account to the *Sydney Herald* of October 23, 1912:

> [O]n Sunday (October 12), I heard that George Summerell, a neighbor of mine, while riding up the track which forms a short cut from Bombala to Bemboka, had that day, about noon, when approaching a small creek about a mile below "Packer's Swamp," ridden close up to a strange animal, which, on all fours, was drinking from the creek. As it was covered with gray hair, the first thought that rose to Summerell's mind was: "What an immense kangaroo." But, hearing the horse's feet on the track, it rose to its full height, of about 7 ft., and looked quietly at the horseman. Then stooping down again, it finished its drink, and then, picking up a stick that lay by it, walked steadily away up a slope to the right or eastern side of the road, and disappeared among the rocks and timber 150 yards away.
>
> Summerell described the face as being like that of an ape or man, minus forehead and chin, with a great trunk all one size from shoulder to hips, and with arms that nearly reached to its ankles.
>
> Hearing this report, I rode up to the scene on Monday morning. On arriving [sic] about a score of footprints attested the truth of Summerell's account, the handprints where the animal had stooped at the edge of the water being especially plain. These handprints differed

from a large human hand chiefly in having the little fingers set much like the thumbs (a formation explaining the 3-1 series of scratches on the white gum tree).

A striking peculiarity was revealed, however, in the footprints: these, resembling an enormously long and ugly human foot in the heel, instep, and ball, had only four toes — long (nearly 5 inches), cylindrical, and showing evidence of extreme flexibility. Even in the prints which had sunk deepest into the mud there was no trace of the "thumb" of the characteristic ape's "foot."

Beside, perhaps a score of new prints, there were old ones discernible, showing that the animal had crossed the creek at least a fortnight previously. After a vexatious delay, I was able, on the Wednesday afternoon, to take three plaster of Paris casts — one of a footprint in very stiff mud, another in very wet mud, and a third of the hand with its palm superimposed on the front part of the corresponding foot. These I have forwarded to Professor David, at the university, where, no doubt, they can be seen by those interested. Anyone acquainted with the nature of mud will not expect to find a cast taken therein three days after imprint as technically perfect as a casting from the regular model, but I believe that any reasonable being will be satisfied by an inspection of these three casts that something quite unknown and unsuspected by science remains to be brought to light.

Jephcott said that the publicity surrounding this sighting had inspired others who feared ridicule to come forward with an "astonishing number of confirmatory cases." The *Sydney Sun* of November 10, 1912, published one such report, with a detailed description by surveyor Charles Harper:

A huge manlike animal stood erect not 20 yards from the fire, growling, grimacing and thumping his breast with his huge handlike paws.... I should say its height when standing erect would be 5 ft. 8 in. to 5 ft. 10 in. Its body, legs, and arms were covered with long, brownish-red hair, which shook with every quivering movement of its body. The hair on its shoulder and back parts appeared in the subdued light of the fire to be jet black, and long; but what struck me as most extraordinary was the apparently human shape, but still so very different.... I saw that the metatarsal bones [of the feet] were very short, much shorter than in genus homo, but the phalanges were extremely long, indicating great grasping power by the feet. The fibula bone of the leg was much shorter than in man. The femur bone of the thigh was very long, out of all proportion to the rest of the leg. The body frame was enormous, indicating immense strength, and power of endurance. The arms and forepaws were extremely long and large, and very muscular, being covered with shorter hair. The head and face were very small, but very human. The eyes were large, dark and piercing, deeply set. A most horrible mouth was ornamented with two large and canine teeth. When the jaws were closed they protruded over the lower lip. The stomach seemed like a sack hanging halfway down the thighs,

● SOURCES:

Bayanov, Dmitri. "The Case for the Australian Hominoids." In Vladimir Markotic, ed. Grover Krantz, associated ed. *The Sasquatch and Other Unknown Hominoids*, 101–26. Calgary, Alberta: Western Publishers, 1984.

Bayanov, Dmitri, Graham C. Joyner, and Colin P. Groves. "Comments and Responses." *Cryptozoology* 6 (1987): 124–29.

Bord, Janet, and Colin Bord. *Alien Animals*. Harrisburg, PA: Stackpole Books, 1981.

———. *The Evidence for Bigfoot and Other Man-Beasts*. Wellingborough, Northamptonshire, England: The Aquarian Press, 1984.

Bottrell, Leigh. "Getting to Grips with a Yowie." *Sydney* [Australia] *Daily Telegraph* (March 16, 1979).

Groves, Colin P. "The Yahoo, the Yowie, and Reports of Australian Hairy Bipeds." *Cryptozoology* 5 (1986): 47–54.

Healy, Tony. "The Riddles of Oz." *Fortean Times* 49 (Winter 1987): 42–45.

Joyner, Graham. *The Hairy Man of South East-*

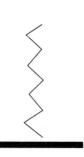

whether natural or a prolapsus, I could not tell. All this observation occupied a few minutes while the creature stood erect, as if the firelight had paralyzed him.

From yahoo to yowie.

Yowie sightings, like the related yahoo traditions, are confined, with few exceptions, to the south and central coastal regions of New South Wales and to Queensland's Gold Coast. The origin of the apparently (though not certainly) more recent word "yowie" is as obscure as that of its predecessor. A modern aboriginal writer remembers that in his youth members of his tribe (the Wiradjuri of southwestern New South Wales) spoke of the "hairy youree — the huge shaggy man-like creature that the whites call 'yowie'." Perhaps "yowie" is a corruption of "youree."

In any case, reports of yowies or yahoos span the entire twentieth century. In 1971 a team of Royal Australian Air Force surveyors landed in a helicopter on top of inaccessible Sentinel Mountain and were astonished to find huge manlike tracks (though too big for a man) in the mud left over from a recent rain. On April 13, 1976, in Grose Valley near Katoomba, New South Wales, five backpackers allegedly encountered a foul-smelling, five-foot-tall yowie — a female judging from its pendulous breasts. On March 5, 1978, a man cutting timber near Springbrook on the Gold Coast reportedly heard what sounded like a grunting pig and went into the forest looking for it. "Then something made me look up," he related, "and there about 12 ft. in front of me, was this big black hairy man-thing. It looked more like a gorilla than anything. It had huge hands, and one of them was wrapped around a sapling.... It had a flat back shiny face, with two big yellow eyes and a hole for a mouth. It just stared at me, and I stared back. I was so numb I couldn't even raise the axe I had in my hand."

Rex Gilroy, who formed the Yowie Research Center in the late 1970s, claims to have collected over 3,000 reports.

None of this has served to shake the skepticism of Australian scientists, who maintain that, as one put it, "The first and only primates to have lived in Australia were human beings." Australian National University anthropologist Colin P. Groves dismisses all the reports as "of little value as evidence." People see, he says, what they expect to see. He rejects the Harper report as "over the top." On the other hand, Graham Joyner, who has written extensively on the controversy, contends — alone among chroniclers of the mystery — that the "Yahoo was an undiscovered marsupial of roughly bear-like conformation, which was referred to intermittently throughout most of the 19th and early 20th centuries.... The Yowie, on the other hand, is a recent fiction which came into being in 1975.... It, of course, has no history, although one has been invented for it."

Certainly it is true that zoologically speaking, the yowie is a most unlikely beast — fully as improbable as the hairy bipeds reported in the American Midwest and comparably unlikely places. Yowies dwell, like so many other creatures with which this book is concerned, at the fringes of cryptozoology, where beasts that cannot possibly exist are reported anyway.

ern Australia. Canberra, Australia: National Library of Australia, 1977.

————. "The Orangutan in England: An Explanation for the Use of Yahoo as a Name for the Australian Hairy Man." *Cryptozoology* 3 (1984): 55–57.

————. "Scientific Discovery and the Place of the Yahoo in Australian Zoological History." *Cryptozoology* 9 (1990): 41–51.

Joyner, Graham C., and Colin P. Groves. "Comments and Responses." *Cryptozoology* 8 (1989): 136–41.

Joyner, Graham C., and Malcolm Smith. "Comments and Responses: The Yahoo: An Improbable Hypothesis." *Cryptozoology* 9 (1990): 116–19.

Maguire, Tony. "Monsters Prowl the Peaks." *Sydney* [Australia] *Sunday* (May 6, 1979).

Raynal, Michel, John Becker, Dmitri Bayanov, and Graham C. Joyner. "Comments and Responses." *Cryptozoology* 4 (1985): 106–12.

Smith, Malcolm. "Analysis of the Australian 'Hairy Man' (Yahoo) Data." *Cryptozoology* 8 (1989): 27–36.